OVID IN THE MIDDI

Ovid is perhaps the most important surviving Latin poet and his work
has influenced writers throughout the world. This volume presents a
groundbreaking series of essays on his reception across the Middle Ages.
The collection includes contributions from distinguished Ovidians as
well as leading specialists in medieval Latin and vernacular literature,
clerical and extra-clerical culture and medieval art, and addresses questions of manuscript and textual transmission, translation, adaptation and
imitation. It also explores the intersecting cultural contexts of the schools
(monastic and secular), courts and literate lay households. It elaborates
the scale and scope of the enthusiasm for Ovid in medieval Europe, following readers of the canon from the Carolingian monasteries to the early
schools of the Île de France and on into clerical and curial milieux in Italy,
Spain, the British Isles and even the Byzantine Empire.

JAMES G. CLARK is Reader in History at the University of Bristol. He
has published widely on the learned culture of later medieval England. His
publications include *A Monastic Renaissance at St Albans: Thomas Walsingham and his Circle c.1350–c.1440* (2004). His research on the reception
of the classics has been supported by fellowships from the British Academy
and the Leverhulme Trust. He is a fellow of the Royal Historical Society.

FRANK T. COULSON is Professor in the Department of Greek and Latin
at the Ohio State University where he serves as Director of Palaeography
in the Center for Epigraphical and Palaeographical Studies. He has published extensively on the medieval and Renaissance manuscript tradition
of Ovid. His books include *The Vulgate Commentary on Ovid's Metamorphoses: The Creation Myth and the Story of Orpheus* (1991) and (with
Bruno Roy) *Incipitarium Ovidianum: A Finding Guide for Texts in Latin
Related to the Medieval School Tradition on Ovid* (2000).

KATHRYN L. MCKINLEY is Associate Professor of English at the University of Maryland, Baltimore County. She has published several studies
on Ovid in medieval England (both in manuscript contexts and vernacular poetry). Her publications include *Reading the Ovidian Heroine:
'Metamorphoses' Commentaries 1100–1618* (2001). She is currently at work
on a study of Chaucer's *House of Fame*.

OVID IN THE MIDDLE AGES

EDITED BY

JAMES G. CLARK
FRANK T. COULSON
KATHRYN L. MCKINLEY

CAMBRIDGE
UNIVERSITY PRESS

CAMBRIDGE
UNIVERSITY PRESS

University Printing House, Cambridge CB2 8BS, United Kingdom

Cambridge University Press is part of the University of Cambridge.

It furthers the University's mission by disseminating knowledge in the pursuit of education, learning and research at the highest international levels of excellence.

www.cambridge.org
Information on this title: www.cambridge.org/9781107526624

First published 2011
Reprinted 2012
First paperback edition 2015

A catalogue record for this publication is available from the British Library

Library of Congress Cataloguing in Publication data
Ovid in the Middle Ages / edited by James G. Clark, Frank T. Coulson,
Kathryn L. McKinley.
p. cm.
Includes bibliographical references and index.
ISBN 978-1-107-00205-0 (hardback)
1. Ovid, 43 BC – AD 17 or 18 – Criticism and interpretation – History.
2. Ovid, 43 BC – AD 17 or 18 – Appreciation – Europe.   3. Ovid, 43 BC – AD 17
or 18 – Influence.   4. Ovid, 43 BC – AD 17 or 18 – In literature.
5. Literature, medieval – Roman influences.   I. Clark, James G.
II. Coulson, Frank T.   III. McKinley, Kathryn L.   IV. Title.
PA6537.O87   2011
871′.01 – dc22   2011008365

ISBN 978-1-107-00205-0 Hardback
ISBN 978-1-107-52662-4 Paperback

Contents

Illustrations

vii

Notes on contributors

ROBERT BLACK is Professor of Renaissance History at the University of Leeds. His most recent books are *Education and Society in Florentine Tuscany, Teachers, Pupils and Schools, c. 1250–1500* (2007) and *Humanism and Education in Medieval and Renaissance Italy: Tradition and Innovation in Latin Schools from the Twelfth to the Fifteenth Century* (2001).

JAMES G. CLARK is Reader in History at the University of Bristol. His research focuses on the books and literary culture of English monasteries in the later Middle Ages. He is the author of *A Monastic Renaissance at St Albans: Thomas Walsingham and his Circle, c.1350–1440* (2004) and has published articles in the *English Historical Review, Speculum* and the *Transactions of the Royal Historical Society*.

FRANK T. COULSON is Professor in the Department of Greek and Latin at the Ohio State University where he serves as Director of Palaeography in its Center for Epigraphical and Palaeographical Studies. He has published extensively on the medieval school tradition on Ovid and is currently completing work for the Ovid volume of the *Catalogus translationum et commentariorum*.

VICENTE CRISTÓBAL is Professor in Latin Philology at Complutense University in Madrid. He has translated and commented on Roman poets including Horace, Ovid, Virgil, and on the Trojan histories of Dares and Dictys. His research is focused on Latin poetry of the Augustan period and especially on the classical tradition in Spanish literature.

MARILYNN DESMOND is Distinguished Professor of English and Comparative Literature at Binghamton University and the author of *Reading Dido: Gender, Textuality, and the Medieval "Aeneid"* (1994) and *Ovid's Art and the Wife of Bath: The Ethics of Erotic Violence* (2006). Her research interests focus on Classics and medieval narrative, Chaucer, feminist and queer theory.

ELIZABETH FISHER is Professor of Classics at the George Washington University in Washington, DC. She has edited the speeches of Michael Psellos for Teubner and has published numerous articles on Michael Psellos, Maximos Planoudes and Manuel Holobolos.

WARREN GINSBERG is Knight Professor of Humanities at the University of Oregon. His books and articles treat classical and medieval literature; he is especially interested in Ovid, Dante, Boccaccio and Chaucer. His current project is *Ovid in Rome: Ovid in the Middle Ages*.

RALPH J. HEXTER is Professor of Classics and Comparative Literature, and Provost and Executive Vice Chancellor, University of California, Davis. He is the author of *Ovid and Medieval Schooling: Studies in Medieval School Commentaries on Ovid's 'Ars amatoria', 'Epistulae ex Ponto', and 'Epistulae Heroidum'* (1986) and numerous articles on the medieval school tradition on Ovid. He is currently completing research on Latin commentaries in print for the Ovid volume of the *Catalogus translationum et commentariorum*.

CARLA LORD is retired as Professor of Art History from the Fine Arts Department of Kean University in Union, NJ. She is the author of 'Marks of ownership in medieval manuscripts: The case of the Rouen *Ovide moralisé*' and 'Illustrated Manuscripts of Berchorius before the Age of Printing'. She is currently working on a survey of lesser-known illuminated manuscripts of Ovid's *Metamorphoses*.

KATHRYN L. McKINLEY is Associate Professor of English at the University of Maryland, Baltimore County. She has published several studies on Ovid in medieval England (both in manuscript contexts and vernacular poetry). Her publications include *Reading the Ovidian Heroine: 'Metamorphoses' Commentaries 1100–1618* (2001). She is currently at work on a study of Chaucer's *House of Fame*.

ANA PAIRET is Associate Professor of French at Rutgers University, NJ. She is the author of *Les mutacions des fables: Figures de la métamorphose dans la littérature française du Moyen Âge* (2002).

SIEGFRIED WENZEL is Professor Emeritus in the Department of English at the University of Pennsylvania and the author of *Macaronic Sermons: Bilingualism and Preaching in Late-Medieval England* (1994) and with Stephen G. Nichols, *The Whole Book: Cultural Perspectives on the Medieval Miscellany* (1996). Most recently, he has published *Preaching in the Age of Chaucer: Selected Sermons in Translation* (2008).

Acknowledgements

This collection offers an introduction to Ovid in the Middle Ages from scholars of diverse expertise with a common interest in medieval culture, both literate and visual, and the cultural legacy of classical antiquity. It is the fruit not only of independent research but also of interactions and collaborations fostered over a number of years: the first cause of the book was a sequence of conference panels convened at, among others, the annual meetings of the American Philological Association and the Medieval Academy of America and the International Medieval Congress. We are grateful to the contributors for their collaborative energy in the development of the volume and their patient forbearance in its final preparation. In the course of their work the contributors have received research assistance from a variety of sources, including the British Academy and the Leverhulme Trust. The editors have also benefited from the time and professionalism of Wendy Watkins in the Center for Epigraphical and Palaeographical Studies at the Ohio State University. Professor Coulson is grateful to Fritz Graf, Chair of the Department of Greek and Latin, and John Roberts, Dean of the College of Humanities at the Ohio State University, who granted him a sabbatical leave during the academic year 2007–8 during which time much of the editorial work was completed. We must also acknowledge the commitment of Michael Sharp at Cambridge which has propelled the project to its completion. We would also like to thank the two anonymous readers for the press who read the manuscript with care and whose comments greatly improved the final draft. In the closing stages, we have also received advice and practical assistance from Elizabeth Hanlon.

The book owes much to the unstinting effort and enthusiasm of Frank T. Coulson. There can be no doubt that Professor Coulson's research has transformed our understanding of Ovid and the manuscripts and textual apparatus that transmitted his *opera* to medieval readers. It is surely a fitting tribute to his contributions in the field that the acknowledged authority on the commentary tradition should now preside over an 'accessus' to the canon as a whole.

Abbreviations

LIBRARIES

BL	British Library
BML	Biblioteca Medicea Laurenziana
BN	Bibliothèque nationale de France
Bodl.	Bodleian Library
SB-PKb	Staatsbibliothek zu Berlin-Preussischer Kulturbesitz

JOURNALS

CQ	*Classical Quarterly*
JWI	*Journal of the Warburg and Courtauld Institutes*
MAev	*Medium Aevum*
MLatJb	*Mittellateinisches Jahrbuch*
PMLA	*Proceedings of the Modern Language Association*
RPh	*Revue de philologie, de littérature et d'histoire ancienne*
StudMed	*Studi medievali*

CHAPTER I

Introduction

James G. Clark

Medieval Europe was shaped not in separation from antiquity – as the polemics of the Renaissance alleged – but in the light of its enduring presence. The cultural, social, economic and political fabric of Christendom was woven with the patterns of the classical world. The people of the West acknowledged, or aspired to, the status of the Latins, they submitted to the authority of competing forms – princely and pontifical – of an ancient *imperium* and they set their confessional, cultural and political boundaries on the same eastern frontier as their Roman forebears. Perhaps above all they appropriated the discourse of the ancients and the textual culture(s), learned, literary, public and personal, that had sustained it for so long. In many regions of Europe, the traces of the ancients were tangible, and city, market, port, road and watercourse all bore the imprint of their ancient infrastructure. Yet it was their textual heritage that left the greater mark upon the medieval imagination. A rich variety of authors and texts, authentic, spurious and often fragmentary, revealed antiquity to Europeans between the sixth and the sixteenth centuries. These authorities were welcomed in the schoolroom, the carrel of the cloisterer, the pulpit and, in time, the *solar* of the recreational reader. A hierarchy emerged, a handful of ancient *auctoritates* accorded the honours generally reserved for the great masters of Christian doctrine and scriptural exegesis. It was not the sober sages of republic and empire – Virgil, Seneca, Cicero – who proved for medieval audiences the most popular and resonant voices of the pre-Christian past. Arguably, it was another and altogether unorthodox Augustan, Ovid (Publius Ovidius Naso, 43 BCE – 17 CE), who provided the greatest number and diversity of Europeans with their most memorable encounter with the classical world.[1] Like the very best of guides,

---

[1] Of course, the Virgilian canon also made an indelible imprint upon the medieval imagination, but it could be contended that Ovid's reach beyond clerical and Latinate culture was especially striking, over the whole course of the European Middle Ages. For the medieval Virgil see Baswell 1995.

Ovid's witness was candid, irreverent and truly independent, not only of the Caesarean regime but also of the political, social and spiritual mores over which it presided. It was also wide in scope. Ovid unfolded a tapestry of high politics, history, myth, social comedy and travelogue, which never failed to reward the returning reader and stimulated a clamour of commentary. Before the recovery of Plutarch, Ovid's reports of lives and letters of the early empire provided a unique point of contact with legends greater than his own. The medieval reader was tantalised by personal anecdotes of those whose names were legendary: 'Virgil I only saw' (*Tristia* 4.10.51). The Middle Ages loved the encyclopaedia as no other genre and in Ovid – particularly in the manuscript compendia that collected his works – were combined the key coordinates of Augustan Rome, its arena, the 'scattered sand of the gladiators' ring' (*Ars amatoria* 1.5), monuments, temples and 'tier' theatres, elegantly rendered in hexameters. Whether schoolboy, learned poetaster, preacher or layperson, when medieval readers conjured the classical past for themselves invariably they did so in the words and images of Ovid. In time, they knew him not only as an authority on a past they had lost but also as a counsellor on their present condition, the exigencies of the human experience and its place in the inexorable programme of the divine.

It was ironic that Ovid's voice should reverberate in the Middle Ages when he was silenced by his own. He was banished in 8 CE for an offence perhaps unintended and passed his remaining nine years at Tomis (now Constanța, on the Black Sea coast, Romania), a satellite *urbs* un-settled with 'fierce, wild and woolly' Getae (*Tristia* 5.7.11–20) that was the antithesis of Rome.[2] His shame was sealed by the public suppression of his works, an act that at least interrupted their transmission and prevented further amendment of his monumental *Metamorphoses*, since 'pluribus exemplis scripta fuisse reor' (*Tristia* 1.7.24); ultimately the *Medea* was forgotten and the *Medicamina faciei femineae* retained only as a fragment.[3] Ovid channelled his creativity into vivid, and often introspective, verses on the lives and loves he had lost, *Tristia*, *Epistulae ex Ponto*, but they failed to efface the trace of scandal among the literati, who, it would appear, had already begun to deepen the blemishes to his reputation and the reception

---

[2] The reason for his 'relegation' is unrecorded. A plausible possibility is his involvement in the sexual scandal which sealed the fall of the younger Julia: Dewar 2002: 388.

[3] Of course, Ovid was an inveterate editor of his own work. The *Amores* as it survives represents an epitome of an original five-book work: 'multa quidem scripsi, sed quae vitiosa putaui / emendaturis ignibus ipse dedi': *Tristia* 4.10.61–2. See also Ovid 1995d: 3–4.

of his poems. Seneca the Elder (54 BCE – 37 CE) scolded him as one who 'did not know when to leave well alone' (*Controversiae* 9.5.17).

There can be no doubt that a certain notoriety, a danger even, surrounded the name of Ovid in the decades following his death. With the conceit characteristic of a following generation, the stylists of the post-Augustan age tempered their evident admiration with a tone of mild reproach. Quintilian (*c.* 35–95 CE) presented him to his pupils as 'frivolous' ('lascivus'), a poet to be praised 'in parts' ('laudandus tamen partibus': *Institutio oratoria*, 10.1.88). Ovid had foreseen such a reception. His *envoi* to the *Tristia* expressed fear for its unprotected entry into the city. It may be a measure of its insecurity that there surfaced several codas to the canon – *Amores* 3.5; *Heroides* 15, Sappho's epistle; the *Consolatio ad Liviam*; *Halieutica*; *Nux* – whose authenticity was suspect.[4] A degree of uncertainty continues to surround the *Heroides*. On the margins of modern criticism is an ascription to Ovid's contemporary, Julius Montanus; perhaps a more plausible speculation is that the so-called 'double' epistles (*Heroides* 16–21) were composed by a subsequent editor.[5] The currency of Ovidian phrases in oral culture in the century after his death, in the epigraphy of the province of Moesia Inferior (the region of Tomis) and Pompei, and in the plays performed in Roman theatres, perhaps also reflects the volatility of his literary profile.[6] Indeed he was 'borne on the lips of the people': ('ore legar populi', *Metamorphoses* 15.878).

It was once believed that Ovid's reputation was steadily eclipsed by the shade of another Augustan, Virgil. Recent reappraisals of the literature of the Claudian and Neronian eras (41–68 CE), however, have revealed the continuing power of the Ovidian corpus. Persius' (34–62 CE) swipe at the 'froth' of his fellow poets (*Satires* 1.92–104) perhaps attests to a pervasive preference for the stylistic display that Ovid pioneered.[7] His creative mastery of metrical form inspired imitative invention: the dactyls of Statius' (*c.* 45–96 CE) *Achilleid* can be interpreted as a debt to Ovid.[8] It was not only his virtuosity that captivated these poets of the so-called Silver Age. His characterisation of classical figures offered a template for new compositions: Statius' Oedipus was drawn from an Ovidian outline.[9] To these inhabitants of a turbulent *urbs* Ovid also transmitted apparent reportage from the birth pangs of the empire.[10] On a different temporal

---

[4] See Ralph Hexter's essay below, pp. 292–5.   [5] Casali 2005: 530–2; Ovid 1995d: 6.
[6] Trapp 1973: 36.   [7] Dewar 2002.   [8] Dewar 2002: 396.
[9] Keith 2002: 383, 394–7.   [10] McNelis 2009: 398.

plane he also provided a conspectus of the mythological inheritance of contemporary Rome.[11]

Such revisionism cannot recast Ovid as the sole stimulus for the poetry of Imperial Rome. Virgil's star never dimmed and Ovid's place was in the ranks – although perhaps the front rank – alongside him.[12] Beyond the literary elite, the signs of his reception are scanty. His exact status in the schools of the empire remains unclear, as does his popularity among the 'reading public' of the wider empire. Certainly there is little in the evidence of papyri to indicate an unusual intensity in transmission at least to the outer reaches of the empire.[13]

By the beginning of the fourth century, Ovid was prominent in the schoolroom, one of the prescribed syllabus authors and a quarry, among many others, for grammarians and their students. Those schooled beyond the Latin hegemony – Claudian, Eutropius, Priscian – even carried an echo of their early Ovidian reading. It was a reflection perhaps of the residual unease over his style and subjects that none of his works apparently was subject to the systematic commentary now prepared for the principal syllabus *auctores*. The residue of a scholial tradition may be apparent in early manuscript glosses; it has been suggested that trace elements are also embedded in the *argumenta*, a critical companion to the mythography of the *Metamorphoses* commonly attributed to Lactantius Placidus.[14] The origin of the text remains obscure although it is often dated to the fifth or sixth centuries; it has been suggested it was composed for a comparable purpose to the *diegeseis*, the prose summaries compiled to support readers of the Greek *Aetia* of Callimachus.[15] Grammarians sought to establish the scope of the Virgilian canon but did not extend the enterprise to his exiled younger contemporary; nor did they offer him his own biography.[16] Christianity caused the *cursus* of syllabus *auctores* to be recast and Ovid, as other pagan authors, again was edged to the margins. The early Christian authorities recognised his value as a pagan point of reference: the *Fasti* and *Metamorphoses* appear as minor authorities in the second-century *Institutiones divinae* of Lactantius Firmianus (*c.* 250 – *c.* 325). His discomfort

---

[11] McNelis 2009: 398; Roberts 2002: e.g. 406.   [12] Wheeler 2002: 341; Roberts 2002: 403.

[13] See Elizabeth Fisher's essay below, p. 28. The exception was perhaps *Metamorphoses*, apparently recalled by Apuleius (*c.* 125–170 CE) in his *Asinus aureus*.

[14] Otis 1936. See also Tarrant 1983: 257–84 at 278.   [15] Knox 2009a: 327–54 at 328–9.

[16] Suetonius' *vita Vergiliana* survives as the only extant section of the fourth-century commentary of Aelius Donatus on the Virgilian canon. His near-contemporary Tiberius Claudius Donatus composed a commentary on the *Aeneid*, the *Interpretationes Vergilianae*. It appears Aelius Donatus' commentary served as the source of Servius' commentary on the *Aeneid*, which was widely circulated in the early and high Middle Ages. See Fowler 1997: 73–8 at 73.

at the challenge which Ovidian chaos posed to the divine programme of creation was explicit: 'nec audiendi sunt poetae qui aiunt chaos in principio fuisse' (*Institutiones* 2.8.8).[17] As a new cadre of Christian poet was preferred for their paradigms in the schoolroom, only doctrinal and moral discourse now attested to a continued awareness of Ovid.[18] A recent study has shown how, successively, the Augustan's creation myth was corrected with the authority of Genesis by Dracontius, (Claudius Marius) Victorius, and Orientius.[19] The fourth-century epigrams of Ausonius cited *Metamorphoses* and are said to have appropriated an Ovidian vocabulary.[20] Perhaps the best witness to his influence at, or after, the fall of imperial Rome (476 CE) was Manlius Anicius Severinus Boethius (c. 480 – c. 525 CE), whose *Consolatio philosophiae* appears to incorporate reminiscences of both the *Amores* and the *Metamorphoses*. Boethius' absorption of these texts prefigured approaches later in the Middle Ages: clearly he was impressed not only by their stylistic facility but also by their figurative capacity.[21] An impression of the persistence of the tradition amid the wreckage of (Christian) Roman culture is provided by Venantius Fortunatus (c. 530–600 × 609) the Italian clerk whose literary career flourished in the ultramontane Merovingian kingdom where the cultural, and perhaps codicological, discontinuities were not so marked. He was also attracted to the figurative models of the Ovidian canon, and in particular the *Heroides*.[22]

   In the East the eclipse of Ovid appears to have been total: as Elizabeth Fisher observes here, the claim that his works were known to the third-century Quintus of Smyrna remains inconclusive; Eusebius (c. 263 – c. 339) omitted him from his *Historia* as did the Hellenist annals of John Malaas, George Synkellos and the Egyptian Nonnos of Panopolis.[23]

   The recovery of Latin culture in the north and, at last, in middle Italy, from the turn of the sixth century, did not significantly alter Ovid's status as an author. The earliest, for the most part monastic, evocations of the classical schoolroom followed a syllabus which would have been recognisable to Boethius. The Christian poets remained the corner-stone; a repertory of pagan authors re-surfaced among which Virgil undoubtedly took precedence. Ovid was occasionally glimpsed in writing generated in this context but rarely if ever did he pass into the foreground. The pseudo-Lactantian *argumenta* on the *Metamorphoses* may have originated in this

---

[17] For Lactantius Firmianus see Roberts 2002: 404–5.
[18] An exception in the literature of this period was the Tuscan Maximianus, whose elegies echoed the figures and phrases of Ovid.
[19] Roberts 2002: 403–6, 411–13.   [20] Keith and Rupp 2007: 26–8.   [21] Claassen 2007.
[22] See also Roberts 2002: 403. See in this volume, p. 294.   [23] See below, p. 29.

period, although the text incorporates earlier scholia and is too slight, and
at times detached from the subject-text, to signify a shift in Ovid's schoolroom status.[24] Perhaps in Byzantium he was better known in this period:
Fisher finds that for John the Lydian (490–c. 565) Ovid was a name to
be dropped before a Greek readership now conscious of Latin *auctores*;
his appearance a century later in the universal chronicle of John of Antioch underlines the East's early advance on this most popular of western
poets.[25]

Ovid's continuing obscurity at the foundation of the medieval Latin
tradition has been seen as a matter of taste: Ludwig Traube saw Ovid's star
wax only after those of Virgil and Horace had begun to wane.[26] Perhaps it
should be connected with the descent of his works in manuscript. There
are indications of an hiatus in circulation between the sixth and the eighth
centuries. After a single witness to Ovid's ancient readership, a solitary
fragment, 25 lines of the *Epistulae ex Ponto*, which dates from the second
quarter of the fifth century and probably originated in Italy, there is no
copy extant which can be dated earlier than the ninth century.[27] This is not
enough to demonstrate a discontinuity, but recent research would suggest
knowledge of Ovid had drifted to the fringes of Europe carried by the
same currents, perhaps, as the cenobitic tradition. The earliest surviving
manuscript of the *Metamorphoses* (London, BL, Add. MS 11967, *s.* x$^{ex.}$),
was written in an Irish script and incorporates erroneous readings that
are redolent of the insular tradition.[28] There is also a suggestion that the
archetype of medieval copies of the amatory verse entered mainstream
circulation at the close of the eighth century from Iberia or even North
Africa.[29] Thus Ovid the Roman citizen returned to Europe from the old
imperial frontier.

Whatever route was followed, Ovid had recovered his early profile in
Europe by (and probably before the beginning of) the ninth century. Traube
located his 'aetas Ovidiana' after 1100 CE but now there can be no doubt the
first stirrings of a new audience for Ovid were seen two centuries before.[30]
The early codices of the amatory poetry, which date between the ninth and
the eleventh centuries, appear to be descended from a common exemplar,
a codex which may have been compiled *c.* 800 and contained each of the

[24] The *argumenta* are preserved in seven early manuscripts; two further copies were known in the sixteenth century: Otis 1936.
[25] See below, pp. 30–1.
[26] Traube 1909–20, vol. II (1911), 'Einleitung in die lateinische Philologie des Mittelalters', 13.
[27] Tarrant 1983: 257–84 at 263.   [28] For this manuscript see Tarrant 1983: 276–82 at 277–9.
[29] See Vicente Cristóbal's essay below, p. 231.
[30] Curtius 1953: 260–1, offers the classic account of the poet's passage out of the shadows.

amatory poems as well as the *Heroides*.[31] The earliest medieval copies of other works are dated to this same period. Monasteries that were the powerhouse of the Benedictine mission in southern and central Europe were pre-eminent in their reception, production and transmission.[32] Early witnesses to the *Amores*, the *Ars amatoria* and the *Metamorphoses* emerged from the scriptorium of Sankt Gallen before the end of the eleventh century.[33] A south German manuscript of the same period, Munich, Bayerische Staatsbibliothek, clm 4610, contains the earliest commentary on *Metamorphoses*: the text has been connected with the master Manegold of Lautenbach (d. after 1103): at the very least it bears witness to the new-found prominence of the Ovidian canon in claustral (and cathedral) schoolrooms.[34] During the reign of the arch reformer Abbot Desiderius (1058–87) Montecassino made and received early exemplars of *Fasti* and *Metamorphoses*: the latter, known as the 'Naples Ovid' (Naples, Biblioteca Nazionale, MS IV. F 3) contains the earliest surviving scheme of images connected with the text, which Carla Lord examines here.[35] It is worth noting the *Ibis* also appears to have entered mainstream circulation from Italy [36] The prominence of these continental centres perhaps explains the paucity of classical exemplars to the north and west: the handful of early Anglo-Saxon inventories does not feature a profusion of *auctores*; of Ovid there is no trace.[37] The century after 1050 witnessed a wider circulation and it would not be a great exaggeration to claim the Ovidian canon as 'the common ornament of libraries' (implied in *Tristia* 1.7.1–4):[38] recent studies of manuscripts and their contemporary witnesses – catalogues, and the identification of better-documented stemma descendants – have brought this into sharper focus. The earliest catalogue of England's premier monastery, the cathedral priory of Christ Church, Canterbury, a twelfth-century document, records copies of each of the principal works combined with other syllabus texts in composite volumes, together with four discrete codices of the 'Ovidius magnus', the common identification for the *Metamorphoses*.[39]

---

[31] Tarrant 1983: 257–84 at 259.   [32] For this phase see also in this volume, pp. 177–9.
[33] Kenney 1962: 1–31.   [34] The commentary is at fols. 61v–84r.
[35] For Montecassino in this period see Cowdrey 1983. For its scriptorial output see Newton 1999. For Lord see below, pp. 257–9.
[36] For the manuscript tradition of *Ibis* see also Reynolds 1983: 273–5; Richmond 2002: 477–80.
[37] Lapidge 2006: 133–4.
[38] 'Siquis habes nostris similes in imagine vultus, / deme meis hederas, Bacchica serta, comis, / ista decent laetos felicia signa poetas, / temporibus non est apta corona meis' (Whoever you may be who possess a portrait of my features, remove from my locks the ivy, the chaplet of Bacchus. Such fortunate symbols are suited to happy poets; a wreath becomes not my temples). 'Ornament' is the widely cited gloss of the Loeb translator, A. L. Wheeler (1924).
[39] James 1903: 7–12 at 11 (no. 159).

The integration of Ovid among other *auctores* in the poetic anthologies of this period is perhaps an index of how widely his works were now reproduced; and as an invaluable *repertorium* has now revealed, the familiarity of Ovid might also be measured in the parallel manuscript transmission of epitomes, extracts and imitative Ovidiana.[40] In the same century, as Vicente Cristóbal recounts here, copies of Ovid passed over the Pyrenees into the learned convents (and courts) of Latin Spain.[41] His passage eastward remains opaque, although a popular reception might be conjectured from the appearance of a distich in a Hungarian (Magyar) charter.[42] The only exception to the unrestricted transmission was perhaps the *Heroides*, which, in spite of a ninth- and tenth-century readership, subsequently appears to have receded from general view until its rediscovery after 1300.[43]

The source of the surge in Ovidian enthusiasm was the schools that flourished not only at major monastic centres but now also affiliated to secular cathedrals and even imperial or royal courts: the significance of these extra-clerical environs has been revealed through recent codicological analysis. Here the amatory poems, in particular, the *Heroides*, *Metamorphoses* and the poetry of exile, reassumed their early role as 'readers' for students of the *artes*, recognised again for their rich repository of grammatical, metrical and rhetorical lore. A remarkable manuscript survival, the so-called 'class book' of Saint Dunstan (Oxford, Bodl., Auct. MS F 4 32, *s.* x*med.*), gives an early glimpse of Ovid in this context: the book contains a copy of the *Heroides* furnished with interlinear glosses both in Latin and the Old English of the marches.[44] The glosses emphasise that the first purpose of Ovid, and other *auctores* in the schoolroom, was to secure and test the linguistic skill of the novice Latinist.[45] Robert Black here describes a comparable manuscript (of Ovid's *Tristia*) a century later in date (Florence, BML, San Marco MS 223, fols. 59r–66v) replete with interlinear glosses.[46] The centrality of Ovid on these curricula is reflected in the sheer intensity of glossed copies that Black records from Tuscan (and other regional) centres. The case of Gunzo of Novara, which Black recalls, confirms that even a gauche courtier could claim familiarity with Ovid.[47]

Here Ovid was regarded not only as a point of reference for those beginning to grasp Latin grammar, syntax and vocabulary, but also a model of fine poetic style. The old exile had expected nothing less: 'your very style will bring you recognition' (*Tristia* 1.1.47–72). Manuscript copies from

---

[40] Coulson and Roy 2000.   [41] See below, p. 231.   [42] Deri 2005.   [43] Tarrant 1983: 268–72.
[44] Hexter 1986: 26–35.   [45] For glossed manuscripts of this period see also Munk Olsen 1995.
[46] See below, p. 134.   [47] See below, p. 123.

this period carry marginal and interlinear glosses – compiled by masters of the clerical or novice *schola* – that elaborate the metrical and rhetorical structures of the text.[48] Clearly the adept student was expected not only to digest the use of these devices but to (attempt to) recreate them in their own compositions. The stylish verse of Théodulf of Orléans (*c.* 760–821) suggests the imitation of Ovid was a feature of scholastic culture already at the beginning of the ninth century.[49] The composition of the pseudo-Ovidian *De pediculo*, apparently of monastic origin, confirms that these exercises were encouraged in claustral *scholae*. By the twelfth century, the impulse to emulate the syllabus *auctores* was intense and it was said Master Bernard of Chartres (d. after 1124) expected of his pupils nothing less than to assume the mantle of the *poetae*.[50] The accomplished pseudo-epic *Alexandreis* of Master Walter of Châtillon (*fl.* 1170) represents the fulfilment of this trend in the third quarter of the twelfth century.[51] The Spanish *Libro de Alexandre* shows that even before 1200 the impulse to imitate Ovid was not confined to the Latin schools of the north.[52] The Ovidian persona was willingly appropriated by his clerical imposters: Théodulf's partner in verse, Modoin of Autun (d. 840 × 843), was known to his schoolroom and courtier contemporaries as 'Naso'.[53]

As an exemplar of Latin style, Ovid was also adopted by the twelfth-century pioneers of the *ars dictaminis*. The Italian Bene da Firenze placed Ovid among the 'philosophos et auctores' of his art; the new masters of medieval grammar and rhetoric – Geoffrey of Vinsauf, Alexander of Villa Dei, Pietro da Isolella – implicitly reinforced Ovid's rising status in this field through their frequent reminiscence of Ovidian phraseology.[54] The particular appeal of Ovidian rhetoric and rhythm remained powerful in the later Middle Ages, long after the climate of the schoolroom had changed. The literary turn taken by masters and students of *dictamen* after 1350 led paradigms from the exile poetry, *Heroides* and *Metamorphoses* to be gathered in preceptive manuals. A new genre of manual on metre, generated by grammar masters in the first and second quarters of the fifteenth century, also privileged Ovidian paradigms.[55] Further analysis of

---

[48] See, for example, the glosses on *Ex Ponto* and *Heroides* in twelfth-century manuscripts connected with Tegernsee, Munich clm 14819, 19475. See also Hexter 1986: 132–6, 143.

[49] Godman 1985: 190–7.

[50] John of Salisbury 1991: 53, *Metalogicon*, 1.24, lines 76–80: 'Quibus autem indicebantur praeexercitamina puerorum in prosis aut poematibus imitandis, poetas aut oratores proponebat et eorum iubebat vestigia imitari, ostendens iuncturas dictionum, et elegantes sermonum clausulas'.

[51] Galteri de Castillione 1978.   [52] See below, pp. 231–2.   [53] Wallace-Hadrill 1983: 263.

[54] For Master Bene see below, p. 124.

[55] Camargo 1991: 37–41; 1995: 20–32, 105–47, 169–221; Clark 2004: 217–20.

these neglected pre-humanist textbooks, which in their reception bridged the divide between the elite *littérateur* and the work-a-day chancery clerk, is long overdue.

Even at the higher reaches of the curriculum, among the arts of the *quadrivium*, master and student recognised Ovid as their guide. His cosmos was a common source for studies that so often elided the distinction between astronomy and astrology; the figures that frequently illustrated astrological compendia in the later Middle Ages were rich with Ovidian reference.[56] The fascination for alchemy that flourished on the fringes of syllabus science also found a stimulus in Ovid: Hermaphroditus (*Metamorphoses* 4) served as a metaphor for the transformation of any matter.[57]

Of course, the status of Ovid in the schoolrooms of the early, and high, Middle Ages should not be overstated. The pedagogic properties of his works were widely appreciated, but their *materia* (as contemporary masters would term it), *amor*, *dolor* and *fabulae deorum*, presented problems for boys, clerks, novices and their custodians. The unease of monastic masters intensified in the age of reform inaugurated by the Benedictine Pope Gregory VII. Conrad of Hirsau (*c.* 1070 – *c.* 1150) questioned the merit of mining nuggets of gold from the filth of Ovid since the student became so mired in the dirt.[58] The Norman monk, Guibert of Nogent (*c.* 1055–1124) perhaps reflected the prevailing monastic view of the twelfth century when he expressed his feelings of guilt for returning to Ovid.[59] Nor was it solely monastic sensibility that was unsettled. The most provocative of peripatetic masters, Pierre Abélard, proved chary of the classical *auctores*.[60] In his *Speculum duorum*, Gerald of Wales (*c.* 1146 – *c.* 1223) dismissed the secular (and pagan) literature of the schoolroom as among the trifles of youth from which the dedicated clerk must detach himself in his maturity, for higher studies.[61] Of course, as contemporary critics of sexual discourse have demonstrated, such discomfort was studiedly disingenuous: pedagogic glosses were not troubled by prudery.[62]

Yet from the time his verses returned to the schoolroom Ovid was also regarded as a reliable authority on themes that ran to the very heart of the higher studies of secular clerk and regular religious. From its first circulation, the narratives of the pagan deities recounted in the *Metamorphoses* were regarded as a complement to Christian studies in mythography. When

[56] Desmond and Sheingorn 2001: 7 and n.   [57] DeVun 2008.
[58] *Accessus ad auctores* 1970: 114. See also Curtius 1953: 49. Conrad's *Dialogus super auctores* rejected the amatory poetry and the *Metamorphoses*, but not the *Ex Ponto* and *Fasti*.
[59] Guibert de Nogent 1984: 87.   [60] Luscombe 2001.
[61] Giraldus Cambrensis 1974: 168–71 at 168–9.   [62] Woods 1996: 65, 81.

the author known to medieval readers as Theodolus composed, perhaps in the tenth century, his account of the conflict between Christian truth and pagan mendacity, called the *Ecloga*, he turned to the *Metamorphoses* as well as the orthodox authorities, Lactantius and Fulgentius: 'the very power of the celestials stirs our hearts'(*Ex Ponto* 1.1.21–46). In the confessional flux of the Gregorian period, the mythographical impulse was reignited and the secular clerks and Cluniac monks of England and Normandy returned to Ovid, alongside his early Christian analogues, Lactantius, Fulgentius and Isidore, to parse, and to neutralise, pagan myth. The compendium attributed to Alberic of London (once known as 'Vatican Mythographer III') originated in this climate and context; the earliest known *genealogia deorum gentilium*, preserved in Oxford, Bodl., Digby MS 221, perhaps should also be assigned to this period and place.[63] The induction of Ovid into the nascent faculties of theology was signalled perhaps by the pioneering commentary of Thomas of Perseigne (d.1190) which turned to the Sulmonian exile to expound the Song of Songs.[64]

The monks and clerks trained in the Ovidian schoolroom of the early and high Middle Ages also returned to the Roman versifier to elaborate, and express, their ethical and philosophical reflections. As early as the turn of the eighth century, Théodulf of Orléans had recommended the verse of Ovid for the philosophical truths that might be recovered from their fabulous *integumenta* (clothing).[65] A deeper engagement with the ethical Ovid was encouraged by the preoccupation of twelfth-century masters with conceptions of the self and self-expression.[66] The amatory and exile poetry, and the *Metamorphoses*, offered figures and insights on joy, sorrow, and love, affective, fraternal, and sexual, that might inform and extend their discourse. Their debt to Ovid was evident not only in the lighter verses on these themes that emanated from Paris and satellite schools – *Architrenius*, *Speculum stultorum* – but also in weightier polemics, such as the *Anticlaudianus* and *De planctu naturae* of Alain of Lille, and scholarship, such as the commentary on Martianus Capella's *De nuptiis Philologiae et Mercurii* attributed to Bernardus Silvestris.[67] These Francophone models were followed elsewhere: as Robert Black shows, Henry of Settimello's *Elegy* was shaped in the image of Master Alain.[68] The masters of the period, at Tours perhaps more than at Paris, also addressed nature as a philosophical

---

[63] Allen 1970. [64] Leclercq 1982: 127. [65] Godman 1985.
[66] Morris 1972: 64–95 is the classic account. See also Spence 1996.
[67] *Architrenius* (1974), ed. Schmidt; Nigel Wireker (1960), ed. Mozley and Raymo; Alain of Lille (1955) ed. Bossuet; Alain of Lille (1980), ed. Sheridan; Bernardus Silvestris (1986), ed. Westra.
[68] See below, pp. 123–4.

problem *per se* under the influence of, among other authorities, the Calcidian commentary on the *Timaeus*.[69] These studies led them into the Ovidian cosmos: Bernardus Silvestris' *Cosmographia* repainted the celestial realm in pagan colours, drawing as much from his Roman as his Greek (i.e. Platonic) sources.[70]

From this scholastic milieu at the turn of the twelfth century there arose a vernacular discourse devoted to the same themes: its formation, scope and critical reception in the generations that followed remains a primary focus for literary scholars.[71] In this regard the *De amore* of Andreas Capellanus, a popular Latin manual of courtly love composed by the educated Aquitainian courtier *c.* 1180, could be considered a transitional text, which conveyed schoolroom Ovidianism to an extra-mural audience. The chaplain's enthusiasm for Ovidian style was unrestrained but his treatment of his theme carried an echo of the earlier scholastic commentaries, perhaps particularly those on Martianus Capella.[72] There were analogues to the *De amore* in the south, as Cristóbal demonstrates: the elegiac verse *Quo modo prius conuenimus*, part of the popular *Carmina Riuipullensia*, is also a reprisal of Ovid's *Amores*.[73] The chaplain's contemporaries, Chrétien de Troyes and the author of the *Lais* of Marie de France, continued the recreation of Ovidian discourse, indeed extended it into the formation of their own fabulous narratives.[74] The *Roman de la Rose*, the first iteration of which was completed by Guillaume de Lorris before 1230, also created an Ovidian landscape but in its form and focus was an analogue of the *De amore*, since it too sought to re-cast the *Ars amatoria* in the light of courtly and Romance literature.[75]

The amatory discourse fuelled and furthered by verses such as these in turn stimulated the vernacular translation of the authentic Ovid. As Marilynn Desmond describes, the thirteenth century witnessed no fewer than four verse translations of the *Ars amatoria*, perhaps more since there is no trace of the text of Chrétien de Troyes, together with prose renderings of the *Ars* and the *Heroides*.[76] The *Heroides* translation served as one of the textual foundations of the second redaction of the *Histoire ancienne*, a French retelling of the Trojan legend whose dramatic set-pieces offered

---

[69] Gersh 1982: 530, 533.   [70] Bernardus Silvestris 1978. For criticism see also Dronke 1974.

[71] Kellogg 1998; Desmond 2006, 2007; Minnis 2001; Fumo 2007.

[72] For *De amore* see Walsh 1982. For textual criticism see Dronke 1994: Minnis 2001: 9.

[73] See below, pp. 231–2.

[74] For Chrétien de Troyes's romances see the critical edition of 1965, ed. Foerster and Hilka. For criticism see Kelly 2002. For Marie de France see Bloch 2003. For the influence of the *Heroides* on the *Salut d'Amour* see Poe 2006.

[75] For the *Roman de la Rose* see Minnis 2001.   [76] See below, p. 110.

further scope for the informed (re)presentation of love. Desmond contends that the circulation of the amatory verse in a vernacular milieu cast Ovidian concepts of gender and sex as normative.[77] There can be little doubt that when, following the Gregorian reform and rise of the secular schools, learned discourse on love, marriage and the nature of women confronted a complex of untamed, ungodly patterns of behaviour, Ovid's amatory advice added to the arsenal of clerical misogyny. Recent scholars have underlined the formative influence of his verse not only in the definition of gender roles but also in the designation of sexual identities, normative and transgressive.[78]

The change of emphasis in the schoolroom, from reading Ovid as a source for grammatical and rhetorical paradigms to recognition of his value as a stimulus for moral, ethical and philosophical reflections, gave rise to a succession of commentaries. Their multiplicity in manuscripts of the twelfth, thirteenth and fourteenth centuries has made them, and contiguous cribs, digests and epitomes, an early and enduring focus for studies of medieval criticism: it is from the prominent and well-preserved apparatus to Ovid that modern scholars have traced the evolution of the critical *schema* that shaped medieval readings of the classical canon as a whole.[79] The earliest systematic commentaries on Ovid addressed the first objective of the schoolmaster, the exposition of the literal sense of the text: Arnulf of Orléans's commentary on the *Metamorphoses*, dating from the last quarter of the twelfth century and described here by Frank Coulson, provides a philological survey of the text.[80] Another Orléans master, William, also provided elementary students and their masters with philological glosses on almost the entire Ovidian canon.[81] Yet the commentators were sensitive to the temper of the schoolroom and in the century after 1180 these student cribs were supplemented with surveys that laid bare the layers of ethical, moral and philosophical meanings. The *Metamorphoses* was always the focus of these works. Arnulf's *Allegoriae* was the earliest but the so-called Vulgate commentary of *c.* 1260 was undoubtedly the most influential: a compendium of criticism, it conflated the allegorical with the philological to provide a multivalent reading of the *Metamorphoses*.[82] The conception of Ovid not only as a stylist but also as a sage, whose authority might equate with those of acknowledged Augustan philosophers, led commentators also to develop biographical notes on the man himself.[83]

---

[77] See below, pp. 108–22 at 108.
[78] See, for example, Calabrese 1994; Desmond and Sheingorn 2001; Desmond 2006.
[79] Minnis and Scott 1991; Minnis and Johnson 2005.   [80] See below, pp. 50–5.
[81] See below, pp. 55–8.   [82] See below, pp. 65–70.   [83] See below, p. 54.

These were transmitted principally in the *accessus* summaries that preceded copies of the verse in many manuscripts and continued to evolve in individual manuscript anthologies even after the commentary tradition itself had receded.

The *accessus* tradition underlined the historical value of the Ovidian canon. In the early Middle Ages only the Hellenist annalists had sought *facta et dicta* from his verse, but the proliferation of universal histories after 1200 established Ovid not only as an authority for the early empire but also in the unfamiliar (and in many respects unsuitable) role as redactor of the ancient history of antiquity, and the Troy story at its heart, the tale of 'aged Priam's towering palace' (*Heroides* 1). Both the *Speculum historiale* of Vincent of Beauvais and the supremely popular *Polychronicon* of the English Benedictine Ranulf Higden shaped their narratives using Ovid.[84] In his *Estoria de España* (also called the *Primera Crónica General*) and his *General Estoria*, Alfonso X, the royal annalist of Spain, drew heavily from the *Metamorphoses* and the *Heroides*. The first instinct of these historians was to interpret the literal sense of the verse; rarely did Alfonso, for example, acknowledge a *fabliella* that might be resolved only allegorically.[85]

Historical interests perhaps provided the impulse for further translations: Maximos Planoudes' Greek texts of the amatory poetry, *Heroides* and *Metamorphoses*, which Elizabeth Fisher examines here, offered a digest of Latin heritage to citizens of fourteenth-century Constantinople.[86] Perhaps it was the prospect of Ovid in life, conversion and death, that provided the pretext for the translation of *De vetula* by Bernat Metge (1340–1413).[87]

The reading of Ovid in the early and high Middle Ages reflected monastic and secular priorities. The form and style of his verse served the practical demands of schoolroom; his subject matter stimulated, and, to a degree, informed, the ethical, moral and confessional (or conversion) discourse in which the cathedrals, courts and monasteries of this period were deeply engaged. Whilst it reinvigorated the religious establishment, the Gregorian movement inaugurated at the turn of the eleventh century did not alter these priorities. Yet the process of reform that followed it in the thirteenth century, initiated at the Fourth Lateran Council of 1215, and underpinned with the formation of the mendicant friars, introduced new imperatives into the teaching and practice of clerks. Its effects on the elementary syllabus were pronounced as the classical and Christian *auctores* were eclipsed by preceptive manuals on the 'primitive sciences' of logic and philosophy.

---

[84] Taylor 1966: 77–9 at 78; Wilkinson 1955: 380; Paulmier-Foucart *et al.* 1990; Lusignan *et al.* 1997.
[85] See below, pp. 232–9 at 234–5.   [86] See below, pp. 32–47 at 45.   [87] See below, pp. 242–4.

The ethical and moral discourse that had burgeoned, particularly among the advanced pupils and masters of the early monastic and secular schools, was now re-directed towards current clerical and pastoral concerns. The impact of this clerical programme on patterns of reading, and pedagogical exposition, has been traced, over the past half-century, in the books and writings of regular and secular scholars in the orbit of Oxford and Paris.[88]

Secular literature again edged to the margins in elementary schools of the thirteenth century – as Black notes here in the case of Italy – and was stifled in the formal studies of schools and universities, but the focus on the pastoral office fostered fresh approaches to the *fabulae poetarum*: the *Parabolae* of Odo of Cheriton (d. 1247) was perhaps the first manual to present the possibility of pagan fables to the post-1215 preacher.[89] Pastors now plundered the poets for *exempla* as readily as early schoolmasters had for their paradigms. Their enterprise has been retraced by modern scholars: there is no doubt Ovid was soon a favourite quarry.[90] His verse offered an abundance of loosely historical tales attractive and recognisable to learned and lay audiences of the later Middle Ages. The poems of exile conveyed lessons on fortune, fraternity, love and loss which matched the priorities of the medieval pastor. The drama, and *dramatis personae*, of the *Metamorphose*s enabled the preacher to explore profound themes, the nature of deity and man's subjection to spiritual and secular powers. It was from a copy of *Metamorphoses* garnered by the mendicant friars of Constantinople presumably for just such a purpose that Planoudes prepared his Greek translation.[91]

The preachers' predilection for literary *exempla* persisted into the fourteenth and fifteenth centuries. In England it was particularly prevalent among the generation of graduate clerks active in the pulpit between the death of Edward III (1377) and the accession of Henry VI (1422). Siegfried Wenzel examines their sermons here. In the age of Chaucer, Gower and Lydgate these *exempla* were surely familiar to the layfolk with whose pastoral care the preachers were charged, but as Wenzel argues, these sermons served an idiom of literary display inclusively fostered in circles of regular and secular clergy.[92] Moreover, it was a schism among the clergy that suppressed these secular influences: the spread of Wycliffite reform at the turn of the fourteenth century aroused hostility to those that 'began

[88] See, for example, Smalley 1960; D'Avray 1984; Baswell 1995.
[89] For Odo of Cheriton see Levy 2004. [90] See D'Avray 1984; Smalley 1960: 247–8.
[91] See below, pp. 32–46 at 33. [92] See below, pp. 169–71.

their theme with a poesy'.[93] It was not exclusive to regions touched by
Wyclif: Black documents the disapproval of the Florentine preacher Giovanni Dominici (1356–1420), dismayed at the return of Ovid to the school
curriculum.[94]

The reading of Ovid with the exegete's eye for moral capital reinforced
the allegorical commentary; inevitably *Metamorphoses* was the prime focus.
The genre was inaugurated by the *Integumenta Ovidii*, an analysis of *Metamorphoses* attributed to a Parisian clerk, John of Garland, active in the
second quarter of the thirteenth century.[95] Garland's removal of Ovid's
pagan garb was continued by the author of the pseudo-Ovidian *De vetula*,
who may have been Garland's near-contemporary. The text – which Ralph
Hexter examines here – represents the exiled Ovid in a mood of self-
reflection, eager to show the reader how he turned from the shallow pursuit
of pleasure to a philosophical mode in which he appeared to have some
premonition of the coming of Christ. As Hexter argues, amid moral sense
commentaries on the authentic Ovid, such *pseudo-epigrapha* should be
understood not as additions to the canon but as additional commentaries,
part of the 'para-Ovidian' *apparatus criticus*.[96] The capacity of this genre to
determine, distort and even eclipse Ovidian (and other) *originalia* is only
now emerging from codicological and textual fragments.

The school commentaries, and perhaps the 'Vulgate' commentary in
particular, presented later medieval readers with an Ovid that was incor-
rigibly plural. As Warren Ginsberg argues here, it was the multiplicity of
Ovids that moulded Dante's treatment of the poet, not only in the *Commedia* but also in earlier compositions including the *Vita nova*.[97] Like the
most severe of the moralising commentators, Dante challenged the *praeceptor* of love and the poet of exile, although as Ginsberg suggests it is not
personal but poetic integrity that is placed under scrutiny. In common
with the commentators on, and re-creators of, Ovid's allegory, Dante also
evinced unease at his metamorphoses but could not suppress them in his
own fictions.

Dante's ties to Ovid underline the fact that Trecento Florentines and
their early followers did not wholly detach themselves from the medieval
mainstream. As Robert Black shows here, the nascent humanist academies
not only of Florence but also Bologna and Cremona continued to venerate
Ovid and offered readings that would have been recognisable to Arnulf
and the masters of the Orléanais: Giovanni del Virgilio's *lecturae* on the

---

[93] See James Clark's essay below, p. 193. For the backlash against pagan literature among theologians
of radical and reformist cast see also now Kerby-Fulton 2005: 230, 350–7.
[94] See below, p. 142.   [95] Rigg 1992: 166–8.
[96] See below, pp. 284–92.   [97] See below, pp. 143–53.

Metamorphoses represent a recapitulation of the *Allegoriae* of Arnulf, refracted through the lens of Garland's *Integumenta* and the Vulgate commentary.[98] There was more than a trace of the preoccupations and methods of high medieval masters also in Petrarch's *Secretum* and Boccaccio's *Genealogia deorum gentilium*.[99] Petrarch's place in the revised preface of Pierre Bersuire's *Ovidius* should remind us there was no palpable partisan separation of Ovidians of this period.[100] Boccaccio's genealogy evokes the earliest investigations of Ovid's mythography in the school environment from which the Theodolan *Ecloga* emerged and connects him with the continuing mythographic researches of northern monastic scholars of the same period.[101]

Of course, the fourteenth century is commonly thought to represent a turning point in attitudes to the literature of antiquity. Scholars at the centre of the academic communities at Oxford and Paris appeared dissatisfied by the strictures of scholastic logic and philosophy and renewed their acquaintance with the authorities of an earlier era; their radical ultramontane counterparts rejected conventional curricula entirely in favour of an undiluted exposure to the lore of the pagans; meanwhile north and south the greater mobility of the monastic orders and the growth of professional book production generated a fresh supply of classical *originalia*. In the generation before the Black Death (1348–50), it might be suggested that ancient authors reached a wider audience than at any time since the inception of the secular schools. And the *cursus honorum* of *auctores* was apparently recast. When the Dominican Nicholas Trevet (d. after 1334) responded to the requests of patrons and colleagues and distilled his erudition in a series of weighty commentaries, he chose Boethius' *Consolatio* and the *Declamationes* and *Tragoediae* of Seneca.[102]

Yet there is no sign that Ovid's own star had fallen. The Ovidian canon had itself been renewed with the advent of the widely popular *spuria*, described here by Hexter. While the origins of *Halieutica* and the Virgilian prefaces were themselves tied to antiquity, others such as the *Nux*, and *De pediculo*, are known only from the advent of the *aetas Ovidiana*. *De vetula*, often attributed to Richard de Fournival (d. 1258), chancellor of Amiens, is distinguished among *pseudo-epigrapha* as perhaps the only example to be accepted beyond question among the authentic *opera*.[103] There are some

---

[98] See below, pp. 127–8.
[99] For Petrarch see 1993 ed. Dotti and Zak 2007, 2010. For Boccaccio's *Genealogia* see Wallace 2002.
[100] Pierre Bersuire 1960–6, which presents the 1509 printed text of the *Ovidius*, inclusive of the preface.
[101] See James Clark's essay below, p. 188.   [102] See Dean 1942, 1945, 1948.
[103] See below, pp. 304–8.

indications that transmission of the authentic Ovid was also reinvigorated. Book-lists from early fourteenth-century England bear witness to a lively turnover of manuscript copies, most notably of the *Metamorphoses*. It was perhaps in this phase of transmission that Ovid entered the non-Christian communities of Christendom: a copy of *Metamorphoses* was recorded in the possession of Jews in 1478, and this may be a late acknowledgement of an earlier acquaintance.[104]

The century after 1300 also saw a succession of influential commentaries. The most original was the *Ovide moralisé*, examined here by Ana Pairet, a work which in its vernacular verse rendered the fifteen books of the *Metamorphoses* into a series of resonant moral tales.[105] The methodology of the *Ovide moralisé* may have recalled John of Garland's *Integumenta*, but in its language and the manner of its exposition it reached out to a contemporary audience comprising both pastors and the lay devout. Yet it would be wrong to represent the *Ovide moralisé* author as purely preceptive. Although fables are re-written to reconcile the *materia* with their spiritual purpose, the rhetorical power of the Ovidian original remains: to read the *Ovide moralisé* was intentionally an aesthetic experience. Its appeal to a readership engaged in public and private devotion is reflected in the schemes of illustration with which it was sometimes associated in manuscript, described here by Carla Lord.[106] A Latin counterpart to the *Ovide moralisé* was composed, and repeatedly revised, before 1362 by Pierre Bersuire, first a friar and subsequently a Benedictine in the Île de France. His *Ovidius moralizatus* also recast the *Metamorphoses* as a compendium of *exempla* primarily for the preacher. The *Ovidius* supplanted earlier criticism and was perhaps the most popular literary commentary of the later Middle Ages.[107]

The *Ovide moralisé* – and, via the pulpit, the *Ovidius moralizatus* – transmitted the *materia* of the *Metamorphoses* to a readership unable to interpret the Latin text for themselves. The *Ovide moralisé* was a popular commission for lay patrons in the period of the Hundred Years War (1337–1443); deluxe copies were prepared for Clemence of Hungary and the prodigious book patron Duke Jean of Berry.[108] The profile of Ovidian figures in this vernacular milieu was raised further by the popular *Roman de Fauvel*, a faux epic attributed to Gervais du Bus, that in structure and (Ovidian) style recalled the Latin entertainments of the twelfth century.[109] Among the same readership, the exposure to Ovidian form and style was also widened

---

[104] See below, p. 278.　　[105] See below, pp. 83–107.　　[106] See below, pp. 261–70.
[107] Engels 1968.　　[108] See below, pp. 261, 265, 270.　　[109] Bent and Wathey 1997.

through the popular amatory poetry of Guillaume de Machaut (1300–77), whose works were sometimes transmitted in manuscript together with a selection of *pseudo-epigrapha* and *originalia*.[110] The familiarity of literate layfolk with the fables of *Metamorphoses* made them ideal figures for the treatment of contemporary themes: the Hainaulter Jean Froissart (*c.* 1337 – *c.* 1405) represented Gaston Fébus, Count of Foix-Béarn (d. 1391), as a demi-god and his death a replica of the twin fates of Callisto and Actaeon.[111]

It was perhaps the capacity of these popular commentaries to serve as surrogates for the *Metamorphoses* that gave rise to the mythographic discourse that was widespread in England, France and northern Italy in the century after 1350. The manuscripts surviving from this period preserve a rich array of mythographic authorities, among them early manuals, such as Fulgentius, later recreations such as the compendia of the second and third 'Vatican mythographers',[112] and the *Fulgentius metaforalis* of the fourteenth-century Franciscan John Ridevall (d. after 1340), and a repertory of anonymous cribs, genealogies and summaries of mythographic lore.[113] These texts were surely a symptom of and a stimulus for the study of Ovid in the shadow of the Black Death. The *anonyma* are often derived from the *Metamorphoses*, at least in part; they are commonly combined with Ovid's text or a prose digest of it. It was in this textual environment, as James Clark reveals here, that the English Benedictine Thomas Walsingham (*c.* 1340 – *c.* 1422) explored the *Metamorphoses* in a commentary of his own.[114] These preoccupations were not only a northern phenomenon. Walsingham's interests might bear comparison with his near-contemporaries Marqués de Santillana, don Íñigo López de Mendoza (d. 1458) and Alfonso de Madrigal (d. 1455), respectively authors of the *Libro mayor de las transformaciones* and the *Las diez cuestiones vulgares*.[115]

The reception of the *Ovide moralisé* and *Ovidius moralizatus* perhaps also reflects the emphatic return of Ovid to his former pre-eminence in the Latin schoolroom. Robert Black traces the second 'aetas Ovidiana' from Bologna in the lifetime of Dante and del Virgilio to Arezzo, Cremona and Padua in the mid fourteenth century, an advance driven by the teaching of Albertino Mussato (1261–1329) and (perhaps especially) Domenico di Bandino

---

[110] See, for example, BN, fonds Francais, 881. A note on the front flyleaf (verso) underlines the substantive link between the ancient master and his fourteenth-century imitator: 'Ovide de la vielle auquel sont contenuz / plusiers nobles ditz et enseignementz / ensemble le livre de l'art d'amour / Davantage les dicts amoureux de Guillaume de Machault' (Ovid's *De vetula* containing many noble poems and lessons; the entire *Ars amatoria*; in addition the amorous *dites* of Guillaume de Machaut). For Machaut see also Butterfield 2002; Cerquiglini and Wilkins 2002.
[111] Fyler 2009: 413.   [112] Bode 1834. For the third Vatican Mythographer see also Sharpe 1997: 35.
[113] See below, pp. 187, 195.   [114] See below, pp. 189, 192.   [115] See below, pp. 245, 247–9.

(d. 1418).[116] Petrarch's preference for Ovidian maxims in *Rerum memo-randarum libri* surely reflects his proverbial presence in the schoolrooms of his own time and that of his first readers.[117] It is possible to see parallels to his Italian resurgence with the reinvigorated interest in Ovid in the claustral *scholae* of England in the fourteenth and fifteenth centuries.[118] There are perhaps further parallels to be found in the teaching of grammar, rhetoric and metre in the monasteries and schools of France and the Low Countries at the turn of the fourteenth century.[119] Of course, the masters of this generation were no less conscious of the controversy that had long surrounded Ovid. The anonymous *Antiovidianus*, once attributed to Petrarch, and certainly of a school origin, condemned him for concealing such ugly matter in so beautiful a cloak.[120]

It was in the same climate in the second half of the fourteenth century that Geoffrey Chaucer and John Gower confronted the Ovidian tradition. As Kathryn McKinley argues here, in his early verse Chaucer regarded Ovid just as his romance forebears had, as *praeceptor amoris* par excellence: 'Venus clerk, Ovide / that hath ysowen wonder wide / the grete god of love's name' (*House of Fame* 1487–9). Chaucer's appetite for the amatory Ovid reflected the tastes of his vernacular milieu: a Middle Dutch contemporary, Dirc Potter (*c.* 1340–1428), compiled *Der minnen loep*, a manual formed from the *Heroides* and *Metamorphoses*, which recalled the foundation of the romance tradition.[121] Yet in the *Canterbury Tales*, incomplete at his death, Chaucer's approach, and appropriations, were not only more nuanced but also more clearly attuned to contemporary clerical readings. In particular, coupling the Ovidian *Manciple's Tale* with the *Parson's Tale*, he uncovers the moral *sensus* of the principal fable (of the first tale), a mode of criticism that connects him – perhaps surprisingly for proponents of a secular Chaucer – with readers of *Ovidius moralizatus* and *Ovide moralisé*.[122] By contrast, Gower was bound only by the intended contemporary import of his verse. While he shared the moral sensibility of his clerical cast – Chaucer commended him as 'moral Gower' (*Troilus and Criseyde* 5.1856) – it is striking how often his Ovidian matter was deployed in a present-minded, political discourse;[123] and while Chaucer's use of *originalia* is speculative, without doubt Gower was deeply bound to the text and frequently fused Ovid's

---

[116] See below, pp. 124–5, 127, 130, 133, 137.   [117] See below, pp. 128–9.   [118] See below, pp. 189–92.
[119] See below, pp. 67, 195–6.   [120] Kienast 1929: 79–111. See also Hexter 1986: 96–9.
[121] Van Buuren 1995.   [122] See below, pp. 221–30. For Chaucer see also Fleming 2003.
[123] For further discussion see also McKinley 2007. The appropriation of Ovidian figures for the purposes of political and public discourse has become a popular theme in contemporary literary criticism: See also Nolan 2004; Peck 2004; and, for the early modern period, Rogers 2005 on Alexander Pope.

words with his own, to underpin his own purpose with the Roman poet's voice.[124]

Their facility with Ovid's imagery and style informed later English poets – John Lydgate (*c.* 1371–1449), for example, a Benedictine also exposed to the mythographic tradition of Walsingham – but the reprisal of Ovidian *amatoria* aroused an aggressive response from Christine de Pizan (*c.* 1363–1434).[125] Her conception of Ovid challenged more than two centuries of courtly tradition: he was the anti-praeceptor, leading his readers away from understanding: 'homs qui vault, selon ce livre faire, n'amera ja' (*Epistre au dieu d'amor* 374–5). Like Chaucer (and Dante) Christine substituted one Ovid for another and from *Heroides* and *Metamorphoses* presented her readers with a prospect of women worthy to be loved virtuously. The role of Ovidian authority in the formulation of a counter-argument to conventional amatory paradigms which were in origin Ovidian is now a primary focus for contemporary critics.

Ovid flourished in a society that knew antiquity only from fragments which aroused in it both fancy and fear. Later medieval movements in art, literature and scholarship – not all of which were ultramontane – transformed Christendom's conception of the classical past and its cultural legacy. Between 1350 and 1500, an abundance of ancient authors, texts and ideas entered European circulation for the first time. Readings in the poetry and prose of republic and empire were no longer confined to the preferences of monastic compilers clumsily captured in manuscript five centuries earlier. The foundations of grammar, rhetoric and metre were revealed from beneath layers of late antique and early medieval accretion following the original guides from Greece and Rome. The monopoly of Latin itself was threatened with an influx of Greek teachers and texts. Moreover, the methods and values of antiquity, in elementary education, in ethics, moral philosophy and, arguably, also theology, were now employed to reinvigorate conventional patterns of thought.

As a larger and more varied canvas of the classical world was revealed, one might expect the reputation of the unorthodox exile to have been revised. Yet there is no indication that Ovid was displaced in the fifteenth century either from the teaching and learning of clerks or the reading patterns of vernacular society. His works continued to circulate in manuscript and

---

[124] The suspicion that Chaucer's knowledge of Ovid was at second hand persists, yet contemporary readers recognised the proximity of Chaucer's readings to the *originalia*: a fifteenth-century Troilus was glossed with line references: Fyler 2009: 420. The manuscript in question is BL, Harley MS 2392. See also below, pp. 197–230.

[125] For Lydgate see Nolan 2004. For Christine de Pizan see Kellogg 1998.

not infrequently were selected for the deluxe codices now prepared for prominent humanist scholars and their patrons. Coluccio Salutati (1331–1406), Chancellor of Florence, as Robert Black relates, made two notable acquisitions, an anthology containing the *Amores*, *Ars*, *Fasti* and *Heroides* (New York, Pierpont Morgan Library, MS M 810) and another of *Fasti* (London, BL, Harley MS 2655). Book-collectors hunted rarities particularly on the periphery of the canon: the *epistula Sapphus* and the *Halieutica* were rediscoveries of the fifteenth century.[126]

There is no doubt the pioneer printers – Pannartz and Sweinheim, Jenson – favoured Cicero, the *magister princeps* of humanist Latin, but editions of the amatory poetry, the *Metamorphoses* and the verses of exile were frequently printed between 1471 and 1525.[127] The earliest printed *Metamorphoses* appeared at Bologna in 1471, the work of editor Francesco dal Pozzo under the patronage of Cardinal Francesco de Gonzaga but perhaps the most influential was Raffaele Regio's text, the first authorised imprint of which appeared in 1493.[128] In England, William Caxton translated one of the two prose renderings of the *Ovide moralisé*, perhaps initially as a personal commission – a single, illustrated manuscript in the Burgundian style survives – but also possibly for an imprint never realised.[129]

The editorial enterprise of this period refreshed the canon and reinforced Ovid's value for a generation of Latinists endowed with a far richer fund of stylistic models than any of their predecessors. The noble poetaster René d'Anjou (1409–80) imagined Ovid as the first occupant of the cemetery at his fabulous *Hôpital d'amour*, where he would also inter Boccaccio and Petrarch.[130] René's taste was more inclined to the *Roman de la Rose* than to contemporary humanism, but his attachment was shared by many of the cultural *avant-garde*. Angelo Poliziano (1454–94) marked his self-imposed separation from the Florence of Lorenzo de Medici (1449–92) with a sequence of Ovidian verses: from *Ex Ponto* and *Tristia* he derived not only the voice of the lonely exile but also the personae of poet and patron, Lorenzo as Augustus *alter*.[131] Lorenzo's own oeuvre was overtly Ovidian.

---

[126] See below, pp. 293n, 294 &n.

[127] The second printed edition of *Metamorphoses*, made by Joannes Andreas, was printed under the device of Pannartz and Sweinheim in 1471 but did not achieve a wide readership before the failure of the press: Steiner 1951: 219–31 at 224.

[128] For dal Pozzo see Steiner 1951: 219–31 at 223. An edition of Regio's *Metamorphoses* printed without the editor's permission appeared at Venice in 1492. The printing of the following year was at the same city. See also Steiner 1951: 219–31 at 22; Davies 1996; Moss 1998; Knox 2009a: 327–54 at 338.

[129] The manuscript is now in two parts held at Magdalene College, Cambridge: Old Library, MS F 1 34 and Pepys Library, MS 2124; see also the cover image of this volume. See also Jung 1997.

[130] Earp 1995: 64.   [131] McGowan 2005: 25–45 at 38.

Ambra recalled the *Metamorphoses*, the eponymous heroine's pursuit by the river god Ombrone an analogue for the transformation of Arethusa.[132] There were contrary voices, of course: perhaps it was the predominance of clerks (regular and secular) at the inception of the northern renaissance that accounts for early discomfort at the *praeceptor amoris*, that '[the] master of love, is [held to be] of greater intelligence than . . . Virgil, father of poets'.[133]

The capturing of the canon in print also stimulated the first systematic criticism for almost a century. Domizio Calderini (1446–78) composed the first printed commentary on *Ibis*, Ovid's exile elegiacs, published in 1474, in which, perhaps inevitably, as a papal courtier himself, he was drawn to the personal dynamics of the poet's expulsion from Rome.[134] Regio's *Enarrationes* recast the *Metamorphoses* for the first readers that were fully conscious of the collateral origins of ancient culture: a Latin memorial to the pioneers of Greek history, myth and poetry, it was a compelling expression of the humanist credo, an 'exemplar totius humanae civilis vitae'.[135] Poliziano himself contributed to a deeper understanding of Ovid's art, correcting Calderini's comically clumsy readings of *Ibis* and delineating the sources of *Fasti* and the distance between the Greek exemplar of (for example) *Fasti* 1.357–8, and its Latin rendition.[136] The philological precision of Ovid's humanist admirers did not efface all trace of earlier critical approaches. In 1510, Regio's *Enarrationes* were coupled in print with a commentary which recalled the moralising compendium of Bersuire and, like its popular predecessor, packaged the *Metamorphoses* primarily as a manual for preachers: its Dominican author, Pierre Lavin, reversed the work of philological restoration undertaken by Regio and Poliziano and revived the prose paraphrases of Ovid's fables which once proliferated in manuscript.[137]

In a social milieu that now sought to surround itself with the forms and styles of antiquity, Ovid attracted renewed interest as a source of artistic inspiration. The rich resources of their classicism are reflected in a range of contemporary pieces, although criticism cannot always easily distinguish

---

[132] Barolsky 1998: 451–74 at 457.

[133] 'magistrum illum amoris Ovidium, quia forsan illi vacat, prefato poetarum, parente Virgilio, prothnefas, ingenii excellentioris asseveravit extitisse' ('Ovid, master of love, is of greater intelligence than our aforesaid Virgil, father of poets'). The voice is that of Jean de Montreuil (1354–1418): *Epistola* 129, lines 18–19: 'dictu mirum et terribile cogitatu, magistrum illum amoris Ovidium, quia forsan illi vacat prefato poetarum parento Virgilio prothnefas . . . ', in Jean de Montreuil 1963–86, vol. 1: 187–91.

[134] Steiner 1951: 219–31 at 229.   [135] Coon 1930: 277–90 at 280.

[136] Grafton 1994: 47–75; Knox 2009a: 327–54 at 335.

[137] Allen 1971: 52, 81–3. Grafton 1985: 615–49 at 620; Moss 2003: 245 &n.

Ovidian influence from those drawn from a common fund of classical reference: the spalliera panels of Giovanni Tornabuoni, recently described, are a case in point.[138] Certainly traces of Ovidian themes are visible in a variety of media, and via canvasses, maiolica and painted panels, they passed from an institutional into a domestic environment. At the Villa Madama, decorated by Romano, Cardinal Giulio de Medici was said to have selected Ovid in preference to the Old Testament.[139] Michelangelo Buonarroti's *Venus and Cupid* was perhaps intended as decoration for a bedchamber.[140] It was in the exclusive circle of Florentine connoisseurs – Lorenzo, certainly, but also his satellites, the patrons of Sandro Botticelli, Piero di Cosimo, Mantegna and Antonio del Pollaiuolo – that his influence was most conspicuous. The fables retained their power and beyond narrative these artists were inspired by the notion of metamorphosis itself.[141]

In fact the figure of Ovid aroused a new fascination in the historical imagination. Commemorative statues were erected: apparently a bust was placed at the city gate at Sulmona, and additional representations were apparent elsewhere; certainly a statue was erected at the Palazzo Pretorio in 1474. Sulmona also employed an Ovidian motto for its seal: 'Sulmo mihi patria est.'[142] Humanists reflected upon, and searched for, his tomb, as they did those of Livy and Virgil.[143]

Perhaps only in the pre-Reformation decades, as the ideals of the humanists became identified closely with the causes of Mother Church, did European scholars question the status of Ovid. Proud of the greater legacy from Greek and Latin antiquity which they enjoyed, they expressed a new doubt over Ovid's claim to be an *auctor* of the first rank. Erasmus of Rotterdam did not 'his proper name forget' in frequent reminiscences in his popular *Adages*,[144] but he confided in a correspondent that he was 'privately indignant' at those that still chose Ovid as their stylistic model in preference to the Christian poets; he acknowledged his 'fluency' but it was to be contrasted with the 'happy rightness of Virgil'.[145] An unnamed scholar of the time of Pope Leo X was said to have translated the *Metamorphoses* into Italian to spare the damage that Ovid's Latin might do to his son's own style.[146] Of course, in the face of perhaps irrevocable schism, stylistic scruples were soon eclipsed by moral imperatives and the integumental

---

[138] For the general problem of criticism see Perlman 2007: 223–38 at 23. For Tornabuoni see Campbell 2007.

[139] Martindale 1988: 152.   [140] Perlman 2007: 225.

[141] Allen 2002; Barolsky 1998: 451–74 at 452–7.   [142] McHam 2005.   [143] Trapp 1973: 41.

[144] See, for example, *Adages*, ii.i.4; ii.i.79; ii.iii.96 (Barker 2001: 59, 79, 187).

[145] Mynors, *et al.* 1974–, vol. i: 97, 103 (Letters 48–9).   [146] Trapp 1973: 39.

Ovid of commentators, preachers and the lay *devotus* was reinvigorated for another generation.

The medieval Ovid is the achievement of a century of modern textual scholarship. The key components in the history of his post-classical reception have all been recovered since the turn of the nineteenth century: the identification and interpretation of the *Ovide moralisé*, the *Ovidius moralizatus* and the Vulgate commentary are landmarks of twentieth-century criticism;[147] the *stemma codicum* of Ovidian *originalia* has evolved over the same course, with key exemplars emerging from codicological and palaeographical analysis over the past twenty years.[148] The transmission and reception of Ovid are now better documented than for any other classical *auctor*. It is not only texts that have been recovered but also critical contexts – the monastic *scholae* of the Anglo-Saxon reformation, the schoolrooms of the Orléanais, the academies of humanist lectors like del Virgilio.[149] The textual traces of Ovid have also revealed the complex of clerical, confessional and personal perspectives that guided readers from the age of reform and renewal in the twelfth century to the resurgence of heresy and schism two centuries on. Bearing the imprint of the cultural and social dynamics of high and later Middle Ages, the Ovidian tradition has served to unlock conceptions of identity, sexuality and even the figuring of the body for a new generation of medievalists. In the pursuit of these studies, the corpus has also proved a fertile ground for the propagation of novel modes of criticism: here historicism, intertextuality and queer theory have each been pioneered; by means of the post-classical Ovid (among other stimuli) Reception Studies has also entered the scholarly mainstream.[150] Of course, we must be cautious of the predominance of Ovid in modern scholarship, as in the surviving manuscript fragments themselves. The medieval Ovid stands not as a monument to the monotone classicism of medieval Europe, but as a symptom of its likely breadth, depth and capacity for reinvention. There are analogues (for other *auctores*) to almost every form of reception evidenced here, many of which are yet to be examined. Ovid, medieval Europe's guide to the classical world, can lead us into the classical Middle Ages.

---

[147] *Ovide moralisé*, ed. de Boer 1915–38; Reynolds 1971, 1978, 1990; Coulson and Roy 2000 (*Ovidius moralizatus*); Coulson 1985, 1987b, 1990, 1991 (Vulgate).

[148] Buttenwieser 1940; Ovid 1951, 1957; Kenney 1962; Ovid 1977c; Tarrant 1983.

[149] Engelbrecht 2006.   [150] Martindale 1988; Burger and Kruger 2001.

CHAPTER 2

Ovid's metempsychosis
The Greek East

Elizabeth Fisher

We know Ovid the mythographer, Ovid the rhetorician, Ovid the poet, Ovid *amator* – but *Ovidius Graecus*? In the thirteenth century Ovid did indeed undergo a sort of metempsychosis, translated into classicising Greek by the Byzantine monk Maximos Planoudes (*c.* 1255 – *c.* 1305). Planoudes transformed Ovid's *Metamorphoses, Heroides* and amatory poems into stylish prose versions for the *Nova Roma*, medieval Constantinople. Although Planoudes is the most familiar Greek author associated with Ovid, he may not have been Ovid's first impresario in the Greek literary tradition. Before examining Planoudes' Byzantine translations, let us take as a prelude the work of scholars who have maintained that Ovid, the shape-shifting poet, influenced the learned literature of late antique Hellenism and early Byzantium.

Modern detectives attempting to catch Ovid in the literature of late antique Hellenism have prowled the epic poetry of the period for evidence of his presence in shared mythological data, common sequences of events or argumentation, similarities in character portrayal, and metaphor. In short, scholars have searched for the evidence of sources that skilful authors tend to reveal only in order to impress an audience familiar with those sources. Lurking in the shadowy background of this continuing investigation is the possibility that Ovid and his putative imitators shared common sources now lost. Although the search for Ovidian influence is fraught with risk, for more than a century scholars have enthusiastically pursued Ovid in Greek epic poetry produced between the late third and the end of the fifth century by poets whose careers brought them to Alexandria, Antioch, Palestinian Caesarea, or Constantinople. In these cosmopolitan centres of the eastern Roman Empire, Greek and Latin coexisted with local languages (e.g., Coptic and Syriac) as the languages of administration and culture.

I am grateful to my colleague Dr Denis Sullivan of the University of Maryland for his sage advice and timely encouragement as I prepared this article.

In this cultural context authors continued the noble tradition of Hellenistic poetry, delving into classical mythology for their subject matter and assuming a polished and sophisticated Greek style in fulsome writings that resembled the literary epics of Rome. Although Virgil has been the primary focus of such research, Ovid too has been the object of investigation and speculation. The 'poets of interest' in this process are Triphiodoros, Quintus of Smyrna and Nonnos.

Triphiodoros of Egypt (third or early fourth century) has left one surviving poem, *The Capture of Troy*, as well as reports of several lost works – the *Story of Hippodamea*, a 'Missing-letter *Odyssey*',[1] a *Marathoniaca*, and a collection of paraphrased Homeric similes; Quintus of Smyrna (third century) supplemented Homer's *Iliad* and *Odyssey* with his own fourteen-book *Posthomerica* describing events bridging Homer's epics; Nonnos of Panopolis in Egypt (*fl.* 450–70) attempted to surpass Homer with his forty-eight book *Dionysiaca* tracing the birth, battles and eventual triumph of the god.[2] Let us now examine the late antique cultural context that might have induced these Greek literati to borrow from such Latin poets as Ovid and Virgil.[3]

Although the *lingua franca* of the eastern Mediterranean was Greek, Latin was the language of law, the army and civil administration, as well as the vehicle chosen by Roman officials for their correspondence with one another. Life in this world is best documented in Roman Egypt, where an abundance of papyrus documents survives, excavated from the trash heaps of settlements abandoned in late antiquity.[4] The small Egyptian towns of Oxyrhynchus and Antinoupolis yield up evidence of some level of Latin culture, possibly encouraged by the presence and prestige of Roman officialdom in Egypt. Papyrus finds indicate that Virgil, Cicero, Sallust and even Juvenal and Lucan were read, perhaps by students aspiring to a career connected with Roman administration. Obscure Latin texts could also travel east with the Roman military, as demonstrated by an astonishing papyrus find in 1978 at the remote desert fortress of Qasr Ibrim in Egyptian Nubia. Nine lines of the first-century Augustan poet C. Cornelius Gallus emerged from the sand on a papyrus dated to 50 BCE – 25 CE, nearly contemporary with the poet's own lifetime. The fragment not only illustrates Ovid's

---

[1] An exercise in mental gymnastics requiring the author to avoid using one letter of the alphabet in paraphrasing each of the *Odyssey*'s twenty-four books; Triphiodoros' predecessor, L. Septimius Nestor (second century CE), composed a 'Missing-letter *Iliad*'.

[2] See the individual entries for these authors in the *OCD³* 1996.

[3] Most recently, Ursula Gärtner has examined this topic (Gärtner 2005: 13–22). I am grateful to an anonymous reader for bringing this book to my attention.

[4] Bagnall 1993: 231–4.

observation in *Tristia* 4.10.53 that Gallus originated the Latin love elegy but also increases the body of his surviving poetry nine-fold.[5] (Previously, Gallus' legacy consisted of only five words: '... uno tellures diuidit amne duas' [... with one river divides two countries]). Because we meet Latin authors in such Egyptian backwaters as Qasr Ibrim, Oxyrhynchus and Antinoupolis, it is at least plausible that Latin literature was available in even greater variety and quantity in Alexandria, the great administrative and cultural centre of Egypt that boasted a long and celebrated tradition of classical scholarship. In fact, in the fifth century Alexandria attracted the philosopher Proclus and Severus, future patriarch of Antioch, to study grammar and rhetoric in both Greek and Latin.[6]

Although Ovid has not yet been identified among the Latin authors surviving on papyrus from Egypt, his learned, lengthy and stylish poems offer obvious attractions to the Greek scholar-poets of late antiquity. In Constantinople, Constantine's freshly 'latinized' capital, or in Alexandria, storehouse of a great treasure of Greek literature now lost, these poets may have encountered and mined the poems of Ovid. Such, at least, is the assumption behind scholarship of the twentieth century that has traced Ovidian influence in the mythological poems of late antiquity. Johannes Irmscher summarised this trend, citing Schanz-Hosius' influential *Geschichte der römischen Literatur* (4th edn., 1935) as a particular locus of the belief that Quintus of Smyrna and Triphiodoros used Ovid's poetry.[7] By mid century, enthusiasm for this idea began to cool and to condense into doubt. Francis Vian[8] denied that Quintus of Smyrna demonstrates any acquaintance with Latin poetry, instead promoting lost Hellenistic poems and mythological handbooks as the common source both for Quintus and for Virgil, Ovid and Seneca, the Latin poets Quintus supposedly imitated. In an extended review of Vian's work, Rudolph Keydell mustered formidable arguments to refute Vian's contention, demonstrating in painstaking detail that Virgil, Seneca and Ovid stood behind passages of the *Posthomerica*; he asserted that Quintus' treatment of Ajax contemplating the arms of Achilles in *Posthomerica* 5.180–236 so closely parallels Ovid's *Metamorphoses* 13.1–127 not only in its theme but also in its argumentation that Ovid was 'extremely likely' (*hochwahrscheinlich*) to be Quintus' source.[9] Despite Keydell's powerful and persistent influence upon scholarly opinion, Irmscher did observe that Ovid's name apparently was not familiar in the Greek East, since Eusebius in the fourth century did not include Ovid in the roster of notable

[5] Anderson *et al.* 1979: 125–8 and 140–8.
[6] Cameron 1965: 494–5.   [7] Irmscher 1974: 28–9.   [8] Vian 1959.
[9] Keydell 1961: 280–1. Ursula Gärtner has recently taken a cautiously optimistic view of Virgil's *Aeneid* as a possible source for Quintus' *Posthomerica* (Gärtner 2005: 279–87).

Latin authors listed in his influential *Chronicle*. Like Eusebius, the later Byzantine chroniclers John Malalas in the sixth century and George the Synkellos in the late eighth century do not mention Ovid. If Ovid had been so important to the writers of late Greek epic, why was he ignored by chroniclers who knew not only Virgil and Livy but also Horace, Sallust, Terence, and Hortensius?[10]

Proponents of Ovidian influence on Nonnos' *Dionysiaca,* however, seemed until recently to be betting on a winner in the Ovidian influence sweepstakes. Julius Braune launched the idea in 1935 and gained Keydell's immediate endorsement of his proposition that Ovid's account of Phaethon's exploits in *Metamorphoses* 1.747–2.398 was the template for Nonnos' narrative in *Dionysiaca* 38.105–434;[11] Peter Knox noted in 1988 that the link between Ovid and Nonnos had become scholarly orthodoxy. Knox, however, argued forcefully and carefully against such a link, citing evidence of multiple lost Hellenistic sources for Phaethon's story and questioning why Nonnos would allude to a Latin author whose works were probably unknown to his audience when Greek sources were readily available.[12] In his recent study of Nonnos, R. Shorrock recognises that Ovid's *Metamorphoses* provides the only parallel for Nonnos' complex coordination of different narratives within a controlling structure but nevertheless considers Ovidian influence on Nonnos 'unproven'.[13] 'Unproven influence of Latin authors!' is the unanimous verdict of a recent conference on late Greek epic, where participants favoured instead lost Hellenistic sources as the missing link between the Latin and Greek epic traditions. The conference organiser observes in his introduction to the published proceedings of the conference: 'As was to be expected, the vexed question of the relationship of later Greek authors with Latin literary texts comes up more than once, but no writer in this volume argues for direct imitation of Latin poetry.'[14] Our playful and elusive Ovid seems to have slipped out of a place in the Greek world of late antiquity, for in no Greek literature of the period have scholars been able to isolate an example of proven linguistic imitation from Latin, a feat 'notoriously difficult', as Mary Whitby observes, 'where translation is involved'.[15]

If we are to catch Ovid in the Greek world of late antiquity, we must turn to Latin authors of the period whose origins and Latin education can be traced to Egypt or Syro-Palestine and whose Latin writings might contain a sure instance of linguistic imitation. Joseph Geiger has assembled several familiar fourth-century Latin authors belonging to this group,

---

[10] Irmscher 1974: 29.   [11] Braune 1935.   [12] Knox 1988: 536–51.
[13] Shorrock 2001 reviewed by Whitby 2002: 283–4.   [14] Paschalis 2005: 2.
[15] Whitby 1985: 512.

i.e., Ammianus Marcellinus, Eutropius and Claudian; he also argues per-
suasively that Priscian (late fifth to early sixth century), dean of Latin
grammarians, should be included as well because the epithet 'Caesariensis'
applied in several manuscripts and by two of his students identifies him
as a native of (Greek-speaking) Palestinian Caesarea.[16] Geiger suggests that
other Greek-speakers of the East wrote learned Latin without achieving the
fame of a Priscian or a Claudian. He illustrates this contention by noting
the anonymous oriental author of *Alcestis Barcinonensis*, a Latin hexameter
poem preserved by happy chance on a recently published papyrus fragment
from Egypt.[17]

That Ovid's poetry may have been familiar to well-educated Greek
authors writing in Latin seems at least plausible in the light of Claudian's
career and literary output. Born in Egypt and educated in Alexandria, Claudian wrote his first poetry in Greek, turning his hand to Latin poetry with
equal ease and skill shortly after arriving in Rome in 394.[18] Almost immediately upon his arrival in the West, Claudian's Latin poetry reveals extensive
and ready familiarity with the works of Ovid as well as of Virgil, Lucan,
Statius, Valerius Flaccus, Silius Italicus and Juvenal; Cameron believes that
Claudian had read and studied these major poets of Golden and Silver Age
Latin while still in Alexandria.[19] Significantly for our investigation Claudian knew Ovid's poetry in sufficient depth to pattern his own metrical
practice on Ovid and to imitate the beginning of the *Metamorphoses* in his
unfinished epic *De raptu Proserpinae*.[20] Recently Brett Mulligan has identified additional verbal and thematic parallels between Claudian's *Deprecatio
ad Hadrianum* and Ovid's *Tristia* 5.6.[21] Peter Knox, however, doubts that
Claudian pursued serious study of Ovid's poetry before arriving in Rome
from the Greek East: 'His [Claudian's] reading of Ovid need not have been
much earlier than his first productions in Latin. For what it is worth, there
is no trace of Latin influence in his surviving Greek verse.'[22] Does the
phrase 'unproven influence' once again frustrate us in our quest after Ovid
in the Greek East? Has our master of illusion once again escaped us?

Since we have encountered so little success in tracing Ovidian influence on the late antique poets of the Greek world, it is startling to find
Ovid paraphrased and cited by name in two prose texts of sixth- and
seventh-century Constantinople. The scholar and antiquarian John the
Lydian (490 – *c.* 565), who obtained a professorship at Constantinople

---

[16] Geiger 1999: 606–17.   [17] Geiger 1999: 613.   [18] Cameron 1970: 2 and 22–9.
[19] Cameron 1970: 316.   [20] Cameron 1970: 344.   [21] Mulligan 2005: 277–80.
[22] Knox 1988: 551 n. 70.

with the support of the Latin-speaking emperor Justinian I, emphasised in his writings Byzantine continuity with the classical Roman heritage.[23] John's single citation of Ovid is to the *Fasti* and occurs in his *De mensibus* (*History of Calendars*), where it illustrates this concern: Ὀβίδιος ὁ Ῥωμαῖος Ἰανὸν ἀλληγορεῖ τὸ χάος εἶναι' (Ovid the Roman allegorically interprets chaos to be Janus).[24] Barry Baldwin first identified this allusion, commenting perceptively that John only cited Ovid by name because he thought his contemporaries would recognise the identity of the poet and admire John's familiarity with this Latin text.[25] A second author of the early Byzantine period who considered Ovid's work prestigious enough to merit direct citation is the early seventh-century chronicler John of Antioch. Umberto Roberto, the most recent editor of John's fragmentary universal history, dates his activity to the first quarter of the seventh century and locates him in Constantinople, where John could draw upon rich library resources to cite liberally both Greek and Latin authors.[26] Roberto's *index locorum* includes one passage from Ovid within an impressive collection of citations from classical and late antique Latin authors.[27] In fragment 2 of his history, John of Antioch alludes to Ovid's *Metamorphoses* 2.151–62: 'τοῦτο ἱστοροῦσι <οἱ Ἕλληνες> καὶ λέγουσι τὸν υἱὸν τοῦ Ἡλίου εἶναι, ὃν Φαέθοντα εἶπον, πεπτωκότα ἐκ τοῦ ἅρματος εἰς τὴν γῆν. Καὶ ποιητικῶς μὲν οὕτω τὴν ἱστορίαν συνεγράψατο Ὀβίδιος, ἀληθέστερον δὲ εἶπεν ὁ Χαιρωνεὺς Πλούταρχος' (<The Greeks> give an account of this fire, and they say that there was a son of Helios, who they said (was) Phaethon, that fell from his chariot to the earth. And thus Ovid described the story in poetic terms, while Plutarch of Chaironea told it more realistically). It is an endorsement of Ovid that John considers his information in the same context as that from Plutarch, for the Greek author enjoyed an excellent reputation in Byzantium.[28]

After that last honourable but brief cameo appearance in a Greek text, Ovid disappears for a time from the literature of the medieval Greek world. The late tenth-century Souda lexicon significantly omits any mention of

---

[23] *ODB* 1991: 1061–2. We may now add the sixth-century historian Agathias (*c.* 532 – *c.* 580) to this select company of early Byzantine authors who incorporated Ovidian texts into their writings; for a persuasive demonstration that Agathias adapted a passage from Ovid's *Metamorphoses*, see Alexakis 2008, which appeared too recently to be incorporated into the argument of this essay.

[24] Cf. Ovid, *Fasti* 1.103, where Janus speaks: 'me Chaos antiqui (nam sum res prisca) vocabant'. Translations into English are my own unless otherwise credited.

[25] Baldwin 1987: 3.   [26] Roberto 2005: xi–xxiii.

[27] Cicero (1), Eutropius (127), *Historia Augusta* (8), Livy (12), Sallust (2), Seneca (1), Suetonius (17), Tacitus (7), Valerius Maximus (2) and Virgil (2).

[28] *ODB* 1991: 1687–8.

Ovid or his writings from its myriad entries elucidating a farrago of biblical, classical Greek, and Roman persons, places and institutions.[29] Some 650 years elapsed until Ovid reappeared emphatically and indisputably in the Greek literature of the thirteenth century, summoned up in elegant Greek versions of the *Metamorphoses*, *Heroides*, and amatory poems translated by the scholarly monk Maximos Planoudes. Current classical scholarship on Ovid tends to take little notice of these translations, as Joseph Farrell recently commented in reviewing *The Cambridge Companion to Ovid*: 'There is passing reference only to Maximos Planoudes' Greek translation of the *Heroides*, but not to his *Metamorphoses*. Admittedly, neither work is the most influential or representative of the many translations and imitations of Ovid's poetry, but any notice of Latin literature in the Greek east in any period is sufficiently unusual to invite some attention.'[30] Indeed, we shall see that Planoudes and his translations from Latin provide an interesting insight into the reception of Ovid in a proudly Greek society generally hostile to and suspicious of the West, its crusaders and the languages, religion and literature associated with them.[31] A brief examination of the role taken by Latin in Planoudes' scholarly activities will serve to introduce in context his Ovid translations. In discussing Planoudes' biography and scholarship, I shall supplement the basic information found in seminal articles by Carl Wendel[32] and by Wolfgang O. Schmitt[33] with more recent studies that have broadened and deepened our understanding of the translations and their significance for the so-called 'Palaeologan Renaissance'.

At some point soon after Michael VIII Palaeologus expelled the short-lived Latin Crusader Kingdom from Constantinople and restored the Byzantines to their ancestral capital, a youthful Planoudes (*c.* 1255 – *c.* 1305) joined the imperial chancery as a scribe. Even at this early stage in his career, Planoudes knew Latin at a fairly sophisticated literary level, as he demonstrated in the sections he copied for a manuscript completed in 1280, Florence, BML Plut. MS 32.16. Planoudes both supervised the team that executed the manuscript and copied sections from Justinian's *Institutiones* in Latin and in the Greek paraphrase by Theophilos Antecessor; he also inserted marginalia supplying the Latin words *nepos* and *vitulus* as gratuitous glosses to Greek words occurring in other parts of the manuscript text.[34] Although Planoudes does not reveal how or why he learned Latin, Constantinople provided both opportunity and incentive for a talented student of the time to learn the language key to diplomatic and ecclesiastical

[29] *ODB* 1991: 1930–1.   [30] Farrell 2004.   [31] *ODB* 1991: 1183 and Kazhdan, 2001: 83–100.
[32] Wendel 1940: 2202–53.   [33] Schmitt 1968: 127–47.   [34] Turyn 1972: 28 and 32–3.

contacts between Byzantine East and Latin West. The obvious locus of such opportunity is the communities of Dominican and Franciscan monks that remained at Constantinople proselytising the Orthodox Greek population after the Crusader Kingdom fell in 1261. In these communities there were Latin books, Latin speakers, and even Latin scholars able to instruct and assist an eager and talented young student like Planoudes. If Planoudes learned Latin among them, he would not be the only Byzantine to do so. His older contemporary Manuel Holobolos, the first Palaeologan scholar to translate into Greek learned Latin writings on rhetoric and philosophy, maintained a cordial and lasting intellectual relationship with Simon of Constantinople, a Dominican admired for his fluency both in Latin and in Greek. We may infer that Holobolos (and perhaps Planoudes as well) learned Latin from Dominicans in Constantinople.[35]

Planoudes' first translations from Latin belong to the period *c.* 1270–85, the earliest stage of his scholarly career, when Michael VIII or his son and successor Andronicus II evidently commissioned Greek versions of Augustine's *De trinitate* and ps.-Cyprian's *De duodecim abusivis*, two Latin texts that were relevant to the debates over ecclesiastical union conducted with the West under imperial auspices.[36] The libraries of the Dominicans and Franciscans at Constantinople are a plausible source for the Latin texts that Planoudes would have needed for his Greek translations. Although imperial Unionist initiatives soon cooled, Planoudes continued to translate various sorts of Latin texts into Greek. He translated and adapted sections from Priscian's *Institutio de arte grammatica* and the collection of moralising verses known as *Disticha Catonis*, apparently for use in the school he supervised at the monastery in Constantinople where he lived, either the Monastery of the Chora or of Akataleptos.[37] His attention as a translator concentrated, however, upon substantial Latin literary texts: Boethius' *Consolatio philosophiae*, Cicero's *Somnium Scipionis* with Macrobius' commentary, and Ovid's *Metamorphoses*, *Heroides* and amatory poems (*Amores*, *Ars amatoria* and *Remedia amoris*); a metrical version of Juvenal's *Satires* 10.19–22 that survives as marginalia in a manuscript of Planoudes' Boethius translation is attributed to him as well. With the exception of Juvenal's *Satires* and Ovid's amatory poems, Planoudes' translations survive complete, and all are available in modern critical editions.[38] Since none appears accompanied by the original Latin text and since none is introduced by a translator's preface, these translations stand as independent works

---

[35] Fisher 2002/3: 95–6.   [36] Beck 1971: 44 and Rigotti 1995: xv–lviii.
[37] Constantinides 1982: 68–70.   [38] Fisher 2002/3: 96 n. 55.

within the Greek literary tradition dissociated from the Latin original and unaccompanied by the persona of a translator, who in effect disappears, allowing the reader to encounter the Greek text seemingly without mediation. Although personally modest and retiring as a translator, Planoudes was energetic and assertive in translating. His Greek *Metamorphoses* and *Heroides* alone represent approximately seven hundred pages of Greek in their modern printed editions.[39]

That Planoudes translated the *Metamorphoses* and *Heroides* into versions elegant both in form and in content can be asserted with confidence because his master copy of the two works survives, providing unimpeachable witness both to the exact text of the translations and to the precise format that Planoudes established for them. Some thirty-five years ago Alexander Turyn declared that the two-volume set Vatican City, BAV, Reg. gr. MS 132 (*Metamorphoses*) and 133 (*Heroides*) is Planoudes' own manuscript, copied in part and corrected throughout in his own hand. Turyn made this extremely important identification in a personal letter to N. G. Wilson but did not publish the basis for it; Wilson privately informed Papathomopoulos, who was at the time engaged in producing his critical edition of the *Heroides* translation.[40] Subsequently scholars tentatively accepted Turyn's identification, awaiting secure palaeographical and codicological demonstration of it.[41] In 2004 Annalisa Rossi published a meticulous and persuasive study mustering the evidence to support Turyn's contention. She demonstrated that the codicology of the two Vatican manuscripts is internally consistent and similar to Planoudes' practice in other manuscripts securely attributed to him;[42] she further established that Planoudes' hand can be recognised in folios 1r–96v of the *Metamorphoses* translation and in the marginalia of both manuscripts.[43] The Greek text with its Lactantian marginalia so exactly replicates details of formatting (e.g., lineation, red marginalia, separation of text into episodes with red initial letter etc.) typical of Ovid's eleventh- and twelfth-century manuscripts that Rossi terms Vat. Reg. gr. 132 and 133 a translation of form as well as of content from Latin West to Byzantine East.[44] The significance of Rossi's work cannot be overstated. It is fundamental for our understanding of Planoudes' *Metamorphoses* and *Heroides* translations and their importance in contemporary and later Byzantine culture.

---

[39] Papathomopoulos and Tsavare 2002 and Planoudes 1976.
[40] Papathomopoulos 1975: 118 n. 18.
[41] Tsavare 1974: 389; Gamillscheg 1981: 391 n. 40; and Papathomopoulos and Tsavare 2002: 12 and 16.
[42] Rossi 2004: 12–13.   [43] Rossi 2004: 69–70 and 75.   [44] Rossi 2004: 16–19.

Only in recent decades has scholarship on Planoudes' translations from Ovid focused upon their positive qualities as works of Byzantine Greek literature. Initially, Latin textual critics searching for Latin manuscripts of the *Metamorphoses* and *Heroides* mined Planoudes' translations for evidence of readings from lost Latin witnesses. A shower of complaint resulted as scholars minutely examined the inadequate and uncritical versions of Planoudes' work available at the time with the expectation that his Greek translations represented exact and literal renderings from his original Latin text. They examined the style and coherence of Planoudes' Greek much less attentively than the correspondence between the translations and Latin phrases or even individual Latin words. Although J. F. Boissonade, *editor princeps* of Planoudes' *Metamorphoses*, conceded the elegant Greek style of the translation, he disparaged the translator's inferior Latin exemplar, scant Latin lexical and grammatical resources, careless lapses in completing an immense translation task, and poor grasp of the Latin language.[45] Alfred Gudeman chastised Planoudes for taking excessive licence in his *Heroides* translation with Latin gerunds, gerundives, ablatives absolute and participles, noting with additional disapproval that Planoudes altered singulars to plurals and *vice versa*.[46] Heinrich Müller followed Gudeman's example in complaining that Planoudes' verb tenses did not accurately reflect those in the text of Ovid's *Metamorphoses*.[47] Louis Purser, introducing Palmer's *editio princeps* of Planoudes' *Heroides*, repeated Gudeman's criticisms and noted tersely the Greek translator's 'very imperfect knowledge of Latin'.[48] In 1963 E. J. Kenney summarised the prevailing assessment of Planoudes' translations: 'literal renderings, an uncertain grasp of Latin vocabulary, idiom and meter, occasional gross errors; balanced . . . by a superior competence in Greek mythology and proper names'.[49] Although Planoudes' inadequacies as a Latinist are well documented and undeniable, his translations are freestanding works of Greek literature adapted from Latin by an accomplished writer of Greek. An assessment of the positive literary aspects of Planoudes' *Metamorphoses* and *Heroides* is essential to a fair and balanced evaluation of these Byzantine translations.

Over the past twenty years such studies have appeared. In 1987 Valentín García Yerba demonstrated that Planoudes applied the standards of Byzantine Greek prose to his translation by supplying connective particles and by translating constructions and usages particular to Latin into equivalent and idiomatic Greek in order to achieve a readable and reasonably

---

[45] Boissonade 1822: ix–xi.   [46] Gudeman 1888: 5–11.   [47] Müller 1906: 2–8.
[48] Purser 1898: xlvii.   [49] Kenney 1963: 219.

accurate version of Ovid's Latin text;[50] Yerba further cited the few passages where Planoudes chose to translate Ovid's verses into freely adapted Greek hexameter versions, evidence of his metrical skills and a contrast with his general practice of conveying the sense of Ovid's poem in prose, a less constraining and thus more accurate medium.[51] In 1990 the present writer's *Planudes' Greek Translation of Ovid's Metamorphoses* detailed the allusive literary vocabulary and rhetorical figures incorporated by the translator to make his rendition of *Metamorphoses* 1.163–208 an elegant example of the mannered and Atticising prose favored by Byzantine literati.[52] Andreas Michalopoulos subsequently examined Planoudes' lapses, variations and omissions from Ovid's Latin text of the *Heroides* while noting as well some of the translation's positive stylistic features, such as hypallage, improved transitions, neologism and word play.[53]

To illustrate both Planoudes' mastery of Greek prose style and his weaknesses as a translator of Latin poetry, let us examine a passage from his translation of *Metamorphoses* 1.700–8, a passage that illustrates not only the sort of alterations from the Latin text so distressing to Latin textual critics but also Planoudes' translation technique, the additions he made for clarity and the rhetorical devices and vocabulary he supplied for aesthetic appeal. In addition, this passage clearly demonstrates a serious mistranslation that Planoudes recognised and later corrected. Since the passage occurs on folio 7r in the section of the manuscript copied by Planoudes himself, it is possible to trace how he mistranslated, attempted correction *in situ* of his flawed version, and later retranslated and completely recopied a final version in the lower margin.[54] Although Planoudes' Latin archetype is unknown, this passage offers no manuscript variants in Tarrant's new critical edition and thus presents no significant questions about the text of the Latin passage that so frustrated its translator. To illustrate the relationship between the Latin text and Planoudes' two versions of it, I shall first supply the Latin text followed by Planoudes' initially flawed Greek translation of it. For the convenience of the reader, I shall break Planoudes' Greek prose into lines corresponding as much as possible with Ovid's lines

---

[50] Yerba 1987: 337–53.   [51] Yerba 1987: 352–53.   [52] Fisher 1990: 69–98.

[53] Michalopoulos 2003: 359–74. Most recently Nóra Fodor has offered two contributions to the discussion of Planoudes as a literary translator; see Fodor 2007 on the bowdlerised version of Ovid's amatory poems sometimes attributed to Planoudes and Fodor 2008, a survey of all Planoudes' translations from Latin. Unfortunately, Fodor's work came to my attention too late to be incorporated into my own discussion.

[54] Planoudes' entire revision covers *Metamorphoses* 1.700–13; for a discussion of the complete revision, a comparison of the passage with Planoudes' translation of *Metamorphoses* 1.543–67 and a photograph of folium 7r, see Fisher 2004: 147–60.

of Latin and translate them into painfully literal English in an accompanying footnote. The ungainly style of my purely functional English reflects the inevitable difference between Greek and English word order as well as Planoudes' awkward first attempt at translating this passage. I hope that my translation will assist readers in comparing the choice of vocabulary, general order of words or phrases, sequence of clauses, and replication or variation of grammatical constructions between Latin original and Greek translation in the discussion that follows. I shall then present Planoudes' revised translation of the same passage followed by discussion of it.[55] Let us begin by plunging into the midst of Mercury's/Hermes' story of Pan and Syrinx at the point where Ovid suddenly switches from direct to indirect discourse at *Metamorphoses* 1.700:[56]

```
        . . . –restabat uerba referre,                          700
et precibus spretis fugisse per auia nympham
donec harenosi placidum Ladonis ad amnem
uenerit; hic illam cursum impedientibus undis
ut se mutarent liquidas orasse sorores;
Panaque, cum prensam sibi iam Syringa putaret,            705
corpore pro nymphae calamos tenuisse palustres;
dumque ibi suspirat, motos in harundine uentos
effecisse sonum tenuem similemque querenti;
```

Vat. Reg. gr. 132 fol. 7r lines 17–22 preserves Planoudes' initial translation of these lines:[57]

```
ὑπόλοιπον ὂν ἔτι καὶ τοὺς λόγους ἀπαγγεῖλαι·                        700
καὶ ὡς τῆς ἱκετείας εἰς κενὸν δαπανηθείσης, δι' ἀβάτων τὴν νύμφην,
μέχρι πρὸς τὸ ἥσυχον ἦλθεν ὕδωρ τοῦ ψαμαθώδους λάδωνος
   πεφευγέναι
κἀκεῖ τὸν δρόμον τοῦ ὕδατος ἀνακόπτοντος
τὰς δ+ὕγρους {sic} ἀδελφὰς ταύτην μεταβαλεῖν ἠντιβοληκέναι·
τόν τε πᾶνα οἰόμενον ἤδη ἑαυτῷ ληφθῆναι τὴν σύριγγα,            705
ἀντὶ τοῦ τῆς νύμφης σώματος καλάμους ἑλείους κεκρατηκέναι.
κἂν τῷ στενάζειν πνεύματος ἐμπεσόντος ἐν τῷ καλάμῳ,
λεπτὸν ἦχον [erasure and scribal flourish], καὶ ἐοικότα θρήνῳ
   πεποιηκέναι·[58]
```

[55] I am grateful to the Vatican Library for the opportunity to examine Vat. Reg. gr. 132, which I used in the summer of 2001 to establish the text of Planoudes' two versions. The text of his first version is a somewhat conjectural restoration based upon his erasures and deletions as he tried unsuccessfully to revise the passage *in situ*.

[56] Ovid 2004: 27–8. See also in this volume, pp. 75–6.

[57] My transcription follows the manuscript in omitting iota subscript.

[58] A functional (though quite awkward) English translation: '[700] yet (it is) remaining still also (his) words to report; / and (that) after his entreaty was as if spent in vain, through untrodden (places)

No less accomplished a Latinist than E. J. Kenney conceded that Ovid's
sudden change from direct to indirect speech in line 700 reveals the poet at
his shape-shifting best: 'Such syntactic variation is one form of the linguistic wit which pervades the poem and in which Ovid took much evident
pleasure.'[59] Even though various additions in the Latin manuscripts at
this point suggest that medieval scribes balked at Ovid's 'linguistic wit',
Planoudes generally negotiates the passage without conspicuous distress
and even produces a passable rendition of difficult portions within it. It
is challenging to follow an extended sequence of accusative subjects and
infinitive verbs and even more problematic to render indirect speech nested
within such a passages as line 704 'ut se mutarent... orasse' and line 705
'cum prensam sibi iam Syringa putaret'. Planoudes' correct Greek translation of these particular passages, however, illustrates several complaints
that Latin textual critics have levelled against him quite unfairly, in my
opinion: (1) Planoudes exercises licence in representing Latin constructions with equivalent but different Greek ones either required by Greek
usage (e.g. the accusative and infinitive replacing an *ut* clause in line 704)
or freely chosen by the translator (e.g. a participle instead of a *cum* clause
in line 705; note also in line 707 an articular infinitive instead of a *dum*
clause and in line 700 an accusative absolute replacing an indicative verb);
(2) Planoudes alters the tenses of verbs (e.g., in line 705 a Greek aorist representing the perfect *prensam* [*esse*]); and (3) Planoudes' vocabulary choices
do not always correspond to the Latin text (e.g. the Greek demonstrative
pronoun ταύτην replacing the reflexive pronoun *se* in line 704). In this
last instance, Planoudes' translation represents Syrinx's plea in a version
close to her own words and avoids repeating the reflexive pronoun in two
successive lines; this is certainly not an instance of mistranslation, because
Planoudes understands *sibi* in line 705 and renders it correctly with its
exact Greek equivalent, ἑαυτῷ.

Sensitivity to Greek vocabulary choices marks the translation overall.
Planoudes explicates Ovid's *spretis* in line 701 with the metaphor 'spent
in vain', emphasised by the particle ὡς = 'as if'. In line 704 Planoudes
corrects his initial choice of a prosaic adjective (διύγρους) into one with
Homeric associations (ὕγρους); he establishes that *amnem* (line 702) and

---

the nymph, / until to the still water of sandy Ladon (she) came, fled / and there, when her flight
the water stopped, / her moist sisters this (girl) to transform (she) entreated; / [705] and (that) Pan,
thinking (that) already for himself was seized Syrinx, / instead of the nymph's body marsh reeds
mastered. / And in his moaning when (his) breath fell on the reed, / a thin voice [erasure and scribal
flourish] and like a lament (he) made'.

[59] Kenney 1986: 384.

undis (line 703) refer to the same 'water' by translating both with the same word, ὕδωρ/ὕδατος (*undis* incidentally illustrates yet another complaint lodged against Planoudes' translation: he exchanges singulars and plurals; see also lines 701 and 707). He accommodates the Byzantine preference for compound words in numerous instances, sometimes by artfully reflecting the elements of the original Latin compound with an equivalent Greek word as he does in line 701, *a-via* = ἀ-βάτων.

Although Planoudes preserves Ovid's word order almost exactly in lines 700 and 703 and generally maintains Ovid's sequence of clauses and their boundaries as well, he adjusts his translation to Greek prose usage by adding connecting particles throughout and by introducing modest stylistic embellishments such as the juxtaposition of two words built on the same verbal root in line 704 (μετα-βαλεῖν ἠντι-βολη-κέναι) and the introduction of hyperbaton between accusative subject and infinitive verb in lines 701–2 ('the nymph . . . fled').

Despite his several virtues as a translator, Planoudes seriously misconstrued the sense of lines 707–8, failing to recognise that Ovid introduced *uentos* as the accusative subject of *effecisse*. He soon realised that his translation had wandered onto treacherous ground, erased approximately twelve letters and filled the resulting space with an extravagant flourish of the pen and a genitive absolute (πνεύματος ἐμπεσόντος) to translate Ovid's *motos . . . uentos*, thus interpreting this Latin accusative with participle as an accusative absolute, possible in Greek (cf. line 700) but not at all regular in Latin. His new version of the passage also requires forcing the sense of *uentos* to represent Pan's breath. Returning later to this vexed passage, Planoudes revised his translation yet again, undoubtedly having gained greater familiarity with Ovid's style and idiom in the course of translating the fifteen books of the *Metamorphoses*. This thorough revision apparently occurred after Vat. Reg. gr. 132 was nearing completion, since Planoudes did not recopy complete folios but rather inserted his retranslation at the bottom of the page as lines 35–9:

τοῦ πανὸς τὸν ἑρμῆν
ὑπόλοιπον ὂν ἔτι καὶ τοὺς λόγους ἀπαγγεῖλαι·   700
καὶ ὡς τῆς ἱκετείας εἰς κενὸν δαπανηθείσης, δι' ἀβάτων ἡ νύμφη
   πέφευγεν,
μέχρι πρὸς τὸ ἥσυχον τοῦ ψαμαθώδους λάδωνος ἦλθεν ὕδωρ·
κἀκεῖ τοῦ ὕδατος ἀνακόπτοντος τὸν δρόμον,
τὰς ἀδελφὰς νηιάδας ἠντιβόλει ταύτην μεταβαλεῖν·
ὁ δὲ πᾶν οἰόμενος ἤδη τὴν σύριγγα εἰληφέναι,   705
ἀντὶ τοῦ τῆς νύμφης σώματος καλάμους κατέσχεν ἑλείους.

καὶ δὴ στενάξαντος [ζ corr. το ξ] τὸ πνεῦμα ἐμπεσὸν ἐν τῷ δόνακι,
λεπτὸν ἦχον ἀποτετέλεκε καὶ ἐοικότα θρήνω.⁶⁰

To clarify the transition from Hermes' direct to Ovid's indirect speech,
Planoudes added as a heading for his revision 'Hermes' as accusative subject of 'to report' and the genitive 'of Pan' to be construed with 'the words'.
He then thoroughly revised his previous translation, abandoning his original attempt to render indirect speech with the accusative and infinitive
option that reflects Ovid's Latin construction and using instead the Greek
construction ὡς = 'that' followed by nominative subjects and indicative
verbs. Gone is the problem of distinguishing accusative subjects from
objects and the challenge of representing indirect statements nested within
the passage. He stabilised his shaky translation of lines 707–8 by recasting
dum... suspirat as an absolute construction with Pan as its implied subject
and *uentos* (still awkwardly wrenched into the sense 'breath') with *motos* as
subject of the verb *effecisse*, now represented by a stylish Greek compound
verb equivalent to Ovid's *ef-fecisse* = ἀπο-τετέλεκε. Once committed to
a thorough revision of the passage, Planoudes refined some portions he
had already translated correctly, rendering Ovid's passive *prensam sibi iam
Syringa* (line 705) with a more forceful and emphatic equivalent in the
active voice and revising vocabulary in his translation; he retranslated
'moist sisters' (line 704) with 'sister naiads', a change in the adjective that
removes the Homeric colour of his earlier choice but incorporates greater
mythological precision for his prose readers. He also chose to reflect the
variation between Ovid's *calamos* (line 706) and *harundine* (line 707) by
introducing the *vox propria* for the reed used in a flute in line 707 (δόνακι),
a nice anticipation of the story's eventual *denouement*. 'Reeds' (καλάμους)
remains in line 706, emphasised by the graceful alliteration of 'κ' that
Planoudes accomplished by juxtaposing the noun with a compound verb
that more closely approximates the sense of Ovid's *tenuisse* (καλάμους
κατέσχεν). Planoudes also increased the rhetorical appeal of his revision
by reordering words to achieve interlocking syntactic arrangements in the
pattern ABA.⁶¹

---

⁶⁰ A functional (and less awkward) English version: '[700] yet (it is) remaining still also the words of
Pan Hermes to report; / and that, after his entreaty was spent in vain, through untrodden (places)
the nymph fled, / until to the still water of sandy Ladon (she) came; / and there, when the water
stopped her flight, / her sister naiads she entreated this (girl) to transform; / [705] but Pan, thinking
(that) already Syrinx he captured, / instead of the nymph's body marsh reeds grasped. / And (when
he) moaned, his breath falling on the flute-reed / a thin voice rendered forth and like a lament'.

⁶¹ See the accusative and genitive elements in line 702 and the accusative elements and verb in lines
706 and 708.

Let us now turn to a broader consideration of Planoudes' two complete translations from the works of Ovid, leaving aside temporarily the fragments remaining from his translation of the *Amores*, *Ars amatoria* and *Remedia amoris*. Attempts to declare Planoudes' *Heroides* translation less skilful and therefore earlier than his *Metamorphoses*[62] have been rendered moot by Rossi's demonstration that the two translations are twins, executed as a set (Vat. Reg. gr. 132 and 133) and copied by a single team under Planoudes' personal direction. Planoudes' translation errors in *Metamorphoses* 1.700–8 confirm that this translation, like Planoudes' *Heroides*, is by no means perfect; Yerba has identified additional passages where the absence of the definite article in Latin caused Planoudes to err in his translation.[63] Rossi sets a date for both translations in the late 1290s on the basis of her codicological comparison of the master manuscript containing them with other manuscripts certainly produced under Planoudes' supervision.[64] She notes as well that Isavella Tsavare's analysis of how Planoudes' hand evolved in manuscripts securely assigned to him supports a date after 1294 for the segment of Vat. Reg. gr. 132 that he copied.[65] Because the four other hands distinguished by Rossi in the master manuscript of Planoudes' *Metamorphoses* and *Heroides* are typical of intellectuals and court bureaucrats, she favours a Constantinopolitan origin for the translations but leaves open the question of their actual provenance.[66] For a group of copyists to collaborate on a shared project is uncommon neither in Byzantium[67] nor in the practice of Planoudes himself. He is known to have served as both coordinator and copyist for Florence, BML, Plut. 32.16 produced in 1280 and for Venice, Biblioteca Nazionale Marciana, Marc. gr. MS 481 (coll. 863) produced in 1299–1301/2.[68] In the particular case of the master copy of these translations, however, the presence of the translator's hand with four others prompts the intriguing question: 'Did the four other scribes serve, like Planoudes himself, as both copyists and translators of portions of the text?' It seems unlikely to me that four translators able to cope with Ovid's eccentric literary Latin collaborated with Planoudes on this project and yet remain unknown; however, the possibility cannot be dismissed unless distinctive translation styles can be demonstrated in the text. Since the passages available for analysis in this case are short and the process of translation reduces the influence of free choice upon each sample, I think it unlikely that individual styles can be characterised. The question, however, invites further investigation.

[62] Dihle 1999: 996, Michalopoulos 2003: 366–74, Planoudes 1976: vi–vii, and Rigotti 1995: xi.
[63] Yerba 1987: 338–40.   [64] Rossi 2004: 80.   [65] Tsavare 1987: 226–7.
[66] Rossi 2004: 69–74.   [67] Canart 1998: 49–67.   [68] Turyn 1972: 28–31 and 90–3.

A second question follows upon the tentative identification of one of the collaborators' hands as that of Leon Bardales, who travelled to Venice in 1296 with Planoudes and other anonymous associates on an unpleasant and protracted diplomatic mission that resulted in a year's detention for the unfortunate members of the embassy.[69] In a recent study of Vatican manuscripts preserving the works of Ovid, Marco Buonocore, unlike Rossi, assigned Vat. Reg. gr. 132 and 133 to an Italian provenance but did not offer any explanation for his attribution.[70] The possibility invites further investigation, since its implications are most tantalising. Could Planoudes, Bardales, and the members of the embassy have whiled away the idle hours of their unwilling stay in Venice by producing the master manuscript of the *Metamorphoses* and *Heroides* translations? Rossi terms this possibility '*intrigante*', while observing that Constantinople remains the most probable site for the manuscripts' production.[71] Further investigation of this intriguing question is a *desideratum* for Planoudean studies.

Planoudes did not confine his interest in Ovid to the mythological poems but also translated his *Amores*, *Ars amatoria* and *Remedia amoris*. Unfortunately, this text survives only in excerpts compiled in the century after Planoudes' death. Without attribution either to Ovid or to Planoudes, two manuscripts preserve different samples of excerpts; the more extensive collection appears in Naples, Biblioteca Nazionale, MS II c 32, published as the *editio princeps* by E. J. Kenney and P. E. Easterling in 1965.[72] Kenney anticipated this publication with a thorough discussion of the text in 1963.[73] Simultaneously J. Lamoureaux reported the existence of the second manuscript, Paris, BN, Supplément grec MS 1194.[74] Both manuscripts are anthologies of various texts useful in composing rhetorical showpieces, and both present the Ovidian material sandwiched between excerpts from Thucydides and from Dionysius of Halicarnassus; in the Naples manuscript, some passages from the fourth-century CE medical writer Oribasius immediately precede the selections from Dionysius. Although textually independent, both manuscripts were apparently based upon similar archetypes.[75] The more extensive Naples selection contains 481 verses of *Ars amatoria* (21%), 434 verses of *Amores* (18%), and 182 verses of *Remedia amoris* (22%), or approximately one fifth of the entire set of amatory poems.[76] Although the excerpts are typically of six to eight lines,

---

[69] Rossi 2004: 20 and Wendel 1940: 2205–6.   [70] Buonocore 1994: 132–3.
[71] Rossi 2004: 80.   [72] Ovid 1965.   [73] Kenney 1963: 213–27.
[74] Lamoureaux 1963: 206–9.   [75] Ovid 1965: 8.
[76] Kenney 1963: 214. See also the recent treatment of 'Ovidiana Graeca' in Fodor 2007.

they range in length from two words to twenty-four lines. Kenney considers the complete Greek translation lying behind these excerpts so similar to Planoudes' version of the *Metamorphoses* and *Heroides* that the complete Greek version of Ovid's amatory poems can reasonably be attributed to him (or to his circle).[77] The editor/excerptor of Planoudes' translation adopted a very different approach to his task. He altered, expanded, compressed, glossed and sanitised the original Greek texts, selecting passages that could be applied to various rhetorical purposes and themes by an author needing inspiration. His activities coincidentally resulted in a collection similar in content and intent to contemporaneous Western *florilegia* that also contain edited excerpts from Ovid's poetry.[78] A brief example will illustrate the sort of interventions he introduced.[79] In *Ars amatoria* 1.755–6, Ovid confides: '. . . sed sunt diuersa puellis / pectora; mille animos excipe mille modis' (. . . but there are different affections to girls; capture a thousand minds in a thousand ways). In the Naples manuscript, the excerptor transforms Ovid's observation into 'ἐπεὶ διάφορα τοῖς ἀνθρώποις εἰσὶν ἤθη, / δεῖ τὸν πολιτευόμενον πρὸς τὰ μυρία ἤθη μυρίας μορφὰς ἐξαλλάττειν' (Since different lifestyles to humans are, / it is necessary for the man in government towards thousands of lifestyles thousands of (his) outward forms to adapt), a useful piece of advice for medieval and modern politicians alike but far from Ovid's original intent.

The seven excerpts preserved in the Paris manuscript all appear as well in the first half of 'Ovidiana Graeca' but represent only slight tidbits of two lines or less that include unusual vocabulary. One passage, however, stands out as an anomaly in this collection. At the conclusion of the selections from *Ars amatoria* 2, a line has been inserted that is pure Ovid in sentiment and style but original in content: 'τοὺς ἔρωτι κάμνοντας μεμφέσθω μηδείς, οὐ γὰρ βουλόμενοι πάσχουσιν, ἀλλὰ πάσχοντες βούλονται' (those from love suffering let no one reprove, for not willing(ly) do they suffer, but (in) suffering they are willing).[80] Although now only a mangled and anonymous survivor of literary adaptation, Planoudes' Greek translation of the amatory poems once inspired some unknown Byzantine to mimic the elusive Ovid's playful voice down the centuries and across linguistic barriers.

Planoudes' Greek translations of Ovid's poetry have left little evidence of their influence on the Byzantine literary tradition. His student Gregorius, however, specifically commended Planoudes' translations in an epigram

---

[77] Kenney 1963: 218–23. [78] Kenney 1963: 223–7.
[79] Texts from Ovid 1965: 24–5. [80] Fisher 1995: 97–8 and n. 32.

apparently written to accompany an unspecified object representing one of them, an eloquent testimonial to the notable impression they made on his contemporaries:[81] 'Αὐσονίης διαλέκτου μ', ὦ ξεῖν', ἐκμετενεγκὼν / Μάξιμος ἀρτίφρων μουσοπόλος σοφίης / ψαύσας ἄκρα γε πείρατα θῆκεν ἐς Ἑλλάδα φωνήν, / δεῖγμα τε ἧς σοφίης, ἐσ<σ>ομένοις δὲ χάριν' (Stranger, in the fullness of his intellectual capacity, Maximus, servant of the Muses, attained wisdom and set its utmost limits by translating me from the speech of Ausonia [i.e., Latin] into the Greek language as a proof of his wisdom and as a joy to future generations).

Planoudes was not the only translator of Latin literature in thirteenth-century Constantinople, although Manuel Holobolos, his older contemporary, cannot fairly be counted with Planoudes among the 'slave(s) of the Muses'. Holobolos translated two of Boethius' rhetorical works and the Latin version of ps.-Aristotle's lost Greek text *De plantis* but did not turn his attention to Latin *belles lettres* as Planoudes did. He does, however, refer briefly to Ovid in the extensive commentary he appended to his translation of Boethius' rhetorical treatise *De topicis differentiis*. In a note mentioning Cicero he compares the Roman orator's skills favourably with those of the eminent Greek rhetorician Themistius, then slides briskly into considering the cognomen 'Cicero' or 'chickpea' in Latin. Holobolos discusses this appellation at some length, explaining that the Roman orator's facial deformity occasioned his name. The onomastic phenomenon prompts Holobolos to mention Ovid:[82] 'ὡσαύτως καὶ ὁ τοῦ μεγάλου ποιητοῦ Βιργιλίου μαθητής, ὁ Ὀβίδιος Πούπλιος, Νάσων παρὰ Λατίνοις ἐπικέκληται. ἑρμηνεύει δὲ παρ' ἡμῖν τὸ Νάσων τὸν μακρόρρινα ἢ τὸν δημολεκτούμενον μυτᾶν' (Just so the student of the great poet Virgil, Publius Ovidius, has also been dubbed 'Nason' by Latin speakers. 'Nason' means among us 'The Big Nose' or, in popular slang, 'The Schnoz'). Holobolos' comment is directed not so much against Ovid as against the disrespectful manner adopted by Westerners in speaking of august literary figures of the Roman past like Cicero and 'the student of the great poet Virgil'. The scholion is consistent with the tone of negative remarks Holobolos makes elsewhere in his commentary about Westerners he encountered in Constantinople.[83]

I can find no secure evidence either that Ovid's name was mentioned or that Planoudes' translations were cited by medieval Greek authors writing later than Holobolos. Ovid's disappearance after Planoudes so diligently

[81] Text and discussion in Fisher 1979: 444–6; translation from Fisher 2007.
[82] Nikitas 1990: 203 lines 21–3.   [83] Nikitas 1990: CVI–CVIII.

introduced his work into the Greek literary tradition prompts the question: 'What was Planoudes' purpose in translating Ovid's works?' Since the letters of Planoudes contain no discussion of his translations and since he, unlike Holobolos, composed no explanatory translator's prefaces for his work, we can only guess at Planoudes' motivation. Scholars suggest either that he translated from purely private motives or that he had broad cultural purposes in mind.[84] Boissonade, the *editor princeps* of Planoudes' *Metamorphoses*, considered the translation a practice exercise for learning Latin, and a more recent suggestion classified the Greek *Metamorphoses* as a complex example of rhetorical paraphrase between languages and genres;[85] the master copy of the *Metamorphoses* and *Heroides*, however, carefully copied and fully annotated, implies that Planoudes envisioned a sophisticated readership well versed in classical mythology for his translations. Several aspects of Ovid's Latin originals would appeal to such an audience: they are based in the Greek mythological tradition treasured by Byzantine literati, they exemplify rhetorical practice at its most polished in an amusing manner, and they offer an insight into the taste and literary tradition of Western culture as Byzantines encountered it in interactions with Latin-speaking scholars. Planoudes' translations are themselves rhetorically sophisticated and elegant by the standards of his time, offering refreshing variety to scholarly readers very familiar with the traditional canon of Greek literature and perhaps a little weary of it.

Whatever motivation or purpose might have spurred Planoudes to translate Ovid's *Metamorphoses*, *Heroides* and amatory poems, the individual manuscript traditions of his three translations demonstrate that each was evaluated separately by later generations of potential readers. As we have seen, Planoudes' translation of the *Ars amatoria*, *Amores* and *Remedia amoris* was not well received. No complete manuscript of the translation survives from the process of excerpting and recasting Planoudes' original work into the few fragments now remaining. His *Heroides* and *Metamorphoses*, however, fared better. The daunting task of copying both these translations did not discourage the production of two sets surviving from the early fourteenth century (Milan, Biblioteca Ambrosiana, MS A 119 sup. and Venice, Biblioteca Nazionale Marciana, Marc. gr. MS 487 (coll. 883)[86]) and of one set from the late fifteenth or early sixteenth century (Paris, BN, gr. MS 2848,

---

[84] Fisher 2002/3: 97–101.   [85] Dihle 1999: 995 and 1002.

[86] Venice, Biblioteca Nazionale Marciana, Cod. Gr. MS 487 (coll. 883) was known neither to Tsavare, who drew up the stemma of Planoudes' *Metamorphoses* manuscripts (Rossi 2004: 9 and 23) nor to Papathomopoulos, who edited Planoudes *Heroides* (Planoudes 1976: viii).

perhaps a copy of the Ambrosian manuscript[87]), a circumstance leading to the conclusion that at least some readers were interested in both these texts soon after Planoudes made them available and for some two hundred years thereafter. Rossi believes that the two volumes of Planoudes' master copy remained together for approximately a century; at the end of the fourteenth century the master copy of Planoudes' *Metamorphoses* (Vat. Reg. gr. 132) and the copy of the *Heroides* (Vat. Reg. gr. 133) went their separate ways. Before they parted, however, two manuscripts containing only the *Heroides* translation were copied in the fourteenth century (Vatican City, BAV, Barb. gr. MS 121 and Escorial, El, Real Biblioteca, MS y iii 13), the only witnesses to survive independent of the *Metamorphoses* translation.[88] Of these, the Escorial manuscript may be nearly contemporary with the master copy, since it preserves marginal notes tentatively identified as belonging to the hand of Demetrios Triclinius, who was himself a major scholar and a close associate of Planoudes.[89] In contrast, Planoudes' *Metamorphoses* survives independently in seven copies, two of the fourteenth century (Florence, BML, Conv. Soppr. MS 105 and the fragmentary Milan, Biblioteca Ambrosiana, MS q 91 sup., fols. 1r–2r), one of the late fourteenth or early fifteenth century (Bucharest, Biblioteca Academiei România, MS 222), three of the late fifteenth or early sixteenth century (Milan, Biblioteca Ambrosiana, MSS b 110 sup., q 91 sup., and Paris, BN, gr. MS 2849), and one of the sixteenth century (Vatican City, BAV, Vat. gr. MS 614).[90] Some of these manuscripts, including Planoudes' master copy, contain marginal glosses in Latin; Rossi ventures to suggest that a few very brief Latin notes in the master copy may be almost contemporary with the production of the manuscript itself, while others are clearly much later.[91] The presence of Latin annotations in the manuscripts of Planoudes' *Metamorphoses* suggests that Western scholars may have used the text to polish their Greek language skills by reading a work they knew very well in Latin. Analysis of the Latin marginalia and of Triclinius' Greek ones might provide useful insights into how readers used Planoudes' translations. Since Rossi demonstrates that details of formatting in most of the Greek manuscripts represent a constant flux among various systems typical of different libraries in the West, we may infer that much of the copying was done in the West.[92]

True to the unpredictable and shape-shifting nature of Ovid himself, it seems that one of Planoudes' translations appeared in a most unexpected

[87] Rossi 2004: 30.   [88] Rossi 2004: 22.   [89] Planoudes 1976: viii n. 20.
[90] Rossi 2004: 22–9.   [91] Rossi 2004: 75–6.   [92] Rossi 2004: 32–3.

context. In the mid-fifteenth century the avid traveller and antiquarian Cyriacus of Ancona noted that the Vatopedi monastery of Mount Athos possessed in its library 'antiquissimam Homeri Iliadem Ovidiumque graece traductum'.[93] Which of Planoudes' translations did Cyriacus see? Although Cyriacus does not reveal the identity of this mysterious text, the apparently unpopular translation of Ovid's amatory poems probably was not in the monastery's library. Shall we then imagine the monks of Vatopedi putting aside their collections of sermons or saints' lives to seek a bit of diversion in the pages of Planoudes' *Metamorphoses* or *Heroides*? This hypothetical scene would surely delight naughty Ovid himself.

Translations of Ovid continued to enrich the post-Byzantine and modern Greek literary traditions. D. Z. Nikitas has opened up this rich but little-studied topic in a preliminary analysis of the eighteenth-century allegorising prose translation of Ovid's *Metamorphoses* by Spyridon Blantzes.[94] Introducing his discussion Nikitas notes an even earlier prose translation of the *Metamorphoses* made in 1698 by John Makolas and as yet unpublished. Both Blantzes and Makolas translated the *Metamorphoses* into the popular dialectical level of Greek, and both worked in Venice's large expatriate Greek community. These pioneering works were followed by a succession of nineteenth- and twentieth-century *Metamorphoses* translations enumerated by Nikitas, all but two into prose. Through the millennia Ovid has indeed continued the metempsychosis of his Latin spirit into a succession of Greek literary bodies.

---

[93] Bodnar 2003: 123 line 7.   [94] Nikitas 1999: 1005–19.

CHAPTER 3

Ovid's Metamorphoses *in the school tradition of France, 1180–1400*
Texts, manuscript traditions, manuscript settings

Frank T. Coulson

Primary evidence for the circulation, reception and study of Ovid's *Metamorphoses* from late antiquity to 1100 is relatively meagre.[1] One branch of the manuscript tradition (the so-called Lactantian family) transmits a series of titles (*tituli*)and summaries (*narrationes*), probably composed in the late antique period and erroneously attributed to the patristic author Lactantius in the Renaissance, that preserve evidence of a once complete commentary.[2] From the fall of the Roman Empire to the revival of learning in the twelfth century, the survival of Ovid's *magnum opus* can be traced only haphazardly in scattered fragments and remnants of once complete manuscripts.[3] The first great revival of interest in the *Metamorphoses* for which we have manuscript evidence occurs in the monastic foundations of southern Germany during the later eleventh and twelfth centuries.[4]

I am grateful to Greti Dinkova-Bruun, Greg Hays, Marjorie Curry Woods, and Ralph Hexter for comments on an earlier draft of this article. The comments of the two anonymous readers for the press also greatly improved the final version.

[1] The best survey of Ovidian influence in the early medieval period remains Munk Olsen 1991.

[2] For a survey of published material on the *Narrationes*, see Coulson and Roy 2000: 37–40, no. 52. Cameron 2004: 4–32 attempts to redate the *Narrationes* to the second century and posits that the *Narrationes* were composed as we have them and do not derive from a late antique commentary. The fullest discussion of the manuscript evidence is now Tarrant 1995. During the Renaissance period, the *Narrationes* were often copied separately from the text of the *Metamorphoses* and were described as a mythological treatise. Annalisa Rossi of the Scuola di Archivistica, Paleografia e Diplomatica of Bari is engaged on a new critical edition of the text. See also in this volume, p. 4.

[3] See, in particular, Tarrant 1983 and Richmond 2002.

[4] The relevant manuscripts (which come from southern German monasteries such as Tegernsee) are Munich, Bayerische Staatsbibliothek, clm 4610, clm 14482, and clm 14809. Other important twelfth-century commentaries on the *Metamorphoses* are transmitted in Freiburg im Breisgau, Universitätsbibliothek, MS 381, and Salzburg, Stiftsbibliothek St. Peter (Abtei), MS a v 4. Meiser 1885 has studied and edited selections from clm 4610, while Coulson 1986a has discussed the relationship of Salzburg, a v 4 to Arnulf of Orléans's *accessus* to the *Metamorphoses*. Young 1944 edits the three *accessus* to the *Metamorphoses* from clm 14482 and Herren 2004 advances arguments for newly identified glosses by Manegold of Lautenbach. For a more general assessment of Manegold and his link to medieval commentary on Horace see Villa 1996.

In the third quarter of the twelfth century, Ovid's poetic corpus was again intensely studied at Orléans, where school masters such as Arnulf of Orléans,[5] William of Orléans,[6] and Fulco of Orléans[7] wrote complete commentaries on individual poems. The Orléanais region continued to be a fruitful centre of scholarship on Ovid well into the mid thirteenth century, for *c.* 1250 an anonymous master compiled the so-called Vulgate commentary,[8] perhaps the most authoritative and widely disseminated commentary on the *Metamorphoses* in Europe during the high Middle Ages. Throughout the later thirteenth and the fourteenth centuries, commentaries, *accessus* (medieval introductions) and allegories on the *Metamorphoses* abound. Some of these commentaries may be attributed to named masters (as is the case with the commentary of William of Thiegiis, extant in Paris, Bibliothèque nationale de France, lat. 8010). More usually, however, such commentaries circulate anonymously and are found in the form of interlinear and marginal glosses surrounding the text of the poem.

In the present chapter, I trace the development of French school commentary on the *Metamorphoses* from its genesis at Orléans around 1180 to 1400. My aim is twofold: first, to provide the reader with a codicological examination of the manuscripts to establish what ancillary school texts were of vital importance to the medieval interpretation of Ovid; and second, to elucidate the varied modes of exegesis and reading adopted by medieval masters, including the allegorical commentary, the philological commentary, the more purely literary explication (best exemplified by the Vulgate commentary) and the prose paraphrase.

---

[5] For studies which treat early masters and the schools at Orléans, see, in particular, Villaret 1876, Delisle 1869 and Cuissard 1871. Engelbrecht 2006 provides statistical analyses proving the importance of Orléans as a centre for the study of Ovid. For manuscripts of the works of Arnulf, see Coulson and Roy 2000: nos. 257 and 333. For previous scholarship on Arnulf, see Ghisalberti, Arnulf 1932.

[6] For a complete listing of manuscripts and relevant bibliography, see Coulson and Roy 2000: no. 13 and Coulson 2002. One new manuscript of William's commentary on the *Metamorphoses* has recently surfaced in Copenhagen, Fabricius 29 2°, fols. 1ra–5vb. The text is now edited in Engelbrecht 2003, who also provides a comprehensive study (in Dutch) of the sources, influences, and approaches used by William to the explication of the text. William's commentary was discussed as early as 1926 by Alton (see Alton 1926), but it was only firmly attributed to him in 1981. Roy and Shooner 1996 discuss William's work in some detail.

[7] Fulco of Orléans was a contemporary of Arnulf at Orléans. His commentaries on the amatory works of Ovid have not yet been edited. For lists of manuscripts of his works, see Coulson and Roy 2000: nos. 56, 71, 94, 161, 173 and 415.

[8] Selections from the Vulgate commentary are edited in Coulson 1991. The manuscripts are catalogued in Coulson 1985, 1987b, and 1990. Discussion of the approaches adopted by the commentary can be found in Coulson 1987a and McKinley 2001.

COMMENTARIES IN THE ORLÉANAIS 1180–1200

From the ninth century onwards, Orléans was known as a centre for the copying and transmission of classical texts. Important manuscripts dating from the ninth to the thirteenth century are associated with the town. For example, a fragment of a manuscript now housed in the University Library of Leipzig (Rep. 1 4° 74), possibly written at Orléans in the ninth century, contains brief excerpts from Martial's epigrams and Ovid's *Metamorphoses*; a ninth-century manuscript of the author Solinus, originally located at Micy, later came to Orléans; and several thirteenth-century manuscripts of Ovid were produced there. Additionally, the two most important *florilegia* circulating in the Middle Ages, the *Florilegium Gallicum* and the *Florilegium Angelicum*, have their origin at Orléans.[9] In the last quarter of the twelfth century, the cathedral school at Orléans produced three remarkable masters, Arnulf, William and Fulco, who composed complete or partial commentaries on the Ovidian corpus that all have a similar appeal and focus.

Arnulf of Orléans

Around 1180, the *Orléanais* master Arnulf wrote two commentaries on the *Metamorphoses* which influenced interpretation of the poem down to the mid fifteenth century. This master spent much of his working life at Orléans and had, by all accounts, an exceedingly problematic and quarrelsome relationship with his contemporaries.[10] A prolific scholar, he not only produced commentaries on select works of Ovid (including the *Fasti*,[11] the *Ars amatoria*,[12] the *Remedia amoris*,[13] and the *Epistulae ex Ponto*[14]) and Lucan's *Bellum ciuile*;[15] he also wrote two distinct explanations of the *Metamorphoses*: one consisted of a grammatical and mythological gloss,

---

[9] Sections from the *Florilegium Gallicum* are edited in Burton 1983 and Hamacher 1975. The texts are discussed in Rouse 1979, where he treats the manuscripts in Richard de Fournival's library thought to have an Orléans origin, and Rouse 1975.

[10] See, in particular, Roy and Shooner 1985–1986.

[11] Now edited by Rieker in Arnulf of Orléans 2005.

[12] Ghisalberti in Arnulf of Orléans 1932: 166–9 edits the *accessus* and brief selections from the commentary. For a complete list of manuscript copies, see Coulson and Roy 2000: no. 252.

[13] Now edited in Roy and Shooner 1996.

[14] Ghisalberti in Arnulf of Orléans 1932: 172–6 edits the *accessus* and select glosses. Hexter 1986: 226–7 provides synopses of the material in the Copenhagen and Wolfenbüttel manuscripts. Coulson and Roy, 2000: no. 306 give a complete list of manuscripts.

[15] Now edited by Marti in Arnulf of Orléans 1958.

introduced by a long and detailed *accessus*,[16] while a second (entitled the *Allegoriae*) provided an allegorical exposition in which the individual stories were explained historically (euhemeristically), morally, or allegorically. The two commentaries were conceived by Arnulf to be read *in tandem* and thereby to provide the medieval reader with what might be termed a 'compleat' approach to the text, that is to say one that embraced both a literal and an allegorical reading. In the two earliest manuscripts of the texts (Munich, Bayerische Staatsbibliothek, clm 7205[17] and Venice, Biblioteca nazionale Marciana, Marc. lat. MS xiv 222 [4007]), both dating to *c*. 1200, the scribes first copy the philological gloss on each book of the *Metamorphoses* and then proceed to the allegorical interpretation (see figure 3.1). By the thirteenth century, however, the manuscript tradition of the two texts diverges sharply so that the philological commentary circulates separately from the allegorical one. The *Allegoriae* during this later period are found primarily with a verse allegory on the poem by John of Garland entitled the *Integumenta Ovidii* (see below).[18] Indeed, the two texts often become so entwined that the relevant verses from the *Integumenta* are displaced from their authorial setting and are copied immediately after the appropriate allegory from Arnulf.

Two other features of the manuscript setting of the philological commentary are of great interest for the history of its transmission and recovery. First, though originally found as a *catena* commentary[19] (that is to say, a commentary written separately from a text manuscript and organised with individual *lemma* followed by gloss), the philological commentary in the thirteenth and fourteenth centuries is disseminated as interlinear and marginal commentary surrounding a text of the *Metamorphoses* (as is the case with St Omer, Bibliothèque municipale, MS 670 and Leiden, Bibliotheek der Rijksuniversiteit, BPL MS 96). Secondly, Arnulf's glosses at times became imbedded within later commentaries and have consequently remained unidentified by scholars.

Arnulf's philological glosses to the *Metamorphoses* are intended as a crib for younger students beginning their reading of classical texts. The glosses,

---

[16] Edited in Ghisalberti in Arnulf of Orléans 1932: 180–1.
[17] Munich, clm 7205 is extensively discussed in Hexter 1987.
[18] Important manuscripts transmitting the works of Arnulf and John *in tandem* include London, BL, Royal MS 12 E. xi; Montpellier, Bibliothèque de la Faculté de médécine, MS H 328; Oxford, Bodl., Hatton MS 92; and Oxford, Merton College, MS 299.
[19] See Ward 1996 and 1998. Ward posits that the *catena* commentary arose in the eleventh and twelfth centuries to meet the needs of students who required copies of masters' glosses and thus affords evidence for institutionalised teaching of classical texts.

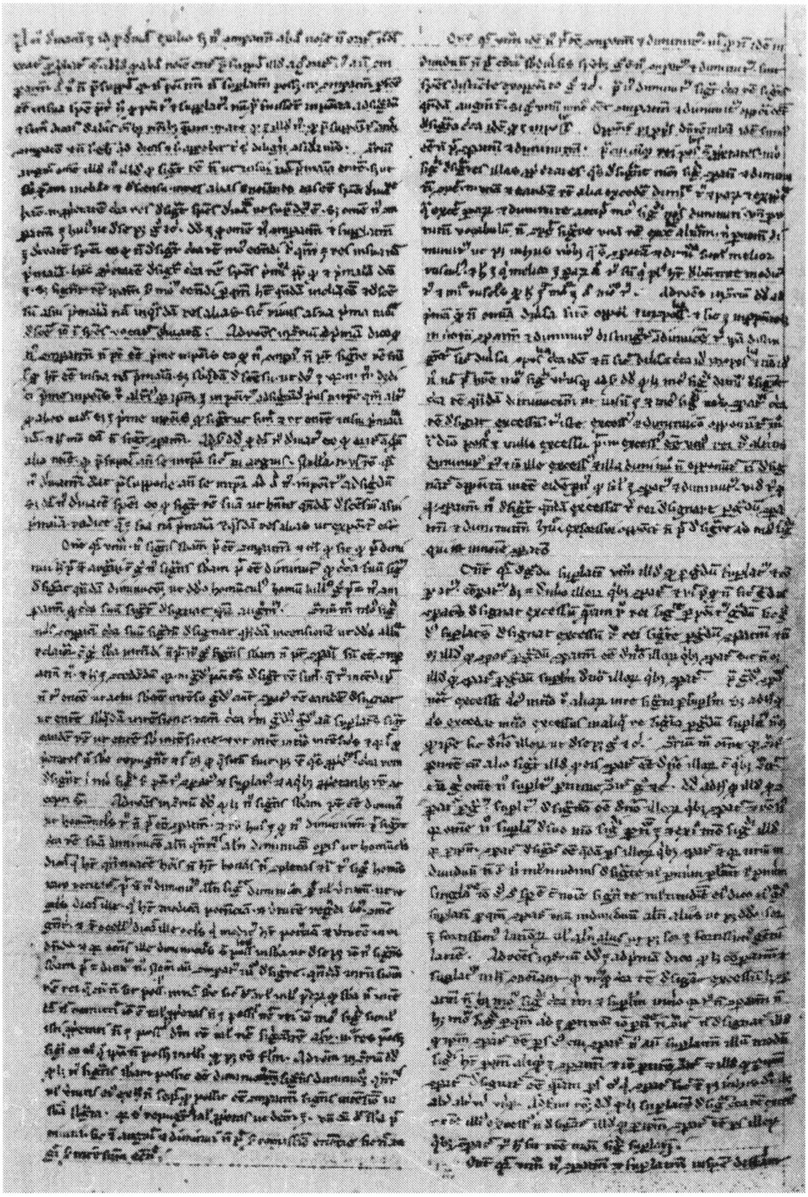

Figure 3.1 Arnulf of Orléans, *Allegoriae* and philological commentary (Munich, Bayerische Staatsbibliothek, Clm 7205, fol. 29v)

which are extensive and comment on nearly every line of the text, are primarily interested in elucidating the grammar of individual passages, explicating abstruse references (particularly allusions to unusual geographical locales), and providing mythological background to individual stories. As such, they must have been a significant help to students as they first confronted the text. Earlier scholarship has judged the philological commentary harshly as the product of a competent but workmanlike grammarian lacking in rigour.[20] A closer examination of the glosses, however, reveals a commentator of somewhat greater abilities, who provides for the medieval reader essential keys to the understanding of the poem in such varied areas as the grammar of individual passages, textual *cruces*, mythological background to the stories, and the overarching structural principles employed by the poet.[21] In addition to his interest in the structure of the poem, Arnulf provides mythological background to the stories, particularly when such information can explicate abstruse allusions made by the poet. At *Met.* 1.669–70, Ovid introduces the story of Mercury and Argus with a somewhat allusive reference to the god Mercury: 'quem lucida partu Pleias enixa est' (he to whom the bright Pleiad gave birth). Arnulf fills in the mythological background, namely that Maia, the mother of Mercury, was one of the Pleiads, who were seven sisters engendered from Atlas and Pleione. Moreover, to his credit Arnulf is aware of textual variants transmitted in the manuscript tradition and attempts to account for them. At *Met.* 1.639–640, for example, Io in her wanderings as a cow comes to the river banks of her father, Inachus: 'Venit et ad ripas, ubi ludere saepe solebat, Inachidas ripas' (and she came to the banks of the river Inachus where she used to play). The medieval tradition at this point gives two variant readings, 'Inachidos' and 'Inachides', both of which Arnulf thinks may be acceptable: '*Inachidos* aque subaudi; vel *Inachides* est litera libri,

[20] See, for example, the comments of Ghisalberti in Arnulf of Orléans 1932: 179: 'Filologo Arnolfo non è, ma è tuttavia sempre un buon grammatico' ('Arnulf is not a philologist, but he is nevertheless a good grammarian'). Ghisalberti in Arnulf 1932: 181–9 transcribes select glosses to Books 1 and 2 of the *Metamorphoses*. Arnulf's glosses to Ovid's creation myth are critically edited in Coulson and Nawotka 1993, but a critical edition of the complete commentary from all extant manuscripts remains a *desideratum*. David Gura of the Department of Greek and Latin at the Ohio State University has announced a forthcoming edition.

[21] See, for example, Arnulf's gloss to *Met.* 2.219: 'Oeagrius mons est qui dividit Macedoniam a Tessalia. Oeagrius dictus est ab Orpheo ibi a mulieribus dilacerato. Sed hoc nondum contigerat, immo futurum erat. Et bene dictus est Oeagrius quia Oeager fuit pater Orphei putativus' (Oeagrius is a mountain which divides Macedonia from Thessaly. It is called 'Oeagrius' from Orpheus who was torn apart there by the women. But this had not yet happened but would take place. And it is properly called 'Oeagrius' since Oeagrus was the putative father of Orpheus) (Arnulf of Orléans 1932: 186).

unde *Inachides ripas*, id est ripas Inachi (*Inachidos*, understand of water, or *Inachides* is the reading, that is to say the banks of her father Inachus).[22]

The long and detailed *accessus*[23] that prefaces the commentary proper, where Arnulf discusses the *Metamorphoses* under six broad headings (*uita poetae, titulus operis, materia, utilitas, intentio, cui parti philosophiae subponatur* – life of the poet, title of the work, subject matter, usefulness, intention and the philosophical category to which the work is to be assigned), served as the prototype for the later medieval tradition of biographical introductions to the epic, influencing the structure and content of many later lives of Ovid. For example, the detailed life of Ovid found in two late twelfth-century manuscripts[24] is essentially an expanded version of Arnulf, as is the *accessus* prefaced to the pseudo-Ovidian poem *De vetula*.[25]

Arnulf's philological commentary and its *accessus* remained a highly influential work, transmitted partially or completely in no fewer than twenty-seven manuscripts dating from the late twelfth to the early fifteenth century.[26] Originally a product of the *Orléanais*, the commentary circulates in many later French, English and Italian manuscripts. Of particular interest here are two Italian manuscripts, one dating to the late thirteenth century, the other to the early fifteenth century, that attest to the continued copying of Arnulf's glosses in Italy well into the Renaissance. Florence, BML, MS 36 18 is a finely produced thirteenth-century manuscript of Italian origin, while Milan, Biblioteca Ambrosiana, MS в 18 inf. is a lavish Italian manuscript written in 1420 at Urbino.[27] The humanistic scholar Zomino of Pistoia (1387–1458) also made extensive use of Arnulf's glosses in his commentary on the *Metamorphoses* extant in Pistoia, Biblioteca Forteguerriana, MS a 46.[28]

Arnulf's second work, the *Allegoriae*, became the most widely circulated and influential interpretation of the epic during the thirteenth and

---

[22] Arnulf of Orléans 1932: 183.

[23] Edited by Ghisalberti in Arnulf 1932: 180–1. For the sources of Arnulf's *accessus*, see Coulson 1986a. For the influence of Arnulf's *accessus* on Italian humanists, see especially Minnis and Scott 1991: 321.

[24] Berlin, SB–PKb, lat. oct. MS 68, fol. 1r and Prague, Národní Knihovna České Republiky, MS viii h 32, fol. 78r. See Coulson and Roy 2000: no. 444 for complete manuscript listings. The commentary is briefly discussed in Peebles 1964.

[25] Edited by Klopsch, Pseudo-Ovidius 1967. For *De vetula* see also in this volume, pp. 305–8.

[26] Complete list of manuscripts in Coulson and Roy 2000: no. 419.

[27] The manuscript is written in a Gothic *textualis formata* bookhand (and not a humanistic bookhand as one might perhaps expect). An anonymous reader for the Press suggested that the script may reflect the antiquarian interests of the commentator. While an intriguing suggestion, I would argue that the Gothic bookhand may merely reflect the speed of dissemination of humanistic minuscule, which only came into being in Florence in the first decade of the fifteenth century.

[28] For Sozomeno, see Coulson 1987c; Martinelli 1991; and Gaisser 2008. For Ovid in this context see also in this volume, pp. 123–42 at 124–5, 130–1, 139–40.

fourteenth centuries. In the manuscripts of the *Metamorphoses*, it was transmitted either as an integral and complete text, often with the *Integumenta
Ovidii* of John of Garland; or alternatively, the individual allegory for
each story became detached from its authorial setting and was placed in
the margins of the manuscript beside the relevant story. This allegorical
mode of reading initiated by Arnulf was to have a long and important history in Ovidian interpretation down to the time of the Renaissance. Such
later authors as the French Vulgate commentator (*fl.* 1250) and the Italian
humanist Giovanni del Virgilio (1323) modified the content of Arnulf's
allegories;[29] the French Dominican scholar Pierre Bersuire greatly enlarged
the scope of this allegorical mode of reading in his *Ovidius moralizatus*,[30] a
work conceived to provide preachers with material for their sermons; and
French Renaissance and German Reformation commentators on the *Metamorphoses*, such as the French Dominican Pierre Lavin[31] and the German
humanist Georg Schuler,[32] pursued the allegorical mode of reading well
into the sixteenth century.

William of Orléans

A generation after Arnulf, William of Orléans (*fl.* 1200) produced at Orléans
a detailed set of philological glosses (the so-called *Versus bursarii*[33]) on virtually the entire Ovidian corpus (see figure 3.2). Like his predecessor Arnulf,
William is clearly writing for a younger, elementary student audience,
and he is primarily, though not exclusively, interested in explicating the

---

[29] For Giovanni del Virgilio see also in this volume, pp. 127–8.

[30] For editions of and bibliography on Bersuire, see Coulson and Roy 2000: no. 2. The best summary
discussion of Bersuire's methodology is Moss 1982: 23–6. For a stimulating discussion of the purpose
behind the work, see Hexter 1989. Selections from the *Ovidius moralizatus* are translated in Reynolds
1971, 1978, and 1990. See also in this volume, pp. 86–7, 180, 184, 191–2, 195, 271–5.

[31] Lavin wrote at Vienne during Easter of 1510 an allegorical interpretation which (perhaps mercifully)
stops at *Met.* 1.451. Printed at Lyons in 1510, the work is most easily accessible in Orgel 1976. For
Lavin, see, in particular, Moss 1982: 31–5 and 1998: 103–21.

[32] Schuler (1513–60) produced his allegories in 1554 for the benefit of his students at Königsberg. See
Moss 1982: 48–53 and 1998: 143–64.

[33] The title derives from the first sentence of William's prologue: 'Quoniam in Ovidianis ex Bur-
sariorum ambiguitate et continuacione sentencie difficultas invenitur, compendiose explanare
decrevimus quid super hoc nostre videtur opinioni. Et quia de Bursariis tractandum est, videndum est quid sit bursarius. Bursarius a bursa, quia in eo diverse inveniuntur explicaciones' (Since
in the works of Ovid difficulty arises both from the ambiguity of the 'bursars' and the train of
thought, we decided to explain fully our thoughts on this. And since it is a question of 'bursars',
we should see what the word means. Bursar is derived from pocket-book, since diverse explanations (or folds) may therein be found). William seems therefore to derive the unusual adjective
bursarius from pocketbook, punning on the double meaning of *explicationes* (folds and solutions
to problems).

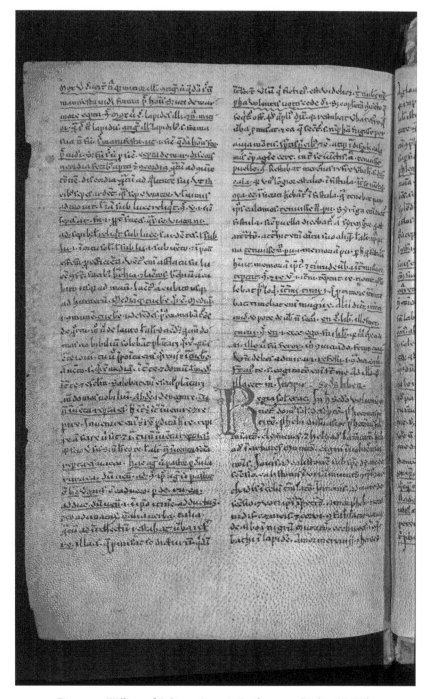

Figure 3.2 William of Orléans, *Bursarii Ovidianorum* (Berlin, SB-PKb, Handschriftenabteilung, lat. qu. MS 219, fol. 83v)

grammar of passages he perceived to be of particular difficulty.[34] William does not allegorise the fables, nor does he reveal a deep interest in Ovidian style.[35] Rather he seeks to explicate the grammar of the poem, to clarify word meanings, to illustrate structural connections between the seemingly loose strands of the narrative, and to furnish mythological background. Further, he is highly selective with regard to the number of lines he glosses in each book. A more detailed examination of the glosses to several books of the *Metamorphoses* will illustrate some of these interests.

William is concerned, in particular, to explicate the meaning of less well-known words for his readers. Hence the gloss to the text at *Met.* 1.13 reads:[36] '*Amphitrites* id est magnum mare, quod circuit mundum ab "amphi" quod est circum, et "triton" quod est mare, sive a "tero, teris"'(*Amphitrite*: that is to say the great sea, which encircles the Earth, from 'amphi' meaning around and 'triton' which means sea, or from 'to wear down'). William also shows some awareness of problematic passages in the text of the poem. At *Met.* 1.700, for example, the narrator reports that Mercury arrests his story in mid stream, since Argus has been lulled to sleep by his soporific tale. Here, unlike Arnulf, William is cognisant of the much vexed question of non-Ovidian lines interpolated into the text:

1.700   *Talia verba refert*: Talia quantum ad intellectum. *Restabat verba referre*, illa scilicet que promiserat se dicturum. Quidam interserunt versum qui ficticius est, videlicet *tibi nubere nimpha volentis votis cede dei*, sed copulata coniunctio que sequitur ostendit quod nichil amplius dixit.

And he says such words: such words as these in sense. *It remained to relate the words*, namely those which he had promised he would relate. Some intercalate a verse which is not Ovidian, namely 'Nymph, accede to the wishes of the god who wants to marry you' but the repetition of the phrase that follows ('uerba referre' to relate the story) shows that he said nothing further.

At *Met.* 2.689, William correctly interprets the manuscript reading *Nili* as an allusion to Nileus, the father of Nestor, and not to the river Nile:

---

[34] In this respect, the commentary is very similar to the Liber Titan, composed by Ralph of Beauvais in the mid twelfth century and now edited in Kneepkens 1991. The classic study on Ralph as a commentator is Hunt 1950.

[35] Parallel passages to other authors are infrequently deduced to explicate the meaning of a phrase but never to illuminate its literary qualities. At *Met.* 8.73, for example, Scylla justifies her course of action with the words: 'Sibi quisque profecto est deus' (each man is his own god), and William comments: 'Hoc dicit secundum sentenciam Stoicorum qui dicunt quod unicuique animus est suus deus [cf. Cicero, *Tusculanae Disputationes* 1.22] iuxta illud Iuuenalis: "Nullum numen habes si sit prudencia"' [Juvenal, *Satires* 10.365] (She says this according to the dictates of the Stoics who say that each man's spirit is his own god, according to that saying of Juvenal: 'you would have no power, if we were sensible').

[36] Quotations are taken from the edited text of the commentary in Engelbrecht 2003: 2.121–68.

2.689 *Herbosaque pascua Nili*, id est Nilei patris Nestoris, qui rex fuit Pylos ciuitatis iuxta quam hoc contigit. Vnde superius 'Pylios memorantur in agros processisse boues' [*Met.* 2.684–5]. Quidam peccant legendo Nili, id est fluuii.

The pasture lands of Nileus, that is to say of Nileus the father of Nestor, who was the king of the region of Pylos, next to which this event took place. And hence above 'The cows, it is said, wandered away into Pylos's fields'. Some here read of the Nile, that is to say of the river, but they are in error.

At other points, William is careful to guide his reader through a word-by-word exposition of the text, scrupulously underlining the connections between its constituent parts.[37]

William's *Versus bursarii* became one of the more important commentaries on the Ovidian corpus circulating in the thirteenth and fourteenth centuries. Many of its glosses were incorporated into the later Vulgate commentary. In particular, William's explication of the *Heroides* circulated widely, often separately from its original setting, and influenced vernacular poets who wrote in imitation of the classical original, such as the Spaniard Juan Rodríguez del Padrón, author of the *El Bursario*.[38]

Manuscripts containing Anthologies

In the thirteenth century, commentaries of French origin, particularly those associated with the *Orléanais*, became anthologised to provide the medieval reader with an overview of school material on the Ovidian corpus. Three of the most important representatives of such anthologies are Copenhagen, Det Kongelige Bibliotek, Fabricius MS 29 2°,[39] Antwerp, Musaeum Plantin Moretus, MS M 85, and Oxford, Bodl., Canon. class. lat. MS 1, all dating to the early thirteenth century. Fabricius 29 2° is a manuscript written in two parts by two roughly contemporary thirteenth-century hands (part one covers folios 1r–45v; part two, folios 46r–59v). The Ovidian commentaries transmitted in the manuscript clearly attest to the continued ascendancy of *Orléanais* masters, for herein we find William of Orléans's glosses to the *Metamorphoses*, Arnulf of Orléans's glosses to the *Fasti*, and two further commentaries, one on the *Heroides* and one on the

---

[37] Examples of this technique can be found at *Met.* 1.403, 493, 746, 2.647, 2.839 etc.

[38] Juan Rodríguez del Padrón wrote the *El Bursario* about 1438. The text is now available in Rodríguez del Padrón 1984, ed. Suàrez-Somonte and Rolàn. Engelbrecht 2003: 2.9–40 lists the parallels between the two works. For the Spanish context see also in this volume, pp. 231–56 at 246.

[39] The manuscript is briefly discussed and described in Lehmann 1935.

Tristia, both of unidentified authorship. Additionally, one finds a collection of *accessus ad auctores* containing introductions to the Ovidian corpus (fols. 5vb–6rb).[40] Antwerp, M 85 brings together the commentaries of Arnulf of Orléans on the *Amores*, *Ars amatoria* and *Metamorphoses*, the commentary on the *Remedia amoris* by Fulco of Orléans, and commentaries on the *Tristia* and the *Epistulae ex Ponto* which may also be attributed to Arnulf. Finally, Oxford, Canon. class. lat. 1, a manuscript of Italian origin, assembles the commentaries of Arnulf of Orléans to the *Ars amatoria*, the *Metamorphoses* and the *Fasti*, the commentary of William of Orléans to the *Tristia*, as well as two further commentaries on the *Heroides* and the *Epistulae ex Ponto* which may be the work of Arnulf of Orléans. Manuscripts that contain anthologies of medieval literary criticism on classical poetry such as the aforementioned provide an important window onto the interests and reading practices of medieval students and scholars.

OVID AT PARIS: JOHN OF GARLAND AND FURTHER ALLEGORICAL READINGS

The Englishman John of Garland[41] was born in 1195 and migrated to the University of Paris about 1217 where he began his teaching career, taking his name from the 'clos de Garlande' in which some of the oldest Parisian schools were established. John remained at Paris for the remainder of his career, except for a brief period as Master of Grammar at the newly founded University of Toulouse from 1229–32. He composed works in varied genres, including poetry, grammar, and rhetoric. His *Integumenta Ovidii* (see figure 3.3),[42] probably written *c.* 1234, consists of 520 elegiac verses wherein John seeks through allegory to uncover the hidden truths of the Ovidian fables:

---

[40] The earliest and most important collection of *accessus* to classical and late antique texts was produced at the monastery of Tegernsee in the late eleventh to early twelfth century. See *Accessus ad auctores* 1970. Selected *accessus* from the collection are translated in Minnis and Scott 1991: 20–30 and Elliott 1980.

[41] For John of Garland's life and works, see in particular, Paetow 1927; Hauréau 1879; and most recently Marguin-Hamon 2006, where the author lists three manuscripts of the *Integumenta* (apparently unaware of the additional nineteen manuscripts of the text listed in Coulson and Roy 2000: no. 333). For a survey of manuscripts of the *Integumenta* in England see McKinley 1998 wherein one can find an excellent overview of Ovid manuscripts circulating in England in the Middle Ages.

[42] The *Integumenta Ovidii* is edited by Ghisalberti, John of Garland 1933, and by Born, John of Garland 1929 (though Born's translation must be used with caution). Quotations from the *Integumenta Ovidii* in this article follow the edition of Ghisalberti. See McKinley 2001: 69–73 and Chance 2000: 236–52. See also in this volume, pp. 94, 102, 105, 237, 239, 300n, 313.

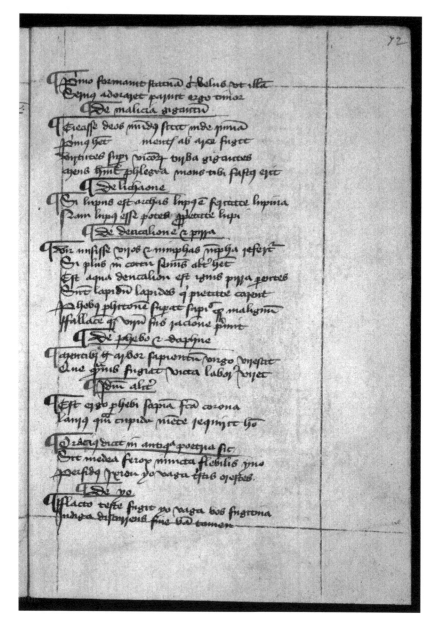

Figure 3.3 John of Garland, *Integumenta* (Oxford, Bodl., Hatton MS 92, fol. 72r)

> Morphosis Ovidii parva cum clave Iohannis
>   Panditur, et presens cartula servit ei.
> Nodos secreti denodat, clausa revelat;
>   Rarificat nebulas, integumenta[43] canit.
>
> (vv. 5–8)

Ovid's *Metamorphosis* is opened up with John's little key, and this little scrap of parchment renders service to it. It unknots secrets, reveals things that are hidden; it disperses clouds and sings of coverings.

The remaining twelve lines of the introduction (vv. 9–20) elucidate John's interpretive strategies: transformation in the *Metamorphoses* may be categorised under four broad categories, namely natural transformation, artificial transformation, transformation by type and magical transformation.[44] Further, John will not allegorise all parts of the story but will deal only with selected episodes – *omnes ficticii partes non discute, summam elige* (vv. 19–20) (Do not enquire into all parts of a fictional story, but choose the essence.)

The *Integumenta Ovidii* overtly (and covertly) draws upon earlier interpretations. Europa's rape by Jupiter, for example, is given a euhemeristic interpretation drawn directly from the *Allegoriae* of Arnulf of Orléans:

> Iuppiter Europam rapuit rate, Taurus in illa
>   Pictus erat, 'taurus' nomine navis erat.
>
> (vv. 151–2)

---

43 The term *integumentum* literally means a covering. During the Middle Ages, it came to denote the hidden or allegorical meaning to be found in a fable or story. The best exposition of the history and use of the term is Jeauneau 1957.

44 John is drawing here on earlier *accessus* to the *Metamorphoses*, all of which divide transformation in the poem into three or four broad categories. Arnulf of Orléans, in his *accessus* to the grammatical glosses, discusses transformation under the headings of natural, magical, and spiritual change (. . . de mutacione enim agit tripliciter s. de naturali, de magica, et de spirituali. Naturalis est que fit per contexionem et retexionem elementorum: per contexionem quando s. elementa coniunguntur ut de spermate fiat puer et de ovo pullus, per retexionem elementorum quando s. retexuntur et dissolvuntur in quelibet corpora vel per ignem vel alio modo in pulverem redigendo. Magica est quando fit per prestigia magicorum, ut de Licaone et Io qui corpore non animo mutati sunt. Spiritualis que fit circa spiritum ut de insano fit sanus, vel e contrario ut Agave et Autonoe que spiritu et non corpore mutabantur (Arnulf of Orléans 1932: 181)). William of Orléans divides transformation into the three broad categories of moral, spiritual and magical transformation (. . . Sed quia de mutacione mencionem fecimus, videndum est quot sint modi mutacionis. Tres scilicet, est enim ethica mutacio et theorica et magica. Ethica est moralis, sicut de animali racionabili ad irracionabile, ut mutacio Lycaonis in lupum. Theorica est spiritualis, ut deficacio Herculis. Magica est de re inanimata ad rem animatam, sciut mutacio ymaginis quam fecit Prometheus (Engelbrecht 2003: 2.122)). The Vulgate commentary includes the four categories of natural, moral, magical, and spiritual transformation (Notandum est quod quadruplex est mutacio: naturalis, moralis, magica, et spiritualis (Coulson 1991: 27)).

Jupiter stole Europa away on a boat on which a bull was painted, and hence the ship was called 'Taurus'.[45]

John directly alludes at v. 97 to Horace's invocation of Io in *Ars poetica*, vv. 123–4:

> Flacco[46] teste, fugit Yo vaga, bos fugitiva (v. 97).[47]
>
> As Horace attests, Io, a wanderer, flees, a fugitive cow.

John's language, at once highly alliterative,[48] elliptical, onomatopoeic and playful, often so obscures the meaning of a given transformation that it may only be understood with recourse to the glosses and commentaries transmitted with text manuscripts of the *Metamorphoses* from 1150–1250 (chief among these being the philological commentary of Arnulf of Orléans and the so-called Vulgate commentary). At *Integ.* vv. 29–33, for example, John, glossing *Met.* 1.52–3, alludes to the numerical proportions employed by the Creator to bind the disparate elements together:

> Nos iuvat hec numeri proportio, mensio terna: –
>   Dic michi bis duo bis ter tria ter tibi sint.
> Hos iungat medio numeros proportio talis:
>   Dic michi bis duo ter ter tria bis tibi sunt.
> Sic numeris elementa ligat,[49] quo cuncta moventur.
>
>   (vv. 29–33)

This proportion of number, this threefold measure, helps us – twice two twice, thrice three thrice. Let such a proportion join these numbers in the middle; twice two thrice, three times three twice. Thus the creator binds the elements in numerical proportion by which the universe is set in motion.

---

[45] Cf. Arnulf, *Allegoriae* 2.13: 'Sed quia navis eius thaurum depictum habebat in priori parte ideo dicitur de specie thauri eam rapuisse. Vel quia navis eius thaurus vocabatur quam ipsa ascendit' (Jupiter is said to have ravished Europa in the form of a bull because his ship had a bull painted on its prow. Or because his boat which she boarded was called 'the Bull').

[46] Ghisalberti's text here reads *fracto*. I adopt the reading from Born, 'The *Integumenta*'.

[47] The allusion parallels the interpretation of the Vulgate commentary to *Met.* 1.727: '*Terruit*: dum sic vagam Io subdidit, Ouidius tanquam bonus poeta proprietatibus materie obseruando doctorem artis Horacium sequitur qui sic fieri docet in *Poetria*' (*He terrified*: Ovid being a good poet, in portraying Io wandering, adheres to the proper handling of his subject matter according to the precepts of Horace, the master of the art, who taught that it should be so in his *Art of Poetry*) (Coulson 1987a: 52).

[48] E.g. v. 35: 'vernat ver, estas estuat, auget et estas' (Ghis. 'escas'); v. 155: 'ut serpens serpit pauper sed pectore prudens'; v. 147: 'vir valet invictus et inexoriabilis esse'; v. 205: 'Tantalides similis tibi, Tantale, vivit avarus'.

[49] 'Sic numeris elementa ligat': the source for which is Boethius, *Consolatio Philosophiae* 3. metron 9.10.

These rather abstruse references[50] cloak an allusion to the creator's use of
numerical proportions as elucidated by Boethius at *Consolatio Philosophiae*
3. metr. 9.10, which the medieval commentary tradition on the *Metamorphoses* expounds upon at some length.[51] Similarly, John's literal explanation of the five zones that divide the earth (*Integ.*, vv. 36–7) owes much
to the commentary tradition accompanying these lines in the medieval
manuscripts.[52] Finally, John's elliptical description of the chariot of the
Sun (vv. 121–2) is once again more clearly understood with reference to the
Latin commentary tradition explicating these verses:

> *Integ.* Themo grammatica, logice nitet axis, adornat
>   Hos resis, decus est quadriviale rote.
>
> (vv. 121–2)

The pole is grammar, the axis gleams with logic, while rhetoric (*rhesis*) adorns
these; the wheels represent the beauty of the quadrivium.

Gloss of the Vulgate commentary to *Met.* 2.107: *Aureus axis*: per currum solis
habet intelligi scientia. Per themonem aureum qui prior est in curru habet intelligi
gramatica que prior est inter alias scientias. Per axem qui sustinet currum intelligitur
logica que est inquisitio veri et falsi, et sustinentur per ipsam alie sciencie quia in
omni sciencia contingit argumentari dialectice. Per crisolitos intelligitur ornatus
tocius sermonis, sicut crisoliti ornant currum. Per quatuor rotas habet intelligi
quatuor artes mathematice que faciunt quadrivium. Et hoc habetur per hos versus:
'Themo' etc.

Golden chariot: by the chariot of the sun one may understand knowledge. By the
golden pole which is at the front of the chariot, one may understand grammar,
which is first among the sciences. By the axle which supports the chariot logic
is understood, which is the investigation into truth and falsehood; and all other
categories of knowledge depend upon it since in every branch of knowledge one has
occasion to argue according to dialectic. By topaz, we understand the adornment
of speech in its entirety, just as topaz adorns the chariot. By the four wheels, one
understands the four mathematical arts which make up the quadrivium. And this
can be understood by these verses: 'The pole' etc.

Most allegories in the *Integumenta* provide a moral interpretation of the
Ovidian fable. So, for instance, the story of Argus represents the clever man
who is ensnared by the riches of the world (vv. 99–102), whereas the story of

---

[50] The exact meaning of the verses remained a mystery to Born, the first editor of the *Integumenta*,
who comments 'What is meant by it at all events I do not know' (John of Garland 1929: 124). The
exact same numerical proportions are found in a twelfth-century commentary on Boethius. See Silk
1935: 161. I am indebted to Greg Hays for this reference.

[51] See, for example, the comments of the Vulgate commentary for lines 1.25 and 1.53.

[52] See, for example, the Vulgate commentary to 1.45.

Narcissus illustrates youth deceived by earthly vanities (vv. 163–4). Certain moral allegories receive a more extended and fanciful development, as is the case with the story of Mercury from Book 1 of the *Metamorphoses*:

> Mercurius mentes curans deus eloquiorum,
> Verbi mobilitas dicitur ala duplex;
> Sermonis virga vis est; sopire tirannos fertur,
> et egrotis mentibus addit opem. (105–8)

Mercury, having care for the mind, is the god of utterances. His two wings represent the rapidity of speech; his wand is the might of speech, which is said to put tyrants to sleep, and aids the sick mind.

The form of the verse allegory on Ovid inaugurated by John exerted a lasting influence on interpretation of the *Metamorphoses* throughout the late Middle Ages. The *Integumenta* itself circulated widely in no fewer than twenty-two manuscripts dating from the thirteenth to the fifteenth century.[53] In addition, individual verses from the *Integumenta* were copied next to the appropriate transformation in virtually every glossed manuscript of the poem during the thirteenth and fourteenth centuries. John's verse treatment spawned numerous contemporary or later imitations. Particularly important are the verse summaries transmitted in Paris, BN, lat. MS 8011 (as yet unedited) and the many verse treatments composed during the Renaissance, including those by Orico da Capriana,[54] Antonio da Asti,[55] Giovanni Francesco Conti,[56] Bartolomeo Bolognine,[57] Pier Candido Decembrio,[58] Folchino de Borfoni,[59] Franciscus Niger Venetus,[60] and the German reformation humanist Johann Spreng.[61] In the early fourteenth century, the Italian humanist scholar Giovanni del Virgilio created his own prosimetric interpretation of the *Metamorphoses* modelled in part on the earlier work of John.[62] And in the school of Alphonso the Wise in Toledo,

---

[53] For a complete list of manuscripts see Coulson and Roy 2000: no. 333.
[54] Edited in Munzi 1990.   [55] Antonio's verse summary is edited in Sabbadini 1905: 74.
[56] Giovanni's verse summary is printed in *Que hoc in libello continentur Jo. Fr. Quintiani Stoae* (Paris: A. Aussonari, 1515).
[57] Bartolomeo's verse treatment is printed in *Epitoma elegiaca in Ovidii libros Metamorphoseon* (Bologna: per Iohannem Iacobus de Fontanensis, 1492).
[58] Edited in Ditt 1932: 89.   [59] Folchino's works are now edited by DeSantis, Folchino 2003.
[60] Franciscus' verse summary is printed in Publius Ovidius Naso, *Opera omnia* (Basel: ex aedibus Henrici Petri, 1544).
[61] Johann Spreng (1524–1601), a pupil of Melanchthon, was a German poet and translator of the classics. His *Metamorphosis Ovidii argumentis quidem soluta oratione, enarrationibus autem et allegoriis elegiaco versu accuratissime expositae* was first published at Frankfurt in 1563. See Moss 1982: 44–8.
[62] For Giovanni del Virgilio, see the comments of Black, below (pp. 127–8) and Ghisalberti in Giovanni del Virgilio 1933.

the redactors of the Spanish vernacular work, *General Estoria*, composed c. 1275, are known to have made use of John's *Integumenta*.

COMMENTARY IN THE ORLÉANAIS C. 1260:
THE VULGATE COMMENTARY

In the third quarter of the thirteenth century, a compiler assembled a commentary on the *Metamorphoses* (the so-called Vulgate commentary[63]) that became the most authoritative 'reading' of the epic in the high Middle Ages. To date, the commentary has not been attributed to a known individual, but it is evident from internal evidence and from certain palaeographical features of the earliest manuscripts that the commentary was produced in the *Orléanais*. These earliest manuscripts (which date to 1250–60[64]) all have an identical layout and decoration – three columns of commentary surround the text of the *Metamorphoses*; the longer allegorical glosses are consistently placed at the top and bottom of folios; flourished initials alternating in red and blue decorate the opening of books and sections (see figure 3.4). Further, the text of the so-called Vulgate commentary is extremely stable, displaying none of the fluidity so characteristic of anonymous commentaries in the later medieval period.[65] The commentary possesses an intimate knowledge of the earlier works of Arnulf and William of Orléans, as well as other twelfth-century commentary to the poem.[66] Extant in twenty-two witnesses,[67] it continued to be copied throughout the fourteenth century in France and Italy and garnered a high degree of *auctoritas*. Though the commentary was not printed, there is evidence for its continued use as late as 1475, since a reader has entered the nearly complete text for Book 1 of the Vulgate commentary into his edition of the *Metamorphoses* printed in that year.[68]

The Vulgate commentary appears to have been used by grammar masters as an authoritative 'reading' of the poem from which they could pick and choose at random according to the level or sophistication of their audience.

---

[63] I have adopted this nomenclature from Castiglioni's reference to the commentary as 'il commentario vulgato' (Castiglioni 1920).

[64] These are the following: Berlin, SB-PKb, Diez. B Sant. MS 5; Leiden, Bibliotheek der Rijksuniversiteit, BPL MS 95; Sélestat, Bibliothèque humaniste, MS 92; Vatican City, BAV, Vat. lat. MS 1598; and Wolfenbüttel, Herzog August Bibliothek, Cod. Guelf. 159 Gud. lat.

[65] For a detailed discussion of the manuscript tradition, see Coulson 1982.

[66] I have traced these borrowings more fully in Coulson 1991.

[67] For a detailed list of manuscripts with bibliography see Coulson and Roy 2000: no. 421.

[68] See Coulson 1995.

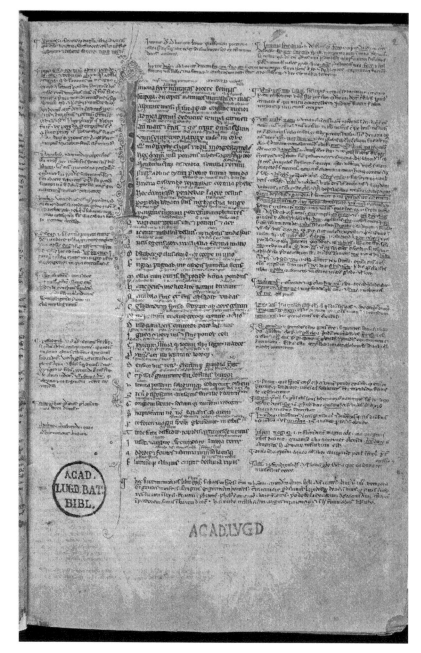

Figure 3.4 Vulgate commentary (Leiden, Bibliotheek der Rijksuniversiteit, BPL MS 95, fol. 2r)

Many of the extant manuscripts of the commentary were owned by teaching masters (see below). In addition, the Vulgate commentary serves as a repository of earlier twelfth-century scholarship on the poem (particularly from Orléans), explicating the poem from multiple perspectives, including the grammatical, the allegorical and the literary. The *magister* could therefore plumb the commentary to meet the needs of the most elementary to the most advanced student.

Individual manuscripts of the Vulgate commentary can tell us much about the circulation of the text. Vatican City, BAV, Vat. lat. MS 1598, one of the earliest manuscripts of the commentary, passed through the hands of a certain Guillelmus Golotii, who in the fourteenth century gave the manuscript to the Augustinian monastery of St Etienne at Dijon as security against a bad debt. It was later acquired by the French cardinal Jean Jouffroi (cardinal of Arras and later of Albi, 1463–71). Further, the manuscript shows evidence of careful reading and correction by a later fourteenth-century hand which alters the original text of the commentary, often introducing readings which are not attested elsewhere in the manuscript tradition, proffering a forcefully worded opinion on the interpretations advanced in the original commentary, or emending the original text.[69] The manuscript presently housed in the Bibliothèque humaniste of Sélestat (MS 92), dating to the second half of the thirteenth century, shows evidence of having been owned by multiple masters and institutions, including Symon Boiseneau, a certain Rollandus and the Regular Canons of Saint Augustin with the date 1329.[70] It was purchased by Beatus Rhenanus, the Alsatian humanist, during his studies in Paris in 1506. Rhenanus wrote a commentary on the *Fasti* at the tender age of 14 (Sélestat, Bibliothèque humaniste, 50), and his purchase of a manuscript of the *Metamorphoses* equipped with the Vulgate commentary may indicate that medieval exegesis was still valued by northern humanists at this relatively late date. Finally, Vatican City, BAV, Ottob. lat. MS 1294, a fourteenth-century Italian copy of the

---

[69] I list several examples of the type of correction provided by the later hand in Vat. lat. 1598. At *Met.* 1.463–4 Cupid replies to Apollo's taunts: 'Your bow may strike all, Phoebus. Mine strikes you' and the Vulgate commentator remarks: '*Figat* concessio ex indignatione, sarcosmos. Hostilis derisio, vel indignacio que pungit usque ad carnem.' The correcting hand adds the comment 'et secundum hoc non suppletur ibi quamuis'. At *Met.* 1.142, the text reads 'war which fights with both' (or alternatively 'on either side') and the Vulgate comments: '*with both*, that is to say on both sides, since you cannot have war except between two people. Or read *in both directions*, in either part. Or understand *with both* because the battle takes place with the sword for gold'. The correcting hand in Vat. lat. 1598 adds: 'Well this reading is a lot better than the others since *with both* is placed materially and causally, since iron is the material from which arms are made with which we fight wars, and gold is the reason for war.'

[70] The manuscript is fully described in Coulson 1985: 126.

Vulgate commentary, contains extensive glossing by at least two later hands, clearly attesting to the reworking of the commentary text by subsequent generations.[71]

The Vulgate commentary is always transmitted as a series of interlinear and marginal glosses surrounding the text of the poem (and never as a separate *catena* commentary, as was the case with the work of the earlier Orléanais commentators Arnulf and William). The interlinear gloss, not surprisingly, functions to elucidate the grammar of the verse, to explain the specific use of cases, to supply a referent for a relative, to provide synonyms for abstruse allusions, to advance alternative manuscript readings, or, more rarely, to comment on metrical anomalies.[72]

The marginal commentary in certain respects reflects the scholarly interests of thirteenth-century masters. For example, the commentator relies principally upon the newly composed verse grammars of Alexander of Villa Dei (*Doctrinale*) and of Eberhard of Béthune (*Graecismus*) for mnemonic verse tags to help students retain essential points of grammar, syntax, and meaning. In addition, like his predecessor Arnulf, he supplies allegorical and moral interpretations that are frequently (though not exclusively) adapted from Arnulf's *Allegoriae* and John of Garland's *Integumenta Ovidii*; and the commentator spends much time elaborating the rhetorical devices Ovid used to embellish his epic.

The Vulgate commentary often directly illustrates the teaching techniques while recording the 'voice' of the medieval master. At *Met.* 8.73, Scylla employs a *sententia* to justify her deed: 'Ignauis precibus Fortuna repugnat' ('Fortune rejects the prayers of the faint at heart'), and the Vulgate commentator explains the phrase with reference to his readership:

Met. 8.73 *Fortuna repugnat* generalis est sententia. Verbi gratia: rogate cotidie deum ut faciat vos bonos clericos, non ideo faciet nisi circa studium intentionem aliquam imponatis. Rogate ergo fortunam, id est deum, non precibus solum set opera.[73]

Fortune rejects: this is a general statement. For example, daily ask God to make you good clerics, but he will not do so unless you put a certain amount of zeal into your studies. Ask therefore fortune, that is to say God, not only with your prayers but with your application.

In other respects, though, the commentary furnishes the medieval reader with a unique and highly sophisticated interpretation of the epic – one that

---

[71] For a detailed description of the manuscript, see Pellegrin *et al.* 1975–91, vol. I.2: 512–13.
[72] For further discussion of the marginal gloss, see in particular Coulson 1991: 8–9.
[73] Coulson 1982: 21 and 1991: 59–61 for further instances.

emphasises to an unprecedented degree the literary qualities of the poem. The commentator is particularly interested in the development of character portrayal, whether it pertains to an individual character in a single story of the *Metamorphoses* (such as the figure of Niobe from Book 6), or as revealed in several Ovidian poems (such as the portrayal of Medea in *Her.* 7 and *Met.* 7).

Further, he is sensitive to smaller, significant details of character. For example, Procne's ruthless slaying of Itys at *Met.* 6.642 is highlighted by Ovid with the words 'nec uultum uertit' (nor did she turn aside her face). The Vulgate commentator notes the savagery in his comment *ad loc.*: 'id est non auertit oculos licet mater esset per quod ipsius impietas permaxima denotatur' (Though a mother, she did not turn aside her eyes, and by this her great impiety is conveyed). The second feature of the Vulgate which clearly sets it apart from other commentaries on the *Metamorphoses* circulating in the high Middle Ages is its intense preoccupation with questions of Ovidian style, word usage, and influence. The commentator lays stress on unusual word usages either invented or coined by the author. To give but two examples of this trait: at *Met.* 2.605, Ovid uses the coined *hapax* 'indeuitato' (that which cannot be avoided) to describe Apollo's arrow. Earlier in the epic at *Met.* 1.458, Apollo describes his own arrows as producing 'certa uulnera' (unerring wounds), and the Vulgate commentator perceptively draws the connection between the two scenes by glossing the adjective in the text 'certa' (sagitta) with the *hapax* 'indeuitata'. At *Met.* 6.275, Ovid similarly employs the adjective 'resupina' (with her head drawn back in a show of pride) to describe the character of Niobe. This meaning of the adjective is virtually unique in Latin, and once again our commentator draws the connection between the adjective and the first entrance of Niobe (*Met.* 6.165), where Ovid emphasises Niobe's pride and disdain. The commentator is both interested in tracing the manner in which Ovid draws upon his epic predecessor Virgil and in elucidating how Ovid influenced the epic tradition of the Silver Age, particularly the writings of Lucan, Statius, and Valerius Flaccus. Virgil's elaborate description of Eurydice's death is set in juxtaposition to Ovid's more compressed account.[74] Ovid's direct influence on Statius' epic the *Thebaid* is duly noted. Most interestingly, in two places, the Vulgate commentary alludes to similarity of presentation in Ovid's 'Argonautica' (*Met.* 7.1–158) and Valerius Flaccus' epic. That the lines from Valerius Flaccus are not attested in the *Florilegium Gallicum* may indicate that a full text of the poem was circulating in the

---

[74] See Coulson 1991: 119.

Loire valley some two hundred years before its supposed rediscovery by
Poggio Bracciolini in 1416.[75]

Finally, I would like to highlight the manner in which the Vulgate
commentator, nearly alone amongst the commentators of the high Middle
Ages, illuminates Ovidian influence on Latin poets of the twelfth century.[76]
At its most basic level, the Vulgate commentary alludes to contemporary
poets to illustrate specifically Ovidian influence on a particular scene.
Reference to twelfth-century poets is also made when explicating Ovid's
extended similes. At *Met.* 8.835–43, Ovid compares Erysichthon's insatiable
hunger to the force of fire and of the sea, and the Vulgate commentator
further develops the imagery:

De duobus insatiabilibus facit hic actor mentionem, de igne scilicet et mari. Sunt
et alia duo, infernus scilicet et connus. De inferno in *Alexandreide*: 'et umbriferi
domus insatiabilis antri' [5.141]. De conno Iuuenalis: 'et lassata uiris numquam sati-
ata recessit' [*Satires* 6.130]; quintum etiam adinuenit Ouidius, scilicet Erisitonem,
cui nichil suffecerat, unde subdit *sic epulas* etc.[77]

Ovid comments here on two things which are insatiable, namely fire and the sea.
There are two others, Hell and the female genitals. [Walter writes] about Hell
in the *Alexandreis*; 'and the insatiable house of the shade-bearing cavern', while
Juvenal writes about the female genitals: 'Tired but never satiated of men, she
slinks home.' To these Ovid adds a fifth, namely Erysichthon, for whom nothing
sufficed, and hence he adds: *Thus dinners* etc.

The Vulgate commentary dominated the exegetical landscape of the
Metamorphoses from 1250 to 1400.[78] Indeed, Fausto Ghisalberti, in a series
of articles published in *Il giornale dantesco*,[79] intimated that the Vulgate
commentary was the probable source for Dante's mythological readings in
the *Divine Comedy* and the *Convivio*. A critical edition of the complete
commentary might shed much light on its influence on other vernacular
authors such as Chaucer.[80]

---

[75] See Coulson 1986b.
[76] See Coulson 1982 for copious examples.   [77] Coulson 1982: 31.
[78] In addition to the twenty-two complete or fragmentary manuscript fragments of the Vulgate
  commentary, there is evidence that the Vulgate strongly influenced the later commentary tradition on the *Metamorphoses*. See, in particular, Coulson 1982: 17–20. See also in this volume,
  pp. 72, 151–2.
[79] See Ghisalberti 1932, 1934 and 1966.
[80] I am currently engaged on a critical edition of the text. My translation of Book I is forthcoming in
  the TEAMS translation series. Numerous scholars in conversation have intimated that the Vulgate
  commentary may be the missing link through which vernacular authors read their Ovid. For
  perceptive analysis of the links between the Latin commentary tradition and vernacular poetry
  (especially Chaucer) see Fumo 2004 and 2007.

During the late thirteenth and fourteenth centuries, manuscripts of the *Metamorphoses* were frequently accompanied by dense interlinear and marginal glosses amounting to an integral commentary. The most striking examples of such glossed manuscripts are Paris, BN, lat. MS 8010 of the early fourteenth century (which contains the commentary of William of Thiegiis); Basel, Universitätsbibliothek, MS F II 28 and Vatican City, BAV, Pal. lat. MS 1667 (which contain an integral commentary henceforward labelled Anonymous Commentary A); Milan, Biblioteca Ambrosiana, MS N 254 sup.; and Vatican City, BAV, Vat. lat. MS 1479.[81]

William of Thiegiis

William of Thiegiis' commentary was brought to the attention of scholars in 1885 by Barthélemy Hauréau[82] from the then single-known manuscript witness, Paris, BN, lat. 8010 of the early fourteenth century, where William, in the gloss to *Met.* 15.871, identifies himself as the author and explicitly alludes to the level of student for whom the commentary has been compiled:

Iamque opus exegi, id est perfeci, et Gullermus de Thiegiis qui hoc fideliter minus prouectis compilauit, ordinauit, et iniunxit, cuiusque scrutantis uel recitantis uel studentis aliquam impetrat orationem in Christo ut ipsius Christus misereatur. (Paris, lat. 8010, fol. 205v)

I have completed a work: that is to say I have brought to completion, and likewise William of Thiegiis, who compiled, and ordered and joined together this commentary for the less advanced students, solicits a prayer in Christ from anyone who peruses, reads or studies it that Christ have pity on him.

Though the precise location designated by 'de Thiegiis' has not been established,[83] research on the French school tradition has added two new witnesses to the list of known manuscripts, namely Oxford, Bodl., Canon. class. lat. MS 72, wherein the text is transmitted as a *catena* commentary with commentaries on Statius' *Achilleis*, Cato's *Disticha* and ps.-Theodolus' *Ecloga*, and Wolfenbüttel, Herzog-August Bibliothek, Cod. Guelf. 5 4.

---

[81] Other manuscripts not discussed in this article but which transmit full commentaries of French origin include Berlin, SB-PKb, Diez. B Sant. 11; Munich, Bayerische Staatsbibliothek, clm 28504; Paris, BN, lat. MS 11315 and lat. 8253; Milan, Biblioteca Ambrosiana, MSS O 3 sup. and S 32 sup.

[82] See Hauréau 1885. The commentary is discussed briefly in Demats 1973: 170, 172, and 191–2 and by Ghisalberti in Arnulf of Orléans 1932: 191–2.

[83] Munari 1957: no. 249 suggests 'Thiais near Paris'.

Aug. 4° (*accessus* and commentary to *Met.* 1.1–219 only).[84] William claims
in his colophon to have 'compiled, ordered and joined together' the glosses.
A perusal of the commentary indicates that William cannot lay claim
to complete originality, for portions bear a striking affinity to the text
of the Vulgate commentary (discussed above). The *accessus*[85] prefacing
the commentary proper is a conflation of numerous earlier introductions, specifically an *accessus* found in numerous twelfth-century commentaries of southern German origin,[86] the *accessus* appended by Arnulf of
Orléans to his commentary,[87] and the introduction of the so-called Vulgate
commentary.[88] The commentary itself draws heavily upon the glosses of
earlier twelfth-century commentaries and of the Vulgate commentary, but
modifies them, often substantially, by adding new material or authorities.
At *Met.* 1.21, Ovid's reference to a god who separated discord ('hanc deus et
melior litem natura diremit') is explicated by William with almost verbatim
copying of a twelfth-century gloss on the poem:

Met. 1.21   *Hanc deus* etc., scilicet deus, quem philosophi togaton, id est summum
deum, dixerunt ut qui ex se noym, id est mentem, generat. Noys enim est mens
siue anima que omnia uegetat. (Paris, lat. 8010, fol. 2v)

A God: that is to say God, whom the philosophers called 'the good', that is the
greatest god, as the one who generates from himself 'nous', that is to say mind.
For 'nous' is mind or soul which brings to life all things.[89]

At *Met.* 1.25, William explains the epithet 'concors', which Ovid applies to
peace, in wording reminiscent of that of the Vulgate commentary:[90]

Pace concordi: epytheton est, omnis pax concors. Bene dicit concors quia licet
discrepant in sui natura, in rebus creandis conueniunt. Pax ista que concordiam
tulit consideratur in qualitate, uel in equo uel in distancia, quia ignis et terra
conueniunt in siccitate, terra et aqua in frigiditate, aer et aqua in humiditate, aer et
ignis in caliditate. Ista iunctura elementorum a diuersis diuersimode nuncupatur.
Macrobius auream cathenam appellat [*Commentarii in Somnium Scipionis* 1.14.15],

[84] Wolfenbüttel, Codex Guelf. Gud lat. 5.4. Aug. 4° transmits three prominent *accessus* on fols. 1r–2v:
the first is that of Arnulf of Orléans; the second begins with the words 'sicut piropus in alto positus';
and a third *accessus* begins, 'Ne prolixitatis fastidio'. The third *accessus* is also transmitted in seven
other manuscripts (listed in Coulson and Roy 2000: no. 271).
[85] Edited in Ghisalberti 1946: 54–6, App. L.   [86] For editions of the text, see Young 1944.
[87] Edited by Ghisalberti in Arnulf of Orléans 1932: 180–1.   [88] Edited in Coulson 1987c: 178–82.
[89] The best discussion of these terms in twelfth-century glosses is Herren 2004.
[90] See Coulson 1991: 47–8: '*Concordi* epiteton est pacis quod sit concors per copulam scilicet ipsius
numeri, quam habuit deus exemplar rebus creandis. Vnde Boecius: "qui numeris elementa ligas".
Concordi quia licet discrepant in sui natura, tamen in rebus creandis conueniunt. Vel pax ista que
concordiam tulit consideratur in qualitatibus: uel in equo pondere, uel in distancia.'

Plato gumphos inuisibiles [*Timaeus* 43a], Boecius sacrum amorem,[91] Lucanus compagem [*Bellum civile* 10.265], actor iste concordem pacem. (Paris, lat. 8010, fol. 2v)

In a united peace: is an [ornamental] epithet; all peace is united. And he well employs the word since, although the elements are at odds in their own essence, they come together in created matter. And that peace which brings unity is considered in its quality, or by its equal weight, or in distance, since fire and earth come together in their dryness, earth and water in coldness, air and water in wetness, air and fire in heat. Various authors speak of this joining of the elements differently. Macrobius calls it a golden chain, Plato, invisible bonds, Boethius, sacred love, Lucan, a seam, while this author calls it united peace.)

William also carefully produces prose transitions which guide the reader through the strands of the narrative. In the introductory section of creation, Ovid moves the reader from primordial chaos to its separation into the four elements, and William carefully maps the transitions by providing summaries of the previous sections. At *Met.* 1.10, our commentator underlines the transitional link between this verse and the initial description of chaos:

Met. 1.10   *Nullus adhuc Titan*: Postquam ostendit actor que materie erant inuolute in illo globo, ostendit unde sit materia celestium corporum dicens quod ex priori yle celestia corpora operatus est deus. *Nullus Titan*, id est nullus sol, et loquitur secundum illos qui dicebant nouiter solem oriri cotidie. Vel *nullus Titan*, id est nullus de genere tytannorum, scilicet nec sol nec luna, qui filii gigantis uel Hyperionis dicti sunt. Gigantes dicebantur quia erant optimi philosophi, uel fortissimi homines, uel illuminatores terre. (Paris, lat. 8010, fol. 2r)

As yet no Titan: After the author described what matter was enveloped in that globe, he shows whence derives the matter for the heavenly bodies saying that from the former Hyle God created the celestial bodies. *No Titan*, that is no sun, and he speaks following those who used to say that the sun arises anew each day. Or *no Titan*, that is to say none from the race of the Titans, namely neither Sun nor Moon, who are said to be the children of a Giant or of Hyperion. And they were called giants either because they were the best philosophers, or the strongest men, or those who shed light on the earth.

At 1.26, William again underlines the narrative progression by viewing v. 26 as a new departure:

Met. 1.26   *Ignea conuexi uis*: Superius ostendit actor materias diuersas esse ab aceruo nature, modo ostendit diuisionem per ordinem elementorum dicens quod ignis minus intensus in contrariis suis prius explicatus est. Vnde Bernardus: 'de confuso et turbido globo prior egreditur uis ignea et uacuas repente tenebras flammis rubentibus interrupit' [*Cosm*. ii.9]. (Paris, lat. 8010, fol. 2r)

The fiery force of heaven's vault: Above the author showed how diverse was the matter from the disordered mass of nature. Now he shows the division of the elements in rank saying that fire less engaged with its opposites freed itself first. Whence Bernard [Silvestris] says: 'The fiery force first leapt from the globe confused and in turmoil and flashed through the empty darkness with its red flames'.

Though partially derivative, William's commentary shows strands of independent and critical comment. The preliminary comments on Ovid's four-line prologue reveal a marked originality, for they comment not only on the metaphor inherent in the Latin verb *deducere*,[92] but emphasise how closely interwoven are the narrative strands of the epic:

Met. 1.3 *Deducite* id est de diuersis compositum et dictum duci concedite. Vel *deducite* id est subtiliter deduci concedite. Et est methaphora tracta a nente lanam quia subtiliter filum a colo deducitur, et sic notatur subtilitas deducendi. *Carmen perpetuum*, in perpetuum enim nulla est interruptio. Vel *perpetuum* id est continuum iuxta illud Horatii [*Ars* 152]: 'Primum nec medio medium nec discrepet imo' [vno MS]. Vel *perpetuum* dicit tangendo quid sit perpetuum et eternum et sic de singulis, set quia per hos versus satis exprimitur non indigent alia expositione: 'perpetuum dat principium set fine carebit' etc. (Paris, lat. 8010, fol. 1v)

Draw out, that is to say allow my song, which is composed and spoken of diverse subjects, to be led. Or *lead down*, that is to say, allow my poem to be led down with subtlety of technique. And the metaphor is derived from weaving wool since the thread is finely drawn from the distaff, and thus the subtlety of the narrative [*deducendi*] is noted. *Perpetual song*, for there is no interruption in what is perpetual. Or *perpetual*, that is to say forming an uninterrupted series according to Horace: 'The beginning should be consistent with the middle, the middle with the end.' Or he says *perpetual* touching upon what is perpetual and eternal, and so on. But I need not expound further on this since it can be explained by these verses: 'Perpetual has a beginning but no end' etc.

Anonymous commentary A

A second important fourteenth-century commentary of French origin is extant in three complete or partial manuscript witnesses, namely Basel, Universitätsbibliothek, F II 28, Vatican city, BAV, Pal. lat. 1667,[93] and (le)

---

[92] Modern commentators have also discussed at great length the programmatic meaning of the verb 'deducere'. See Kenney 1976.

[93] Now catalogued in Pellegrin *et al*. 1975–91, vol. II.2: 319–20.

Puy en Velay, private collection.[94] As is the case with many fourteenth-
century commentaries, our glossator compiles and incorporates many earlier interpretations into his analyses, specifically the glosses of William of
Orléans, Arnulf of Orléans' *Allegoriae* and John of Garland's *Integumenta
Ovidii*. He demonstrates a relatively limited interest in exploring literary
and stylistic features of the epic, primarily restricting his citation of classical
parallels to Lucan. The commentator, however, is not without a certain
innate intelligence, particularly evident in his treatment of Ovid's rather
complex narrative structures. A telling example of this trait can be found
at *Met.* 1.689–723, wherein Mercury narrates the story of Pan and Syrinx
to Argus in direct speech to the middle of verse 700, after which the narrator (Ovid) reports the remaining section in indirect speech.[95] Modern
critical editions can readily indicate this narrative shift through quotation
marks, but medieval scribes lacked any such mechanism, and the changes
in speakers and constructions had to be signalled through the interlinear
and marginal gloss. Both types of gloss carefully construe for the reader the
speakers (who in verse 700 change in mid sentence from Mercury to our
omniscient narrator [Ovid]):

Interlinear gloss: *Talia uerba refert* que dixerat Pan ad Siringam; *Restabat* Mercurio
uerba referre. (Vatican City, Pal lat. 1667, fol. 10r)

Mercury relates the following words: which Pan had related to Syrinx. *It remained*
for Mercury *to relate the words.*

Marginal gloss: *Talia uerba refert*: Pan. Vel Mercurius siquidem uolens dare uerba
Panis et mutacionem Siringe uidit Argum sompno penitus degrauatum et destitit
a sermone. Incipiebat Mercurius referre dicens *Pan uidet hanc* et *restabat referre
uerba* et cum hoc diceret Mercurius tacuit. Ouidius uero suplet hoc ex parte sua
quod Mercurius erat dicturus narrando fabulam quia incognita erat.

He relates such a story: Pan. Or indeed Mercury, wishing to relate the words of Pan
and the transformation of Syrinx, saw that Argus was deep in sleep and stopped.
Mercury began the narration saying *Pan sees her*, and *it remained to relate*, and
when Mercury was saying this, he fell silent. Ovid from his part in fact supplies
what Mercury was going to relate by narrating the story that was unknown.

Interlinear gloss: *Restabat uerba referre* debet preponi omnibus clausulis sequentibus et ad *fugisse* et ad *orasse* quod sequitur postea.

---

[94] I am grateful to the Institut de recherche et d'histoire des textes for providing me with reproductions
of select folios from this manuscript. Passages discussed in this article are transcribed from Pal. lat.
1667.

[95] For further discussion of the episode, see the essay by Fisher, above, pp. 37–8.

It remained to narrate should be placed before all the following clauses, both before *she fled*, and before *she prayed*, which follows subsequently.

At *Met.* 1.713, where the narrative resumes with the marker *talia dicturus* (intending to tell such a tale), our commentator remarks, 'que ego suppleui' (which I have supplied) (Vatican City, Pal. lat. 1667, fol. 10v).

The commentator is also quite astute at drawing out the embedded structural connections cleverly inserted by Ovid into his narrative. For example, Book 1 ends with Phaethon eager to visit his father the sun. He makes for the regions of the Ethiopians, who are described as his own (*suos*) – a fleeting reference which connects this section of the narrative to Phaethon's later chariot flight:

Suos dicit quia in oriente sunt et ipse erat orientalis. Vel *suos* id est quos ipse postea fecit nigros ut in sequentibus habetur [*Met.* 2 236]. Vel *suos* quia ipse erat rex Ethiopum. (Vatican City, Pal. lat. 1667, fol. 11v)

His own: he says this since they are in the east and he (Phaethon) was an easterner. Or *his own*, that is to say those whom he later made black as is narrated subsequently. Or *his own*, since he himself was the king of the Ethiopians.

Similarly, the commentator details how Ovid's passing allusion to the river Cayster at *Met.* 2.253 foreshadows the transformation of Cygnus, destined to take place some 130 lines later:

Met. 2.253   Cahister est fluuius Antiochie qui currit per Meoniam ubi habundant cigni. Vnde infra: 'quae colat eligit contraria flumina flammis' [*Met.*, 2.380]. (Vatican City, Pal. lat. 1667, fol. 14v)

Cayster is a river of Antiochia which flows through Maeonia where swans abound. Hence below: 'He chooses rivers, the opposite of flames, for his abode.'

Embedded stories which momentarily arrest the narrative momentum are demarcated for the reader, as is the case at *Met.* 2.272–302 where the Earth addresses Jupiter:

Met. 2.279   In hac oratione intendit tellus inpetrare a Ioue quod si per ignem debeat perire quod per fulmen Iouis perire et non huiusmodi igne. (Vatican City, Pal. lat. 1667, fol. 15r)

In this speech Earth intends to beg Jupiter, should she have to be destroyed by fire, to destroy her by his thunderbolt and not by fire of this kind.

Met. 2. 302   Ita locuta fuerat tellus ad Iouem et dixerat ei quod omnia laborabant et quod ipsa terra erat exusta, et aer exustus, aqua desiccata *At pater.* (Vatican City, Pal. lat. 1667, fol. 15v)

Thus the earth had spoken to Jupiter and had told him that everything was in turmoil, and the land and the air were scorched, and water dried up. *But Jupiter.*

Like the earlier Vulgate commentator, Anonymous commentary A frequently takes account of Ovidian influence on twelfth-century poets. At *Met.* 2.254–5, the river Nile, scorched by the heat of the sun, 'retreated in terror to the world's end and hid his head, still hidden' (Nilus in extremum fugit perterritus orbem / occuluitque caput, quod adhuc latet), and the commentator references Walter of Châtillon's and Lucan's use of the same motif:

Met. 2.255   *Quod adhuc latet*: Vnde in *Alexandreide* 'querere nescitum Nili mortalibus ortum' [9.507], et Lucanus in ultimo: 'Archanum natura caput non prodidit ulli' [10.295] et dicit ibidem 'et nulli contingit Gloria genti ut Nilo sit leta suo (10.284)' id est aput se orientem. (Vatican City, Pal. lat. 1667, fol 14v)

Which still lies hidden: Hence in the *Alexandreis*: '[he prepares] to seek out the source of the Nile unknown to mankind', and Lucan says in the last book 'Nature reveals its hidden source to no one', and Lucan says in the same book 'And no nation can boast that it takes pride in the Nile', that is to say, arising in its territory.'

Several lines later within the same episode, the river Tiber, destined to inherit the world's riches, is threatened with destruction. The commentator skilfully alludes to the manner in which Bernard Silvester has incorporated this motif into his epic, the *Cosmographia*:

Met. 2.259   *Cuique fuit rerum promissa*: Hic dicit auctor quod Romani potentissimi erant. Bernardus: 'Romanas habiturus opes et culmina rerum / distulit obliquas ad mare Tibris aquas' [*Cosmographia* iii.253–4]. (Vatican City, Pal. lat. 1667, fol. 14v)

To whom world dominion was promised: Ovid here says that the Romans were most powerful. As Bernard Silvester [says]: 'The Tiber, destined to possess Roman riches and world dominion, bore its winding waters to the sea.'

The commentary also imparts background to historical events alluded to in the narrative. At *Met.* 2.538, in a learned aside, Ovid incorporates a reference to the geese which saved Rome during the city's sack by the Gauls in 390 BC, and the commentator dutifully explicates the line:

Met. 2.538   *Vigili capitolia uoce*: Tangit Ouidius historiam in hoc loco. Sciendum quod quidam obtulit anserem in templo Iunonis qui erat in Capitolio. Cum autem senones Galli inuasissent Capitolium, Iuno per anserem Mallium Torquatum custodem Capitolii excitauit, quapropter in honorem Iunonis fuit quidam anser argenteus in Capitolio constructus. Vnde Iuno a monendo dicta est moneta. (Vatican City, Pal. lat. 1667, fol. 18v)

Destined to guard the Capitol with their vigilant honking: Ovid touches upon history here. One should know that someone donated a goose to the temple of Juno which was on the Capitol. And when the Senones, a Gallic tribe, had attacked the Capitol, Juno by means of the goose woke up Manlius Torquatus, the guardian of the Capitol. And on this account in honour of Juno a silver goose was constructed on the Capitol and Juno was called 'Moneta' on account of warning.

Milan, Biblioteca Ambrosiana, MS N 254 sup.

Ambrosiana MS N 254 sup. transmits an integral commentary largely independent of other commentaries circulating in the fourteenth century. One evident indication of this independence lies in the transformation lists which precede each book, for they share no affinity with those composed by either Arnulf or William of Orléans. Unlike the Vulgate commentary, which evinces a strong literary interest in the poem, the commentator of Ambrosiana N 254 sup. adopts a relatively more mundane approach, pointing out such features as metaphor or imagery, but eschewing more complex literary features such as characterisation, word usage, or Ovidian influence on later authors. Such preoccupations probably indicate that the commentary is aimed at the intermediate student who is still grappling with comprehending the basic elements of the storyline. The commentator also assists the reader through the relatively complex narrative structure of individual passages or books (for example, Book 5, in which the songs of the Pierides possess multiple narrators). At *Met.* 1.190, Ovid employs a metaphor taken over from surgery to describe the cure needed to remedy mankind's ills, and our commentator underlines this connection:

Vulnus tractum est a bono cirurgio qui carnem putridam uulneris eradit ne peioretur caro uiua et bona. (fol. 5r)

The wound: [A metaphor] drawn from [the image of] a good surgeon who cuts away the putrid flesh of the wound so that the living and good flesh may not be infected.

Likewise, the adjective *lymphata* (maddened), applied to the Maenads at *Met.* 11.3, is explained as derived from rabies which drives dogs mad:

Limphata id est vesana, et tractum est a quadam vena que est in capite canis que quando nimis est plena humoribus fit canis insanus ita quod non potest uidere limpham quin nimis moueatur ad insaniam. (fol. 108r)

Enraged, that is maddened, and the word comes from a certain vein in the head of a dog which, when it is too full of humors, makes a dog mad, so that each time it sees water it is made quite insane.

At *Met.* 1.144, the impersonal use of the verb *uiuo* (to live) is explained (*uiuitur* impersonaliter tenetur, fol. 4r). The commentator is also concerned to underline the structural links within (or between) stories, as is the case at *Met.* 1.398, where the commentator stresses the connection back to *Met.* 1.382:

Velant caput ad hoc quod superius dictum est concordat actor quia superius dixerat 'et velate caput' [*Met.* 1.382], modo dicit 'uelantque caput'. (fol. 8r)

They cover their head: the author connects his text with what was previously stated, since above he said, 'Cover your head' and now he says, 'they cover their head'.

Lastly, narrative strands of the narrative are clearly identified. At *Met.* 8.236–59, Ovid inserts the story of Perdix within the central narrative of Daedalus and Icarus, only returning to the central narrative at *Met.* 8.260. Our commentator carefully marks out the digression for the reader:

Facta digressione, redit auctor ad materiam dicens 'ita intumulato filio suo abibat Dedalus' et *iam* venerat scilicet in Siciliam *Iamque fatigatum*. (fol. 80v)

Once the digression is complete, the author returns to his subject matter saying 'Having buried his son, Daedalus departed' and he had *already* reached Sicily, *weary*.

Vatican City, BAV, Vat. lat. MS 1479

Vatican City, Biblioteca Apostolica Vaticana, Vat. lat. MS 1479[96] transmits a collection of texts (accompanied with commentary) used as primary teaching tools in the Middle Ages and frequently designated by the term *liber Catonianus*.[97] The interlinear and marginal gloss to the *Metamorphoses* (fols. 53r–182v; incomplete 1.1–14.50) represents a stratum of gloss largely original and independent of the Vulgate commentary (see above). Each book is preceded by a list of transformations drawn directly from Arnulf of Orléans's *Allegoriae* and by the appropriate verses from the *Integumenta Ovidii* of John of Garland (see above). The glossator seeks to elucidate the literal sense of the poem for the reader and to provide an allegorical

[96] Now catalogued in Pellegrin *et al.* 1975–91, vol. III.1: 60–4. The commentary is briefly mentioned by Ghisalberti in Arnulf of Orléans 1932: 191, n. 4. Nogara 1910: 423–31 provides a summary discussion of the contents of the manuscript and edits the life. For updated bibliography see Pellegrin *et al.* 1975–91, vol. III.1: 64 and Coulson 1994: 11, no. 333.

[97] See Boas 1914; Sanford 1924; and Pellegrin 1957. The *Liber Catonianus* usually consisted of the *Disticha Catonis*, the *Ecloga Theoduli*, the *Fabulae* of Avianus, the *Elegiae* of Maximianus, the *De raptu Proserpinae* of Claudian, the *Achilleis* of Statius, and the *Ilias latina*.

and explicitly Christian framework in which to read the fables.[98] So, for example, in the opening segment of the epic, wherein Ovid details the creation of the world and of man, the commentator repeatedly enumerates the direct parallels with the Book of Genesis. I list below selected examples of this trait from the commentator's exposition of the creation myth (*Met.* 1.1–150):

Met. 1.21   *Hanc deus* etc. Ouidius sentiens unum deum esse a principio, non tamen ausus dicere, uocauit ipsum melior natura. (fol. 53v)

Though Ovid realized there was one god from the beginning, yet he did not dare to name him but called him better nature.

Quod chaos mutatum fuit in species non indiget expositione quia uerum est cum uniuersa essent in loco uno in principio, uidelicet in inspiratione diuina. Confuso modo dicitur propter oppositionem elementorum. Quod dicit quod deus diuisit, uerum est sicut in Genesi continetur et apellatur melior natura quia ille est natura naturans omnes res. (fol. 53v)

The transformation of chaos into species requires no explanation since it is true, because in the beginning all things were in a single place, namely in the divine inspiration. It is said that they were in a confused manner because of the opposition of the elements. Ovid's assertion that God divided them is true just as is found in Genesis, and God is called 'better nature' because he is nature creating all things.

Like Arnulf, John of Garland and the Vulgate commentator, the commentator is partial to allegorical interpretation, providing allegories strongly influenced by the earlier *Allegoriae* of Arnulf for most transformations. The allegory on the creation of man, which Vat. lat. 1479 appends to the story of creation, well illustrates this tendency:

Allegoria talis est. Iste Prometenus (*sic*) dicitur primus deus qui de limo terre hominem fecit et in eo spiraculum uite spiritu oris sui aspirauit ut in Genesi continetur. Fabula talis est: Promotheus filius Iapeti qui alio nomine dicitur demogorgon,[99] fuit primus et summus deorum, et de limo terre formauit ymaginem terream et eam in igne et sole dissicauit et illa desiccata mutata est in hominem et inde pro tali facto in Caucaso monte a posteritate missus fuit in exilium. Historia talis est: Promotheus re uera quidam fuit qui in Caucaso monte studens primo naturam hominis duplam considerauit, scilicet corpus terreneum unde dicitur corpus de limo terre siue de terra fecisse, et animam celestem, unde

---

[98] Such an anachronistic reading of the poem was perpetuated well into the Renaissance, particularly in reformation Germany. Georg Schuler, the son-in-law of Melanchthon, in his *Interpretatio fabularum Ovidii*, which he wrote in 1554 for the benefit of his students at Königsberg, employed such a procedure, as did Veit Dietrich, whose commentary on the *Metamorphoses* written at Wittenberg in 1534, is extant in Zwickau, Ratsschulbibliothek, MS 123.

[99] For the god Demogorgon, see especially Pade 1997 with bibliography.

dicitur spiraculum uite celestis in eo imposuisse. Quod dicitur iecur eius a uul-
turibus corrodi nichil aliud est dictum nisi quod cum cura studebat et corrodit
cura corpus humanum et maxime corpora studentium sicut adhuc facit. Hoc est
quod dicit. (fol. 54r)

This is the allegory: This Prometheus is said to be the first god who made man
from the mud of the earth and breathed life into him from the breath of his own
mouth, just as is found in Genesis. The myth is as follows: Prometheus, the son of
Iapetus who is also called Demogorgon, was the first and greatest of the gods, and
he formed a physical image from the mud of the earth and dried it out with fire and
the sun, and once it was dried, it was transformed into man. Afterwards, because
of this deed he was cast into exile for eternity on a mountain of the Caucasus.
This is the historical interpretation: Prometheus in fact was a certain man who,
while studying on the mountain of the Caucasus, discovered that man's nature
was twofold, namely an earthly body, hence his body is said to be made from the
mud of the earth or from earth, and a heavenly soul, hence Prometheus is said to
have breathed divine life into him. The fact that vultures are said to have eaten
his liver can be interpreted as follows: He studied assiduously, and care chews up
the human body and most of all the bodies of those who pursue studies, just as it
does to the present day, and this is what he states.

Vat. lat. 1479 is also keen to impart the mythological background to
each story, drawing his information primarily from the Third Vatican
Mythographer:[100]

Met. 1.113   *Postquam*: Fabula talis est: Saturnus fuit primus deus et audiuit in
responsis quod haberet quemdam filium qui eum de regno suo eiceret unde iussit
Opi uxori sue quod quicquid pareret sibi daret. Vnde cum ipsa peperisset Iouem,
uoluit tradere patri suo ad interficiendum sed cum uellet tradere, Iupiter risit
matri sue; unde illa miserata filii sui tradidit marito suo albestum[101] lapidem et
sic defraudauit illum et fecit puerum nutriri, conuocans illum Iouem siue Iupiter,
qui interpretatur risus.[102] Cum magnus esset iste Iupiter, collegit exercitum contra
patrem et ipsum expulit de regno et illi successit. Vnde peiorate fuerunt gentes in
tantum quantum argentum est peius auro. (fol. 54v)

After: The myth is as follows: Saturn was the first god and he heard from the
oracles that he would have a certain son who would cast him from his kingdom.
Hence he ordered his wife Ops to hand over to him any child she gave birth to.
Hence when Ops had given birth to Jupiter, she prepared to hand him over to his

---

[100] The identification of the Third Vatican Mythographer remains inconclusive, though he has been
identified with Alberic of London. The text of the First, Second and Third Vatican Mythographers
was published in Bode 1834, and newly translated in Pepin 2008.

[101] 'Albestum' is a rarely attested word. I suspect it cloaks an allusion to 'Abaddir', the name given to
the stone proffered by Juno to Jupiter. See Hexter 2002a: 222.

[102] I have not found the source for this statement, which does not seem to make sense in context. The
name of Isaac has this derivation. See Isidore, *Etymologiae* 7.7.3.

father for slaughter. But as she was handing him over, Jupiter smiled at his mother and she took pity on him and gave to her husband the stone 'albestus', thereby cheating him. She had the boy brought up and called him Jove or Jupiter which means 'smile'. And when Jupiter became a man, he collected an army against his father, expelled him from his kingdom, and succeded him. Thence the races became worse to the same degree as silver is less precious than gold.

* * * * * * *

Latin school commentary on the *Metamorphoses* written in France from 1180 to 1400 confronts the modern reader with a multiplicity of approaches in explicating the text that served the needs of varied audiences. The earliest commentaries, composed at Orléans by masters Arnulf and William for the more elementary student, explicated the literal sense of the poem and provided a preliminary framework in which to interpret the work allegorically. The later Vulgate commentary, assembled in the *Orléanais* in the mid thirteenth century, furnished a relatively sophisticated reading of the text and became the standard commentary on the *Metamorphoses* during the high Middle Ages. During the later thirteenth and fourteenth centuries, production of commentaries, which were transmitted as interlinear and marginal glosses in text manuscripts, multiplied. While nearly all manuscripts of the *Metamorphoses* from this period contain some glossing, the four commentaries studied above show evidence of a careful, sustained and detailed reading of the text.

CHAPTER 4

Recasting the Metamorphoses in fourteenth-century France
The challenges of the Ovide moralisé

Ana Pairet

In the first third of the fourteenth century, an anonymous poet writing in the French Burgundian vernacular ventured to translate into verse and to moralise Ovid's 'fables de l'ancien temps' (fables of antiquity) (1.61).[1] The spirit of this vast undertaking, which was likely completed between 1316 and 1328, is summarised by the opening lines that in Pierpont Morgan Library, MS M 0443 (*c.* 1400) set apart the *Ovide moralisé* from its Latin model: 'Cy commence en rommant, / Les fables Ovide le grant, / Reportes dessoubz verite, / Reduittes a moralite' (Here begin in Romance the fables of the great Ovid, told according to truth and aligned with morality).[2] At slightly over seventy thousand lines, or six times the length of the *Metamorphoses*, the *Ovide moralisé* was to provide the first complete French translation and commentary of Ovid's poem.[3] Stretching to the limit the evolving conventions of medieval translation, it amplifies aggressively and rewrites selectively its Latin source. Each of Ovid's fables is paraphrased, glossed in historical or physical terms (*estoire*), and read as moral *exemplum* or spiritual allegory (*sens, entendement, exposicion, allegorie*), even as the poem eschews a strict exegetical program.[4]

Brought to the attention of modern scholars in the 1890s by Gaston Paris, edited by Cornelis de Boer from 1915 to 1938, and further studied by Joseph Engels (1943) and Paule Demats (1973), the *Ovide moralisé* has become a touchstone for the study of mythographic writing and late

---

[1] *Ovide moralisé*, ed. de Boer 1915–38: 1.61. All further references to this five-volume work will be included parenthetically in the text.

[2] Quoted in de Boer (ed.) 1915–38, vol. 1: 45.

[3] On dates of composition and a classification of extant manuscripts, see de Boer (ed.), vol. 1: 44–7; Jung 1996a: 253; and Jung 1994: 170–2.

[4] The didactic and allegorical framework supplied by the vernacular translation had a lasting impact on interpretations of the classical author throughout the late medieval and early modern periods. On allegorical readings of Ovid in the French Renaissance, see Moisan and Malenfant 1997: xix–xxxvi, and Moss 1984 and 1998. Renaissance treatments are also discussed in Moog-Grünewald 1979.

medieval poetics as well as for the reception history of Ovid.[5] Its glosses on specific fables reveal how late medieval interpretive strategies measure up to classical mythology, while non-classical materials introduced in the poem's frequent satirical and scientific digressions and manuscript iconography compose a rich cultural encyclopaedia. The hybrid generic status of the medieval poem, which draws on the mythographic, commentary and encyclopaedic traditions, presents an impediment for critics, and despite a surge in critical interest since the 1990s, the sources, themes, levels of meaning and architecture of the *Ovide moralisé* remain insufficiently studied, owing in no small part to the sheer volume of the text.[6]

As Marc-René Jung notes,[7] any interpretation of the *Ovide moralisé* and its reception history must be grounded on thorough textual description, including the rubrics and marginalia which de Boer regretfully excluded from his historic edition. My intent here is not to provide such a comprehensive philological description, a task which could only be achieved via systematic confrontation of textual and paratextual variants for all twenty-one extant manuscripts. I wish rather to survey some challenges posed by the work's unique narrative and thematic structure; to examine the ways in which scholars have addressed the vernacular rendering of Ovid's fables; and to suggest areas where future investigation of the fourteenth-century poem and its manuscript tradition promises to be most fruitful, such as the vocabulary of hermeneutics and the relation between metamorphosis as a narrative motif and as a poetic principle.

THE *OVIDE MORALISÉ* IN ITS MANUSCRIPT CONTEXT

The narrative poem known as the *Ovide moralisé* is preserved in twenty-one manuscripts composed between *c.* 1320 and the end of the fifteenth century. De Boer's edition, based on Rouen, Bibliothèque municipale, MS O 4 (*c.* 1320), includes variants from Lyons, Bibliothèque municipale, MS 742 (*c.* 1390) and from one of four manuscripts in group Y.[8] Copenhagen, Det Kongelige Bibliotek, Thott MS 399, composed about 1480, which is not included in de Boer's classification, contains a twenty-five folio preface in prose derived from 'De formis figurisque deorum', Pierre Bersuire's

[5] Blumenfeld-Kosinski 1997: 90–109.
[6] The only comprehensive study to date of the *Ovide moralisé* is Possamaï-Pérez 2006. See Possamaï-Pérez 2009.
[7] Jung 1994: 149.
[8] De Boer's classification of group Y includes Paris, BN, fr. MS 871, London, BL, Add. MS 10324 (both *c.* 1400), the fourteenth-century Paris, BN, fr. MS 872 and the fifteenth-century Rouen, Bibliothèque municipale, MS O 11 bis.

introduction to Book 15 of the *Reductorium morale*.[9] Two independently composed fifteenth-century prose versions have also transmitted the materials in the *Ovide moralisé*. The earlier of the two (Vatican City, BAV, Reg. lat. MS 1686) was written in 1466 or 1467 for René d'Anjou, while the later version, preserved in three manuscripts, including Paris, BN, fr. MS 137, was produced in Bruges around 1475.[10] This second prose reworking is of particular importance in the reception history of Ovid as it was likely one of the main sources for the first French printed adaptation of the *Metamorphoses*, Colard Mansion's *Bible des poètes* (1484) and also for Caxton's influential Middle English translation (1480).

Jung has pointed out the limitations of the only available modern edition of the *Ovide moralisé* and rekindled interest in those material aspects of the manuscripts neglected by de Boer, such as tables of contents, rubrication, marginalia and iconography.[11] Jung's lexical study of rubrics referring to the *translateur* sheds light on the purposes and reception of the medieval work. Following de Boer, Jung divides extant manuscripts into two main families, X and Y,[12] represented by thirteen and seven manuscripts respectively. In the Y group, the translation adheres closely to Ovid's text; two copies in this family, Paris, BN, fr. MS 870 and fr. MS 19121, systematically eliminate Christian allegories. The textual reorganisation, additions and omissions in the Y group suggest that from the end of the fourteenth century onwards, a significant segment of the readership was interested more in *les fables d'Ovide* and their historical explanation than in their moral or spiritual interpretation.[13] Comparison of textual and paratextual variants highlights the very composite nature of what we have come to call the *Ovide moralisé*, of which de Boer's editorial labour of love is but one possible instantiation.

Among the more striking features of the manuscripts of the French poem are their magnificent mythological and allegorical illustrations of a type rarely attested in Latin manuscripts of Ovid's works.[14] Since we possess scant historical and textual evidence on the circumstances of the vernacular poem's composition, iconography is a crucial area of study where competing medieval moralisations of Ovid are concerned.

---

[9] Van T'Sant 1929. On the 'double prologue' of the Copenhagen manuscript and its iconography, see Clier-Colombani 2001: 60–2.

[10] The text in Vatican City, BAV, Reg. lat. MS 1686 is edited by de Boer, *Ovide moralisé* 1954. On the second prose version and its prologue, see Jung 1997. For selective comparisons of verse and prose versions, see Ehrhart 1994 and Mora 2002.

[11] Jung 1996b.

[12] A third branch of the manuscript stemma derives from X but contains elements of the Y group. See de Boer (ed.) 1915–1938, vol. 1: 48–9.

[13] Jung 1996a: 274.   [14] Lord 1975: 161.

At present, save the inventory established by Jung, no full description of illustrations contained in the twenty-one manuscripts of the *Ovide moralisé* and its two prose versions is available. Perhaps this lack of emphasis on text–image interplay can be attributed to the philological zeal of de Boer, who in his prefatory description fails to mention that his base manuscript, Rouen, Bibliothèque municipale, MS O 4, contains over 450 illustrations, which make it the most lavishly illuminated of the work's extant manuscripts. Art historian Carla Lord, who corrected this oversight by surveying the Old French poem's rich iconography, has identified two groups among illustrated manuscripts.[15] In the earlier tradition exemplified by the 453 miniatures of Rouen, O 4, the 302 miniatures of Paris, Bibliothèque de l'Arsenal, MS 5069 and the 57 miniatures of the incomplete Lyons, Bibliothèque Municipale, MS 742, imagery and text are closely intertwined. More than half of the miniatures reflect the narrative content of Ovid's fables, while up to a fifth of them relate to the allegorical *exposicion*. This first group of manuscripts, whose redaction dates from 1315 to 1390, shows a decreasing focus on religious and allegorical iconography and a corresponding increase in the weight given to Ovid's fables proper. The majority of extant manuscripts of the poem, however, fall into a later, second group crafted in the *imagines deorum* tradition as described by Panofsky, in which each book is headed by an illumination representing a mythological god or goddess.[16]

What little we know about the composition of the *Ovide moralisé* we owe to its Latin counterpart, Bersuire's *Ovidius moralizatus*, written in Avignon between 1337 and 1340. In the 1342 revised version of his *Reductorium morale*, of which Book 15 contains the Latin moralisation of the *Metamorphoses*, Bersuire acknowledges having only recently learned of the existence of the vernacular poem, composed, he claims, 'ad instanciam Johanne quondam regine Francie' (at the request of Joan, Queen of France).[17] The chronological proximity of the vernacular and Latin works confirms the groundswell of interest in moralisations of Ovid in fourteenth-century France. While the two Ovidian *summae* address distinct audiences, they draw on common sources and provide several complementary interpretations which later would be integrated both in vernacular mythographical works and in Latin marginalia to translations of the *Metamorphoses*.[18]

---

[15] The Rouen manuscript is also discussed with copious illustrations in Desmond 2007. Jung 1994: 170–2.

[16] Blumenfeld-Kosinski 2002: 71–2.

[17] Quoted in de Boer (ed.) 1915–1938 vol. 1: 10. According to de Boer, the Queen of France mentioned by Bersuire was likely Joan of Burgundy, who died in 1329. For the *Ovidius moralizatus* see also in this volume, pp. 180, 184, 187, 194, 270–5, 314.

[18] Early editions of translations of the *Metamorphoses* loosely based on the *Ovide moralisé* attest to the influence of Bersuire's glosses. Colard Mansion's 1484 *Bible des poètes* thus opens with a translation

Bersuire's *Ovidius moralizatus* and the Old French poem would remain influential sourcebooks well into the Renaissance; tracing their influence is crucial to understanding the cultural and linguistic hierarchies that governed reading and writing in the late Middle Ages. The text and iconography generated by the verse translation of Ovid's poem over two centuries, and the subsequent transformation of the medieval French poem through prosification and the advent of print, open up a host of questions whose limits we can hardly ascertain until updated critical editions of all texts concerned are made available.

RECREATING OVID'S *METAMORPHOSES*

The retelling of Ovid's fables 'en romans' (in the French vernacular) (1.16) is an unprecedented attempt to recast not simply the text of the *Metamorphoses*, but the history of its successive readings. The vernacular author draws on a long line of commentary to shape the fables' narration and *exposicion*. As a privileged site for authorial self-representation, the prologue deserves particular attention, as do those transitional passages where the poet-narrator provides metanarrative or procedural commentary.

In the opening of his poem, which is replete with terms borrowed from Latin academic prologues like 'espondre' (lines 11, 75), 'exposicion' (line 48) and 'sens' (lines 9, 12, 13), the author states, following the theory of *integumentum*, that he aims to uncover the truth hidden beneath the fables: 'La veritez seroit aperte / Qui souz les fables gist couverte' (The truth that lies underneath the fables would stand revealed) (lines 45–6). Rita Copeland situates the poem's first seventy lines in the context of the medieval Ovidian *accessus*, a codified introduction supplying biographical information on the author (*vita auctoris*) and identifying the work's title, subject matter, purpose and usefulness.[19] By the fourteenth century, such academic prologues to Ovid had become sophisticated exercises that provided endless variations on three major prologue types.[20] According to Copeland, the opening seventy lines can be read as 'a composite of topics' that blend the 'common *accessus* form' and 'the scholastic or Aristotelian prologue, including some Romance equivalents for Latin exegetical terminology'.[21]

---

of Bersuire's 'De formis figurisque deorum'. On Bersuire's moralisation, see S. Vervacke 1999. The genealogy of Mansion's edition is retraced in J. C. Moisan and S. Vervacke, 'Les *Métamorphoses* d'Ovide et le monde de l'imprimé: La *Bible des Poëtes*, Bruges, Colard Mansion, 1484', in Bury 2003: 217–38.

[19] Copeland 1991: 108–10. For biographies of Ovid in the *accessus* to commentaries or as independent lives, see in particular Ghisalberti 1946, and Coulson 1987c and 1997b.

[20] See Hunt 1948. The three types of *accessus ad auctores* are discussed in Minnis 1988: 15–29.

[21] Copeland 1991: 108–9. See also Coulson 1991: 12–13.

But the *Ovide moralisé* stands out among Latin and vernacular introductions to Ovid's works in that its prologue employs, in a self-referential key, vernacular equivalents of the introductory terms and topics commonly used in academic prologues. It thus can be said to comprise a witty variation on the tendency of medieval academic prologues to the *Metamorphoses* to turn into an *accessus ad commentatorem*.

This critical angle sheds light on the vernacular poet's announced subject matter, namely 'les mutacions des fables' (the transformations of the fables) (1.53). While both nouns in the latter expression are associated with the *Metamorphoses* in vernacular literature, rarely do they appear *in tandem*.[22] In the context of Ovidian commentary, 'mutacions' invariably recalls the twelfth-century Arnulfian division of the *Metamorphoses* into a series of *mutationes*, each of which can be explained in allegorical, moral, or historical terms.[23] The use of the term *mutacions* and the allusion to academic *expositio* ('Ne puis pas faire mencion / De chascune exposicion / Des fables, quar trop i metroie' (I cannot mention all the explanations of each fable, for it would take too much space), 1.47–9) implies that if the vernacular poet cannot hope to compile all the individual interpretations of commentators, he can at the very least adhere to their segmentation of Ovid's poem. Hence the ambiguous genitive in 'les mutacions *des* fables' applies equally to the transformations recounted *in* Ovid's fables and to the discursive transformations *of* the fables; in other words, how does the interpretative process give rise to meaning? Contrary to previous philological commentaries of the *Metamorphoses*, which aimed to preserve the meaning of the letter by dispelling rhetorical obscurity, the vernacular gloss will enlist verbal invention – a poetics informed by the principle of metamorphosis itself – in the service of disclosure.

The poet justifies his enterprise at the outset of the prologue by offering the failsafe rhetorical argument that 'Se l'escripture ne me ment, / Tout est pour nostre enseignement' (If scripture does not deceive me, everything exists for our edification) (1.1–2). Even immoral tales serve a moral purpose when properly handled, and those whom God blesses with the capacity for understanding are obliged to reveal the knowledge they gather: 'Quar nulz ne doit son sens repondre, / Quar ne vault sens que l'en enserre / Ne plus qu'avoirs repost en terre' (Nor should one hide what he knows, for meaning locked away is worth no more than riches buried in the ground) (1.12–14). Presenting himself as the last in a long line of *expositores*, the

---

[22] The term *mutacion* was commonly used in the French vernacular to refer to changes of appearance, shape, state, gender, species as well as physical location. On the interpretation of 'mutacions des fables' see Blumenfeld-Kosinski 1997: 90; Pairet 2002: 97–134; and Possamaï-Pérez 2006: 657.

[23] Hexter 1987: 69–70.

anonymous poet renews the challenge of past generations of scholars in an assertive *captatio benevolentiae*: 'Pluiseur ont essaié sans faille / A fere ce que je proupos, / Sans acomplir tout lor proupos' (Many have certainly tried to do what I now attempt, but failed to accomplish their project) (1.20–2). Following the customary humility topos, the prologue closes with the idea of textual transmission as emendation. Even as the vernacular poet revises tradition, he acknowledges that he will accept corrections from his readers provided that they conform to ecclesiastical teachings. Profession of faith in the Church shields the poet against the accusations of impiety that the translator of a pagan work might otherwise attract (1.67–70).

The translation proper is set off from the prologue by the authorial tag 'Or vueil comencier ma matire' (Now I wish to begin my subject matter) (line 71). Before translating the Ovidian *prooemium*, the poet brings to mind the name and purpose of the classical *auteur*:

> Ovides dist: 'Mes cuers vieult dire
> Les formes qui muees furent
> En nouviaux cors'. Aucun qui durent
> L'autour espondre et declairier
> S'entremistrent de l'empirier,
> De l'auteur reprendre et desdire,
> Disant que li autours dut dire:
> 'Les cors qui en formes noveles
> furent muez', mes teulz faveles
> Ne doivent audience avoir.   (1.72–81)

Ovid says: 'I feel I must tell about the forms that were changed into new bodies.' Some, whose task it was to explain and illuminate the author's meaning, began to make it obscure, correcting and contradicting the author, saying that the author meant to say: 'The bodies that were changed into new forms.' Such flights of the imagination are not to be listened to.

Where Ovid addresses the gods as he presents his subject ('In nova fert animus mutatas dicere formas corpora'[24]), the vernacular poet offers instead a lesson in philology, taking issue with previous exegetes whose readings, he feels, revise or contradict the literal meaning of the Latin poem's *incipit*. The criticism voiced here seems to target commentaries inspired by Arnulf of Orléans, who had construed the jumbled syntax of Ovid's *incipit* to make it say 'the bodies that were changed into new forms' rather than 'the forms changed into new bodies'.[25] As the diminutive noun 'faveles'

---

[24] Ovid 1984, tr. Miller and Goold: 1.3. All subsequent references to this edition will appear in the body of the text.

[25] 'fiat ipallage sic: formas mutatas in nova corpora id est corpora mutata in novas formas', Arnulf of Orléans 1932, lines 181–2, quoted in Engels 1943: 87.

(1.80) suggests, the rhetorical distortions produced by commentators are no less misleading than the *fabulae* on which they are based. By inverting the subject and predicate of the sentence, medieval commentators misinterpret what the Latin poet wished to say, only to arrive at a nonsensical proposition incompatible with the Christian idea of creation:

> Que bien dist, ce croi, li autours,
> Quar, ançois que li Creatours
> Creast le monde, il n'iert encors
> Ne ne pooit estre nul cors
> Qui nove forme receüst.
>
> (1.83–7)

The author, I believe, speaks the truth, for since the Creator created the world, there has never been and there cannot be any body that receives a new form.

The vernacular translator gets at the hidden truth of Ovid's apparently paradoxical phrase. If his commentary claims to adhere to the letter of the Latin poem, it arguably distorts the latter's spirit by relating the 'formes qui muees furent en nouviaux cors' (forms that were changed into new bodies) (1.72–3) to the idea of divine creation. Taking full possession of his *matire* (1.51), the medieval poet aims to disclose less the truths lying within Ovid's text than the meanings that the work of translation and exegesis can produce. Rendering Ovid's poem in the vernacular allows the medieval clerk to settle scores with prior interpreters and to underscore the originality of his project, which he characterises at once by a greater fidelity to the letter of the text and by significant latitude in its interpretation.

Paradoxically, this liminal gloss on literal interpretation will enable the author of the *Ovide moralisé* to steer clear of the poem's very subject: if he comments on 'nova . . . corpora', he provides no gloss on the problematic adjective 'mutatas' that qualifies 'formas'. Such selective use of gloss is emblematic of the Christian *translatio*. Let us recall, for instance, the apostrophe in the second half of the *prooemium* where Ovid compares the transformative power of poetry to that of the gods (*Metamorphoses* 1.2–4): 'Ye gods, for you yourselves have wrought the changes, breathe on these my undertakings, and bring down my song in unbroken strains from the world's very beginning even unto the present time.' This passably irreverent prayer is echoed by the medieval poet's own introduction of his subject matter, now piously inscribed within a Christian temporality.[26] When commenting on Ovid's apostrophe, the medieval poet dwells exclusively

---

[26] 'Des le premier comencement / Du mont jusqu'à l'avenement / Jhesu Christ' (From the beginning of the world until the coming of Jesus Christ) (1.34–40).

on the plural *di* (*Metamorphoses* 1.107–46), saying nothing of the metamorphoses the gods provoke. To justify the use of the plural, the poet recalls the doctrine of the Holy Trinity, stating that a single divine essence may present itself under three *samblances* (line 136) or *guises* (line 140):

> Sans deviser lor unité,
> Et sans muer lor deïté,
> Se muerent en un moment
> En trois guises sensiblement.
> Pour ce pot em pluralité
> L'autors prier la Trinité.
>   (1.137–42)

Without dividing their unity or changing their divine nature, (the divine persons) were instantly transformed into three visible figures. This is why the author can pray to the Trinity in the plural.

In using the vocabulary of appearances to refer to Christian mysteries, the poet claims that only faith can dissipate the illusion of bodily change by revealing the true essence behind the shifting play of the senses.[27] It is significant that word play – here, the paranomasia *sans muer* / *se muerent* – is used to encapsulate the Christian perspective on metamorphosis, for the poet thereby demonstrates, if only unconsciously, the usefulness of poetry in domesticating pagan concepts of change. But there is an important structural element at work as well. By commenting on the *prooemium* in two steps, the *Ovide moralisé* not only breaks with the Ovidian framework of the *carmen perpetuum* or 'uninterrupted song' but also effectively erases the deceitful metamorphoses of the pagan gods.[28]

Such efforts to extract Christian truth from the fables subtend the retelling of Ovid's cosmography, whose vernacular description closely follows the portrayal in the *Metamorphoses* of primeval chaos:

> Tout iere envolepez en tasse
> Li mons en une obscure masse.
> 'Chaos' avoit non li monciaux,
> Dont Dieus traist la terre et les ciaux;
> Ce n'ert fors un moncel de forme,
> Sans art, sans devise et sans forme,
> Ou toute estoit en discordance.
>   (1.151–7)

---

[27] Harf-Lancner 1985.
[28] At the doctrinal level the idea of forms contained in God's thought (1.90–3) may attest to the influence of St Bonaventure, as suggested by Possamaï-Pérez 2006: 753.

Everything in the world was piled up in an obscure mass. 'Chaos' was the name given to this heap from which God created the earth and the heavens. It was but a heap of forms with neither craft, nor distinction, nor shape, where everything was discordant.

Against the backdrop of elemental confusion, the creation narrative appears proleptically via such terms as 'forme', 'art', 'devise' and 'semence'. Whereas the Latin poem mentions both the mythic gods who watch over the threshold of the *Metamorphoses* and the anonymous god to whom the author attributes the origins of the world ('deus et melior . . . natura' (God – or kindlier nature), line 21), the medieval cleric establishes the uncontested primacy of the 'Crierres' (Creator) (line 111) by identifying Ovid's demiurge as 'Deus naturans nature' (God creator of nature) (line 182).[29] In the subsequent gloss, Ovid's energetic cosmogony is transformed into didactic allegory. The medieval poet reminds his readers of an etymology included since the thirteenth century in Latin *accessus* to Ovid's works: 'Pour manifester clerement, / Et pour donner entendement / Coment vait li ordenemens / Et l'assise des elemens, / A ce veoir nous avisa, / Ovides, qui l'œuf devisa' (To make manifest and convey a sense of the order and foundations of the elements, Ovid cracked open the egg so that we may see the truth) (lines 199–204). Ovid's name would derive, then, from the fact that he exposed ('devisa') the elemental structure of the world, here compared to a hard-boiled egg.[30] Just as the egg contains 'trois choses / Qui sont dedens la quoque encloses' (three things enclosed by the shell) (lines 209–10), so does the world present three elemental layers: the yolk ('le moieuf'), which designates the earth, is enclosed by the white ('l'aubun'), or water, which is in turn covered by a thin layer of air ('la pelete') (line 211). From what at first would be an odd, if hardly original, onomastic gloss, the medieval poet derives a cosmological lesson similar to those included in the thirteenth-century French didactic treatise *Placides et Timeo*. By placing the cosmic egg 'similitude' (line 205) immediately after Ovid's depiction of elemental discord and divine separation, the author of the *Ovide moralisé* underscores the value of Ovid's poem as natural philosophy and announces the theory of the elements that he will later expound in Book 15.

[29] On the opposition between the Creator (*natura naturans*) and creation (*natura naturata*) present in Vatican City, Vat. lat. 1479 and the *Integumenta Ovidii*, see Engels 1943: 89. It is also attested in the Vulgate commentary, see Coulson 1991: 39.

[30] The *accessus* to the Vulgate commentary (*c.* 1250) glosses Ovid's name in allegorical terms, see Coulson 1991: 13, 25. On the etymology of Ovid as 'ovum dividens' see Demats 1973: 161–2. Medieval renditions of the myth of the cosmic egg are discussed in Dronke 1974: 79–80, 154–66. Illuminated manuscripts of the *Ovide moralisé* reflect the didactic purpose of the simile by juxtaposing images of Creation with those of Ovid holding an egg. See Clier-Colombani 2001: 64–5.

Informed by prior readings of the *Metamorphoses*, the prologue of the *Ovide moralisé* situates the work in a long tradition of *exposicion*. The opening creation narrative exemplifies this rich interplay of the vernacular translation and the Ovidian commentary tradition. Rather than attempting to reconcile competing explanations of Ovid's most problematic verses, the vernacular poem tends to reinvent their meaning, permitting itself latitude towards not only the Latin *auctor* but also its successive commentators. Only careful analysis of prior commentaries would allow us to measure fully the originality of the readings the *Ovide moralisé* provides and the role of the poet's wit in establishing the work's genealogy.

FROM COMPILATION TO TRANSFORMATION

The vernacular poet composes a complex authorial figure which plays, according to Copeland, the twofold role of *compilator* and *expositor*. 'The *Ovide moralisé* seems to contain and rehearse within its own boundaries the very practice and history of the textual transmission of Ovid in the Middle Ages.'[31] I wish to pursue this idea by examining how Ovid's narrative of endless transformation is both amplified and modified in its basic structure. Through omissions and additions, the medieval poet turns his 'mutacions des fables' (1.53) into a vast mythographic synthesis. In adopting segmentation techniques used by earlier mythographers,[32] he prefers amplification to summary, both in the narration of the fables and in their commentary. These predispositions generate a poetic flux that rivals and recasts Ovid's *carmen perpetuum*.

The amplification of Ovid's fables and the practice of mythographical digression betray the poem's status as vernacular compilation. To the Ovidian tapestry the medieval poet adds numerous figures and episodes. Noteworthy among these interpolated narrative segments are the castration of Saturn (1.513–718), the myths of the Danaids (2.4587–4795), Phrixus and Helle (4.2786–2928), Hero and Leander (4.3150–3584), the revenge of Medea (7.1365–1508), Theseus' descent into hell (7.1684–1730), the history of Thebes (9.1437–1838) and several episodes from the Trojan War, recounted in Books 11–13. Since the medieval author had likely read the *Metamorphoses* in an annotated manuscript whose margins and interlinear glosses would have reflected a long tradition of commentary, it is difficult

---

[31] Copeland 1991: 116.
[32] On the segmentation of Ovid's poem by early mythographers see Hexter 1987: 63–82.

to establish his source or sources for each fable.[33] Having contrasted sections of the vernacular poem with John of Garland's *Integumenta Ovidii* and Arnulf of Orléans's prose commentary, Fausto Ghisalberti concludes that neither of these prior allegorisations of the *Metamorphoses* was directly available to the anonymous author.[34] Rather, he surmises, the medieval poet must have used a manuscript of the *Metamorphoses* whose marginalia combined the *Integumenta Ovidii* with Arnulf of Orléans's prose commentary, as is the case of Vatican City, BAV, Vat. lat. MS 1479.[35] As shown by Demats, the poet uses mythographical materials variously to enrich his translation, to expand on allusions in Ovid's text and to construct a cohesive narrative out of Ovid's sometimes fragmentary notations. When telling the fable of Coronis, for instance, he expands across twenty lines (2.2221–44) an allusion made by Ovid to the birth of Erichthonius, 'proles sine matre creata' (the child born without a mother) (*Met.* 2.553).[36]

The French translation draws extensively from other works attributed to Ovid, in particular the *Heroides* from which are borrowed the legend of the Danaids and the myth of Iole, the stories of Hero and Leander, Jason and Medea, and Paris and Helen, as well as Dido's complaint.[37] The vernacular poet finds in Ovid's love poetry not simply a source for added material, but a means of conveying psychological and sentimental notes sometimes missing from the characters' depictions in the *Metamorphoses*. Compilation may take place at the expense of narrative coherence, as in the story of the Danaids, interpolated at the end of Book 2 between the fable of Aglauros and Invidia and that of Europa. Here, the medieval poet-storyteller unabashedly announces that he will break with the *auctor*'s narrative:

> Mes ançois que plus vous en die,
> Pour mieux acomplir ma matire,
> Vous vaudrai raconter et dire
> Un dit, qui n'est pas en cest livre
> Sans l'ordre de l'auctor ensivre.
>
> (2.4582–6)

---

[33] De Boer, Engels, and Demats have noted possible borrowings from Hyginus, Fulgentius and the Third Vatican Mythographer.

[34] For these commentaries see also in this volume, pp. 49–65, 311–13.

[35] Ghisalberti in Giovanni del Virgilio 1933: 8–15. For further discussion of Vat. lat. 1479, see Coulson above, pp. 79–82.

[36] The fable is present in Hyginus' *Fabulae* 224. See de Boer (ed.) 1915–1938, vol. II: 168, n. 1.

[37] Completing Demats' study of Book 4 in *Fabula*, 73, Jung charts the main additions and their sources in all fifteen books: Jung 1994: 152–3. As suggested by Léchat 2002, the digressive structure of Book 4 in the *Ovide moralisé* may well have been inspired by the Minyeïdes, whose tales this book recounts.

But before saying any more, to better develop my subject matter I would like to tell you a story that is not in this book, without following the order of the *auctor*.

To justify this patent digression, the poet refers his audience to the point in Book 1 where he had recounted Epaphus' birth and his challenge to his playmate Phaethon, as recounted in Ovid (*Met.* 1.748–54), followed by the story of how Io's son became King of Egypt and founded Memphis according to 'l'estoire escripte' (the written record) (1.4238). This brief addition, which Engels attributes to Hyginus' *Fabulae* 149,[38] is expanded in Book 2, where the poet adds that Epaphus' male heir fathered eight sons, 'si com l'estoire nous retrait' (as history tells us) (2.4594)). One wonders in light of such disruptions to the original structure of the *Metamorphoses* whether passages are added in the interest of compilation alone, or whether they play a more fundamental role in the process of medieval rewriting. Indeed, the anonymous poet seems to amplify not simply Ovid's fables but, more radically, the underlying narrative patterns of the *Metamorphoses* themselves.

The poet of the *Ovide moralisé* is not always eager to amplify and comment; he may grant only a few lines to a given allusion or fable, contenting himself to refer to glosses of Ovid's poem or to the mythographic literature. Digressions from the text risk steering the vernacular poet into unfamiliar territory, as is the case with the first major interpolation, that of Saturn's castration which leads to the narrative of Venus' birth.[39] There, the poet moves briskly from his euhemeristic explanation of the Golden Age myth, where Saturn, a Cretan king, is worshipped as a god, to the narrative retracing the fate of the male heirs whom Saturn decides to put to death after he is told that his throne will be usurped by one of his sons. A later segment dedicated to Jupiter (1.513–718) is prompted by the historical interpretation of the myth of the Golden Age, yet it remains within the purview of the fable via the motif of Venus' birth:

> Par force d'armes et de guerre
> Le desherita de sa terre;
> Les genitaires li trencha,
> Et dedens la mer les lança;
> De l'escume de mer salee
> Et d'eulz fu la grant Venus nee.
>
> (1.649–54)

[38] 'Iuppiter Epaphum quem ex Io procreaverat, Agypto oppido communire ibique regnare iussit. Is oppidum primum Memphim et alia plura constituit', Hyginus, *Fabulae*, quoted in Engels 1943: 142.
[39] The castration of Uranus and birth of Aphrodite are recounted in Hesiod's *Theogony*.

By the strength of arms and war he took away his land; he cut off his genitals and threw them in the sea; from out of the sea's salty foam and from them Venus the great was born.

This scene is likely inspired by Jean de Meun's rendering of the castration episode in the *Roman de la Rose*. The first metamorphosis of the *Ovide moralisé* would hence be a vernacular borrowing, one which suggestively portrays the manner in which the work of *translatio* gives renewed impetus to the *carmen perpetuum*.[40] Rather than attempt to arrest the *Metamorphoses'* 'uninterrupted song', the translator seeks in the history of the poem's transmission those narrative models which best accommodate change.

The interpolation of the Saturn myth, which, for Demats, exemplifies the intrusion of euhemeristic glosses in the fable, helps us appreciate how the vernacular poet patches together Ovidian fables and mythographic materials. On the one hand, the euhemeristic commentary gives the fable an historical aura; on the other, a myth of origins seems to lend the fable its narrative principle. The tale of Venus' birth calls forth a development on the genealogy of the gods in a passage that alludes to the children born to Jupiter by his own daughter and closes with the evocation of the sterile union of Vulcan, son of Juno, and the goddess of love. References to painting suggest that the genealogical development following the Saturn episode is inspired by the iconography of the gods.[41] Here, the author evokes Venus' weapons and glosses the iconography of her children in allegorical terms:

> Jocus et Cupido sont point
> Au pointures nu, sans veüe,
> Quar fole amours et jex desnue
> Les musars de robe et d'avoir,
> D'entendement et de savoir,
> D'onnor et de bones vertus:
> Pour ce sont il paint desvestus.
>   (1.672–8)

Jocus and Cupid are depicted naked and blind in paintings, for crazy love and games deprive fools of their clothing and riches, reason and wisdom, honour and good virtues: hence are they painted naked.

---

[40] Ovid mentions only that the Golden Age ends with the fall of Saturn: 'Postquam, Saturno tenebrosa in Tartara misso, Sub Ioue mundus erat, subiit argentea proles', *Metamorphoses* 1.113–14. On the myth of Saturn's castration and its role in the *Romance of the Rose*, see Fritz 1988: 43–60.

[41] The poet provides a euhemeristic explanation of the iconography of the gods. Saturn is depicted 'Tenans la faucille en deus poins' (1.700) (Grasping the sickle with two hands), since he taught the people of Lombardy to wield that implement.

Not all additions to the Latin poem are so striking as these. More often than not they merely allow the medieval clerk, who willingly fills up the gaps in Ovid's text, to flaunt his erudition and his talents as a storyteller as part of his grand mythographic project.

If the medieval poet explicitly contrasts the *Ovide moralisé* to its Latin models, including the classical mythography and medieval commentaries, he is less forthcoming about his debts to vernacular sources. Few explicit references occur to Old French texts, and no vernacular writers are mentioned by name, with the exception of Benoît de Sainte-Maure (12.1715 and 12.1734), who is made the object of a unfavourable comparison between the Old French *Roman de Troie* and the version contained in the *Ilias latina* of Baebius Italicus (referred to as 'Homers' in 12.1725). When prior vernacular renditions of Ovid's fables are available, the writer generally defers to them and respects their textual integrity. The tale of Pyramus and Thisbe (4.229–1149), for example, is borrowed in extenso from a twelfth-century Anglo-Norman poem:[42]

> Or vous raconterai le conte
> Et la fable sans ajouster,
> Sans muer et sans riens oster,
> Si comme uns autres l'a dité,
> Puis i metrai la verité.
>
> (4.224–8)

I will recount the tale and the fable without adding, changing, or removing anything, just as another has told it; then I will explain its truth.

Other vernacular citations include the anonymous twelfth-century Old French poem on Philomela (6.2217–3684), of particular interest to medieval scholars as it is commonly identified as the lost Ovidian tale that Chrétien de Troyes mentions in the prologue to *Cligès*.[43] Two references to the presumptive author of the *conte*, 'Crestiens' (6.2212–16 and lines 3685–6), frame the interpolated tale, while a third reference to 'Crestiiens li Gois' (6.2950) occurs at the tale's narrative midpoint, where it immediately precedes the amputation scene. Since the *Ovide moralisé* is the only medieval text to preserve *Philomena* and since it also contains the least corrupt

---

[42] In addition to the text preserved in the *Ovide moralisé*, three thirteenth-century manuscripts contain Old French versions of the Pyramus and Thisbe myth. For an electronic edition of the four renditions, see Penny Eley, ed. and trans., *Piramus et Tisbé*, Liverpool Online Series/Critical Editions of French Texts 5 (2001).

[43] Chrétien de Troyes 1974. For the interpretation of the Procne and Philomela story in the Latin commentary tradition, see Coulson 2008.

version of the twelfth-century Old French tale of Pyramus and Thisbe, the poem effectively becomes a vernacular anthology of Ovidian fables.

Although it is possible through lexical comparison to identify possible vernacular sources or intertexts, precise borrowings are difficult to prove. In rare cases, intervernacular allusions can be located on the level of key phrases or expressions; one noted example commented on by Blumenfeld-Kosinski is the expression 'li mireoirs perillous' (3.1925) in the fable of Narcissus, where Guillaume's poem is unmistakably the intertext (*Roman de la Rose*, line 1569).[44] This is but one in a series of echoes of the *Roman de la Rose*. Two lines not glossed by de Boer are lifted from Guillaume's text: compare 'Bien se sot lors amours vengier / dou grant orgueil et dou dangier' (1.1577–8) and 'Lors se sot bien Amors venchier/ dou grant orguil et dou dangier' (*Roman de la Rose*, lines 1487–8) (Then Love found a good way to take vengeance against (Narcissus') great pride and resistance).

In a poem of such vast scope as the *Ovide moralisé*, tracing such direct borrowings and distant verbal echoes would afford a firmer grasp of vernacular intertextuality in its relation to the treatment of Latin sources.

THE HERMENEUTIC FRAMEWORK AND THE POETICS OF METAMORPHOSIS

It can be argued that the fundamental novelty of the *Ovide moralisé* as Ovidian commentary is the poem's refusal to instigate a firm hierarchy between the narration of the fables and their various *mutacions*. While comparison of the Latin and vernacular texts that inform the medieval French commentator provides insight in this domain, source study alone cannot explain what makes the *Ovide moralisé* a metamorphic text in its own right. The poem's coherence can perhaps best be ascertained if fable and commentary are read as a part of a poetic continuum, not as two distinct modes of discourse placed in juxtaposition. In what follows, I will first concentrate on the translation and commentary of the Lycaon myth to illustrate how the *Ovide moralisé* reworks its models into a sophisticated metamorphic exercise.

Often quoted in the *accessus* is the transformation of Lycaon, the first of the metamorphoses in Ovid's text to affect a human being.[45] The medieval tradition retains the myth's exemplary character: changed into a wolf because he has acted like one, Lycaon merely becomes what he already

---

[44] Blumenfeld-Kosinski 1997: 125.   [45] See Coulson 1991: 27.

was in essence. However, if the *Ovide moralisé* underscores Lycaon's ferocity, it downplays the continuity between man and beast that is central to
Ovid's poetics of bodily change:

> Fit lupus et ueteris seruat uestigia formae;
> canities eadem est, eadem uiolentia uultus,
> Idem oculi lucent, eadem feritatis imago est.
> (*Met.* 1.237–9)

He turns into a wolf, and yet retains some traces of his former shape. There is the
same grey hair, the same fierce face, the same gleaming eyes, the same picture of
beastly savagery.

In Ovid's narrative, as he undergoes metamorphosis Lycaon retains not
only his cruelty but his physical traits, as the repetition of the adjective
eadem suggests. By contrast, the vernacular translation erases all traces 'of
his former shape' such that the similarity between man and beast takes on
strictly moral dimensions:

> Il est fais leuz malz et nuisans;
> Encor a il les ieus luisans,
> S'est plains de rage et de mauté,
> Si come il otançois esté.
> (1.1385–8)

He is made into a wolf, mean and destructive; he still has gleaming eyes and is as
full of rage and malice as he had been before.

Where Ovid foregrounds identity in and through transformation ('eadem
feritatis imago est'), the medieval poet splits bodily change into two
moments whose juxtaposition, contained in an analogy (line 1388), counters
the paradoxical aspect of Lycaon's metamorphosis.

Consecutive analogical sequences will be the building blocks of the poet's
multifold *exposicion* that further transform Ovidian fables into unambigu-
ous *exempla*. The first explanation proposed of the Lycaon myth describes
the King of Arcadia's sacrilegious crime in terms of feudal revolt. Wishing to test the power of Jupiter, Lycaon attacks him in his sleep. When
Jupiter invades his lands and sets fire to his property, the tyrant hides in
the forest, where he pillages and plunders the poor. The first gloss seems to
demystify the passage by describing pagan fables as clumsy transpositions
of historical events: 'Pour ce fu dit, selonc les fables, / Qu'il fu leuz glouz
et ravissables' (That's why it is said according to the fables that he was a
gluttonous and destructive wolf) (1.1443–4). After presenting an analogy
between Jupiter's wrath and the story of the Flood, the author compares

Lycaon's crimes to the Massacre of the Innocents: 'Des sains aus meres esraçoit / Li glouz leus ceulz qu'il escachoit, / Si lor espandoit les cerveles, / Les entrailles et les boëles' (The bloodthirsty wolf tore his prey from their mother's breast, spreading their brains, innards and bowels) (1.1555–8). As punishment, God takes away Lycaon's kingdom and throws him into hell. The poet attributes yet another meaning ('autre sens') to the fable by comparing the character to a wolf who 'escorce' (skins), 'desrobe' (steals from), 'despoulle' (fleeces) and 'devore' (devours) the poor. Among these verbs only the last denotes animal ferocity, suggesting that the true target of the comparison is human society. By the close of the anaphoric development based on the words 'Leu[s] qui' (The wolves who), the predator has taken on an unmistakeably human visage:

> Ha, Dieus, com de telz leus sont ore!
>
> . . .
>
> Leu qui des povres gens menjucent
> Char et sustance, et le sanc sucent,
> Leus qui sor povres gens forsenent,
> Leus qui tout desrobent et prennent;
> Baillif, bedel, prevost et maire
> Ne pensent qu'a l'autrui soustraire;
>
> (1.1574–84)

Oh God, how many such wolves are there now! . . . Wolves who eat the poor folks' flesh and marrow, and suck their blood, wolves who steal and take all. The bailiff, the officer, the provost and the mayor think of nothing but stealing from others.

These lines employ the same terms through which Jean de Meun's Faux Semblant explains how the rich dispossess the poor (*Roman de la Rose*, lines 11507–18). The lexical similarity suggests that the poet's satirical intent motivates the moralised reading: the lupine metaphor reveals the true face of the flesh-eaters. Where Ovid speaks only of Lycaon's thirst for blood, in his paraphrase the medieval poet pointedly introduces the metaphor of torture via the verbs *acorer* (disembowel), *escorcer* (flay) and *desrober* (undress); this development finds its rhetorical culmination in the poet's critique of the *escorceor* (line 1586), or those rich and maleficent merchants and magistrates who fleece the poor. The moralisation's power derives from the poet's word choice, for the literal and figurative meanings of each term are simultaneously preserved.[46]

---

[46] The central element in this metaphoric field, *escorcer*, is a keyword of medieval exegesis, where the image of the shell and the nut designates the opposition between literal and figural meanings of Scripture.

The medieval poet's commentaries exhibit even greater structural diversity than do his renditions of Ovid's fables. The poet enlists the methods of demystification to establish the falsehood of fables, which are presented as allegories of the natural world or as crude transpositions of historical events.[47] On first reading, recurrence of lexical items such as 'estoire', 'sentence' or 'alegorie' may suggest that interpretation inexorably moves from physical and historical to moral to spiritual interpretations: 'La premiere fable autrement / Puis espondre naturelment, / Selonc phisique' (I can explain the first fable in natural terms, according to physics) (14.5314–15). In this respect, the *Ovide moralisé* would propose a method for interpreting myth akin to the practice of deciphering Scripture. However, this assumption about the poem's hermeneutics does not take into account the distinction between sacred and profane exegesis and significantly distorts the medieval commentator's actual techniques. It is rare in fact that we encounter four systematic interpretations of the same myth, and when four are present, they need not reflect the four levels of Biblical exegesis defined by Lubac. As Jung notes, only physical and historical explanations ordinarily lead to term-to-term interpretation.[48] Spiritual interpretations, by contrast, are structured by the unfolding of one or more lexical fields in a manner that recalls medieval predication more than Biblical exegesis.[49]

In her study of the vernacular poet's practice of moralisation, Possamaï-Pérez clearly shows the 'saut herméneutique' or interpretive leap from 'concrete' meanings to spiritual interpretations, where tropological, typological and anagogical elements are combined in a flowing yet highly structured manner.[50] To establish an 'acceptable literal meaning',[51] the poet must first decipher fabulous materials by using those types of discourse that fall under the general rubric of 'estoire': history, exempla, literary or legendary materials, and Biblical history.[52] To illustrate the complex articulation of fable, demystification and allegoresis, I will concentrate here on Daphne's metamorphosis in Book 1 (lines 2737–3064), a passage that has attracted the attention of critics because of a reference to the 'Integument'

[47] On demystification in Ovidian commentary, see, in particular, Barkan 1990: 104–9.
[48] Jung 1994: 150–1.
[49] On the resemblance of rhetoric in the *Ovide moralisé*'s commentaries to that of the *Ars praedicandi*, see Tilliette 1996 and Ribemont 2002: 13–24.
[50] See Possamaï-Pérez 2006: 367–493. In her study of the work's didactic construction, Possamaï-Pérez shows how 'sensual relays' are progressively abandoned on behalf of spiritual explanations. This is particularly true of physical glosses, which are not represented in Books 5–9 (2006: 642–7).
[51] Possamaï-Pérez 2006: 371.
[52] On the different meanings of the term 'estoire' in the *Ovide moralisé*, see Blumenfeld-Kosinski 1997: 103–7 and Possamaï-Pérez 2006: 383–95.

(line 3126), which de Boer construes as meaning John of Garland's *Integumenta Ovidii*.[53] Daphne's metamorphosis follows a digression on the history of Babylon and Palestine after the flood (lines 2365–2622): 'De ces etoires vous lairai, / Et des fables vous retrairai, / Si comme Ovides les recite' (I will leave aside these stories and tell you the fables just as Ovid narrates them) (lines 2623–5). Expanding on Ovid's allusion to Phoebus' tree ('nondum laurus erat', *Met.* 1.450), the medieval poet presents his tale as an aetiological myth: 'Se nulz quiert pour quoi ne comment / Li loriers vint premierement, / Je le li dirai sans demour' (If anyone wonders why and how the bay tree came to exist, I will tell him straightaway) (1.2737–9). He expands Ovid's narrative with an amplification (lines 2867–77) on 'vaine esperance' (foolish hope); a second, playful digression on how love can turn the head of the wisest men (lines 2952–65) occurs when Daphne's flight forces Apollo to break off his 'sermon' (line 2969).

After providing a physical interpretation of the fable where Apollo makes bay trees multiply on the banks of the Peneus River, the poet reads the myth as the transposition of an historical event in which a young girl chose to die rather than surrender her virginity and was buried under a bay tree. As noted by Possamaï-Pérez,[54] the transitional formula suggests the superiority of the historical interpretation, which can be read as a moral exemplum: 'Autre sentence i puet avoir, / Par istoire acordable a voir' (It may hold another lesson that can be aligned with truth through history) (lines 3075–6). These first two lessons are presented as being embedded in the fable, perhaps as shaped by commentary. By contrast, the fable's Christian morality or tropological lesson results from the poet's external interpretive activity: 'Mes or donons a ceste fable / Autre sentence profitable' (Let us now give to this fable an edifying meaning) (lines 3109–10). The daughter of a frigid river, Daphne remains unresponsive to the sun, which is held to personify the cardinal virtues of 'sapience' (wisdom) and 'charité' (charity). To support this association of the sun with wisdom, the poet invokes the authority of the 'Integument', stating: 'C'est Phebus, que l'Integument, / Selonc la paienne creence, / Apele dieu de sapience' (The *Integumentum* calls Phoebus, in keeping with pagan belief, the god of wisdom) (lines 3126–8). Next, he condemns the 'cold' virgins who preserve their bodies but not their hearts, invoking the parable of the foolish virgins (Matt. 25:1–13) ('De teulz dist Dieus, en l'Evangile' (About these (virgins) God

---

[53] After examining de Boer's meagre evidence, Ghisalberti, in Arnulf of Orléans 1932, contests this identification. In his view, neither John of Garland's *Integumenta Ovidii* nor Arnulf of Orléans's commentary are direct sources for the anonymous poet.

[54] Possamaï-Pérez 2006: 376.

says in the Gospels . . .), line 3156), which he glosses as a prefiguration of the Last Judgement. In a further interpretation where the bay tree figures the Virgin Mary (line 3215), Phoebus' embrace represents the mystery of Christ's incarnation. This spiritual allegory is followed by a final gloss of the dispute between Cupid and Phoebus, which includes an extended allegoresis of the arrows of Christian love (lines 3261–3407). Arguably, the five interpretations set forth here are driven by semantic associations to the notion of virginity as figured by the bay tree rather than by a codified method of exegesis.

What Ralph Hexter writes of Arnulf of Orléans can be said to apply equally to the construction of meaning in the *Ovide moralisé*: 'there is no one, all-embracing "allegory" of the *Metamorphoses* here, but allegories which shift ground from story to story'.[55] Progression of the medieval poem's shifting patterns of interpretation calls for close analysis, all the more so given that the anonymous author may alter the hierarchy of internal narrators or narrative structure from book to book.[56] Book 15 is a case in point, where, contrary to the pattern he has followed throughout the poem, the vernacular author intervenes as commentator only after having translated the final book in its entirety. Shifts in the medieval poet's hermeneutic can further be appreciated through lexical variation, whether of individual items or of recurrent transitional formulas. Metalanguage runs through the poem and is particularly in evidence in Book 1, where 'fable(s)' appears thirty-three times and 'estoire(s)' or 'istoire', nine. This second term generally announces an euhemeristic explanation of the myth or refers to Biblical history, while 'sens', 'sentence', 'entendement', 'exposicion' and 'allegorie' point to moral and spiritual interpretations. From one occurrence to the next a term such as 'allegorie', which appears three times in the opening book, may exhibit functional and semantic nuances. In 'Tel allegorie y puis metre' (I can put forth another allegory) (line 1185), the term announces the tropological interpretation of the Giants as proud men who challenge God. In 'Allegorie i puet avoir / Qui bien est acordable a voir' (The allegory it contains can be aligned with the truth) (lines 3905–6), it introduces a negative exemplum where Io stands for a pious virgin who surrenders to worldly temptations. The term finally appears in a typological reading of Phaethon's flight, which is compared to the fall of Lucifer. This brief 'alegorie' (lines 4245–60) is followed by a gloss in which the myth of Phaethon illustrates God's forgiveness towards the repentant sinner and the fall of the proud into the depths of hell.

---

[55] Hexter 1987: 65.   [56] Blumenfeld-Kosinski 1997: 119–21 and Possamaï-Pérez 2006: 638–53.

Discursive formulas used to stitch together interpretive sequences in Book I emphasise the manifold nature of interpretation. 'Autre sens puet avoir la fable' (The fable can have another meaning) (line 1568) bridges the identification of Lycaon's crimes with those of Herod, to produce a reading of the fable as social satire; 'Or vous dirai que senefie/ Cele fable, qu'avez oïe' (I will now say what the fable that you have just heard means) (lines 2159–60) introduces a physical reading of the stones that Deucalion and Pyrrha throw over their shoulders as male and female sperm ('jerme', line 2171; 'semence', line 2178). More elaborate transitions outline the approach to be followed in aligning the fables with truth: 'Qui ceste fable veult savoir, / Bien en puet ramener a voir / La sentence en mainte maniere' (Whoever wants to understand this fable truthfully can approach its lesson in many ways) (lines 3797–9). A second, euhemeristic reading of Io's story is introduced by an image that reinforces the idea of a progression towards truth: 'Mes or tornons en autre fueil / Ceste fable, et par autre estoire / Veons comment la fable est voire' (But let us now turn this fable in another manner and let us see through another story how the fable holds true) (lines 3830–2). It should be noted that discursive tags or interpretative terms do not necessarily highlight the moral value of the *exposicion*. The nonspecific 'Esponnons la fable autrement' (Now let's explain the fable differently) (line 2185) fronts an extended allegoresis of the myth of Deucalion and Pyrrha which includes a diatribe against a topsy-turvy social world where evil is rewarded and goodness is soiled; following Deucalion and Pyrrha's lead, we must cover our heads with the scarf of salvation and leave behind, through confession, the vices that taint our soul. When properly interpreted, like Themis' oracle, fables can provide 'example et enseigne / Et signe et vraie demonstrance' (example, teaching, sign and truthful demonstration) (lines 2298–9). An emphasis on interpretative freedom brings the poem's reader to a finer understanding of allegoresis as poetic technique; the gloss derives its authority not from a strict adherence to levels of meaning, but from the progressive transformation of material signs into spiritual meanings.

Pagan fables remain inherently deceitful, and as such call for interpretation. Beyond historical or moral truth, it is with Holy Scripture they must be reconciled: 'La devine page et la fable / Sont en ce, ce samble, acordable' (Holy Scripture and the fable are in this respect, it seems, in agreement) (1.2139–40). Selective exegesis allows the poet to turn pagan motifs into vehicles for Christian edification. While transforming the Ovidian fable remains at the poem's core, there is not necessarily an end to the hermeneutic process or a moment where truth would stand revealed, as announced in the prologue ('La veritez seroit aperte / Qui souz les fables gist couverte', 1.45–6). Shifts in meaning in transitional formulas ultimately suggest that discontinuities are not only inherent in interpretation, but perhaps beneficial to it, for they remind us that reading and writing are contingent practices. Returning to the prologue, for instance, one notes how the author transforms the modesty topos. While he initially presents his poem as the continuation of work that others had undertaken but were unable to finish (1.20–4), he also asks that others rework and correct his own text: 'Proi tous ceulz qui liront cest livre, / Que, se je mespreng a escrire / Ou a dire que je ne doie, / Corrigent moi' (I beg my readers to correct me if I write something wrong or say something I shouldn't) (1.61–4). Beyond the fundamental distinction between concrete and spiritual meanings, interpretative hierarchies are perhaps themselves subjective. The poet ranks different ways of reading a specific fable, labelling one interpretation as 'meillour' (better), 'plus noble' (nobler), 'plus digne' (worthier), 'plus saine' (healthier) than another.[57] This introduction of evaluative gradations breaks with prior Ovidian commentaries, including the allegories in John of Garland's *Integumenta Ovidii*. Rather than offer an exegetical method based on levels of meaning, the *Ovide moralisé* tends to construct a moral hierarchy of poetic readings. Claiming to write with God's guidance, the poet ultimately controls the ways each fable should be read: 'En Dieu me fi de cest afaire' (I trust God in this matter) (1.26).

The effect of commentary in the *Ovide moralisé* is, then, to set up a discursive mechanism that allows for endless analogical amplification. If there is no single hidden meaning to be unveiled, but only a series of signifiers subject to multiple glossing, nothing in principle need put an end to the commentary. As interpretative technique, analogy seems never to stray from the fable whose terms it borrows the better to transform them. This continuous change in perspective, akin to pictorial techniques of anamorphosis, can be coupled with a play on the polysemy of individual terms since the coherence of any analogical network rests on the possibility of opening up new semantic fields. The poem's hermeneutics makes room for structural echoes and thematic variations that amplify the Ovidian paradox of constant change.

To sum up, analysis of the vocabulary of interpretation allows us to measure how the medieval author recasts, through analogy, the models

---

[57] Blumenfeld-Kosinski 1997: 119–20.

of commentary provided by biblical exegesis and academic commentary. Placed in relation to a discourse built around the theme of metamorphosis, this practice is innovative. Twelfth- and thirteenth-century academic commentators, when reading the pagan text, tend to ascribe to each metamorphosis individual glosses that make its meaning apparent; in this framework, interpretation is meant to put an end to the daunting chain of metamorphoses. Analogical commentary in the *Ovide moralisé* seems to work to opposite ends, since its discursive force – founded on unstable ascriptions of meaning – derives from the seductive power of narratives of metamorphoses themselves. Recourse to analogy thus takes on a new dimension: the commentary arrests the tale's metamorphosis only to reproduce, in its linear progression, the permanent variation proper to Ovid's central theme.

The sheer variety of the *exposicion* provided by the *Ovide moralisé* suggests that there is no single key that would allow us to unlock the poem's system of meaning, and no level of analysis where multiple interpretations of each fable neatly coincide. Were we to attempt to provide a unified interpretative grid for the *Ovide moralisé*, we would only efface the tense and productive interaction that ensues between the narration of the fables and their commentary. Moreover, by imposing such a grid on the poem we would risk minimising the impact of prior glosses on the medieval poet's approach to individual fables and silencing intertextual echoes that are traceable on the stylistic level. A more fruitful approach may be to examine the dynamics of interpretation by following the trajectory of key words or stylistic features – how they migrate from fable to commentary and back again – and those lexical, thematic and formal connections that lead from one interpretation to the next.

The fundamental challenge posed by the *Ovide moralisé* to medieval readers concerns the Ovidian paradox of the instability of being and of identity in change.[58] The poem both enacts and reflects a contradiction between doctrine and practice. At the doctrinal level, the Church Fathers' crusade to domesticate metamorphosis by reaffirming the omnipotence of God against the shifting play of the senses found in the fourteenth-century anonymous French poet one of its most staunch allies. Moralisation of Ovid effectively dissociates the theme of bodily change from the domain of the marvellous which had dominated vernacular representations of 'mutacion' since the twelfth century. At the rhetorical level, however, there remains

---

[58] Bynum 2001.

a strong continuity between Ovid's narrative and the medieval French poem, which cautiously avoids any single, unifying *exposicion*. In contrast to prior commentaries that sought to counter Ovid's narrative of endless metamorphosis by segmenting and decoding it, narrative and hermeneutic choices in the *Ovide moralisé* unabashedly reflect the flowing spirit of Ovid's *carmen perpetuum*.

CHAPTER 5

Gender and desire in medieval French translations of Ovid's amatory works

Marilynn Desmond

The reception and translation of Ovid's texts made available a language of desire that contributed to the emergence of a heteroerotic ethic in medieval literary cultures. While Ovid's *Metamorphoses* provides a storehouse of anecdotes that vividly depict sexual escapades, it is Ovid's amatory works that develop and elaborate on the structures of desire. The medieval reception of two Ovidian texts – the *Ars amatoria* and the *Heroides* – was critical to the development of an erotic discourse in medieval textual traditions. The *Ars amatoria* and the *Heroides* circulated widely in Latin from the twelfth century onwards, and the reception of these texts left traces throughout medieval genres, perhaps most visibly in medieval romance. In the thirteenth century, the *Ars amatoria* begins to circulate in French verse, and both the *Ars amatoria* and the *Heroides* exist in late medieval prose versions that attempt to provide verbatim renditions of Ovid's Latin. These prose translations participate in a vast cultural effort in the thirteenth and fourteenth centuries aimed at making Latin texts available to vernacular readers by producing readable French versions of Latin *auctoritas*.[1] In their efforts to provide *verbum ex verbo* renditions of Ovid's Latin, these prose translators render Ovid's categories for desire as normative categories of gender. As a consequence, the trajectory of these texts from Latin elegiac couplets into French prose – the *lingua franca* of medieval textual cultures from England to Italy – contributed to the construction of normative sexual regimes and even sexual identities.

The *Heroides* and the *Ars amatoria* represent formal innovations in Latin literary history, and both texts – one pedagogical, one performative – call attention to the rhetorical basis of Latin love elegy and its highly self-conscious evocation of erotic desire. Ovid's initial composition in elegiac metres, the *Amores*, exemplifies the heterosexual contract that emerges

---

[1] On French translations of Latin texts in the thirteenth and fourteenth centuries, see Lusignan 1986: 129–71.

in the literary conventions of Roman amatory poetry: the *Amores* situates its narrator as a male lover who addresses a female object of desire.[2]
After producing the *Amores*, however, Ovid proceeded to compose two
texts in elegiac metre that belabour the categories of desire constructed in
Latin love elegy: the *Ars amatoria*, which didactically expounds on every
aspect of heterosexual performance to the exclusion of same-sex desire,
and the *Heroides*, a collection of heteroerotic letters ostensibly written by
the lovelorn and abandoned women of ancient myth, several of which are
paired with responses from their lovers.[3] The narrators of the *Ars amatoria* and the *Heroides* presuppose a connection between gender and desire,
if only ironically: the pedagogical structure of the *Ars amatoria* provides
detailed instruction regarding the *habitus* of heterosexual *amor*, and the
female narrators of the *Heroides* perform a highly gendered discourse of
female longing for an absent male lover.

Ovid composed both the *Heroides* and the *Ars amatoria* as ironic commentaries on Roman politics and literary values; such literary irony, however, depends heavily on the social context of a text.[4] The medieval *fortuna*
of Ovid's texts, particularly their translation into the vernacular, removes
them from their original context. From the twelfth century on, medieval
Latin manuscripts address the cultural alterity of Ovid's poetry through
the inclusion of introductory material, collectively known as the *accessus ad
auctores*, as well as marginal prose glosses and commentary.[5] Such a reading
apparatus worked to authorise the Latin texts of Ovid's poetry as didactic
treatises or as disquisitions on ethics.[6] French translations of Ovid's poetry
frequently include a translation of the ancillary material alongside the text.
For instance, an adaptation of the *Metamorphoses* in French verse – the
Ovide moralisé (1316–28) – appends allegorical commentaries to each unit
of narrative translated from Ovid's text.[7] The prose translation of the *Ars*

---

[2] On elegiac discourse, see Holzberg 2002: 16–20.
[3] *Heroides* 1–15, the female voiced epistles, are known as the single letters, and *Heroides* 16–21, which includes pairs of lovers and letters sent by men, are known as the 'double letters'.
[4] Ovid composed the *Heroides* after the *Amores*, followed by the *Ars amatoria*. On the chronology of the Ovidian corpus, see Holzberg 2002: 16–20.
[5] On the commentary tradition, see Gillespie 2005; Hexter 1986; Coulson 1991; McKinley 2001; and Ghisalberti in Arnulf of Orléans 1932.
[6] On Latin texts of the Ovidian corpus in the medieval classroom, see Hexter 1986, 2006; and McGregor 1978. On the reception of Latin texts of Ovid's amatory works, see Toury 2003; Hagedorn 2004; Allen 1992; Baldwin 1992; Bond 1995; and Nolan 1989. For the manuscript tradition, see Kenney 1962. For an overview of Ovid in the Middle Ages, see Dimmick 2002; Rand 1926; Wilkinson 1955; Battaglia 1959; and Munari 1960.
[7] De Boer (ed.), 1915–38. On the *Ovide moralisé*, see Blumenfeld-Kosinski 1997: 90–135; Copeland 1991: 107–30; and Desmond 2007.

amatoria – the *Art d'amours* – likewise includes commentary as a supplement to the prose version of the text, thus creating a didactic register in place of the irony of Ovid's original. While the translations of the *Heroides* do not incorporate any material from the commentary tradition, they are presented as part of the history of Trojan War, thereby emphasising the narrative component of the *Heroides*.

The *Amores* do not appear to have been translated into the vernacular in the Middle Ages; the French versions of the *Heroides* and the *Ars amatoria*, however, were widely disseminated. As a result, vernacular translations of the *Ars amatoria* and the *Heroides* greatly influenced the reception of Ovidian amatory poetry and the consequent constructions of desire in medieval vernacular literature. Indeed, the process of *translatio* appears to be critical to the vernacular reception of Ovid. When Chrétien de Troyes states in the prologue to *Cligès* (1176) that he has translated the *Ars amatoria* into French, he acknowledges the significance of Ovid's poem for the *translatio studii* of Latin erotic rhetoric into medieval romance. In a distinct departure from his earlier romance, *Erec et Enide* (*c.* 1170), Chrétien developed an elaborate heteroerotic ethic in *Cligès* that is derived from the *Ars*, and the Ovidian discourse developed in *Cligès* is apparent in all his later romances. Though no copy of Chrétien's twelfth-century translation has been preserved, five French versions of the *Ars amatoria* – four in verse and one in prose – survive from the thirteenth century.[8] Like much that purports to be 'translation' in medieval vernacular culture, these verse adaptations are not literal renditions of Ovid's text but poetic explorations of the premises of the *Ars amatoria*. Such repeated efforts at *translatio* testify to the centrality of the *Ars amatoria* to the development of an erotic discourse in medieval francophone cultures. The anonymous prose version of the *Ars*, the *Art d'amours*, offers the most extensive treatment of Ovid's text.[9] The first two books of the *Ars amatoria* – the books directed to a male audience – were translated as Books 1 and 2 of the *Art d'amours* during the first third of the thirteenth century. The final book – the book specifically addressed to female readers – was translated somewhat later towards the end of the century. The *Art d'amours* presents a prose rendition of Ovid's Latin text designated by the rubric *texte*, followed by commentary identified by a rubric, *glose*. Taken together, the three books of the *Art d'amours* provide a close French translation of Ovid's Latin, accompanied

---

[8] For the four verse translations of the *Ars amatoria*, see Lucas 1970: 241–2; Gaston Paris 1885: 455–525; Desmond 2006: 75–9; and Ovid 2008.

[9] On the *Art d'amours* and medieval vernacular culture, see Desmond 2006: 73–164.

by extensive explanations of the mythological or cultural references of Ovid's text, often drawn from the *Metamorphoses* or the *Heroides*. Such ancillary material frames the *Ars amatoria* as a serious treatise on the art and artifices of love: in the *Art d'amours*, Ovid's playful proposition that lovers might cynically manipulate desire becomes an authoritative text on erotic performance.

The Latin text of the *Heroides* circulated widely in the medieval West from the twelfth century onwards, though medieval Latin collections of the *Heroides*, with one exception, never include *Heroides* 15 (Sappho).[10] Although the *Heroides* as a complete collection of texts did not appear in French until the translation by Octavien de Saint-Gelais in 1496, translations of individual letters appear as part of larger texts. The *Ovide moralisé*, for instance, included a loose translation in verse of *Heroides* 7 (Dido); this adaptation of *Heroides* 7 is presented as a complaint rather than a letter.[11] The *Histoire ancienne jusqu'à César*, a compendium of universal history in French prose, includes prose translations of the *Heroides* which are inserted at various points in the narrative.[12] The first redaction of the *Histoire ancienne*, produced in the thirteenth century, included a translation of *Heroides* 1 (Penelope). The second redaction, produced in the middle of the fourteenth century, included versions of *Heroides* 2 (Phyllis), 3 (Briseis), 4 (Phaedra), 5 (Oenone), 8 (Hermoine), 10 (Ariadne), 11 (Canace), 13 (Laodamia), 16 (Paris), 17 (Helen), 18 (Leander) and 19 (Hero). As performative interludes inserted into larger narrative contexts, these translations of the *Heroides* enact longing and loss as constitutive features of female subjectivity and desire. Since the *Art d'amours* and the fugitive texts of the *Heroides* in the *Histoire ancienne* survive in significant numbers of medieval manuscripts,[13] these vernacular versions of Ovid's amatory texts appear to have circulated in place of the original Latin version.

The ancient world classified *amor* not by the gender but by the social class of the subject as well as the object of desire, and the adult Roman male citizen was always supposed to play the active role.[14] Latin amatory poetry,

---

[10] Tarrant 1983: 268–73; on the *Heroides* and the Latin culture of the Middle Ages, see Hagedorn 2004: 21–46.

[11] See *Ovide moralisé* 14.343–473.

[12] On the translations of the *Heroides* in the *Histoire ancienne*, see Barbieri 2005; Chesney 1942: 46–67; Meyer 1885; and Monfrin 1972. There exists a medieval Italian translation of the *Heroides* into Italian that is roughly contemporary with the French translation, see Barbieri 2005: 44–51.

[13] The *Art d'amours* survives in four manuscripts; the prose *Heroides* survive in nineteen manuscripts; see Barbieri 2005.

[14] As Holt N. Parker summarises Roman sexualities, 'The Romans divided sexual categories for people and acts on the axis of 'active and passive . . . the one normative action is the penetration of a bodily

as a consequence, does not idealise desire as such, and heterosexual *amor* did not have a normative status in ancient Roman culture or literature. In the *Ars amatoria*, the pedantic lessons of the *praeceptor* on the gestures, attitudes and rhetorics of *amor* treat heterosexual *eros* as a performance that does not come easily or naturally to the uninitiated. The rhetorical excess of the *Ars amatoria* ironically suggests that the mechanics of seduction must be taught and learned. As Thomas Habinek put it: 'Ovid invents the category of the heterosexual male.'[15] As a poem that unapologetically promotes adultery and promiscuous sexuality, the *Ars amatoria* starkly contradicts the value placed on chastity and marital sexuality that constitutes the dominant discourses on desire in the Christian Middle Ages. In the prologue to the *Art d'amours*, the translator acknowledges that 'il [Ovid] ne pense mie a traictier des honnestes' (he does not want to talk about chastity) (line 238);[16] the translator nonetheless states his intention to translate the 'moralité et la sentence' (line 21) of Ovid's text. Drawing on the Latin tradition of academic prologues – the *accessus ad auctores* – the translator notes that Ovid composed the *Ars amatoria* to teach his readers how to acquire the love of women and girls.[17] In approaching the *Ars amatoria* as a didactic text, the translator puts his faith in the efficacy of a text to inculcate normative desire in its readers: 'tel puet lire et oïr l'art d'amours qui, s'il ne l'eüst leü, ja n'eüst talent ne volanté d'amer; et si n'est mie deffendue du tout pour ce que aucuns qui avoient esté navrés d'amours ne savoient querre leur santé ne leur guarison, si en venoient a droite mort et en villains pechiés contre nature' (some, if they never read about the art of love, would never have the desire or the will to love. Another reason is that some who are heartbroken over love would not know how to seek their health or their cure and thus would go straight to their death from it in their wicked sins against nature) (lines 105–6). While the glosses repeatedly note that Ovid's text is not directed at virtuous or married women, the translator expresses no disapproval of the *praeceptor*'s advice that the prospective lover should employ deception and trickery in the pursuit of *amor*. The translator, however, expresses a purpose that differs

---

orifice by a penis', Parker 1997: 48. See also, Walters 1997: 29–43. For a general discussion of Ovid and issues of gender and sexuality, see Sharrock 1994: 97–122, Sharrock 2002; Ginsberg 1989; and O'Gorman 1997.

[15] Habinek 1977: 31.

[16] For text see Roy 1974; for English translation, see Ovid 1987.

[17] On the *accessus ad auctores*, see Gillespie 2005; Alton and Wormell 1961: 73; *Accessus ad auctores* 1970; Quain 1945; Coulson 1987, 1997; and Ghisalberti 1946. For translations of the accessus ad auctores see Elliot 1980; and Minnis and Scott 1991.

from the Latin original: the translator's goal is to offer an art of love that will keep those wounded by desire from falling into 'sins against nature' out of ignorance of the arts by which one might pursue heterosexual *amor*. For the medieval translator, Ovid's text offers instruction on how to channel desire into a normative sexual performance, one that the translator considers 'natural'. Ovid's mockery of categories of desire in the *Ars amatoria* does not survive in the *Art d'amours*, which consequently becomes a treatise on normative sexuality.

The vernacular tradition of the *Ars amatoria* privileges the first two books of Ovid's text – the two books addressed to male readers – and tends to exclude or abbreviate the third book, which Ovid addresses to women so that they might be 'armed against the men'. The verse translations of the *Ars amatoria* include little or nothing of *Ars amatoria* 3, and in the case of the *Art d'amours*, as we have noted, the third book was translated much later than the first two books. Thus, the vernacular tradition of the *Ars amatoria* constructs heterosexual desire around masculine agency, a gendered assumption that the flat prose of the *Art d'amours* reiterates and explicitly endorses in the glosses. In Book 1 of the *Ars amatoria*, Ovid's *praeceptor* evokes and then undermines the notion of a masculine prerogative in love in order to mock the mechanics of heterosexual performance, as in the couplet: 'conueniat maribus ne quam nos ante rogemus, / femina iam partes uicta rogantis aget' (Were it not suitable for men that we entreat first, the woman, having already been conquered, would play the role of the suitor) (1.277–8). The translator renders this couplet as 'Et appartient aus hommes que ilz prient les dames et aus dames qu'elles soient priees et vaincues' (It is appropriate for men to court women, and it is appropriate for women to be courted and conquered) (lines 920–1). Likewise, at the beginning of Book 2, the translator takes Ovid's predatory metaphors at face value and renders them programmatically when he says: 'la proye est prise que nous avons chassié' (the prey is taken which we have chased) (line 2242). The purpose of Book 2 is asserted in similar terms: 'Il ne souffist mie que tu aies quise t'amie par mon art et par mon engien, car ainsi comme elle est prise par mon art, aussi est elle a retenir par mon art' (It is not enough that you have sought your sweetheart by my art and by my devices, for as she is taken by my art, so she must be kept by my art) (lines 2268–70) (cf. *Ars am.* 2.11–12). In the glosses to the third book, however, the translator often expresses dismay that Ovid would teach artifice to women: 'Aucuns pourroient reprendre Ovide de ce qu'il enseingne les femmes, car elles de leur propre nature sont soubtilles et malicieuses' (One could reprimand

Ovid for what he teaches women, for women are by nature subtle and malicious) (lines 3603–4). Indeed, the French translator who produced the third book of the *Art d'amours* often expresses anxiety regarding female desire. The categories of desire playfully deployed in the *Ars amatoria* – whether the hypermasculinity proposed in Books 1 and 2 or the feminine artifices cynically proposed in Book 3 – are treated as ethical assumptions by the translator and evaluated accordingly.

If the glosses in the *Art d'amours* delineate all aspects of heterosexual seduction promoted by the *praeceptor*, the topic of same-sex desire is routinely excoriated. Throughout the *Ars amatoria*, Ovid nonchalantly refers to same-sex desire as one of the erotic categories available to his readers, though he suggests that the love of boys is too one-sided to count as passion (2.683–4), and in keeping with Roman sexual codes, he explicitly rejects the subject position of the passive adult male. For instance, when the *praeceptor* advises the male lover in pursuit of women not to indulge in excessive grooming, he suggestively evokes gendered identity in a move designed to satirise contemporary practices of self-adornment.[18] He advises men seeking women not to curl their hair nor shave their legs; he suggests that any attention to self-presentation beyond basic hygiene is not compatible with rustic Roman masculinity: 'cetera lasciuae faciant concede puellae; / et si quis male uir quaerit habere uirum'[19] (Leave the remaining things for lustful girls to do and any half-man who wrongly seeks to have a man) (1.523–4). In the process of satirising Roman urbanity, the *praeceptor* explicity connects gender and desire. In the *Art d'amours* the Ovid's excluded category of 'men seeking men' becomes performative: 'de ces autres cointises laisses convenir aus dames et a ceulx qui sont de mais mestier' (Of other customs let it be suitable to women and to those who practise evil customs) (lines 1654–5). The *glose* proceeds to equate these 'evil customs' with the identity of the Sodomite:

c'est a dire ycestui mauvés mestier qui fu exercités en cinq cités qui en furent perrez, si comme nous tesmoingne la saincte escripture. Et pour ce sont ilz en aucuns lieux appellés sodomites pour une d'icelles cités qui fondi, qui avoit nom Sodome . . . et ce doit savoir chascun que c'est si grant pechiez que Dieux le het tant que les cinq cités qui pour ycelui pechié fondirent puent tant qu'il n'est nul qui d'icelles peüst aprocher. (1655–63)

He means the evil custom that was practised in five cities that were lost because of it, as the Holy Scripture testifies to us. Because of this sin, in one place they are

---

[18] On this passage in Ovid, see Habinek 1977.   [19] Text of the *Ars amatoria* from Ovid 1995b.

called Sodomites, for one of these cities that fell had the name Sodom . . . Each person should know that this is a great sin and that God hates it so much that the five cities fell because of this sin and that they stank so much that no one could approach them.

In attaching the identity of the Sodomite to the category of 'a great sin', the language excludes not only specific practices but also the individuals who practise them. As Mark Jordan has demonstrated, the Sodomite emerges in medieval theology as an identity attached to specific sexual practices which by their exclusion define the normative.[20] In appealing to scriptural authority, this gloss evokes theological categories in order to classify Ovid's discourse of desire as a discourse of identity.

The passage in *Ars amatoria* 1 on the basics of grooming for men is closely echoed in *Ars amatoria* 3 when the *praeceptor* advises women to avoid men who are too interested in their looks: 'sed uitate uiros cultum formamque professos / quique suas ponunt in statione comas' (But shun men exhibiting finery and a handsome appearance and who put their hair in place) (*Ars am.* 3.433–34). Though the Latin passage only suggests that such dandies are likely to be promiscuous, the French translation reads this passage in light of the distinctions between these categories of desire – men who love women and men who love against nature – established in the first book of the *Art d'amours*:

Que vaulra il a la dame de amer tel qui est si curieux a sa beaulté monstrer? Certes nient, car par aventure pourra il plaire mieux a aucuns sodomitez que ne feroient les dames, et pour ce affiert il mieux que les dames mectent grant cure de elles aorner que les hommes, afin que eiles plaisent plus. (4559–63)

What will it be worth to a lady to love a man who takes a lot of trouble to show his good looks? Certainly nothing, for, perhaps, he will be able to please some Sodomites better than he would the ladies, and because of this it is more appropriate that women take greater care to adorn themselves than men, so that they are more pleasing.

In drawing on the identity of the Sodomite already established in Book 1, The translator classifies adornment as a gendered behaviour, so that the man who is interested in his looks becomes effeminate and consequently more likely to attract a 'sodomite' than a woman. While the excluded Sodomite is classified by name, the unnamed heterosexual becomes legible as normative.

[20] Jordan 1996; see also Burgwinkle 2005. On the classification of Orpheus as a sodomite in the *Ovide moralisé*, see Desmond and Sheingorn 2003: 101–12.

Having identified the Sodomite by his erotic desires, the translator proceeds to elaborate on the nature of Sodomitic desire in both heterosexual and same-sex contexts. In *Ars amatoria* 2, the *praeceptor* advises the would-be lover to seek privacy for his love-making: 'conueniunt thalami furtis et ianua nostris' (Bedrooms and closed doors suit our secrets) (*Ars am.* 2.617). The translator casts the issue of privacy in the language of secrets: 'Gardez bien que vous cellés les deduiz de vos secrez' (Be very careful that you conceal the pleasures of your secrets) (lines 3328). Even though there is nothing in the Latin text about the specifics of sexual practices at this point in Book 2, the *glose* slips from the topic of secrecy to the identity of the Sodomite:

GLOSE: Ilz sont trois manieres de dommages: li uns est a nous, li autre si est de ce qu'elles ne sont plus gardees que autre n'y puisse avenir, et l'autre si est grant pechié et grant vice aux demoiselles sans raison. Pour ce dit bien cil qui dit ce que nous avons autresfoiz dit:

> «De mauvais oisel lait cry,
> Et de felon maleveuillance,
> N'onques de vaissel pourri
> Nulle bonne oudeur n'issit».

Et ceste maniere ont volentiers li sodomite, qui font contre nature: ilz se vantent des femmes, dont ilz n'ont cure, pour estaindre la fumee de leur mauvaistié et de leur vice, et pour ce qu'il s'en vantent, de mauvaistié leur vient. (3339–3350)

GLOSSARY: There are three types of harm: one is what is done to us, another is what happens because the lovers are not more careful lest another come upon them, and another is the great sin and great vice of the maidens which they do without reason. Because of this he speaks well who says what we have said before:

> 'From a bad bird comes an ugly cry,
> And from a criminal, ill-will;
> No good odour ever
> Comes from a rotten jar.'

Sodomites like this type of love, and they practise it against nature. They boast of women of whom they have no care in order to put smoke over their evil and their vice, and because they brag about it, evil comes to them.

The *glose* explains that 'acts against nature' can be practised by both sexes, since maidens (demoiselles) do it. The Sodomite, however, is identified as a man who performs such an act within the context of same-sex desire, since the Sodomite pretends to pursue women as a cover for 'mauvasité et ... vice'. As in the earlier passage, the identity of the Sodomite clarifies by contrast the identity of the heterosexual lover. The *Art d'amours* thus represents heterosexual *amor* as a *habitus* that requires the would-be lover to develop a predatory practice as a pursuer and seducer of women; in the process, it glosses the text with a commentary on the normative and deviant categories for sexual practices. In its attention to the mechanics of sexuality as well as the gestures and attitudes suitable to heterosexual seduction, the *Art d'amours* rendered the *Ars amatoria* a didactic treatise on the erotic potential of starkly gendered subject positions.

Among the various performances of desire promoted in the *Ars amatoria*, the *praeceptor* emphasises the erotic efficacy of epistolary rhetoric. In the first book of the *Ars amatoria*, the *praeceptor* advises the prospective male lover that the seductive potential of a letter depends on the rhetorical skill of its author: 'sit tibi credibilis sermo consuetaque uerba, / blanda tamen' (Let your language be credible and your words familiar, even coaxing) (1.467–8). In *Ars* 3, the *praeceptor* specifically addresses this advice to women and urges his female disciples to adopt the level of style most appropriate to the expression of desire (3.479–82). The *Art d'amours* glosses this exhortation to epistolary desire with an assessment of women's use of rhetoric: 'Toute la fin principale a quoy femmes tendent, soit par escripture ou autrement, si est pour decevoir ceulx qu'elles ont en leur las; et afin que elles mieulx puissent leurs amis plumer, elles escripvent aucunesfoiz tant de si doulces paroles et amoureuses qu'il semble aux musars que elles les aiment de tres loyal amour' (The very last principle to which women have an inclination is, be it by writing or otherwise, to deceive those whom they have in their snares. Therefore, they fleece their lovers better, they sometimes write so many sweet and amorous words that it seems to the foolish that they love them with a very loyal love) (lines 4695–9). In the context of the third book of the *Art d'amours*, which emphasises the dangers of female desire in any form, this *glose* endorses the Ovidian assumption that letters and letter-writing constitute an erotic performance.

As an exercise in verse *suasoria*, the *Heroides* thus exemplify the precepts of the *Ars amatoria*; however, most of the *Heroides* put these amatory arguments not in the voice of a male lover, but in the female voice, since the majority (*Her.* 1–15, 17, 19, 21) purport to be letters written by women to their absent lovers. If the *praeceptor* in the *Ars amatoria* recommends letter-writing to lovers of both sexes, Ovid's *Heroides* equate epistolarity with female desire. The epistolary structure requires that the opening couplets of each poem identify the speaker as a woman, and the body of each letter develops an argument aimed at persuading her recalcitrant or wandering lover to return to her. The epistolary format situates these female speakers as honorary authors who attempt to arrange rhetorical arguments to make their case. The direct address situates the reader in an intimate exchange with these eloquent female speakers; such intimacy implies that the text of each fictional letter offers a glimpse of authentic female subjectivity. Because all the women are immediately recognisable as figures from well-known narratives, their predicament would be utterly familiar to the ancient or medieval reader, and the outcome of each case is always already known: while Odysseus returns to Penelope, Phyllis and Dido commit suicide, and Oenone, Ariadne, Hypsipyle and Hermione are abandoned.[21] However authoritative their arguments, their letters do not change the course of their love affairs, and the doomed status of most of these letter-writers stands in stark contrast to the force of their appeals. In contrast to the *praeceptor*'s faith in the efficacy of letter-writing in the *Ars amatoria*, the *Heroides* suggest that the female lover might not find her epistles to be persuasive. Given their status as failed rhetoric, the *Heroides* script an excess of desire, expressed in the most familiar and cajoling terms, as the *praeceptor* advises in the *Ars amatoria*. Such intense expressions of female heteroerotic desire expressed in the *Heroides* would have been considered transgressive for a Roman matron who was expected to experience desire only in the most moderate terms. Thus the language of desire in the *Heroides* is more appropriate to a *meretrix*, a woman of the *demi-monde* who occupied a liminal space in the social hierarchy.[22] The rhetorical excess of the *Heroides* offered its Roman audience an ironic, even theatrical exploration of the amatory predicaments of these mythical heroines.

The medieval reception of the *Heroides* treats these dramatic monologues as *exempla* of female desire.[23] The schoolboys and poets who read the *Heroides* in Latin were instructed by the *accessus ad auctores* to read these epistles for the ethical judgements they might offer on the pursuit of love.[24] Given the prevalence of the *ars dictaminis* in clerical cultures, the *Heroides* were also read as formulae for love letters, so that the inflated and self-indulgent desire of Ovid's heroines becomes a model for medieval letter-writers. One medieval commentator considered the *Heroides* to be an extension of the mechanical advice offered by the *praeceptor* in the *Ars amatoria*: 'Aliter, intentio sua est, cum in preceptis de arte amatoria non ostendit quo modo aliquis per epistolas sollicitaretur, illud hic exequitur' (Since in the precepts on the art of love he did not show in what way one might be seduced through epistles, it is his intention to demonstrate

---

[21] Farrell 1998. See also Hagedorn 2004.   [22] See Parker 1997: 55–6.
[23] See Hagedorn 2004.   [24] See Hagedorn 2004, and Hexter 1986: 136–302.

that here).[25] Given the transmission of the *Heroides* as rhetorical models in medieval Latin culture, their reception in vernacular cultures emphasises their formal status as epistles and the rhetorical properties of the desire they explore.

Medieval French translations of the *Heroides* appear as non-narrative interludes inserted into longer narrative texts; not only does this placement emphasise the epistolary status of the *Heroides*, but it also guarantees that these fictional epistles would be read in the context of the classical legend to which they belong, a context that emphasises the failure of these letters to arrive, as Jacques Derrida would put it.[26] The twelve *Heroides* that are added to the second redaction of the *Histoire ancienne* are all contextualised by the Troy story, since the *Heroides* were inserted into the *Histoire ancienne* as part of the expansion of the Troy story in the second redaction. This redaction of the *Histoire ancienne* originates in the francophone court of Robert of Anjou, king of Naples from 1309 to 1343. During his reign, Robert of Anjou commissioned numerous Latin translations of Greek medical and scientific texts, translations that relied on the practice of *verbum ex verbo* renditions in order to transmit accurate versions of these treatises.[27] The compiler who produced the prose versions of Ovid's *Heroides* as a means of developing the plot of the Troy story in the second redaction of the *Histoire ancienne* similarly aspired to produce literal French translations of the Latin text of the *Heroides*. French prose of the fourteenth century, however, did not offer adequate equivalencies for Latin vocabulary or syntax, and the resulting French translations are often laboured. Unlike the elegiac couplets of Ovid's Latin text, a poetic form that relies on a series of sharp, succinct assertions, the elasticity of the French prose in the *Histoire ancienne* expansively elaborates on the pain and loss of unrequited desire. The bathos of the Latin is lost in translation, to be replaced by an earnest simplicity that results from such paratactic prose. Most significantly, in the French version, Ovid's heroines are defined by their subjectivity rather than their rhetorical agency. Emotions and expressions that suggest agency are frequently excluded from the translation; couplets that express anger, for instance, are often omitted altogether, despite the line-by-line practice of the translator.[28]

---

[25] Text from *Accessus ad auctores* 1970: 32. Translation is my own.   [26] See Derrida 1987.

[27] Weiss 1977 and Lusignan 1986: 129–30.

[28] Neither Dido's letter (*Her.* 7), nor Medea's (*Her.* 12) appear in the *Histoire ancienne*; the section on Medea and Jason includes the narrative detail regarding a different letter that Medea sends Jason, and the section on the Troy material in this redaction does not include the narrative of the *Aeneid*, which constitutes a different section of the text. The epistles of both Dido and Medea are dominated

If the *Art d'amours* equates heterosexual performance and predatory masculinity, the French translations of the *Heroides* reify longing as the constitutive feature of female heteroerotic desire. The reiterations of desire in Oenone's letter to Paris, *Heroides* 5, illustrate this discursive effect. Oenone's letter is inserted into the narrative of the Troy story at the point where the text recounts how the news of Paris's marriage to Helen has spread throughout the world. The narrator notes that this report caused Oenone – Paris's first love when he was in exile as a shepherd – such great pain that she sent a letter to Paris. A rubric introduces the letter 'ceste epistre envoia Oenona a Paris son ami' (5.4) (Oenone sent this epistle to Paris her lover).[29] The translation that follows offers a verbatim version of Ovid's Latin that closely follows the sequence of the original. Following the structure of Ovid's text, Oenone exclaims that she does not know what she did to deserve to be set aside in favour of Paris's new bride, Helen: 'et quel pechié et quel blasme et quele malaventure me fist que je ne soie toe? Je doi bien souffrir en gré tous les maus que tu me fais, car je les ai biens deservis, et si me vienent de ma droite merite: l'en se doit plus doloir et plus a enuis recevoir, que l'en n'a mie deservi' (What sin or what misdeed or crime caused me not to be yours? I would suffer fully and willingly all the evil that you do me, if I fully deserved it and I had merited it; that which is not deserved causes more sorrow and hardship) (5.11–15). This passage renders two Latin couplets:

> Quis deus opposuit nostris sua numina votis?
>   Ne tua permaneam, quod mihi crimen obest?
> Leniter, e merito quicquid patiare, ferendum est;
>   quae venit indignae poena dolenda venit. (5.5–8)[30]

What god put his power in the way of our desires? What is my crime, that I cannot remain yours? Whatever we have deserved must be suffered lightly; when undeserved punishment happens, it brings pain.

The translator provides three phrases in order to render *Quis deus*: 'Quel diex et quela fortune, quela diverse aventure' (5.10). *Crimen* is likewise expanded into three phrases. The impersonal and proverbial force of the

---

more by anger than desire for an absent lover; their absence allows for the erasure of anger from the *Heroides* inserted into the text.

[29] The text of the French versions of the *Heroides* comes from Barbieri 2005; translations are my own. The 2005 edition in Italian was republished in a French edition in 2007 wherein the line numbers of the text have changed.

[30] Latin text of the *Heroides* from Dörrie, Ovid 1971. Translations are my own.

second couplet (5.7–8) is transposed into a first person statement that takes on a narcissistic tone. The effort to provide equivalences in French leads to a laboured elaboration on the original Latin statement.

Oenone proceeds to catalogue Paris's debts to her, and she emphasises that she took Paris as a husband when he was nothing but a 'serf' (5.19). She also points out that her love – unlike Helen's – will not bring an invading army to his land. She concludes by rendering Ovid's pithy couplet that only Paris can cure Oenone: 'Ha, biaus amis, tu seuls me pues donner ce que Phebus li diex ne herbe ne medecine ne me pourroient donner, ce est santé et aide et confort' (Ah, dear beloved, you alone are able to give me the health and aid and comfort that the god Phoebus with his herbs and medicine could not) (5.133–5). In both the Latin and the French versions, Oenone measures the intensity of her love for Paris by her despair at losing him. However, the simple sentence structure of the French version cannot fully convey Oenone's arguments as they are rehearsed in Latin. The more the translator attempts to provide word-for-word equivalences in French, the less the rhetorical register of the Latin survives. The translation appears to lack artifice and to seem more authentic as a result. In translation, Oenone's letters becomes an endless repetition of statement of unfulfilled desire.

Expressions that equate feminine desire with suffering and female subjectivity with loss are scattered throughout these translations of the *Heroides*. Ariadne's epistle (*Her.* 10), for example, narrates in excessive detail the material facts of her abandonment on Naxos. She describes how she became aware of Theseus' departure, and with each detail, she anatomises the pain and suffering that result: 'Je ne pensse mie tant seulement a ce que je doi souffrir, ains pensse a tout ce que puet soffrir fame qui a son mari perdu' (I think not only about what I must suffer but about all that a woman who has lost her husband can suffer) (8.55–6). At the end of her epistle (*Her.* 3), Briseis declares to Achilles: 'Et saches que ma vie et ma soustenance est en toi, et que je ne vif se par toi non' (And know that my life and my sustenance are in you, and that I do not live except through you) (3.89–90). Likewise, in *Heroides* 2, Phyllis programmatically connects femininity with an inclination to excessive love when she tells Demophoon: 'sum decepta tuis et amans et femina verbis' (*Her.* 2.65) (Both a lover and a woman, I was deceived by your words). The French translation renders Phyllis' statement in equally categorical terms: 'et je, fame et amant, sui deceüe par tes paroles' (And I, a woman and a lover, was deceived by your words) (2.54). In *Heroides* 19, Hero tells Leander: 'car plus fort est la substance de vertu es malles que es femeles, et espeťialment es puceles qui ont le cuer humble et la substance tendre et poi de vie. Ma vie deffaudra du tout se tu demeures longuement' (The quality of virtue is stronger in males than in females, and especially in a maiden who has a humble heart and a tender and compassionate nature. My life is completely empty unless you remain for a long time) (14.7–10). Each of these passages attempts a literal rendition of Ovid's Latin, but the syntax of the French prose version results in simple and unadorned statements that assert a connection between gender and desire that is only suggested in the Latin original. The heteroerotic discourse scripted by the *Heroides* in the *Histoire ancienne* achieves legibility as female desire through expressions of loss and longing.

Medieval vernacular versions of Ovid's *Heroides* and the *Ars amatoria* together transmit a gendered paradigm for the performance of desire. French translations and adaptations of the *Ars amatoria* emphasise a version of masculinity that is predatory and manipulative; this reception of the *Ars amatoria* proposes that heteroerotic performance defines masculinity. This notion is especially evident in the *Art d'amours* and its rejection of the desire that it attaches to the identity of the sodomite. The translation and commentary of the *Art d'amours* consequently endorses the erotic potentials of a normative heterosexual desire. The French versions of the *Heroides* in the *Histoire ancienne* offer transcriptions of female desire in narrative contexts – a rhetorically gendered discourse that is rare in both classical and medieval textual cultures. However, the translator of these letters in the *Histoire ancienne* was neither interested in nor capable of preserving the elaborate twists and turns of Ovid's rhetorical poetics. Consequently, these French versions of the *Heroides* suggest that female heteroerotic desire is measured by its masochistic intensity. In their ironic attention to the mechanics and emotions of *amor*, Ovid's *Ars amatoria* and the *Heroides* emerge as rhetorical explorations of the queer status of heterosexual desire in the context of ancient Roman culture. The medieval vernacular reception of these texts paradoxically renders them as normative statements on the gendered nature of desire.

CHAPTER 6

Ovid in medieval Italy

Robert Black

During the Middle Ages, Ovid's poetry was a pervasive ingredient of civilisation wherever culture was based on the Latin language, and Italy was no exception. Gunzo of Novara, when arriving at St Gall in 965 as courtier of Otto I, was mocked by the local monks for misusing a Latin case in conversation,[1] but he could have protested a direct acquaintance with Ovid, evidence of which has subsequently emerged.[2] Italy, of course, lagged behind Northern Europe and especially France in the study of the Latin classics after the millennium; nevertheless, in the eleventh century, among the fundamental copies of texts by Latin authors made at Montecassino, Ovid's verse was scarcely neglected.[3]

It is true that, ultimately south of the Alps, the triumph of *ars dictaminis* resulted in a less classicising approach to rhetoric, but this anti-classical direction emerged only gradually in Italy. Alberic of Montecassino (d. 1105), usually seen as the parent of *dictamen*, still focused on 'the traditional rhetoric of the schools',[4] making use, among other classical authors, of Ovid.[5] Adalberto Samaritano (*fl.* 1115–25), often cited as first among Alberic's successors,[6] opened his *Praecepta dictaminum* with a citation 'from Ovid's *Metamorphoses*'.[7] The great Italian Ovidian of the twelfth century was Henry of Settimello (near Florence), whose renowned *Elegy* (1193) invokes Ovid by name in the seventeenth verse: 'If Ovid . . . commend[s] men, then my fortune will be just barely assured.'[8]

In content, Henry's poem is modelled on Boethius' *Consolation of Philosophy*: the author, denied an ecclesiastical preferment and railing against the old hag Fortune, was then consoled by Lady Philosophy; in language and sentiment, however, the *Elegy* is neo-Ovidian. It consists of five hundred

---

[1] Curtius 1953: 33.   [2] Novati 1899: 31ff.; Taylor 1925: 258–9; Bullough, 1964: 131; Riché 1979: 153.
[3] Reynolds 1983: xxxiii, 191–2, 418. For Ovid in such monastic contexts see also in this volume, pp. 177–96 at 177–9.
[4] Camargo 1988: 169.   [5] Miller *et al.* 1973: 132.   [6] Murphy 1974: 211.
[7] Ward 2001: 181.   [8] Edited in Henry of Settimello 1949: 26 (1.17–18); translated in Gehl 1993: 180.

elegiac couplets,[9] a verse form in which Ovid was, needless to say, particularly well practised. Henry consciously followed in the footsteps of the contemporary French Ovidians, Alain of Lille and Walter of Châtillon,[10] even directly adapting figures from medieval Ovidian predecessors.[11] His complaints about maltreatment and misfortune, and particularly his propensity to dwell on personal sentiments, recall more the world of the *Tristia* and *Epistulae ex Ponto* than of the *Consolatio philosophiae*; moreover, as in Ovid, there is no neo-Platonic, metaphysical, theological superstructure, such as emerges with Boethius, nor any hint of providential determinism. Henry can justifiably be seen as a precursor of the stoicism of some subsequent Italian humanism: although it is debatable to what extent Ovid took his own misfortunes stoically, nevertheless Henry, who never sought solace in the hope of a Christian afterlife, found a kindred spirit in Ovid's secular reaction to his fate.[12]

In the thirteenth century, Bene da Firenze (d. before 1242), professor of *dictamen* at Bologna, expected his students to read 'philosophos et autores', among whom would have been Ovid, citing in his *Candelabrum* the first two lines of the pseudo-Ovidian *Nux* as an example of personification (*prosopopeia*):

Quintum genus extendendi materiam est prosopopeia, id est informatio nove persone, que inter colores dicitur conformatio, iuxta illud:

> Nus ego iuncta vie cum sim crimine vite
> A populo saxis pretereunte petor.[13]

The fifth way to elaborate material is *prosopopeia*, that is, the representation of a new person, which among rhetorical colours is called personification, as in this quotation: 'I am a roadside walnut-tree, and although my life is blameless, I am pelted with stones by passers-by.' (tr. Martin Pulbrook, ed., *Ovid Nux*, Maynooth Co. Kildare, Ireland, 1985: 46)

In his *Tesoretto*[14] (v. 2373), the Florentine *dictator* and chancellor Brunetto Latini (d. 1295) introduced Ovid of the *Remedia amoris*, speaking to him, so Latini declared, using the Tuscan vernacular.[15] But the principal Italian Ovidian of the Duecento was Lovato Lovati (d. 1309), now usually regarded as the first Italian Renaissance humanist. Indeed, in his first surviving example of Latin poetry (c. 1268), Lovato complained of an illness to his friend and Paduan compatriot, Compagnino, lacing 227 lines of elegiac

---

[9] Monteverdi 1962.   [10] Monteverdi 1962: 315.   [11] Bianchini 1989: 861–2.
[12] See Dickinson 1973.   [13] Bene da Firenze 1983: 217.   [14] Brunetto Latini 1981.
[15] Brownlee 1997: 259–61.

verse with borrowings from the *Metamorphoses*; recalling Ovid's exile at Tomis on the Black Sea, Lovato consoled himself with the opportunity for literary activity afforded by his indisposition:

> Naso Tomitana metro spatiatus in ora
> Flebilis exilii debilitabat onus.[16]

Ovid, walking around on the shores of Tomis, used to lessen the burden of his wretched exile with verse.

More significantly for the history of the classical revival, credit may be due to Lovato for reintroducing the *Ibis* to Italian readership.[17]

Other early humanists with a penchant for Ovid were Lovato's fellow Paduans Albertino Mussato (d. 1329), one of whose elegies was 'a cento from Ovid's *Tristia*',[18] and Geremia da Montagnone (d. 1320 or 1321), whose citations of Ovid (including the *Ibis*,[19] possibly thanks to Lovato) in his widely circulated book of quotations *Compendium moralium notabilium* lagged behind only those of Aristotle, the younger Seneca and Cicero.[20]

But in the early fourteenth century it was their immeasurably greater contemporary, Dante, for whom Ovid assumed a truly exceptional role.[21] Near the beginning of his descent through Hell, four shades come forward to greet his guide Virgil:

> Onorate l'altissimo poeta;
> l'ombra sua torna, ch'era dipartita.
>
> (4.80–1)

Honour the great Poet! His shade returns that was departed. (Tr. Carlyle and Oelsner, Dante 1964b: 41)

Dante's teacher, Virgil, introduces the group:

> Mira colui con quella spada in mano,
> che vien dinanzi ai tre sì come sire:
>   quelli è Omero poeta sovrano;
> l'altro è Orazio satiro che vene;
> Ovidio è 'l terzo, e l'ultimo Lucano.
>
> (4.85–90)

---

[16] Sisler 1977: 67, vv. 215–16; translation also from Sisler. On Lovato, see most recently Witt 2000.
[17] Billanovich 1958: 159.   [18] Curtius 1953: 220.   [19] Reynolds and Wilson 1991: 126.
[20] B. L. Ullman, 'Hieremias de Montagnone and his citations from Catullus', in Ullman 1955: 81–115, at 82.
[21] For Dante see also in this volume, pp. 143–59.

Mark him with that sword in hand, who comes before the three as their lord: that is Homer, the sovereign Poet; the next who comes is Horace the satirist; Ovid is the third, and the last is Lucan. (Tr. Carlyle and Oelsner, Dante 1964b: 41) These constituted the fair school of the lord of loftiest song, 'la bella scuola di quel segnor de l'altissimo canto', who soars like an eagle above the rest:

> Così vid'i' adunar la bella scola
> di quel segnor de l'altissimo canto,
> che sovra li altri com'aquila vola.
> (4.94–6)

Thus I saw assembled the goodly school of those lords of highest song, which, like an eagle, soars above the rest. (Tr. Carlyle and Oelsner, Dante 1964b: 43)

Dante, putting aside false modesty, declares that these five bards invited him to join their select company as the sixth supreme poet:

> E più d'onore ancora assai mi fenno,
> ch' e' si mi fecer de la loro schiera,
> sì ch'io fui sesto tra cotanto senno.
> (4.100–2)

And greatly more besides they honoured me; for they made me of their number, so that I was a sixth amid such intelligences. (Tr. Carlyle and Oelsner, Dante 1964b: 43)

For Dante, Ovid was thus a brother literary creator. But he was a rival too: depicting the transformation of a thief into a reptile and vice versa, he boasts to have outdone the supreme metamorphoser, who had never contemplated the simultaneous exchange of form and substance:

> Taccia di Cadmo e d'Aretusa Ovidio:
> ché se quello in serpente e quella in fonte
> converte poetando, io non lo 'nvidio;
> ché due nature mai a fronte a fronte
> non trasmutò sì ch' amendue le forme
> a cambiar lor matera fosser pronte.
> (*Inferno* 25.97–102)

Of Cadmus and of Arethusa be Ovid silent: for if he, poetising, converts the one into a serpent and the other into a fount, I envy him not: for never did he so transmute two natures front to front, that both forms were ready to exchange their substance. (Tr. Carlyle and Oelsner, Dante 1964b: 281)

Ovid was a model as well. For the highest poetic style, the *Metamorphoses* were, according to Dante, to be imitated, alongside Virgil, Statius and Lucan:

Et fortassis utilissimum foret ad illam [supremam constructionem] habituandam regulatos vidisse poetas, Virgilium videlicet, Ovidium Metamorfoseos, Statium atque Lucanum . . . (*De vulgari eloquentia* 2.6.7)

And perhaps it would be most useful, in order to make the practice of such constructions habitual, to read the poets who respect the rules, namely Virgil, the Ovid of the *Metamorphoses*, Statius, and Lucan . . . (Tr. S. Botterill, Dante 1996a: 67)

Dante's correspondent and poetic sparring partner, the Bolognese Giovanni del Virgilio (*fl.* 1321–6), has a special place among medieval Italian Ovidians. Giovanni may owe his surname to a contemporary reputation for devotion to Virgil, but the classical poet to whom he dedicated the most attention, at least according to surviving evidence, was Ovid. On 16 November 1321, Giovanni was appointed to lecture at Bologna on four 'great' authors: Virgil, Statius, Lucan and Ovid, for the last of whom his brief was to elucidate the *Metamorphoses*. His lecture course occupied at least two years, 1322 and 1323, before he transferred himself to Cesena by the end of 1324. His teaching of Ovid is reflected in two separate works: a conventional scholastic *expositio*, which consists of an *accessus*, organised according to the usual four Aristotelian causes and providing the normal opportunity to recount Ovid's biography and to list his works, and a lemmatic commentary, offering a detailed and often minute philological analysis not significantly diverging from standard medieval commentary practice. Giovanni went further, however, also writing a separate work, entitled *Allegorie librorum Ovidii Metamorphoseos*, which he seems to have composed as a complementary treatment simultaneously with his *expositio*. Here Giovanni drew directly on previous allegorical commentaries by Arnulf of Orléans and John of Garland,[22] but he did so in an entirely new format for Ovidian commentary, alternating expository prose sections with mnemonic verses. This was a practice which he doubtless derived from the medieval Italian grammatical tradition, as it had developed in the thirteenth century: there is hardly a Latin textbook by an Italian Trecento grammar teacher that does not copiously lace prose exposition of the standard topics of the secondary theoretical Latin syllabus

---

[22] For these commentaries see also this volume, pp. 49–65, 311–13.

with mnemonic verses, borrowed either from works such as Alexander of Villa Dei's *Doctrinale*, Eberhard of Béthune's *Graecismus* or the manuals of other recent grammarians, or composed for the occasion by the writer of the treatise himself.[23] Giovanni often revised or rejected the allegories of Arnulf, his principal source, and John of Garland was similarly, if less insistently, treated. In general, Giovanni's tended, more than his sources, to favour naturalistic, moral and historical comment: this was a propensity typical of Italian grammarians in contrast to their transalpine predecessors and counterparts.[24] Both his *expositio* and his allegories achieved a notable circulation in manuscript during the fourteenth and fifteenth centuries.[25]

Ovid was an important author for Petrarch too. He figures prominently in his list of favourite books, where the *Metamorphoses* is especially prized:

Ovid(ius) p(re)s(er)ti(m) i(n) maiori.[26]

Ovid especially in the *Metamorphoses*.

Among the authors cited in his works, Ovid comes between Horace and Lucan; in Petrarch's copy of Virgil, he is quoted 32 times (28 from the *Metamorphoses*).[27] In his *Rerum memorandarum libri*, Ovid is praised (following the *Controversiae* of the elder Seneca) not so much for practical guidance in the art of love-making but for his numerous uplifting maxims (*sententiae*); Ovid could, without exaggeration, be proud of his prolific poetic gifts:

... puto nullum equari posse Nasoni poete, qui – ut est apud Senecam [*Controversiae* II.ii.8] – hoc seculum [*sc.* Cesaris Augusti] amatoriis non artibus tantum sed sententiis implevit. De exundanti quidem facultate carminum Ovidius ipse gloriatur, nec mendaciter. (*Rerum memorandarum libri* 2.20)[28]

I think no one can be the equal of Ovid the poet, who – as according to Seneca – filled their age [*sc.* of Augustus] not only with the amorous arts but also with wise sayings. Ovid himself boasts of an overflowing abundance of poems, and not falsely.

---

[23] See Black 2001: 87ff.   [24] See Black 2001: 327ff.; Black and Pomaro 2000: 14–33.

[25] Fundamental is Ghisalberti in Giovanni del Virgilio 1933: 3–110, who publishes the *accessus* to the *expositio* (13–19) and the entire *Allegorie* (43–107). But Marchesi 1909 and Wicksteed and Gardner 1902: 314–21 still have some value, if only because they cite a now lost manuscript of the *Allegorie* from S. Gimignano. More recently, see especially Ballistreri 1976; Coulson 1986c and 1996; Coulson and Roy 2000: 125–8.

[26] Ullman, 'Petrarch's favorite books', in Ullman 1955: 117–37, at 122.

[27] Ullman, 'Petrarch's favorite books', in Ullman 1955: 130–1.   [28] Petrarca 1945: 56.

Prominent among the series of Latin poets celebrated in Petrarch's tenth eclogue was Ovid:

> Inde alius gelidi Sulmonis alumnus
> multa iocans . . . [29]

Another son of icy Sulmona with a fecund wit.

Of course, Ovid figures conspicuously among the Roman amatory poets extolled in the *Triumph of Love*:

> Virgilio vidi, e parmi ch'egli avesse
> compagni d'alto ingegno e da trastullo,
> di quei che volentier già il mondo lesse:
>   l'uno era Ovidio, e l'altro era Catullo,
> l'altro Properzio, che d'amor cantaro
> fervidamente, e l'altro era Tibullo.[30]

I saw Virgil, and it seems to me that he had highly intelligent and amusing companions, among those whom the world read willingly already: one was Ovid, and the other Catullus, the other Propertius, who fervently sang of love, and the other was Tibullus.

But in a more sombre work, such as the *Secretum*, Ovid was one of the classical Latin authorities who provided Petrarch with the wisdom needed to overcome human misery: for this purpose he cited *Remedia amoris* (579–80) on the necessity of companionship to comfort the lovelorn, *Amores* (1.10.13) on the need to accompany carnal with spiritual love, *Epistulae ex Ponto* (3.1.35) on will-power and *Metamorphoses* on the brevity of worldly life (10.522–3) and the inevitability of death (10.34).[31] Similarly in his late invective *On his own ignorance and that of many others* (dedicated in 1371), he cited a maxim from *Epistulae ex Ponto* (3.3.102), to the effect that envy does not rise up to embrace high minds but slithers on the ground like a viper:

Quanquam enim iners malum sit invidia et altos in animos non ascendat, sed vipere in morem, iuxta Nasonis sententiam, humi serpat . . . [32]

Envy is an inert evil; it does not rise into exalted souls but 'creeps on the ground like a viper', as Naso [Ovid] puts it.

It is a commonplace that Boccaccio's early vernacular works were, at least in part, inspired by Ovid, the poet of love, whereas later, as a more serious humanist scholar under Petrarch's influence, he was spurned as 'lascivious': 'In his youth, Ovid somewhat went to his head, and in his old age was

---

[29] Petrarca 1968: 27.   [30] Petrarca 1951: 502.   [31] Petrarca 1955: 154, 128, 24 and 160.
[32] Petrarca 2003: 356. Tr. H. Nachnod in Cassirer *et al.* 1948: 128.

somewhat banished from his heart.'[33] Thus the infatuation of Florio and Biancofiore, lovers appearing repeatedly in his early works, is fed by reading Ovid ('saper leggere il santo libro d'Ovidio').[34] Ovid has been seen as the inspiration for the scenes showing hunting nymphs in his first narrative poem, *La caccia di Diana*,[35] while the obvious models for Fiammetta, spurned and deserted by her lover Panfilo in *Fiammetta*, were the forsaken heroines of the *Heroides*. In another early work, *L'amorosa visione* (1342), Ovid appears repeatedly in the course of the allegory,[36] while in his early prose romance *Filocolo* (*c.* 1331) there are many near-verbatim appropriations, especially from *Metamorphoses* and *Heroides*.[37] Despite his protestations against Ovid's prurience after his Petrarchan conversion, Boccaccio continued to exploit his poems without restraint for the rest of his writing career. In *De mulieribus claris* (begun in 1361 and revised over the rest of his life), prominent among the sources for the mythological figures were the *Fasti*, *Metamorphoses* and *Heroides*,[38] while for the *Genealogia deorum gentilium* (a repertory that preoccupied Boccaccio during his last twenty-five years), Ovid ranked behind only Virgil as a mythological treasure trove.[39] His passion for Latin rarities led him beyond even Petrarch's ambit, not only to the *Appendix Vergiliana* but also to the *Ibis* and *Priapea*, a collection stamped by Ovidian influence and perhaps containing a rare *Ovidianum* (n. 3), the oldest surviving manuscript of which (Florence, BML, Plut., MS 33 31) Boccaccio copied himself.[40]

For Coluccio Salutati (1331/3–1406), it was Ovid of the *Metamorphoses* who first kindled his passion for Latin literature:

I owe many things in fact to Ovid, who for me served as a kind of gateway and teacher, when, as though through divine inspiration, my enthusiasm was first sparked by this kind of study. Indeed, without a teacher to lead the way and utterly without formal instruction [nullumque penitus audiens], I studied [legi] all the poets on my own, and, as though it was a gift from God, I gained an understanding of them, after this Ovid of ours came into my hands.[41]

As Ullman suggests, this first interest in classical literature, inspired by Ovid, occurred after he left Bologna and the lessons of Pietro da Moglio

---

[33] Rand 1926: 152, repeated Robathan 1973: 204.   [34] Robathan 1973: 204.
[35] McLaughlin 1995: 61.   [36] Boccaccio 1939: 134, 230, 240.   [37] Robathan 1973: 204.
[38] Boccaccio 2001: 481–91.   [39] Boccaccio 1951: 880–2; see Robathan 1973: 204.
[40] Reynolds and Wilson 1991: 133. For these rarities see also in this volume, *Appendix Vergiliana*, 285, 299; *Ibis*, see pp. 7, 23, 125, 197 n.2, 295 n.43, 303nn.
[41] 'Multa quidem sibi [Ovidio] debeo, quem habui, cum primum hoc studio in fine mee adolescentie quasi divinitus excandui et accensus sum, veluti ianuam et doctorem. Etenim nullo monitore previo nullumque penitus audiens a memet ipso cunctos poetas legi et, sicut a Deo datum est, intellexi, postquam noster Sulmonensis michi venit in manus': Ullman 1963: 45.

in 1350–1. Salutati went on to obtain copies of the *Fasti* from a Florentine bookseller, Maffio da Figline, in 1357 (London, BL, Harley MS 2655[42]), and of the *Fasti* and *Heroides* (both with commentary) as well as the *Amores* and *Ars amatoria* (New York, Pierpont Morgan Library, MS M 810[43]). Salutati was also possibly familiar with Giovanni del Virgilio's allegories.[44] According to Ullman, Ovid remained one of his favourite authors:[45]

> he is quoted hundreds of times. The *Metamorphoses* is the most quoted, especially in *Lab[ores]Herc[ulis]*. All of the genuine works are cited except *Epistulae [ex Ponto]* (those after the *Heroides*), and *Medicamina faciei*. Also cited are the verse summaries of Virgil, attributed to Ovid and the pseudo-Ovidian *Philomela* . . . He must have had other manuscripts of Ovid's works that he annotated. It is unfortunate that his *Metamorphoses* is lost.[46]

Petrarch, Boccaccio and Salutati were not, of course, grammar masters (although Boccaccio did lecture on Dante in Florence), but several important teachers followed their predecessor Giovanni del Virgilio's lead and used Ovid in their lessons. Folchino de' Borfoni taught grammar in his native city of Cremona during the last two decades of the fourteenth century; he was a salaried communal teacher there in 1401. His theoretical grammar, entitled *Cremonina*,[47] was designed for use at secondary schools, consisting of a treatise on nouns and another on verbs, a long section on syntax and on orthography, concluding with a brief tractate on prosody.[48] In this work, he showed a penchant for citing classical Latin authors, one of whom was Ovid, 'quoted 7 times, of which 5 are independent citations and 2 arrive through Alexander of Villadei and Pietro da Isolella'[49] (da Cremona, the thirteenth-century author of a widely circulated school grammar). Giovanni Conversini da Ravenna (1343–1408) worked during the 1370s as schoolmaster in Conegliano and then in Belluno, where he composed his first major work, the *Dialogus inter Johannem et literam*,[50] written over Christmas 1378 and dedicated to his uncle, the Franciscan Tommaso da Frignano, in commemoration of his elevation to the cardinalate on 18 September 1378.[51] This work, revealing the kinds of sources he was reading and using during his early teaching career, cites not only the *Metamorphoses*:

---

[42] See Ullman 1963: 199 for the ownership note and further details.
[43] See Ullman 1963: 202–3 for the ownership note and further details.   [44] Ullman 1963: 233.
[45] Ullman 1963: 258.   [46] Ullman 1963: 238.   [47] Edited by DeSantis in Folchino 2003.
[48] On the Italian secondary-level curriculum, see Black 2001, ch. 2.
[49] Folchino 2003: 69   [50] Conversini da Ravenna 1989.   [51] Conversini da Ravenna 1989: 1–8.

> opes scelerum semina [13.433–4], ut Naso ait . . .

riches the seeds of wickedness, as Naso [Ovid] says . . .

> madidis Nothus evolat alis [1.264], ut ait poeta.

'Forth flies the South-wind with dripping wings', as the poet says. (Tr. Miller in Ovid 1984: 21)

but also the *Epistulae ex Ponto*:

> semel piscis fallaci lesus ab hamo omnibus unca cibis era subesse putat (2.7.9–10)[52]

The fish once wounded by the treacherous hook fancies the barbed bronze concealed in every bit of food.

The use of Ovid by these three prominent fourteenth-century schoolmasters suggests that his poetry had found a place in the medieval Italian grammar curriculum, and indeed since the twelfth century grammarians in Italy had been citing Ovid in their textbooks. In his elementary grammar from the late twelfth century entitled *Donatus*, Paolo Camaldolese explicitly cited lines from Ovid.[53] In 1225, the Piedmontese Mayfredo di Belmonte wrote a grammar entitled both *Doctrinale* and *Donatus*; in the oldest manuscript (Venice, Biblioteca Nazionale Marciana, lat., MS XIII 19 (4470), *s.* XIV[in.]) – a copy that has escaped the notice of previous scholars such as Capello, Gasca Queirazza and Capellino[54] – there are passages from Ovid, cited with the name of the author.[55] Bene da Firenze, who was teaching at Bologna by 1218, wrote a Latin grammatical *Summa* in which he too cited Ovid.[56] A striking thirteenth-century example is the anonymous treatise in two parts, *De differentiis nominum* and *De differentiis verborum*, found in Florence, BML, Plut. MS 52.26. With nominal and verbal homonyms for its subject, the work was originally copied in the middle of the thirteenth century, the second part then restored and recopied at the turn of the fourteenth century; the texts provide abundant citations of Ovid.[57] The tradition of citing classical authors in Latin grammars – and

---

[52] Conversini da Ravenna 1989: 80, 90, 98. Translation from Ovid 1988: 351.

[53] Paulus 1990: 156–7.

[54] Capello 1943: 45–70; Gasca Queirazza 1966; Gasca Queirazza 1977; Capellino 1984.

[55] Fol. 4r: unde Ovidius, unde Ovidius; 7r: unde Ovidius; 8r: unde Ovidius; 20r: unde Ovidius; 23r: unde Ovidius.

[56] Venice, Biblioteca Nazionale Marciana, Marc. Lat. MS XIII 7 (4031), fols. 1r–63r (*s.* xiv[in.]): Bene da Firenze, *Summa*, Inc. Incipit summa Magistri Boni sive Magistri Bene. Gerundia dicuntur quasi duo gerentia scilicet activam et passivam significationem. f. 6r: Ovidius de Ponto; 23r: unde Ovidius; 30r: unde Ovidius; 45r: unde Ovidius.

[57] (a) fols. 1r–31v (*s.* xiii[1/med.]) Inc. 'De nominum ac verborum nec non aliarum partium orationis differentiis tractaturi.' (b) fols. 35r–92v (*c. a.* 1280–1320) Inc. 'Dictis incidenter que dicenda erant

not least Ovid – continued in the second half of the thirteenth century, as demonstrated by the most widely diffused Italian grammar of the period, the *Summa* by Pietro da Isolella da Cremona, written between 1252 and 1286.[58] Pietro cites Ovid in both the purely grammatical sections of the work,[59] while the chapter dealing with prosody is illustrated on several occasions with his verses too.[60]

In the fourteenth century, several schoolmasters besides Giovanni del Virgilio, Folchino or Giovanni Conversini used Ovid in the classroom as well. Pietro da Asolo was a grammarian active in the Veneto (especially in Treviso and Conegliano) during the second half of the century.[61] His *Constructiones*, which survive in manuscript Florence, BML, Ashburnham MS 241, cite Ovid more than any classical author, or indeed any authority whomever.[62] Another example is Domenico di Bandino (b. 1335), grammar teacher at Florence, Bologna, Città di Castello and also Arezzo, his native city, before his death in 1418.[63] Like many other schoolmasters of the period, Domenico wrote a grammar for his own pupils, 'ad rudium utilitatem' (fol. 3r). The work, uniquely surviving in Venice, Biblioteca Nazionale Marciana, Marc. lat. MS XIII 47 (4220), was entitled *Rosarium* because

rosarium est rosarum collectio et locus ubi habunda[n]t rose et ubi ponuntur; ergo merito intitolabitur liber iste propter flores rosarum id est regularum que ibi compendiose sunt locate. (fol. 3r)

A *rosarium* is a collection of roses and a place where roses are in abundance and where they are placed; therefore with good reason this book is entitled thus, on account of the rose flowers, that is, the rules which are copiously to be found there.

Among the 'flowers' illustrating grammar rules were citations from Ovid.[64] Moreover, in a Friulian exercise book datable to the second half of the fourteenth century, Ovid appears as one of the standard school authors.[65]

de nominis defferentiis, secundario vero quoniam verbum in ordine tractandi ponitur.' (a) fol. 2r: et Ovidius . . . unde Ovidius . . . 6r: unde Ovidius; 8r: unde Ovidius . . . unde Ovidius; 12v: unde Ovidius Metamorphoseos in VI; 15v: unde Ovidius; 20r: unde Ovidius; 30r: unde Ovidius. (b) fol. 37v: Ovidius in VI Metamorforseon; 45r: unde Ovidius; 57r: unde O[vidius]; 65v: ponit Ovidius in quarto Metamorfoseos; 72r: unde Ovidius; 74r: unde Ovidius.

[58] Ed. Fierville 1886.   [59] Fierville 1886: 63.   [60] Fierville 1886: 96–104.   [61] Gargan 1965.

[62] Bible (fol. 51v), Donatus (32r), Boethius (32r, 32v, 34r, 51r), Priscian (3v, 31r, 54r, 56r), Hugutio (56r, 63r, 64r), *Graecismus* (57v), Aquinas (43v), Lucan (4v, 5r, 32v, 51v), Ovid (5r, 32r, 34v, 47r, 48v, 49r, 69r) and Virgil (51r, 51v).

[63] For his biography, see A. T. Hankey 1963: 707–9; Jaitner-Hahner 1993: 208, 214, 227, 232–3, 260–1, 271–2, 289; Black 1996: 334–5, 371–7, 402, 410–20.

[64] 5v: ut in Ovidio, 7v: sicut mostravit Ovidius, 29r: Ovidius, 49r: Ovidius, 106v: Ovidius li. XIII Methamorfoseo.

[65] Schiaffini 1922: 24.

The evidence for school use of classical authors such as Ovid is not limited to citations in grammatical works by (mainly) known grammarians. Indeed, many medieval manuscripts of Ovid were actually produced or used as schoolbooks in the classroom either by teachers or pupils, or by both. The school manuscripts now surviving in Florentine libraries[66] provide a window onto the chronology and use of Ovid in the Italian schoolroom beginning in the eleventh century. An evidently Italian school-type manuscript from this early period is a fragment of Ovid's *Tristia* (Florence, BML, San Marco MS 223, fols. 59r–66v) dating from the end of the eleventh century; in the past some doubts have been raised about its Italian provenance,[67] but a transcription of a later note of possession (fol. 66v, end of the thirteenth century) leaves little doubt about the West Tuscan origins of the fragment.[68] This section of the manuscript, written by at least three hands, includes sparse contemporaneous interlinear glosses. Another school-type manuscript, containing the *Metamorphoses*, possibly from central/southern Italy and dating from the turn of the twelfth century (Florence, BML, San Marco, MS 225), has light school-type interlinear vocabulary glosses, as well as occasional normally brief philological marginalia by a number of different hands dating from the period in which it was copied.[69]

Outside Florence there is one Ovid manuscript so far identified as an Italian schoolbook datable before the twelfth century. This is a copy of the *Tristia* (fols. 23r–40r) in Vatican City, BAV, Ottob. lat. MS 1469. Its origin is clearly Italian; its date seems to be the turn of the twelfth century.[70] An obvious schoolbook, it was heavily glossed interlinearly, mainly by copyists but also by some twelfth-century glossators, with one or two marginalia.[71]

Ovid is well represented among twelfth-century schoolbooks in Florentine libraries. A Tuscan manuscript of the *Metamorphoses*, forming part of a subsequent composite codex and dating from the early twelfth century

---

[66] On the criteria used for identifying school manuscripts, see Black 2001: 386–90.

[67] Munk Olsen 1982–1989: II: 135: 'Allemagne (ou Italie)?'

[68] Die XX mensis nov(em)bris B< . . . e>ne(m) qui dicitur < . . . >sthinus <?> Thomas<i> pignoraverunt d< . . . >am< . . . to> hunc librum pro III sol. pisano(rum) hac (con)<ditione> et pacto q(uod) < . . . > ad duos menses possit < . . . >ll< . . . > recoligere. Testes fuerunt Mag(iste)r Gratianus, Yustinus < . . . et> Cardutius.

[69] The manuscript continued to have school-type use during the twelfth and thirteenth centuries, but there is no sign of similar activity in the fourteenth or fifteenth centuries.

[70] Munk Olsen 1982–9 (xi[ex.]; 'Italie'); Questa 1959: 217–32 (xi/xii); Pellegrin *et al.* 1975: I: 579–80 (xi/xii, 'probablement italienne'). Origin: typical Italian abbreviation for 'qui' as 'q', written on pigskin with a characteristically rounded script. Date: ct ligature, 7-shaped 'et' throughout, 'g' with separate lower loop, script leaning to right without any tendency to verticality, diphthongs with cedilla.

[71] No xiiic. or subsequent use evident; completed in xv², when other works by Ovid were added.

(Florence, BML, San Marco MS 223, fols. 4r–9v, 13r–v, 16r–56r), contains school-type glosses by a twelfth-century hand, including a simple grammatical annotation (fol. 26r: 'quia nominativus pluralis regit nominativum singularem') showing the early influence in Italy of Northern European grammatical terminology.[72] Another *Metamorphoses*, probably from central Italy and datable to the third quarter of the twelfth century (Florence, BML, Plut. MS 36 10), was glossed from beginning to end by a number of near-contemporary hands,[73] while a third *Metamorphoses*, probably Italian dating from the turn of the thirteenth century (Florence, BML, San Marco MS 238), was not only glossed by three hands contemporaneous with the copyist (see fol. 34r for all three) but also has word-order marks written soon after the production of the text (fols. 107r, 112r, 143r).[74] A fourth manuscript, containing the *Heroides*, probably Italian and datable to the turn of the thirteenth century (Florence, BML, San Marco MS 235), has contemporary simple philological interlinear and marginal annotations (e.g. fols. 18v–19r).[75] Finally, a fifth manuscript, containing

---

[72] See Black 2001: 72ff. This section of the manuscript seems to have been the object of continual school use, and especially of interlinear vocabulary glossing, from the twelfth to the fifteenth century. Other texts in the codex (*Medicamina* and ps.-Ovidian *Nux*) show no signs of school use.

[73] After the initial twelfth and thirteenth-century phase of glossing, this manuscript shows little distinctive school-type glossing until the early Quattrocento, when a series of simple marginal paraphrases (cf. esp. fols. 9r–25v) were added. The manuscript had heavy school use in the earlier Quattrocento, when two hands made a dense series of paraphrase/summary glosses (cf. esp. fols. 38r–60v). The manuscript shows little sign of use in the later fifteenth century, when restorations were made (fols. 1–8, 129). The manuscript may have a North Italian provenance, in view of the Latin orthography (fol. 9r: dissuaxionem, alliam; 19r: specialli; 19v: generalli; 23r: confuxa; 24r: responssionem) of a glossator writing at the turn of the fifteenth century; however, the initial and final restorations were Florentine.

[74] After this initial glossing, the manuscript shows no further signs of use in a school context, despite the fact that it later passed through the hands of two fifteenth-century grammar teachers, Filippo Pieruzzi and Giorgio Antonio Vespucci. For Pieruzzi's ownership, see the erased ownership note on fol. 150v: 'Liber mei Philippi Ser Ugolini Peruzii notarii'; for Vespucci's interventions, see fols. 1r–2v and 151r, which were restored and copied by him (for Pieruzzi's and Vespucci's association, see Ullman and Stadter 1972: 38). The manuscript did not appear in the fifteenth-century catalogue of S. Marco, probably because it did not yet belong to the library, although it could be n. 942: 'Eiusdem [sc. Ovidii methamorphoseos] de sine titulo, in volumine parvo albo in membranis' (Ullman and Stadter 1972: 235).

[75] Although there seems to be only one vernacular interlinear annotation (fol. 7r: *la gelada*, XIV[c]), the manuscript showed continuous relatively low-level school-type use from the time of its copying until the end of the fourteenth century. Particularly interesting are the following grammatical exercises on the changing cases of nouns and adverbs of place, written on fol. 35v by a XIII[2] Italian hand: 'Romam Rotomagum Vernone[m] tendit Atenas; / Rus tendebat humum miliciamque domum. / Roma [corrected from 'Romam'] Rotomago Vernone redibat Atenis; / Rure [corrected from 'rus'] redibat humo miliciaque domo. / Roma Rotomago Vernone meabat Atenis; / Rure meabat humo miliciaque domo. / Rom(e) Rotomagi Vernone moratur Atenis; / Ruri [corrected from 'rure'] moratur humi miliciaeque domi [corrected from domo].'

This exercise corresponds closely to some near contemporary French verse glosses on Horace (Paris, BN, lat. MS 8216) as well as to Ralph of Beauvais's *Verba preceptiva* (BL, Add. MS 16380): see Reynolds 1996a: 117.

the *Metamorphoses* and produced in North Italy at the end of the twelfth century (Florence, BML, Plut. MS 36 14), was lightly glossed by one of its several copyists.[76]

Outside Florence, Italian twelfth-century Ovid schoolbooks include several copies of the *Metamorphoses*. British Library, King's Collection 26 is a *Metamorphoses* datable to the second half of the twelfth century.[77] This was an obvious schoolbook, with heavy marginal and interlinear glosses in all periods from the twelfth to the fifteenth century; fol. 126r has glosses written by an unformed schoolboy hand, datable to the turn of the thirteenth century. Naples, Biblioteca Nazionale, MS IV F 2 is another *Metamorphoses* (with a few lines from the *Tristia* added at the beginning), datable to the second half of the twelfth century.[78] The manuscript shows consistent, sometimes intensive marginalia throughout, and there are instances of dense interlinear glossing too; the glossing is continuous from the time of production until the end of fourteenth century. Rome, Biblioteca Vallicelliana, F MS 25 is another Italian school-type *Metamorphoses*, this time datable to the very end of the twelfth century.[79] Dense interlinear and marginal glossing begins contemporaneously with production, continuing in the thirteenth, fourteenth and earlier fifteenth centuries. Vatican City, BAV, Vat. lat. MS 1593 is an Italian *Metamorphoses*, datable originally to the

---

[76] This manuscript's North Italian provenance is clear from its earliest surviving note of possession, written in elongated *cancellaresca* script datable to the later Duecento: (fol. 115v) 'Iste liber est Magistri Jacobi de < ... > de Viglevano; qui est bonus puer d<ebet ... >'. Further indications of continued school use of the manuscript are the added Trecento colophon written in an immature hand (fol. 116r: 'finito libro < ... > qui me furat<ur ... >'), as well as on fol. 116v both the sketch of a 'labe<rinthus>' and the mention of 'Magistro Martino', also written by Trecento hands. The manuscript moved to Florence in the Quattrocento, as is suggested by the restoration of fol. 1, written in a Cennini-style humanist cursive script. The manuscript was glossed at a school level in all periods from its production to the fifteenth century; this annotation tended to consist of persistent but brief interlinear and marginal glossing. Particularly prominent are the glosses of one of the copyists (cf. fols. 7r, 9v, 13v with 109r), the omnipresent interlinear and occasional marginal glosses of a tiny hand writing at the turn of the Trecento (cf. e.g. fols. 34v, 36v–37r) and an early Trecento hand which added metric allegories by Giovanni del Virgilio to Books 1 and 2 (fols. 5v, 7v–8r, 11v, 13r–14v).

[77] Munk Olsen 1982–9 ('xii[1]'; 'Italie'). Date: ampersands alternate with 7-shaped 'et'; 'ct' ligatures; diphthongs with cedilla predominate, slants slightly to right. Origin: pigskin; qui = q; rounded script; Italian xiiic. and later glossators.

[78] Munk Olsen 1982–9 (xii[ex.]; 'Italie'), but 'ct' ligature used by both scribe and early glossators suggests earlier dating. Munk Olsen's suggestion of only rare marginalia is inaccurate.

[79] Munk Olsen 1982–9 (xii[ex.]; 'Italie'); Petrucci 1970: 1068–9 (xii[ex.]). Date: 'g' tending to be compressed, ampersands and 7-shaped 'et' alternate, diphthongs with cedilla, 'ct' ligature. Origin: q = qui, pigskin, 7-shaped 'et' regularly of Italian type, although occasionally a glossator's 7-shaped 'et' is not so characteristically Italian: e.g. fol. 126r, but some XIII[c] glossing looks distinctively Italian: e.g. fol. 119r–v.

second half of the twelfth century.[80] An annotation may suggest a Tuscan origin or provenance for the manuscript.[81] There are dense interlinear and marginal glosses throughout the manuscript by many different hands from the second half of the twelfth to the later fifteenth century, with every period in between represented.

Outside manuscripts now in Florence the range of Ovid texts used as schoolbooks in the twelfth century is wider than is suggested by Florentine copies. Milan, Biblioteca Ambrosiana, MS E 74 sup. is a *Fasti*, datable to the second half of the twelfth century and originating in northern Italy, possibly Padua.[82] There were two main school-type glossators here, both leaving copious interlinear and marginal glosses: the first is contemporaneous with the copyist, using light brown ink, while the second uses dark ink and writes in the later thirteenth century. Rome, Biblioteca Angelica, MS 1060 (fols. 33r–95v) is an *Heroides*, datable to the second half of the twelfth century;[83] it was a low-cost product, prepared as a schoolbook on reused parchment. The manuscript was heavily glossed, marginally and interlinearly, from the time of its production to the end of the fourteenth century. Vatican City, BAV, Vat. lat. MS 1606 is a *Tristia*, datable to the second half of the twelfth century;[84] there are a few twelfth-century interlinear and marginal glosses,

[80] Fols. 1r–118v: xii[2], written as a collaborative effort by various hands (all have 'g' with separate lower loop, no 'ct' ligature, diphthongs with cedilla, no ampersands, 7-shaped 'et' throughout). Munk Olsen 1982–9 (xii/xiii; 'Italie'); Nogara 1912: 87–8 (xii[ex.]); Munari 1957: 65 (xii); Pellegrin *et al.* 1975–91: III.1: 175–8 (xii[fin.]; 'paraît italienne'). Fols. 119r–147r: xiii[1], apparently a restoration of missing final fascicles, all written by one hand, who no longer indicates diphthongs with cedilla and whose 'g' is simplified, with lower loop compressed and some indication of diagonal stroke from lower left to upper right, characteristic of *duecentesco* Italian hands. Origin: qui = q, pigskin, xiii[c] Italian glosses, annotations and additions.

[81] Fol. 1r: 'Guidattus Lucchesis de Pentolina comitatus senensis quondam in XXV libr. pro furto in folio < . . . > in libro cleri<coru?>m'. This is part of an inferior script of a folio used as a flyleaf: Fol. 1[v]–11[r] also contains similar annotations, where 'Lucchese' is legible once and possibly twice.

[82] Munk Olsen 1982–9 (xii ex.; 'France ?'), but Italian origin is indicated through use of pigskin with typical three-hole hair marks, through copious glosses by an Italian XIII[2] glossator and through early XIV[c] historical references to North Italy (fol. 59r: 'MCCCXI° die XV° apprilis gens imperatoris Henrici habuit Vincentium Paduanis expulssit. MCCCXIIII de mensse septembris Canis de Scalla vicit Paduanos in Burgo Sancti Petri. MCCCXX de mensse augusti Canis fuit victus ad Bassanelum per Henricum Comitem Gu[ce] (?). MCCCXXVIII de mense septembris Carrariensses dederunt Paduam Cani de Scalla. MCCCXXIX de mensse iullii. Obiit Canis de la Scalla XXII° dicti mensis iulii') written by a hand contemporaneous with events (evidently from Padua; consonant duplications indicate North Italian provenance).

[83] Munk Olsen 1982–9 (xii[2], 'Italie'). Date: no 'ct' ligature, diphthongs with cedilla, 'g' showing tendency to compression but lower loop still distinct, 7-shaped 'et' throughout, no ampersands. Origin: qui = q, pigskin, xiii[c] Italian glossators.

[84] Munk Olsen 1982–9 (xii[ex.]; 'Italie'); Nogara 1912: 94–5 (xii); Pellegrin *et al.* 1975–91: III.1: 199–200 (xii; 'italienne'). Date: no 'ct' ligatures, ampersands alternate with 7-shaped 'et', bottom loop of 'g' separate, diphthongs with cedilla. Origin: qui = q, pigskin.

then nothing further till the Quattrocento. Vatican City, BAV, Vat. lat. MS 3254 (fols. 46r–86v) is an *Heroides*, datable to the second half of the twelfth century;[85] it has light contemporaneous interlinear and marginal glossing, then nothing till the fifteenth century (except perhaps one *duecentesca probatio pennae* on fol. 80v).

The thirteenth century saw a sharp decline in the use of classical Latin authors in Italian schools,[86] but Ovid seems to have remained in the curriculum, albeit in an attenuated state. In Florence there are two thirteenth-century Italian school-level copies of Ovid. One is a codex of the *Metamorphoses*, dating from the mid-Duecento and completed at the turn of the fourteenth century (Florence, BML, Plut. MS 36 5), with school- type glossing both before and after its restoration.[87] The other is a manuscript of his *Epistulae ex Ponto*, dating from the first half of the thirteenth century, possibly from northwest Italy (Florence, BML, Plut. MS 36 32), and glossed by a number of hands contemporary with the copyist's. Outside Florence, thirteenth-century school activity with Ovid can be seen in Milan, Biblioteca Ambrosiana, MS R 22 sup., a text of the *Metamorphoses* with a brief extract from the *Tristia* (fol. 130v). Datable

---

[85] Munk Olsen 1982–9 (xi/xii; 'Italie'). Date: 'g' with separate lower loop, some 'ct' ligatures, rounded script, diphthongs with cedilla and occasionally fully written out, ampersands alternate with 7-shaped 'et'. Origin: qui = q, pigskin, rounded script.

[86] Black 2001: 192ff. For reflections on this shift see also in this volume, p. 15.

[87] This manuscript consists of two sections: A (fols. 1r–138v) and B (fols. 139v–212r). A is datable to the mid-Duecento, and B to the turn of the fourteenth century. B follows A without any kind of textual adjustment or alteration, and so the most likely hypothesis is that B was a restoration to a pre-existing fragmentary text. The decoration throughout the codex is uniform and seems to have been added soon after the restoration took place. As has been shown by Anderson 1977: 255–88, A was 'a virtual diplomatic copy' of a Beneventan manuscript Naples, Biblioteca Nazionale, MS IV F 3 (N), extending not only to the text but also to the glosses; B, on the other hand, had no relation to the Naples manuscript. However, the correspondence of A and N is, in fact, limited to the text and the interlinear glosses, as is clear from the photographs published by Anderson; the copyist of A also provided generally brief marginal comments throughout his section which do not correspond to N. These marginalia to A consist of the simple, low-level type of commentary (mythology, grammar, geography, figures) typical of schoolbooks (including one allusion to Virgil on fol. 128v), and it seems not unreasonable to hypothesise that the copyist of A added these for teaching or study purposes: they do not correspond either to Arnulf of Orléans' commentary (cf. Arnulf 1932: 157–234) or to the so-called vulgate commentary (see Coulson 1987a: 29–62). There is also a school-type commentary throughout B provided by a hand datable to the first half of the Trecento; like the marginal commentary of A's copyist, this principal glossing of B consists entirely of simple philology, with, however, a much greater prevalence of simple paraphrase. This hand also reappears in the margins of A, most notably in an allegorical gloss on fol. 2r; there are also occasional allegories by this hand in section B. There are also numerous other Trecento school-type glossators of B, some of whom also seem to reappear in A. There is no fifteenth-century glossing in the manuscript. There is an ownership note of Maestro Pellegrino da Pisa (fol. 212r: Liber Magistri Peregrini de Pisis).

to the turn of the thirteenth century[88] and possibly northern Italian in origin,[89] this manuscript was glossed marginally and interlinearly by a succession of thirteenth-, fourteenth- and early fifteenth-century Italian glossators; but the most regular and consistent glossing by a considerable variety of hands occurred in the Duecento, indicating intensive school use in that period.

A number of former standbys of the grammar syllabus resumed a leading position in the curriculum in the fourteenth century, including Ovid's *Metamorphoses*. One Tuscan or even Florentine manuscript dating from the third quarter of the century (Florence, BML, Conv. Soppr. MS 186) is glossed by two readers: one writing still fully in the Trecento manner, provides philological glosses of the school type, also citing a few other authors[90] – a practice certainly not unknown at the school level;[91] the other, writing near the end of the century, provides, among normal school-type philological glosses, a few allegorical mythologies[92] – again a procedure not unknown among school readers.[93] Another *Metamorphoses*, this time from the very end of the century (Florence, BML, Conv. Soppr. MS 340), is glossed mainly by the copyist himself overwhelmingly in the standard philological school manner, notably taking three allegorical moralities from Giovanni del Virgilio (fols. 3r and 11r).[94] A third *Metamorphoses*, datable to the second half of the century and possibly northern Italian or even Bolognese (Florence, BML, Plut. 36.17),[95] is glossed in an entirely standard school manner by the copyist, including simple lexical paraphrase and philological marginalia.[96] The glossing and copying of a fourth

---

[88] Various scribes collaborated, all contemporaneous; occasional ampersands but 2-shaped 'et' predominates, 'ct' ligatures used by only one copyist, diphthongs usually omitted but sometimes indicated with cedilla. Munk Olsen 1982–9: XII[ex].

[89] Inside front cover: 'Hunc codicem ob antiquitatem 560 circiter annorum et propter notas viri docti, quibus adspersus est, multas faciendum emimus una cum multis aliis, ab heredibus Francisci Ciuci Aegii olim in hac urbe Mediolanensi eloquentiae praeceptoris. Felicibus auspiciis Ill.mi Federici Borrhomei Archiepisopi Mediol. et Bibliothecae, necnon scholae Ambrosianae fundatoris Antonius Olgiatus primus eius Bibliothecarius scripsi anno 1604.'

[90] Fol. 2v: Ovid, *Fasti*; 3v: Claudian, Juvenal; 10r: Virgil, *Bucolics*; 11v: Ovid, *Heroides*, 38r: Lucan; Ovid, *Ars amandi*.

[91] See Black 2001: 301ff. and Appendix VI.

[92] Fol. 26r: 'Nota allegoriam dei descendentis pro salute humani generis...; 40r: nota quod moralis est ista fabula. Per Martem intelligendum est virum virtuosum et probus [sic]...; 41r: Nota quod ista mutatio Phebi... est moralis. Nam per Phebum intelligendum est virum sapientem [sic].'

[93] Black 2001: 324–5.

[94] Black 2001: 326. The school-type glossing throughout the manuscript is mainly from the earlier Quattrocento. There is also a learned glossator from the later fifteenth century, leaving long marginalia.

[95] On the basis of the some of the watermarks, identifiable with Briquet n. 3227.

[96] After the glossing by the copyist, the manuscript remained in light school use in the first half of the fifteenth century; the sophisticated reader who makes occasional glosses including Greek (e.g.

Metamorphoses (Florence, BML, Plut. MS 36 16) are particularly well documented: not only is it known that the glossator, Nofri di Angelo da San Gimignano, undertook his work in at least two phases, one completed in 1398, the other in 1403,[97] but also that he was the communal grammar master in Colle Valdelsa between 1393 and 1395, and 1402 and 1403[98] (as well as in 1398[99]), besides serving in San Miniato in 1401 and 1403[100] and San Gimignano between 1395 and 1396;[101] the conclusion seems hard to avoid that the simple interlinear paraphrases, the philological marginalia (mainly paraphrase, explication) and the allegories borrowed from Giovanni del Virgilio, in which each transformation is narrated and interpreted,[102] all related directly to his work in the classroom.[103] A fifth *Metamorphoses*, of northern Italian provenance and datable to mid-century (Florence, BML, Acquisti e doni 387),[104] had only slight possibly school use in the Trecento (fols. 2r, 109r, 125v).[105]

Finally, Ovid's *Heroides*, occasionally represented up to the end of the twelfth century but then disappearing in the thirteenth, continued to languish in the fourteenth, the only pre-fifteenth-century schoolbook in Florence being the famous BML, Plut. MS 36 28, a copy datable to the second half of the century and owned by Messer Luca Buondelmonti, from whom it was purchased by Cosimo de' Medici (b. 1389) for use

---

fol. 221r) was writing in the sixteenth century. Apart from a few simple interlinear glosses on fol. 252r, there seems to have been no further school-type use of this manuscript after the earlier fifteenth century.

[97] Fol. 202v: 'Et sic liber iste explicit glosari atque corrigi a me Dompno Honofrio Angeli de Sancto Geminiano, ibidem die 21 mensis septenbris anno domini millesimo trecentesimo nonagesimo octavo, existendo horam quasi vespertinam et diem dominicam. Christo sit laus. Amen.' Added in the same hand: 'Item 1403, die sabbati XI augusti, Colle'. Published previously by Angelis 1984: 128, n. 45.

[98] Siena, Archivio di stato, Colle Valdelsa, MSS 132, fol. xxxiii recto; 133, fol. xiiii recto, xliii verso, xlv recto, lviii verso – lx recto; 134, fol. xxxvi recto; 137, fols. 56v–57v, 58r–v; 138, fol. viiii verso – xi recto.

[99] Siena, Archivio di stato, Colle Valdelsa, MS 135, fol. xxviii verso – xxviiii recto.

[100] Siena, Archivio di stato, Colle Valdelsa, MS 137, fol. 58r–v; 138, fol. xi verso.

[101] San Gimignano, Archivio comunale, MS 156, fol. xxviii recto–verso.   [102] Black 2001: 326.

[103] Apart from the glossator writing in 1407, who is different from Nofri (indeed, criticising Nofri's gloss on fol. 200r), who expresses anti-Florentine sentiments and whose philologically critical comments are not those of a school-type reader, there is no further use of this manuscript.

[104] The manuscript seems to have been the collaborative work of several copyists.

[105] Thereafter the first two books were given lexical/philological marginalia in the mid-Quattrocento (fols. 1r–20r), and there was occasional further school-type activity at about the same time (e.g. fols. 78v–83r, 93v–95v, 98v–106r, 107v–114v) until eventually there is a direct reference to a lecture course on Ovid, possibly in Verona, beginning on 15 April 1473: fol. IIr: 'Maistro Columbino V(er)oniso comenzò el *Metamorphoseos* a dì 15 de aprillo 1473; Ma<i>stro Colonbino Veroniso comenzò el *Morphoseos* a dì aprillo 1473.' The manuscript has copious fifteenth-century *probationes* on the front and rear flyleaves, as well as on the inside back cover.

at the school of Maestro Niccolò di Ser Duccio d'Arezzo.[106] Cosimo's glossing probably took place at the turn of the fifteenth century, when Niccolò di Ser Duccio was teaching in Florence: he was in fact given an official appointment by the Studio officials for the academic year 1401–2.[107] All the annotation on the manuscript is typical grammar-school fare. The codex contains intermittent marginal comments in the hand of the copyist, possibly extracted in the normal school manner from a larger commentary on the text. After the scribe, the first reader of the book seems to be a tiny, fine cursive hand which provides frequent simple interlinear paraphrases (e.g. fol. 1r) especially at the beginning of the work. There was also another early reader who provided a couple of marginalia on fol. 1r. Both these preceded Cosimo de' Medici, who rewrote the latter marginal glossator's comments on fol. 1r and wrote over the interlinear commentator's glosses on the same folio. Cosimo's glosses are not difficult to pick out, writing as he did with a distinctively dark ink. His interlinear glosses are typical simple lexical equivalents;[108] his marginalia are the normal basic philology.[109] Roughly contemporaneous with Cosimo were several other glossators, one of whom amended his gloss on Laertes.[110]

Cosimo de' Medici's school fare would be typical of the changing school curriculum noticeable in the fifteenth century. In a famous passage of his *Regola del governo di cura familiare*, written between 1401 and 1403, the

---

[106] This information is contained at the end of the text in the ownership note on fol. 57v, which has been published in part by Bandini 1774–7: II, col. 237; the same partial transcription is republished by Hankins 1992: 71, n. 4; de la Mare 1992: 140, gives a full transcription of the note, of which she publishes a photograph (plate 1[b]): 'Iste liber est Cosme Iohannis de Medicis morantis ad scolas d. Magistri Nicholai de Aretio et eum Emi a d. lucha de bondalmontibus de Florentia. costitit uno flor(en)o s(olidi) octus videlicet.' But several re-examinations of the original manuscript have led me to the view that the letter at the end of 'octu' is not an 's' but rather an '8', possibly rewritten from an 'o', in which case the phrase would read literally 'costitit uno flor° soctu8 vz'; this would then be transcribed as 'costitit uno floreno s(olidis) octu, 8 videlicet'. According to the proposed reading, the cost of the book was one florin, eight *soldi*.

[107] Gherardi 1881: 376.

[108] E.g. (fol. 1r) Lacedemona = Grecia, deserto = relicto, querenti = petenti, spatiosam = longam, leto = morte.

[109] E.g.: (fol. 1r) Penolope fuit filia Ycarii; Antilocus fuit filius Nestoris quem Paris interfecit; Trilolomus fuit filius Erculis interfectus ab Ethore; Pat(ro)colus fuit filius Meneaci interfectus ab Ethore. (1v) Resus fuit rex Traice; epitetum. (2v) Telemacus fuit filius Ulixis. (3r) Anteas erat quidam mons a quo lignis ortis naves fiebant. (7r) Traicus fuit Orfeus, repertor lire. (38v) Pliasdis uxor Athamantis que habuit VII filias cum quibus omnibus concubuit Iupiter et eas mutavit in gallinella[m] signum celeste.

[110] Cosimo had written simply (fol. 2v) 'Laertes fuit pater Ulixis'; the subsequent glossator added to the beginning 'hic tangitur mos antiquus' and to the end 'et filius consueverat claudere oculos patris post ipsius mortem', so that the whole gloss now reads: 'Hic tangitur mos antiquus: Laertes fuit pater Ulixis et filius consueverat claudere oculos patris post ipsius mortem.'

Although there were a number of apparently school-type readers working at about the same time as Cosimo, the book shows little sign of any type of reading later in the Quattrocento.

Florentine Dominican preacher, Giovanni Dominici, declared that, in the good old days, Florentines had read the traditional school texts, consisting of the so-called minor authors such as Cato's *Distichs*, Aesop's *Fables*, Prosper of Aquitaine's *Epigrams*, Prudentius' *Dittochaeon*, Theobaldus' *Physiologus* and Theodulus' *Eclogue*, as well as Boethius' *Consolation*, but now children were reading immoral texts (from the so-called major authors[111]) including Ovid's *Metamorphoses*, *Heroides*, *Ars amatoria* and other lascivious works (presumably the *Amores* and *Remedia amoris*).[112] Dominici did not say that the classics had not been read by 'nostri antichi', nor that the minor authors and Boethius were no longer being read at school; what he actually said was that Ovid (as well as Virgil and Seneca) constituted new additions to the curriculum. In fact, Dominici is relatively precise in depicting the changing curriculum of schools at the turn of the fifteenth century. From his chronological perspective, Ovidian works such as the *Heroides* as well as the *Tristia* or *Fasti*, represented marginally in the Italian school curriculum during the twelfth century, had not been traditionally used (i.e. in the thirteenth or fourteenth centuries). The principal Ovidian text in the Trecento had been the *Metamorphoses*, not the *Heroides*, nor the *Ars amatoria* nor *Remedia amoris*. These latter works would now assume the front ranks at the upper levels of the grammar curriculum in the fifteenth century.[113] A conservative, even reactionary voice such as Dominici's would not be able to halt the changes to the Italian school curriculum accompanying the rise of humanism.

---

[111] On the minor and major authors, see Black 2001: 173–4.
[112] Garin 1958: 72.   [113] Black 2001: 248ff.

CHAPTER 7

Dante's Ovids

Warren Ginsberg

Ovid: *magister amoris*, poet of passion, banished from the Rome he loved because he taught Romans how to love; *Ovidius Metamorphoseos*, poem of transformation, encyclopaedia of myths and the causes of things, history of the world. In the Middle Ages, Ovid was many things to many people; to Dante, however, he was, above all, the '*alter poeta*', a figure whose vita and verse came to share enough in common with Dante's own to cause him to turn the Roman bard into the rejected model, the not-Virgil, of poetic accomplishment. At various moments in his works, Dante emulated and suppressed the various Ovids he knew. In this essay, I will discuss how in each instance Dante made his appropriation and erasure of these Ovids – the erotic, the mythographic, the exiled Ovid – part of his self-fashioning as an author and an authority.[1]

Near the centre of *Vita Nova*, Dante recounts a nightmarish hallucination in which he hears that Beatrice has died. A few days later, Love appears in a vision and says that Dante should bless the day the god took him captive ('Pensa di benedicere lo dì che io ti presi', 24.2). Shortly after, the poet sees a lady approaching him, whose name is Giovanna but whose beauty is such that she is called Primavera; close behind her comes Beatrice. After the one and the other have passed him, Love informs Dante that the first lady acquired her nickname for the sole reason that she would come before (*prima verrà*) Beatrice this day, just as John the Baptist had prepared the way for Christ's advent. Amor then concludes: 'Anyone of subtle discernment would call Beatrice Love, so greatly does she resemble me' ('E chi volesse sottilmente considerare, quella Beatrice chiamerebbe Amore per molta simiglianza che ha meco', 24.5, translations of this text following Dante 1992, tr. Musa).

---

[1] On Dante's understanding of himself as author and authority, see now Ascoli 2008. My debt to this brilliant study is impossible to overstate.

In the sonnet Dante wrote about this encounter, 'Io mi sent' svegliar', the details differ more or less greatly. Here 'monna Vanna' and 'monna Bice' are both miracles who pass Dante in turn ('l'una appresso de l'altra maraviglia'), but the Christian glosses of the prose account, which comes before the sonnet, are missing. The God says only that the first lady is called Primavera and that the name of the second, who so resembles him, is Love: 'Quell'è Primavera, / e quell'ha nome Amor, sì mi somiglia.'

Dante then notoriously suspends all movement, narrative and otherwise, to answer a hypothetical critic who objects, not as one might have expected, to the effrontery of his theology, but to his lending Love a body. Amor, the accusation would run, appears in Dante's *libello* as if it were a free-standing being, able to move and speak, rather than as what it really is, 'an accident in a substance', a condition brought about in someone. Dante defends himself by maintaining that a vernacular poet should have a freer hand in choosing modes of representation than 'prosaici dittatori', even as Roman poets had greater licence than prose writers. He supports his point by noting that

> Virgil . . . says that Juno, a goddess hostile to the Trojans, spoke to Aeolus, god of the winds . . . [and] has an inanimate thing (the shrine of Apollo) speak to animate beings; in Lucan, [an] animate being [the poet] speaks to the inanimate object [Rome]; in Horace a man speaks to his own inspiration as if to another person, and not only are the words of Horace but he gives them as if quoting from the good Homer . . . (25.9)

Last in this list of authorities is Ovid:

> Per Ovidio parla Amore, sì come se fosse persona umana, ne lo principio de lo libro c'ha nome Libro di Remedio d'Amore, quivi: 'Bella michi, video, bella parantur, ait'.

> In Ovid, Love speaks as if it were a human being, in the beginning of the book called *The Remedy of Love*: 'Wars, I see', he [i.e. Love] said, 'wars are being prepared against me'.

Since Love has appeared as an autonomous character from the beginning of the *Vita Nova* and internal spirits have sighed, wept and spoken throughout, Dante's justification of his use of prosopopoeia at this particular juncture in the work underscores its connection with the episode that immediately precedes it. Only now, at the moment when Dante makes explicit the astounding equation of Beatrice and Christ, does he insert an equally astounding lesson in literary history, whose purpose, it would seem, is to place Dante among the renowned poets of antiquity.[2] The

---

[2] For a reading of this chapter with a full survey of the critical literature, see Ascoli 2008: 178–201.

first two citations from the *Aeneid* pointedly mirror the events Dante had just related: even as Juno once commanded Aeolus, so the God of Love commands Dante, who obeys Amor's injunction as willingly as the wind god obeyed Juno's; even as the shrine on Delos trembled before issuing its momentous prophecy, so Dante trembles at Love's coming and hears his startling pronouncement. Dante does take pains to hedge the suggestion that he and Virgil are on equal footing; his claim, he makes clear, is simply that in relation to prose writers a vernacular poet has the same right to figurative expression that a Horace had but a Varro did not. But the deference of this analogy, which is real, is immediately nudged aside by the audacity of the analogy it supports, in which an accident, a happenstance of order, *is* substantive, indeed supersubstantive, an epiphanic disclosure of more-than-human essence. In his commentary, Love insists that Giovanna not only precedes Beatrice, but that she precedes her as John the Baptist preceded Christ. She not only is like the Baptist, she is the Baptist, because Beatrice, who so resembles the God of Love, not only is like Christ, she is Christ, since she shares with him the name Amor. In the afterglow of copulas such as these, which function both as analogies that preserve distinctions and homologies that dissolve them, Dante can fully acknowledge the linguistic and cultural differences that distinguish classical '*poete*' such as Virgil and Horace from '*dicitori per rima*', who 'are simply poets writing in the vernacular' (25.7), and imply that they share the same identity.

Ovid plays a special role in this tableau of parity and priority, where Latin eminence and Italian prepossession have been invited to the same banquet but find themselves seated at opposite ends of the table. The passages from Virgil, Lucan and Horace, by corresponding more or less closely to situational or thematic elements in Dante's *mise-en-scène*, lend his poetic practice what one might call metonymic esteem, status by association. But when he cites the *Remedia amoris*, Dante is less interested in yoking the prestige of classical tradition to vernacular poetry than in exercising authority over both. In his role as reader and commentator, Dante discriminates between the ethical and the erotic Ovid, so that he can excise the latter. As poet, Dante nods towards the *Remedia*'s opening *jeu d'esprit*, where the God of Love initially balks at but subsequently embraces the poem, so that he might set himself apart from vernacular love poets in general and from Guido Cavalcanti in particular.[3]

The plunge from the high pitch and presumption of the twenty-fourth chapter of the *Vita Nova* to the dry pedantry of the twenty-fifth is so

[3] On the antagonism this passage exhibits toward Guido, see especially Durling 2001: 2003.

precipitate, a reader might be forgiven for overlooking an incongruity nearly as stupefying: immediately following Love's deification of the woman he loves, Dante quotes a treatise that purports to teach men how to fall out of love. An instance, one might have thought, from Ovid's poems about winning and keeping love would have better fit the occasion. Amor is in fact personified in the *Amores* and *Ars amatoria*; either could have provided Dante apt illustrations of prosopopoeia. But these works are unabashedly prurient; their carnality ill suits the kind of love Dante has come to profess for Beatrice, a love whose expression he says has increased in merit in proportion to the extent that it has captured and praised the sublimity of her qualities. From this point of view, the choice to cite the *Remedia* becomes meaningful in itself. It repositions the revelations Dante has just staged so that they are also now an announcement of self-reformation, in which the poet repudiates, if only by means of allusion, whatever had been lustful in his desire.

The strategic value of the *Remedia* for Dante, in other words, has little to do with its content and much to do with the fact that Ovid presents it as a recantation of the *Ars*. The poem begins, in fact, by staging its own near cancellation; in the line that precedes the one Dante repeats, Love looks over Ovid's shoulder and expresses displeasure at what he sees:

> Legerat huius Amor titulum nomenque libelli:
> Bella michi, video, bella parantur, ait.

Love read the name and title of this book; 'Wars', he said, 'wars are being planned against me.'

The complete couplet, which Dante expects his reader to recall, reveals that he is looking over Ovid's shoulder as well. Dante, however, carries out Love's threat, not by expunging the *Remedia*, but by silencing the pornographic Ovid of the *Ars amatoria*. Deleting Ovid by adopting him, Dante authorises himself as writer by the way he reads Ovid; changing what he imitates, he indicates through his quotation of the *Remedia* that the new in his new life overwrites the old, that Dante's first book is already a palinode.

The poet-speaker of the *Remedia*, of course, soon convinces Amor that the book will contain little that will vex him. Dante effectively seconds Love's ultimate endorsement of Ovid's poem by citing it by name. Yet Dante would be appalled if, at this point in the *Vita Nova*, someone should think he would follow any of its precepts. As long as Beatrice lives, he never would fall out of love; at the same time, however, he makes sure we know that Guido Cavalcanti, to whom he had sent 'Io mi sent' svegliar', has. The Giovanna who preceded Beatrice, Dante tells us, at one time had been his best friend's beloved ('e fue già molto donna di questo primo mio amico', 24.3). Even though he says later that he believes Guido 'still much admired this noble Primavera's beauty' ('credendo io che ancor lo suo cuore mirasse la bieltade di questa Primavera gentile', 24.6), the absolute past 'fue' confirms that his 'primo amico' is the Ovidian that Dante is not: Guido has learned how to cool his ardor. On one hand, Dante joins Guido in holding that they are entitled to deploy the same devices Ovid deployed in the *Remedia*; on the other, by associating Guido with Ovid's *Remedia*, Dante dissociates himself from both. The Roman and the older Florentine poet may have gone before him, but in terms of precedence, Dante comes first.

We do not know for certain if, as Michelangelo Picone has argued, Dante read the *Remedia* with the accompanying medieval commentaries.[4] It seems likely that he did, or that he at least would have encountered the kind of *accessus* that usually introduced the poem. If so, though, my guess is that he was as ambivalent about what he found as he was about the *Remedia* itself. In an earlier exchange of sonnets with the physician Dante da Maiano, Dante had already indirectly cast doubt on the high-mindedness of Ovid's palliatives, which often are every bit as sexual as the indispositions they are supposed to treat.[5] Even as a young man, Dante's temper was such that he may well have thought the commentators had found more ethical import in Ovid's cures than they actually had.[6] In any event, Dante never names the *Remedia* again. From now on, whenever he refers to Ovid, it is *Ovidio maggiore*, the *Metamorphoses*, that he cites.

Composed in the first half of the 1290s, *Vita Nova* is the only book certainly by Dante that we know he wrote before he was banished from Florence. Some time during the earlier years of his exile, probably between 1302 and 1308, he produced three works: the unfinished *Convivio*, like *Vita Nova* a prosimetrum in Italian; *De vulgari eloquentia*, a Latin tractatus, which is also unfinished; and *Epistle 3*, a letter of Latin commentary on a

[4] Picone 1993, 2003.
[5] Dante had asked Dante da Maiano what is the greatest suffering that love causes. The physician responded that a lover experiences nothing more painful than to love unloved. This, he says, certainly has been his own experience. He tried at first to cure himself by reading the *Remedia amoris*; dosing himself with Ovid, however, proved a poor physic. Dante disagreed. When the heart's ardor is slighted or ignored, he says, the lover should rely on 'natural wit and acquired skill', not to try to fall out of love but to seize the occasion to demonstrate the virtues that conquer the distress it brings. For text, translation, and commentary, especially on the problem of attribution of the poems, see Dante 1967, ed. Foster and Boyde, II: 1–3, 6–9.
[6] On the view in medieval commentaries that Ovid's erotic poems fall under the heading of ethics, see Ginsberg 1998; Hexter 1986. More generally, see Allen 1982.

sonnet in Italian, both of which answer a question about love that Cino
da Pistoia, Dante's poet-friend and likewise an exile, had asked him to
adjudicate. Although critics have debated the order of their composition,
these texts are clearly related by the concerns they share and the manner
in which they are treated.[7] In them Dante expands the quest for authority
he had begun in the *Vita Nova*. He continues to exhibit the personal
qualities an author had to have; he now also strives to secure the social
and institutional status of the vernacular he employed. In the *Convivio*
and *Epistle 3*, Dante again comments on his poems in prose, as if they had
issued from a Roman quill; compared to the *Vita Nova*, however, as Albert
Ascoli has said, Dante has moved much closer to Latin encyclopaedic
traditions.[8] In the *De vulgari eloquentia*, Dante set himself the apparently
contradictory goal of proving the superiority of his vernacular not only
to all other varieties of Italian but to Latin as well. Once again, the Ovid
Dante cites and the Ovid he does not cite are important strategies in his
campaign to realise his literary and cultural ambitions.

In the *Convivio*, Dante refers to Ovid frequently. The *favola* of Orpheus
(*Met.* 10.1ff.), 'as Ovid shows' (sì come quando dice Ovidio, translations
of this text following Dante 1990, tr. Lansing), demonstrates that poetry
can hide allegorical truth beneath its cloak of fiction (*Conv.* 2.1.3). In
Convivio 2.5.14, Dante explains why the third heaven is associated with
love; he quotes first Virgil, then Venus' words to Cupid from 'the fifth
book of the *Metamorphoses*' (5.365). In *Convivio* 2.14.5, he says he believes
the Pythagoreans who held that the sun once strayed from its course were
influenced by the fable of Phaethon, 'which Ovid tells at the start of the
second book of the *Metamorphoses*'. In *Convivio* 3.3.7, he cites both Lucan
and the *Metamorphoses* (9.183–4) as sources of the story of Hercules' battle
with Antaeus. In the fourth tractate (*Conv.* 4.15.8), Dante cites Ovid's
Prometheus (*Met.* 1.78–83) to prove that even Gentiles maintained that
man was created alone. In *Convivio* 4.23.14, Dante again calls on Ovid's
Phaethon (2.153–4) to account for the Gentiles' notion that the Sun had
four horses.[9] Finally, in *Convivio* 4.27.17–20, he commends at length Ovid's
Cephalus (*Met.* 7.474ff.), who possessed the prudence, justice, generosity
and affability a man should have in the third stage of life, old age.

[7] For a full review of the bibliography on the dating and order of composition of these texts, see Ascoli
2008: 135.
[8] Ascoli 2008: 202.
[9] Fausto Ghisalberti 1934 has argued that this allusion reveals that Dante's manuscript of the *Metamorphoses* contained an allegorising commentary of the sort associated with Arnulf d'Orléans. See also
Ghisalberti 1932.

As a group, these allusions reveal that Dante's regard for Ovid is tempered by a certain detachment from him. Beyond the number of times he adduces the *Metamorphoses*, the points Ovid is used to support show that, like the *accessus* commentators, Dante considered the epic a repository of ethical, even metaphysical knowledge.[10] Just as clearly, by bypassing Ovid's other works, Dante suggests they no longer, if ever, had such standing. In a sense, then, this turn to *Ovidio maggiore* corresponds to the greater maturity Dante says the *Convivio* ought to exhibit: in the *Vita Nova*, which he wrote on the threshold of youth, he was properly 'fervid' and 'passionate'; now that he has entered adulthood, his writing has grown more *'temperata e virile'* (1.1.16), more tempered, manly, self-controlled. The foregrounding of gender, however, which the adjective *virile* makes hard to ignore, strongly implies that just as Dante had muffled the *Ars* by quoting the *Remedia* in his earlier work, in the *Convivio* he mutes the *Remedia* by referring only to the *Metamorphoses*. In the *Vita Nova*, Dante related that after Beatrice's death he was greatly attracted by a *donna gentile* who seemed to pity him, until a powerful vision of Beatrice caused him to rebuke himself and return to her. In *Convivio* 2.2.1–9, though, he tells us that after long struggle and in great anguish, he yielded to this kind gentlewoman, whom he later identifies as Lady Philosophy (2.12.5). The forsaking of Beatrice, the overt reversal of the record set down in the *Vita Nova*: both on the level of plot and by deliberately reversing himself, Dante would appear to have joined Guido as Ovid's poetic outpatient. Dante, of course, would have expected Cavalcanti to admit that the circumstances of their *disinnamoramenti* differed radically; unlike 'monna Vanna', Beatrice, after all, was dead, and Philosophy, though a lady, is only the figure of a woman. By this time, however, Guido had also died. Nevertheless, the message Dante sends through Ovid is meant in part for him. By acknowledging only the *Metamorphoses*, Dante dislodges the *Remedia,* not only as a text that authorises prosopopoeia but as an authority of any sort, as if to say his change of heart, far from an Ovidian abandonment, is an elevating transformation.

The tensions and contradictions that result from this use of one of Ovid's works to push another aside are similar to the tensions and contradictions that characterise Dante's authorial self-presentation in the *Convivio* generally.[11] From 1302 on, however, his refusal to recollect the *Remedia* in

---

[10] The authority Dante accords the *Metamorphoses*, however, does seem qualified. Dante rarely cites Ovid alone; when he does, he is usually the last text quoted. On the *accessus* to the *Metamorphoses* generally, see Coulson 1986a, 2007; Ghisalberti 1946; Minnis 1984. On the particular kind of commentary Dante read, see Ghisalberti 1966; Picone 1993.

[11] On these tensions see especially Ascoli 2008: 67–226.

situations that invite allusion to it masks a second, more fraught occlusion of Ovid: a refusal to acknowledge, except in the faintest way possible, the increasing coincidence between the Roman exile's biography and his own.

Banishment transformed Dante's idea of Ovid's authority by removing his life from literature and relocating it in history. In *Vita Nova* 25.6, Dante had said that 'composition in the vernacular from the beginning was intended for treating of love'. The Ovid he would have had to confront, not simply because he was a leading love-poet, but because, unlike his lyric contemporaries, he had woven his love poems into the larger narrative of his life, was the Ovid who claimed his experiences had made him '*praeceptor amoris*'.[12] The triumphs and setbacks from which he had gained his expertise, however, were chronicled only in his poems; moreover, to show that his know-how was comprehensive, the incidents and settings he recounted were all commonplaces of elegiac tradition. As lover, Ovid's vita is deliberately generic; nor would Dante have learned anything more specific about it from the medieval commentaries on the *Amores*, *Ars* and *Remedia*.[13] Notwithstanding this vagueness, which would have allowed Dante to call any resemblance between Ovid's exploits and his a coincidence of convention, the poet of the *Vita Nova* was unwilling to associate his amatory career with any part of Ovid's except that one instance when Dante renounced, or seemed to renounce, the connection between his poetic art and the art of fornication.

Ovid's exile, however, was real, the unfortunate outcome of a collision between cultural and political authority which Dante, as poet, could not ignore. In the fourth book of the *Convivio* (6.5–6), Dante discusses at length the meaning of 'authority' (*autoritade*), which, he says, 'is nothing more than the pronouncement (*atto*) of an "author" (*autore*)'. 'When spelled this way, without a c', Dante continues, 'the word has two possible derivations. One is a verb that has very much fallen out of use in Latin and which

---

[12] *Ars amatoria* 1.25–30: 'Non ego, Phoebe, datas a te mihi mentiar artes, / Nec nos aëriae voce monemur avis, / Nec mihi sunt visae Clio Cliusque sorores / Servanti pecudes vallibus, Ascra, tuis: / Usus opus movet hoc: vati parete perito; / Vera canam: coeptis, mater Amoris, ades! (I will not lie and say I received my art from you, O Apollo, nor did the voices of birds in the air instruct me, nor did Clio and her sisters appear to me, grazing my herds in your valleys, O Ascra. Experience guides my work; learn from the poet made expert by it. The things I sing are true; O Mother of Love, be present at my undertaking).
   Dante would have been impressed not only by the ironic contradictions that Ovid foregrounds in making his claim, but also by the fact that they in no way seem to detract from the fervour with which he makes them.

[13] As Ghisalberti 1966: 15 notes, the *accessus* for these poems do not include full accounts of Ovid's life. They tend only to say that the poems record Ovid's experiences as lover.

signifies more or less "to tie words together", that is, *auieo*'. This sense is reserved for the work of poets:

> Anyone who studies it carefully in its first form will observe that it displays its own meaning, for it is made up only of the ties of words, that is, of the five vowels alone, which are the soul and tie of every word, and is composed of them in a different order, so as to portray the image of a tie. In so far as 'author' is derived and comes from this verb it is used only to refer to poets who have tied their words together with the art of poetry.[14]

The second source of authority is

> a Greek word pronounced *autentin* which in Latin means 'worthy of faith and obedience'. Thus 'author', in this derivation, is used for any person deserving of being believed and obeyed. From this comes the word which we are presently treating . . . hence we can see that authority means 'pronouncement worthy of faith and obedience'.

Although Dante follows Hugutio of Pisa, from whose *Derivationes* he drew these etymologies, in applying this sense to philosophers, Ascoli has shown that the poet would devote the rest of his life to ascribing it to himself.[15] There is, moreover, a third derivation in Hugh, which Dante does not note in *Convivio*, that nonetheless is equally central to his thinking: *auctor*, with a c, from *augeo* ((I) increase). This meaning, Hugh says, is political; it applies to emperors like Augustus, whose name is cognate with *augere*, who are 'augmentors' of the imperium.

　　From this perspective, Ovid had to be a special problem for Dante; his life was at odds with his authority. The latter was not in doubt; by the thirteenth century, the *Metamorphoses* was considered a 'pagan Bible', and academic commentators had discovered ethical import even in the erotic elegies. Yet Ovid the man had gained Augustus' enmity for a poem (the *Ars amatoria*, according to medieval commentaries) and for a fault (having seen something he should not have seen), as he tells us in the *Tristia* (2.207). Dante knew the *Tristia*, which includes many details about Ovid's birth and youth, his forced departure from Rome, and the hardships of his years in Tomis, well enough to adopt, tacitly, phrases from it.[16] Moreover, if Dante's manuscript of the *Metamorphoses* contained medieval glosses, as Fausto Ghisalberti has strongly argued[17] (glosses that may have derived from the *Vulgate* commentary), its *accessus* would also have provided a

---

[14] Complicating this explanation is an alternative account of *autore* from *aueio* in *Convivio* 4.6.3–4. For a definitive discussion of the significance of Dante's transformation of Hugutio's etymologies, and the only apparent omission of *auctor* in *Convivio*, see Ascoli 2008: 67–129 and passim.

[15] Ascoli 2008.　　[16] Picone 2003.　　[17] Ghisalberti 1966.

more or less full, more or less fantastic version of Ovid's life and career.[18] How, then, could such a person, disgraced and an outcast, command faith or obedience, especially for a Dante who, with his praise for Frederick II in the *Convivio*, seems intent on investing his poetry with the Emperor's as well as the philosopher's authority? The *Metamorphoses* was impossible to ignore in either endeavour; to press it into the service of his art, however, Dante would have to separate the man from his epic. To keep the Latin Ovid he would banish the Roman Ovid a second time by silencing his poems of exile.

The idea that the book of his life might turn out to be a palimpsest, that beneath his own history Dante's readers would be able to see more and more of Ovid's, was too disconcerting to go unremarked. The response he provided in *Epistle 3*, which is addressed to Cino da Pistoia, cuts in sharply different directions. Cino, whom Dante would praise as the exemplary poet of love in the vernacular (*De vulgari eloquentia* (2.2.7)), had asked Dante to resolve a much debated issue: whether the soul can be transformed from one passion into another ('utrum de passione in passionem possit anima transformari').[19] The diction is scholastic, but the subject – if you have fallen out of love with someone, can you fall in love with someone else – is clearly Ovidian. Instead of citing the *Remedia*, however, undoubtedly the poem that not only speaks directly to the issue but also supports Dante's position on it – you can – he quotes the *Metamorphoses*:

Auctoritatem vero Nasonis, quarto *De Rerum Transformatione*, que directe atque ad litteram propositum respicit, superest ut intueare; scilicet ubi ait, et quidem in fabula trium sororum contemtricium in semine Semeles, ad Solem loquens, qui nymphis aliis derelictis atque neglectis in quas prius exarserat, noviter Leucothoen diligebat: 'Quid nunc, Yperione nate', et reliqua.

It remains to consider the authority of Ovid in the fourth book of the *Metamorphoses*, which bears directly and literally upon the proposition; namely when in the fable of the three sisters who were contemptuous of the son of Semele, he addresses the Sun, who, having deserted and neglected other nymphs for whom he had burned, was newly in love with Leuconoë: 'What now, Son of Hyperion', and what follows.

<hr>

[18] In private correspondence, Frank Coulson has made this suggestion to me. It is definitely worth further research. For the Vulgate commentary see also in this volume, pp. 65–71, 313. In this regard, we should also note Picone's arguments 1992, 2001 that Dante knew, and made use of, the pseudo-Ovidian *De vetula*, which contains the startling story that, rather like Dante's Statius, Ovid converted to Christianity. On the *De vetula*, see Hexter 2002b; Pseudo-Ovidius 1967; Robathan 1968; and in this volume, pp. 305–8.

[19] Cino's request does not survive. Dante is responsible for the way the question is framed. For a general analysis of the *Epistola*, see Ascoli 2008: 122–9.

Dante calls this an argument from 'authority'; it immediately follows a philosophical proof in which he makes full use of the resources of dialectic and faculty psychology.[20] The shift from reason to myth is jarring, especially since Dante says Phoebus' relevance here is not figural; its abruptness perhaps caused Cino to pause, and as he paused to notice that Dante refers both to Ovid and to his poem in ways that are unusual for him. Everywhere else the poet is *Ovidio* or *Ovidius*; only here does he appear as *Naso*.[21] With one exception, everywhere else the poem is called *Metamorphoseos* or *Ovidio maggiore*; here is it *De Rerum Transformatione*.[22] These departures from his normal nomenclature are, I think, signals that Dante thinks substitution itself is part of what is at issue here. By transforming the *Metamorphoses* into 'On Transformation', he obviously prepares the ground for the epic Ovid to judge the matter of whether the soul can be transformed (*transformari*) from one passion to another. But the transformation in question is predicated on falling out of love, the subject of the *Remedia amoris*. Cino, who knew the *Vita Nova*, and would readily remember that Dante cited Ovid's poem there to support the vernacular poet's rights to prosopopoeia, may well have wondered why Dante did not let Ovid appear here as the *magister amoris*.

Dante would have expected his friend to agree that the greater prestige of the *Metamorphoses* makes it a better buttress for his reasoning generally; he would also have wanted Cino to connect his leaving the lesser for the greater Ovid to his particular transfer of affection from Beatrice to Lady Philosophy. His inconstancy, one is to infer, has nothing to do with low passion, the sort of skirt-chasing an Italian might call *seguire le gonelle*, for which Dante elsewhere reproved Cino, twice. It is rather, he suggests, a supersession, an Apollonian ascent from eros to a higher form of love. But the allusions to the daughters of Minyas and to the story that Leuconoë tells have darker implications. The three sisters, who alone remained in Thebes after everyone else, including their father, had left it for Dionysian revels, were turned into bats; Leuconoë's father buried her alive when he found out she was the Sun's lover. Because they refused to change the object

---

[20] Dante's phrasing, although conventional, invites further comment: 'Et fides huius, quanquam sit ab experientia persuasum, ratione potest et auctoritate muniri' (3) (And the truth of this, although it is proved by experience, may be confirmed by reason and authority). On one hand, experience effectively makes further explanation unnecessary. On the other, it supports both Dante's dialectical argument, which stipulates love as a passion of the sensible soul, and his argument from authority; each in its own way recalls Ovid's boast that his authority was based on his experience.

[21] If it were not so recherché, one would think Dante and Cino were sharing a private joke here. Alan of Lille (*De fide Catholica* 1.30, *PL* 210, col. 333) had famously said that 'authority has a wax nose, which means it can be bent into taking on different meanings'. Quoted by Minnis 2001: 138.

[22] The exception is *Monarchia* 2.7.8, referred to below. The dating of *Monarchia* is controversial; no one, however, thinks Dante composed it before *Convivio* or *Epistle 3*.

of their passion, to worship Bacchus in lieu of Pallas, Minyas' daughters first shut themselves up inside their palace, in effect exiling themselves in their own city, and then were exiled from daylight when Bacchus exacted his revenge. Because his daughter fell in love, Orchamus first banished her from his affection and then made his house a sunless tomb to his alienation from her. These are strange stories for Dante to adduce, for together they imply there is a price to pay no matter whether one's heart changes or remains loyal. Dante certainly seems ready to defend the ethical propriety of his own realignment of affection; in the sonnet (III) he attaches to his commentary, 'Io sono stato con Amore insieme / de la circulazion del sol mia nona' (I have been together with Love since my ninth revolution of the sun), Dante attempts to justify his love for Lady Philosophy by pointedly reconfiguring the astronomical and metaphysical fireworks of his falling in love with Beatrice. The circlings of the heaven of light and fixed stars that dated his childhood enamourment here appear as the 'circle' (cerchio) of Love's arena; the internal spirits' scholastic proclamation in the *Vita Nova* that the Amor has come to take up residence in Dante's heart finds its counterpart in his heterodox doctrine that in Love's arena 'free will was never free' ('liber arbitrio già mai non fu franco'). But the Ovidian women reveal the strain of these revisions. Dante invokes their stories to vindicate his lack of steadfastness; but however much they suggest that passion is irresistible, it is hard to avoid thinking that these Theban daughters also function as apotropaic surrogates, onto whose shoulders Dante shifts some of the blame and chastisement he continues to feel he deserves for his lapsed allegiance.

For Dante's eviction of Beatrice from his heart coincides with his expulsion from Florence. The salutation of *Epistle 3* begins 'Exulanti Pistoriensi Florentinus exul inmeritus' (to the exile from Pistoia a Florentine undeservedly in exile). Despite this twofold emphasis, first on Cino's banishment, then on his own, when Dante evokes Ovid's, the echo is so faint, one suspects he wanted no one to hear it. Dante tells Cino he quite understands why he asked him to address a matter that Cino would have had little trouble resolving himself: it is so that 'by the solution of this much debated issue you might enhance the renown of my name' ('ut in declaratione rei nimium dubitate titulum mei nominis ampliares', 2). As a number of scholars have noted,[23] Dante's locution recalls a phrase from *Tristia* I: 'donec eram sospes, tituli tangebar amore, quaerendique mihi nominis ardor erat' (1.1.53–4) (While I was secure, I was touched by love

---

[23] Frugoni and Brugnoli in Dante 1979: 533; cf. Ascoli 2008: 124.

for fame and I burned to win a name for myself). By reassigning his desire for glory and honour to Cino's love for him, by proudly proclaiming himself *exul inmeritus*, Dante distances his renown as outcast from Ovid's. The faults for which he was forced to leave Florence were not his own, either as poet or as a man worthy of authority. Florence has uprooted him from her heart, but the fame and glory of name he bears, which now includes the title of 'unmerited exile', he has conferred on himself and wears as a crown of honor. In the face of dispossession, such sentiments are brave and noble; yet it is equally true that Dante has burnished his resolution by dimming Ovid's. He trumpets Ovid as the poet of the *Metamorphoses* at the same time that he lowers the volume of Ovid's poetry of exile to a whisper. Once again Ovid becomes a sort of textual totem, through whom Dante expresses the divisions of his soul – an open embrace of solitude, on the one hand, in defiance of his unjust extirpation from his native city; a barely audible hope to return, on the other, in which, perhaps unintentionally, he has buried doubts about himself. Unable to countenance any substantive similarity between Ovid's ouster and his own, unable to ignore the correspondence, Dante in effect turns him into an alter-Leuconoë, interring the man of the *Tristia* alongside the poet of the *Remedia*, but indemnifying his burial of both by embracing the encyclopaedic authority of Ovid *De Rerum Transformatione*.

Thus in *De vulgari eloquentia* 1.2.7, Dante makes a point of saying that the talking magpies of *Metamorphoses* 5 do not contradict his claim that only humans speak, because Ovid is 'speaking figuratively and means something else'. And in *De vulgari eloquentia* 2.6.7, *Ovidius Metamorfoseos* joins Virgil, Lucan and Statius as one of the four *regulati poetae*, poets who respected the rules of their art. Similarly, Dante quotes Ovid in the later tractate *Monarchia* (2.8.4), to prove that the Babylonian empire was more limited than Rome's, which truly encompassed the whole world. In *Monarchia* 2.7.10, Ovid's account of Hercules' battle with Antaeus supports Dante's argument that Rome was elected by God to win the battle for world hegemony.[24] He also compares the contest for empire to a race; Rome's victory was prefigured in Ovid's account of Atalanta and Hippomene.

In the *Comedy*, however, the scope and art of *Ovidio maggiore* are reconfigured. The *Metamorphoses* is everywhere in it; Dante imports characters or loci from each of Ovid's fifteen books. At the start of *Inferno*, Dante meets the poet himself in Limbo (*Inf.* 4.90); in the closing lines of

---

[24] Dante repeats here the pairing of Ovid and Lucan as sources of the story that he had made in *Convivio* 3.3.7.

Paradiso, Ovid's description of the Argo supplied material for a simile of the pilgrim's astonishment when he sees God face to face (*Par.* 33.94–6). Every reference to Ovid's poem, however, is part of an extended meditation on the reach and the shortcomings of its idea of metamorphosis. In Hell, Dante refitted the conceit of 'forms changed into new bodies' ('in nova . . . mutatas . . . formas / corpora', *Met.* 1.1–2) so that it could underwrite the exhaustion of form in the damned and their dissolution into the inert matter of non-being. In Purgatory he baptised it, so that it subtends the soul's reformation. In Paradise, he sanctified it, so that it dimly foreshadows the perfection of bliss the resurrected will enjoy after the Second Coming. Many excellent studies have examined the specific nature and operation of each of these transformations of Ovid, but I lack the space to rehearse their arguments here.[25] I will instead discuss what I think is the most exemplary Ovidian encounter in the *Comedy*, Dante's silencing of him; I will restrict my analysis, however, to the ways in which this muting of the authority of the *Metamorphoses* recall and modify the ways in which Dante had circumscribed the *Ars*, the *Remedia* and the *Tristia* in his earlier works.

In the sixth pit of *Malebolge*, the eighth circle of Hell, thieves undergo horrific transformations. In one, a man and a snake merge into an unidentifiable amalgam of matter; in another, a man takes the form of the snake that has bitten him while the snake becomes the man he bites. In the middle of his description of this last mutation, Dante stops to challenge to Ovid:

> Taccia di Cadmo e d'Aretusa Ovidio,
> ché se quello in serpente e quella in fonte
> converte poetando, io non lo 'nvidio;
> ché due nature mai a fronte a fronte
> non trasmutò sì ch'amendue le forme
> a cambiar lor matera fosser pronte.
>
> (25.97–102)

Let Ovid be silent about Cadmus and Arethusa, for if he poetically converts the one into a serpent and the other into a fountain, I do not envy him; for two natures face to face he never transmuted so that both forms were ready to exchange their matter. (Translations of this text are the author's own.)

Dante makes it difficult to overlook the paradoxes that shape this apostrophe. At the same moment he commands Ovid to be silent about Cadmus and Arethusa, he implicitly rehearses their transformations by confessing

---

[25] The bibliography is extensive. I cite as representative examples the fine essays in Sowell 1991 and Jacoff and Schnapp 1991. See also Barkan 1990; Brownlee 1986; and Wetherbee 2008.

that he does not envy Ovid's depiction of them. Peremptory yet self-effacing, the address in fact so openly foregrounds the incongruity between its own outspokenness and the muteness it decrees, one suspects Dante wanted to call attention to its status as a trope. One reason why he may have done so is to suggest that in the discourse of salvation, Ovidian metamorphosis can never be more than a figure of speech. The rhetorical ostentation of the apostrophe, in other words, is part of its point. It exemplifies Dante's sense that transformations in which nothing is transformed except the external frame are merely stylistic, little more than superficial shape-shiftings whose significance does not extend beyond a play of surface differences. Without correction and supplement, they cannot claim to be even an inferior image of substantive Christian change, of conversion, transfiguration, resurrection.[26]

The specific limitation Dante identifies in Ovid's metamorphoses is that they are always singular. In Hell, two natures, one human, the other not, lose or exchange their forms simultaneously. In part, Dante underlines this tandem participation in order to expose the inner distortions of theft, which Aquinas had condemned as a violation of particular justice. Particular justice, he taught, regulates 'the due coordination of one person with another' (*Summa theologica* 2.5.8). Theft thus is an offence against the proportions of reciprocity that make social relations possible; it is the immolation of ethics that the ego demands that has no regard for anyone besides itself. Dante therefore punishes the brazen footpad and secret defalcator by taking from them all title to the material form which identified them as particular individuals and their intercourse with others as human. By insisting on the duality of the thieves' mutations, however, Dante offers more than a theological reading of their sin; he critiques the narcissism of Ovid's poetics as well. Relation, the tie that binds components together, is the essence of *aueio*, Dante's etymon of poetic authority. In Ovid, Cadmus remains Cadmus, Arethusa Arethusa; the serpent and the spring the one and the other become are in effect accidental alterations; nothing substantial joins them to the form they once had or to the new form they assumed. First by highlighting their disconnectedness, their lack of attachment even to themselves, then by setting this lonely autonomy against the copulatives of infernal deformation, Dante's thieves more than imply that Ovid has tied his words together in a way that at best is skin deep.

In enjoining Ovid's silence, Dante would have him overtly do to the *Metamorphoses* what Dante had already done covertly to the *Ars* in the *Vita*

---

[26] These points are argued more extensively in Ginsberg 1999: 115–59.

Nova, to the *Remedia* in the *Convivio*, to the *Tristia* in the *Epistle* to Cino. Indeed, in many ways, Dante's apostrophe revisits his first invocation of Ovid in the *Vita Nova*. There Dante quoted Ovid to justify his making a personification talk as if it were a person. Here he would strike dumb an Ovid who is a personification of the text he has written. The Ovid Dante addresses in *Inferno* 25 is *Ovidio maggiore*: the man who actually lived has been poetically converted into the poem he wrote.

The solitary hermeticism that Dante sees in Ovidian transformation is the mirror image of the integrated *auctoritas* he had always sought for himself.[27] In the *Comedy*, the authority of prose commentary and poetry, of reader and writer, of writer and man, are unified in the figure of Dante *poeta-personnaggio*, the pilgrim-poet whose life is his poem, whose poem is his life. In the metamorphoses cantos, Dante's apostrophe makes visible, quite on purpose, I think, the seamless ligature of all aspects of his narrative 'I'. The startling transformation of Francesco and Buoso he narrates as pilgrim; he addresses Ovid as poet. But in contrast to the merged mass that Agnello and Cianfa become, pilgrim and poet are both unmistakably Dante, even if it is impossible to tell where the one leaves off and the other begins. By making himself two and one, in contrast to the thieves, who are 'neither two nor one' ('né due né uno', *Inf.* 25.69), Dante becomes no less similar to the commutative metamorphoses he recounts than his single-dimensioned Ovid is like his idea of Ovidian transformation.

What ultimately lies behind Dante's compulsion to refashion Ovid at various moments in his life? I personally feel that Dante censored Ovid less for moral than for poetic reasons; he never found Ovid's obscenity as objectionable as his irony. The *Ars amatoria* in fact so thoroughly dismantles the logic of love it professes to teach that it directly imperilled Dante's understanding of himself as a poet. Whether he was claiming the right to make Love talk in his poems, or announcing that he exists on earth as an embodied metaphor of the Love that inspired him to write, as he tells Bonagiunta in Purgatory (24.52–4), Ovid raised the possibility that all figurative language, including the incarnational tropings of the *Comedy*, emerges not from the doubled speech of allegory but from the nullifications of irony.[28] Dante's own suppression of the erotic and the exilic Ovid have, to my mind, their own weird propriety; they are responses in kind, though Ovid, ironically enough, not Dante, is their ultimate author. For Ovid,

---

[27] Stillinger 1992; Ascoli 2008.   [28] I treat these issues at greater length in Ginsberg 2002: 29–57.

who anticipated his critics' urge to scrape clean his rolls, does talk back to Dante.[29] Of all the unreported conversations Dante says he had with the poets in Limbo, that is the conversation I most of all would want to hear.

[29] For a reading of how especially in the *Ars amatoria* Ovid endorses and invalidates all ethical interpretations of him, see Ginsberg 1998.

CHAPTER 8

Ovid from the pulpit

Siegfried Wenzel

That Ovid was read and quoted by medieval religious men and women will not come as a surprise – 'Ovid... *belonged* to these men as personal property', as Jean Leclercq has said.[1] And he belonged not only to the *aetas Ovidiana* – the twelfth and thirteenth centuries – or to Benedictine monks alone, but was shared among Christian readers of various religious affiliations until the end of the Middle Ages and beyond. This includes preachers, men whose direct, immediate task and mission it was to bring the word of God to people inside and outside the Church and to teach them the basics of Christian faith and morals. I have elsewhere discussed their appropriation of the Classics during the later Middle Ages.[2] In this essay I wish to focus on Ovid and examine the extent to which we find him quoted in surviving sermons from fourteenth- and fifteenth-century England, and then ask what we may be able to tell about the preachers who quoted his works, about their audiences, and about their engagement with the Roman poet.

In the roughly 2,500 sermons I have examined for this essay,[3] I have found over one hundred references to or quotations from Ovid which mention the poet either by name ('Ouidius') or call him 'the poet', with the citation leaving no doubt that Ovid is meant. Such citations occur in

---

[1] Leclercq 1982: 119; I owe the quotation to Stapleton 1996: 46.   [2] Wenzel 1995a: 127–43.

[3] These include the collections I have described in Wenzel 2005: especially 395, which were made in England between roughly 1350 and 1450. (In the following notes the sermons are cited by the sigla listed at the end of this essay with the respective sermon number.) To them I have added two collections from the first half of the fourteenth century: the 119 dominical sermons by Robert Holcot, OP (d. 1349; in Cambridge, Peterhouse College, MS 210), the 155 *Distinctiones* by John Bromyard, OP (d. 1352; in Oxford, Bodl., Bodley MS 859, also discussed in *Latin Sermon Collections*, 137–8), and the unusual Benedictine Chapter sermon of, perhaps, 1423 (see note 5 below). I have also, for comparative purposes, checked the 122 *de tempore* homilies by the twelfth-century French theologian Radulfus Ardens, which appear in several English manuscripts of the fourteenth and fifteenth centuries (see Wenzel 2005: 197–9), and the temporal and saints' sermons attributed to Thomas de Lisle or Thomas Brito, who is now thought to be a French Dominican of the late thirteenth century.

eighty-nine different sermons spread over twenty-eight collections.[4] The overwhelming majority come from the *Metamorphoses*, often cited as *De transformatis* (59 citations); but Ovid's love poetry is likewise fully represented, as are, in smaller numbers, his *Fasti*, *Tristia* and *Epistulae ex Ponto*.[5] As a major authority in the schools, in literature, and as we shall see in preaching, Ovid also inspired, and was claimed to be the author of, a number of medieval imitations, and thus several pseudo-Ovidian works appear with his name in sermons as well. The thirteenth-century *De vetula* is quoted six times.[6] Medieval preachers were particularly attracted to this poem's praise of the Blessed Virgin[7] and the astronomical prediction of the birth of Jesus;[8] these occur in four sermons. Similarly, the critique of pursuing lucrative sciences, in *De vetula* 1.691f. ('Omnes declinant ad sciencias lucratiuas'), is used by two preachers.[9] Another pseudo-Ovidian work quoted by some preachers is *De mirabilibus mundi*,[10] which has been called a proto-bestiary and is preserved in at least five English manuscripts.[11] Lastly, there are quotations from a work entitled *De fallaciis*

---

4 As indicated, one sermon stands by itself, in London, BL, Cotton MS Titus C IX, fols. 26r–27v, a sermon for the Benedictine general chapter.

5 *Metamorphoses*: 59; *Amores*: 6 (once quoted as 'Ouidius in libro de sine titulo'); *Ars amatoria*: 7; *Remedia amoris*: 5; *Heroides*: 4; *Fasti*: 4; *Tristia*: 4; *Epistulae ex Ponto*: 3.

6 To which should probably be added C-66: p. 58: 'Ouidius *Methamorphoseos* sol propter dignitatem exaltatam habet tres planetas supra se et tres infra.'. The reference may be rather to *De vetula* 2.164–6. For this and the other *pseudo-epigrapha* discussed in this paragraph see in this volume, pp. 304–8.

7 Praise of the Virgin from *De vetula* 3.772ff. ('O virgo felix') in BR-9 (three lines) and Padua-55 (the equivalent of fifteen lines, somewhat garbled, followed by two more hexameters with internal rhyme); a similar praise of the Virgin from *De vetula* 2.202–3 ('Unus erat totus nature vultus in orbe') in Bodley MS Auct. F infra 1.3/2–18.

8 Prophecy of the Virgin birth, from *De vetula* 3.613–15, 637, in O-37: 182. Notice that in this context *De vetula* cites Albumasar, whose prediction that a virgin would give birth at the conjunction of Jupiter and Venus occurs separately elsewhere in late medieval sermons.

9 The remarks against studying lucrative sciences instead of theology, from *De vetula* 1.691f. are quoted verbatim in D-13: fol. 30v and alluded to in C-93, p. 80.

10 'Hec luxuria notari potest per herbam venenosam, de qua loquitur Ouidius *De mirabilibus mundi* dicens: "Hec fera tam sevum prebuit natura venenum, / vt quicumque bibat vitam ridendo relinquat" ' (RE-22: fol. 166vb (see note 12 below)). Problematic is the following passage from a sermon on the Incarnation: 'Quamuis enim poete fabulantur Iouem per ymbrem aureum Danem inpregnasse, necnon et auicula quedam, auis paradisi dicta, celesti rore gustato sine mare credat concipere. Sed quod recitat Alexander in commento super Ouidium *de mirabilibus*: hoc ecce tercium, hoc recens est et omnibus admirandum, ut virgo filium, femina deum, ancilla dominum, eua enixa[?? or -um?], quos Eua suo vicio fecerat dampnatos Maria mater triplici miraculo tuo Deo nos reddat acceptos' Padua-35: 67. It is not clear whether 'de mirabilibus' here is a book title or belongs to the following clause. Finally, V-18: fol. 21v retells the Aesopian fable of the crab and its mother (or 'The Two Crabs') and locates it 'inter fabulas Ouidii'.

11 Edited by James 1913: 286–98; see Pfaff 1980: 233 and notes. There was a copy in the medieval library of the Austin Friars at York; see Humphreys 1990: 129. The first quotation cited in the previous note occurs in James 1913: 290.

fortune[12] and from another called *De Iano*,[13] both attributed to Ovid but evidently by a non-classical author: 'Quod fuit oblitum rectum facit equat iniquum' O-39: fols. 174v–175r. More verses of this kind follow both attributed to Ovid, but appearing in definitely non-classical metrical garbs.

Several of these collections are by known authors, of whom several were mendicants: the Dominicans Robert Holcot (d. probably 1349), John Bromyard, (d. probably by 1352), William Jordan (*fl.* 1350s/1360s) and a 'Frater Guillelmus de Bay'lewyk', and the Augustinian Friar John Waldeby (d. probably soon after 1372). Others belonged to monastic orders: the Benedictines Bishop Thomas Brinton (d. 1389) and Robert Rypon (d. after 1419), and the Augustinian canon, Bishop Philip Repingdon (d. 1424).[14] The same mixture of mendicant and monastic authorship appears in those anonymous collections that can, with different degrees of certitude, be affiliated with either mendicant (the Franciscan collection Q and the Dominican collection D) or Benedictine (O, R, W) milieux. Sermons with quotations from Ovid are about evenly distributed between the two milieux. To what extent Ovid quotations were included in the sermons by preachers from the secular clergy is harder to determine. The twelfth-century French theologian Radulfus Ardens, archdeacon of Poitiers, whose sermons I have included for comparison with an earlier age, presumably was a secular priest. But the authorship of the interesting pieces in collection A, for example, or of the university sermons given at Cambridge in the second and third decades of the fifteenth century remains quite uncertain. In any case, citation of Ovid was not limited to one particular religious order.

It would be good to know before what audiences such quotations were used. Unfortunately this question encounters two major problems stemming from the written and therefore literary nature of the evidence and from the fact that late medieval sermons are notoriously devoid of clear indications of their intended audiences. First, we can never be certain how close the preserved text of a given sermon was to the actual words spoken

---

[12] 'Ouidius *De fallaciis Fortune* dicit quod Domina Fortuna solebat depingi ut ymago pulcra habens in manu sua tria, scilicet a rose valuyng, a lyly þe leuys fallyng, and a rode worte flowr at eve closyng;' N-106: fol. 211, a funeral sermon).

[13] A sermon on St Edmund, king and martyr: 'Ouidius de / Iano recitat ad regem autem qui digito percussit nasum uel saltem super nasum posuit digitum dicuntur isti versus:

> Princeps qui digito nasum feriendo minatur
> Penset quod subito quod prominet incineratur.

De lege autem que secundum Ouidium de Iano fuit cum bursa dicuntur isti versus:

> Bursa regem regens tollit condit sibi leges
> Quod fuit oblitum rectum facit equat iniquum.   (O-39: 174v–175)

More verses of this kind follow.

[14] For the use of Ovid by authors of the monastic authors see also in this volume, pp. 177–96.

from the pulpit. To be sure, one can distinguish between formal sermons that were written as integral parts of model collections, and actual or 'real' sermons. The former smell of the lamp – or perhaps rather of the compiler's sweat in opening hefty tomes and copying relevant material – while the latter tend to vibrate with the rhythms and devices of oral delivery. But between these two poles – academic model collections like that made by Philip Repingdon and stylistically much looser sermons that are full of local references and of direct addresses and such – lies a vast middle ground of sermons whose verbal texture shares aspects of both extremes. In general, it is prudent to keep in mind that all medieval sermons that have come down to us are products of a literary activity, an activity during which a reference to Ovid could have easily been slipped in, a quotation which the preacher himself may or may not have used in the pulpit. In any case, Ovid quotations occur through the entire spectrum, from Repingdon's regular cycle of Sunday sermons to sermons that are full of oral devices including different types of macaronic mixture.

The second problem, determining the precise audience before whom a sermon was delivered or for whom it was intended, while never solvable to our complete satisfaction, is a touch less forbidding. Even where a sermon does not bear a clear rubric that would assign it to a specific audience (such as 'ad clerum', 'in visitatione', or 'ad populum'), address forms can give us a clue (such as 'Reverendi' or 'Reverendi domini' addressing the clergy, although the frequent 'Karissimi' is probably not very decisive). Of the about one hundred sermons that cite Ovid, two are rubricated as having been given to the clergy,[15] nineteen are addressed to 'Reverendi' or 'Venerandi', and about half a dozen more can on internal evidence be inferred to have been directed to clerical ears. An additional five sermons were explicitly given to a university audience, and two more to students, probably young Augustinian friars. The remaining approximately seventy sermons are addressed to 'Karissimi' or have neither addresses nor clear internal indications of their intended audience. It would seem, then, that Ovid quotations were largely directed to a learned, clerical audience. This is borne out by the learned company Ovid quotations keep. To give but one example: the funeral sermon for the Benedictine abbot Walter Froucetur, given in 1412, quotes Alexander Nequam, Aristotle, Augustine, Avicenna, Basil, Constantinus Africanus, Grosseteste, Isidore, Johannes Balbus (*Catholicon*), Socrates, Solinus and Vegetius together with Ovid.[16] In other cases that have a similarly rich texture of quotations Ovid finds himself in the company of such classical authors as Cicero, Horace, Livy,

---

[15] BR-11 and 14.   [16] R-03, edited by Horner 1977: 147–66.

Pliny, Seneca, Trogus Pompeius, Valerius Maximus, Vegetius, Virgil and others, while elsewhere we find him together with Arabic scientists (Albumasar, Alfraganus, Averroes) or with St Thomas Aquinas. Clearly, in late medieval preaching Ovid lived in learned environments.

Nonetheless, Ovid is also quoted in sermons that have a decidedly popular flavour. Thus, a sermon on *Heu, heu, heu* (Ezekiel 6:11) begins:

Heu, casus accidit dolorosus: punctus qui erat in circuli medio non contentus tali loco tam abcessit rupto circulo. Anglice sic:

> Alas, her is ifalle a reuful cas:
> A poynt was by-lokyn in a compas.
> Þe poynt þat was þar in bi-loken
> Al þe compas haþ to-broken.

Moraliter: Homo punctus est modicus tam paruitate molis quam virtutis respectu tocius vniuersi respectu cuius tota terra eciam quasi punctus est. Vnde refert Seneca *Ad Lucillum Epistula* 91 quod cum Alexander Magnus addisceret geometricam . . .[17]

Alas, something painful has happened: the point that was in the centre of a circle, not content with that place, has left and thus broken the circle . . . Morally speaking: Man is a point, moderate in its size as well as in its power in comparison with the whole universe, in regard to which the whole earth also is as it were a point. Hence Seneca reports in his Letters to Lucillus, letter 91, that when Alexander the Great was learning geometry . . .

With many further English rhymes[18] the sermon utilises as its central notion material that suggests a non-learned, non-clerical audience: three tricks that a wrestler uses to throw his opponent. Were this a modern sermon, one would think the preacher had been watching Saturday night wrestling and got his inspiration from there. But this is a late medieval discourse, and the wrestling tricks (with English terms) are accompanied by quotations not only from the Bible but from Seneca, Augustine, Bernard of Clairvaux, Gregory the Great, Isidore (*Soliloquia*), Aelred on the life of cloistered nuns, Alan of Lille (*Anticlaudianus*), Chrysostom and eventually Ovid (*Tristia* 2.179–82).[19] Was the audience, then, a group of clerics or a lay parish? As

---

[17] A-24, fol. 85.

[18] Including the well-known 'Atte ston casting my lemman i ches', fol. 87 [old], which has been taken to be a popular dance song: Greene 1977: xlix–l and cxlvii. The sermon also contains a story about people digging 'in a cemetery in England' and finding an uncorrupt body with an inscription at his head lamenting his evil life; cf. Erb 1971: 63–84, at 78.

[19] Earlier in the sermon the preacher reports ('fertur') Hercules' fighting with Antaeus (here 'Anicodes'), who stood up with greater strength every time he was thrown to the earth, but does not mention Ovid.

I have argued elsewhere, even the presence of popular elements cannot be taken as proof that the sermon was directed *ad populum*.[20] What we can say about this particular sermon is that its verbal texture would place it among genuine, real sermons (rather than pieces in a systematic cycle), but its precise audience remains undecided. Like many of its companions, it can be safely assumed to have been written down for the inspection and use of preachers, who then might have used it before whatever audience they deemed suitable. As far as the intended audience of Ovid quotations is concerned, it would therefore make best sense to say that basically they were intended for learned readers and listeners, and that now and then a preacher may well have carried them with him to the pulpit before an unlearned lay audience.

What values, then, would a late medieval preacher have found in quoting Ovid? Examining one sermon that is unusually rich in classical quotations will provide a number of clues. The sermon (B/2-67) is anonymous and bears no indications of the occasion for which it was made or its audience. Its author clearly was a learned and sophisticated man: for his *thema* he chose contiguous words from two successive gospel verses: 'He is troubled who does not answer.'[21] His lengthy introduction, which spans nearly half of the sermon, begins with the general observation: 'It is commonly said by people who use reason that the harder one is aggrieved in his heart, the more reluctantly does one show one's inner pain in external signs, such as words, tears, or acts of vengeance.'[22] Conversely, grief that is not shown externally becomes ever so much harder to bear. This is then applied to man's moral life: anyone who consents to mortal sin accumulates in himself matter of great grief, since he becomes unable to do any good and meritorious work. The point leads the preacher to deal with the question of an individual's responsibility for his or her sin, and in making the point that no matter how much one may be tempted by the devil, consent is always a matter of one's own responsibility, the preacher adds:

'Narrat Ouidius *Epistularum* suarum, Epistula 2, quod Phillis quedam regina <Tracie> que adamauit Demofontem recedentem de bello Troiano propter

---

[20] Wenzel 2005: 9–10 and 242–4.

[21] Matthew 15:22–23, on the Canaanite woman begging for help for her daughter: 'My daughter is grievously troubled by the devil. Who answered her not a word' ('Filia mea male a daemonio vexatur. Qui [i.e., Jesus] non respondit ei verbum'). Wrenching thus words out of context was frowned upon in contemporary *Artes praedicandi*, and enough examples have survived to explain the cause of such frowns.

[22] 'Vt communiter racione vtentibus exprimitur quod quanto quis dure et ex corde grauatus fuerit, remissius dolorem interiorem exterioribus signis ostendit, vtputa verbis aut lacrimis vindictis' B/2-67: 256ra).

munera promissa. Qui proficiscens in patriam suam pactum decepte non tenuit. Phillis vero m[ult]o amore illius flagrans dolore concepto quod iste non rediit, mortua est. Cuius mortis causam breuiter in fine perstringit Ouidius sic dicens:

> Phillade Demofon leto dedit hospes amantem.
> Ille necis causam prebuit, illa manum.
> (*Heroides* 2.147–8)

Hec ille. Vult dicere quod quamuis ille fuit causa parcialis, idest per suam suggestionem quod ipsa fuit corrupta per eum et post mortua, tamen nisi ista assensisset volendo, non fuisset corrupta nec occisa, quia ille tantum incepit, ipsa consummauit. Sic moraliter: Quantumcumque tentetur quis grauiter a diabolo, nusquam corrumpi potest per mortale nec occidi nisi ipsemet prebeat manum, idest voluntatis assensum' (fol. 256va–b).

In his *Epistles*, epistle 2, Ovid reports that Phyllis, queen of Thrace, was deeply in love with Demophoon on his return from the Trojan War, because of promised gifts. As Demophoon went into his own country, he did not keep his pact with the deceived [queen]. But Phyllis, burning with love for him, was overtaken by grief that he did not return and died. Ovid briefly summarises (*perstringit*) the cause of her death at the end and says:

> Demophoon killed Phyllis: a guest, he stole her love
> and by this theft caused the death that came from her hand.
> (*Heroides* 2.147–8)

So far Ovid. Which means that although Demophoon was partially responsible through his suggestion that Phyllis was corrupted and then died, nevertheless unless Phyllis had agreed willingly, she would not have been corrupted or killed. He only started it, she carried it out. Thus morally: however gravely a person is tempted by the devil, he can never be corrupted in mortal sin nor be killed unless he himself furnished his hand, that is, the assent of his will.[23]

This being the case, so the preacher concludes his exposition, it also follows that whoever wishes to eliminate the grief of his sin has the responsibility to do penance and confess.

Then follows the sermon's main division. The words of the chosen *thema* – 'He is troubled who does not answer' – suggest two things: an intense pain ('trouble') and an immense remedy ('answer'). The first point is again subdivided into two parts: Scripture speaks of two kinds of tribulation: for the elect here in this life, and for the damned in hell. Both are then developed, the first briefly, the second at greater length, leading the preacher to speak of four evils that are found in contemporary society: avarice, falsehood, pride and oppression of the poor. Again it is only the

[23] The translation is taken from Ovid 1990a: 16.

first of these, avarice, which then keeps the preacher's attention to the end of the sermon.

But in the briefer section on the tribulation of the elect, Ovid appears when the preacher declares:

Sextus Iulius *Stratagematum* libro 2, capitulo 1, refert quod Fabius consul maximus Romanorum pugnaturus contra Gallos et sciens eos tantum primo impetu valere imperauit suis militibus quos infatigabiles nouit vt hostium sustinerent primos congressus vt eos eciam mora fatigaret. Quo facto cum iam fessis Gallis recentes ad bellum essent, Romani Gallos sine aliqua difficultate subiecerunt. Cui concordat Ouidius 1 *De arte amoris*:

> Cede repugnantem, cedendo victor abibis.

Hec ille. Moraliter: Fortitudo huius mundi solummodo est in primo impetu et quasi in ictu oculi, idest in vita presenti, quia amplius non durat. Milites autem Christi, idest electi, sunt milites infatigabiles'. (fol. 257rb–va: see Sextus Julius Frontinus, *Stratagemata* 2.1.8)

In Book 2, chapter 1, of his *Stratagemata* Sextus Julius reports that Fabius, the Consul Maximus of the Romans, was about to fight against the Gauls. He knew that they were powerful only in their first onrush. So he ordered his soldiers, whom he knew to wear out easily, to endure their enemies' first assault, so that the enemies would be worn out by the delay. And this is what happened. As the Gauls were tired out, the Romans, still fresh for combat, managed to overcome them without any difficulty. With this Ovid agrees in Book 1 of his *Art of Love*:

> Yield to resistance, yielding wins the day.
>   (*Ars amatoria* 2.197)

So far our author. In moral terms: the World is strong only in its first assault and, as it were, for the twinkling of an eye, that is, during our present life, which does not last longer. But the soldiers of Christ, that is, the elect, cannot be worn out.[24]

Further on, in dealing with avarice, the preacher once more uses a line from Ovid. All men desire the friendship of the World, he declares, but it cannot be had without riches, for as someone says in verse,

> While you are safe, the friends you'll count are many.[25]

In this case, Ovid is not cited by name, which probably means that the preacher knew or remembered the verse only as a general proverb or saying.

---

[24] The translation is by Melville in Ovid 1990b: 113.
[25] 'Sicut dicit quidam metricus: "Cum fueris felix, multos numerabis amicos" ' (fol. 257va). Cf. *Tristia* 1.9.5. The same line with the next pentameter appears also in 25v. The translation is taken from Ovid 1992: 19.

This unusually rich sermon shows, first of all, medieval preachers' fondness for Ovidian tales found mostly in the *Metamorphoses*, but also in the *Heroides*, which are briefly retold and moralised for the purpose of illustrating a moral point the preacher was trying to get across. Thus, the story of Argus and Mercury warns against flatterers,[26] tempters,[27] or the allurements of the devil trying to rob our soul.[28] Similarly, the infant Hercules strangling two serpents sent by Juno into his cradle illustrates the strength that a true child of God has to overcome the flesh and the world,[29] or else the power of a truthfully ordained and promoted churchman.[30] Atalanta and her swiftness also appear in several sermons and symbolise the human soul, which is 'caught' with the three golden apples, either of the three laws (of nature, Moses and Christ)[31] or else of the false goods of sensual delights, worldly honours and riches.[32] The stories of Phaethon and Icarus warn against pride, ambition and disobedience,[33] while Narcissus exemplifies those who take too much pride in their physical beauty.[34]

In retelling or alluding to and moralising some of these and other Ovidian tales, preachers mention Ovid by name, in others they refer only to 'the poet' or 'poets' (often with a line from Ovid), and in still others they quote without any attribution. At this point Ovid's poetry fades into the large field of ancient and medieval mythography, the collections of myths and fables made by writers from Hyginus and 'Lactantius' through Fulgentius and the Vatican Mythographers to Bersuire and beyond. Not only their moralisations, so freely used in sermons, but even narrative details were known to medieval preachers from this mythographic tradition and presented under Ovid's name. For example, Hercules' strangling two serpents is based on a single line (*Metamorphoses* 9.67), but Brinton gives further details:

As an illustration, Ovid tells in *Metamorphoses* 11 that, as Jupiter after leaving Juno had sired a son on Alcmene, Juno secretly wanted to kill the boy. She sent him two serpents as he lay softly at rest in his cradle. But he fought them with his strength and strangled them in his hands and so killed them. And thereby it was shown that he was truly the son of Jupiter.[35]

---

[26] Titus: 27v.   [27] RE-53: 277rb, from Peraldus.
[28] W-97: 188v; W-107: 207v–208; Z-09: 30rb.   [29] BR-14: 56, W-125: 235vb.
[30] BR-14: 56; W-125: 235vb.   [31] W-89: 166ra.
[32] BR-11: 41; O-09: 56v. See further Auct. F infra 1.3/2-01: 44va–b.
[33] Phaethon: D-41: 110v–111; D-69: 200. Icarus: Titus: 27.   [34] BR-49: 220; BR-106: 489.
[35] BR-53: p. 239. Brinton used the same passage in BR-14, and the story further appears in Holcot-10 and W-125. These three sermons give the story with Ovid's name but refer to the 'penultimate' of his *Epistles* (i.e. *Heroides*).

A similar expansion of a brief allusion in Ovid's poetry is the account of the 'Roman Triumph' (see below).

Besides his stories about gods and heroes Ovid also appealed to preachers with narrative material of a slightly different kind. One instance is his account of the four ages in *Metamorphoses* 1.89–150. In a sermon for the first Sunday in Lent, on 'Command that these stones be made bread' ('Dic ut lapides isti panes fiant', Matthew 4:3), Holcot dwelt on the account at some length, showing that 'the longer we live, the worse it goes with the world' and then adding that today we live in a fifth age, that of stone. The idea and apparently Holcot's text of the sermon introduction were taken over for the initial paragraph in a later Easter sermon on 'They saw the stone rolled back' ('Viderunt reuolutum lapidem', Mark 16:4), and the notion of social deterioration, now in three ages, was further used by Rypon, though here attributed to 'poets'.[36] Another instance of Ovidian narrative that does not involve a story proper is the 'Roman Triumph': in ancient Rome, a general returning victoriously from foreign wars was carried in triumph to the Capitol in a car drawn by four horses, where he received three honours and three acts of shame. The *exemplum* is widespread in medieval religious literature and occurs in many sermons. In at least two instances it is attributed to Ovid, with citation of *Ars amatoria* 1.214, 'Quattuor in medio aureis ibis equis.'[37]

But it is not only Ovidian narrative that attracted preachers as useful material for their work. The second Ovid quotation in the sermon 'He is troubled' enriches an account from Frontinus' *Stratagemata*, with a line from Ovid's love poetry (*Ars amatoria* 2.197). Surely this line is not simply probative but, in its succinct formulation of a moral truth, held for the preacher an added rhetorical or aesthetic appeal. This is true of many instances in which one or several lines from Ovid's love poems or from *Tristia* and *Ex Ponto* are quoted, usually with the author's name, to formulate a general, usually moral truth. One of Repingdon's model sermons is particularly rich: it strings together four separate distichs from *Ex Ponto* (two), *Tristia* and *Ars amatoria* to illustrate that there are 'many who would not preach or teach as readily unless they were urged on by their desire for vain glory'.[38] And two folios later, still in the same sermon,

---

[36] RY-08: 27r–v.
[37] A-46: 144v, and Worcester, Cathedral Library, F 126 [131], fol. 148rb. For the *exemplum* see Tubach 5084 and 4126. Brinton uses the story in three sermons (BR-7, 36 and 106) without mention of Ovid and attributing it to Isidore.
[38] 'Multi enim nisi eos inanis glorie inpelleret appetitus fructus in genere bonorum nec tam cito predicarent vel docerent.' Ouidius: 'Excitat auditor studium . . .' (RE-33: 263va).

Repingdon expands on a quotation from St Paul with two distichs from *Ars amatoria*.³⁹ The twelfth-century Radulfus Ardens similary extends a quotation from the Sermon on the Mount with a line from the *Amores*.⁴⁰

Another sermon writer who was fond of Ovid quotation is the unknown author of a collection in Oxford, Merton College, MS 236. Besides using several Ovidian tales, he also incorporates individual lines from Ovid's love poetry. Some of them are simply descriptive, as when he tells us that by nature man walks erect,⁴¹ or that some kinds of fever can be healed while others must lead to death, 'for as Ovid testifies, "it doesn't always lie in the doctor's power that a sick man is helped" '.⁴² Others are more directly concerned with man's moral life. Thus, 'when the honey of smooth flattery is given to evil people, it takes away their reason, for then they do not know who they are or what they are doing. Hence Ovid says in his *Book Without Title* [i.e. *Amores*]: "Sweet honey hides the poison down below".⁴³ Or, one must not only know God's commandments but keep them, as the poet says: "To keep's no less a virtue than to find." '⁴⁴ Still other citations are expressly hortatory, such as the admonition to 'stop at the start, if you've the least unease'.⁴⁵

The various purposes for which Ovid is quoted in Merton 236/2 can likewise be found in other sermon collections. To their descriptive and hortatory functions may be added that of complaint at moral depravity or decay. The lament at the misuse of knowledge for personal gain voiced in *De vetula* appears in two different collections,⁴⁶ as of course Ovidian

---

³⁹ 'In laboribus erumpna, in vigiliis multis, in fame et siti', etc., quorum meritis vitam capere intendant. De hiis dicit Ouidius: 'Scit bene venator . . . ' (RE-33: 265vb). The biblical quotation is 2 Corinthians 11:27, the Ovid, *Ars amatoria* 3.45–8. Repingdon may or may not have found this material in his source, an unspecified *postillator*, who has not been identified.

⁴⁰ 'Unde ipse Dominus ait: "Qui viderit mulierem ad concupiscendam eam, jam moechatus est in corde suo." Et poeta: "Et si servetur bene corpus, adultera mens est." Requirit ergo Dominus a suis non solum innocentiam corporis, sed etiam mentis' (*PL* 155: 1997). The biblical quotation is Matthew 5:27, for the Ovidian line see *Amores* 3.4.5. None of the four Ovid quotations I have found in the *de tempore* sermons of Radulfus Ardens mentions Ovid by name.

⁴¹ Mert 236-52: 203ra, 'vnde Ouidius', quoting *ex Ponto* 1.3.17. The same quotation was used by Radulfus Ardens, without Ovid's name, at *PL* 155: 1815.

⁴² 'Nam vt testatur Ouidius: "Non est in medico semper releuetur vt eger" ' (Mert 236-26: 160rb), from *ex Ponto* 1.3.17.

⁴³ 'Mel blande adulacionis, quando malis propinatur, racionem illis aufert, quia non se cognoscunt qui sunt et quid faciunt. Unde Ouidius in libro *de sine titulo*: "Impia sub dulci melle venena latent"' (Mert 236/2-24: 157rb), quoting *Amores* 1.8.104. Translated by Melville in Ovid 1990b: 17.

⁴⁴ Mert 236/2-25: 158vb, quoting *Ars amatoria* 2.13; translated by Melville, 108.

⁴⁵ 'Melius et leuius resistitur in principio. Ouidius: "Dum licet et medici [*read* modici] tangunt precordia motus, Si sapis in primo limite, siste pedem." Psalmista . . . ' (Mert 236-20: 151ra). The quote is from *Remedia amoris* 79–80; translated by Melville in Ovid 1990b: 153.

⁴⁶ See above, note 9.

myths and fables often furnish examples of vices that are far surpassed by the modern age, such as Phaethon, who

in his pride wanted to drive the car of his father, Apollo, as the poet described in his book *On Transformations*. None of these [examplary figures], I say, surpassed in their various actions the many proud people of our time.[47]

Finally, lines from or attributed to the classical poet may even have specifically religious functions. The praise of the Blessed Virgin from the end of *De vetula* was mentioned earlier. Even more remarkably, the 'wrestling' sermon on *Heu, heu, heu*, also discussed above, closes with an exhortation to pray, in which the preacher first adduces the examples of the three youths in the fiery oven and of the Ninivites confessing their sins and pleading for God's mercy, and then concludes:

And we, too, should ask for this, for the love of the saints of the New Testament, the apostles, martyrs, and confessors, and we should say with Ovid who, in his book of *Epistles*, persuades Caesar:

> Spare me, I pray, and lay aside your lightning,
>> Fierce weapon I, poor soul, too well have known.
> Great Father of my fatherland, oh spare me
>> And, mindful of that title of renown.[48]

Hardly could a pagan poet find himself in a more saintly, Christian company and context!

In all these cases, whether an individual quotation merely exemplifies and illustrates or carries some additional stylistic, aesthetic pleasure, Ovid quotations serve the general purpose of proof texts. They do so with myriads of citations from accepted 'authorities' that range from the Bible and the Church Fathers, theologians, natural and systematic philosophers, historians and classical and medieval poets, to contemporary stories and everyday experience. In selecting and using them, one can assume that a preacher's mind moved from the notion he was dealing with to finding appropriate material for its illustration in the many sources at his disposal.

---

[47] After listing proud rulers from the Bible and the *Historia Alexandri*: 'Nec Feton, qui ob superbiam detestandam currum Appollinis patris / sui ascendere rege[re?] volebat, poeta libro *De transformatis* sonante. Nullus inquam horum miris[?] et variis superborum modernos multos in superbia superauit' (D-14: 110v–111).

[48] 'Et hoc vtique debemus nos petere propter amorem sanctorum noui testamenti apostolorum, martirum, confessorum, et dicamus cum Ouidio libro *Epistularum* inducente Cesarem: "Parce, precor filiumque tuum fera tela repone. Heu inicium misero cog'ta tela mihi parce patrie ne memor huius. o si." etc.' (A-24: 88v). This at the end of the sermon's third principal part. The main division had announced six parts, and the text of A-24 ends with the marginal remark 'Non plus in copia.' The quote is *Tristia* 2.179–82; translation by Melville in Ovid 1992: 30–1.

Was this thought process ever the reverse – that is, could a preacher's thinking have started from an Ovidian text and then be led to a point he developed further in the sermon? Second-guessing late medieval thought processes is of course very hazardous. Yet I believe there is some evidence to suggest that in quite rare instances that may indeed have been the case. The best case in my experience is the sermon given at the occasion of the enclosure of Alice Huntingfield.[49] The sermon's *thema* is from 'today's epistle': 'Enter the city' ('Ingredere civitatem', Acts 9:7), the epistle lection for the feast of the Conversion of St Paul. The preacher begins by analysing and dividing the notion of 'city', declares that the city of religion is the most perfect, and closes his introductory section with exhorting Alice to enter this city bravely. For the main part of the sermon he returns to the notion of 'city' and treats three kinds of city that he finds in Scripture: those of our mind, of the religious life, and of heavenly joy. Beginning with the city of the human mind, he summarises Ovid's account of the house of the Sun (*Metamorphoses* 2.1–18), whose details he moralises, one after the other. Ovid's 'sublimibus alta columnis', for instance, means that our soul stands elevated on the three theological virtues; the 'caeli fulgentis imago' signifies its dignity, which 'carries in it a likeness of heaven, earth, and all creatures';[50] and the image of the *ambiguus* Proteus painted in the house of the Sun indicates that sinners change the image of God into that of the devil. The preacher then ends this section by saying that four things support this house of the soul: 'amor Dei, laus Dei, ymago Dei, et sapiencia' – whose initial letters spell ALYS, the name of the woman about to be enclosed!

As he begins his second main part, on the city of holy religion, the preacher returns to Ovid, but now to 'the city of Alcathous, which had a very strong tower, in which Nisus, king of that city, enclosed his daughter called Scylla' (see *Metamorphoses* 8. 7–8, 14–18, 91).[51] The punning continues, for the preacher finds that 'Sylla' spells 'Alys' backwards. And he promptly proceeds to allegorise other details of the Ovidian narrative, such as Apollo with his lyre bringing comfort to the enclosed woman. This moralisation is in no way different from moralisations of Herculus, Argus, Antaeus and so forth. Nor is the punning on Alice's name unusual, as late medieval

---

[49] I have discussed this sermon previously in Wenzel 1995a: 127–43, especially 137–42. The Sermon has been translated in Wenzel 2008: 283–97.

[50] 'Dignitas enim humane anime est tanta quod representat similitudinem celi et terre et omnium creaturarum' (J/S-18:) 80v. See *Metamorphoses* 8. 7–8, 14–18, 91.

[51] 'Ciuitas Alchose habuit turrim fortissimam, in qua turri Nisus rex eiusdem ciuitatis inclusit filiam suam, que vocabatur Silla', fol. 81v.

preachers fondly used such punning in funerary sermons and academic speeches that contained personal names. What makes this sermon unusual is this preacher's familiarity and engagement with Ovid. His moving from the notion of 'city of religion' to the Nisus and Scylla story is remarkable; I know of no parallels to the use of the story of Nisus and Scylla in the sermons I have scanned (in contrast to Hercules, Argus, the house of the Sun, etc.). Further, the verbal and notional connection here reaches deeper than the mere word *civitas*: the previous punning on Alice's name continues, and Apollo, who brings her comfort, would of course have been known to the preacher as Phoebus Apollo, the Sun, whose house was described in the first main part of the sermon.[52] This preacher appropriates a classical story, not because part of it illustrates a single word or notion, but rather because its totality connects with what has been said and at the same time moves the development of his discourse forward.

We can be quite sure that Wyclif would not have approved of any of this. 'But alas, these days', he laments in a sermon that deals at length with preaching, 'if a preacher speaks, he will not preach as it were the words of God but, for the sake of illustration, stories, poems, and fables from outside Scripture', and then launches into a lengthy analysis and condemnation of the use of exempla and of other rhetorical devices of contemporary preaching (divisions, rhymes, etc.).[53] Wyclif's negative attitude was shared not only by his followers but also by some orthodox preachers.[54] The thirteenth-century Dominican William Peraldus, author of very popular *summae* on the vices and virtues and of model sermons, in dealing with or interpreting the gospel lection of the woman who is healed of her haemorrhage and who had 'bestowed all her substance on physicians' (Luke 8:43), explains that 'those especially bestow their substance [on physicians] who exhaust the power of their intelligence in studying the books of the poets'.[55] Some of his followers of the fourteenth and fifteenth centuries thus condemn not just the study of presumably pagan poetry but its use in sermons. One sermon writer declares that when a preacher 'tries too hard to show his knowledge in subtle devices, such as elegant introductions of his *thema* or elegant divisions of his sermons, or a strange narrative from poetic fables', he 'speaks from himself'.[56] And another says:

---

[52] Thus the first Vatican Mythographer, in Bode 1834, vol. I: 36; and in later mythographers, including Thomas Walsingham, Bersuire, etc.

[53] Wyclif 1887–90, vol. IV: 262–75, at 265.   [54] See also Wenzel 2005: 343, 345.

[55] Guilelmus Peraldus 1499, sermon for 24 Trinity.

[56] 'Ille enim a seipso loquitur qui nimis nititur ostendere scienciam suam in subtilitatibus, sicut sunt curiose introducciones thematis siue curiose diuisiones sermonum, uel extranea narracio fabularum poeticarum' (M4-13: 316ra).

This reading [of the gospel] is more necessary to man's soul than Horace or Ovid or all the poets that ever were. Even if you don't look into Terence or Scotus you can come to the kingdom of heaven. Even if you don't know Euclid or [*blank*], you can be saved. But if you don't know the text of faith, you will without doubt be damned. This is the reading that Christ taught us, to know him and to come to the kingdom of heaven.[57]

And yet another preacher, in an academic sermon in praise of theology, claims that the views of philosophers and poets are without merit, like those of the followers of Pythagoras,

who was so deluded that he maintained he had been a certain Euphorbus in the time of the Trojan War and remembered the lance of Atreus' son by which he was wounded, and the shield which he then carried on his arm, as Ovid testifies in *Metamorphoses* 15 when he writes in his person:

> I was Euphorbus, son of Panthous, in whose opposing breast
> Hung the spear of the younger son of Atreus.

But why should I talk of the poets' fables in which almost as many lies are woven together as there are stories? In their works they openly lie about boys transformed into flowers, such as Narcissus and Hippolytus, or girls into trees, as Daphne and Heliades, or men into animals, as Lycaon and Hippomenes . . . [58]

But these are warnings against uncritically and literally accepting fables as truth, and against overindulgence in studying them. Orthodox preachers were perfectly happy to quote a good story or line. Thus, Peraldus in the quoted passage calls philosophy and poetry *sirens*, and a few pages later explicitly quotes Ovid on sirens and on the *fistula* of Mercury. And the preacher of W-22 not only quotes Ovid in the same breath as he queries the use of fables but had, earlier within the same sermon, quoted a line from *Remedia amoris*. Holcot even begins his sermon on 'The Father himself

---

[57] 'Ista leccio est magis necessaria humane anime quam Oracius uel Ouidius, uel omnes poete qui vmquam fuerunt. Licet non respicias Tere[n]cium uel Scotum potes peruenire ad regnum celorum, licet ignoreris Euclidem nec [*blank*] poteris saluari, si nesciueris leccionem fidei indubitanter dampnaberis' (O-03: 17v).

[58] 'In tantum delusus erat ille eximius philosophorum Pictagoras, vt diceret seipsum tempore Troiani belli fuisse quendam militem nomine Euforbium meminisseque lancee Attride qua extitit vulneratus et scuti quod tunc manu gestabat, prout testatur Ouidius *De transformatis* libro 15, in eius persona sic scribens:

> Pantoydes Euforbus eram cui pectore leuo
> hesit ab aduerso [*Ovid adds*: gravis] hasta minoris Attride.'

Sed quid de vanis poetarum fabulis referam, in quibus tot fere inseruntur mendacia quot ibi historie referuntur? Cum nunc pueros conuersos in flores, vt Narcissum Ypolitum, nunc virgines mutatas in arbores, vt Dafnem et Eliades, nunc viros transformatos in pecudes, vt Lycaonem et Ypominem, sparsim in suis tractatibus publice menciuntur'. (W-22: 76ra.) The preacher quotes *Metamorphoses* 15.161–62. For the whole sermon see Wenzel 1995b: 321–9.

loves you' (John 16:27) with: 'Beloved, after the *sententia* of the poet Ovid, in book I of *De arte amandi*, only he can become a teacher of love (*preceptor amoris*) who first had been wounded by love's darts and firebrands.'[59]

Finally, where would late medieval preachers have got their Ovid quotations from? It is plausible that most of them drew this material from systematic sermon cycles or from other aids for preachers, such as the fourteenth-century *Fasciculus morum*[60] or the fifteenth-century collections made by John Wheathampstead, abbot of St Albans.[61] Textual analysis of the story about the infant Hercules strangling the serpents sent by Juno, which occurs in several different collections, suggests that it was taken from a common intermediate source, not from Ovid directly. The story is repeatedly attributed to Ovid's *Epistles* (i.e. *Heroides*) rather than the *Metamorphoses*.[62] Likewise, the already noted expansions of Ovid's own words point to a common source between the poet's works and the preachers. The same is true of factual errors, such as claiming that Jason had to confront 'terrible lions', which in Ovid are definitely steers (*tauri, Metamorphoses* 7.29, 104–5, 210).[63] Having said this, one must add to the contrary that some preachers, such as the author of the sermon for Alice Huntingfield, used quotations in a way that suggests that they may well have drawn on their memories of what they had learned in the Arts course,[64] or they may even have gone directly to Ovid.

In any case, there is no doubt that Ovid continued to live in sermons during the last medieval centuries. On the evidence of surviving texts, preachers were far more attracted to him than to Virgil or Horace.[65] His fables especially gave them rich grist for their mills, whether for merely decorative or structural purposes, and his love poetry furnished many a *bon mot* of moral import. It was evidently not simply the matter but also

---

[59] 'Karissimi, secundum sentenciam poete Ovidii primo *De arte amandi*, solus ille debet fieri preceptor amoris qui prius eiusdem iaculis et faculis per experienciam fuerat wlneratus' (Holcot-97, referring to *Ars amatoria* 1.17 and following).

[60] In the edited text Ovid's name appears seven times, and five more passages are quotations without his name or probably based on his poetry; see Wenzel 1989: Index, 751.

[61] Especially his *Pabularium poetarum* (London, BL, Egerton MS 646), which gathers a vast amount of material in alphabetical articles containing many references to Ovid. For instance, the article on *Domus Solis* cites *Metamorphoses* 2. See also below p. 185 &n. In the later thirteenth century John of Wales, OFM, similarly gathered a good deal of Ovidian material in his several aids for preachers; see Swanson 1989: Index, 305 (for '199' read '198'). For Ovid quotations in the various preachers' aids written by William de Montibus (d. 1213), see Goering 1992: Index, 635.

[62] Thus in Holcot-19, BR-14: p. 56, and W-125: 235vb.

[63] 'Narrat enim Ouidius quod contra Iasonem erant ordinati leones terribiles', W-27: 80vb.

[64] For the teaching of Ovid in the Arts curriculum at Oxford, see Fletcher 1992: 323.

[65] In the collections examined I have found a little over thirty citations of Virgil with his name; the largest number is found in the monastic collection W. Horace appears considerably less often; I have found his name in some eight sermons, almost all of them also citing Ovid.

the form, the metrical crispness of a quotation, that appealed to their rhetorical sense, as the example of Phyllis and Demophoon quoted above demonstrates. In the years between the twelfth and the sixteenth centuries, Ovid's poetry continued to strike receptive ears and gave delight even in the most prosaic of rhetorical enterprises.

LIST OF SIGLA

A: Cambridge, University Library, MS Ii.3.8

Aberdeen: Thomas de Lisle, in Aberdeen, University Library, MS 154

Auct: Oxford, Bodleian Library, MS Auct. F. inf. 1.3

B/2: Cambridge, University Library, MS Kk.4.24

BR: Thomas Brinton, OSB, bishop of Rochester, in London, British Library, MS Harley 3760; edited by Mary Aquinas Devlin, *The Sermons of Thomas Brinton, Bishop of Rochester (1373–1389)* 2 vols. (London, 1954)

Bro: John Bromyard, OP, *Distinctiones*, in Oxford, Bodleian Library, MS Bodley 859

C: Cambridge, Gonville and Caius College, MS 356

D: Toulouse, Bibliothèque Municipale, MS 342

E: Hereford, Cathedral Library, MS O.iii

F/1: Oxford, Bodleian Library, MS Auct. F. infra 1.2, fols. 85–103

F/5: Oxford, Bodleian Library, MS Auct. F. infra 1.2, fols. 340–401

Holcot: sermons by Robert Holcot, OP, in Cambridge, Peterhouse College, MS 210

J/5: Cambridge, Jesus College, MS 13

M: Manchester, John Rylands Library, MS 367

Mert236: Oxford, Merton College, MS 236

O: Oxford, Bodleian Library, MS Bodley 649

P2: Cambridge, Pembroke College, MS 257

Padua: Padua, Biblioteca Antoniana, MS 515

Q: Oxford, Bodleian Library, MS Lat. th. d. 1

R: Oxford, Bodleian Library, MS Laud. misc. 706

Radulfus: Radulfus Ardens, homilies for Sundays and saints' feasts, edited in PL 155: 1667–2118 and 1301–1626

RE: Philip Repingdon, OSA, bishop of Lincoln, homilies on the Sunday gospels, in Oxford, Corpus Christi College, MS 54

RY: Robert Rypon, OSB, sermons, in London, British Library, MS Harley 4894

S: Oxford, Balliol College, MS 149

Titus: General Chapter sermon, in London, British Library, MS Cotton Titus C IX, fols. 26r–27v.

V: Oxford, Trinity College, MS 42

W: Worcester, Cathedral Library, MS F 10, with new foliation.

WA: John Waldeby, OESA, *Novum opus dominicale*, in Oxford, Bodleian Library, MS Laud.misc. 77

X: Worcester, Cathedral Library, MS F 126

Z: Arras, Bibliothèque de la Ville, MS 254

CHAPTER 9

Ovid in the monasteries
The evidence from late medieval England

James G. Clark

The monasteries formed the crucible of classical studies in medieval Europe. It was in the monastic scriptoria of northern Italy and western France that the few remaining fragments of antiquity were finally broken and recast in the forms – *florilegium*, schoolbook – that would determine their reception throughout the medieval centuries. To these pioneers of monastic classicism can be credited the recovery of some of the masters of Roman poetry and prose: Virgil, Horace, Persius and Juvenal.[1] Another Augustan master, Ovid, at first appeared only of secondary interest and the transmission of texts was intermittent.[2] Aldhelm of Malmesbury (639–709) perhaps knew passages of the *Metamorphoses* well enough to echo them in his prose, but a generation later Bede (673–735) knew Book 1 of the text only from Isidore's *Etymologiae*.[3] In barely a century, however, and certainly before the advent of the *aetas Ovidiana*, Ovid's works were well established in the monasteries of the Benedictine mission.[4] It was these monastic readers of the ninth, tenth and eleventh centuries who transformed the remains of the Roman poet into the medieval Ovid. It was principally in their revived scriptoria that key parts of the canon were recovered and transmitted: prominent in the stemma of the *Amores* is the Corbie codex (Paris, BN, lat. MS 8242 (*s.* ix$^{ex.}$)); an early example of the *Epistulae ex Ponto* was made at Tegernsee (Munich, Bayerische Staatsbibliothek, clm MS 19476 (*s.* xii)); and valuable witnesses to, respectively, the *Heroides* and *Fasti*, are from the fount of Benedictinism, Montecassino (Eton College, MS 150 (*s.* xi$^{ex.}$) and Vatican City, BAV, Vat. lat. MS 3262 (*s.* xi).[5] Montecassino was also the provenance (but not the origin) of one of three earliest, complete

Research for this chapter was assisted by awards from the British Academy and the Leverhulme Trust.

[1] Bischoff 1994a: 142–7. For a classic account of the transmission of texts in the early period see Lowe 1947.
[2] Tarrant 1983: 260, 264, 266; Richmond 2002; Bischoff 1994b: 134–60 at 135–51.
[3] Lapidge 2006: 67, 98, n. 34, 115 and n.   [4] Bischoff 1994b: 157–8.
[5] Tarrant 1983: 260, 264, 266. For Eton 150 see also Newton 1999: 112–13, 247.

texts of the *Metamorphoses*;[6] two earlier fragments of the same text are also possibly of monastic provenance, Paris, BN, lat. MS 12246 and Vatican City, BAV, Urb. lat. MS 342, fols. 77–8, attributed to Fleury.[7] It was the early masters of claustral *schola* who also transformed the shorter texts, the amatory poetry and the *Heroides* into textbooks. The so-called 'Dunstan classbook', (Oxford, Bodl., Auct. MS F 4 32), passed through other hands before reaching Benedictine Glastonbury, but perhaps it was principally the monks there, indeed Dunstan himself, who prepared its partial copy of the *Ars amatoria* for study.[8] It was these same masters, and their *discipuli*, who formed the foundations of Ovid criticism, which grew incrementally from the forms of interlinear and marginal gloss that cluster in the Dunstan classbook, to the concise *accessus* found in an eleventh-century anthology of introductions to the curriculum authors, into fully formed commentaries, such as the exposition of the *ex Ponto* preserved in manuscripts from (again Benedictine) monasteries of St Gunneram (Regensburg) and Tegernsee. In the centuries of greatest monastic expansion – *c.* 950 to *c.* 1150 – Ovid emerged as the pre-eminent Latin master of the cloister, the companion of the schoolboys, novices and juniors, and also the corruption of their senior colleagues, who still stole moments with the poet in the solitude of their carrels: 'I was so far guided by my folly', wrote Abbot Guibert, abbot of Nogent-sur-Seine, in *c.* 1125, 'as to give first place to Ovid ... By love of it I was taken captive, being snared both by the wantonness of the sweet words I took from the poets and by those which I poured forth myself'.[9]

The monasteries of England – and, briefly, their Celtic neighbours – were an important source and stimulus for this early classical enthusiasm in European cloisters. It is possible that exchanges between English and Irish (i.e. Columbanian) monks and their French and German counterparts even extended to exemplars of classical authors and texts.[10] Ovid attracted attention from monks in England perhaps even earlier than their counterparts on the European mainland: not only Aldhelm, but also Abbo of Ramsey (originally a Fleury monk) and Wulfstan of Winchester; Alcuin's knowledge of Ovid was perhaps as much a reflection of his native culture as of his adopted monastery of St Martin, Tours.[11] The *aetas Ovidiana*

---

[6] Naples, Biblioteca Nazionale, MS I F 3. The late eleventh-century manuscript was at Montecassino from the early twelfth century. See Newton 1999: 248.

[7] Tarrant 1983: 277, 279.   [8] Hexter 1986: 26–35.

[9] Guibert de Nogent, *De vita sua*: 'ad hoc ipsum, duce mea levitate, iam veneram, ut Ovidiana et bucolicorum dicta praesumerem et lepores amatorios in specierum distributionibus epistolisque nexilibus affectarem ...': Labande 1981: 134. See also Guibert de Nogent 1984: 87.

[10] Bischoff 1994b: 134–60 at 136–7; Lapidge 2006: 127–32 at 128–9.

[11] Lapidge 2006: 183, 245, 248–9; Bischoff 1994a: 106–7, 138–9, 142–3.

itself offers significantly fewer expressions of Ovidian enthusiasm from England than are to be found in contemporary continental cloisters. There is nothing to compare to the candour of Abbot Guibert. The handful of pre-1200 catalogues surviving from English Benedictine houses suggests Ovid remained somewhat in the second rank of authors: at Christ Church, Canterbury, where Horace, Juvenal, Persius, Statius and Terence were held in multiple copies (no fewer than nine for Persius), the works of Ovid were scattered elsewhere, sometimes incomplete, with the exception of a quartet of the *Metamorphoses*.[12] Although Abbot Alexander Nequam of Cirencester (1157–1217) expressed alarm at the presence of Ovid in the cloister, anecdotal evidence would suggest he was hardly typical of English monks of the second half of the twelfth century.[13] Another abbot of a greater abbey, Henry of Blois, of Glastonbury (1126–71), was 'a man distinguished by literary skill'.[14] 'The trifles of the Muses are not incompatible with the devotion of the cloister', declared the St Albans monk, Ralph of Dunstable, in his verse *vita Albani* (c. 1170).[15] The atmosphere (1182–1211) at nearby Bury St Edmunds was apparently even more unabashed: 'they [the literary brethren] have declined *Musa, Musae*, so often that they are all accounted bemused'.[16] The stimuli for such diversions are not specified, but the works of Ovid were surely among them.

The place of the monasteries in the early history of medieval classicism – and of the medieval Ovid – has never been in doubt, but it has always been understood that even in the twelfth century their importance was already fading and the focus of these studies had shifted in favour of the secular schools. As individuals, the monks may have been enthusiastic readers of Ovid, but it was the secular masters of Orléans, and also Tours (at least in the time of Bernardus Silvestris), who began to expound his work and to imitate his imagery and style.[17] The Ovidian moment in the schools itself

---

[12] James 1903: 9–11 at 11. See also the earliest extant catalogue of the library at Durham Priory, which recorded single copies of the principal works, including *Metamorphoses* (i.e. Ovidius 'magnus'), Raine 1838: 5; also the earliest catalogue from Rochester Priory, *c.* 1202: Sharpe *et al.* 1996: B79.213 (497–526 at 522).

[13] Alexander Nequam, 'placuit tamen viris autenticis carmina amatoria cum satiris subducenda esse a manibus adolescencium ac . . . librum fastorum non esse legendum nonnullis placet': Haskins 1924: 372. See also Hexter 1986: 18.

[14] 'vir quem habundans literature pericia illustrauit morumque honestas apprime decorauit': John of Glastonbury 1985, ed. Carley: 164–5.

[15] Ralph of Dunstable, *Vita Albani*, prologue: 'pieridum ludis claustri laxare rigorem non est emeritae religionis opus'. See also McLeod 1980: 412.

[16] 'tantum declinaverunt musa, muse quod omnes musardi reputati sunt': Jocelin of Brakelond 1949, ed. Butler: 130.

[17] For Ovid in the twelfth-century schools, see Arnulf of Orléans 1932: 157–234. See also the authorities cited in Frank T. Coulson's essay in this collection pp. 50–5.

soon passed, and as patterns of grammar teaching were transformed (and rhetoric pushed to the margins), it is generally understood the greatest enthusiasm for Ovid was to be found only in the extra-clerical context of Guillaume de Lorris and Jean de Meun,[18] and in the following century, Geoffrey Chaucer and John Gower.[19] The success of the *Ovide moralisé* and Pierre Bersuire's *Ovidius moralizatus* between the Great Famine and Black Death and its aftermath may have caused a resurgence of the *Metamorphoses* (if not other works of Ovid) in clerical circles but not, it is thought, a general revival of their early enthusiasm.[20] Beryl Smalley read the fragments she recovered from the regulars of fourteenth-century England as the records of a failed renaissance.[21]

The conviction that the monasteries abandoned the classics, together with other of their early traditions, after the turn of the twelfth century has proved so persistent that many monastic manuscripts and fragments from the thirteenth, fourteenth and fifteenth centuries remain unexamined even today. While the culture of continental convents in these centuries is still uncharted territory,[22] however, recent research has brought their English counterparts into sharper focus. The recovery of catalogues and other inventories of books and book collections, for the first time, has made it possible properly to assess the intellectual resources of the monasteries in the later Middle Ages.[23] As important as the institutional inventories are the two extant union catalogues (for want of a better term), which, after painstaking analysis, now enable us to construct a conspectus of the holdings of monasteries at the beginning and the end of the fourteenth century.[24] These discoveries have coincided with the publication of catalogues, hand-lists and *repertoria*, which have drawn attention to the textual

---

[18] Horgan 1994; Strubel 1984.

[19] For Chaucer's knowledge of Ovid see Minnis 1982; Fyler 1979. For Gower's knowledge of Ovid see Harbert 1988: 83–97.

[20] For the *Ovide moralisé* see ed. de Boer 1915–38. The classic study of the text remains Engels 1943. See also Lord 1975: 161–75; Jung 1996b: 75–98; Delaney 1999. For Bersuire's *Ovidius* see the pioneering efforts of Engels 1968: 102–7; (1969): 73–78; (1971): 19–24. See also Coulson 1997a: 164–86; Rivers, 2006: 92–100. The text awaits a critical edition.

[21] Smalley 1960: 5.

[22] Recent studies of the books and book collections of French monasteries have focused rather on the Renaissance period, or later, e.g. Le Minor 2002; Bondéelle-Souchier 2000–6; the late medieval manuscripts of German monasteries have attracted greater attention, e.g., Rothe 1977; Freckmann 2006; in neither case, however, has there been a synthetic study.

[23] See, for example, Bell 1995; Sharpe *et al.* 1996; Watson and Webber 1998; Stoneman 1999; Friis-Jensen and Willoughby 2001.

[24] Rouse and Rouse 1991; Rouse and Rouse 2005: a re-working of Professor R. H. Rouse's PhD dissertation (1963). The interpretation of this latter document has evolved over more than fifty years, and a number of other scholars have contributed to the process, e.g. Mynors 1957: 199–217. Ovid is witnessed at two libraries (Bury St Edmund's, Aldgate): Rouse and Rouse, 2005: 412 (376–8).

discoveries that might be made in late medieval manuscripts of monastic provenance.[25] At the same time, a number of new (and *ab initio*) editions of monastic texts of this period have served to underline the intellectual vigour, and originality, still to be found in the English monasteries of the fourteenth, and even the fifteenth centuries.[26] The sources bear witness to studies in a wide variety of disciplines. The influence of the schools is striking.[27] Yet there is also evidence of a return to earlier monastic traditions, to hagiography, historiography and, to an extent that eclipses these others, the *studia litterarum*. In a cross-section of English cloisters it seems readers revisited the literary landmarks so familiar to their forebears, and looked upon some with a new intensity; Ovid especially.

* * * * * * *

The assumption that classical studies faded fast from European cloisters has always been underpinned by the impression that after 1300 the monasteries no longer maintained their scriptoria, played a significant role in the transmission of texts, nor curated their book collections with the watchfulness which in earlier centuries had ensured the survival of so many ancient codices.[28] In the climate of reform that prevailed after 1215, it is often suggested the neglect of early books was reinforced by a narrowing of monastic attitudes to secular literature, and the pagan classics in particular.[29] Such views owe much to the testimony of the early humanists, for whom the monasteries' contempt for books was both an article of faith and a disingenuous defence against their own dubious conduct.[30] Theirs was a trope retailed as frequently in England as it was in Europe, perhaps first by Richard de Bury (*c.* 1345), but subsequently by Thomas Gascoigne (*c.* 1440), and most memorably by John Leland (1536).[31] The recently

---

[25] For example, Sharpe 1997: which brings into focus a number of hitherto unnoticed monastic authors of the post-Black Death period. See also the succession of new, or revised catalogues of the medieval manuscripts of the cathedrals and university colleges, which are rich in monastic material, for example: Thomson 2001; Watson 1999; Hanna 2002. A new online catalogue of the medieval manuscripts of Queen's College, Oxford was published in 2004: www.queens.ox.ac.uk/library/ms.

[26] For example, John of Glastonbury 1985; Henry Knighton 1995; Thomas Walsingham 2003. See also Siegfried Wenzel's valuable calendar of monastic sermon collections of the fourteenth and fifteenth centuries, 2005: 403–671 (calendar from 409).

[27] See, for example, Greatrex 1991: 555–83; 1990: 213–25; 1994: 396–411; Dobson 1991: 151–72; Coates 1999: 87–107; Thomson 2007.

[28] For example, 'the isolation and inaccessibility of texts in various monasteries' asserted by Sweeney 1971: 29–36 at 31.

[29] For example: 'copies of the *Ars* and *Amores* were . . . destroyed, as many a zealous abbot, solicitous for the morals of his monks, weeded out the cankerous volume from his library', wrote Buttenwieser 1940: 45–51 at 50 n. 25.

[30] The classic instance is the correspondence of Niccolò Niccoli and Poggio Bracciolini, as especially the latter searched monastic libraries north of the Alps: Gordan 1974: 31–77 at 34–6, 42, 46.

[31] Richard de Bury 1950: 90–1; Gascoigne 1881: 72–3 at 73; Hearne 1715, vol. III: 60.

recovered, and rediscovered, books and book-lists, however, have cast a very different impression of the condition of monastic collections in this period, one not primarily of neglect but of a new vitality. Monastic libraries grew, in some cases on a grand scale.[32] Some houses initiated a programme of stocking, or re-stocking, into which substantial institutional resources were diverted.[33] There are also indications of at least a partial return to in-house book production.[34] Collections were reorganised (rationalised even) and there is no doubt that books, some of them early ones, were loaned or removed, frequently for sale.[35] Clearly they were also subject to the same dangers (fire, theft) that had always threatened them, but instances of deliberate destruction or dispersal of manuscripts are rare and should be set alongside the rising number of books now donated by patrons, both clerical and lay.[36] One obvious consequence of these trends was the new prominence of academic authors and texts in English cloisters.[37] Yet it seems they also served to bring earlier texts, and textual traditions, to a new audience. After a century and a half of comparative obscurity, the Latin classics were once again distributed in significant numbers throughout the community, in the cloister (carrels and cupboards), the *librarium* and the *camera* of the monks.

The works of Ovid themselves assumed a prominence in this period per-haps greater than they had ever known, at least among English monks. Only a partial impression of the favour they enjoyed in the fourteenth and fif-teenth centuries is provided by the surviving library documents themselves. The catalogues from the Benedictine houses at Dover (dated 1389) and Peterborough (before 1400) record copies of each of the principal works – the amatory poetry, *Fasti*, *Tristia* and the *Metamorphoses* and some pseu-doepigrapha, but nothing more perhaps than one might have expected to find in their foundation collection.[38] Likewise, the catalogue of the

---

[32] For example, Christ Church Cathedral Priory, Canterbury, the earliest (*s*. xii) extant catalogue of which records 200 books, and the latest (*s*. xv*ex.*) 1800. The expansion, diversification and subdivision of book-collections are also attested at, among other houses, Durham, Evesham, Glastonbury, St Albans and Westminster: Sharpe *et al.* 1996: B30 (Evesham); B43 (Glastonbury); Norwich (B57–8); B86–90 (St Albans) 138–48; 220–32, 293–304, 553–84. For Durham see Raine 1838: 10–116.

[33] A post-1300 programme of purchases is evident at Glastonbury, and Norwich Cathedral Priory was re-stocked after a devastating fire in 1272: Carley and Coughlan 1981: 498–514; Ker 1949: 1–28; Sharpe *et al.* 1996: B43 (220–32).

[34] For example: Dobson 1973: 377–8; Carley 1988: 138–44 at 138–41; Coates 1999: 61–86; Gransden 1998: 228–85; Clark 2004: 79–123.

[35] Piper 1978: 213–49; Clark 2004: 79–123. See also Sharpe *et al.* 1996: B27 (Ely) (129–30).

[36] See, for example, Sharpe *et al.* 1996: B18 (Thomas Lexham); B21 (Richard of Chester) (101–2, 106–7).

[37] See, for example, Dobson 1973: especially 375–6; Piper (1978): 213–49; Coates 1999: 87–107; Thomson 2007: *passim*.

[38] Stoneman 1999: BM1. 203e, 397a, 403a, b, 410c, 418 (106, 157, 159, 162, 164); Friis-Jensen and Willoughby 2001: B21. 95b, 97c, 127gh, l, 142ab, c, x, 143a, 144b, 145a (91–2, 102, 108–9).

Augustinian abbey at Leicester (1477 × 1494, but a summation of earlier acquisitions) records single copies of each of the known works, including the comparatively scarce *Heroides*, but no multiple copies, and the catalogue from the Cistercian abbey at Titchfield (*c.* 1400) contains only the staple schoolroom texts.[39] These lists offer few surprises but at least it might be inferred from them that the monasteries' early (i.e. pre-1200) collections of Ovid remained largely intact even at the beginning of the fifteenth century. Another document from the early fifteenth century might indicate that early copies not only remained on the shelves in many houses but were also consciously redeployed to meet the demand of a new generation of readers. In an indenture of *c.* 1396 × 1420, the custodian of the library at St Albans Abbey recalled a group of books that had been on permanent loan to the dependent priory at Hertford, among them a copy of the *Fasti*.[40] This generation of St Albans monks also sought to make good the losses suffered by their library in earlier decades, recovering several early manuscripts of classical texts (works of Ovid possibly amongst them) previously sold to the bishop of Durham.[41] An early twelfth-century manuscript from St Swithun's Priory, Winchester, bears witness to this process of recovery and re-use: the codex, an anthology of poetry containing the pseudo-Ovid *Nux*, was glossed and repaginated in the fourteenth century and finally re-bound (in red leather) in the first half of the fifteenth century.[42] The indications of early books being re-commissioned to meet the demand from a new generation of readers might be corroborated further by the migration of two Ovid manuscripts from their monastic home in the period after 1350: Oxford, Balliol College, MS 142 (*s.* xii), originated at Westminster Abbey and quite probably reached Oxford in the hands of a student monk to whom it had been assigned; Eton College, MS 91 (*s.* xiii), which may have belonged to the library at Christ Church, Canterbury, passed into the library at Winchester College at some point after 1400; again the point of contact may have been Oxford where both institutions maintained a *studium* (i.e. Canterbury College, and New College).[43]

The signs of change are perhaps more conspicuous in the records of the monks' own book collections. The catalogue of the library at St Augustine's

---

[39] Watson and Webber 1998: A20.1053 (Leicester: 303); Bell 1995: P6.144c, d (221). See also McKinley 1998: 41–86 at 58, 67.

[40] Sharpe *et al.* 1996: B86 (552–3).   [41] Walsingham 1867–9: II. 200.

[42] Oxford, Bodl., Auct. MS F 2 14, fols. 104r–107v.

[43] Mynors 1963: 121; Ker *et al.* 1969–2002: ii.705–7. Ker suggested a Canterbury provenance for the Eton manuscript on the grounds that it carries the title 'omnes libros Ovidii', as did the volume recorded in the early fourteenth-century catalogue of the library at Christ Church: James 1903: 72 (no. 632). There are no marks of provenance on the manuscript. The extant marginalia, much of it fourteenth-century, is indicative of intensive use prior to its migration to Winchester.

Abbey, Canterbury, compiled in the final quarter of the fifteenth century, offers a conspectus of new accessions over the preceding century and half, many of which were books assimilated from the personal libraries of past monks. Among its 1800 entries are the collections of three scholars active between the first and final quarters of the fourteenth century. No fewer than three manuscripts of the *Metamorphoses* were recorded as the former property of one John of London whose status, monastic or secular remains unresolved, although his ties to the abbey are clear. One of these codices held a prose summary, with incipit 'Cum omnis generi humani eiusdem . . .'[44] A near-contemporary, William Welde, who had studied as a monk at Oxford and subsequently served as abbot (1387–1405), also owned a copy of the *Metamorphoses*.[45] Another graduate, John Hawkhurst (*fl.* 1400), owned a number of anthologies of Latin poetry and prose, which included copies of *Amores*, *Remedia amoris* and the pseudonymous *De cuculo*.[46] John of London's multiple copies are suggestive of a critical approach to author and text; the prose *Metamorphoses* perhaps served him as a digest of the original poetry. He was not the only clerk of the period in this context to acquire, or compile for himself an Ovid 'reader'. William Seton, a monk of Durham Priory active in the first half of the fifteenth century, made his own anthology of Ovidian works, including an *accessus* to Ovid and copies of the pseudonymous *De vetula*, and the *Ovidius moralizatus* of Pierre Bersuire, a work which, like John of London's prose, served as a surrogate for the *Metamorphoses* itself.[47] There appears to have been a general interest in the shorter works and *pseudo-epigrapha* among monastic readers of this generation. Seton's book was one of two containing *De vetula* to enter Durham Priory after 1350.[48] Copies of *De cuculo*, *Nux* and *De pulice* entered the Canterbury collection under Prior Henry Eastry (*d.* 1331), perhaps the gift of Prior Eastry himself.[49] Some personal acquisitions of the period suggest a positively antiquarian interest in the scarcest texts and the earliest copies. A late twelfth-century manuscript containing, among other

[44] James 1903: 366 (no. 1453). John of London's manuscript survives as Cambridge, St John's College, D 22 (97). See also Coulson and Roy 2000: 80, 45. For the enigma surrounding John of London see Knorr 2004.
[45] James 1903: 366 (no. 1455, second folio, 'os homini').   [46] James 1903: 368 (no. 1480).
[47] Cambridge, Sidney Sussex College, MS 56 (Δ.3.11): *De vetula* is at 149–65, *Ovidius moralizatus* at 175–330: Seton's signature, 'quod Willelmus Seton . . .' is given in the colophon of several texts, e.g., 170, 330; Seton copied the text from 145–382. The codex passed into the personal libraries of a succession of Durham monks: William Law added a table of contents on the verso of the front flyleaf; it passed to Richard Bell, prior of Durham, who bequeathed it to the conventual library. See Coulson and Roy 2000: 167, 63.
[48] See also Cambridge, Jesus College, MS 70 (Q. G. 22) (*s.* xv^in.), fols. 111r–22r; Coulson and Roy 2000: 167, 318, 400 (63, 98, 116).
[49] James 1903: 72 (no. 632). N. R. Ker observed a similarity between the codex in this catalogue entry and the extant Eton College, MS 91 (*s.* xiii).

texts, *Ex Ponto* was acquired, apparently for 16d, by William Coverdale, a fifteenth-century monk of St Mary's Abbey, York.[50] The early twelfth-century *Metamorphoses* at Westminster Abbey before 1487, may have been the acquisition of the monk, Richard Teddington, who died in that year.[51] An early twelfth-century manuscript fragment of the *Heroides* bought by Hugh Legat (*fl.* 1410) as a gift for his conventual library at St Albans may not have been the first copy to enter the collection but was perhaps prized for its scheme of early glosses.[52] It was perhaps a similar impulse that persuaded William Charyte (*fl.* 1439 × 1502), canon prior and precentor of Leicester Abbey, to purchase a twelfth-century text of the *Fasti.*[53] These acquisitions cluster around the turn of the fourteenth century, but the interest of monastic readers in manuscript copies of the classics endured perhaps even a century later; a composite manuscript containing the *Remedia amoris* and brought together by the Carmelite Nicholas Cantelowe (d. 1441) had passed into the library at Worcester Priory by (and probably before) *c.* 1530, when the convent's usual label was pasted onto the back cover.[54]

These fragments suggest that in some late medieval English monasteries at least, knowledge of Ovid extended beyond the standard works in the standard repertories. Works which had been missing, or were underrepresented, in earlier times, were sought out or supplemented. In addition to Charyte's early copy of *Fasti*, the Leicester canons also acquired *Heroides* (a work still lacking in some collections) and as many as four copies of the *Metamorphoses.*[55] Although sketchy in their descriptions, catalogue entries hint at some significant rarities. The scale and scope of the codex recorded at Canterbury in the time of Prior Eastry was surely not commonplace: catalogued as 'omnes libros Ovidii', a title perhaps displayed on the horn label on the front board, it contained as many as thirteen works, of which one third were *pseudo-epigrapha.*[56] John Wheathampstead of St Albans clearly consulted 'omnes libros Ovidii' for the extracts in his *Pabularium poetarum.*[57]

Another measure of the renewed enthusiasm for Ovid among monastic readers is the quantity of 'Ovidiana', i.e. the *accessus*, epitomes, commentaries and other forms of critical apparatus that were now to be found in their anthologies. The *accessus* had assisted readers of Ovid since the

---

[50] London, BL, Burney MS 220 (*s.* xii^ex.): fols. 33r–46v. See also McKinley 1998: 71.
[51] Oxford, Balliol MS 142 (*s.* xii^in.).
[52] Oxford, Bodl., Rawlinson MS G 99 (*s.* xii): fols. 21r–65v. Legat's *exdono* is at fol. ix ult.
[53] Edinburgh, National Library of Scotland, Advocates Library, MS 18 5 13 (*s.* xii). See also Buttenwieser 1940: 45–51 at 47; Cunningham 1973: 64–90; Watson & Webber 1998: 107.
[54] Worcester Cathedral Library, MS Q 55 (*s.* xiii, xiv). See also Thomson 2001: 154.
[55] Watson and Webber 1998: A20. 1027–31; 1053 (301, 303).   [56] James 1903: 72 (no. 632).
[57] BL, Egerton MS 646, fos. 1r–117r, incorporating an entry on the poet himself at fos. 49v–50r.

eleventh century, but the number surviving in later medieval manuscripts suggests it was in the century after 1350 that they achieved their widest circulation. There are examples found in almost every one of the surviving literary compendia known to have been connected with a monastic reader. William Seton copied two *accessus* into his anthology.[58] Another Durham anthology of this period contains an *accessus* to Ovid and a preface to the pseudo-Ovid *De vetula*.[59] John Wylde (*fl.* 1460), a canon of Waltham Abbey, added (stitched) a bi-folium containing an *accessus* to an anthology that also included a prose summary of the *Metamorphoses* and the only surviving copy of Thomas Walsingham's *Dites ditatus*.[60] John of London appended a series of *accessus* to his prose *Metamorphoses* in Cambridge, St John's D 22 (97).[61] The interest among monastic readers in the *accessus* tradition was perhaps an impulse in the St Albans monk Thomas Walsingham's collection of *accessus* to twenty-nine Latin authors (Ovid amongst them), the *Prohemia poetarum*.[62] Not only *accessus*, but also examples of early commentaries attracted the interest of this generation of monastic readers. An anonymous Worcester monk of the fourteenth century recovered an early (*s.* xii[ex.]) probably French copy of Arnulf of Orléans's commentary on *Fasti* and combined it with a copy of the Sentences of Peter Lombard; indeed of the ten surviving copies of Arnulf's commentary, the majority are of English origin.[63]

Readers were clearly also drawn to the rich, and expanding, variety of commentaries on the *Metamorphoses* and on the mythographical tradition which it represented. John of Garland's *Integumenta* is not attested in any contemporary monastic library catalogue, but it does feature in surviving anthologies compiled by monastic readers.[64] There was perhaps something of a resurgence of interest in Fulgentius' *Mitologiae*, a work which the catalogue evidence would suggest had not always been widely available. George Penshurst, abbot of St Augustine's, Canterbury (1430–57), gave (or bequeathed) a copy to his conventual library, one of two copies that appear in the late fifteenth-century catalogue, both perhaps acquisitions intended

---

[58] Cambridge, Sidney Sussex, 56 (Δ. 3. 11): 165–70.

[59] Cambridge, Jesus College, MS 70 (*s.* xv[in.]): fols. 111v–119v.

[60] Oxford, Bodl., Rawlinson B 214 (*c.* 1460): fols. 200r–201v; Coulson and Roy 2000: 419 (122). See also Rigg 1977: 281–330; Coulson 1998: 122–3.

[61] James 1903: 366 (no. 1453).

[62] Walsingham's *Prohemia* survives uniquely in BL, Harley MS 2693, fols. 131r–177r; Coulson and Roy 2000: 319 (99).

[63] Worcester Cathedral Library, MS Q 88, fols. 153r–160r. See also Thomson, 2001: 179–80 at 179.

[64] See, for example, Oxford, Bodl., Auct. MS F 5 16 (Worcester Cathedral Priory: *s.* xiv): 161–204; Oxford, Bodl., Digby MS 104 (Coventry Cathedral Priory: *s.* xiii[ex.]): fols. 161r–167r; See also Coulson and Roy 2000: no. 257, 333, (83–4, 101–2).

to meet a contemporary demand.[65] Contemporary, or near contemporary, criticism also attracted close attention in the cloister. Generally the work of the early fourteenth-century 'classicising' friars – Robert Holcot, Thomas Waleys – appears to have had little impact upon the literary scholarship of the monks, but John Ridevall's re-casting of Fulgentius was widely circulated, a product again of the popularity of the *Metamorphoses*.[66]

The monks were also perhaps the first English scholars to show an interest in the *Ovidius moralizatus* of Pierre Bersuire, the final recension of which was complete by 1362. Certainly the text entered English circulation at an early date. It is first attested in a library catalogue of 1374 and the earliest surviving manuscript can be dated to within the same decade.[67] The majority of the extant English copies date from the half-century 1375–1425, an indication perhaps of the intense interest it aroused. The survivors include turn-of-the-century examples from the cathedral priories of Durham and Norwich and the Cistercian Abbey at Fountains.[68] Some of the unassigned survivors may also be of monastic provenance, such as Oxford, Bodl., Bodley MS 571, an anthology which combines the *Ovidius moralizatus* with Garland's *Integumenta* and one of the common prose summaries in circulation in England, and Worcester Cathedral Library, MS Q 93, a copy of Bersuire's *Reductorium morale*, incorporating the *Ovidius* as Book 15 of the larger text. These manuscripts show how rapidly Bersuire's apparatus came to shape monastic readings of Ovid: the surviving copies are not, generally, discrete codices, but appear alongside a repertory of texts associated with the *Metamorphoses* and its mythographic content. The status of the *Ovidius* is also attested in an anonymous commentary surviving in an early fifteenth-century anthology probably of monastic origin. The

---

[65] James 1903: 369 (no. 1484).

[66] See, for example, London, BL, Royal MS 7 C 1 (*s.* xiv) fols. 309ra–335rb: a book which belonged to, and was perhaps compiled by, William Kettering, a monk of Ramsey Abbey; Worcester Cathedral Library, MS 154 (*s.* xiv): fols. 26r–42r, an anthology compiled at Worcester Cathedral Priory, in which Ridevall's work was found together with pseudo-Alberic of London's *Mythologia* (i.e. Third Vatican Mythographer). For the reception of Holcot and Waleys, see Smalley 1960: 88–100, 133–48 at 146–7.

[67] A copy of the *Ovidius* was among books given to Merton College, Oxford from the library of Bishop William Rede of Chichester in 1374. See also Garrod and Highfield 1978: 9–19. Of the surviving English copies, perhaps the earliest was that copied by Adam Stocton, an Augustinian friar of the Cambridge convent, in the course of a preaching tour undertaken between *c.* 1375 and 1377 and incorporated in an anthology of his own compilation, now Dublin, Trinity College, MS 115, 55–154; Coulson and Roy: 2 (25).

[68] Cambridge, University Library, MS Ii 2 20 (*s.* xiv^ex.); Durham Cathedral Library, MS B iv 38 (Durham Cathedral Priory: *s.* xiv^ex.); London, BL, Add. MS 62132A (Fountains Abbey: *s.* xiv^ex.). See also Coulson and Roy 2000: no. 2 (24–5).

text in BL, Cotton, MS Titus D xx, an unattributed *Libellus deorum gentilium*, cites 'Waleys super fabulas Ovidii' as its principal source.[69] Bersuire's *Ovidius* appears to have eclipsed all other critical apparatus to Ovid in English cloisters; indeed it was regarded by some readers as a substitute for the text of the *Metamorphoses* itself.[70] It is worth noting there is no trace, textual or otherwise, of its near contemporary, the *Ovide moralisé*.[71]

The remarkable resurgence of interest in early eleventh- and twelfth-century Latin poetry and prose evident in English books of the period 1350–1400, might also be interpreted as a by-product of the growing popularity of Ovid in the monasteries. The *Ecloga* attributed to the pseudo-Theodolus, a mythographic manual of only minor importance in the schoolrooms of the eleventh and twelfth centuries, found a new audience in fourteenth-century England and appears to have been regarded not only as a companion reader to the *Metamorphoses*, but also as a guide both to the *materia* and the poetic style of ancient authors in general. An anthology dating from the turn of the fourteenth century, which may be of monastic provenance, and certainly contains material of monastic origin, combined the *Ecloga* with a fragment of the pseudo-Ovidian *De mirabilitus mundi*.[72] No fewer than four copies of the text were added to the library at St Augustine's Abbey, Canterbury, in the course of the fourteenth and fifteenth centuries, and in each case it was combined either with classical *originalia*, or preceptive texts on the *ars poetria*.[73]

The monks of late medieval England appear to have been far better equipped than their forebears for the reading and interpretation of Ovid, even perhaps than those of the monastic 'golden age'. Nonetheless it is worth noting that alongside a growing number of *originalia*, monastic readers also continued to come to Ovid at one (or more) remove from the original, through *lemmata*, and sometimes longer extracts, found in *florilegia*, or the themed collections of the *sententiae* that appear to have been more popular, for the purposes of preaching, in this period. St Peter's, Gloucester, was surely not the only monastery to possess at least one anthology whose flyleaves were clustered with verses from a wide variety of Latin authors: the Gloucester example contains scribbled extracts from the *Tristia*.[74] The appearance of Ovid alongside Seneca in a collection of

---

[69] BL, Cotton Titus D xx, (s. xv^in.): fols. 97r–104v, 'Waleys' cited, for example, at 103v, 104v.
[70] In the *explicit* to his copy of the *Ovidius*, Adam Stocton identified the text as 'liber Ovidii metamorphoseos': Dublin, Trinity College, 115, 154.
[71] A single copy of a French vernacular *Metamorphoses* survives in a manuscript owned originally by the monks of Norwich Cathedral Priory, and now London, BL, Cotton MS Julius F VII, fols. 6r–13v.
[72] Oxford, Bodl., Digby MS 100 (s. xiv^ex.) fols. 75r–112r (text r and commentary from 76r).
[73] James (1903): 360, 368 (nos. 1408, 1478–9).
[74] Hereford Cathedral Library, MS P I 15 (s. xii^med.): fols. ii–iv^v at iii^r.

moral *dicta* (BL, Royal MS 7 C I: Ramsey Abbey) may have been typical, but might also be encountered by monastic readers in the guise of medical *magister* in a compendium concerning the natural sciences (BL, Royal MS 12 F xv: Bury St Edmunds). The diversity, and instability, of the sources of Ovid in use in English cloisters in this period are underlined by occasional quotations incorporated in other monastic narratives. Even Thomas Walsingham, himself the author of a commentary on the *Metamorphoses*, clumsily misquoted the text in a laboured image in his *Chronica maiora*.[75]

* * * * * * *

The growing interest in Ovid and *Ovidiana* among monastic readers was generated by variety of intellectual impulses. The return to Ovid, as to other classical authors and texts, was at least in part a product of a new approach to elementary education. Reforms of the thirteenth and early fourteenth centuries had required the monasteries in England to make more formal provision for the teaching of grammar in the cloister, not only to prepare the ablest novices for academic study in the schools, but also to provide the majority with the requisite skills to fulfil their routine liturgical, pastoral and administrative responsibilities. It appears their response was to improvise a syllabus of studies which in some of its essentials resembled patterns of teaching in the earliest monastic schoolrooms. The curriculum authors were again made the mainstay of the novice manuals, and the poetry and prose of the pagan classics (alongside those of the early Middle Ages) served again as 'readers', a source of grammatical paradigms and a test of reading proficiency. Several of the attested and surviving manuscripts containing works of Ovid were evidently prepared for such a purpose. A codex recorded in the catalogue of Christ Church, Canterbury, joined elementary dictionaries and glossaries (Papias' *Elementarium*, John of Genoa's [Johannes Balbus] *Catholicon*) with unspecified extracts from Ovid entitled 'gramatica Ovidii'.[76] It seems it was the *materia* of Ovid, as much as his style, which monastic instructors understood to be particularly useful for their pupils. Thus it seems even the surrogate Ovids might serve: a turn-of-the-century anthology from Fountains Abbey combined grammars and a guide to the compilation of charters with a copy of Bersuire's *Ovidius*.[77] It is worth noting when the St Albans monk, Thomas Walsingham (*c.* 1340–1422), first compiled his commentary on the *Metamorphoses*, he offered it to his brethren as a companion to their studies in the 'subtleties of grammar'.[78]

Ovid was now recruited not only as a grammar reader but also as a guide to the principles of rhetoric. The cloister curriculum of this period appears

---

[75] Galbraith 1937: 9.   [76] James 1903: 158 (no. 159).
[77] BL, Add 62132A, fols. 4r–17v, 18r–53v, 199v–204r.
[78] London, BL, Lansdowne MS 728, fols 16r–175v at fol. 40r. See also Engels 1968: 103.

to have given far greater emphasis to the *ars rhetorici* than in contemporary secular schools, still less the arts course of the universities.[79] This must reflect the monks' rediscovery of their own tradition of the *studia litterarum*, although it might also be seen as a response to the practical imperative to provide proficient proctors and preachers. The amatory poetry, the *Metamorphoses* and the pseudonymous *De vetula* all appear in anthologies of the period bound together with well-known guides to rhetoric, rhetorical colours, etc. There were two such collections recorded in the fifteenth-century catalogue from St Augustine's, Canterbury, one combining *De vetula* with Geoffrey of Vinsauf's *Poetria nova*, the other obscure extracts 'principium misteriorum librorum Ovidii' and an unspecified liber 'de coloribus rethoricis'.[80]

The monks of this period not only studied the rhetoric of the poets *per se*, but were also encouraged, and, it seems, sometimes required, to master its practical application in the *ars dictaminis*. The growing burden of routine administration in the monastery, and the great expansion of litigation over both their spiritual and temporal properties, appear to have persuaded convents to incorporate the *ars dictaminis* in their cloister curriculum. There is an account from the early fourteenth century of a young monk being dispatched to a distant priory for the expressed purpose of studying *dictamen*, so that he might compose conventual letters 'as well as any from the papal chancery'.[81] Given the subject of some of their model letters – from an abbot to a prior, from a novice to his novice-master, etc. – it seems probable that the secular schools of *dictamen* also accepted monks as their students.[82] In the cloister, the students of *dictamen* were equipped with a wide variety of preceptive treatises, from twelfth- and thirteenth-century authorities, such as Geoffrey of Vinsauf and Thomas of Capua, to the contemporary textbooks of London and Oxford masters, such as John Leyland and Thomas Sampson.[83] As the manuscript evidence attests, these works were combined with examples of the Latin classics. Ovid was a popular companion text, if not the only one. William Seton's Durham codex containing *De vetula* and Bersuire's *Ovidius* opened with the *Tria sunt* of Geoffrey of Vinsauf.[84] A manuscript from Dover Priory, which appears to have been prepared as a dictaminal manual, combined the

---

[79] For the curricula of contemporary grammar schools see Orme 2006: 86–127. For the curriculum of the arts courses at Oxford and Cambridge see Fletcher 1992: 315–45.

[80] James 1903: 366 (no. 1456).   [81] Walsingham 1867–9, vol. II: 374; See also Clark 2004: 42–78.

[82] Camargo 1991: 37–41 at 37; 1995: 20–32 at 25–7; Clark 2004: 214.

[83] See, for example, Sharpe *et al.* 1996: B10.107; B76. 13b (32, 463); Watson and Webber 1998: A17. 46; A20. 829c (101, 265); Bell 1995: P6. 171g, 207c, 218b (236, 248, 251).

[84] Cambridge, Sidney Sussex, 56 (Δ. 3. 11): 1–148.

Metamorphoses with the work of Peter of Blois on epistolary *amicitia* and a sequence of sample letters from conventual and diocesan sources.[85] The monks' use of Ovid, and other classical authors, as models for epistolary style was in tune with changing approaches to the art among contemporary dictaminal masters. The generation of masters active at the turn of the fourteenth century appears to have abandoned the established teaching method, founded on 'real' or quasi 'real' documents which modelled the various forms of address, in favour of literary paradigms culled from classical (and later) Latin literature.[86] The monks became eager advocates of this approach: one turn-of-the-century Benedictine, Thomas Merke, of Westminster Abbey, composed his own *Formula moderni et usitati dictaminis*, in which many of the paradigms were drawn from the works of Ovid.[87]

Ovid was the pre-eminent master of the schoolroom for the monks of this time, as he had been for their forebears. Yet what set this period apart from the monastic 'golden age' was the extent to which Ovid also became a preoccupation for readers past their probation, engaged in the professional occupations of the senior monk – preaching, pastoral care – or pursuing self-determined programmes of private study. For many of these mature readers, Ovid was a source of, and stimulus for, moral reflection. Extracts from the canon had always found a place in collections of moral *dicta* and *exempla*, and from the first, the commentators, from Arnulf of Orléans, to John of Garland and John Ridevall, had privileged the moral readings of Ovid's *materia*. The commentary on the *Metamorphoses* composed by Walter of Peterborough, monk of Revesby, in the middle years of the fourteenth century was apparently overtly moralistic in its approach: Walter recalled his work in a panegyric to the Black Prince, claiming he had scrutinised (*vigilavi*) the pagan fables for the honour of the Church.[88] In the second half of the fourteenth century, however, it was the *Ovidius moralizatus* of Pierre Bersuire that served as the principal guide, and model, for monastic readers. The work was frequently combined not only with the *Metamorphoses* but also – for example, in William Seton's anthology – with other works in the canon, including *pseudo-epigrapha*. It also inspired readers' own rudimentary attempts at textual analysis, serving as the model for several prose summaries, and tables of Ovidian *fabulae* preserved in manuscripts of monastic provenance. Monastic readers shared

---

[85] Stoneman 1999: BMI. 203 (106).   [86] Camargo 1995: esp. 24–6, 122–41, 169–221.

[87] Camargo 1995: 105–47 (text 122–41); Ovid at 145. See also Sharpe 1997: 668–9.

[88] Wright 1859–61, vol. I: 97–122 at 98. See also Sharpe 1997: 739. Sharpe records Walter's work as lost but A. G. Rigg identifies it as the prose rendering of *Metamorphoses* preserved in Oxford, Bodl., Rawlinson B 214, fols. 203r–233r, an identification accepted by Coulson and Roy 2000: 290, 92.

the moral imperative of Bersuire, but it was a measure of how detached many of them remained from the culture of the schools that their own readings of the *Metamorphoses*, and other works, owed less to formal theological discourse than to traditional monastic homiletics. The glosses in William Seton's copy of the *Ovidius moralizatus* cluster around expositions of specifically monastic interest, such as the exemplum of an abbot and a monk (8.2), and those expositions that transmit the kind of casual misogyny that was the stock-in-trade of monastic moralisation.[89] In his own exposition of the *Metamorphoses*, which owed much to Bersuire, Thomas Walsingham eschewed the Frenchman's overtly theological expositions but retained those which referenced monastic religion.[90] As he explained in his preface, Walsingham intended his *Archana deorum* to guide the independent reading of individual monks; William's Seton's octavo volume was also prepared for private study.[91]

There were perhaps a growing number of monastic readers of this period, however, for whom the moral exposition of Ovid served a practical purpose, in the preparation of sermons. The fourteenth century saw an expansion in monastic preaching in England, as, under their own capitular and papal reforms, the monasteries were required to engage lectors (as in any secular cathedral); the growth of graduate monks with the advent of the monastic *studia* at Oxford also projected a greater number into the ranks of the episcopate.[92] A number of substantial sermon collections of monastic origin survive from the century 1350–1450, and among other features, they make regular recourse to exempla derived from classical sources.[93] The works of Ovid were an obvious favourite. The Benedictine Bishop of Rochester, Thomas Brinton (1373–89), whose sermons delivered in both public and monastic contexts survive in a single manuscript, showed a particular preference for the *Metamorphoses*, and incorporated fables in no fewer than four sermons.[94] He employs the figure of Narcissus twice to exemplify the sin of pride; in another sermon the parentage of Hercules provides an allegory for the affiliation of the ecclesiastic or religious ('virum

[89] Cambridge, Sidney Sussex 56 (Δ. 3. 11): 234, 280, 287.
[90] Clark 2004: 163–208. The text of one recension of Walsingham's *Archana* was transcribed by Van Kluyve, Walsingham 1968.
[91] Walsingham 1968: 3; Cambridge, Sidney Sussex MS 56 (Δ. 3. 11). Seton's codex is cluttered with glosses, the legacy of the three, or more, fifteenth-century monks who in turn took possession of the anthology.
[92] For these developments see Greatrex 1994: 396–411; Clark 2004: 42–78.
[93] For these collections see Wenzel 2005: 26–30, 45–9, 66–73, 84–90, 151–8, 278–87; Wenzel (1995a): 127–43.
[94] Devlin 1954, vol. I: 31, 41, 56, 107, 220; vol. II: 489.

ecclesiasticum vel religiosum') to God the Father and to Mother Church; in a fourth the fleet-footed virgin Atalanta is 'anima Christiana... hec anima est tante agilitatis quod affectibus et cogitacionibus nunc est Rome nunc est Avinione, nunc in terra nunc in cello, nunc in paradiso, nunc in inferno' (the Christian spirit of such vigour that in spirit and understanding it is at once at Rome, Avignon, earth and the heavens, paradise and the inferno); three of the four appear to have been addressed to Brinton's own monastic community at Rochester, a reason perhaps for the preference for moral readings which carried (at the moment the papacy descended into schism) a clear contemporary resonance.[95] Brinton was a scholar of some stature, and although his exposition of the *Metamorphoses* is reminiscent of Bersuire, there are no direct borrowings and he appears to have worked from the *Metamorphoses* itself. Bersuire's *Ovidius* did serve as a surrogate Ovid for other monastic preachers. Hugh Legat, a monk of St Albans already noted, appears to cite Bersuire directly in one of his (macaronic) sermons, which refers to the figure of Apollo, as expounded in *De formis figurisque deorum*.[96] The reading of Ovid in this context is also suggested by the arrangement of a (now lost) anthology from the library of Christ Church, Canterbury: the volume was labelled 'sermones diebus festiuis per annum' and in addition to 'sermones diversorum doctorum' also contained 'notule psalterii' and a copy of the *Remedia amoris*.[97] In fact by the beginning of the fifteenth century, an obsession with Ovidian exempla may have become a marker of monastic sermon for English audiences: one anonymous text from a collection connected with Worcester Cathedral Priory opened with the apology 'I saye noght at I red in ouidie...Vor þe last tyme þat I was her ich was blamyd of som men word because þat I began my sermon wyt a poysy.'[98]

Clearly there were many monastic readers of this period whose enthusiasm for Ovid, as for other classical authors, carried with it the same caveats, the same eagerness to clothe the pagan fables with moral teaching, as the early commentators. Yet there are also indications in main text and margins of the surviving manuscripts of readers more inclined to suspend these sensibilities, and to engage critically with these texts. As with their approach to Bersuire, these monastic readers did not conform closely to contemporary trends in literary criticism. There is scarcely a

---

[95] Devlin 1954, vol. I: 41 (Atalanta): 56 (Hercules) 220 (Narcissus); vol. II: 489 (Narcissus).
[96] 'Thus auteres þat treten *de picturis deorum* tellen þat Apollo deus sapientie, was peyntid with a bowe & an arwe in his on hond, an harpe in his oþur & on is heuid a chapelet with grene lori leues in tokeninge þat bi his wit & bi his discreciun...': *Three Middle English Sermons*, 1939: 13.
[97] James 1903: 69 (no. 592).   [98] *Three Middle English Sermons*, 1939: 22.

trace in the manuscripts of the strict analytical schema adopted by, for example, Nicholas Trevet (1275–1330) in his Senecan commentaries (which were widely circulated in late medieval England).[99] If monastic readers expressed any preference, it was for the categories of the earliest *accessus* and analytical prologues, examples of which they entered into their anthologies. Generally, however, their analyses followed no single scheme but drew freely from critical, historical and even further literary authorities. The distinctive character of Thomas Walsingham's 'commentaries' not only on Ovid but also on the matters of Alexander and of Troy, which has often been depicted as detached from the contemporary trends, was in fact quite typical of monastic criticism.[100] There are several other schemes of glosses, or short commentaries, preserved in monastic manuscripts of the period which share these characteristics: John Wylde, canon of Waltham, who did much to recover the remains of Walsingham's work, produced his own scheme of glosses on Ovid, and other classical works in his Rawlinson compendium; the author of an anonymous *Libellus deorum* preserved in BL, Cotton MS Titus D XX adopted the same approach, combining quotations from Bersuire's *Ovidius*, and other commentaries with extracts, and prose paraphrases, from the *Metamorphoses* and other classical and later Latin works.[101] This idiosyncratic approach to criticism surely reflects both the conservatism of monastic culture, and the uneven levels of learning in the late medieval English cloister. Yet it is worth noting that a number of these monastic readers of Ovid – those named, and those whose traces are preserved in the margins of manuscripts – were also receptive to the currents of classical learning emanating from Italy. John Wheathampstead (*c.* 1390–1465) of St Albans Abbey, a younger contemporary of Thomas Walsingham, incorporated references to Boccaccio's *Genealogia deorum gentilium* in a scheme of glosses on Ovidian themes incorporated in his *Palearium poetarum*; Wheathampstead also matched the humanists in the sheer scope of his Ovid references in this text and his *Pabularium*.[102] The *Genealogia* attracted the attention of a number of early monastic readers between the first and third quarters of the fifteenth century and was one of the first examples of the early humanists' Latin scholarship to enter English

[99] For Trevet as commentator see Smalley 1960: 58–65, 88–92; Minnis and Scott 1991: 318–20, 324–7.
[100] For discussion of Walsingham's techniques see Rigg 1992: 297–8.
[101] Oxford, Bodl., Rawlinson MS B 214; BL, Cotton MS Titus D XX (*s.* xv*ᶦⁿ·*). The latter manuscript is unprovenanced but its codicological features, and the contents of the anthology, are typical of a monastic book of this period.
[102] For Wheathampstead's *Palearium* see BL, Add. MS 26764. Boccaccio's *Genealogia* is cited, for example, at fol. 33v, in a gloss on Demogorgon, 'deorum omniun parens'. For Wheathampstead's compilations see also Sharpe 1997: 344–5.

cloisters. The progression from Ovid to Boccaccio is obvious in a codex from (and probably compiled at) Norwich Priory, which bears the *ex libris* of a fifteenth-century monk, Robert Yarmouth, where the *Genealogia* is combined with an original compilation of extracts from Ridevall's *Fulgentius metaforalis* and Bersuire's *Ovidius moralizatus*.[103]

* * * * * * *

A critical engagement with the works of Ovid, and a wider awareness of both early, and contemporary commentary traditions is most conspicuous in manuscripts connected with the 'great and solemn' monasteries of late medieval England, such as the Canterbury convents, Durham, Glastonbury, St Albans, Westminster and Worcester.[104] It was not only that these houses, both in their libraries and their sense of their intellectual heritage, best preserved the literary traditions of earlier centuries, but also that they had been profoundly affected by the reform movement of the late thirteenth and early fourteenth centuries. The reformers' prime concern was to create a cadre of graduate monks which might combat the growing influence of the mendicants and the secular clergy, but their rhetoric of a return *ad fontes* had encouraged a general reflection on the foundations of monastic culture, scholarly as well as spiritual, and their requirement to ready novices for university had made the return of the traditional schoolroom *auctores* to the cloister a practical necessity. The twin spectres of Wyclif and the papal schism perhaps provided the monks of these premier houses with a further rationale for their literary tastes, since Ovid (and others) might now serve both as a source, and a proving-ground, for their own rhetorical flourishes, particularly from the pulpit.

It is worth noting that the signs of resurgence of interest in Ovid, and other classical *auctores*, are also visible in several contemporary continental convents similarly affected by the spirit of monastic reform. The mid fifteenth-century revival of Clairvaux was signalled among other symptoms by a return to in-house book production. One of the most productive compilers and copyists of the period, Jean de Vepria, showed a particular interest in the Latin classics. One anthology, with Bersuire's *Ovidius moralizatus* as its centrepiece, is a close counterpart of William Seton's Durham codex.[105]

---

[103] The Norwich codex is now Norwich Cathedral Library, MS 2 (*s.* xv); the *Genealogia deorum* is at fols. 23r–152v, the extracts from Ridevall and Bersuire at, respectively, fols. 188r–189r, 190r–191r. Another copy of the *Genealogia* is preserved in Exeter Cathedral Library, MS 3529 (*s.* xv$^{ex.}$), fols. 1r–166v: a volume which passed from a fifteenth-century donor to St Augustine's Abbey, Canterbury. For both codices, see also Ker *et al.* 1969–2002, vol. II: 836–7; vol. III: 529–31.

[104] The phrase was employed by the royal commissioners during the dissolution of the monasteries (1536–40) to pinpoint the earliest and best endowed of the country's abbeys and cathedral priories.

[105] For Jean de Vepria and the manuscripts of fifteenth-century Clairvaux see Mews 2001: 8–15, 181–4.

A study of fifteenth-century manuscripts of the monasteries of the Nether-
lands might also suggest a connection between currents of monastic reform
and the revival of classical studies.[106] It may be a measure of how widespread
was this enthusiasm by the final quarter of the fifteenth century that a new
generation of monastic reformers (and the first fully to embrace *Christian
humanism*) were moved to stifle it. 'There are some monks', opined Abbot
Johann Tritheim of Sponheim [1466–1516], who [still] apply their minds to
the phantasms of the gentiles.'[107] His colleague and correspondent, Jacob
Wimpfeling (1450–1528) was more outspoken and specific in his condemnation: 'there are many among your monks who sometimes take delight
in the amorous writings of Ovid and in other exceedingly sordid epistles
and the like by pagan poets'.[108]

These criticisms recall the concerns of Abbot Nequam, and certainly
the place of Ovid in pre-Reformation cloister was not unlike that in the
monastic 'golden age'. His works returned to the reinvigorated schoolroom
and again served as a source of grammatical and rhetorical paradigms.
The appeal of his imagery and poetic style was perhaps heightened given
the greater importance attached to the practice of preaching. Moreover, the
monks of this period did not detach themselves from Ovid as they departed
the schoolroom. His works were a favourite among mature monastic readers. They were perhaps more prominent in their libraries than in centuries
past, and if the monasteries no longer played a direct role in the descent
of any text, the growing mobility of monastic manuscripts meant the
approach to Ovid of many clerical readers was still shaped by anthologies,
and critical apparatus, that originated in the cloister. For the majority of
monks, Ovid served as a source of routine historical and moral reflections,
but for a minority, at the turn of the fourteenth century, the exposition of
his works, and the *Metamorphoses* in particular, also encouraged an engagement with contemporary literary criticism, and even a brief encounter with
the literature of the early Renaissance.

---

[106] Oberman 1996: 151–65.   [107] Brann 1981: 135.
[108] Jacob Wimpfeling, *De vita et miraculis Johannis Gerson* (Paris, 1506) sig. B iv^r, cited in Brann 1981:
266.

CHAPTER 10

Gower and Chaucer
Readings of Ovid in late medieval England

Kathryn L. McKinley

If the Loire Valley was the centre of classical studies in thirteenth-century France and Ovid was widely represented in France both in Latin texts and in the vernacular up through the fifteenth century, England itself saw a modest but steady increase in the texts of Ovid between 1200 and 1500.[1] It has often been said that England lagged behind the Continent in terms of humanist activity; while this is no doubt true, one can nevertheless see copies of Ovid surfacing in many English libraries throughout the period. In medieval England, manuscript evidence reveals that there were many 'Ovids' from which to choose, whether Latin 'school texts', Latin prose summaries, or Latin or French moralised versions.[2] Since my essay will focus on John Gower's and Geoffrey Chaucer's engagements with Ovid's works, it is worth considering as well who else was reading and drawing upon Ovid in late medieval England. Ovid also appears, if fleetingly, in a wide array of types of writing from high to later medieval England, from chronologies to political writings, and finally, to literary works. In non-literary texts in medieval England Ovid is often present: the clerk William Fitz Stephen, for example, draws upon Ovid among other classical authors in his description of the city of London (1173–5), which was used as a preface to his life of Thomas Becket;[3] John of Salisbury also quotes from Ovid in the *Policraticus*, even at times to explain a Biblical verse.[4] Likewise, Boethius' *Consolation of Philosophy*, which was read and translated

---

[1] McKinley 1998: 41–85.

[2] In the fourteenth century, there are 8 copies of the *Metamorphoses* in England, with, in addition, eight *Met.* commentaries of different sorts; 7 copies of the *Fasti*, 8 of the *Epistulae ex Ponto*, 5 of the *Heroides*, 7 of the *Ibis*; and 2 of the *Ars amatoria*. Figures for the fifteenth century (which do not duplicate any of the above numbers) are respectively: *Met.*, 10; *Met.* commentaries, 14; *Fasti*, 1; *Epistulae ex Ponto*, 6; *Heroides*, 5; *Ibis*, 3; *Ars amatoria*, 5; McKinley 1998: 80.

[3] Gransden 1972: 46.

[4] Examples of quotes from Ovid in the *Policraticus*: Book 4: a couplet from Ovid's *Epistulae ex Ponto* 1.2.123–4; Book 6, brief references to *Ars amatoria* 2.233 and *Heroides* 4.75; Book 7: a twelve-line section from Ovid's *Fasti* 1.297–308; in Book 8, John glosses St Paul (Romans 7.11) with Ovid (*Ars amatoria* 3.4.17; 2.19.3) immediately afterwards.

in medieval England, contains quotations from Ovid's poetry.[5] In many cases these quotes may reflect use of *florilegia*; however, Ovid's verses and *topoi* are nevertheless frequently drawn into many forms of discourse in high and later medieval England.

Elsewhere in this collection James Clark shows that Ovid was widely read within late medieval English monastic culture; and Siegfried Wenzel demonstrates the frequency with which lines from 'the grete clerc Ovide'[6] could be heard in Latin sermons in fourteenth- and fifteenth-century England.[7] Chroniclers such as Matthew Paris (*c.* 1200–59) and Thomas Walsingham (*c.* 1340–1422) regularly quote from Ovid in annals; Walsingham himself was moved to write his own commentary on the *Metamorphoses*, the *Archana deorum*.[8] Ovid surfaces very rarely in the works of William Langland or the Gawain-poet; his influence can be seen perhaps to a greater extent in some of the Middle English romances, such as *Sir Orfeo*, *Floris and Blancheflour*, and others which employ the ubiquitous Ovidian arts of courtly love. Of all the Ricardian poets, Gower and Chaucer are the most influenced by Latinate culture; they also may have written most for a learned, Latinate audience,[9] one which would have had a greater familiarity with Ovid. Gower and Chaucer are the most Ovidian of the Middle English poets, but more remains to be said about the nature and extent of their Ovidianism. Gower can help to situate Chaucer as 'England's Ovid' by having Venus call Chaucer 'mi poete';[10] for all of Gower's own considerable Ovidianism, it may finally be of a different kind from Chaucer's. The reception of the two poets in the fifteenth century (Gower's much greater fame, later to be eclipsed by Chaucer's) may reflect something not only of the nature of that century, but the nature of the two poets' relative Ovidianisms.[11]

Ovid was the classical poet *par excellence* for both Gower and Chaucer. If for Gower Ovid is useful in constructing an ideal world – a coherent, but highly stratified *mundus* of political, ethical and theological

---

[5] Boethius, *Consolation of Philosophy*, Book 2, poem 5. See further Claassen 2007: 1–35.

[6] Gower 1901; *Confessio Amantis* VIII.2266.   [7] See also in this volume, pp. 160–76, 177–96.

[8] On Matthew Paris's use of Ovid, see Marshall 1939: 467ff.; for Walsingham, see Clark 2004: 191; 200–5. Both chroniclers evince enough interest in Ovid to have drawn from full texts of Ovid rather than (only) *florilegia*. Walsingham's *Archana deorum* is found in Oxford, St John's College, MS 124 and London, BL, Lansdowne MS 728; see McKinley 2001: 113–27; Clark 2004: 198–208, for discussion of the commentary. See also in this volume, pp. 192, 194.

[9] For reading circles in late medieval London, see Kerby-Fulton and Justice 1997: 59–84. Kerby-Fulton argues that scholars have underestimated the extent to which Latinate clergy may have formed the main intended audience for Gower's, Chaucer's and Langland's poetry.

[10] I am grateful to the Press's anonymous reader for this point.

[11] For discussion of Chaucer's relatively more subversive Ovidianism (with regard to literary authorities), see McKinley 2011.

dimensions – for Chaucer Ovid is useful in exploring the larger, often open-ended, moral and ethical questions that one should ask while making one's way through a rather less clearly delineated world. Yet both poets display medieval 'habits of thought' in their responses to the classical poet. In the Middle Ages, clerical readers, including poets, had been trained to interpret and understand classical authors in specific ways within the medieval curriculum,[12] and 'Ovidius ethicus' was a paradigm familiar to Chaucer and Gower. As will become clear in the discussion that follows, both Gower and Chaucer avail themselves of a wide range of possible forms of Ovids, whether Latin 'school texts' of the *Metamorphoses* or the *Heroides* or moralised versions. In some cases, Gower will opt for a moralised version as it suits his narrative purposes better; in others, he will work directly from an unmoralised Latin text of Ovid's verse. The same holds true for Chaucer; however, Chaucer seems to resort less frequently to the moralised apparatus in his use of Ovid's texts. In the case of Gower, it seems clear that he had some form of an 'omnibus Ovid' at hand, or had borrowed a full range of texts of Ovid; he certainly was not restricted to only the *Ovidius moralizatus* or other moralised version available to him. As is evident in his composition process in the *Vox Clamantis*, Gower frequently incorporates large segments of Ovid's verse wholesale into his own poetic structure – even freely changing Ovid's Latin – to an extent that rules out the use of florilegia. By the same token, as can be seen in Chaucer's *Legend of Thisbe*, in *The Legend of Good Women*, Chaucer was quite able, when he chose, to translate directly from Ovid's Latin and eschew any moralising or summarising alternative. Both poets, it is clear, worked with a range of forms of Ovid's poems, from the unmoralised, to the moralised, text.

Gower's and Chaucer's imaginative adaptations of Ovid elicited a steady stream of scholarly studies throughout the twentieth century.[13] In Chaucer, for example, some of the classic Ovidian explorations are the *House of*

[12] Coulson 1991; Hexter 1986; McKinley 2001. For general studies of the medieval reception of classical literature, see Wetherbee 2005; Minnis and Scott 1991: 314–72; Minnis 1988: 15–16, 55–7; Baswell 1995; Reynolds 1996b.

[13] In the present essay I do not aim to offer a detailed survey of the ubiquitous reworkings of Ovid in Chaucer's and Gower's extensive bodies of poetry (something akin to discussing in an essay the influence of Homer on Virgil and Ovid!). I seek, rather, to move past the conventional wisdom on Ovidian motifs and *topoi* in these poets, to explore dimensions of their engagement with Ovid not previously discussed in the scholarship, and thus to extend the conventionally described parameters for the ways in which Chaucer and Gower drew upon Ovid. There has been very little discussion of the rich and varied uses of Ovid in Gower's Latin poetry, for example; of Gower's use of Ovidian myths *per se* as a means of political discourse; or of Chaucer's purposeful engagement of Ovid *per se* to explore theological themes at the close of his major work, *The Canterbury Tales*. To do justice to Ovid's complexity, and the complex range of responses to his poetry by medieval poets, we need finally to move past the encyclopaedic (and therefore necessarily superficial) approach seen in such early works as Hoffman 1966. It does not, therefore, seem prudent to me – or very illuminating

Fame, the *Book of the Duchess*, the *Wife of Bath's Prologue* and *Troilus and Criseyde*.[14] The *Legend of Good Women* itself is modelled on Ovid's *Heroides*, and the *Legend's* Prologue, in which the poet-narrator is arraigned by Venus and Cupid,[15] also reworks many Ovidian motifs and themes.[16] Helen Cooper has treated some of these works in her excellent assessment of Chaucer's uses of Ovid.[17] Jeremy Dimmick has elucidated the ways Ovid's enduring appeal for medieval literary culture was a function of his role as classical *auctor* – but an *auctor* who resisted different forms of authority.[18] In this essay I will not reiterate for readers what other scholars have so admirably discussed already. To highlight some other aspects of Gower's and Chaucer's responses to Ovid, I will discuss four main narratives: Gower's construction of Latin verse in part from lines of Ovid in *Vox Clamantis* Book I; the tales of Pyramus and Thisbe and Theseus/Ariadne in the *Confessio Amantis* and in the *Legend of Good Women*; and lastly, Chaucer's *Manciple's Tale*, the penultimate narrative of the *Canterbury Tales* and the only exclusively Ovidian tale in that work. Close analysis reveals poetic achievements that complicate our standard working assumptions about how the two poets might recast Ovid. Gower draws on Ovid at times to extend the subjectivity of both narrators and characters as a means to offer veiled counsel to the king or to explore the ethical implications of oath-keeping. Further examination reveals a Chaucer indeed, in Cooper's words, 'critical, not subservient'[19] in his uses of Ovid, but even intent occasionally on the appropriation of Ovid to project a moral and theological vision.

VOX CLAMANTIS BOOK I

Gower's *Vox Clamantis* illustrates in striking ways late medieval traditions of poetic composition in Anglo-Latin.[20] Gower drew on complete Latin

---

for readers already somewhat familiar with Chaucer's and Gower's uses of Ovid – to reiterate here what is already available in published studies. Readers seeking overviews might start with the best such recent study, Dimmick 2002. For studies specifically on Ovid and Gower, see Simpson 1995; Sadlek 2004; Harbert 1988; Mainzer 1972; Hiscoe 1985; Beidler 1982; Callan 1946. On Ovid and Chaucer, see Calabrese 1994; Fleming 1990; Cooper 1988; Wetherbee 1984; Kiser 1983; Minnis 1982; Fyler 1979; Ginsberg 1983; Shannon 1929.

[14] On the Wife of Bath and Ovid, see Desmond 2006; on Ovid in the *Wife of Bath's Tale*, see McKinley 1996c: 40–59.

[15] For further discussion of the charges brought against Chaucer in the Prologue, see Percival 1998: 11–14; 96–148.

[16] See the discussions by Edwards 2006; Simpson 1998; Copeland 1991: 186–98.

[17] Cooper 1988: 71–81.   [18] Dimmick 2002: 264–87.   [19] Cooper 1988: 72.

[20] Gower composed one of the longest of surviving Anglo-Latin poems of the later Middle Ages in the *Vox*; see Rigg 1992: 287–90; Rigg and Moore 2004: 153–64; and Carlson 2004: 389–406.

texts of some of Ovid's works, in addition to moralisations. According to G. C. Macaulay, Gower's 'knowledge of Ovid seems to have been pretty complete, for he borrows from almost every section of his works with the air of one who knows perfectly well where to turn for what he wants'.[21] Frederick Mish has identified some 750 lines from Ovid in the seven books of the *Vox Clamantis*, with the great majority found in Book 1.[22] As my first example, I examine a little-discussed aspect of Gower's poetic process, his assembling of lines of Ovid's Latin verse into his own composite whole.[23] One can see his active appropriation of Ovidian verse in a passage which occurs late in *Vox Clamantis* Book 1: the dreamer/narrator's vision of an encounter with the divine on an island (1.2021–50).[24]

Well into the dream-vision that makes up *Vox* Book 1, the narrator lands on a shore where he sees crowds of people, and is met by an old man who describes the people of the land through the verses of Ovid's *Tristia* and *Epistulae ex Ponto*. The narrator seems to have landed, after the storm at sea (i.e. the Rising), on an island that is England.[25] His apprehension at the barbarity of the inhabitants is consistent with Gower's larger view of the country after the Rising, a realm in chaos with social classes disregarding both their duties and the laws themselves. The *visio*'s dreamer/narrator is one of shifting identities,[26] a characteristic also of Ovid's narrators.[27] The wildness of Britain is the wildness of the body politic driven by sin and not by reason. The narrator is again filled with turmoil and wonders why he was not allowed to die earlier. Gower invokes the experience of John, exiled to the island of Patmos, and the account of his vision in Revelation chapter 1. John relates his awe at seeing the divine person: 'et cum vidissem

---

[21] Gower (1904–12), vol. 1:xxxiii; Macaulay also observes that the *Vox Clamantis* is 'written in elegiac verse, more or less after the model of Ovid', vol. 1:xxx; Simpson 1995: 150, 154. See also Mish 1973.

[22] Mish 1973: 130. Mish adds newly identified lines to those earlier found by Macaulay and by Stockton in Gower 1962.

[23] On Gower's possible use of *cento*, see Yeager 1989: 113–32; also Yeager 1990: 47–60. Scott McGill defines *cento* as 'the stringing together of discrete lines of classical Latin verse to create a narrative' (definition provided in private correspondence). He also states that 'including a long, unchanged passage from Ovid, would not' constitute *cento*. Gower's incorporation of extended passages from Ovid, as in *Vox Clamantis* 1.1675–84, is thus not *cento*, but the passage quoted below, the speech of the divine figure, does apparently qualify as a form of *cento*. See McGill 2005. On Gower's construction of the Latin verse of the *Vox Clamantis* in part from Latin excerpts of other authors, see Carlson 2003: 293–317.

[24] For a study of a later section of *Vox* Book 1, in which Gower depicts the narrator's reflections on the attack on the Tower of London, see McKinley 2008.

[25] Gower may be invoking a similar scene in Geoffrey of Monmouth's *Historia Regum Britanniae*, chapter 20, where Brutus, having arrived on an island, receives a vision from the goddess Diana foretelling what kingdom he is to occupy. On Brutus in *Vox* Book 1, see Federico 2003: 11–12.

[26] For the unstable identity of many medieval narrators, see Spearing 2005.

[27] See Sharrock 2002: 150–62, and Barchiesi 2002: 182–97.

eum cecidi ad pedes eius tamquam mortuus' (and when I had seen him, I
fell at his feet as though dead; Revelation 1.17).[28] Gower's narrator, although
seeing no divine figure, similarly falls into a swoon, overcome with sorrow:
'In terram cecidi mortis ad instar ego' (I fell to the ground as if dead; 2012).
When Gower's narrator wakes, crowd and ship have disappeared and he
is alone on shore. At this point a second dream seems to be incorporated
within the longer dream; this second dream may belong to the category of
somnium coeleste or possibly oracular dream, in which 'truth is revealed by
an austere figure of authority . . . 'even a god clearly reveals what will or will
not transpire, and what action to take or to avoid'. It may also qualify as an
admonitio, 'a dream of divine counsel'.[29] As Gower's narrator despairs, he
hears the voice from heaven. In the next chapter the narrator will identify
the voice as that of God: 'Thou Who kindly didst advise me to live when
love of death was in my grief-stricken breast' (95).[30]

In the passage below, I have highlighted the lines from Ovid which
Gower incorporates within the speech of the God-figure:

Vox Clamantis I.2021–50	Lines from Ovid or other sources
Nil tibi tristicia confert; si dampna per orbem	
Circuiendo mare te timuisse liquet,	
Immo tibi pocius modo provideas, quia discors	
Insula te cepit, pax ubi raro manet.	
Te minus ergo decet mundanos ferre labores,	
Munera nam mundus nulla quietis habet:	
Si tibi guerra foris pateat, tamen interiori	
Pace, iuvante deo, te pacienter habe.	
Dum furor incurrit, currenti cede furori,	dum furor in cursu est, currenti cede furori;

[28] *Biblia sacra iuxta vulgatam versionem* (1969), vol. II: 1883.   [29] Kruger 1992: 28.
[30] Gower deliberately situates the entire *visio* of Book I in the tradition of Revelation: at the end of
the Prologue to Book I, he prays that John of Patmos give him direction in the writing of the
work 'Insula quem Pathmos suscepit in Apocalipsi, / Cuius ego nomen gesto, governet opus' (*Vox
Clamantis*, Prologue, lines 57–8).

Vox Clamantis I.2021–50	Lines from Ovid or other sources
Difficiles aditus impetus omnis habet;	difficiles aditus impetus omnis habet.[31] (*Remed. amor.* 119–20)
Desine luctari, referant tua carbasa venti,	desine luctari; referant tua carbasa venti,
Utque iubent fluctus sic tibi remus eat.	quaque vocant fluctus, hac tibi remus eat. (*Remed. amor.* 531–2)
Sive die laxatur humus seu frigida lucent	Sive die laxatur humus, seu frigida lucent
Sidera, prospicias que freta ventus agit:	sidera, prospicio, quis freta ventus agat (*Her.* 2.123–4)
Tempora sicut erunt sic te circumspice, nulla,	
Sint nisi pre manibus, secula visa cape:	
Ludit in humanis divina potencia rebus,	Ludit in humanis divina potentia rebus
Et certam presens vix habet hora fidem.	et certam praesens vix habet hora fidem. (*Ex Ponto* 4.3.49–50)
Semper agas timidus, et que tibi leta videntur,	
Dum loqueris fieri tristia posse putes:	
Qui silet est firmus, loquitur qui plura repente,	
Probra satis fieri postulat ipse sibi.	
Ocia corpus alunt, corpus quoque pascitur illis,	Otia corpus alunt, animus quoque pascitur illis
Excessusque tui dampna laboris habent	inmodicus contra carpit utrumque labor. (*Ex Ponto* 1.4.21–2)

---

[31] Gower's Latin at times departs from that of Ovid's text. The Latin text quoted in the right column (which is taken from the Loeb editions cited in the next note) has been confirmed in a manuscript of Ovid known to be in England in Chaucer's time: Eton College, MS 91 (*s.* xiii). Eton 91's Latin text is identical to those in the five quotes in the right margin, with a few exceptions: it has 'vocent' (fol. 45r) in place of Ovid's 'vocant' (*Remedia Amoris* 531–2); the spelling 'presens' (fol. 165r) for Ovid's 'praesens' (*Ex Ponto* 4.3.49–50); the spelling 'lassatur' (fol. 2r) in place of Ovid's 'laxatur' (*Heroides* 2.123). Oxford, Bodl. canon. class. lat. 1 (*s.* xiii) has the spelling 'laxatur' (fol. 2v). There has not been sufficient time, unfortunately, to identify the manuscript traditions of Ovid Gower was using; but for discussion of his tendency to alter existing texts of Ovid, see Mish 1973: 170–87.

Vox Clamantis I.2021–50	Lines from Ovid or other sources
Gaudet de modico natura, set illud habundans	
Quod nimis est hominem semper egere facit:	
Te tamen admoneo, tibi cum dent ocia tempus,	scribe ergo quae vidisti et quae sunt et quae
Quicquid in hoc sompno visus et auris habent,	oportet fieri post haec (Revelation 1.19)
Scribere festines, nam sompnia sepe futurum	
Indicium reddunt.	

Sadness is not going to help you. If it is the case that you were afraid of losses when the sea surrounded you, now you should take even greater care for yourself. A contentious island has received you, where peace rarely remains. Therefore you must put away earthly struggles, for the world has no gifts of rest. If an outer battle besets you, still, with God's help, possess yourself patiently, with an inner tranquillity. When its madness strikes, yield to the rushing frenzy; every attack has a harsh approach. Stop toiling, let the winds carry your sails backwards, and as the waves bid, so let your oar obey. Whether the ground is loosened in the day or the cold stars gleam, see how the wind drives the sea. Reflect upon future events; lay claim to only those that are at hand. Divine power gambles with human experience, and the present moment hardly offers certain faith. Always act with care, and what seem joys to you even while you are speaking may seem to become sorrows. He who is silent is unwavering; he who speaks many things rashly, asks for aspersions against himself. Rest nourishes the body, and the body feeds upon it, and too much effort takes a toll on you. Nature delights in the mean, but that abundance which is excessive always makes one needy. Still, I advise you, while leisure gives you time, whatever you have seen or heard in this dream, write it down quickly, for dreams often bring an indication of future things.[32]

The inhabitants of the island are equated with turmoil, quarrelling, disturbance. The narrator is to look within, to self-control (with God's help), to a type of regulation which is supremely rational. Aquinas addresses this issue when commenting on Aristotle:

---

[32] Quotations and translations from Ovid in this essay are from the following editions: *Remedia amoris*, from *The Art of Love and Other Poems*, Ovid 1985; *Tristia: Ex Ponto*, from Ovid 1988; *Heroides* and *Amores*, from Ovid 1977a; *Metamorphoses*, from Ovid 1984). The translation of Gower's Latin in the divine figure's speech is my own. For an analysis of Gower's incorporation of lines of Ovid earlier in *Vox* Book I, see Yeager 1990: 49–52.

And thus the Philosopher speaks wisely when he suggests in *Politics* book 3 [ch. 11], that in a right government not a beast, but God and the understanding should rule; for a beast rules when a king tries to rule others not by reason, but by passion and lust, in which we share with the beasts; but God rules when in ruling others the king does not deviate from right reason and from natural law.[33]

It is as if, in the *Vox* passage, the heavens open and God reads Aristotle's *Politics* to the bedraggled narrator, but with lines of Ovid intermingled. Yet whether Ovid writes in the *Heroides* or the exile poetry, self-control is not, to put it mildly, his narrator's most pressing objective. Gower thus employs the Ovidian text at times to ends nearly diametrically opposed to those of the Roman poet, yet this narrative practice is one that is widespread in medieval poetry.

The first two excerpts in this speech come from the *Remedies of Love*. In Ovid, the narrator counsels his readers to check new growths in love, to put out small fires before they grow too large to contain. But Ovid's passage then offers a humorous, and counterproductive, concession to the fact that sometimes love cannot be withstood. Gower quotes the next line: 'When its madness strikes, yield to the rushing frenzy; every attack has a harsh approach' (*Remedia amoris* 119–20). In contrast to Ovid's text, the narrator of the *Vox* is not to succumb to the storms and stresses around him but to be of calm mind.

Another quote from Ovid which Gower incorporates is, 'Divine power gambles with human experience, and the present moment hardly offers certain faith' (*Ex Ponto* 4.3.49–50), words that can hardly be reassuring to the dreamer, coming from heaven itself. Again the heavenly speaker is made the mouthpiece for a type of secular, rather than Christian, wisdom.

Finally, Gower adapts a verse from *Ex Ponto* 1.4.21–2, a verse again made to serve as a call to moderation. The speech ends with the Biblical injunction from Revelation for the narrator to commit to writing what he has seen and heard, and thus we near the end of the longer *visio* of Book I as well. The vision ends, the narrator awakens from his deep sleep, and Gower commences chapter 21, the final chapter of Book I, which celebrates God's power over the rebellion and His mercy to the upper classes.

Despite the explicitly Christian prayer of the narrator in the preceding chapter, which seems to avert the catastrophe, and despite the previous

---

[33] Fisher 1965: 181 (trans. Fisher). Thomas Aquinas, *De Regimine Principum*, 3.2.29. Gower does make some reference to Aristotle in his works, and may have had one of Aquinas' commentaries on Aristotle. Even if he did not, Aquinas' passage illustrates the kind of principle which is at work in the *Vox* passage. See Simpson 1995: 7, 168, 269 n. 35; and Yeager 1990: 28n., 163n., 206, etc., for discussions applying Aquinas to Gower.

episode's emphasis on repentance and contrition,[34] Gower enacts a shift to a more classical form of discourse in this passage, in which the heavens open and the narrator is given instruction. Ovid is made a proponent of the virtues of self-mastery, of *ratio* over *amor*, in a startling reversal. It is possible that a late medieval English poet believed that such interpolated lines were superior to his own Latin verse. What of Gower's use of excerpts irrespective of their larger narrative contexts? One answer may be that classical Latin verse carried its own authority, even apart from any larger context. Like a part of a bone from a saint's body, the classical Latin couplet has been partitioned off from its larger sacred body with the belief that its presence will bring life and power to its new poetic environment. How then does the divine figure's speech fit within the larger vision of Book I? In Gower's view, the upper classes need to watch more responsibly over the lower and middle classes, to prevent such an unseemly rebellion, so 'detrimental' to the common good. Ovid is brought into the service of these ideals, as even God himself speaks through the Roman poet.

NEGOTIATING OVID: THE *CONFESSIO AMANTIS* AND THE *LEGEND OF GOOD WOMEN*

When we turn to Gower's *Confessio Amantis*, we find a wealth of Ovidian episodes; it may be worth pausing to consider more broadly Gower's framework for that poem: a collective poem, in some ways, like the *Metamorphoses*. Gower uses the Ovidian art of love in the *Confessio Amantis* principally as a mechanism to express a political vision, educate the princely reader, and approach the concept of self-rule. Amans must begin to understand self as subservient to other selves, and love as something ethical, not as something only intrinsic or aimed at gratifying one's own desires. The framework of the *Confessio Amantis*, a merging of the *praeceptor amoris* tradition with the medieval rite of confession, illustrates Gower's highly innovative use of the Ovidian matter of love, subordinated to a larger vision of the body politic. Gower takes up the widely used theme of the ne'er-do-well lover/learner/narrator and his need for guidance (a popular device also in Chaucer's poetry) but sets it within a strongly didactic frame. The lover, Amans, is a representative variously of 'Gower' the poet, the lover himself, and even Richard II, as others have observed.[35] Gower did not always rely on moralised versions of Ovid, as Macaulay and others have amply demonstrated; he also drew from Latin school texts of Ovid

---

[34] On this episode, see Wetherbee 1999: 596.   [35] Burrow 1983: 23; Porter 1983: 147.

complete with glosses.[36] But regularly throughout both the *Vox Clamantis* and the *Confessio*, Gower fits the Ovidian text within his larger programmatic, didactic purpose; he creates, in effect, an *Ovidius ethicus* of his own. Amans' encounter with Venus, Cupid and Genius in Book 1 is a widely known Ovidian segment of the *Confessio*; however, for the sake of space, I will not treat what others have perceptively discussed already.[37]

As James Simpson and others have shown, the *Confessio* itself takes up the project of educating the lover about the nature of love; this love, as it turns out, is one that is ultimately defined and understood in the largest possible social, even political, sense. Since Richard II is said to have commissioned a poem from Gower, and the *Confessio* is the logical fulfilment of that request, the poem has often been read as a *speculum principis*. Amans is thus a figure for the erring monarch, who, ironically, was to be notorious for his refusal to heed counsel. I have treated elsewhere several episodes from the *Confessio* (Jason; Tereus) that suggest Gower's interest in educating the king, and doing so through Ovidian exempla.[38] These seem to cluster most strongly in Books v and vii of the *Confessio*; Book vii has increasingly been seen as the poem's mini-*speculum principis*.[39] Here I would like to discuss two other Ovidian tales from the *Confessio*, to show further Gower's methods of engaging the classical poet: the stories of Pyramus and Thisbe from Book iii; and Theseus and Ariadne from Book v. Both of these Ovidian stories have their counterparts in Chaucer and the difference in the poets' handling of the stories reveals much.

The tale of Pyramus/Thisbe

In Ovid, the story of Pyramus and Thisbe (*Metamorphoses* 4.55–166) reveals perhaps the author's wry assessment of the overall storyline;[40] whatever his motivation, his telling of the myth is farcical in several scenes. Elsewhere in the *Metamorphoses* Ovid shows himself capable of producing genuinely

---

[36] Mainzer 1972: 215, 221.

[37] See Burrow 1983: 5–24; Butterfield 2004: 165–80; Simpson 1995: 139–48.

[38] McKinley 2007, 1996a.

[39] For Gower's borrowing of the classical ekphrastic model to structure Book vii of the *Confessio Amantis*, see McKinley 1996a. Book vii is an excellent illustration of Gower's imitation of Ovidian narrative structures of subversion within the larger framework of the confession. Space in the present essay does not allow me to discuss more than a limited number of tales having counterparts in Ovid and Chaucer; for analysis of some of the more subversive story-matter in the *Confessio*, see Watt 2003.

[40] Anderson in Ovid 1997: 417–18, notes that 'we do not feel compelled' by the story of the couple's love. Galinsky 1975: 128, also observes Ovid's 'refusal to be truly compassionate with the woes of the characters'.

tragic narrative.[41] But in many ways the Pyramus and Thisbe story receives the same treatment by Ovid as the mock-tragic suicide of the centaur Hylonome over her beloved Cyllarus' death (Book 12), the latter of which seems to be a parody of Dido's suicide in *Aeneid* Book 4. There are numerous comic details in Ovid's tale of the young star-crossed lovers,[42] beginning with Pyramus' reaction when he finds Thisbe's bloody veil. He cries out, in rhetoric worthy of high tragedy, 'una duos ... nox perdet amantes' (one night shall bring two lovers to death; line 108). He blames himself for her death, and summons all the lions to come and consume him. He checks himself, and says, 'sed timidi est optare necem' (But 'tis a coward's part merely to pray for death; line 115). He kisses the veil and, weeping, cries out, 'accipe nunc ... nostri quoque sanguinis haustus!' (Drink now my blood too!; line 118). When he stabs himself with the sword, Ovid provides a particularly vivid simile:

> quoque erat accinctus, demisit in ilia ferrum,
> nec mora, ferventi moriens e vulnere traxit.
> ut iacuit resupinus humo, cruor emicat alte,
> non aliter quam cum vitiato fistula plumbo
> scinditur et tenui stridente foramine longas
> eiaculatur aquas atque ictibus aera rumpit.
>   (*Metamorphoses* 4.119–24)

He drew the sword which he wore girt about him, plunged the blade into his side, and straightway, with his dying effort, drew the sword from his warm wound. As he lay stretched upon the earth the spouting blood leaped high; just as when a pipe has broken at a weak spot in the lead and through the small hissing aperture sends spurting forth long streams of water, cleaving the air with its jets.

The sky-high water imagery cannot help but puncture the supposed 'seriousness' of the scene; several scholars have commented on the simile's inappropriately comic effect.[43] Next Thisbe emerges from hiding for fear of the lion and notices that the mulberries now are strangely darkened in colour. She 'sees somebody's limbs writhing on the bloody ground' ('tremebunda videt pulsare cruentum membra solum'; lines 133–4) and steps back; on recognising Pyramus, she beats her arms and then embraces his body. She kisses him, 'now cold in death' ('gelidis in vultibus oscula figens'; line 141), and calls out repeatedly to him. Pyramus, although first flailing

---

[41] See for example the Ceyx/Alcyone story of Book 11; Hecuba's tragedy in Book 13; Cephalus' monologue on the loss of his wife, Book 7.

[42] Throughout this essay, classical spelling of characters' names has been used, since often the same medieval author presents a multiplicity of spellings for the same name (Adryane, Adriane, etc.).

[43] Newlands (1986: 144) comments on the irony of this description; Galinsky 1975: 153, and Anderson in Ovid 1997: 425, also observe the inappropriateness of the image.

his legs and only a few lines later 'chilly' in death, revives to open his eyes at the sound of her name, and promptly expires. Thisbe takes his sword and, after a dramatic soliloquy, plunges it into her breast. There are many incongruous moments which, even if they are not full-blown comedy, are surely highly inappropriate. Ovid's tone, in short, is bathetic; yet this some-times sardonic humor, even delight in the grotesque, is a long-recognised part of Ovidian poetic style.[44]

Gower changes much of this. The story of Pyramus and Thisbe is situated within *Confessio* Book III (lines 1331–1530), thus falling under the sin of wrath. In Gower the story, drawn from the *Ovide moralisé*,[45] is presented as illustrating the dangers of rash actions: Pyramus' misconstruing of the bloody wimple and his resultant anguish lead him to end his life. Gower identifies Pyramus' actions as those of 'folhaste' (III.1447). Genius concludes the tale with a warning to Amans not to be the cause of his own misery (*bale*, 1496): the person who acts in *folhaste* may like Pyramus unnecessarily forfeit his own life. In placing Ovid's story within the rubrics of a book on wrath, it is clear why Gower would prefer the *Ovide moralisé*'s very different version of Ovid's story. Gower often drew on French intermediaries and sources of all kinds. In this case, however, the *Ovide moralisé* conveniently removes many details from Ovid's account which create a mock tragedy.[46]

All Thisbe finds when she comes upon Pyramus is his 'bledende' body (III.1469). The shooting water effect has been omitted, as have the thrashing limbs and the nearly simultaneously ice-cold lips/face. Gower prefers a more dignified rendering, more appropriate for his larger purposes with Book v. One can see similar judgements guiding the shaping of other Ovidian tales in the *Confessio*. In his retelling of the Jason and Medea story in Book v, Gower draws often on Benoît de Sainte-Maure's version of it in *le Roman de Troie*; as a result, the Medea in Gower is more courtly and demure than her namesake in Ovid.[47] These choices at times result in Gower's delivering a very different Ovid from the one found even in complete Latin editions of his day. When one speaks of 'Gower's Ovid', then, one must understand an Ovid sometimes (not always) considerably reconstituted through moralising traditions. It is clear both from his own composition of Latin and from his use of Latin editions of Ovid for other stories in the *Confessio* that Gower was not drawing on the French versions because of his lack of fluency in Latin. They may have been somewhat

---

[44] Solodow 1988: 101–9, 118–19; Galinsky 1975: 142–3.   [45] Mainzer 1972: 217.

[46] All quotations from the *Ovide Moralisé* are from the edition by C. de Boer 1915–38. For discussion of several Anglo-French poems dealing with the Pyramus and Thisbe story (but which neither Gower nor Chaucer appears to have used), see Glendenning 1986: 51–78; esp. 54–63.

[47] McKinley 2007: 310–19.

easier for him to read, but Gower seems to have chosen the French (or Latin) moralised intermediaries mainly for their changed emphases. At times, then, Gower opts to incorporate a more dignified or courtly version of Ovid's story-matter than that found in Ovid's own text.

The same does not appear to be as true for Chaucer. Although it has been clearly demonstrated that Chaucer used the *Ovide moralisé* and other moralised versions of Ovid,[48] it is also evident that he at times preferred to draw directly from Latin editions. This is the case with the Pyramus and Thisbe story, which he remakes as the *Legend of Thisbe* in the *Legend of Good Women*.[49] Chaucer's larger programme with the *Legend of Good Women*, as announced by Alceste in the Prologue, is to relate the tales of many virtuous women, so as to compensate for the 'falsehoods' of his representation of the femme fatale, Criseyde.[50] In the *Legend of Thisbe*, however, it is clear that Chaucer wants to retain all of the incongruities of Ovid's original story; he fully embraces its ironies, even adding to the comic send-up the story presents. Since Chaucer does not set his tale within the larger moral hermeneutic we find operative in the *Confessio* – despite Chaucer's claims with the *Legend* – he is freer to adopt the full emphases of the tale, including bathos and the grotesque. The moral Chaucer offers at the end is one extolling both Thisbe and Pyramus for their singular devotion to one another; indeed the narrator comments upon the rarity of Pyramus' sort of fidelity among men, and notes that this justifies his conclusion in the legendary. And although this makes the tale of Thisbe ostensibly fall within the larger programme of the *Legend*, and within its larger rationale (the defence of women as penance for his maligning of women through the portrait of Criseyde), there are many ways in which the story falls short of its ostensible purpose. The tale of Thisbe offers us an excellent example of Chaucer's very close adherence to Ovid's Latin; in fact there are many scenes which appear nearly as Middle English translations of the passages in Ovid. The result of this close translation is that Chaucer brings in all of the parodic scenes present in Ovid's narrative, and at times elaborates upon them. There are other instances in which Chaucer adds his own lines into the story, and these sometimes function to increase character depth; but elsewhere such additions may heighten the sense of bathos which pervades the latter half of the tale. The result is an uneasy

---

[48] Lowes 1918; Meech 1931; Wimsatt 1967; Minnis 1979.

[49] For a fifteenth-century English response to Chaucer's and Ovid's tales of Pyramus and Thisbe, see John Metham's poem *Amoryus and Cleopes* (*c.* 1449), Metham 1999; also ed. Hardin Craig, EETS o.s. 132 (London, 1916), 1–81 (Princeton University Library, Garrett MS 141).

[50] Chaucer (1987): *Legend of Good Women*, Prologue, F 435–41.

mix of ostensible tragedy, undercut with highly incongruous, if not comic detail; the bathos is so frequent that it is ultimately fatal for the tragedy.[51]

Chaucer provides a number of additions to the storyline as he finds it in Ovid. One addition early on presents Thisbe's choice to desert friends for the love of Pyramus: she goes out to meet him disguised in a wimple:

> For alle hire frendes – for to save hire trouthe –
> She hath forsake; allas, and that is routhe
> That evere woman wolde ben so trewe
> To truste man, but she the bet hym knewe.
>
> (798–801)

The narrator's comment on the untrustworthy nature of men, ostensibly in keeping with the larger programme of the *Legend of Good Women*, will in fact fail to materialise in Thisbe's case; it is part of the narrator's general polemic against the falsehood of men, a polemic which is part of the larger fiction Chaucer employs in the poem. Thisbe in fact goes out to meet a very devoted lover; she will be disappointed, but for other reasons. Once Thisbe has seen the lioness and run for cover to the cave, dropping her wimple, Chaucer adds only minor details to Ovid's account: 'And tok no hed, so sore she was awhaped, / And ek so glad that that she was escaped; / And thus she sit and darketh wonder stylle' (814–16). These lines may develop the representation of her sense of fear, but not significantly.

Pyramus arrives and for many lines Chaucer presents a very literal translation of Ovid's scene. Pyramus sees in the sand the tracks of a lion and is filled with fear. He then sees the bloody wimple and makes his lament:

> Allas . . . the day that I was born!
> This o nyght wol us lovers bothe sle!
> How shulde I axe mercy of Tisbe,
> Whan I am he that have yow slayn, allas!
> My biddyng hath yow slayn, as in this cas.
> Allas, to bidde a woman gon by nyghte
> In place there as peril falle myghte
> And I so slow! Allas, I ne hadde be
> Here in this place a furlong wey or ye!
> Now what lyoun that be in this forest,
> My body mote he renten, or what best
> That wilde is, gnawe mote he now myn herte!
>
> (833–44)

---

[51] This mixing of tone has frequently been noted in the *Legend of Good Women* in general, although critics have attributed it to different causes: Percival 1998: 6; Frank 1972: 206. Percival does not discuss the *Legend of Thisbe* in her study.

A comparison of Chaucer's rendition with Ovid's Latin shows Chaucer translating much of the speech quite closely.[52] But when Chaucer reaches the point where Ovid's Pyramus makes his mock-tragic outburst to the veil, 'Drink now my blood too!' (*Met.* 4. 118), Chaucer seems to capture Ovid's tone, and gives Pyramus a drawn-out address to the wimple:

> And with that word he to the wympel sterte,
> And kiste it ofte, and wep on it ful sore,
> And seyde, 'Wympel, allas! There is no more
> But thow shalt feele as wel the blod of me
> As thow hast felt the bledyng of Tisbe!'
>
> (845–9)

What was already a one-line histrionic outburst is taken into the realm of absurdity. Chaucer includes as well the broken water-pipe image, as Pyramus lies dying: 'The blod out of the wounde as brode sterte / As water whan the condit broken is' (851–2).

Chaucer, unlike Gower, includes the scene of the thrashing limbs, since he is intent on rendering much of Ovid's comedic emphasis. Thisbe emerges from the cave (not Gower's, and the *Ovide moralisé*'s bush) and comes upon her dying beloved. This is Chaucer's rendering of the passage:

> And at the laste hire love thanne hath she founde,
> Betynge with his heles on the grounde,
> Al blody, and therwithal a-bak she sterte,
> And lik the wawes quappe gan hire herte,
> And pale as box she was, and in a throwe
> Avisede hire, and gan hym wel to knowe,
> That it was Piramus, hire herte deere.   (862–68)

Derek Pearsall also observes the 'grotesquely comic effect' of Pyramus' palpitating heels.[53] The next lines Chaucer draws closely from Ovid, but shapes into a highly rhetorical anaphoric passage, repeating the 'How . . . how . . . how' ostensibly as a means of building pathos for Thisbe's discovery.

> Who coude wryte which a dedly cheere
> Hath Thisbe now, and how hire heer she rente,
> And how she gan hireselve to turmente,
> And how she lyth and swouneth on the grounde,
> And how she wep of teres ful his wounde;

---

[52] For further discussion of Chaucer's direct use of the *Metamorphoses* here, see Burns 1997: 637–47.
[53] Pearsall 1992: 196.

How medeleth she his blod with hire compleynte;
How with his blod hireselve gan she peynte;
How clyppeth she the deede cors, allas!
How doth this woful Tisbe in this cas!
How kysseth she his frosty mouth so cold!

(869–78)

Though many details seem to create a sympathetic rendering of her loss, some work directly against it: if his heels have just been beating the ground, how is his mouth now 'frosty'? And what could it mean that Thisbe is now painting herself with his blood? There is no correlative line in Ovid or in the *Ovide moralisé*. Short of any other reasonable explanation, the passage is depicting Thisbe as momentarily having lost her wits. The excesses of Thisbe's grief, as those of Ariadne (to be discussed below), tax the reader's good faith; they fail to convince in this tale, partly because of the incongruous mixing of details, and because of her seeming loss of sanity (the painting of a deceased loved one's blood on one's body being a particularly macabre effect). The remainder of the tale follows Ovid fairly closely, with the exception that just prior to her own suicide, Chaucer extends the speech Thisbe's namesake gives in Ovid. The added lines include a moral which is a poor fit to the story, and thus present not only the narrator (earlier), but even Thisbe as a poor reader of her own experience:

And ryghtwis God to every lovere sende,
That loveth trewely, more prosperite
Than evere yit had Piramus and Tisbe!
And lat no gentil woman hyre assure
To putten hire in swich an aventure.
But God forbede but a woman can
Ben as trewe in lovynge as a man!
And for my part, I shal anon it kythe.

(905–12)

In Ovid, Thisbe's suicide (though never presented as high tragedy) is somehow honorable because for her to die with Pyramus is better than to live. In Chaucer, however, Thisbe's decision to die has been diminished through her determination to prove her own extremity of devotion worthy of that of any man. That is, her thoughts are made to fit the *Legend of Good Women's* larger framework of justifying women, in a kind of competition with men. But in the context of the story Chaucer tells, there is no reason why Thisbe should need to feel this urge to prove herself; her final outburst, in which she will 'kythe', 'show', or 'illustrate' that she is as willing to die for love as are men, fits uneasily into the larger story. Pyramus has always been faithful to her and Chaucer provides no earlier narrative grounding for her shift in point of view.

Chaucer, like Ovid, may have seen the tale as one incapable of tragic treatment, and so develops, like the Roman poet, a mixture of comic and tragic to burlesque the myth's inherent inanity. Chaucer also shows (like Ovid) that he is capable of presenting the most serious tragedy, with its profound impact on its sufferers (Troilus), and the story of Thisbe, by contrast, can only appear as a form of burlesque. But Chaucer's rendering of the myth is different from Gower's because of the vastly different hermeneutic frame within which Chaucer presents his tale. If Chaucer does not intend wholly seriously the *Legend of Good Women* as a type of penance for his portrait of Criseyde, then the individual legends will not operate as effective 'proof texts' on the virtue of woman. It is true that Thisbe is virtuous, but she and Pyramus are also extremely rash in their judgements, and the reader impressed with their 'honourable' suicides over love has had to overlook Pyramus' hasty misconstruing of the evidence. In short, the tone of Chaucer's tale can be mixed, if not outright parodic, because his tale does not need to operate to support the larger 'argument' of the *Legend of Good Women*, an argument which is itself a fiction. At best Chaucer would have been very doubtful about the need to 'repent' of his portrait of Criseyde; and one of the ironic outcomes of the *Legend of Good Women* as a whole is that by sheer contrast, the characterisation of Criseyde emerges as a tour de force. A. C. Spearing for one observes Chaucer's achievement in representing the 'shimmering complexity of her inner life'.[54]

Florence Percival, in her study of the *Legend of Good Women*, argues that the criticism Chaucer says he received regarding Criseyde is a fiction, and that Criseyde functions as a symbol of unfaithfulness.[55] Percival points to the arraignment of the poet as a topos often employed in literary tradition. Chaucer was using this topos as a convenient device, therefore, to launch the subject matter of the *Legend of Good Women*. Percival's argument is convincing, yet even if Chaucer manufactured the story (as he manufactures much else in the poem), it is not unlikely that Chaucer developed the *Legend* in part as a way to broach the late medieval 'woman question' and his particular track record on the subject. This record, from a modern perspective, is fairly flawed, yet from Chaucer's own perspective, Criseyde might well have seemed to be much more than the generic faithless woman. The net effect of the intentionally abysmal quality of the

---

[54] Spearing 2005: 96.   [55] Percival 1998: 98–112.

Legend is that Criseyde's portrait is even somewhat improved. It is not impossible that Chaucer does in fact engage the many legends of 'good women' so as to throw even greater light on what he knew was a great accomplishment: Criseyde's complex subjectivity. He reworks Ovid's heroines, in part, therefore, as a means of drawing attention to his own earlier narrative performance. Whether there was actual criticism of *Troilus and Criseyde*, as the poem alleges, is a moot point.[56]

The tale of Theseus/Ariadne

In *Confessio Amantis* Book v, Gower treats the sin of avarice, under which fall the sins of perjury and oath-breaking. Among other stories in *Confessio* Book v, the tales of Jason and Tereus receive extended treatment; between them is Gower's rendition of the story of Theseus and Ariadne (5230–5504).[57] The myth is told briefly in *Metamorphoses* 7.456–8 and 8.152–76;[58] likewise, the *Ovide moralisé*, an important source for Gower, offers only a brief version of the tale. Gower, however, expands upon the tale in ways that reveal his own poetic originality. According to Genius, the tale of Theseus and Ariadne illustrates the vice of 'unkindeschipe', that is, cruelty or faithlessness (with the root of the word, *unkinde*, emphasising its unnatural quality). As in the tale of Tereus, Gower develops the reader's empathy for the victim through additional passages and speeches which heighten the pathos. Tellingly, perhaps, Gower follows this tale of betrayal with a preface to the tale of Tereus, which focuses upon 'extorcion' (line 5511), a crime hardly attributable to Tereus. Instead in the tales of Jason and Tereus Gower highlights strongly the theme of oath-breaking, and even adds the crime of extortion into the prologue to the Tereus tale; in the 1380s the climate at court was extremely tense because of Richard II's committing of both such violations (violations with which he would be charged in his final deposition as well).[59] In any case, Book v seems to offer a cluster of tales with important political resonances, reflecting the many failures of the monarch to fulfil his own oaths and promises.[60]

---

[56] For further discussion of the charges brought against Chaucer in the Prologue, see Percival 1998: 11–14; 96–148.

[57] Bakalian 2005: 118 discusses the Ariadne/Theseus story in Gower, focusing mainly on truth in love relationships.

[58] Ovid also treats the story in *Ars amatoria* 1.509–10 and 527–64, and in *Heroides* 10.

[59] McKinley 2007: 319–21, 324.

[60] In this respect, the study of Bakalian, while useful on the nature of love in the *Confessio*, seems to fall short. Bakalian does not engage the larger political framework within which Gower situates the love stories in Book v.

Once Theseus has beheaded the Minotaur and escaped from the labyrinth, Gower develops the narrative of Ariadne's betrayal and abandonment on the island Chios with great empathy (lines 5368–5504). In the *Metamorphoses*, Ariadne loves Theseus and saves his life with the thread, but there is no promise of marriage; this detail is found in the *Heroides* 10.92, where Ariadne says that she was 'tibi pacta' (betrothed to you). In the *Ovide moralisé* 8.1144–1249, Ariadne engages in a long introspective monologue (not found in the *Metamorphoses*) before she approaches Theseus. When she offers to help him, she asks that he reward her if he is successful. When he agrees to give her himself as her vassal, she asks that he take her to his country and marry her (1298–1303). Gower follows the tradition of the promise of marriage so as to heighten Theseus' villainy, but markedly changes the *Ovide moralisé's* presentation of Ariadne. She does not engage in a monologue, nor does she barter with Theseus. Instead, both fall in love immediately, and Ariadne commences to instruct him how he should extricate himself from the labyrinth with the 'clue of thred' (5343). After she gives him the instructions and the 'pelote', a detail Gower takes from the *Ovide moralisé* ('Un poleton compost li baille / De glus, de saijn et de cole'; 1308–9),[61] Theseus proceeds to slaughter the Minotaur. Next Gower relates that Theseus promised to marry Ariadne, and that 'Al prively betwen hem tweie / The ferste flour he tok aweie' (5381–2). Theseus also promised his enduring love and that 'as his ogne hertes lif / He scholde hire love and trouthe bere' (5386–7). Gower develops the pathos as he describes Ariadne's response: 'And sche, which mihte noght forbere, / So sore loveth him ayein, / That what as evere he wolde sein / With al hire herte sche believeth' (5388–91). Again Gower emphasises the word 'trouthe' – central to the oath-breaking theme of Book v – when he describes Theseus' inward thoughts: 'And thus his pourpos he achieveth, / So that assured of his trouthe / With him sche wente, and that was routhe' (5392–4). Theseus leaves Ariadne on Chios 'alonde', sailing off with Phaedra (5433).

In the *Confessio*, Gower at times presents empathetically the pain of the innocent, who from naïveté offer their trust to those who later abuse it. Ariadne, when she awakens, discovers the ship sailing in the distance, and cries out against Theseus in a speech loosely taken from the *Ovide moralisé*. She decries his 'Senne', saying she thought 'I hadde his love boght, / And so deserved ate nede' (5448) when he offered her his promises. She demands to know how he could forget his own words, declares that the world will learn of his treachery, and, in a line not in the *Ovide moralisé*, she laments

---

[61] Meech 1931: 197.

that 'He yaf his trouthe bodily, / That he myn honour scholde kepe' (lines 5460–1). Although it is clear that the medieval Ariadne suffers in part because she has lost her 'ferste flour' to Theseus, this complaint shows that she is not just concerned about the loss of her virginity. Her sense of betrayal by Theseus is heightened because of the love she felt they shared. Gower's early details, in which Theseus and Ariadne are 'al on' (5339) in their love before she ever offers the solution to the labyrinth, present a slightly less draconian Theseus; however, even his early claims of love for Ariadne (the daughter of the hostile King Minos) evoke opportunistic motives. In the later scenes Gower reveals the stark difference in Theseus' and Ariadne's perspectives, but does so without condemning Ariadne; her willingness to trust is presented as worthy. Ariadne is described then as suffering so much that 'sche betwen the deth and lif / Swounende lay fulofte among' (5467–8). Gower, in a rather striking phrase, condemns Theseus' abandonment of Ariadne, as a wrong that will always 'Stond in Cronique of remembrance' (5471). Theseus' love for Ariadne was 'unkinde' (5469); and 'he the lawe of loves riht / Forfeted hath in alle weie' (lines 5476–7). Genius then warns Amans not to show such 'Unkindeschipe' to his beloved (5485), and the tale comes to a close, followed by the prologue to the tale of Tereus.

Gower develops his tale of Ariadne partly through his uses of the *Ovide moralisé*. He chooses this version in part because the French version includes the element of the negotiations over marriage (less developed in the *Heroides*), and this connects the tale more effectively to the marriage vows that are made and broken in the tales of Jason and Tereus which precede and follow it. One can see similar judgements guiding the shaping of other Ovidian tales in the *Confessio*. In his retelling of the Jason and Medea story in Book v, Gower draws often on Benoît de Sainte-Maure's version of it in *le Roman de Troie*; as a result, the Medea in Gower is more courtly and demure than her namesake in Ovid.[62] At times, then, Gower opts to incorporate a more dignified or courtly version of Ovid's story-matter than that found in Ovid's own text.[63]

---

[62] McKinley 2007: 310–19.

[63] Such choices place in stark relief the question how medieval poets such as Gower or Chaucer perceived their Ovidian source material. The preference for Ovid's 'own Latin' over a range of intermediaries may be a post-nineteenth-century perspective, resulting from the development of the discipline of textual editing. Although they do appear to employ medieval school texts of Ovid's Latin frequently, Gower and Chaucer are clearly quite comfortable with French, Italian, and Latin adaptations and moralisations, which seem to furnish them with additional narrative opportunities. And although Gower may have held Ovid's Latin verses in higher regard, qua Latin, than his own, it does not seem clear that he or Chaucer necessarily saw the medieval Latin edition of Ovid's work as a superior text to that of the medieval translation or moralisation.

As with the Jason and Medea story, Gower alters the details of the Theseus/Ariadne narrative so that the lovers are presented initially as sharing a mutual love. Gower often presents the victims of love with considerable tenderness, and this is evinced through his own shaping of Ariadne's experience.[64] His Ariadne is both more courtly than the conniving, bartering Ariadne of the *Ovide* tradition who also initiates her own betrothal (after the pattern of Medea); and also more outspoken in her final soliloquy. Gower also makes Ariadne a somewhat more tragic figure, as he ends her story without any trace of the Bacchus who arrives to marry her in both Ovid and the French poem. His emphasis, as with the framing Jason and Tereus tales, is finally on the importance of keeping one's *trouthe*, with implications not only for Amans, but perhaps for a royal reader as well.

Chaucer's version of the story in the *Legend of Good Women* has many different emphases,[65] and is drawn from a combination of sources, including the *Metamorphoses*, the *Heroides*, the *Ovide moralisé* and an Italian translation of the *Heroides*.[66] The case for Chaucer's use of the *Ovide moralisé* has long been advanced,[67] and although he appears to work in part from the French poem here, in other cases (such as the Legend of Tisbe) he seems to draw directly from a Latin school text of the *Metamorphoses*.[68] What makes Chaucer's recasting of the Ariadne tale most Ovidian, however, is his adoption of the ironic, shifting tone pervasive in the *Heroides*.[69]

In the *Legend* (as in the *Ovide moralisé*), Theseus swears his humble service to Ariadne, and she in turn answers that he should wed her, take her and Phaedra to his country, and marry Phaedra to Hippolytus.[70] Robert Frank observes that 'There is remarkably little talk of love, almost none in fact.'[71] Chaucer also shifts in his use of sources mid-way: he relies upon the *Ovide moralisé* up to Theseus' vow of fidelity to Ariadne the day before he slays the Minotaur, and then shifts to the *Heroides*' version of Ariadne's

---

[64] For similar comments about Gower's portrait of Philomela, see Yeager 1990: 155.

[65] Sheila Delany discusses the story 1994: 147–9 and 208–13.

[66] Meech 1930; Meech 1931: 182–204.

[67] Lowes 1918; Meech 1930; Meech 1931; Young 1944: 1–13, esp. 3 and 11; Wimsatt 1967; Delany 1968: 254–64; Minnis 1979; Minnis 1982: 17–20; Pearsall 1985: 238–9; Pearsall 1992: 33, 241; Percival 1998: 196, 219; and Fumo 2004: 365. Since Gower also drew from the *Ovide moralisé* (Mainzer 1972: 217, 218, 220ff.), it is more likely to have been available in late medieval London. On balance it seems better to allow for Chaucer's probable use of it.

[68] Chaucer 1987: 1067, notes on *The Legend of Thisbe*; see especially in Chaucer lines 833–44.

[69] For more on the *Heroides* and Chaucer, see Percival 1998:173–5.

[70] Sanford Meech notes that Chaucer found this variant (the betrothal of Phaedra) in the Italian translation of the *Heroides* (c. 1320–30) by Filippo (Ceff?) he was using. Meech 1931: 199; also Meech 1930, 117; for Filippo, see G. Bernardoni, ed., *Epistole Eroiche di Ovidio Nasone volgarizzate* (Milan, 1842): 31.

[71] Frank 1972: 119.

hardship for the remaining narrative.[72] In Chaucer, the two sisters hear Theseus lamenting from his jail cell at night, and Ariadne expresses pity for him. As Frank has noted, the mention of the 'foreyne' (privy; F 1962) adjoining his prison cell is one of many anti-romance elements Chaucer employs in the story.[73] Phaedra then advises Ariadne that they go to the jailer for help, and suggests that they give Theseus the device of the ball of wax and thread to choke the Minotaur, and then follow the thread backwards out of the labyrinth.[74] Yet Phaedra's role and actions are not new with Chaucer.[75] Theseus agrees to the plan, and offers to be Ariadne's servitor. In the *Ovide moralisé*, which Chaucer used for this section of the story, Theseus promises his word first to serve her, but he does not give a speech as long and obsequious as the one Chaucer has him deliver, kneeling, in the *Legend* (F 2055–73). Ariadne answers in the same way as her counterpart in the *Ovide moralisé*; she proposes their marriage. In Chaucer we do not find an Ariadne who has fallen in love, but a heroine who, like her French counterpart, negotiates to better her own future in practical terms. The Ariadne of the *Ovide* is notably shrewd and strategising: she thinks of how Theseus will be forced to marry her once she presents him with the only 'engin' of his escape (line 1201). The French heroine also, before she ever addresses Theseus, imagines herself returning to Athens with Theseus, as his 'dame' (1228). Chaucer does away with some of this, making Phaedra the originator of the escape plan, and removing some of the scheming, almost manipulative, nature of Ariadne from the French model.

Once Ariadne proffers the betrothal plans to Theseus, he readily agrees. Although this is their first meeting, he states that he has loved Ariadne for seven years even from Athens (F 2120), a claim which although not unparalleled in medieval romances, contributes to the larger tone of irony Chaucer is building in the story.[76] After Theseus agrees to her plan, Ariadne announces to her sister,

> Now be we duchesses, bothe I and ye,
> And sekered to the regals of Athenes,
> And bothe hereafter likly to ben quenes;

---

[72] Meech 1931: 200.   [73] Frank 1972: 115.

[74] Chaucer also developed the new detail of the jailer in his story from Filippo's translation (*Epistole eroiche*, 31); Meech 1931: 198–9.

[75] For discussion, see Percival 1998:175–6; Meech 1931: 197 n. 82 notes that the choking object can be traced back through the *Ovide moralisé* (lines 1308–9) to a gloss to the *Metamorphoses*. Meech cites Munich, clm MS 7205, fol. 45.

[76] See further Percival 1998: 184–5.

> And saved from his deth a kynges sone;
> As evere of gentil women is the wone
> To save a gentyl man, emforth hire myght,
> In honest cause, and namely in his ryght.
> Me thynketh no wight oughte us herof blame,
> Ne beren us therfore an evil name.   (2127–35)

Her speech reflects in part the machinations of the French Ariadne's monologue. Chaucer presents this as something that Ariadne will reflect upon
(privately or publicly) only after Theseus' vows. From this point onward,
the narrative moves quickly through Theseus' success with the Minotaur
and his escape with the two women from Crete. The narrator rails at Theseus for his desertion of Ariadne, and we are left finally with the lamenting
Ariadne of the *Heroides* (2211–17), her divine rescue and transformation
into a crown in the heavens.

What is most strikingly absent in the legend of Ariadne is the love
interest. In Chaucer's reworking of the Ariadne tale, we see a noble, virtuous
heroine, moved by pity to save the life of a young king. She has not seen him,
but has only heard his complaints from a prison cell; thus the circumstances
of their meeting are sharply different from those in Gower. Even her
negotiations with Theseus for marriage reflect the reality of many arranged
marriages in the Middle Ages: often loveless arrangements based on family
networks, bloodlines, land-holdings, inheritance and dowry. The greater
emphasis in the legend seems to be on the emptying out of the story's *sens*
(the love interest long associated with Ariadne's misfortune) so as to subject
the larger project (the ostensible penance 'Chaucer the poet' has taken on
himself for his misdeeds in the representation of women) to ironic scrutiny.
There are many aspects of the *Legend*, as critics have observed, which call
into question Chaucer's announced plan with the poem. As Percival has
argued, Chaucer's *Legend of Good Women* may well be the working out
of an ironic palinode 'whereby Chaucer ostensibly performs penance for
his sin, at the same time doing exactly what he was originally condemned
for'.[77] Although Ariadne weeps and rails at the unfaithful Theseus, we have
not been given sufficient grounds to truly empathise with her in her loss, or
to imagine the subjectivity she might possess. While displaying Ariadne's
prudence, business sense and far-sightedness, Chaucer intentionally fails to
produce a heroine whose love for Theseus has been devastated by betrayal.

---

[77] Percival 1998: 193.

This is because Chaucer's purposes are otherwise with the *Legend of Good Women*.

My final illustration of Chaucer's transformation of Ovid, is his rendition of the tale of Apollo and the crow (*Metamorphoses* 2.531–632), in the *Manciple's Tale*. The *Manciple's Tale* is the only tale from the *Canterbury Tales* which is based entirely on an Ovidian myth, and Chaucer positions it as the final 'fictional' tale in the poem. Placed as such, it has naturally garnered much critical focus in recent years.[78] Although I find some recent readings of this tale persuasive, none sufficiently addresses Chaucer's strategies in employing Ovid *per se* last in his series of fables in the *Canterbury Tales*, and particularly *in conjunction with* the very sombre *Parson's Tale*. This discussion is designed to address Chaucer's accomplishments in situating a stark Ovidian tale last and adjoining it to his final exploration, a treatise on penitence. The *Manciple's Tale* becomes an exploration of the nexus of language, truth and silence, in ways that have mesmerised, and troubled, readers. The *Manciple's Tale* follows on the *Canon's Yeoman's Tale*, and as others have noted, as Chaucer approaches the conclusion of the tales, the story-matter becomes increasingly seedy, remorseless and dark. The two final tales stage corruption in two medieval institutions: church and marriage, respectively. If the *Canon's Yeoman's Tale* offers a marvellously detailed manual on methods canons might use to fleece their flocks through alchemical sleight of hand,[79] the *Manciple's Tale* offers an abject world of adultery and murder. Narrated by a 'sneering' Manciple who sees life 'for the warfare of self-interest that it is',[80] the tale strips Ovid's story of much of its pathos and presents us with a Phoebus who 'keeps' both bird and wife, a wife who easily shifts to a disreputable lover, and a bracing scene of brutal murder. Chaucer paints the last two fictional tales of the *Canterbury Tales* in the sombre hues of smoky, cloak-and-dagger *film noir*. The *Manciple's Tale*, in particular, is a cold, stark world. A look at Ovid's version of the story shows how much Chaucer changed.

Although in Ovid the tale (*Metamorphoses* 2.531–632) begins somewhat simply as a beast fable, it grows more serious and tragic in tone towards

---

[78] Fumo 2004: 355–75; Kensak 1999: 190–206; Wallace 1997: 247–60; Herman 1991: 318–28; Fradenberg 1985: 85–118; Dean 1985.

[79] For discussion of the *Canon's Yeoman's Tale*, see Fyler 2007.   [80] Pearsall 1985, 241.

the end, when Phoebus discovers his beloved's infidelity, and slays her in his rage. In Ovid, Coronis of Larissa is no sooner praised for her beauty than she is found unfaithful to Apollo. Apollo himself, having failed in his pursuit of Daphne earlier in Book I, is presented as a jealous lover. The raven (Apollo's bird), en route to inform his master, is stopped by the crow, who warns the raven against such a course. The crow tells another tale, of how he was punished by Minerva for informing her of the truth on one occasion; the raven, disregarding the warning, informs Apollo of Coronis' infidelity. Apollo, enraged, strings his bow and mortally wounds Coronis. She admits her wrongdoing, but informs him that now he has killed their unborn child as well. The scene's details evoke tragedy: 'And while she spoke her life ebbed out with her streaming blood, and soon her body, its life all spent, lay cold in death' (2.610–11).[81] Though the story is relatively brief in Ovid, nevertheless the poet captures the agony of Apollo in his remorse over his passionate anger, dealing with the terrible duty of preparing Coronis' body for the funeral pyre, a body he had rashly deprived of life. Despite Ovid's presumably ambivalent response to the emperor's favourite deity,[82] in this scene the poet powerfully conveys the grief of Apollo. Ovid even accentuates the pain of the god by highlighting the paradoxical limits of the divine body, unable to weep, but only to emit groans. Perhaps most tellingly Ovidian is the psyche in torment: the Apollo caught in a paroxysm of grief, self-hatred and regret, after his rash show of anger. The scenes of Phoebus' murder of Coronis, up to and including the rescue of his son, reveal an Ovid capable of rendering powerfully tragic narrative.

Before moving to Chaucer's complex reworking of the tale of the crow, however, it is useful to consider Gower's version of the story. Genius relates the tale to Amans to illustrate the dangers of 'janglyng' and of *cheste* (or 'contention') within Book III of the *Confessio*, which is devoted to the sin of wrath. The story (III.783–816) is very briefly told, as follows: Phoebus loved Cornide, Cornide took a lover ('a yong kniht'; 790), and the 'fals' white bird Cornide kept in her room was a witness to their love affair. Corvus, the white bird, informed Phoebus, who 'for wraththe . . . Cornide anon he slowh' (800–1). Regretting his actions, Phoebus punished the bird for its 'wicke speche' (805), changing its colour from white to black. Gower follows the tradition after Ovid that henceforth the bird's cries are

---

[81] Galinsky 1975: 143, remarks on this passage as an instance of Ovid's depicting 'the pathos of human agony and suffering without travestying it'.

[82] Barchiesi 1997: 212; Wallace-Hadrill 1993: 27–8.

harbingers of some ill fortune. Genius' lesson for Amans is that he should not 'jangle and telle tales so', nor should he 'chyde' (832, 833). The tale is a truncated form of the same in Ovid, and functions in part to introduce the sin of hate, which is elaborated at much greater length.

Chaucer's story of the crow is 258 lines in length to Gower's 34 and Ovid's 98.[83] Gower and Chaucer may have been drawing on a similar version of Ovid's tale; Chaucer at least appears to have relied in places on the *Ovide moralisé*, among other sources.[84] In Chaucer, Phoebus is no longer a god, but a knight: 'the flour of bachilrie' (IX.125). What accounts for the greater length in Chaucer is his insertion of a string of exempla on the inevitable faithlessness of women (IX.163–95), and the Manciple's mother's 44-line speech of advice at the end (318–62).

Chaucer's tale, as many have observed, ironically tells – through excessive *janglyng* – the dangers of *janglyng*. The tale is highly self-reflexive on matters of speech, song, music, language. Not only is Phoebus extraordinarily gifted in music and 'mynstralcie' (IX.113), he has a crow whose abilities in singing, and in counterfeiting human speech, are beyond comparison. But soon after the tale begins, with its successive passages praising Phoebus and his crow, the story turns as Phoebus' wife is introduced. Chaucer makes Coronis a 'wyf' (139), and although the Middle English word 'wyf' can mean 'woman', the tale's many exempla on 'wyves' strongly imply the context of marriage. Thus Chaucer changes an act of infidelity to an act of adultery, only one of many changes contributing to the *Manciple's Tale's* sharper edges.[85] Also new in Chaucer are the exempla, following the detail of the wife's infidelity, on the natural propensity of women to be unfaithful (148–95).[86] The Manciple's reflections on the wife's infidelity leads to a digression (175–82) on the difficulty of keeping a 'shrewe' under lock and key, and he provides many animal analogies (some derived from the *Roman de la Rose*) which ostensibly prove the difficulty of restraining the libido of a bad wife.

---

[83] W. F. Bryan and Germaine Dempster (1958: 701) sum up the ways both Gower's and Chaucer's versions differ from Ovid's: 'ignoring all reference to cornix and her story, to corvus' journey to Phoebus, to the pregnancy and lament of Coronis, to Phoebus' vain attempts to save Coronis, to the cremation of Coronis, and to the birth of Aesculapius'. See also Fumo 2004: 355–75.

[84] Chaucer 1984: 4–9; Bryan and Dempster 1958: 699–722; Pearsall 1985: 238.

[85] One of Chaucer's analogues, *The Seven Sages of Rome* (Bryan and Dempster 1958: 717), features a wife. In Ovid and some Latin commentaries on the *Metamorphoses*, the word 'adulterium' is used, or its French equivalent in the *Ovide moralisé*. But Gower does not use the word 'wyf' in his rendition of the story.

[86] Similar instances could be found in St Jerome or Theophrastus. For examples, see Hanna and Lawler 1997; Blamires 1992.

Next the Manciple returns to the story itself, and remarks on Phoebus' deception and the tawdry nature of such sexual relationships. For the Manciple, class is no issue, when a wife has been unfaithful; language cannot elide the facts of the matter. After this jumble of moral assessments, the Manciple backs away, saying that he is not a 'textueel' man (235; that is, not learned in textual matters), and returns to the story. The crow, that 'heeng ay in the cage', observes Phoebus' wife's dealings, and reports them to him. For the first time, the crow communicates on its own (up until this time it had either sung or mimicked human speech) to Phoebus. He reports that Phoebus has been tricked by 'oon of litel reputacioun' (253), a man of little social standing, a phrase used twice in the tale (previously at line 199).

Phoebus, feeling that 'his sorweful herte brast atwo' (263), places an arrow in his bow and 'in his ire his wyfe thanne hath he slayn' (265). Chaucer adds the further acts of destruction by Phoebus: the breaking of his 'mynstralcie / Bothe harpe, and lute, and gyterne, and sautrie; / And eek he brak his arwes and his bowe' (267–79). Next Phoebus addresses the crow, giving a lament not in Ovid or the *Ovide moralisé*:

> Traitour . . . with tonge of scorpioun,
> Thou hast me broght to my confusioun;
> Allas, that I was wroght! Why nere I deed?
> O deere wyf! O gemme of lustiheed!
> That were to me so sad and eek so trewe,
> Now listow deed, with face pale of hewe,
> Ful giltelees, that dorste I swere, ywys!
> O rakel hand, to doon so foule amys!
> O trouble wit, O ire recchelees,
> That unavysed smyteth gilteles!   (271–80)

Chaucer develops the intense regret and self-loathing that characterised the wrathful Phoebus in Ovid. Phoebus likens the crow to a *scorpioun* which, according to *The Riverside Chaucer*, was 'a common symbol of treachery'; in the Wycliffite Bible is found this description: 'A scorpioun that maketh fair semblaunt with the face and pricketh with the tail; so a wicked woman draweth by flateryngis, and prickith til deth.'[87] In Chaucer, Phoebus' lament focuses mainly on his own actions; he reimagines his wife as 'Ful giltelees', an apparent debt to Guillaume de Machaut's *Le Livre du*

---

[87] Chaucer (1987) 954 n. 271; 972 n. 636–41. The scorpion is also paired with serpents (likened to the powers of evil and the enemy), as beasts to be trod underfoot by the seventy-two, in Luke 10:19 (perhaps an echo of Genesis 3:15).

Voir Dit,[88] one of Chaucer's sources for this tale. 'Rakel ire' becomes the
key focus of regret, to the extent that, paradoxically, this Phoebus even
considers taking his own life. Despite the Manciple's earlier emphases, the
focus becomes not the wife's wrongdoing but the greater wrongdoing of
Phoebus himself in slaying her. Phoebus, moreover, destroys now all the
instruments and weapons which have heretofore defined him. His revenge
continues as he punishes the truth-speaking bird with not only a change
of colour, but more importantly a loss of voice, language.

The tale ends with the speech of the Manciple's mother (318–62), which
runs for forty-five lines, offering a litany of proverbs and *sententiae* which
puzzlingly constitute the closing passage of the final 'fictional' tale of the
Canterbury Tales. Critics have offered various suggestions here, including a
primal 'return to the mother'.[89] Yet Chaucer's tactic resembles more closely
his strategies in the dazzling *Tale of Sir Thopas*, in which inappropriate
narrative moves all too clearly call attention to themselves, and to the
clear determination of their author to create a form of 'bad fiction'. As
to the length of the speech, in Ovid the crow's speech of advice to the
raven is forty-seven lines long (2.549–95). Chaucer may have settled on the
number 45 in part through his response to medieval Ovid commentaries:
both Arnulf of Orléans offers the Vatican Mythographer's gloss that the
raven was sacred to Phoebus because the bird possessed 'LXIIII^{or} vocum
interpretationes' (64 interpretations of voices).[90] Thomas Walsingham also
transmits this reading, but changes the number to 44: 'quadraginta quattuor
vocum interpretationes' in his *Archana deorum* (London, BL, Lansdowne
MS 728, fol. 54r; 'XLIIII^{or}' in Oxford, St Johns College, MS 124, fol. 45r). I
will return to Chaucer's possible use of the *Archana Deorum* below. Words
of advice that foolishly go unheeded by the raven in the original tale are
transferred to the mother in a way that cannot help but be noticed by all
readers. However, what might have been gained in dramatic intensity and
near-pathos, by the lament of Phoebus, is somehow lost in this final passage
with its emphasis on *not* speaking the truth.[91] The Manciple's mother warns
her son with an opening phrase reminiscent of Gower's Genius:

> My sone, be war, and be noon auctour newe
> Of tidynges, wheither they been false or trewe,
> Whereso thou come, amonges hye or lowe,
> Kepe wel thy tonge and thenk upon the crowe.
> (359–62)

---

[88] Lines 8098–9 (Bryan and Dempster 1958: 715). [89] Travis 2003: 317–24; Wallace 1997: 255–6.
[90] Arnulf of Orléans, *Allegoriae*, 1932: 157–234; II.7 and n. [91] Cf. Craun 1997: 201–8.

As Derek Pearsall characterises it:

The 'moral' for the story, therefore, when it comes, is vile . . . The thing to do . . . is to learn the tricks (to learn how to call black white) and use them for one's own advantage, and not be carried away by passion or idealism or that shibboleth called truth.[92]

As a final stance on language, and truth, and their relations, this is a disturbing note to reach at the conclusion of one ending of the *Canterbury Tales*. And in lines that are a precursor to a treatise on penitence, it is especially unsettling to be urged to *conceal* whatever truth one might know, rather than to express it.[93]

The Ovidian story in itself offers the counsel of keeping silence when one knows of a potentially damaging truth. In Ovid, the tale is suggestively linked to the poet's own situation with Augustus (who frequently associated himself with Apollo in Rome), and his subsequent exile. With Chaucer, too, one might view the crow as a figure for a poet who has been even indirectly silenced by an angry Phoebus; there are many ways in which the *Manciple's Tale* could function as a cynical, despairing statement by a Ricardian poet on the dangers, and futility, of 'speaking truth to power' – particularly in the decade of the 1390s.[94] Although political readings illuminate important aspects of the *Manciple's Tale*, they frequently fail to address adequately the *Manciple's Tale*'s relation to the *Parson's Tale*. In the textual tradition of the *Canterbury Tales*, there is little doubt that the order and sequential nature of fragments IX and X were intended.[95]

Chaucer constructs a moralising hermeneutics through his strategic placement of the Ovidian tale in conjunction with the *Parson's Tale*.[96] We are led, as it were, to agree with the Parson, and to find the language, the treatment of human relationships, and the 'truths' of the *Manciple's Tale*, wanting.[97] Chaucer takes an extraordinarily eloquent Ovidian tale

---

[92] Pearsall 1985: 239–40; 241.

[93] Although critics have remarked on the possibility of Chaucer's parodying of Gower's *Confessio Amantis* in this passage, I do not see that the speech of the mother functions mainly to this end.

[94] A number of critics have explored the political contexts for, and meanings of, the *Manciple's Tale*: Fradenburg 1985: 85–118; Herman 1991: 318–28; Wallace 1997: 247–60.

[95] Pearsall 1985: 16; Chaucer 1987: 951; Dean 1979. But cf. Blake 1981.

[96] I do not accept the position that the *Parson's Tale* is intended as the measure against which all of the earlier tales should be judged, or that Chaucer in every sense embraces the Parson's rejection of literary art. For a useful summary of the multiplicity of recent interpretations on the tale, see Wenzel 2000: 1–10.

[97] Kensak 1999:190–206, has presented a powerful case for Chaucer's final 'silences' in the tradition of Dante and the *Anticlaudianus*. It should be noted, however, that although the *Parson's Tale* represents penitential discourse, it is very much Chaucer's own making. Though the 'voice' of the *Parson's Tale* represents a distinct shift from the voice of the *Manciple's Tale*, the former is yet

about the dangers of truthful speech, rids it of its empathetic qualities, and situates it just prior to the Parson's instruction of the soul.[98] If the idea of Chaucer 'moralising' Ovid seems unlikely, that is because much criticism in the twentieth century has emphasised Chaucer as the 'secular' reader of classical poetry.[99] Although there is a good deal of truth to this description, in cases it is anachronistic, and particularly unconvincing when one considers Chaucer's strongly moral choice in ending the *Canterbury Tales* with a treatise on penitence (to which he devoted a considerable amount of time).[100] That the Ovidian tale just adjacent to Chaucer's most overtly religious text should also ultimately partake of a moralising hermeneutics is not surprising. Any discomfort in considering this hermeneutics is a modern reader's, not Chaucer's.[101]

Many critics have noted the sneering tone of the crow's speech, as one which provokes Phoebus' just ire.[102] I would argue that this addition by Chaucer complicates considerably the question of Phoebus' own culpability in the tale. Early on Phoebus demonstrates the 'watching' behaviour of the fabliau husband that results in the inevitable cuckolding. Phoebus' actions of murder and destruction create a terrifying spectre and reduce him later to overwhelming remorse. Yet if Phoebus offers a speech of contrition (of sorts), Chaucer makes ambiguous the source of his sin. By changing the crow's way of presenting the news to Phoebus, Chaucer highlights the problem of intention in the tale, and the ways in which an evil intention in the delivery of the 'truth' can precipitate a host of new forms of wrongdoing (the crow arguably has a more originary malicious intent in his actions than the suddenly angered Phoebus does). Thus Chaucer is preparing for the extensive examination of sin in all its forms, and the respective remedies for it, in the *Parson's Tale*. Elsewhere Chaucer endows beasts with moral agency: the fox in the *Nun's Priest's Tale*, who deceptively praises and

another fiction of Chaucer's, employed to close the *Canterbury Tales* with yet another speaker and worldview.

[98] See for example, Ferster 2000; Bestul 1989: 600–19; Dean 1985; Patterson 1978.
[99] After the period of D. W. Robertson's exegetical 'school' of criticism, A. J. Minnis contributed a much-needed study of Chaucer's 'historical' understanding of, and response to, classical *auctores* (Minnis 1982 generally, but here, 15–25); his emphasis on Chaucer's historicist sense and Cooper's on Chaucer's form of 'humanism' (Cooper 1988: 77) are still powerful and convincing assessments of Chaucer. However, many other critics asserting Chaucer's 'secular' approach do not do so within the framework Minnis and Cooper provide.
[100] Patterson 1978; and the excellent work on the tale by Richard Newhauser in 2000 and 2002.
[101] I should note that in most cases Chaucer does not moralise his Ovid, and as many scholars have shown (for example, Cooper 1988: 75–6), Chaucer routinely omits the moralisations he finds in medieval commentaries on Ovid. In the case of the *Manciple's Tale*, however, Chaucer chooses to situate an Ovidian tale just prior to the closing *Parson's Tale*; the net effect is that the treatise on penitence in some sense comments upon the tale of human betrayal, sin, and anguish that precedes it.
[102] Cooper 1996: 393–4; Scattergood 1974; Herman 1991: 323–4.

misleads the cock so that he may finally kill him; and the speaking birds
in *The Parlement of Foules* and in the *House of Fame*. In medieval beast
fables and other writings, therefore, beasts are at times accorded powers
of volition and moral agency, as a vehicle for exploring these elements in
humans.[103]

Once Phoebus returns home, he asks the crow to tell him 'what song'
he has to tell him. The crow replies,

> By God ... I synge nat amys.
> Phebus ... for al thy worthynesse,
> For al thy beautee and thy gentilesse,
> For al thy song and al thy mynstralcye,
> For al thy waityng, blered is thyn ye
> With oon of litel reputacioun,
> Noght worth to thee, as in comparisoun,
> The montance of a gnat, so moote I thryve!
> For on thy bed thy wyf I saugh hym swyve.
>
> (248–56)

The crow, albeit not extensively developed by Chaucer, clearly has a kind
of vindictive delight in exposing the infidelity of his master's wife. And if
Phoebus will go on to commit a range of sins, including wrath and murder
(and thoughts of suicide), the crow betrays his own 'distortion' of will in
this scene.

Edward Craun has fascinatingly examined the phenomenon of late
medieval 'clerically sanctioned fraternal correction' in a study on Margery
Kempe. He also discusses the 'three deviant sisters' of fraternal correction:
'improper reproof/rebuke, slander, and chiding'.[104] Although the crow is
clearly not aiming any direct rebuke at his master, his speech does fall into
the category of chiding; at the very least it illustrates the evil intention
in speech that is frequently condemned by the clergy. *The Parson's Tale*
discusses 'chidynge and reproche':

For certes, chidynge may nat come but out of a vileyns herte. For after the
habundance of the herte speketh the mouth ful ofte. / And ye shul understonde
that looke, by any wey, whan any man shal chastise another, that he be war from
chidynge or reprevynge. For trewely, but he be war, he may ful lightly quyken the
fir of angre and of wratthe, which that he sholde quenche, and peraventure sleeth
hym which that he myghte chastise with benignitee. (x.626–7)

---

[103] Cooper 1996: 385, notes the use of beast exempla in medieval sermons; also Ziolkowski 1993.
Ziolkowski notes the medieval tradition of using a bird to represent the soul (107).
[104] Craun 2003: 191. Cf. also Craun 1997: 187–216 for discussion of the *Manciple's Tale*. Craun argues
that the crow's 'character is not realized at all' (195) and sees the crow as type of mouthpiece for the
Manciple's own manipulation of language (194–7).

The crow revels in the low-class status of the lover Phoebus' wife has taken, although appearing to flatter Phoebus in the same breath: 'With oon of litel reputacioun, / Noght worth to thee, as in comparisoun, / The montance of a gnat'. He finishes off the speech with the coarse verb 'swyve', which can only exacerbate Phoebus' wrath. The question of the wife's adultery aside, what Chaucer seems to explore is the way in which ill-intentioned speech can itself precipitate the sins of others. In fact, in Machaut's *Le Livre du Voir Dit*, the narrator condemns the ill-will of the exulting bird (there a raven): 'il faurra à son entente' (line 7997).[105] Even earlier, a commentary on this passage of the *Metamorphoses* remarks on the malevolence of one who enjoys reporting bad news: Pierre Bersuire's *Ovidius moralizatus*, for example, has 'gaudet talia referre' (Oxford, Merton College, MS 989, fol. 28v).[106] Chaucer seems interested in examining the complex relations of intention and action, not just in Phoebus, but also in the crow who now, it can be argued, has become a moral agent in part responsible for the blood-letting that follows. What is the origin of Phoebus' wrongdoing? Is sin a collective enterprise? Lynn Staley has argued that

In positioning the Parson's Tale where he does and giving it such authority, Chaucer may be elaborating upon Langland's decision to end *Piers Plowman* with Conscience. Conscience is that faculty operative in penance and, for the Parson, an agent of social change.[107]

For Chaucer, in the tale of Apollo and the crow, the question is not only, as it is in Ovid, the dangers of speaking truth, but also the complex terrain of moral agency. In his exploration of the multiple causes and agents in Phoebus' crimes/sins, he introduces the larger undertaking of the *Parson's Tale*. Thomas Walsingham's *Archana deorum*, a late fourteenth-century commentary on Ovid (with which Chaucer may have been familiar) offers a provocative rendering of the scene. Walsingham first paraphrases Ovid's Latin (2.612) to describe Phoebus' intense regret after slaying Coronis, before quoting Ovid's line (613): '*mox ductus penitencia licet nimis cera seque quod audierit quod sic exarsit odit*' (*soon led by penitence although it was too late*, he hated himself because he became so enraged at what he had heard; Oxford, St Johns 124, fol. 44v; emphasis added).[108] Ovid had

---

[105] Bryan and Dempster 1958: 713.
[106] Although this manuscript is dated to *s.* xv[in.], nine copies were available in late fourteenth-century England (Clark 2004: 183n.80).
[107] Staley 2005: 331.
[108] The earlier copy of the *Archana deorum* (London, MS Lansdowne 728), does not contain as extended a discussion of the story of Apollo and the crow, and thus does not contain the word 'penitencia'. However, Clark notes that the later copy (Oxford, St Johns 124) or a version similar to it may well have been available to Chaucer.

used the verb 'paenitet' (2.612), but Walsingham appears to be the first commentator to incorporate the Latin word 'penitencia' (with its medieval associations) in this context; if Chaucer was aware of this reading, it may help explain his decision to place the *Manciple's Tale* as a type of 'ante-room' to the treatise on penitence which is the *Parson's Tale*. Chaucer positions the *Manciple's Tale*, and its rough-hewn way of relating the worst side of human nature (adultery, murder, destruction, removal of the bird's own means of communication), from within the hearing of the Parson as a way of introducing rather starkly the problems of sin, intention and their complex relations.[109]

* * * * * * *

From apocalyptic vision to dark beast fable: these are some of the forms in which Gower and Chaucer 'remake' their Ovids. What emerges is a rich diversity in treatment even by the same poet. Gower considers ways of incorporating Ovid's own verse into a speech from the heavens, directed to a distraught narrator who has discovered himself on a strange island surrounded with many unfamiliar people. At the close of the second vision of *Vox* Book 1, even the divine speaker ventriloquises as he counsels moderation and self-rule. Gower often reshapes Ovid's myths in the *Confessio Amantis* so as to highlight larger principles of self-restraint and oath-keeping, central to both Amans and to (perhaps) the listening monarch. One result of this reshaping is Gower's development of a hero-ine's inner world, in the case of Ariadne. For his part, Chaucer purges the Ariadne tale of its traditional *sens*, tragic heartbreak, so as to disable the larger 'project' of the *Legend of Good Women*. Chaucer also selects for his final fictional tale in the *Canterbury Tales* Ovid's tale of the raven/crow, and reworks the whole imaginatively to project a harsh, cynical world of violence and betrayal, and yet thereby to complicate its moral valences, in anticipation of the approaching *Parson's Tale*. What appears as a disturbing 'shutting down' of voice, language, and truth in the *Manciple's Tale* is at the same time an opening up of a new vein of exploration in the poem: the analysis of intention in relation to sin; thus we discover in startling ways Chaucer 'moralising' his Ovid. From this study it should be clear that Gower and Chaucer availed themselves of Ovids Latin and French, both Latin school texts of the day and moralisations. Yet both poets show extraordinary creativity in their own 'glosynge' of Ovid.

---

[109] On the idea of Chaucer's development of a spiritual progression or ascent from the latter part of the *Canterbury Tales*, into the *Parson's Tale*, and finally to the *Retraction*, see Bestul 1989: 617–18.

CHAPTER 11

Ovid in medieval Spain

Vicente Cristóbal

Ovid was well known and widely recognised in medieval Spain, particularly from the thirteenth century onwards, both for his works about love and about mythology. Spanish literature indeed played an important role in the so-called *aetas Ovidiana*, which spread through Western Europe during the final centuries of the medieval era.

The presence of Ovid in the Spanish literature of the thirteenth to the fifteenth century confirms the existence of manuscripts of his work, as do the references to manuscripts of Ovid in the extant lists of medieval book catalogues.[1] Such manuscripts, many of which no doubt contained *accessus* and abundant glosses, probably came to Spain from France. Unfortunately, no trace of these manuscripts remains, as all Ovidian manuscripts preserved in Spain at present come from Italy and were acquired by means of sales or donations.[2] However, according to Tafel's hypothesis,[3] the archetype of Ovid's amatory works was of Spanish or African origins, and it was taken to France from Spain by Theodulf of Orléans by the end of the eighth century.

Before considering the historiography of Alfonso X ('The Wise'), two works must first be mentioned: the *Carmina Riuipullensia* and the *Libro de Alexandre*. The *Carmina Riuipullensia*, an anonymous Latin verse collection dating from the last third of the twelfth century (or perhaps even earlier), can be considered an early example of the Iberian *aetas Ovidiana*. In particular, the elegiac poem entitled *Quo modo prius conuenimus* is written in imitation of Ovid's *Amores* 1.5.[4] In Spanish romance, the first evidence for the impact of the *Heroides* and the *Metamorphoses* can already be found in the anonymous *Libro de Alexandre* (first third of the thirteenth century). Schevill and subsequent critics have signalled the indebtedness of the poem

---

The author would like to thank Ana González-Rivas Fernández, who translated the text from Spanish into English.

[1] Díaz y Díaz 1991: 80–1 and 273–4. [2] Arcaz 1992; 1996.
[3] Tafel 1910: 32–45 and 73. [4] Raby 1997, II: 236–47; Moralejo 1986: 84; Ovid 1989: 143.

to its Ovidian original,[5] though some of these echoes may also be due to the influence of the *Alexandreis* of Walter de Châtillon, another primary source of the *Libro*.

In the second half of the thirteenth century, the historiographical works of King Alfonso X (1256–84), namely his *Estoria de España* (also entitled *Primera Crónica General*)[6] and his *General Estoria*, emerge as outstanding examples of Ovidianism, which show not only engagement with the ancient poet's text, but also a deep knowledge of the most recent commentaries and interpretations of the Latin work.

A major part of Ovid's poetry, in particular more than half of the *Heroides* and multiple passages of the *Metamorphoses*, was translated into Spanish by the circle of scholars surrounding Alfonso, who adapted these verses to contemporary needs using the different glosses and interpretations included in the text.[7] The *Estoria de España* and the *General Estoria*, both written between 1270 and 1280, promoted the double political agenda of Alfonso X: the consolidation of national sovereignty and the acquisition of an imperial crown.[8] Their composition coincides with the collection of the literary sources on which the works are based; we know that at the beginning of 1270 Alfonso X borrowed from the Collegiate Church of Albelda and the monastery of Santa María de Nájera (both in Rioja) certain ancient books (obviously *codices* recently arrived from France), among which there was a Lucan, a *Thebaid* of Statius, a Boethius, a Virgil manuscript containing the *Eclogues* and *Georgics*, and a copy of Ovid's *Heroides*.[9]

The compostion of the *Estoria de España* initially required much greater effort on the part of Alfonso, and indeed he later incorporated many sections from it into the *General Estoria*. In his work on his native land, Alfonso X maintains the same pattern as that found in the Latin chronicles written before Rodrigo Jiménez de Rada and Lucas de Tuy. As was the norm in these Latin chronicles, Alfonso, when he wishes to recall the most ancient events in the history of Spain, does not hesitate to use the mythical legends related to the peninsula, especially that of Hercules. Among

---

[5] Schevill 1913: 18–22; Solalinde 1928; Casas Rigall 1999: 44.
[6] Menéndez Pidal and Catalán 1977.
[7] Lida de Malkiel 1975: 339–97; 1958–9; 1959–60. Neither Schevill 1913 nor Highet 1949 alludes to the reception of Ovid in Alfonso X's work.
[8] Gómez Redondo 1998–2007, 1: 643–5 and 686–9.
[9] Díaz y Díaz 1991: 80–1 and 273–4 and Gómez Redondo 1998–2007, 1: 669.

the various invaders, he includes the Carthaginians and the founding of Carthage by queen Dido (chapters 51–61). First, he relates the version of the story of Dido transmitted by Justinus in Pompeius Trogus' summary (*Historiae Philippicae* 18.4–6), according to which Dido never met Aeneas and committed suicide in order to escape the marriage demands of the king of Libya. Subsequently, an alternative version is offered, namely Virgil's poetic version (with many cuts and alterations), where the poet presents the love relationship between the queen and Aeneas, and the suicide of the former due to the Trojan's departure. Nevertheless, there is no evidence of direct use of the Virgilian text, but only of intermediate sources, especially the *Historia Romanorum* by Jiménez de Rada. At no point in Alfonso's narration are the ancient authorities mentioned, but only the 'estoria' or 'estorias'. In addition to the second version of the legend of Dido, the queen's letter to Aeneas, which appears as epistle 7 of Ovid's *Heroides*, is translated (chapter 59), a clear sign of the influence of the Latin poet in this work, perhaps due to the manuscript borrowed from Nájera. The writers associated with Alfonso primarily use the technique of *amplificatio* to explain what is obscure in Ovid's text, to make a moral judgement on the characters' attitudes, or for stylistic reasons.[10] In any case, the evident pleasure taken in the rhetorically excessive prose is characteristic of this text. Dido's letter, therefore, is a very special chapter in the *Estoria de España* because of its highly sentimental tone, which highlights this particular episode among the other historiographical contents and imitates the contemporary 'jarchas' and 'cantigas de amigo', as Impey states.[11] Ovid's poetry was one of the main sources of this account. In the *Estoria de España*, this elegy is the only one of the *Heroides* that is translated and integrated into the whole of the historical narrative, and the only one that has a thematic relationship with the Spanish past.

Alfonso X's *Grande e General Estoria* constitutes a very broadly conceived and unique historiography, quite without equal. In addition to the contents taken from the Bible and the translation of the *Heroides*, this work includes a rendering in prose of a large part of the *Metamorphoses*, intertwined with a number of prolix explanations derived from medieval sources.[12] With his *Grande e General Estoria*, Alfonso took on the task of creating a universal history, which, in fact, became a vast encyclopaedia wherein he aimed to encompass all knowledge in keeping with the spirit of the comprehensive aim of science at that time. To understand the structure of the *Grande e General Estoria*, we have to go far back to the model of the ancient

---

[10] Impey 1980a.   [11] Impey 1980a: 4.   [12] Ginzler 1987 and Brancaforte 1990.

Chronicles of Eusebius and St Jerome (the latter is a Latin translation and amplification of the former), where the events of the sacred history of Israel and of the ancient world are recounted. Closer to King Alfonso's epoch, Peter Comestor's *Historia Scholastica* (*c.* 1170) is another key source. It is based on the Bible and the *Jewish Antiquities* of Flavius Josephus, and it provides an even more effective model for the insertion of events into an extra-biblical ancient history. The events of ancient mythology, narrated by Ovid in the *Metamorphoses* in a somewhat chronological sequence, are therefore interpreted as history. As Lida de Malkiel points out,[13] the aim of Alfonso's writers, starting from the framework provided by Peter Comestor, is very ambitious: to include every ancient event ever recorded, and to narrate each as meticulously and extensively as possible. They frequently reference the rather prolix nature of Ovid's narration. One example is the passage about Arcas, the son of Jupiter and Callisto (*GE*,[14] first part: 595: 'Ouidio cuenta . . . mas complida mientr': (Ovid narrates . . . in a more detailed manner)).

That Ovid as a poet was not obliged to respect the strict truth escaped neither Alfonso X nor his collaborators. Consequently, the writers often turn to allegorical interpretations, considering that poets usually hide the truth under the veil of a fable;[15] once this veil is lifted, it is possible to discover the real facts therein or the fruitful and ennobling truth that underlies the imaginative narratives. This allegorical approach serves to uncover the hidden meanings of Ovid's fables, which turn out to be historical, natural or moral truths. On the other hand, it does not matter that this unveiled truth goes beyond the realms of historiography, because, as mentioned before, the *General Estoria* has an encyclopaedic and pedagogical aspiration in every sense, and this is also made manifest in many of its digressions. So, when dealing with Io and her metamorphosis from woman to cow, and then from cow to woman, Alfonso's historians point out the seriousness of the theme (*GE*, first part, Genesis, Book 6, ch. 26: 163):

Aquello que Yo fue por el ruego de Juppiter mudada de uaca en mugier et de todo en todo, e dada dalli adelante a todas buenas costumbres, e en el cabo fecha deessa de Egipto, non lo tenga ninguno por fabliella, por que es delas razones de Ouidio, ca el que las sus razones bien catare e las entendiere fallara que non ay fabliella ninguna, nin freyres predigadores e los menores que se trabaian de tornarlo en la nuestra theologia non lo farien si assi fuesse, mas todo es dicho en figura e en semeiança de al.

[13] Lida de Malkiel 1958–9: 112.   [14] *GE* = Alfonso el Sabio 1930.   [15] Seznec 1983: 77–104.

Regarding the account that narrates Io's transformation, limb by limb, into a cow at Jupiter's request, and explains that subsequently she gave herself up to good habits, and was eventually made goddess of Egypt, don't think it is a lie for the sole reason that it belongs to Ovid's discourse; because if you read the text carefully, you will find no lie there, and the preacher and other minor friars that try to make it part of our theology would not do so if it were a lie; actually, everything is used as an image and a symbol of another reality.

Very seldom is the fantastic character of the mythological narrative shown and the conclusion drawn that in the text there is no mystery to reveal, but only a display of imagination. It is possible that neither the glosses nor the auxiliary sources on which Alfonso X relied provided any allegorical explanation of a passage. As a result, certain narratives were set aside or summarised only briefly, as is the case in the episodes of the flood and the fire provoked by Phaethon, which were extensively narrated by Ovid in the first two books of the *Metamorphoses*. Alfonso summarised these episodes in just a few words, because he considered them a 'fabliella' (fable) in which Ovid presents himself as a poet and, therefore, a liar whose statements have no true basis (*GE*, first part Exodus, Book 13, ch. 15: 368–9). The *Metamorphoses* therefore only provides the material for the incidents highlighted in the basic structural sources (St Jerome, Peter Comestor), while the glosses and commentaries on Ovid's work, to which I shall return shortly, add material to the original text. The same process occurs in some of the *Heroides*, a collection of letters from heroines that, once translated using a periphrastic style, are inserted into the corresponding legendary account, thereby completing the process of *amplificatio*. Ovid's epic work, however, is referred to only once by its original title: 'Dize Ouidio en el su Libro mayor, que a nombre Methamorphosis' (Ovid says in his 'Greater Book', titled *Metamorphosis*) (*GE*, first part, Genesis, Book 7, ch. 42: 199). In the remaining allusions, the writers refer to this work only as 'Libro Mayor' ('Greater Book');[16] it is compared to the Bible in meaning and, since it deals with gods and gentile heroes, it is also defined as a compendium of pagan theology (*GE*, first part, Genesis, Book 6, ch. 26: 162–3).

There are constant references to the Roman poet's work in the mythographical sections, either by mentioning the poet's name, or the poet's name and that of the work ('Libro Mayor'), or the name of the poet and the work, and also the number of books. Sometimes the writers even quote

---

[16] During the Middle Ages, the *Metamorphoses* was usually entitled the *Ovidius maior*, hence the Spanish title.

some verses in Latin, followed by translations. In sum, a substantial portion of the *Metamorphoses*, in a somewhat dismembered form, is transferred into Alfonso X's work. In the first part of the *General Estoria*, the writers adapt material from Book 1, specifically the narrative about the Golden and later Ages, that of Deucalion's flood (summarised), Io and Jupiter, Argus and Mercury, Pan and Syrinx; from Book 2, the accounts about Phaethon (only alluded to briefly), and about Jupiter, Callisto and Arcas. In the second part of the *General Estoria*, they refer to the fables of Jupiter and Europa (Book 2 of *Metamorphoses*); from Book 3 they take into account the stories of Cadmus and Harmonia, Actaeon, Jupiter and Semele, Tiresias, Narcissus and Echo, and Pentheus; from Book 4, the narrations about Minyeides, Pyramus and Thisbe, Leucothoe and Clytie, the adulterous relationship between Mars and Venus, the stories of Hermaphroditus and Salmacis, Ino and Athamas, and finally, the figure of Perseus as the killer of Medusa and the saviour of Andromeda; from Book 5, everything to do with Proserpina's kidnapping (together with the passage of the same story in the *Fasti*);[17] from Book 6 Alfonso takes the fables of Niobe, Tereus, Procne and Philomela, and Boreas and Orithyia; from Book 7, the entire story of Medea and Jason, Minos, the prodigious origin of the Myrmidons, and the story of Cephalus and Procris; from Book 8, the accounts of Scylla, Ariadne and Theseus, Daedalus and Icarus, Meleager and the Calydonian boar, and Hercules' struggle with the river Achelous, though the beautiful (but historically irrelevant) episode of Philemon and Baucis, which is an outstanding example of virtue and piety at the very heart of paganism, is omitted; from Book 9, Alfonso's collaborators take the stories of Hercules and Deianira, Hercules' death, and many other elements that provide material for the so-called 'Estoria de Ercules', inserted in the second part of the *General Estoria*; however, in this same second part they omit the account of Lygdus, Telethusa and Iphis (also narrated in Book 9 of the *Metamorphoses*), in which pagan religious sincerity is very clear, and the thorny theme of female homosexuality shows itself; from Book 10, they adapt the fable of Orpheus and Eurydice, which is entirely based on Ovid's work without any insertions from Virgil's account in the *Georgics*, but they leave out the episodes of Pygmalion, Adonis, Hippomenes and Atalanta, as well as the whole story of Orpheus' invention of pederasty, for obvious reasons of moral censorship; from Book 11 they extract the stories of Midas and Laomedon; and from the content of the last four books material of a very different kind is taken (such as the judgement of Achilles' armour and Ajax's and Ulysses' discourses), which are inserted in

[17] See Castro Jiménez 1993: 361–5.

the course of the second and third part of the work, in Ulysses' account and the corresponding section of the 'Estoria de Troya', derived from the narrations of Dyctis and Dares.[18]

The view of Ovid adopted by the writers of the *General Estoria* may be conditioned by the glosses transmitted in the manuscripts of Ovid's work, as well as the independent, and for the most part moralistic, commentaries on the *Metamorphoses*. Some of the details of Alfonso's versions of the Ovidian myths not present in the Latin text may derive from these glosses, as Lida has demonstrated.[19] Two commentaries transmitted independently of the *Metamorphoses* are frequently used and quoted in the *General Estoria*: the first is that of 'maestre Johan el Inglés' (teacher John, the Englishman), identified as 'Iohannes Anglicus' or 'Iohannes de Garlandia' (i.e. John of Garland) since Solalinde's edition,[20] who wrote in 1234 the *Integumenta Ovidii*, an allegorical commentary to the *Metamorphoses* composed in elegiac distichs.[21] The second commentary is by a 'frayre' (a friar), who is said to be one 'de los frayres menores' (one of the friars minor, i.e. Franciscans) and 'que trabaio de tornar las razones de Ouidio mayor a theologia' (who works to turn the thoughts of the *Metamorphoses* to theology) (*GE*, first part Genesis, Book 4, ch. 9: 91); despite the divergences in many areas between his testimony and the French work, Solalinde identified this friar with the anonymous author of the *Ovide moralisé*, a long exegetical-allegorical poem that was dated by its editor, C. de Boer, to the beginning of the fourteenth century.[22] Since this dating is incompatible with the fact that it was used, as is generally believed, as a source for the *General Estoria*, Solalinde suggests that the French poem originated in an earlier period.[23] This synthesis of materials may be better understood if we take into consideration the open nature of the medieval commentaries.[24] Moreover, Engels affirms that Arnulf of Orléans was a source for the French work, a fact that would explain the sporadic parallels between the two later works and the *Allegoriae*. Many other ancient and medieval texts shape, fix and interpret the contents of Ovid, among which we find Pliny's *Natural*

---

[18] The Ovidian materials of the third part do not appear in the editions of Solalinde 1930 and Solalinde *et al.* 1957–61, but they can be found in the collection edited by Brancaforte 1990: 333–73.

[19] Lida de Malkiel 1958–9: 114.   [20] Alfonso el Sabio 1930: xiv.

[21] For John of Garland's *Integumenta*, see also in this volume, pp. 59–65.

[22] For the *Ovide moralisé* see also in this volume, pp. 83–107.

[23] Solalinde 1925. Engels 1943: 5 offers a solution to this problem, positing that under the pseudonym of 'the friar' Alfonso's writers allude to a group of textual commentaries collected together in only one *corpus* of manuscripts, among which we find the *Integumenta Ovidii* by John of Garland (1933) and, mixed with other sources, the *Allegoriae super Ovidii Metamorphosin* by Arnulf of Orléans (1932) (twelfth century; to whom Alfonso X never refers by name).

[24] Coulson 1985 and 1991.

History, St Augustine's *City of God*, Orosius' *History*, a mysterious *Libro de las generaciones de los dioses*, and Godfrey of Viterbo's *Pantheon*.[25]

Lastly, we must highlight the interpretative method of the *General Estoria*. Ovidian myths had to be reduced to purely human dimensions in order to be incorporated into Alfonso X's historiographical work. To accomplish this, the writers employed euhemerism, whereby mythological accounts are treated as a reflection of actual historical events shaped by retelling. The divinities' supernatural powers and ability to transform themselves are explained as acts of magic and witchcraft. They can indeed cause transformation in other beings, or make them believe they have taken on a new shape. In a culture which accepted the reality of witchcraft, Ovid's mythical stories suffered a systematic change, completed by an occasional allegorical interpretation. Whereas the euhemeristic interpretation is usually inserted into the main body of the narrative, the allegory, which is a more typical strategy of the textual commentators (either the 'maestre Johan el Inglés', the 'frayre' or any other 'esponedor'), is inserted later as a complement added to the bare fable.

In addition to material from the *Metamorphoses*, ten of the letters from Ovid's *Heroides* (the book that Alfonso calls the 'Libro de la duennas') are translated in Alfonso's work, where they are inserted in the body of the corresponding mythical narrative.[26] The translations made from the *Heroides* were much more elegant and faithful than those from the *Metamorphoses*, although they also depend more on *amplificatio*, and there is also less exegetical material than that collected for the 'Libro mayor'. However, it is evident that the originals used by Alfonso's writers were generously glossed, and that sometimes these glosses provided the authors of the *General Estoria* with material that was wrongly attributed to Ovid's authority.

The *Metamorphoses* and the *Heroides* are, therefore, very much present in Alfonso X's historical works, but the rest of Ovid's works, except for the *Fasti*, were of little interest for the work's purposes because of their amatory or exilic content. From the *Fasti*, however, there are at least two recurrent motifs: one in the first part of the *General Estoria* (*GE*, Genesis, Book 8,

---

[25] Lida de Malkiel 1958–9: 115–22.

[26] The first part contains none, but the second has eight: epistle 2 (from 'Ypermestra' to 'Lino', corrupted name of Linceus – this sort of corruption of proper names, usually the result of faulty transmission, is common in medieval texts and in Alfonso's works, as can be seen in several cases); 4 ('Adriagna' to 'Theseo'); 6 ('Phedra' to 'Ypolito'); 9 ('Daymira' to 'Ercules'); 10 ('Ysifile' to 'Jason'); 12 ('Medea' to 'Jason'); 14 ('Oenone' to 'Paris'); and 3 ('Fillis' to 'Demofon'). The third part includes two more letters: epistle 1 ('Penalope' to 'Vlixes'), and 8 ('Herminone' to 'Orestes'); as regards the remaining ten letters, in the second part there are some allusions to 3, 16 and 17 (detected in Ashton 1944), and in the fifth part we find references to 18 and 19 (detected in Rodríguez del Padrón 1984).

ch. 2: 205), specifically when Ovid's work is quoted as a source for Proserpina's genealogy ('assi com diz Ouidio en el libro de Fastos' (as Ovid says in his book of Fasti)),[27] and the other in the second part of the work (*GE*, Jueces, ch. 36: T 163),[28] concerning the genealogy of Juno and her sisters. In the latter case, the writers even quote the Latin verses to which the content refers, explaining the meaning of the work's title (*Fasti*), and comparing the pagan holiday calendar to the Christian rituals consecrated to the Saints. Finally, Alfonso refers to the *Remedia amoris* (*GE*, Numbers, Book 21, ch. 16: 605), a work that is called, in a very Spanish way, 'Sanidades del amor' ('Cures of Love').[29] From this work, the authors quote, translate, and gloss verse 150 ('Da vacuae menti, quo teneatur opus' (Give an idle mind a task to do)). The reference originates in the commentaries of John of Garland and the mysterious 'frayre' on Callisto's transformation into a bear; consequently, it is quite probable that this reference to the *Remedia* was taken from the commentators on Ovid's texts. This passage discusses the dangers of idleness, through which Callisto lost her virginity, and concludes that the best defence against the traps of the devil is to have an occupation of some kind.

Alfonso's historiographical work thus constitutes the most important chapter of Spanish Ovidianism in the Middle Ages.

OVID IN THE IBERIAN *HISTORIA TROYANA*

At the time that Alfonso X began his vast historiographical work, there appeared in Spain the anonymous work known as the 'polymetric' *Historia Troyana*,[30] based on the *Roman de Troie* and dated by Menéndez Pidal to around 1270. This work only covers a small part of the material condensed in the long French poem, specifically from the defection of the seer Calchas to the Greek side up to Andromache's lament for the death of Hector. The prose passages of the version of the legend of Troy (which are relatively faithful to the source) alternate with passages of verse that are more independent and original, and therefore constitute a very interesting example of poetry at a very early stage in Spanish literature.[31] The work relates primarily the story of Briseis, Troilus and Diomedes, as related by Benoît de Sainte-Maure. Consequently, most of the material in verse has to do with the sentimental adventure involving these three characters.

[27] Castro Jiménez 1993: 361–5.
[28] Solalinde *et al.* 1957–61.   [29] Ovid 1989: 144–5.
[30] Gómez Redondo 1998–2007, vol. I: 803–17; Menéndez Pidal 1934; Castro Jiménez 2007: 130–3; Arcaz 2007: 146–9.
[31] Menéndez Pidal 1934: ix.

The anonymous author of the work adds some passages and amplifies others from the *Roman*. One instance of this approach is related to our search for traces of Ovid: in order to support the argument about the traditionally fickle character of women, the author mentions one of the verses from the *Remedia amoris* (463: 'successore nouo uincitur omnis amor' (All love is defeated by a new love that succeeds it)), which does not appear in the French source. Ovid's influence, however, reveals itself in a deeper and more direct way: the versified amplifications, especially in the passages about love, tend to be constructed as discourses of love in the manner of the *Heroides*, with much the same rhetorical technique. Ovidianism was already present in the French work, so the Spanish author takes on this influence through dual channels: one direct, and the other indirect. This same Ovidianism, however, is particularly highlighted in a certain passage from the Castilian work, which, in this episode, is very faithful to the *Roman*: the moment when Briseis arrives among the Greek troops, Diomedes demands her love, and she, though first denying him, eventually consents to his amorous overtures:

E bien cred ende una cosa, e sed ende çierto, que sy en guisa me copiese que yo ouiese de fazer aquesto, non querria ningund omne por amigo mas que a uos; mas non he ende sabor, nin me lo de nunca el nuestro señor.

And do believe – and take it for certain – that, if I felt like doing it, I wouldn't like any other lover but you. But I don't fancy it now, and pray God this never happens.

In this passage of the *Historia Troyana*, one may trace the impact of the last epistles of the *Heroides*, crossed letters between heroes and heroines. Especially relevant here are the parallels in the contrasting 'question-and-answer' discourses between Diomedes and Briseis on the one hand, and the Ovidian letters of Paris and Helen on the other. In Helen's letter the rapid changes in her spirit are clearly perceived by the reader, as she shifts from an initial rejection of Paris's proposal to total consent to his plan. There is no doubt that Sainte-Maure created the character of Briseis as a reflection and projection of the ancient Ovidian Helen.[32]

THE LATER MIDDLE AGES

Whereas during the thirteenth century writers draw predominantly on Ovid's mythographical works (a fundamental aspect in the historical

---

[32] Menéndez Pidal 1934: x–xi and Ovid 1950: 51–2.

writing of Alfonso X), during the fourteenth century the more influential works are those on love (*Amores*, *Ars amatoria* and *Remedia amoris*).
These had a major impact on one of the most significant poems in Spanish
literature: the *Libro de buen amor*, by Juan Ruiz, Archpriest of Hita, who
lived in the first half of the fourteenth century. Nonetheless, this impact
occurred through an indirect route: that is to say, the twelfth-century Latin
play *Pamphilus de amore*, the most famous and influential of the medieval
elegiac comedies, especially in Spain. *Pamphilus de amore* was probably
written in France, though some scholars have attributed a Spanish origin
to it.[33] The plot of the comedy revolves around Pamphilus' love for Galatea,
and the mediation between the two of a procuress (*alcahueta*), the heir of
Ovid's procuress in *Amores* 1.8. In other examples, the influence of Ovid is
more direct: the didactic intentions of the *Ars amatoria*, sometimes with
an autobiographical tinge, are closer to the *Libro de buen amor* than to the
dramatic form of *Pamphilus*.[34] Moreover, the combination of advice and
exempla (with a mythical background in the *Ars*, and a fabulist one in Juan
Ruiz) also has its precedent in Ovidian didactics. Both Ovid and Pamphilus
are quoted at the same time by the Archpriest (stanza 429), when the character of Love refers to these two advanced students in his school ('Pánfilo,
cual Nasón, por mí fue amaestrado' (Pamphilus, like Naso, was taught by
me)). At the end of the account about don Melón and doña Endrina, the
writer confesses his dual sources (stanza 891: 'pues lo feo de la historia es
de Pánfilo y Nasón' (because the ugly part of the story comes from Pamphilus and Naso)). At other times, Ovid is quoted alone, as in stanza 612
('De Ovidio don Amor fue maestro en la escuela' (Lord Love was Ovid's
school teacher)[35]). Reacting against the thesis supported, for instance, by
Cejador,[36] on the Archpriest's indirect knowledge of Ovid, Schevill draws
our attention to a number of parallels which seem independent from the
account of the *Pamphilus*.[37]

Juan Ruiz translates and rephrases many verses of the *Pamphilus*.[38] It can
sometimes be instructive to observe the evolution of the same passage in the
three texts: that of Ovid, the *Pamphilus*, and the work of the Archpriest. For
example, the consideration of the *ars* as a way to access love is present in *Ars
amatoria* 1.3–4, *Pamphilus* 82–7, and *Libro de buen amor*, stanzas 618–19.

---

[33] *Pamphilus de amor*, ed. Rubio and González Rolán 1977: 21–4.   [34] Lida de Malkiel 1973: 297.
[35] The identification of Amor as Ovid's *maestro* seems to be a precise inversion of the relationship of
Ovid as *praeceptor* and love as unruly pupil at the start of the *Ars amatoria*. I am grateful to one of
the anonymous referees for the Press for this observation.
[36] Cejador in Ruiz 1913: xxvii.   [37] Schevill 1913: 28–54.
[38] List of coincidences in *Pamphilus de amor*, ed. Rubio and González Rolán 1977: 33–8.

The three passages maintain the anaphora of *ars*/art, and the enumeration displays a casuistry that is progressively multiplied: three cases in Ovid's text, six in the anonymous narration, and nine in the Archpriest's work. The content of the examples differs in Ovid and in the *Pamphilus*, but is almost identical in the *Pamphilus* and the *Libro de buen amor*, with a few additions in the latter. In this case, the dependence of the *Libro de buen amor* on the *Pamphilus* is very evident, but the tradition of these procedures goes back to the work of Ovid himself. Lida de Malkiel concludes that the repetitive use of the anaphora in the Spanish work is in response to the influence of Ovid.[39] Finally, Dagenais points out that the introductions (*accessus*) to the Ovidian corpus collected in the manuscripts had a great influence on the prologue of the Archpriest's book, which manifests a purely ethical vision of literature.[40]

The *Sumas de historia troyana* is attributed to a mysterious Leomarte, though it is obvious that the work is anonymous, and Leomarte is only one of many adduced authorities.[41] In this work, the legend of the Trojan war appears once more, in the manner of the *Roman de Troie*, but intertwined with many other sources. Following the pattern of Alfonso X, five letters from the *Heroides* are intercalated in this work: numbers 6 (Hypsipyle), 12 (Medea), 9 (Deianira), 5 (Oenone) and 7 (Dido), the latter with many amplifications taken from Justinus' anti-Virgilian version.[42] Achilles' love for Polyxena is narrated in a passionate tone and in a language derived from Ovid, as Gómez Redondo points out. Many of the chapters in this work are also dedicated to examining the heroes' adventures in love and are fashioned after Ovid's mythographical works and his works on love.[43]

Bernat Metge (1340–1413) is perhaps the most outstanding figure in the literature written in Catalan during the fourteenth century. He was an author steeped in humanism who was well acquainted with the classics. There are many excellent examples of the influence of Ovid in his prose,[44] including the work entitled *Ovidi enamorat*, which is actually a Catalan translation of part of the second book of the pseudo-Ovidian Latin poem *De vetula* (dating from the thirteenth century), written in hexameters. *De vetula* is a fictional autobiographical narrative recounted by Ovid himself, in which he narrates his own love affairs, detailing how he resorted to a procuress (the *vetula* of the title) in order to achieve success. The Catalan author may have become familiar with Ovid's erotic poetry through this

---

[39] Lida 1973: 14.   [40] Dagenais 1986–7.
[41] Leomarte 1932; Gómez Redondo 1998–2007, vol. II: 1632–49.   [42] Ovid 1950: 35–6.
[43] Gómez Redondo 1998–2007, vol. II: 1637–8 and 1644–5.   [44] Metge 1983.

indirect source. It is curious to see how the enchantment of *Amores* 1.5 (the first encounter between the lover-poet and Corinna) and the enthusiastic description of the beloved's body are filtered through the anonymous medieval poem, confirming the enduring impact of that pentameter, so charged with sensuality (*Amores* 1.5, 20: 'forma papillarum quam fuit apta premi!' (how suitable was her breast to be pressed!)):

Los altres membres de les vestidures eren coberts, mas bé podia hom devinar que ço que era cobert esa assats bell e gentil per ço que hom veïa descobert. En lo seu pits se llevaven dues coses redones, ço és dues mamelles, que paria que desijassen ésser premudes de dolços abraçaments.

The rest of her body was covered with the dress, but it was possible to guess that what was hidden was really beautiful and fine-looking – considering what could be seen. In her breast there were two rounded shapes, that is to say, the two breasts, which seemed to be longing to be pressed by sweet embraces.

The procuress introduced by the author of the *De vetula* and by Metge was derived from the other procuress depicted by Ovid in *Amores* 1.8, who also served as the model for the one in *Pamphilus* and for the large entourage of literary procuresses that followed her. We can see this lineage in Metge's version of the bawd: 'una velletona, pobra e molt poderosa de llengua, veïna de ma germana, a la qual doné sovent almoina per pietat; e era estada nodrissa, al temps passat, de la dita donzella de mi amada' (a very old woman, poor and very talkative, my sister's neighbour, to whom very often I gave alms for mercy, was the wet-nurse of my beloved's aforementioned maid).

Metge's most famous work, *Lo somni* (1399), echoes Ovid's poetry, in particular the *Metamorphoses*,[45] more directly. The Catalan author resorts to the dream vision as the framework for his exposition, and bases the entire work on a dialogue which revolves around the immortality of the soul. The historical king Juan I, and the legendary Orpheus and Tiresias all take part in this dialogue. In Book 3, Orpheus narrates the vicissitudes of his own life, drawing on Book 10 of Ovid's *Metamorphoses*, and Book 4 of Virgil's *Georgics*. Orpheus' address to the divinities of Hell is clearly modelled on *Metamorphoses* 10.17–39:

No són vengut ací per mirar les tenebres infernals, a les quals necessàriament tota cosa mortal ha a davallar, ne per encadenar lo coll de Cèrbero, així com alguns han fet; sola causa de la mia venguda és ma muller, la qual, estant en la flor del seu jovent, una serpent ha morta ab son verí.

---

[45] Badia 1993: 56–67 and Butinyà 1994.

I have not come here to behold the hellish darkness, which every mortal being will necessarily face; neither to chain Cerberus' dog, as others did; the only aim of my coming is my wife, who, being in the prime of her life, was killed by the poison of a snake.

Further, the description of the attack on Orpheus by the Maenads and of the musician's death clearly shows affinities with Ovid's account. This story, recounted by Orpheus, allows Tiresias to narrate a number of scenes from the fables found in the third book of the *Metamorphoses*, in particular his temporary transformation into a woman and his participation as a judge in the discussion between Juno and Jupiter concerning the extent of sexual pleasure in men and women. The rest of Book 3 consists of a long description of Hell, mainly extracted from Book 6 of the *Aeneid*. Book 4 opens another controversy, partly based on Ovid's *Heroides* and Renaissance authors such as Boccaccio, regarding women, in which positive and negative opinions are expressed.

THE EARLY RENAISSANCE

During the first half of the fifteenth century, a nascent humanism developed in Spain, reflected in the notable scholarly activity centred on the classical authors. For example, translation of ancient texts became more frequent, and some authors, such as Virgil, were known directly, whereas previously they were seen as remote authorities that could only be consulted via intermediate sources. Figures such as Enrique de Villena (1384?–1434)[46] and Alonso de Madrigal (1410–55)[47] are illustrious examples of this new era.

The didactic prose of Enrique de Villena (to whom we owe the first Spanish translation of the *Aeneid*)[48] is scattered with quotations, translations, exegesis and reworkings of Ovid. In his *Tratado de la consolación*, for example, he refers to the narratives of the *Metamorphoses* on Medea and Pelias, Hercules and Deianira, Priam, Thyestes, Proserpina, Jupiter and Danae, Jupiter and Europa, Cinyras and Myrrha, and Nisus and Scylla.[49] The *Metamorphoses* is one of the ancient texts that Villena uses expressly for the composition of his work *Los doze trabajos de Hércules*,[50] quoting Ovid as a source for six of the twelve Labours of Hercules: the first (centaurs), the fifth (Cerberus), the eighth (Achelous, here 'Atheleo'), the tenth (Cacus),

[46] Gómez Redondo 1998–2007, vol. IV: 2473–2516.
[47] Gómez Redondo 1998–2007, vol. IV: 2643–2661.   [48] Cátedra 1989.
[49] Enrique de Villena 1976.   [50] Enrique de Villena 1958.

the eleventh (the lion), and the twelfth labour (where he had to hold the sky on his shoulders, according to Boethius). Villena's acquaintance with Ovid and his works, as well as his respect for Ovid as a poet, is shown in his autobiographical sketch, which constitutes a gloss on the 'prohemio' (introduction) of his translations and glosses on the *Aeneid*,[51] a passage analysed by Schevill:[52]

Éste fue poetha laureado después de Virgilio e fizo los argumentos a la Eneyda dicha e tenido fuera de Virgilio por mayor de los otros latynos, e, por ende, su testimonio faze mayor el loor de Virgilio conosçiendole mayoría por su boca, mayormente en sus escriptos; e por eso lo alego aquí. E déste se fallan doze obras poéthicas en estas partes de España, que son: el *Methamorphoseos*, el *De ponto*, el *De faustys*, el *De vetula*, el *De arte amandi*, el *De remedio amoris*, el de las *Epístolas*, el de las *Eroydas*, el *De lupo*, el *De mensa*, el *De pulice*, el *De viçibus* ['vocibus' creo que debería editarse] *animalium*, aunque dizen más fizo.

This poet was crowned with laurel after Virgil. He wrote the stories of the already mentioned *Aeneid*, and, apart from Virgil, he was considered the greatest among the Latin authors. For this reason, his testimony makes Ovid's glory become greater, since most of the people know him, and talk about him and about his texts. This is why I mention him here. There are twelve poetic works in these regions of Spain, that is: the *Metamorphoseos*, the *De Ponto*, the *Fasti*, the *De vetula*, the *De arte amandi*, the *De remedio amoris*, the *Epistles*, the *Heroides*, the *De lupo*, the *De mensa*, the *De pulice*, the *De vicibus animalium*, although he is said to have composed others as well.

Alfonso de Madrigal, also known as 'el Tostado' or 'el Abulense', was a prolific author of the fifteenth century also very well acquainted with ancient classical culture.[53] Two of his works are especially significant for this study: the *Comento a Eusebio* and *Las diez cuestiones vulgares*. The former is a wide-ranging commentary to Eusebius-Jerome's *Chronicle*, translated by Madrigal and divided into five parts, and published in Salamanca in 1506 and 1507, at the request of cardinal Cisneros. It is a universal history in the style of the *General Estoria*, where the author narrates a number of mythical events, for which Ovid was often the source. *Las diez cuestiones vulgares* was published in the same period in the same city,[54] as a supplement to the *Comento*.[55] *Las diez cuestiones vulgares* can be defined as the first Spanish mythographical work, depending as it does to a great extent on the mythographical handbook of Boccaccio, although the *Genealogia* is only quoted twice. The author also, however, appeals to Ovid's authority in the *Metamorphoses*, as can be seen in the fourth 'cuestión' about Narcissus.

[51] Cátedra 1989, I: 58–9.   [52] Schevill 1913: 239–40.   [53] Fernández Vallina 1988.
[54] Tostado de Madrigal 1995.   [55] Crosas López 1997.

There is no complete extant translation of the *Heroides* before Juan Rodríguez del Padrón's translation of Ovid's work in the *Bursario*,[56] written in the first half of the fifteenth century. Rodríguez del Padrón adds three original epistles, which surprisingly he also attributes to Ovid, and which are written according to the Ovidian pattern; the letters from Madreselva to Mauseol, Troilus to Briseis and Briseis to Troilus.[57] In the two latter epistles we can see that the author has recourse to the medieval tradition of the *Roman de Troie*, but the epistolary form and the discourse of love are entirely Ovidian, and even certain material elements can be considered as such (there are many echoes of Ovid's letter of Briseis, *Her.* 3.7–8 and 45–8). As Dagenais points out, in the brief prologue to the work there is evidence that the author translates a preliminary commentary (*accessus*) to the Ovidian text.[58]

Another work by Rodríguez del Padrón that deserves our attention because of its Ovidianism is the *Triunfo de las donas*, a book that follows the protofeminist tradition of Boccaccio's *De mulieribus claris*, where the text advances several arguments for women's superiority over men. A particularly Ovidian element of the *Triunfo* occurs in the episode where the author grants an encomiastic speech to a fountain, in the context of a visionary landscape. Only at the end of the treatise does a conceit created by the author himself, in imitation of Ovid's *Metamorphoses*, explain the true identity of the fountain. Long ago, Alisio had fallen in love with a nymph called Cardiana; despairing at being ignored by her, he committed suicide and was transformed into a tree. The nymph saw this and cried, and she was changed into a fountain. The author also employs one of the 'tricks' learnt in the *Heroides*: that of the interposed voice of the character who forms the framework for the story. It is therefore evident that his contact with Ovid as a 'translator' became very fruitful for Juan Rodríguez del Padrón, as far as his literary education was concerned.

The *Heroides* strongly influenced the first examples of the sentimental novel in Spain,[59] not only in their epistolary form but also in the development of a particular use of amatory language. Clearly, the *Cárcel de amor*, by Diego de San Pedro (see Leriano's letter to Laureola), and the novel by the above-mentioned Rodríguez del Padrón, *Siervo libre de amor*, are heavily indebted to Ovid. The translation of Ovid was probably good training for this work, and Rodríguez del Padrón doubtless put into practice what he

---

[56] Schevill 1913: 115–16; Rodríguez del Padrón 1984.
[57] González Rolán and Saquero Suárez-Somonte 1984.   [58] Dagenais 1985–6.
[59] Schevill 1913; 117–19. Impey 1980b; Brownlee 1990.

had learnt from the original. Ovid's indirect influence, through Boccaccio's *Fiammetta* and Eneas Silvio Piccolomini's *Historia de duobus amantibus*, should also be taken into account.

The Marqués de Santillana, don Íñigo López de Mendoza (1398–1458), was afforded the broadest possible humanistic education, expending considerable energy on the acquisition of books.[60] This vast culture is reflected to varying degrees in his poetic work.[61] Whereas the Marqués' famous 'serranillas' and his religious poetry and songs are exempt from any mythical allusion, the same is not true of his lyrical sayings (*decires*), nor of his sonnets 'al itálico modo', in which the stylistic ornament and the use of the names from legends endow his work with touches of conscious erudition. His narrative *decires*, on the other hand, are even more influenced by mythical material, in particular the works of *El triumphete de amor*, *El sueño*, the *Defunsión de don Enrique de Villena* and the *Comedieta de Ponça*. Though in these poems Santillana only resorts to mythology on certain occasions, these take up so much space that there is hardly room left for the main message of the text. Some of the allusions made in his *Proverbs* are explained afterwards in the *Glosses* with great erudition. One finds the same delight in mythology in *Bías contra Fortuna* and *Favor de Hércules contra Fortuna*.

Apart from literary material on Troy, the saga of Hercules and the *Aeneid*, Ovid's *Metamorphoses* and *Heroides* are the main sources used regularly by López de Mendoza.[62] In a letter to his son, he attests that he ordered Ovid's *Metamorphoses* to be translated, since he was keen to acquire direct knowledge of this poetic work, which he refers to as the *Libro mayor de las transformaciones*.

But the Marqués also uses the Spanish translation of Bersuire's *Ovidius moralizatus* ('*Morales* de Ovidio'), especially in the *Glosses*. This work already formed part of his library,[63] as did Boccaccio's *Genealogia deorum gentilium* (translated by Martín de Ávila), which provided him an easily accessible indirect source of information on certain Ovidian themes.

The mark left by the enormous influence of Ovid on the Marqués' poetry is very difficult to assess; nevertheless, I shall try to give an overall perspective of the main areas of influence, following the order of stories found in the *Metamorphoses*. The description of the origins of the world, with the separation of the four elements and the evolution of life from

[60] Schiff 1905; Reichenberger 1969; López de Bascuñana 1977, 1978. [61] Santillana 1988.
[62] Crosas López 1995: 171–92, esp. 178–81. [63] Schiff 1905: 86.

Chaos, is expressed in *Bías Contra Fortuna* 101–9, and the comparison
with the nymph Daphne, unreceptive to Apollo's advances, is referred to
in several places (sonnet 12, quoting the original source: 'de quien Ovidio
grand loor esplana', *Comedieta de Ponça* 41, *Proverbios o Centiloquio* 54,
with the corresponding erudite gloss, pointing out the sources). Phaethon
and Deucalion are quoted in *Bías* 26, the search for Europa by her brothers
is recorded in *El Sueño* 36, Cadmus and his adventures in founding Thebes
are alluded to in *Infierno de los enamorados* 23, and Actaeon appears in
El Sueño 43 and in *Com. Ponça* 46 (quoted this time as Antheon).[64] In
Book 12 (where Troy is one of the main topics), and in the following ones
the echoes become scarcer, probably because the Marqués preferred to use
other sources for the remaining events.

The pair of lovers in the *Heroides*, and especially the women writers of
the letters, provide famous cases for comparisons, and prestigious names
for lists of examples: in the *decir* 'Quando la fortuna quiso', stanza 7 points
out that 'Qual del cisne es ya mi canto / e mi carta es la de Dido' (my song
is already like swan's song, and my letter is like Dido's letter), referring to
the beginning of *Heroides* 7 ('Sic ubi fata vocant, udis abiectus in herbis /
ad vada Maeandri concinit albus olor...' (as the white swan sings when
his fate calls him, thrown on the humid grass close to the stream of the
river Meander...)). The preliminary considerations of Phaedra's letter to
Hippolytus (*Her.* 4) are reflected in sonnet 7, the reaction of Hypsipyle
on being informed by a messenger about Jason's treason (everything is
explained in *Her.* 6.9–40), Canace and Macareus (*Her.* 11), Aeneas and
Dido (*Her.* 7), Paris and Helen (*Her.* 16 and 17), and Hero and Leander
(*Her.* 16 and 17) are sufficient references to prove Santillana's liberal use of
Ovid's work. As an example of Ovidian feminine names, the passage of *El
triumphete de amor*, 129–44 stands out. In a retinue of Cupid in celebration
of the god's triumph, the poet contemplates a large group of legendary
women, whose stories are narrated in the *Metamorphoses*, as well as in the
Heroides or the Trojan cycle (Medea, Adriana, Braçaida, Dido, Penelope,
Andromaca, Poliçena, Felix de Redope, Ansiona, Philomena... with the
usual medieval corruption of proper names). Finally, stanza 12 of this
composition constitutes a curious passage, as far as Ovid is concerned;
Santillana twice mentions the Roman poet, with a double authority: his

---

[64] Other examples of this technique include: Semele's death in *Com. Ponça* 67; Echo (here 'Equo')
in *El sueño* 38; Narcissus in the *decires* 'Calíope se levante...' 4, 'Gentil dueña, tal paresce...' 8,
'Quando la fortuna quiso...' 1, *Inf.* 19 and *Com. Ponça* 48; Pentheus in *El sueño* 60 and *Com. Ponça*
48; Pyramus and Thisbe in *Inf.* 56; Perseus and the Gorgons in *Inf.* 23, the Gorgons again in *Com.
Ponça* 5, with an explicit allusion to the Ovidian source; and Perseus and Medusa in *Com. Ponça* 48.

erotic work (the *Ars amatoria*, usually called 'De Amante' or 'D'Amante' in the fifteenth century) and his mythographic work (the *Metamorphoses*). Since the latter used to be interpreted in an allegorical way, it is mentioned with his author's appellative, 'Naso metaforisante'.[65]

The Cordoban Juan de Mena (1411–56) uses myths more frugally than his contemporary the Marqués de Santillana, although, paradoxically, his learning was greater than the latter's, at least as far as ancient sources are concerned: he was himself the translator of Latin works of the early Empire (such as the *Ilias Latina*), whereas the Marqués de Santillana had to depend on the translation of others.[66] His erudite and exegetical work based on classical mythology, the results of which are represented in his *Glosses* to *La Coronación del Marqués de Santillana*, is more wide-ranging and representative than the use made of mythology by the Marqués (see, especially, his compositions on love, as well as other works like *La Coronación* or *Laberinto*). His didactic prose (*Tratado de amor*, *Tratado sobre el título de duque*) is ornamented with digressions and references to antiquity, which frequently go beyond the limits of myth.

As a commentator on mythology in his *Glosses* to *La Coronación*, Mena, starting from his own poetic references (generally reduced to proper names), provides a complete narrative of events in order to extract the historical truth and to offer an allegorical-moral application of this. In the narrative itself, he reworks, especially in form and details, the account of the source, greatly enhanced with some particulars of his own invention, which bring the story to life and make it more appealing, warmer and more novelistic. This can be seen in the passage inserted in the large explanation about the name Tereus (stanza 5).

Although Mena always quotes the primary sources from antiquity, he does not rely directly on the *Metamorphoses* (despite the Latin quotations from this text which Mena includes), but on the romance refashioning of the Latin work in the *General Estoria* by Alfonso X.[67] Thanks to the precedent of Alfonso, Mena's prose has a foundation on which to rest, which makes his work more fluid and ornamented. Alfonso's mythical accounts also favour resorting to prestigious names, as can be seen in the development, within the poem *La Coronación*, of myths concerning Athamas, Ino and Melicertes, Cadmus, Jason, Penelope, and Narcissus (stanza 6), Actaeon, Hector, Meleager, and Phineus (stanza 7), Ixion, the Danaids, and Amphiaraus (stanza 8), Orpheus (stanza 16, in which Mena shows his lack

[65] For the textual problems of this passage, see Cristóbal 1989. [66] Juan de Mena 1989.
[67] Reichenberger 1975; Parker 1978.

of knowledge of Book 4 of Virgil's *Georgics*, since he only refers to Ovid's and Boethius' text), Clytie (stanza 25), and Salmacis (stanza 34). Ovid's texts about metamorphoses, as well as the characters and themes of the *Heroides*, were very recent in Mena's memory, and he had easy access to these sources, as can be demonstrated in many of the allusions made in his other poems. Ovidian names, albeit generally changed significantly, are scattered throughout amatory poems such as 'El sol clarecía los montes acayos...' (in stanza 3 there is mention of Cephalus' magic javelin, Daedalus and his wings, Cadmus...), and 'El fijo muy claro de Yperión' (in stanza 15 of which we can read the account of Tereus' adultery and Thisbe's mourning before the dead Pyramus). In *El Laberinto*, his longest and most famous work, Mena offers some riddles, mainly taken from Ovid (102–4: Clytemnestra and Aegisthus, Cinyras and Myrrha, Tereus and Philomela, Canace and Macareus, Ixion and the cloud, Pasiphae and the bull, and Scylla and Nisos). One should also observe that the epithet 'Penatígero' (*Laberinto* 31) is Ovidian and not Virgilian, although it refers to Aeneas: the adjective *penatiger* is applied to the Trojan hero in *Metamorphoses* 15.450, since he is the saviour of the *penates* of his motherland.

Finally, we have in a geographical description (*Laberinto* 41) an echo of Ovid's *relegatio*, derived from his scholarly formation and which may imply an acquaintance of his elegiac work written in exile ('... tierra de Ponto, / do Naso e Clemente fueron relegados' (the land of Pontus, where Naso and Clement were exiled)).

Thanks to his own testimony as recorded in the *Coplas de los pecados mortales*, we know that at the end of his life Mena felt disappointed with his eager application of erudition and humanism to classical literature, and, considering this a trivial subject, he chose to focus on a more ascetic, religious poetry (a change also found in Juan del Encina). This testimony reveals his intentions, ensuring that, from that moment, the poet will accept the pagan fables, not in terms of form and ornament – something that he considers trivial – but as everlasting lessons. He insists on an allegorical-moral interpretation, redirecting the ancient fable 'a la catholica vía', from a more confessional perspective:

> Usemos de los poemas
> tomando dellos lo bueno,
> mas fuigan de nuestro seno
> las sus fabulosas temas;

Let us take the good part of the poems; but let their fabulous themes escape from our bosom.

This declaration, like the one made years later by Juan del Encina or by Ovid's critics themselves, who condemned his worthless fables (a judgement which was read by other poets of the same period), renewed the ancient mistrust that the Church Fathers felt towards pagan mythology and literature, representing the reaction of a very broad clerical sector, faced with an ever-greater burgeoning of pagan literature, as the Renaissance took hold.

To Juan de Mena is also attributed the *Tratado de amor*, a didactic work in prose.[68] Lida de Malkiel and Street, who have studied the question of authorship, believe that the work is authentic.[69] This is relevant to our study, since, although the *Tratado* was written with a more serious and edifying purpose than Ovid's works, it forms part of the tradition of the Latin poet, and quotes, translates and imitates certain passages from the *Ars amatoria*, and, above all, from the *Remedia amoris*. The doctrinal exposition is marked out by mythical examples and other ancient authorities besides Ovid. If we are to seek out the mark of the Sulmonese poet in this work, however, we will find that at the beginning of the treatise, as at the beginning of the *Ars amatoria* (1.31–2), mothers and pure women are advised to set this work aside: 'Por ende vos otras, fuid lexos de aquí con vuestras guardadas fijas . . . ' (therefore, go far away from here, and take your daughters with you . . .). The writer usually refers to his model in Latin, translating the sentences with one or more glosses. Much of the advice given in the *Remedia amoris* reappeared in Mena's treatise regarding how to avoid a troublesome love, how to evade the interaction, how to stop the relationship at the beginning, how to ask the beloved for a demonstration of those skills she lacks, etc. In accordance with the intentions of the work and the author's point of view, in the *Tratado* quotations and allusions from the *Remedia* prevail over those from the *Ars*, and the vision of the former (against love) over the latter (for love). Street expresses the opinion that the *Tratado* was Mena's first composition, with evident traces of his school education, and a very close dependence on the sources.[70] Pérez Priego, however, believes it is more or less contemporary with *Laberinto*, a work with which it shares many themes in common.[71]

Names of Ovidian mythological characters are also present in other poets of the fifteenth century; not only in the main figures, such as Santillana and Mena, but also in the most humble poets, whose verses were collected in *cancioneros* such as Baena and Estúñiga. Crosas López' study[72] is most

---

[68] Juan de Mena 1989: 379–91.   [69] Lida de Malkiel 1950: 153–6 and Street 1952.
[70] Street 1952.   [71] Juan de Mena 1989: xxix.   [72] Crosas López 1995.

illuminating on the question of the literary debt these poets owed to Ovid. Nonetheless, there is also some proof of the continuing struggle concerning the validity of mythology, a debate engaged in during the first centuries of Christianity. In the context of this debate, there are also some examples of intolerance and negative views of the *Metamorphoses*, as is the case in Fernán Pérez de Guzmán's verses of *Loores de los claros varones de España*:

> Ovidio poetizando
> el caso de Filomena,
> e cómo engañó a Almena
> Júpiter se transformando,
> vaya sus trufas cantando,
> ornando materias viles
> con invenciones sotiles,
> su alto estilo levantando.
> Aquestas obras baldías
> parecen al que soñando
> falla oro, e despertando
> siente sus manos vacías:
> asaz emplea sus días
> en oficio infructuoso
> quien sólo en fablar fermoso
> muestra sus filosofías.

When Ovid writes verses about the story of Philomena and about how Jupiter cheated Alcmena by changing his shape, he sings these lies embellishing these not very worthy themes with subtle inventions and using his accustomed high style. These vain works are like the one who in his dreams finds gold, but has his hands empty when he wakes up: the person who only shows his intelligence in his beautiful speech dedicates his days to a work of fruitless endeavour.

Despite his claim here, Guzmán very often resorts to Ovidian myth. Nevertheless, such a declaration manifests a decided anti-aestheticism, and, at the same time, a symptom of the medieval mentality. From a medieval point of view, 'fablar fermoso' ('speaking beautifully') is completely worthless, whereas historical truth and the indoctrinating example are the greatest of values.[73]

Although the poets tend to have recourse to the mythographical rather than the erotic works, there are some allusions to the latter, above all in order to confirm Ovid's authority in erotic matters. In this sense, the use of the title 'De Amante', instead of *Ars amatoria*, is very curious. This title appears, for example, in the *Cancionero de Baena*, where, together with

---

[73] Green 1950.

other authors quoted only by their names, Ovid is referred to by his name and by his work.[74] Sometimes the title of the work is quoted alone and is confused with the author's name, as can be seen in a passage by Ferrant Manuel, also inserted in the *Cancionero de Baena* (n° 372: 645 Dutton-González Cuenca: 'Segunt los actores Vergillo e Demante' (According to the authors Virgil and Demante)). It is a use we have already seen in Santillana's verses.[75]

LATE MEDIEVAL VERNACULAR

This period also witnessed a flowering of literature in the Catalan vernacular. The anonymous novel *Curial e Güelfa* (dated to the mid fifteenth century),[76] constitutes a blend between the sentimental and the chivalric. In the third book, where the author displays great meta-literary erudition as regards ancient writers, there is a reference to Ovid's *Metamorphoses*, in the context of the Muses' legendary confrontation with and victory over the Pierides, who were then transformed into magpies:

E sobre aquestes fabuliza Ovidi, en lo quint llibre, que altres nou germanes, nades en Grècia, de Pierus, pare seu, e de mare Evipta (e per ço son dites Pièrides), aprengueren sonar e cantar maravellosament . . . Tantot les dites Pièrides foren per los déus convertides en piques, que en comun llenguatge català són dites garses, e són ocells garruladors . . .

About them, Ovid narrates in his fifth book the fable about the nine sisters born in Greece. They were daughters of Pierus and Evipta (and called Pierides, for this reason), and they learned to compose music and to sing wonderfully . . . The Pierides were soon transformed by the gods into magpies, which in common Catalan is 'garses', very talkative and noisy birds.

The hidden meaning of the fable is then unveiled, in accordance with medieval practice, other authorities invoked, and the account expanded with moralisations and etymologies. Later on in the same book, one of the most important female characters, the Moor Cámar, who became acquainted with some classical authors thanks to the main character, Curial, shows remarkable wisdom, which is difficult to explain given the short time she had to learn. She not only quotes Plato and St Jerome, but also a long list of women from legend, victims of unfortunate loves, almost all of whom are characters from Ovid: Pasiphae, Phaedra, Semiramis, Jocasta, Myrrha,

---

[74] 'e con ellos calle Ovidio D'amante' (and, beside them, Ovid De amante should shut up) (no. 231, Baena 1993: 280).
[75] No. 372, Baena 1993: 645.   [76] Ed. Gustà, Anon. 1979.

etc. A little later, Cámar, who continues to recall female characters from
Ovid like Medea, Procne and Philomela ('Filomena'), compares them with
her own situation.

Beside these passages, which are derived from Ovid, there is a recasting
of the Virgilian love of Dido and Aeneas: Cámar falls in love with the
foreigner Curial; since her love was never returned, she commits suicide,
invoking Dido. This evocation of Ovid and Virgil, together with the
comparison between Homer and Dictys and Dares – all three witnesses to
the war of Troy (as is recounted in the third book) – show the wide-ranging
humanistic culture of the anonymous author of the novel.

In the context of fifteenth-century Catalan humanism, the work of the
Valencian Joan Roís de Corella (1435–97) stands out. The *Metamorphoses*
and the *Heroides* are especially significant here,[77] as Corella wrote prose
narratives whose plots were drawn from the latter poems. The stories of
many of his works were derived from the *Metamorphoses* (which at the time
had still not been translated into Catalan, as this was only completed in
1494 by Francesc Alegre). Among these are the *Rahonament de Thelamó
e de Ulixes* ('Reasoning of Telamon and Ulysses'), a copy of the so-called
'judgement of arms' narrated by Ovid in Book 13; the *Lamentación de
Biblis* ('Byblis' lamentation'), derived from the episode about incestuous
love between siblings in Book 9; and the *Lamentations* ('Lamentations'),
a book that refers to three other narratives from the same source: those
of Myrrha, Narcissus, and Pyramus and Thisbe. Another example is the
Parlament, a book in the manner of Boccaccio's *Decameron*, in which on
the occasion of a banquet, five speakers narrate mythical stories told by
Ovid: Cephalus and Procris in which we have a letter from Procris (an
example of the formal influence of the *Heroides*), Orpheus,[78] Scylla and
Minos, Pasiphae, and Tereus, Procne and Philomela. The influence of the
Heroides on the content of the work is quite obvious in *La istòria de Leànder
i Hero* ('Story of Leander and Hero'), which shows the influence of letters
18 and 19. Formal and generic influence, on the other hand, appears not
only in the above-mentioned letter from Procris, inserted in the *Parlament*,
but also in the *Letra fengida que Achilles scriu a Policena* ('feigned letter
from Achilles to Polixena': actually two letters, like the double *Heroides*
of the Sulmonese poet), a work where the material is derived from the
medieval tradition regarding Troy (Dictys Cretensis and Dares, *Roman de*

---

[77] Martos 2001; Trilla and Cristóbal 1996.
[78] The speaker, however, sets aside – or is perhaps ignorant of? – the Virgilian testimony of the *Georgics*,
and follows only the model of the *Metamorphoses*.

Troie, Guido de Columnis). Corella's *Medea* and *Plant dolorós de la reyna Ècuba* ('Painful elegy of the queen Hecuba') are derived from the *Heroides* and from Seneca's tragedies, and finally, *Lo johí de Paris* is a dramatised reworking of this legendary event, based on several sources, including the *Heroides* (epistle 16), accompanied by an allegorical-moral interpretation of it.[79]

* * * * * * *

To conclude this account of the influence of Ovid in medieval Spain, certain salient points emerge. First, two large groups of Ovid's poetry played a significant role in his reception in medieval Spain: the texts on love (*Amores*, *Ars amatoria* and *Remedia amoris*), and the mythographical texts (*Heroides* and *Metamorphoses*). The elegies on exile and, to a great extent, the *Fasti* were not the object of great interest in this period.

These two groups of texts had a dual influence: in form and in content. The mythographic content of the *Metamorphoses* and *Heroides* lent itself to historiographical and moralising uses; they were of interest for their narrative plots and for the characters that populate them, providing examples of virtue and vice (see Alfonso X, Bernat Metge, Roís de Corella, the Castilian lyrical poets of the fifteenth century). These texts, however, also proposed different forms of narrative expression, and became resources for the presentation of objective and subjective information, ways to engage in literary introspection, and a language of concepts and images that serves to clarify certain mental processes, especially the phenomenology of love (as can be seen in Alfonso X, the 'polymetric' *Trojan Chronicle*, Roís de Corella, the sentimental novel). The *Amores*, *Ars amatoria* and the *Remedia amoris* became an important source as regards love, advice and general principles on relationships between men and women, but they also formed a model for the formalisation of sentimental language (as we can see in the *Libro de buen amor*, in the sentimental novel, and in *La Celestina*).

On the other hand, the influence of Ovid was not always direct and free from intermediate sources. Ovid's works were frequently transmitted to the Middle Ages via other works, which refocused the poet's message in different directions, manipulated it, truncated it, forged and distorted it, or

---

[79] As a sample of Corella's prose, which is elegant and highly expressive, despite his debt to his sources, we shall quote the following lines from *La istòria de Leànder i Hero*, which correspond to the moment before the lover's despairing death at sea: 'E, si un poch espay lo cap de les ones alçava reclamant lo nom de Hero, escupia l'aygua salada, la qual, ab terrible porfídia, volia entrar en lo cos de Leànder. Però l'amor de Hero axí tot lo occupava, que a les amargues aygües la entrada defenia . . .' (And if he raised his head a bit from the waves screaming out Heros' name, he spat out the salty water, which, with a terrible obstinacy, wanted to enter Leander's body. However, the love for Hero filled him so much that it blocked the path of the bitter waters).

even served as an essential support to make it more comprehensible (as, for instance, in the case of the *accessus*, and glosses on the manuscripts or moral interpretations such as the *Integumenta* or the *Allegoriae*, the *Pamphilus de amore*, Alfonso X's histories, the *De vetula*, Bersuire's *Ovidius moralizatus*, or the works of Boccaccio).

It is only too clear that these two groups of Ovidian texts underwent certain shifts and changes in the way they were received in Spanish medieval literature: the reception of the mythographical work shows a certain continuity from the thirteenth to the fifteenth century (with a small break in the fourteenth century), whereas the works on love were largely ignored during the thirteenth century, but found greater popularity in the fourteenth and fifteenth centuries. In any case, in our opinion, the apogee of Spanish medieval Ovidianism is the vast body of work of Alfonso X, called the Wise.

In the fifteenth century, views of Ovid were affected by a curiously varied phenomenology. The old prejudices against Ovid's poetry reappeared, given currency by some of the Fathers of the Church and medieval writers, either because of a presumed immorality or materialism in his approach to love, or because of an aesthetic that moved away from any kind of fiction. These prejudices, however, were not entirely dominant in literature, and in some authors (for example, Juan de Mena, Pérez de Guzmán and Juan del Encina) they even coexist with an acceptance of Ovid. The rhetorical essence of the *Remedia amoris* became less important, since this work was valued primarily as a moral and edifying text (see the *Tratado de amor*), and Ovid's attention to the world of women in the *Heroides* (an attitude partly learnt from Euripides) also contributed to enriching the debate about the goodness and evil of woman present in several works of the fifteenth century (Rodríguez del Padrón's *Triunfo de las donas*, for one).

Finally, these different relationships with Ovid's work imply a closeness to it, to a greater or lesser extent, as well as a variable degree of originality and innovation in the translation (there are versions of the *Heroides* in Alfonso X's works and in the *Bursario*, as well as in many passages of Roís de Corella's narrative texts), including amplified re-creation and the creation of new material inspired by the ancient model, as occurs in the fiction (or pseudomyth) of Cardiana and Aliso in Rodríguez del Padrón's *Triunfo de las donas*.

CHAPTER 12

A survey of imagery in medieval manuscripts of Ovid's Metamorphoses *and related commentaries*

Carla Lord

Patrons of illuminated manuscripts of Ovid in the Middle Ages are not always identifiable. Whether the text was meant for prelates or princes – in Latin commentary, or in vernacular and/or moralised interpretations – the quality and the content of the imagery fluctuated. This essay attempts to sort out what we know about the patrons, focusing mainly upon the readers of what are now France and Italy and on illuminated manuscripts relating to the *Metamorphoses*.[1] A few codicological matters, including rubrication, may lead us to locate the patrons, as well as to clarify the imagery. Some of the historiated codices contain dozens of scenes. One or two illustrations may have to suffice as a hint of further riches, and about half of the illustrations here included are hitherto unpublished. I shall limit examples to a few themes that have meandered through many of the codices, namely the tale of Diana and Actaeon and also that of Io, Mercury and Argus.

So far the oldest surviving group of illustrations to the *Metamorphoses* hovers in dating between the late eleventh and early twelfth centuries and can be found in one codex that was created in Italy: Naples, Biblioteca Nazionale Vittorio Emanuele III, MS F IV 3.[2] The manuscript is important, not only for its early date, but for its profusion of imagery. The orderly system of interlace initials in the Naples manuscript that opens thirteen of the

My thanks to the astute editors of this volume for their corrections, and to the staff of the Warburg Institute, University of London for their helpfulness in both the photographic collection and the library. In particular I am grateful to the late J. B. Trapp for his advice and for the excellent collection of Ovidiana that he acquired for the Warburg Institute when he was librarian.

[1] For illustrations of the *Heroides* see Zaggia and Ceriana 1996.

[2] For the earliest surviving imagery in the *Metamorphoses* in Naples, Biblioteca Nazionale, IV F 3, see Orofino 1993: 5–18. Orofino discusses the illustrations, e.g., of Phaethon, as they relate to the Aratean tradition of the zodiac, and the subject matter of other figures closely related to the text of the *Metamorphoses* itself. See also Orofino 1998, for the facsimile of Naples, Biblioteca Nazionale, IV F 3, text volume: 103–9, and the essay by Magistrale 1998: 41–101, who, 42–6, traces the readership of the heavily used codex, from its time in the library of the abbey at Montecassino through some distinguished Renaissance readers up until its entry in the collection of the present-day library; he discusses the non-figurative initial ornament on 67–72; and the text and interpolation of the so-called Lactantius, 75–82. For early readership of this manuscript see also Newton 1999: 247.

Figure 12.1 Argus (Naples, Biblioteca Nazionale, MS IV F 3, fol. 16r)

fifteen books of the *Metamorphoses* contrasts with a wild menagerie in the margins. This combination of neatly arranged initials and fanciful 'images at the edge' will not give rise to a tradition, at least not in Ovid. Centaurs, griffins and harpies may be extraneous to the *Metamorphoses* or may serve as pictorial glosses,[3] or as a kind of psychomachia, suggesting contention in the text. Some of the animals from the zoomorphic marginalia in the Naples codex are relevant to the text of the *Metamorphoses*.

Giulia Orofino has contributed the most important scholarship on the imagery in the Naples Ovid, deftly analysing over twenty motifs linked to Ovid in the codex, but she just occasionally strains the relationship of image to the text. Dogs are not included in Arachne's tapestry (*Met.* 6.102ff.), where the challenger of Minerva has woven all sorts of species, but none canine.[4] More à propos to Ovid are indeed the dogs that have devoured the unfortunate hunter Actaeon, which are seen over two folios (fols. 35v and 36r) (*Met.* 3.231ff.). Other animals, such as the snarling camel next to the text of Narcissus, as a personification of arrogance, are more convincingly tied in with the bestiary tradition.[5] The motif of the eagle devouring a hare may well allude to the inner conflict of Scylla having to choose between the fortune of her father and that of her lover.[6] Many of the more bizarre creatures are inexplicable in terms of the text but can be found in Apulian sculptural decoration, while other fantasy figures come from Islamic motifs, as do the pseudo-Cufic ornamental borders surrounding the interpolated text of the so-called Lactantius.[7] It has been argued that the Beneventan script and the manuscript itself had been produced in Bari and the codex was then housed in the abbey at Montecassino.[8]

Another somewhat later twelfth-century work of Italian or Spanish provenance is Vatican City, BAV, Vat. lat. MS 1596,[9] which also has its share of animal decoration. The illustrator of Vat. lat. 1596 gives up after the third book of the *Metamorphoses*, but until then, not surprisingly, he shares or draws upon some of the same themes that Ovid provided. In the Naples manuscript, the hundred-eyed Argus, sent by Juno to guard Io (*Met.* 1.625ff.) is shown nude but clad head to toe in multiple eyes (figure 12.1), whereas in Vat. lat. 1596 Argus (figure 12.2) is discreetly

---

[3] See Camille 1992: 106.   [4] Orofino 1993: 8 and 9.   [5] Orofino 1993: 8 and 9.

[6] Orofino 1993: 8 and 9, and her fig. 13. See Wittkower 1939: 293–325, also for the eagle and hare variation found in several examples *c.* 1200 in Apulia, 318 and pl. 52.

[7] Orofino 1998: 105.

[8] Both Magistrale 1998 and Orofino 1998: 41–2 and 106 note the arguments for the production of the manuscript either in Bari or the scriptorium at the abbey of Montecassino.

[9] See Tristano in Buonocore 1996: 226–8, cat. no. 30 and figs. 140–2. She lists the thematic contents of about a dozen images and refers to the Iberian owner and/or scribe 'Fernandus,' who in the colophon proclaims his name and pride at completing 6,000 lines.

Figure 12.2 Callisto; Argus (Vatican City, BAV, Vat. lat. MS 1596, fol. 8v)

dressed as a shepherd with just the face grimly covered in ocular gear. Above him stands the vexed Io, transformed into a cow. Equally disparate are the renderings of Actaeon. He is not depicted at all in the Naples codex, but instead, his own two dogs, having devoured him, are seen scampering across two folios. The ill-fated hunter in Vat. lat. 1596 is changed into a stag set upon by three of his dogs (figure 12.3). In art it is difficult to represent the continuity of a metamorphosis[10] and in most medieval imagery of the scene, the transformation is presented as a *fait accompli*. There is no pictorial relationship between these two manuscripts except for the common dependence upon the text of Ovid. Whether Vat. lat 1596 was illustrated in Spain or Italy is still not known, and indeed illustrations of Ovid manuscripts in both Spain and Germany need more investigation. In terms of pictorial milestones for the *Metamorphoses* in the rest of the thirteenth century, our knowledge is quite patchy.

NARRATIVE IMAGERY IN THE *OVIDE MORALISÉ*

The fourteenth century presents a new efflorescence of Ovidian manuscript adornment, as well as considerable transalpine traffic. For problems of circulation we must return to Naples IV F 3, first discussed as the oldest decorated *Metamorphoses* on the cusp of the twelfth century, a manuscript that was heavily used in the library of Montecassino. It must have lost the fifteenth and last book, which was rewritten in the fourteenth century, when the codex was rearranged, as well as amended to add French or Angevin-style Roman numeral chapter divisions and lists of chapter contents, familiar to readers of fourteenth-century French romances in manuscript format (figure 12.4).[11]

Much has been written about the French influence in southern Italy from Norman times onwards.[12] In the next link, the traffic will flow the other way. For patronage of the best-known and most beautiful example of the moralised Ovid, we turn to the well-travelled Clemence of Hungary. She was brought up at the court of her uncle, Robert of Naples. When she became of suitable age, Clemence was sent off to Paris to marry the first son of Philip IV, Louis Hutin, whose short reign as king of France lasted from 1314 to 1316. Probably it was Clemence, rather than Jeanne de

---

[10] See Pairet 2002: 113 and n. 31. See also Possamaï-Pérez 2006: 54–113, for an exhaustive analysis of the transformations.
[11] Magistrale 1998: 53–63 also notes fourteenth-century additions to the manuscript, including a table of contents, interpolated chapter headings, and a rewritten fifteenth book.
[12] See Orofino 1994: 375–89.

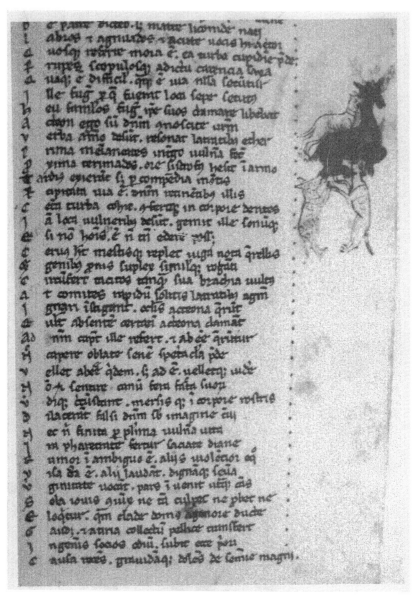

Figure 12.3 Actaeon (Vatican City, BAV, Vat. lat. MS 1596, fol. 25r)

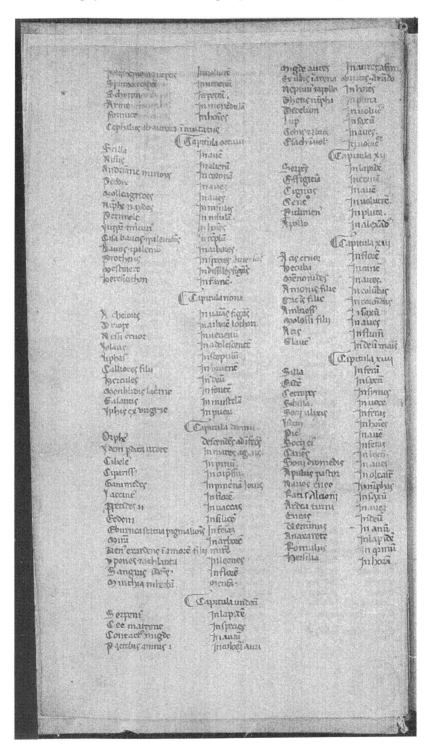

Figure 12.4 List of chapter contents (Naples, Biblioteca Nazionale, MS IV F 3, fol. IV)

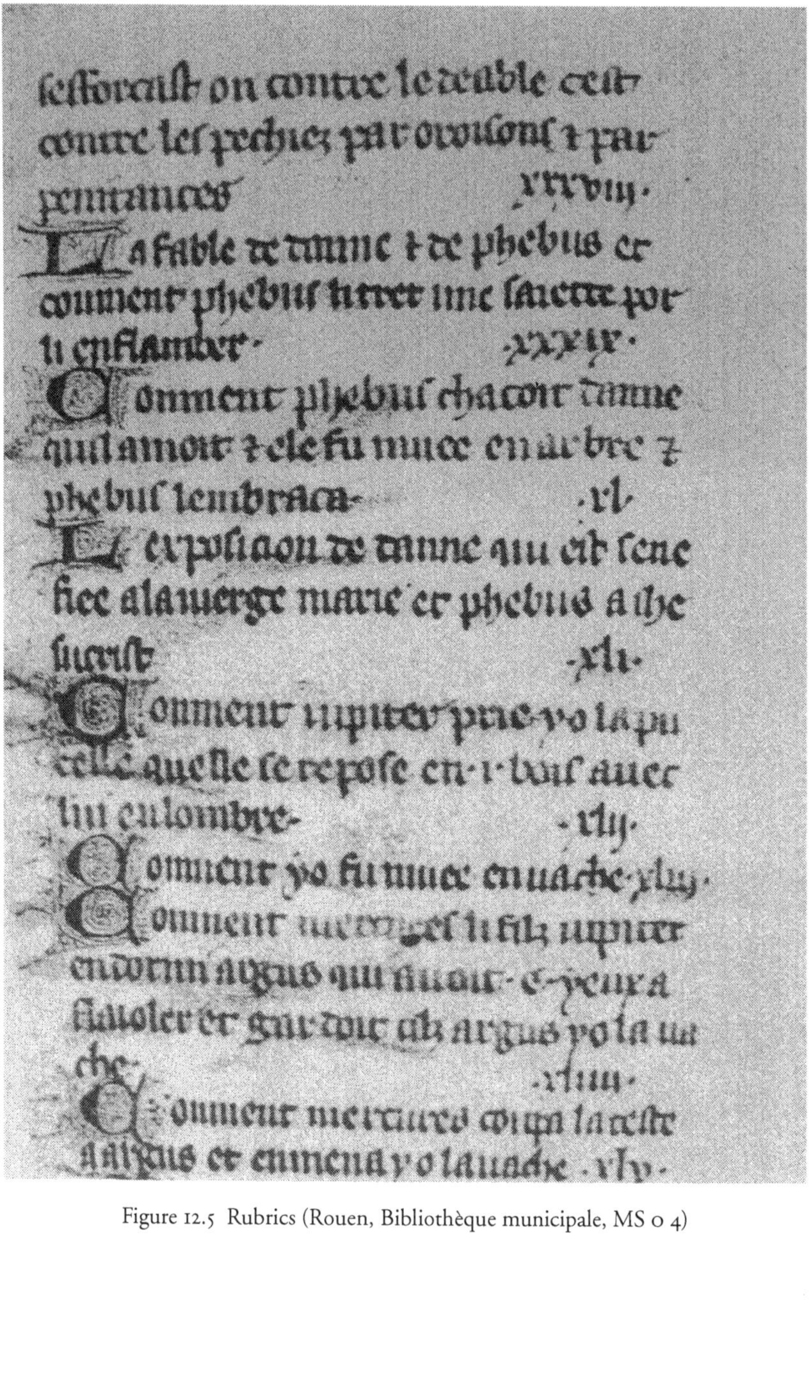

feſſorcent on contre le ꝛcable ceſt
contre leſ pechieꝫ par oroiſonſ ꞇ par
penitanceſ   xxviij·

La fable ꝛe ꝛanne ꞇ ꝛe phebus er
coument phebus tiret une ſaiette por
li enflamber·   xxxix·

Comment phebus chacoit ꝛanne
qu'il amoit ꞇ ele fu muee en arbre ꞇ
phebus lembraca·   ·xl·

L'expoſiaon ꝛe ꝛanne qui eſt ſene
fiee ala uierge marie er phebus a ihe
ſucriſt   ·xli·

Comment jupiter prie yo la pu
cele quelle ſe repoſe en·i·boiſ auec
lui en lombre·   ·xlij·

Comment yo fu muee en uache·xliij·
Comment uircargeſ li filz jupiter
endormit argus qui ꞇluoit· e·yeux a
flauoler et gar ꝛoit celi argus po la ua
che·   ·xliiij·

Comment mercure coupa la teſte
a argus et emmena yo la uache·xlv·

Figure 12.5 Rubrics (Rouen, Bibliothèque municipale, MS o 4)

Bourgogne, who then commissioned the splendid manuscript now known as the *Ovide moralisé* in Old French verse with 453 or 454 illuminations (Rouen, Bibliothèque municipale, MS o 4). This codex would then have been executed between 1314 and Clemence's death in 1328, when it was bought by King Philip VI.

The Rouen manuscript has profuse flourished initials of 'C' and 'L', alternating between the initial of Clemence and that of her husband Louis, though 'C' soon becomes more prevalent.[13] The initials adorn a descriptive list of contents, thirteen double-sided folios, which are gathered together in rubrics at the beginning of the manuscript. Not so coincidentally the descriptions open with blue and red initials, usually beginning with 'Comment' and sometimes with 'Li'. The rubrics preview the subject matter of the images and are still valuable for identifying some of the equivocal scenes. It is difficult to know how the reader used them in the Middle Ages. Grouped separately at the beginning of the manuscript, the rubrics are far ahead of the text and pictorial cycle of the *Ovide moralisé*.

Below is one of the more straightforward sets of rubrics, which coordinate quite well when matched with the pictorial cycle of four scenes: an excerpt, once again from the tale of Io (figure 12.5).

Comment iupiter prie yo la pu	
celle quelle se repose en-i-bois avec	
lui en lombre –	-xlii-
Comment yo fu muee en vache	-xliii-
Comment mercures li filz iuppiter	
endormi argus qui avoit-c-yeux a	
flaioler et gardat cilz argus yo la va	
che.	-xliiii-
Comment mercures coupa la teste	
a argus et enmena yo la vache	-xlv-

How Jupiter took Io the maiden, who reposed in the woods with him, into the shadow [our figure 12.6]. How Io was changed into a cow [our figure 12.7]. How Mercury the son of Jupiter put 100-eyed Argus to sleep with his flute playing and Argus guarded thus Io the cow [our figure 12.8]. How Mercury cut the head off of Argus and led away Io the cow [our figure 12.9].

The Io cycle is typical of patterns found in the Rouen MS o 4: small and simple two or three-figured images of great elegance, ranging from a delicate and decorous rape scene to mild violence, as in the beheading of

---

[13] The importance of the rubrics was indicated by Jung 1996b: 75–98, especially 76–7. See also Lord 1998: 7 –11.

Figure 12.6 Jupiter and Io (Rouen, Bibliothèque municipale, MS O 4, fol. 37r)

Figure 12.7 Juno, Jupiter and Io as Cow (Rouen, Bibliothèque municipale, MS o 4, fol. 38r)

Figure 12.8 Mercury, Argus and Io (Rouen, Bibliothèque municipale, MS o 4, fol. 38r)

Figure 12.9 Mercury slays Argus (Rouen, Bibliothèque municipale, MS o 4, fol. 38v)

Argus. Jupiter in figure 12.6 quietly advances on an acquiescent Io, whose submissiveness is apparent in her lost headdress, though there is little other indication of distress. They are framed by trees that represent both the forest and the dark shade that Jupiter has cast over them. In the next scene (figure 12.7) Juno, strongly suspicious, exhibits gestures of outrage when she asks Jupiter for control of the cow into which he has instantly transformed Io. Next (figure 12.8) follows Mercury's performance on the flute, raptly attended by the guardian Argus, his headgear covered with eyes. Finally (figure 12.9), with Io as cow looking forward to being liberated, Mercury slays the hapless Argus.

This montage of four scenes does not include an image from the long and complicated allegories on Io, in which she is identified serially as a prostitute, then a queen of Egypt (as Isis), or as the inventor of the alphabet and finally as the redeemed St Mary of Egypt.[14] Allegorical scenes of redemption in the Rouen manuscript tend to rely on Biblical imagery.

The readership of Ovid's tales had thus expanded into the vernacular, becoming more accessible to the public, and certainly with its illuminations had an added appeal to the French court. The *Ovide moralisé*

---

[14] For explanations of the allegories on Io, see Pairet 2002: 111–13; Desmond and Sheingorn 2003: 217–20, who see the positive light of Io's role in literacy carried on into the court art and text of Christine de Pizan. For other myths, allegories and colour illustrations from the Rouen manuscript, see now also Desmond 2007 and figs. 3.1 and 3.8.

accrued in Valois inventories throughout the fourteenth century in multiple manuscripts.[15] The explosion in the sheer numbers of images matches the use of French rather than Latin as a political as well as a cultural phenomenon.[16] There is also a codex of the moralised Ovid in French, probably of the 1320s, which resembles the manuscript in Rouen, but which lacks the deluxe royal touch: Paris, Bibliothèque de l'Arsenal, MS 5069.[17] In both manuscripts the pictorial zoo of the previous centuries is long gone. Instead, hundreds of tiny scenes reveal the gods and heroes of the Ovidian plot with decorum, verve or sometimes violence.[18] Periodically a scene of the Crucifixion or other religious theme appears in order to remind the reader that this is a moralisation.[19] The last in the series of narrative French scenes to the *Ovide moralisé* in French verse, Lyons, Bibliothèque municipale, MS 742, and made for the royal circle, came from the collection of Jean, duc de Berry. It was executed *c.* 1385–90, updating both the courtly Gothic costumes and the settings, which include expansive landscapes, rather than diaper-patterned backgrounds. In the Lyons manuscript, the allegories have shrunk both in text and image.[20]

PIERRE BERSUIRE AND IMAGES OF THE GODS

Of the various Latin commentaries on Ovid's *Metamorphoses* since the twelfth century, I am not aware of any that are illustrated, with the exception of the Benedictine Pierre Bersuire's.[21] Thanks to him and/or the writer of

---

[15] For the composition and reception of the *Ovide moralisé* see also in this volume, pp. 83–107.

[16] A discussion of the politics of the vernacular under Philip IV can be found in Cerquiglini-Toulet 1997: 6–7.

[17] For the narrative miniatures in Rouen and the Paris codex, Bibliothèque de l'Arsenal, MS 5069, written in the 1320s, and others, see Lord 1975: 161–75. The author has been justly criticised for not including the full repertory of 453 scenes in Rouen, MS O 4 or in the other manuscripts in the appendix.

[18] See Desmond and Sheingorn 2003, especially 166–8. Also for scenes similar to Io: a restrained view of Pasiphae embracing the bull, Rouen, fol. 204 and the abduction of Helen by Paris see 141 and their figs. 3.26 and 152, fig. 3.33, and ch. 4 'Engendering Violence' 157–93. See also Wolfthal 1999: especially 2, 12, and 129 for 'sanitized rape'. Most of her examples from the *Ovide moralisé*, such as Philomela, Paris and Helen and Bellerophon (132) come from Arsenal 5069, which is less courtly and conversely more frank in its expression. For allegories of Arsenal 5069, see also Blumenfeld-Kosinski 2002: 71–82.

[19] See Lord 1985: 95–102.

[20] See Jung 1996b: 78. For an incomplete listing of themes in Lyons 742, see Lord 1975: 171–5 and for imagery, Seznec 1953: 110.

[21] For studies of the Ovid commentary texts and allegorical tradition see Desmond 1989; Coulson and Molyviati-Toptsis 1992: 134–202; McKinley 1996b: 117–49 and Coulson 2007: 33–60. For Bersuire in particular see Hexter 1989: 51–84, and Coulson 1997a: 164–86. See below, n. 26. See also in this volume, pp. 48–82.

Figure 12.10 Mercury (Treviso, Biblioteca comunale, MS 344, fol. 4r)

the *Fulgentius metaforalis*,[22] a whole new pictorial approach to mythology came into being during the second half of the fourteenth century. In the fifteenth book of the *Reductorium morale*, before he went on to summarise Ovid's plots and moralise them, Bersuire set somewhat fanciful descriptions of the Greco-Roman gods: their attributes, and sometimes their special means of transportation. The descriptions were meant for readers who were unfamiliar with the appearance of the gods. His *De formis figurisque deorum* was intended for royal, religious and general lay readers.[23] It spread throughout Europe.

The Bersuire codices do not often have illustrations, but those that do need more attention. In some manuscripts, as in Treviso, Biblioteca comunale, MS 344, the descriptions and illustrations of the gods took on their own separate identity, and the rest of the narrative is lost or abandoned. The text in the Treviso manuscript is highly abridged and forms part of a miscellany. Amongst the medieval 'snapshots' of the gods, Mercury (figure 12.10) in the Treviso manuscript stars with the now familiar sleeping Argus, who appears not in the context of a narrative, but as background

---

[22] Liebeschütz 1926. See also in this volume, pp. 187, 195.
[23] See Avril 1996: 87–98. See also in this volume, pp. 18, 23, 55, 55 n. 30, 84, 86 n. 18, 180, 180 n. 20, 184–9, 192–5, 229, 247.

for the god's kit of attributes. Of the objects specified in the text, Mercury sprouts winged headgear, holds his staff and curved sword. His flute lies on the rocky ground. In another miscellany, a fifteenth-century English manuscript, Oxford, Bodl., Rawlinson MS B 214, fol. 198v, one finds an even more expressive view of Mercury with similar and greatly enlarged feathery attributes.[24] For these features Bersuire cites his authorities first mainly as Rabanus Maurus and Fulgentius, going on to explain Mercury's connection with the planet and with eloquence.[25]

In a few other manuscripts, the display of gods and narrative illustrations from the *Reductorium morale* remains integrated, as in the most interesting, but somewhat clumsy draftsmanship of Bergamo, Biblioteca civica Angelo Mai, Cassaf. MS 3 4.[26] The series of gods and the narration comprising 209 scenes can be epitomised in one miniature, fol. 32v, with three episodes of continuous narration depicting Actaeon's plight (figure 12.11): at left a group of Diana and her amorphous-looking followers bathing in the fountain, followed by the hunter Actaeon in the centre who has stumbled into the scene of nude bathers, followed at the right by his punishment, a rare instance where he is shown in the process of transformation into a stag. His hind legs are still human; his forelegs are cloven. A scene follows (fol. 33v) in which his friends astride horses come looking for him, but his dogs, not recognising Actaeon as a stag, have already made a meal of him. Images are not used to convey the allegories that follow.[27]

Amongst Bersuire manuscripts that need further exploration, there is above all the illumination of Gotha, Forschungs- und Landesbibliothek, MS I 98: a beautiful, if unfinished work. The Treviso and Gotha manuscripts are northern Italian and suggest the diffusion of Bersuire beyond France.[28]

[24] My thanks to Frank T. Coulson for the reference to Oxford, Bodl., MS Rawlinson B 214. See Saxl and Meier 1953, part I: 395–8 and for illustration of Mercury, part 2, pl. VI, fig. 19. For Rawlinson B 214, see also Scott 2002: 43, no. 821; Rigg, 1977: 281–330; McKinley 1998: 41–86, especially 68 for its localisation to the Augustinian Abbey in Waltham, Essex; see also Coulson 1998: 122–3. See also in this volume, pp. 186 & n, 191n, 194 & n. Another insert of Bersuire's parade of gods executed later in the fifteenth century and extant in Ghent Cathedral, MS 12 deserves further study: see Derolez 1979: no. 28, 161–8.

[25] For variants and transcription of the diplomatic text of Brussels, Bibliothèque royale MS 863–9, see Engels 1966: 25–8. Here are transcribed the meanings that Bersuire attached to the assortment of attributes of the gods, including Mercury: the staff signifies prudence; the sword, justice; the flute, eloquence, and the cock, vigilance, with citations from Timothy and Apostles. After the Images of the Gods, see also Hexter 1989: 59–61 for the narrative, which gives six shifting forms of exegesis by Bersuire for the Io legend and further subdivisions plus Bersuire's citations from scripture.

[26] For Andrea Spiriti's summary of the 209 scenes of this MS, see Gatti Perer 1989: 286–310, cat. no. 122.

[27] For Bersuire's allegories on Actaeon, see Levine 1989: 197–221.

[28] See Lord 1995: 1–11, and also critique by Hexter 1999a: 75–88. See also below, n. 32.

Figure 12.11 Diana and Actaeon (Bergamo, Biblioteca civica, Cassaf. MS 3.4, fol. 32v)

The series of fifteen gods and goddesses then re-emerged in a cluster of French *Ovide moralisé* manuscripts, executed mainly between 1380 and 1390. Still based on Bersuire's prescriptions for depicting the gods, the deities have been reduced in number and rearranged. A different god opens each of the fifteen books of the *Ovide moralisé*. The deities can best be seen in Vatican City, BAV, Reg. lat. MS 1480.[29] To pick one god out of the ensemble, Apollo (fol. 290r: figure 12.12) stands decorously wearing his turreted crown and fashionable tunic, bearing what Bersuire recommends: a cithara in one hand, a bow, arrows and quiver in the other. Furthermore, he stands over a monster, described by Bersuire as serpentine. On one side

[29] See Manzari in Buonocore 1996: 289–94, cat. 58, and her figs. 221–35 in colour, with illustrations of fifteen gods and their descriptions by Bersuire. Each of the gods opens one of the fifteen books of the *Ovide moralisé*. Also in the cluster of three manuscripts of the *Ovide moralisé* with images of the gods is one in Geneva, Bibliothèque Publique et Universitaire, MS 176: see Gagnebin 1976, cat. no. 30 and fig. 77, who discusses, 76–7, the problem of attribution by Pierre Bersuire of the patronage of the *Ovide moralisé* to a former queen Jeanne. If a queen of France named Jeanne did commission the first (lost?) manuscript, it would have had to be Jeanne de Champagne-Navarre, wife of Philip IV. The last manuscript in the series of images of the gods is Paris, BN, fr. MS 373, which was owned by the duke of Berry. The order of the gods varies in manuscripts that are discussed by Jung 1996a: 259–61. Panofsky's eloquent footnote remains relevant: Panofsky 1960: 78–81, n. 2. He also cites, 81, and lists another rare instance of English sketches of the gods (London, BL, Cotton MS Julius F VII).

Figure 12.12 Apollo (Vatican City, BAV, Reg. lat. MS 1480, fol. 290r)

is his tree, the laurel, and on the other a black crow. Bersuire goes on to remind us that Apollo is the best judge or prelate; the serpent or Python represents the evil sinners; the laurel tree connotes wisdom, and the crow poverty.

Whereas the figure of Apollo assimilates nicely into what might be a court scene during the reign of Charles V of France, and would look suitably heroic to the courtly reader, he does stand near the end of an era of regal Gothic icons. Towards the end of the next century the Apollo Belvedere will take over as the model from classical antiquity, adopted by readers and artists alike.

ITALIAN NARRATIVE IMAGERY OF THE TRECENTO

Running parallel to the diffusion of Ovid in the vernacular *Ovide moralisé* during the fourteenth century is an early unmoralised translation of the *Metamorphoses* into Italian by Arrigo Simintendi, translated after 1333.[30] This Italian version appears in nineteen manuscripts with exactly one known illustrated example, Florence, Biblioteca Nazionale Centrale, Panciatichi MS 63. After the earliest Latin manuscript discussed above (Naples IV F 3), this is the next most important Ovid codex in Italy.[31] It is still full of puzzlements, especially in terms of its dating and attribution, but Panciatichi 63 should also have a facsimile edition. It has seventy or more illustrations of the *Metamorfosi* on paper,[32] but even the watermark is equivocal. Degenhart and Schmitt have listed and illustrated more than half of the contents, though in a somewhat scattered manner.[33] This is the first manuscript that consistently labels its characters in highly expressive bas-de-page scenes. In some scenes (e.g. figure 12.13) the illustrator has not

---

[30] See Ciaranfi 1977: 177–83. She discusses the translation and its dating, and lists and illustrates some of the themes.

[31] For Ovid in Italy see also in this volume, pp. 123–42.

[32] Degenhart and Schmitt 1980: part 2, vol. II: 358–69, cat. no. 710, figs. 579–86; part 2, vol. III, plates 177–84 for Panciatichi 63. Their erudition is apparent in the outlining of the tradition of the moralised Ovid (though without apparently knowing the manuscript in Rouen with hundreds of images) and they give an impressive account of Pierre Bersuire, illustrating, part 2, vol. II, the manuscripts in Treviso (figs 588–9, 593); Bergamo (figs 587, 597); and Gotha (figs 598–600). Another manuscript of Bersuire that is typical of a large body of manuscript decorators: the amateur, rather than professional illuminator, is signalled by Damangeot-Bourdat 2007: 68–9 and fig. 8. She describes BN, lat. MS 5703 and its mediocre but expressive marginal drawings as they illustrate the *Ovidius moralizatus*. Damangeot-Bordat suggests that they date to *c.* 1400 and are the work of a man who later became clerk (greffier) in the parlement de Paris, Clément de Fauquembergue.

[33] Lazzi in Buonocore 1996: 249–51, catalogue no. 42, gives a succinct account, listing the subject matter of Simintendi's Italian translation of the *Metamorphoses* as it appears in the Panciatichi manuscript.

Figure 12.13 Diana and Actaeon (Florence, Biblioteca nazionale centrale, Panciatichi MS
63, fol. 26r)

judged the space properly and the figures are cut off at the bottom. The
labels are not by the same hand as the regular script, which is also hard to
date.[34] Eleanora Mattia has valiantly analysed the problems of attribution.
She has also effectively argued that the codex was made for private use
and is typical of those secular manuscripts that have not yet been as thoroughly examined as manuscripts with religious illumination.[35] Illustration
in manuscripts of Dante and of Ovid's *Heroides* are similar in style and
might point to a Tuscan workshop of secular manuscript production,[36]
but it would be nice to find documentary evidence of such a scriptorium. Characteristic of Panciatichi 63 is the scene of Diana and Actaeon
(figure 12.13). Actaeon the accidental voyeur is seen first at the left, spying
upon Diana whose nymphs have brought her water from an urn. The nude
figures are unabashedly nude and almost classical in their contrapposto and

[34] Some time in the 1960s no less a connoisseur of manuscripts than Paul Oskar Kristeller, when
confronted with photographs of the script, thought that it was 'mercantile', but when asked to date
it, he smiled wrily and suggested that one try art historical methods. See also n. 35.
[35] Mattia 1996–7: 45–54. Her communication from Armando Petrucci (her n. 23) agrees with that of
Kristeller in terms of the somewhat humbler mercantile script.
[36] Mattia 1996–7: 51 and 53, n. 15. For the manuscript of the *Heroides*, Milan, Biblioteca Ambrosiana,
MS SP 13 bis, see Zaggia and Ceriana 1996: 23–38 and their fig. 5.

Figure 12.14 Apollo and Daphne (Florence, Biblioteca nazionale centrale, Panciatichi MS 63, fol. 12v)

proportions. Nearby is the natural arc-shaped grotto famously described by Ovid, *Met.* 3.155–62 and in the Simintendi translation,[37] but rarely depicted until the time of Titian. In other illustrations, the costuming of Panciatichi 63 is quasi-classical, as in the scene of Daphne fleeing Apollo (figure 12.14), her drapery bunched at the hip like a chiton, rather than flowing loosely.[38] The Panciatichi paper codex was evidently not made for the luxury market, though by the sixteenth century it began to have some distinguished Florentine collectors.[39] Everyone agrees that the manuscript itself is Florentine or at least Tuscan. Its landscape of Aeneas in Fiesole,[40] with the local river labelled Mugnone, may be a cartographical first, but perhaps that very landscape might lead to some closer dating. Scholars have accorded Panciatichi 63 a chronological range from the second half of the fourteenth century to possibly the beginning of the fifteenth century, as vague a span as the above-described North Italian manuscripts of Bersuire, but we do not yet know more. Copious in their narrative imagery, these fourteenth- or early fifteenth-century Italian or moralised Latin renditions of the *Metamorphoses* do not seem to have survived in great quantities.

---

[37] Basi and Guasti 1846–50: I, 14.   [38] Mattia 1996–7: 48 and her n. 19.
[39] Mattia 1996–7: n. 7.   [40] Mattia 1996–7: 50–1, and her fig. 11.

Two more illustrated manuscripts containing the *Metamorphoses* are dated, but do not otherwise evoke much art historical interest: One is Vatican City, BAV, Vat. lat. MS 2780, dated 1415, which has a few scattered pen drawings, but no consistent iconographical or professional approach. It is more interesting for its text.[41] The other is in Trent, Castello del Buonconsiglio, MS 1364, which is dated 1426, but disappointingly has only the frontispiece and some initials that are decorated, though not historiated. The arms of the bishop de Metis are also on the bottom margin of the frontispiece. We learn from the colophon both the date (1426) and the name of the copyist, Lorenzo, son of Antonio de Castro. We also learn from a note on fol. 11r that the manuscript belonged to Iohannes Hinderbach, bishop of Trent and that it was confiscated in 1478 from Jews, along with other books and goods.[42]

There are probably missing links, but the next major collection of full-fledged Ovid scenes in Italy will not occur until the fifty-three woodcuts from the 1497 Giovanni Rosso edition of the *Methamorphoseos* in Venice, illustrating the highly popular rendition of the poem into Italian completed by Bonsignori some 120 years earlier. Very likely the 1497 edition has a missing visual model since Giovanni Bonsignori wrote it in Città di Castello in 1377. Meanwhile MS Panciatichi 63 points the way or is in the midst of a trend in Italy towards smaller, more discreet decoration: initials. At least it had space left for initials, though they were not completed.[43]

HISTORIATED INITIALS

We need not leave Florence in order to find the category of book illustration that became far more widespread than large narrative pictures. I shall not deal with purely ornamental initials, which were appropriate to any form of literature. It is the historiated or figurative initials that became prevalent, such as those found in Florence, BML, Plut. MS 36 8. This manuscript of the *Metamorphoses* came from the Medici Collection, although it has been described as being created in the Venetian orbit of the late thirteenth or early fourteenth century.[44] The male costuming is probably more typical

---

[41] See Tristano in Buonocore 1996: 336–40: cat. no. 81, who illustrates two of the motifs: Europa (fig. 307) and Cadmus combatting the Dragon (fig. 309). She describes a few more of the figures. See also Munzi 1990: 331–63.

[42] See Casagrande Mazzoli 1996: cat. no. 60 for other possessors of the book, real and fictive.

[43] Mattia 1996–7: 51, n. 6.

[44] See Ciardi Dupré Dal Poggetto 1976: 72–9, who (78, no. 61) describes BML, Plut. 36 8 as being in the Venetian ambiente of the late thirteenth or early fourteenth century. This review is cited by Mattia, below, note 46.

Figure 12.15 Phaethon (Florence, BML, Plut. MS 36 8, fol. 14r)

of the short, close-fitting tunics from the mid fourteenth century onwards. These initials stand as an incipit to each of the fifteen books of the *Metamorphoses*, once again in Latin. Typical is the view of the courteous Phaethon (figure 12.15), a single figure, supplicating his father, who is not present. A ceremonious god or hero within the initials usually hints at a major story in each book, but these are not action scenes and the architecture of the initials themselves tends to overwhelm the diminutive figures.[45]

---

[45] The subject matter of the initials in BML Plut. 36 8 is as follows: Book 1, fol. 1: drôlerie of a nude man crawling up the initial 'I'; Book 2, fol. 14r: Phaethon kneeling (figure 12.15); Book 3, fol. 28v:

As scriptoria near the University of Paris tended to dominate the production of secular manuscript illumination in France in the fourteenth century, so in Italy the University of Bologna was the centre of much of the pictorial output. Nicola di Giacomo da Bologna and his numerous disciples, documented in the last quarter of the fourteenth century, or grouped as anonymous masters by later art historians, are here the focus of attention for the dynamic initials that they created. They produced lively scenes within these initials for manuscripts of classical literature and for official government and hospital documents.[46] Among the Ovid manuscripts attributed to Nicola di Giacomo or his circle is a fine manuscript in Venice, Biblioteca Nazionale Marciana, Zan. lat. MS 449a (1634). The *Metamorphoses* with the initial 'I' for 'Iamque' opens with the first rousing combat of Book 3: Cadmus vs. the Dragon (figure 12.16). Into a corner no more than the space of eight lines, the illuminator has fitted in the stalwart hero, his ferocious opponent and the many heads of companions whose deaths he seeks to avenge.

Mattia discusses another manuscript of the *Metamorphoses*, Cesena, Biblioteca Malatestiana, MS MXXV 6, which is replete with unidentifiable bust figures, some of which are portrayed as reading.[47] Similarly there is a group of bulky readers, again each introducing a book of the *Metamorphoses*, in Vienna, Österreichische Nationalbibliothek, MS 127 (figure 12.17),[48] who are seen in lost profile with their backs turned, almost in preview of the massive prophets of the Sistine Ceiling.

With a cut-off date of 1450 for this anthology, we cannot discuss several later fifteenth-century Flemish illuminated manuscripts, which have

the crested serpent whom Cadmus fought entwined in initial; Book 4, fol. 41r: perhaps Thisbe in a long red gown; Book 5, fol. 54: Perseus in a green tunic holding the head of Medusa in his left hand and a sword in his right hand; Book 6, fol. 65v: crowned Minerva seated about to enter contest with Arachne; Book 7, fol. 77v: Jason (?) dressed as a monk; Book 8, fol. 92: Famine; Book 9, fol. 107: Hercules with club and lion skin ready to fight Achelous; Book 10, fol. 120v: Hymen flying away from wedding of Orpheus and Eurydice; Book 11, fol. 132v: Orpheus playing a viol; Book 12, fol. 146: Calchas with bird flying overhead, prophesying the future victory of the Greeks; Book 13, fol. 164v: Ajax or Ulysses with sword and shield; Book 14, fol. 172: Glaucus asks Circe for help; Book 15, fol. 187: Crowned Numa enthroned holding sceptre.

[46] See Medica 1999: 62–70 and cat. nos. 17, 21, and 22. See also Mattia 1990–1: 63–73.

[47] Mattia 1990–1 for analysis and illustrations of eight more initials from the Marciana manuscript and also figures from Cesena MXXV 6. The Marciana manuscript and others will be discussed in a forthcoming article.

[48] See Hermann 1929: vol. VIII, part 5: cod. 127, pl. 92 and cat. no. 115. He describes the codex as Lombard, of the last quarter of the fourteenth century, noting (221) sixteen initials and the representation of professors with books in Bolognese art. Hereby a belated acknowledgment to Munari for his pioneering *Catalogue of the MSS of Ovid's Metamorphoses* and further supplements in Coulson 1988, 1992, 1994 and 1995b.

Figure 12.16 Cadmus (Venice, Biblioteca Nazionale Marciana, Zan. lat. MS 449a (1634), fol. 21v)

familiar moralised variants of the *Metamorphoses*.[49] The decoration of Ovid manuscripts in Italy will change noticeably in the fifteenth century with the development of the more abstract white vine scroll framework, although initials all' antica will still play a strong role.[50]

Many Ovid manuscripts have doodles in the margins showing hands, which perhaps served as medieval or later bookmarks. Dragons and drôleries also stand in the margins.[51]

There are probably more illuminated manuscripts of the *Metamorphoses* waiting to be discovered equipped with more annotations by elusive readers. Patrons and owners are easier to document than other casual or even

[49] For a discussion of the late fifteenth-century Flemish manuscripts of the *Metamorphoses*, the moralised versions and their relationship with the first illustrated and printed edition of Colard Mansion in Bruges, see Arnould and Massing 1993: 218–20, cat. no. 76, which refers to Holkham Hall, MS 324, as well as Copenhagen, Kongelige Bibliotek, Thott MS 399, and Paris, BN, fr. MS 137, all of whose links could be pursued further, including those with London, BL, Royal MS 17 E IV. See Saxl and Meier, 1953, part 1: 213–15. For a discussion of northern manuscripts of the Ovid tradition, see Koble 2002.

[50] See Armstrong 1981: 59–68, and cat. no. 47.

[51] Berlin, SB-PKb, Hamilton MS 490 contains fine fifteenth-century examples of hands and dragons. See Boese 1966.

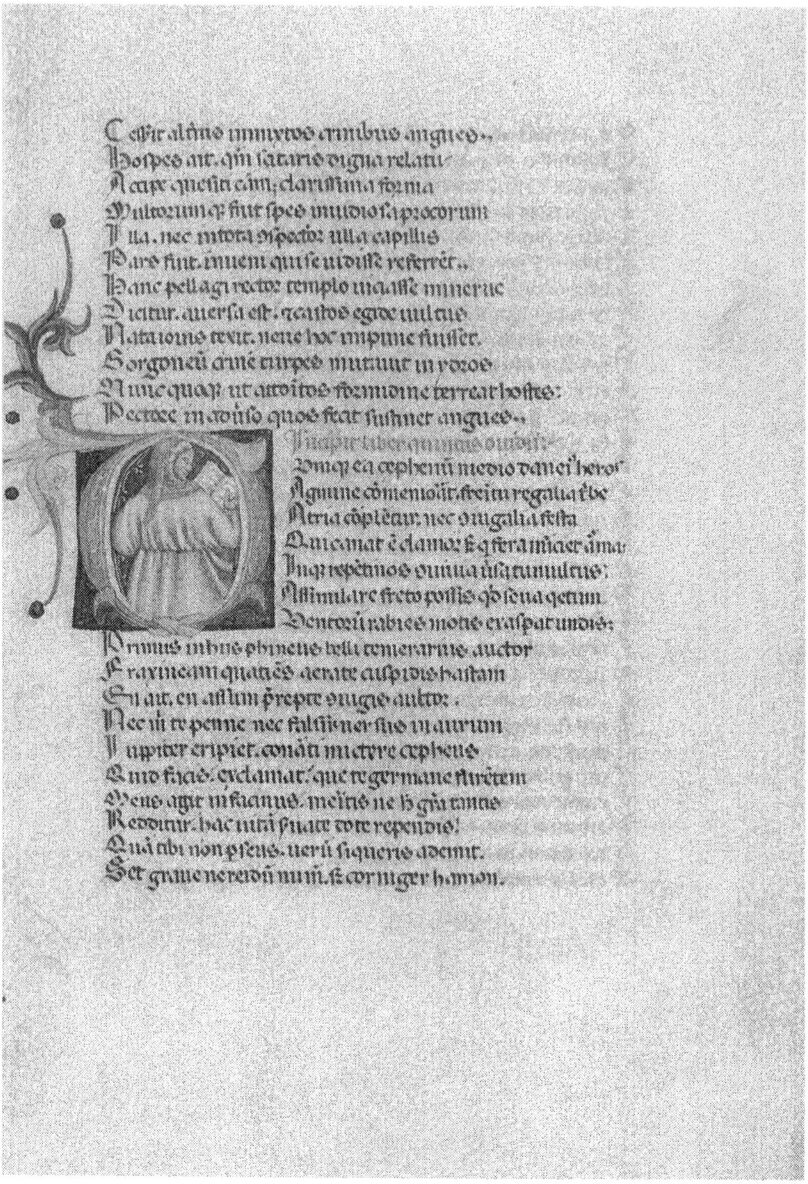

Figure 12.17 A reader (Vienna, Österreichische Nationalbibliothek, MS 127, fol. 55r)

serious readers. In their demand for illumination patrons veered towards the vernacular – moralised as in the *Ovide moralisé*, a favourite text at the French court; or Simintendi's fairly straightforward translation into Italian, which seems to have appealed to the mercantile class, though we have only one illustrated example. In Latin Bersuire's *Ovidius moralizatus*, perhaps intended for clerical use, was rarely illustrated and it may be that the few illustrated manuscripts were executed by clerics. More widespread was the adoption of his pictorial introduction *De formis figurisque deorum*. Otherwise those who preferred the *Metamorphoses* in Latin with discrete initials, either as animated scenes or as simple attractive book dividers, could turn to illuminators in and around Bologna, who offered a range of decoration to the well-off scholar. For four centuries mega miniatures or micro miniature initials attracted readers across European borders.

CHAPTER 13

Shades of Ovid
Pseudo- (and para-) Ovidiana in the Middle Ages

Ralph J. Hexter

OVIDIANUS POETA
HIC QUIESCIT[1]

An overview of 'Ovid in the Middle Ages' or the 'medieval Ovid' such as the present volume offers would be incomplete without an account of the 'pseudo-Ovidiana', a working definition of which might run 'works not authored by Ovid that circulated under his name'. The supposititious works taken by medieval readers to be Ovid's at once contributed to and testify to medieval understandings and perceptions of the poet. Some of these texts merely gained Ovidian attribution in the Middle Ages, while others were not just reproduced but produced by medieval pens, so that one might well say that these Ovidian *pseudo-epigrapha* are the most distinctly medieval Ovid we could ever hope to have.[2]

While not a few scholars have made significant advances in identifying, editing and interpreting individual poems that can be described as pseudo-Ovidian, only a few have tried to bring conceptual order to the entire

---

For responding to an earlier draft with many valuable suggestions, I thank Professors Wilken Engelbrecht and Jan Ziolkowski. I thank Dr Uwe Vagelpohl for his able assistance and, in particular, for the rapid development of a working database of the manuscripts that could not have come about without his energy, discipline and organisational skills.

[1] An inscription found in Itri; *Corpus Inscriptionum Latinarum* 1863: X 6127; *Inscriptions Latinae Selectue* 1892–1916: 2955.

[2] Indeed, I have said this in Hexter 1999b: 341. Recent surveys of Ovid in the Middle Ages have not often included review of the pseudo-Ovidiana. For example, Dimmick 2002 briefly touches on *De vetula* (273, 275–6). (Oddly, the index to the volume, s.v. 'pseudo-Ovidian works', refers only to one page (32) in another article where the term does not appear but where there is mention of *Epistula Sapphus*, *Nux* and *Halieutica* and to the pseudo-*Met.* episode first published by Anderson 1974 (and discussed below), although no reader without extensive knowledge of the topic would understand that this is what was meant.) A generation earlier, Dorothy Robathan, an editor of *De vetula* (discussed below) also offered brief remarks in Robathan 1973. Though many of the details have since been superseded, Ghisalberti 1946 does give appropriate place to the pseudo-Ovidiana as part of a full picture of 'the medieval Ovid', more in fact than one might at first expect from an article entitled 'Mediaeval Biographies of Ovid'. Ghisalberti's article has received important additions and corrections by Frank T. Coulson in a series of articles (Coulson 1987c, 1997b).

set.[3] The image of wrestling the shape-shifting Proteus comes to mind, and no surprise, since the pseudo-Ovidiana contain works that are 'Ovidian' in a variety of senses. The challenge facing any would-be organiser is to devise a system of categories and definitions such that each of the non-genuine works attributed to Ovid would find its place somewhere on the grid. Far to one side there would be out-and-out forgeries, far to the other side works that were simply drawn into the gravitational field of 'planet Ovid' and ever after orbited under his name. Somewhere in the design one would find a place for works that were intermittently Ovidian, i.e., in terms of attribution,[4] or for interpolations in otherwise authentic texts by Ovid, such as the *Heroides* (on which more below) and even sections of works by Ovid himself that were excerpted and then reattached to Ovid as if each were a separate and distinct minor work.[5]

I say Ovid, but the problem would in theory apply to the case of Virgil or of any classical author with a lively history of reception from antiquity through the Middle Ages to the Renaissance. Indeed, I have often looked ruefully at the *Appendix Vergiliana*[6] on my shelf and wondered why one could not assemble an 'Appendix Ovidiana' to set beside it. Part of the greater tractability of the Virgilian material stems from the fact that production of the major Virgilian *minora* fell in a much earlier period.[7] To be sure, the Middle Ages and Renaissance, rich in both study of and popular legend about Virgil, saw at least two dozen new poetic accretions

[3] Early on Manitius 1899, followed by Lehmann 1927. The many works by Friedrich Walter Lenz taken together constitute perhaps the most formidable contribution by any single scholar. For an overview, see Lenz 1959a. Knox 2009b recognises the need for renewed scholarly engagement.

[4] For example, the *Conflictus veris et hiemis* (also at times attributed to Virgil; see below, n. 7), the *Birria* (or *Byrrhia*) of Vitalis of Blois, ascribed to Ovid in one Berlin manuscript (Lenz 1959a: 182), or Maximian's *Elegies*, inscribed *Ovidius de senectute* by one hand in the fourteenth-century Diez в Sant. 4 (Winter 1986: 18–22).

[5] Of this three examples from the *Amores* serve neatly: *Am.* 1.5 circulated under the title *De meridie* (cf. Walther 1959, no. 632; Schaller and Könsgen 1977, no. 406), 2.15 as *De anulo* (cf. Walther 1959, no. 1345; Schaller and Könsgen 1977, no. 919) and 3.5 as either *De somno* or *De rustico* (cf. Walther 1959, no. 12342; Schaller and Könsgen 1977, no. 10626).

[6] E.g., the Oxford Classical Text volume bearing that name (Clausen *et al.* 1966). In a new edition of the second volume of the Loeb *Aeneid* (Virgil 1999–2000), G. P. Goold offers a fresh introduction to the *Appendix Vergiliana* (II: 370–85). The term *appendix* seems to go back to J. J. Scaliger and the title of his Lyon, 1573 edition.

[7] Already Donatus could list eight and Servius nine titles that largely overlap with what ultimately emerged as the canonical Virgilian appendix. Reeve documents the nine works listed as appearing in a manuscript described in a ninth-century catalogue from Murbach (Reeve 1983: 437). There are many treatments of the *Appendix Vergiliana*; in addition to the introduction by Goold mentioned above, see Pette 1991, Holzberg 2005, and, briefly, Putnam and Ziolkowski 2008: 25–27. On issues of transmission (and of more than the canonical set), Reeve 1983 offers a good starting point and further bibliography.

to the Virgiliana, whether by new composition or wild attribution,[8] but in richness and interest they do not match the poems of the received 'Appendix' much less the pseudo-Ovidiana, a mirror, in a certain sense, of the marvellous variety of Ovid's own output.

So far I have somewhat blithely used both the terms '*pseudo-epigrapha*' and 'forgeries'. In fact, there are both variety and complexity in the vocabulary of pseudonymous texts, depending – for starters – on the field in which one is operating, so that even finding a way to talk about the history of works falsely ascribed to texts from Ovid's own times to, say, 1500, constitutes a challenge. A scholar working in this area needs to be sensitive not only to the discipline-specific nuances and the often unarticulated assumptions behind the concepts the terms represent, but also to the histories of those very terms,[9] concepts and disciplines. It might be easiest to illustrate this need for caution with a term that has only infrequently been applied to the pseudo-Ovidiana: forgery. Money is forged, and so is artwork, especially in times and places when the latter, if believed to be the work of a specific individual, can bring the seller a great deal of the former. Texts have been forged as well, even when the monetisation of a single exemplar is not an issue,[10] but there is a great deal of difference, in motives and impact, between the forging of a sacred text, a letter of Clement, for example, or even Peter or Paul, which might well be regarded as canonical;[11]

---

[8] For example, Ademar of Chabannes (*c.* 989–1034) classed the above-mentioned *Conflictus veris et hiemis* as Virgilian (Putnam and Ziolkowski 2008: 26), which is particularly interesting because the same poem is intermittently regarded as pseudo-Ovidian. The standard starting point for the medieval Virgil remains Comparetti 1997 and for popular legend, Spargo 1934, now joined by the rich compendium of texts and translations with invaluable contextual introductions and commentary of Putnam and Ziolkowski 2008. Although the poems of what one might call the canonical Virgilian appendix have received the most attention, by the Renaissance one could read a good two dozen more bits of Virgiliana.

[9] For example, I have not yet come across a complete history of the use of the prefix 'pseudo' specifically as attached to an author's name or an adjective derived from that name (e.g. pseudo-Ovid, pseudo-Virgiliana). In looking at catalogues, one must be careful to distinguish between precise citations of title pages and later summaries. (A good example is the 1480 Calderinus volume cited in the preceding note; it is frequently listed as *Commentarii in quaedam pseudo-Vergiliana*, but the title page has *quaedam opuscula Vergiliana*.) 'Pseudonym' itself appears as early as the commentary on Salvian's ninth epistle in the 1688 edition by Rittershausen (cited by Haefner 1934: 14, n. 16). The first appearance of 'pseudo-Ovidius' I have so far been able to document is in the second edition of *Lexicon Latinae Linguae Antibarbarum Quadripartitum: Cum . . . Recensione Scriptorum Latinorum Critica. Iterata Hac Editione . . . Emendatum Ac Locupletatum* (Leipzig, 1744) of Johann Friedrich Nolte (1694–1754), s.v. 'pontificare'. The article on 'pontificare' is substantially shorter in the first edition of 1730 and does not include the term 'pseudo-Ovidius'. (The expanded second edition is accessible online at www.uni-mannheim.de/mateo/camenaref/nolte.html.)

[10] On the history of literary 'forgery', see, for instance, Ruthven 2001 and Haywood 1987. Indispensable is the meditation of Grafton 1990.

[11] 'Forging' as a term may be provocative in the context of the study of scripture. Creating texts and passing them off as products of earlier and more famous figures is part of scripture in many

the 'Epistles of [the sixth-century BCE Sicilian tyrant] Phalaris', a production of the Second Sophistic presumably recognised as fictions at the time of its confection, taken as genuine by many much later readers and ultimately proved spurious by Bentley in 1697 and 1699; the so-called 'Donation of Constantine', unmasked by Lorenzo Valla; the *Protocols of the Elders of Zion*, incredibly still in circulation, and more incredibly still, still credited in many parts of the world; the diaries of Hitler, which for a time took in a Regius Professor of History at Oxford; and a counterfeit copy of Dan Brown's *The Da Vinci Code* for sale in China.

Two clear principles, it seems to me, must inform any historical study of pseudo-Ovidiana today:

1 'False authorship', or what renders a given authorial attribution 'false', can only be determined in relation to the concepts of author, authorship and attribution that obtain at a specific historical moment in a specific time and milieu.[12]

Throughout the high Middle Ages, and thus perforce during the *aetas Ovidiana*,[13] when there was a great increase in the depth of attention to Ovid's style and manner in the world of Latin textuality,[14] the concept of the *auctor* was embedded in a complex and very specific matrix of text production and reproduction. By definition, any sense of what we would call pseudonymous authorship needs to be inflected with an appreciation of

---

traditions. Out of the (as one might imagine) vast literature on the Judaeo-Christian deuterocanonical literature and *pseudo-epigrapha* (to use some prettier words at home in the disciplines), I have found most helpful Speyer 1971 and Baum 2001. In Salvian's ninth epistle one has precious fifth-century testimony of someone who has crafted a letter and attributed it to the apostle Timothy; the Latin original is in *Corpus Scriptorum Ecclesiasticorum Latinorum* (*CSEL*) 8 (1883): 217–23; for a partial English translation, see Haefner 1934.

[12] 'Milieu' is an intentionally capacious term; I mean not to exclude either 'audience' or 'genre' – either alone or in combination – but do wish to bypass, given the constraints of the current context, the extensive discussion, with extensive literature, that both would require.

[13] The phrase was coined by Ludwig Traube in his account of the successive poetic models for medieval Latin poets, according to which the *aetas Vergiliana* of the eighth and ninth centuries is succeeded by an *aetas Horatiana* in the tenth and eleventh centuries, which then gives way to the *aetas Ovidiana* of the twelfth and thirteenth centuries (Traube 1909–20, vol. ii: 113). Of the three 'ages', it is only the Ovidian that gained significant traction. On this exclusive focus on the *aetas Ovidiana* and the ever-expanding era(s) to which subsequent scholars have applied it, cf. Hexter 1986: 2–3 and Hexter 2002b, esp. 413; Gallo and Nicastri 1995; Holsinger and Townsend 2000: 242–3.

[14] In the current study I remain, a few exceptions apart, in the Latin world; the vernacular will enter only peripherally. Of course the membrane between these two 'worlds' was not impermeable. Is it provocative to remind readers that the topography suggested by the temporal phrase 'high Middle Ages' reflects a Latin orientation and that any lumping of Latin and 'the' vernacular (not to mention the individual vernaculars) forces a synchronization of the definitionally asynchronous (and, usually, yet another anachronism, whereby multiple medieval vernaculars are themselves lumped into variant precursors of later national languages no matter how false that is to contemporary realities or understandings).

that conceptual system. As Alastair Minnis and others have well described, *auctor* was the name for a role that stood at one end of a scale of functions that began with *scriptor* (scribe) and proceeded through *compilator* and *commentator* before arriving at the *auctor* proper.[15] Even more important – and this is by no means merely a medieval attitude – the mark of the '*auctor*' was not first and foremost 'originality' (much less sincerity). Instead, it was accomplishment and skill. Reading and study of earlier texts was the prerequisite to the first rung on the ladder of writing, which one achieved through a series of exercises based on *imitatio*.[16] I will return to this point shortly.

The second principle is really a corollary of the first that becomes necessary as we shift from a synchronic to a diachronic perspective:

2 In order truly to reconstruct the history of the pseudo-Ovidiana over the entire course of their 'existence', one would have first to construct the literary system prevailing at every point along the way, with contemporary concepts of the author, authenticity and pseudonymy – see principle (1) – and then present them as if in a film made out of the sequence of still photographs.

I merely make explicit what is implicit in both principles when I put 'existence' in scare-quotes, for not only is the 'falseness' of one or more pseudo-Ovidian works subject to changing perspectives, definitions and values, but the very idea of a coherent, consistent, continuous and self-evident category of 'pseudo-Ovidiana' – that imaginary volume '*Appendix Ovidiana*' – is a retrojection from a philological world based on a modern concept of authorship.[17]

---

[15] Minnis 1988, esp. 94–103. One runs the risk of generalising of course across the 'Middle Ages'; in those pages he is explicating an essentially thirteenth-century perspective, although one by no means restricted to that century. See also Minnis and Scott 1991 and Zimmermann 2001.

[16] Still valuable for the Roman system is Reiff 1959; more accessible will be West and Woodman 1979. There were of course limits not to be crossed; Stemplinger 1912 is still worth consulting on 'plagiarism' (in the Greek context); more recent, D. A. Russell in West and Woodman 1979: 1–16. There is now an entire bookshelf on 'intertextuality', but I consciously cite bibliography on 'imitation' that might otherwise seem outdated since my approach demands in the first instance a focus on the activities of confectors of verse.

[17] It is our modern view, founded on a modern (but not post-modern; see immediately below) sense of authorship, that makes a text 'pseudo-Ovidian' if the 'pseudo-' implies the intent to deceive. One might argue that the post-modern (i.e. Barthesian, Foucauldian) position of literature 'after the death of the author' might return us to a world closer in some ways to the textual universe in which the 'Ovidiana' described here had their place, but I would be wary of too swift or easy an equation, for, as I discuss shortly, in the medieval system of authorship, the *auctor* was not dead; he was not necessarily, however, a 'genius' and utterly sundered from others involved in the production and transmission of texts (Barthes 1977; Foucault 1977). Neither did he (or his designees) have the same kind of 'rights' of ownership that the institution of copyright law, which emerged and

I by no means wish to suggest that there were not earlier conceptions of authorship or even debates about authenticity and inauthenticity that would make us modern scholars feel right at home. For example, Hellenistic scholars were quite ready to distinguish between authentic and inauthentic, not only in authorial ascriptions of entire works but even within texts.[18] Adherents of specific philosophical schools were quite advanced in their discussion and categorisation of pseudonymy, even as to its motivations.[19] Buyers of medical treatises also had cause for concern: not all books ascribed to Galen were by Galen. Roman scholars working in the wake of Greek experts operated in the same manner: Lucius Aelius and, following in his footsteps, the more famous Varro created lists (*indices*) of what, in their view, were, respectively, the 25 or 21 authentic plays of Plautus out of the roughly 130 that were transmitted under his name.[20]

The very process of establishing the canon of the Bible also involved debates about authorship and authenticity, although here the process of documenting a text as 'authentic' and thus 'canonical' was not solely one of determining which texts were actually written by the persons to whom they were ascribed and which were not and then systematically including all the former and excluding all the latter. As Jerome's prefaces to the major portions of his Latin translation of the scriptures (eventually called the 'Vulgate') make clear, sometimes the issue of authorship (as we would frame it) was decisive, but at other times, the standards for authenticity and catholicity involved other elements.[21]

---

was codified in stages in Europe in the modern periods, afforded and which is inextricably bound up with our modern sense of authorship. Cf. Derrida 1978. Two recent books, Coombe 1998 and Saint-Amour 2003, give some taste of the variety of questions being debated along with reference to further secondary literature.

[18] The authenticity of many passages of Homer was denied by one Alexandrian critic or another, often on the grounds of their not being 'fitting' (*ou prepon*). This serves as a very striking reminder that the criteria Homeric scholars have applied to discriminate between the authentic and the inauthentic have varied widely over more than two millennia.

[19] Müller 1969. The Greek *notha biblia* (a phrase of Ammonius and others; *op. cit.* 120) offers an attractive metaphorical field: these are, literally, 'bastard books' (on which, cf. Grafton 1990: 12).

[20] Aulus Gellius, *Noctes Atticae* 3.3. This chapter is a repository of contemporary vocabulary surrounding issues of authenticity: [*fabulae/comoediae*] *ambiguae, dubiosae, incertae, genuinae*. Cf. Donatus' phrase *de qua ambigitur* on the *Aetna* of the Virgilian Appendix; Reeve 1983: 437; Putnam and Ziolkowski 2008: 191.

[21] For example, the *Prologus Hieronymi in libris Salomonis*, in which Jerome applies the Greek term *pseudepigraphos* to the Sapientia Salomonis and notes that the church reads Judith, Tobit (or Tobias) and the books of the Maccabees even if it does not consider them canonical ('sed inter canonicas scripturas non recipit'), Weber *et al.* 1969: 957. Cf. further relevant remarks in his prologues to Tobias (677), Judith (691) and Daniel (1341–2). Jerome does not shy away from such debates even within the 'New Testament'; in his *Prologus in epistulis Pauli apostoli* (1748–9), he addresses the debate over the Pauline authorship of the Letter to the Hebrews (1748). He takes up the argument that the

All the above-mentioned perspectives were at play during the first few hundred years of the transmission of Ovid's poetry, when (as I will discuss below) some 'Ovidian' works were added to the mix, in most cases only much later being added to manuscripts along with what we today regard as genuine. Indeed, the evidence of manuscripts – not only ascriptions in manuscripts but what is included, what is not, and what is grouped with what (and sometimes in what sequence) – can give precious indications of what works were considered 'Ovidian', and even how Ovidian, at different times and places.

Now many things – about the institutions of literature, Latinity, the breadth and depth of appreciation of subtle differences in Latin style and metrics, schooling and the attitudes toward *auctores* – change radically when one goes 800, 1000, 1200 and 1400 years out from the date of Ovid's death. I do not intend to give even a crude and jerky version of that stop-action film I imagined above, but I do want to emphasise that one needs to appreciate the historicity of such concepts and practices as one engages seriously with this body of literature. For example, in the monastic and cathedral schools of the high Middle Ages, there was a near-tautological understanding of authenticity: a work is 'authorial' and 'authoritative' if it is by an *auctor*, i.e. one of those whose works were on the prescribed reading list of texts.[22] And yet the practices of study could change from one generation to the next. Wilken Engelbrecht has suggested to me that in the later Middle Ages, especially the fourteenth and fifteenth centuries, when teachers and students relied for their study of the *auctores* increasingly on *florilegia* and excerpts, imitations of Ovid crafted only two centuries earlier could more readily be mistaken as ancient productions, and sometimes were.[23]

It is not surprising if we do not have terminology that applies equally well to all the stages in this development. Alas, we have yet to hit on a

Greek of 2 Peter is, on stylistic grounds, not likely to be from the same pen as the author of 1 Peter at *de viris illustribus* 1. Jerome's explanation – that the two letters had different *interpretes* (*Epistula* 120, *ad Hedibiam* = *PL* 22, col. 1002), which normally means 'translators' but more likely in Jerome's mind here refers to amanuenses who responded differently to Peter's dictation – places before us yet another example of the difference in conceptions of 'authorship' that different cultural practices and expectations produce. Here, not only does dictation intervene in a concept of authoring that modern students often assume requires the author to put pen to paper (or finger to keyboard) but a dictation that did not always guarantee or presume the transcription of the speaker's *ipsissima verba*.

[22] Battaglia 1959: 195–9 already offered an important discussion of the etymological linkages between *auctor*, *augeo* and *autentin* based on Isidore, Dante (*Convivio* IV) and important glossators such as Hugutio of Pisa and Papias.

[23] Personal communication. He asks, rhetorically, 'how many of our modern students, used to read[ing] authors only in syllabuses, would be able to discern a text written in the style of James Joyce from a genuine text of James Joyce?'

vocabulary that could make what might seem like the most fundamental of distinctions, between works that were written to be taken for Ovid's and those that were written in emulation of Ovid. Although the false-ness that the prefix 'pseudo' points to does not always involve intentional deception on the part of a human agent,[24] when human agency is involved, that falseness is readily, almost inevitably read as deceptive. For that rea-son, it might be better to replace 'pseudo-Ovidiana' as the most inclusive term with a more value-neutral one, for example, 'para-Ovidiana'. In what follows I have not systematically discarded traditional terminology. It is almost certain that we would discover that 'para-Ovidiana', like most new terminology, would have its own deficiencies and inconveniences. It may well be, though, that the epicyclical twisting and turning I put us through as I attempt to survey and anatomise the 'pseudo-Ovidiana' may itself con-stitute a strong argument in favour of 'para-Ovidiana' as a better category, albeit one that would require a new and even more capacious survey.

Whichever term one uses, one can agree that the act of creating such texts involves masquerading. The important question is: what sort of mas-querade? At the height of education in the *auctores*, imitation was an essential tool in the pedagogic process and a central element in a writer's self-fashioning.[25] Appreciation of this fact is key to understanding a good number of the texts I survey, especially if one is of a mind to speculate (as I will only rarely) on what was in authors' minds when they wrote and put these texts into circulation. Did they anticipate that their verses just might or likely would be ascribed to Ovid? Did they intend them to be? If so, did they consider what they were doing as in any way a deception? It seems fairly obvious to me that within a system of literary production, reproduction and transmission that was based at its most fundamental level on imitation, masquerade and ventriloquism, 'forgery' is not the best or even most accurate term for what writers were doing when they created new Ovidian texts.[26]

---

[24] Jan Ziolkowski adduces its use in a compound such as 'pseudopod' (personal communication).

[25] E.g. Bernard of Chartres demanded that his students imitate Latin poets (John of Salisbury 1991, *Metalogicon* 855b; I thank Wilken Engelbrecht for the reference). And while 'self-fashioning' origi-nally gained currency in the context of modern studies on the Renaissance, I think no medievalist would deny its applicability to a poet like Baudri of Bourgueil, discussed below, or Hildebert of Lavardin.

[26] Obviously, sometimes capturing an author's style so that it would seem to be a text of that author's but also not be ascribed to him is the point. The parodist will have succeeded too well by half if the gap between the texts and authors is not clearly discerned. In a fuller account, the category of 'parody' would have to be anatomised as well. Bibliography here, too, is extensive. I mention above all, Lehmann 1963, as its author is a major scholar of the pseudo-Ovidian tradition. Recent and helpful (again, in the medieval Latin context) is the study of Bayless 1996.

Finally, as I have already suggested, we must not be trapped by thinking that appreciation of the Latin classics and the means by which students encountered them were uniform throughout the 'Middle Ages', or even that developments ran in one direction only. The average twelfth-century Latin student might have been more finely attuned to Ovidian style than the average fourteenth-century student (even if there may have been more of the latter), but of course, the fourteenth century could also produce a Petrarch.

* * * * * * *

Just as pseudonymy in literature is a function of reception, so any full account of the pseudo- or para-Ovidiana would have to track the reception history of Ovid, a vast project to which the present article cannot possibly aspire. In the following, I strive to mention nearly all the works that can reasonably be thought to belong to the universe of Latin pseudo-Ovidiana to the end of the Middle Ages, and although limited space does not permit me to give more than a superficial sense of each text, I aim to offer readers sufficient information to explore further on their own. In general my survey moves in a largely historical fashion, but there is good reason not to follow chronology slavishly. For one thing, given the uncertain dating of a number of poems, to strive for precise chronological exactitude would be an exercise in futility. Furthermore, some of the pseudo-Ovidian poems respond not merely to Ovid's canonical works but to other pseudo-Ovidiana, so that in a few instances incipient sub-genres spring up. It makes sense to recognise thematic complexes within an overarching historically oriented sequence and to discuss these groupings together.

Let me effect the transition to this inevitably partial history with one final disclaimer: I will not attempt to address what scholars identify as issues of 'authenticity' within what are universally recognised as 'authentic' works of Ovid, even if the establishment of a passage as not the work of the author Ovid renders it pseudo-Ovidian in a very real (if rarely recognised) sense. Every interpolation would constitute an intervention in the text, every (conscious) interpolation a forgery.[27] The *Heroides* would provide the best

---

[27] It is of course possible that some of these were not really intended as forgeries. For example, if a reader and 'fan' of Ovid who was sufficiently gifted as a versifier were, in an ecstasy of readerly responsiveness, to dash off a line or couplet and scribble it in his margin, with no intention that it ever be taken as anything other than a personal supplement or homage, a subsequent reader or scribe might nonetheless insert it into the text. This is offered only to suggest that 'intent' may be beside the point, or at least beyond our capacity to ferret out. – It would be an interesting extension of my argument here to consider variants as constituting what one might term degree zero examples of pseudo-Ovidiana.

example.[28] Scholars actively question whether several epistles transmitted in the twenty-one constituting the work as it has been published for some 500 years now are in fact Ovid's.[29] I phrase it thus because the medieval collection itself looked somewhat different.[30] If the impugned letters are not by Ovid, they have been read as (unrecognised) pseudo-Ovidiana all along.[31] Of somewhat different status are the introductory couplets to many of the *Heroides*, which seem to have been penned to standardise the openings of the letters.[32] Of course, there were many other imitations of the epistles, starting (so we hear) with Julius Titianus in the third century and with an extant remake, likely also third century, of Dido's letter to Aeneas

[28] The dialogic nature of the epistles inspired works of response that are 'Ovidian' in a certain sense but in no sense pseudo-Ovidian: Ovid himself reports (*Am.* 2.18.27–34) that his friend Sabinus penned responses to six of the initial *Heroides* (1, 2, 4, 6, 7, 15; I must here leave aside the debate that rages about the interpretation of these very lines). These are lost, but in the Renaissance there circulated three letters now regarded as virtually certainly the creations of a fifteenth-century Angelo Sani Di Cure or, in Latin, Angelus de Curibus Sabinis; Dörrie 1968: 104–6; cf. Knox 2009b: 216). In ch. 4 of his study, White 2009 analyses these as well as a series of French responding letters. (White does allow for the possibility that these might not be pseudo-Sabinus.) Another Latin letter of Ulysses to Penelope attributed to Sabinus (whether by the same humanist or another) has now been edited (Mecklenborg and Schneider 2002; cf. Knox 2009b: 216). For the vast European culture of responding (in multiple senses) to the *Heroides*, Dörrie 1968 remains indispensable.

[29] On the authenticity of some of the first fourteen epistles (*Her.* 8–10 and 12–13 the most consistently impugned), see Tarrant 1981:152; Ovid 1995d: 5–14; Knox 2002: 118–22; Knox 2009b: 211. On the question of the double letters, 16–21, Kenney 1996: 20–6 has, for now at least, turned the tide in favour of Ovidian authorship, suggesting they may date from the years prior to Ovid's exile (cf. Knox 2002: 211). For the possibility that the paired letters were the work of Ovid's period of exile, see Gaertner 2007, esp. 155 n. 4 and 161 n. 37 (with further bibliography). *Heroides* 15, or the *Epistula Sapphus* (*ES*), is another matter altogether: the medieval period barely knew it; until its fifteenth-century rediscovery, *ES* likely could have been read in only one Frankfurt manuscript (Barth. 110, discussed below, n. 86).

[30] It comprised, by our numeration, *Her.* 1–14, 16 (less vv. 39–144) and 17–21.14. On the peculiar problems of *Heroides* 16, 20 and 21, see Hexter 1986: 141; Kenney 1996: 20–6; Ovid 1995d: 6.

[31] The same is often said for *Amores* 3.5. It is perhaps worth observing the irony that the *Heroides* themselves pose a challenge to any stable concept of authenticity, since Ovid the *author* prides himself on masquerading in turn as Penelope, Phyllis, Briseis, Dido, Oenone *et al.* (For this reason the *Heroides* appear as a key example in the 'dramatic' type of pseudonymy as described in Candlish 1891: 96). As often, Ovid anticipates and offers the most challenging theoretical critique in his own work far in advance of any of us 'theorists'.

[32] On the additional introductory couplets and other detachable couplets in *Heroides* 1–15, see Ovid 1995d: 36, with the bibliography there in n. 99, and Kirfel 1969: 1–10, 112–19. Richmond 2002: 465 observes: 'It is impossible to be sure that any one explanation will cover all the cases.' The 'modular' nature of the *Heroides* invited not only additions and responses but intrusions, all the easier to pass off in the vernacular; cf. the three non-Ovidian letters – the *Carta de Madreselua a Manseol*, *Troylos a Brecayda* and *Brecayda a Troylo* – in the *Bursario* of Juan Rodriguez del Padrón (1390 – c.1450), in other ways unusual but still a 'translation' according to contemporary standards of the medieval *Heroides* as studied in schools (Hexter 2007b: 1317).

and, then, in the sixth century, Venantius Fortunatus' fictional epistle of a nun to Christ.[33] But none of these is actually intended to be taken as Ovid's, and none was.

At least two works of the first century that hover at the edges of the Ovidian corpus must be mentioned here, for unless they are by Ovid himself, they must be accounted veritable pseudo-Ovidiana. The one is the *Halieutica*.[34] Pliny the Elder knew and cited verses from this work;[35] he further believed it to be by Ovid.[36] For Pliny, Ovid the Pontic ichthyologist is a potential source of scientific lore.[37] But the text we have, and to judge by his quotations, that Pliny had, too, is in suboptimal shape and, to many, not at all Ovidian. Could Pliny have been misled by a counterfeit or simply a false labelling?

The other such text is the *Nux*[38] that 'comes to light in several parts of Europe in the decades before and after 1100'.[39] Conrad of Hirsau (*c.* 1070 – *c.* 1150) considered it a work of Ovid's and found it worthy of study,[40] and it received a commentary from no less a humanist than Erasmus.[41] Modern scholars vary in their assessment. Tarrant, by calling it 'the most accomplished of pseudo-Ovidian poems', makes clear that he denies to Ovid its authorship, and though Richmond's final stance is agnostic, he admits that there are no utterly insuperable arguments against Ovidian authorship.[42] Of course, we should not imagine that every work must be ascribable to a great author; that would be to fall into the very logic behind a good many ascriptions, to Ovid and other poets, over the centuries. Still, if it is not truly Ovid's, it is Ovidian. When it first entered into the class

---

[33] Titianus: reported by Sidonius Apollinaris, *Ep.* 1.1.2 in Anderson 1980–4; the Dido letter: from Paris, BN, lat. MS 10318 (the 'Salmasianus'), fols. 64–74, collected as *Anthologia Latina* 71 (1972– (= 83 Riese)); Venantius Fortunatus 8.3.227–48 in Reydellet 1994–, discussed in Schmid 1959: 253–63. On all three, see Dörrie 1968: 96–7.

[34] Schaller and Könsgen 1977, no. 86, edited by Richmond 1962. Once discovered by Jacopo Sannazaro at the start of the sixteenth century, the work was initially known as *Versus de piscibus et feris*; see Reeve 1983: 181.

[35] *Natural History* 23.11 and 152–3.   [36] 11.152. Richmond 2002: 450 is certain it is not by Ovid.

[37] While it may perhaps be odd that we do not possess more first-century testimonia to Ovid's exile, it is wrong to claim (as some have) that there are none; Pliny (*Natural History* 32.152; cf. Knox 2009b: 212) and Statius ('nec tristis in ipsis / Naso Tomis', *Silvae* 1.2.254–5) place him there.

[38] Schaller and Könsgen 1977, no. 10797; the best edition is Lenz 1956, though Tarrant 1983 is less than enthusiastic about his apparatus and use thereof.

[39] Walther 1959, no. 12505; Schaller and Könsgen 1977, no. 10797. Cf. Tarrant 1983: 285.

[40] *Accessus ad auctores* 1970, lines 1331–5.

[41] 1524 saw two printings: Johannes Frobenius in Basel and Joannes Soter in Cologne. It was reprinted frequently through the following forty years and well past Erasmus' death (1536).

[42] Tarrant 1983: 285; Richmond 2002: 468–9; Richmond 1981: 2765–7; Knox 2009b: 212.

of pseudo-Ovidiana, in other words, when it was first ascribed to Ovid, cannot be said with any certainty.[43]

One of the most widely dispersed and among the most frequently copied pseudo-Ovidian poems has almost nothing to do with Ovid at all, if by that is meant his life or works. The function of attributing to Ovid both introductory verses to Virgil's major works and summaries of the individual books of the *Aeneid* was to express and inscribe Ovid's subordinate status in every manuscript of Virgil in which they appear. Ovid is 'number two', Virgil 'number one', Virgil the *ne plus ultra* of canonicity, Ovid the 'also ran'.[44] At least one strain of these Virgilian paraphernalia (the so-called *Argumenta*) might date from as early as the third or fourth century, although the strict *terminus ante quem* is provided by the famous 'Vergilius Romanus' (Vatican City, BAV, Vat. lat. MS 3867) of the fifth century. These and other major strains were also often copied apart from texts of Virgil, most notably in the witnesses to the so-called *Anthologia Latina* starting with the 'Salmasianus' of the eighth century.[45] It is so far not determinable when exactly these poems became pseudo-Ovidian, i.e. prefixed with Ovid's name, but likely when they were made to follow the '*Praefatio*', the first couplet of which runs: 'Vergilius magno quantum concessit Homero, / tantum ego Vergilio, Naso poeta, meo'.[46] As Marpicati points out, no extant manuscript of these ten prefatory verses predates the ninth century.[47]

---

[43] Richmond also points to another interesting question: if it is Ovid's (or intended to be believed to be Ovid's), when did Ovid write it? ('When did pseudo-Ovid write it?' would mean: when in Ovid's career do those who think it Ovidian imagine Ovid wrote it?) Slight oddities or imperfections can lead scholars either to call it a work of Ovid's youth or extreme old age (particularly if, credulous, they believe in Ovid's own testimony to his waning powers at Tomis). In the case of the *Nux*, there seems to be no reason to see it as a work of Ovid's youth (the period in which Virgil's *minora* are placed). If it is Ovidian, the argument that it, like the *Ibis*, is also a product of his years in Tomis, has attractions. See the comments of Richmond 1981: 2765 on the mode of ascribing works to poets' youth. Two works that also seem best dated to this period, the *Elegiae in Maecenatem* and the *Consolatio ad Liviam (de morte Drusi)* I will not treat here; on them, see Knox 2009b: 213–14. Neither was associated with the Ovidian corpus very often and then only very very late, in the sixteenth century. (They had only been recovered in the fifteenth.)

[44] It will support but does not demand the opposition of ultimate insider/ultimate outsider, a position in which Ovid has often been placed and which in my view ultimately does a greater injustice to Virgil than it does to Ovid.

[45] The three major sets are printed as *Anthologia latina* 1.1–2a (Shackleton Bailey), 1–2 and 654 (Riese). The second, the *Tetrasticha in cunctis libris Vergilii*, do not begin with a comparable proclamation of Ovidian authorship, but they are attributed to Ovid in Vatican City, BAV, Vat. lat. MS 1575 of the tenth or eleventh century (Shackleton Bailey, 11 and x).

[46] *Anthologia latina* 1.1 (Shackleton Bailey); Putnam and Ziolkowski 2008: 22.

[47] Marpicati 2000: 150–1. As one follows Marpicati through his evaluation of the 'emendations' modern editors have made in the preface (and, in his Marpicati 1997, other of the arguments), one realises that in a certain sense, the work of crafting pseudo-Ovidiana is an ongoing industry.

They might be older, of course, but it seems that only once the 'Praefatio' had been prefixed to the poem did the other collections become provably pseudo-Ovidian. It would certainly make sense if this gesture, at once bringing Ovid on the scene but relegating him to a subordinate status, is datable to the *aetas Vergiliana*.[48]

The crafting of Ovidiana that are worthy tributes to the Augustan poet would not arise again until the system of literary education based on the study of Latin authors was restored under the Carolingians and, after several generations, sufficiently stable such that writers of medieval Latin had the capacity and inclination to write quantitative verse in imitation of Roman poets. An example of both inclination and skill would be Baudri of Bourgeuil's crossing of the form of *Heroides* 16–21 (the double letters) with the thematic of Ovid's exile to produce *Florus Ovidio* and *Ovidius Floro*.[49] In the latter, Baudri dons the mask of Ovid, but this is a fictive exchange, and no one has ever thought otherwise. It is a good example of what is Ovidian, even fictively Ovidian, but even if in a certain sense pseudo-Ovidian, it never entered the stream of received pseudo-Ovidiana.[50]

Baudri's life span – 1046–1130 – coincided with the beginning of the *aetas Ovidiana*. As I have noted, Traube originally applied the term to the twelfth and thirteenth centuries in a context very much oriented to Latin poetic *imitatio*,[51] but scholars have broadened it not only temporally but expanded its signification to describe a wider cultural movement which certainly began before 1100. By this time, a school-based familiarity with Ovid had begun to inspire new works, particularly in the erotic and

[48] I.e. the eighth and ninth centuries according to Traube's scheme; cf. n. 13 above.
[49] 97–8 in Baudri of Bourgeuil ed. Hilbert 1979, as well as the superior edition, with French translation, ed. Tilliette 1998–2002; Tilliette follows Hilbert's numeration. This epistolary pair has been subjected to much criticism, from Schuelper 1979, through Bond 1989 and, more recently, Bond 1995; in my own most recent discussion (Hexter 2007a: 225–30), I comment on the debate between Ratkowitsch 1987 and Tilliette 1994. Baudri's paired epistles *Paris Helenae* and *Helena Paridi* (7–8 in Baudri ed. Hilbert 1979), however much inspired by *Her.* 16–17, have not generally been considered examples of pseudo-Ovidiana, presumably because their reception was limited to the (not vast) reception of Baudri's own oeuvre. They might be compared to the eleventh-century *Deidamia Achilli* edited by Stohlmann 1973, Ovidian in inspiration but not actually ascribed to Ovid, in which the anonymous author gives voice to another Trojan woman besides Briseis who had occasion to write to Achilles.
[50] Manitius 1911–1931, III: 891–2 uses the word 'pseudo' (in the index of the volume) much more narrowly than the way I use the term and even writes that Baudri wanted his Paris–Helen epistolary exchange to 'replace' (ersetzen) *Her.* 16–17. Even more emphatically do I reject Kurt Smolak's use of the term *Fälschung* (forgery) to describe Baudri's epistolary interchange between the imaginary 'Florus' and an imagined 'Ovidius': Smolak 1980, esp. 165, 167. To express what is going on here via the metaphorics of celestial mechanics with which I have sometimes toyed, one might say that Baudri himself as a poet has sufficient mass to keep these poems orbiting around him and thus not permit them to be drawn into an Ovid-centric orbit.
[51] On Traube's schema, see n. 13, above.

eroto-didactic realms, where masquerading might have attractions beyond a desire to imitate Ovidian style (and show off at doing so). Not all who received a schoolroom education in Latin went on to be churchmen like Baudri or Hildebert of Lavardin. Some of the *clerici* were indeed *vagantes*, whose characteristic goliardic ribaldry is reflected in a text such as *Ovidius puellarum* that Peter Dronke has dated to about 1080 and which partakes in part of the world Ovid described in the *Amores* and *Ars amatoria* but even more of medieval fabliaux.[52] The poem narrates the seduction of the *puella* for a handsome young man through the offices of the *nuntius*, a male go-between; hence its alternative title, *De nuntio sagaci*.[53] Very much in the same vein is the immensely influential *Pamphilus* (*c.* 1100).[54] The *Pamphilus* clearly belongs to the same world as the Ovidian works of the period; note the appearance of an *accessus* to it in Tegernsee, Munich clm 19475 and the reference to it by Arnulf of Orléans in his commentary on Ovid's *Remedia amoris*. That it was not claimed in the school tradition to be by Ovid would suggest that we not admit it to the ranks of pseudo-Ovidiana, and perhaps it does not at first belong among them. Yet if one looks at the reception history of the *Pamphilus* in vernacular literatures – I think of French and Spanish above all, e.g. Juan Ruiz's *Libro de buen amor* – it is brought into contact with both Ovid the Roman author and the 'Ovid' of *De vetula* (on which, see below), so that ultimately it may be considered a naturalised pseudo-Ovidianum, or possibly a pseudo-pseudo-Ovidianum.[55]

One does not have to leave Latin to observe a similar process occur in the case of *Facetus* '*moribus et vita*' which should probably be dated *c.* 1130–40.[56] The final line in some of its many manuscripts suggests that

[52] Dronke 1979: 230.

[53] Walther 1959, nos. 18441, 18787. Edited by Alton 1931, now replaced by the edition of Rossetti 1980. We have precious indication of the reading of this text as Ovidian in the Tegernsee love letters (clm 19411). I cite from Dronke 1976: 130, n. 10: 'Suo sua sibi se. Dicit quidam sub nomine Ovidii de amore, Sperabam c.f.f.f.', where the last bit ('Sperabam c.f.f.f.') renders *Ovidius puellarum* v. 2 (after the fashion, I might add, common for quotations of lemmata in commentaries also emerging in southern Bavarian monasteries at this time).

[54] Texts: Becker 1972; *Pamphilus*, ed. Rubio and González Rolán 1977; Pittaluga 1980. Schotter 1992 provides references to English translations as well as further bibliography. For the date, again Dronke 1979.

[55] One manuscript now in Berlin offers us a thirteenth-century interlinear Venetian version of the *Pamphilus*; Hexter 2007b: 1320, with further bibliography. Even earlier it had been translated into Old Norse prose; see Hexter 2007b: 1318.

[56] Walther 1959, no. 11220; Dronke 1976 and (for the date) 1979; translation: Elliot 1977; cf. Baldwin 1994: 20–1, with the bibliography on 276, n. 69. In Hexter 2007b I failed to mention the Catalan translation of the *Facetus* known from one manuscript miscellany dated c. 1400; see Cantavella 1998: 304.

the author may be an otherwise unidentifiable 'Aurigena'. The *Facetus* is
Ovidian in its disposition, and Ovid himself was called '*facetus*' by Hugh
of Trimberg,[57] but there is otherwise no direct connection. However, while
many manuscripts contain the whole, there are some manuscripts that
contain sections cut out from it as, first, a pseudo-Ovidian *Ars amatoria*
and then a pseudo-Ovidian *Remedia amoris*.[58]

These examples are clearly pseudo-Ovidian. Whether or not the *Facetus*
as a whole should count as belonging to the pseudo-Ovidiana, it nonetheless instructively stands, one might say, at a crossroads where at least two
Ovidian 'streets' intersect: Ovid the teacher of manners and Ovid the eroto-
didact. The former is well represented by the *Doctrina mense*, a seventy-line
poem in elegiacs dating likely from the thirteenth century but certainly
no later than the first half of the fourteenth.[59] We might also regard the
Elegia de ludo scacchorum[60] as belonging to this 'courtly' stream, although
a not insignificant impulse may well have been Ovid's own mention of
instruction manuals for dice and other games.[61]

Alongside the 'courtly' stream, there developed a yet cruder strain within
the general field of Ovidiana, already quite frank in *Ovidius puellarum*
(and *Pamphilus*), whether actually ascribed to him or not. With the so-
called 'elegiac comedies',[62] the corpus of pseudo-Ovidiana bleeds into

---

[57] 'letus et facetus', *Registrum multorum auctorum*, v. 125; Langosch 1942; cf. Klein 1978: 184. On *facetus*
as 'courtly', see Elliott 1977: 27.

[58] These sections are fairly stable. They are edited together in Thiel 1968, with further commentary in
Thiel 1970 and Schnell 1975. They were also known as distinct poems to Lehmann 1927: 11. Notice
that they in fact comprise portions of another, larger work was provided by Dronke, who writes: 'In
A. Morel-Fatio's edition of this poem (*Romania* xv, 1886, 224–35), the "Pseudo-Ars" (190 lines in
Thiel's text) constitutes *Facetus* lines 131–320; the "Pseudo-Remedia" (60 lines in Thiel), following
without a break in *Facetus*, comprises lines 321–84; Thiel's lines 1–29 are *Facetus* 321–39, his 30–60
are *Facetus* 354–84. *Facetus* 350–53 are omitted in Thiel's text: even though, as he notes (1968: 130–2),
they do occur in one of his groups of manuscripts, he dismisses them as an interpolation. Thiel's
edition also contains one line (33) that completely alters the *Facetus* text (357) – though again the
Facetus version of the line, as Thiel's apparatus shows, is found in two of his manuscript groups'
(1976: 126–7).

[59] Walther 1959, no. 10925. Edited on the basis of seven manuscripts in Klein 1978; for the date, 185. It
is interesting that the manuscripts fall into two groups, one Spanish (three manuscripts) the other
German (four manuscripts), the earliest witness of the former group *c.* 100 years before the second
(185). Explicit attribution to Ovid appears in three manuscripts and alternative titles include *Liber
de facecia mense* and *Carmen faceciarum comedencium*. On two other manuscripts, see Stohlmann
1979.

[60] Ed. by Pascal 1907: 137–41 and Murray 1913: 515–16. Winter 1986: 18, notes that the poem is Walther
1959, no. 15455, not 15440.

[61] *Tristia* 2.471–82. The gaming tradition will be picked up and expanded in *De vetula*, discussed
below. Note that in the catalogue of contemporary leisure pursuits and their publishing gurus that
Ovid includes, there appears 'hic epulis leges hospitioque dedit' (488): a *doctrina mense*, as it were,
from Roman times.

[62] Original corpus of these dialogues, in elegiac meter, was Cohen 1931. Replaced by Bertini 1976–.

the fabulistic and at times obscene realm of William of Blois's *Alda* and Vitalis of Blois's *Geta*.[63] Another bit of obscenity was inspired by a famous poem within the *Appendix Vergiliana*. Just as Virgil was supposed to have written the witty tale of the *Culex* (the 'gnat'),[64] so Ovid is given a poem – a versified dirty joke, really – on the *Pulex* (the 'flea').[65] Modular and imitative composition functions in the ongoing production of *pseudo-epigrapha*. As the gnat 'begat' the flea, so to speak, so the flea begat the louse: *De pediculo*.[66]

Dating is quite treacherous, and one may never be completely confident that one has caught the first attribution, but by about this time or shortly before some older brief poems about animals were drawn by the gravitational force of 'planet Ovid' into the Ovidian system. Prime examples are *De cuculo*[67] and *De philomela*.[68] Then there is the odd case of what most of its manuscripts term *Ovidius de mirabilibus mundi*. The material is bestiary lore, drawn in large measure from Solinus. Its first editor, M. R. James, argues that the seventy-nine 'sections' 'were meant to serve as explanations of pictorial representations'.[69]

---

[63] Baldwin 1994 rightly emphasises the remarkably graphic presentation of male nudity in the *Alda* (98, 108–10) and of female nudity in the pseudo-Ovidian *De tribus puellis* (98–110), adducing contemporary and comparable vernacular frankness. For the most recent text of the latter, consult Pittaluga 1976. Vital de Blois's *Geta* has now been edited in Bertini 1976–, vol. III: 139–242.

[64] *Culex* belongs to the canonical *Appendix Vergiliana*; see above, nn. 7–8.

[65] Walther 1959, nos. 8072, 13745 and 13752; edition: Lenz 1962. An Italian translation of the pseudo-Ovidian *De pulice* is found in multiple manuscripts; see Hexter 2007b: 1321, with further references.

[66] Walther 1959, nos. 8890 and 10257; edition: Lenz 1955 (and further, Lenz 1959a). Lenz dates the poem before 1250 and argues that the louse is a teacher and monk who was particularly nasty in the way he forced his students to write Latin hexameters and who was further excessively carnal. This interpretation, though possible, is hardly an obvious construction of the poem's modest seven elegiac couplets. As Jan Ziolkowski observes, 'from another vantage, the ring poem begat both the flea and the louse' (personal communication); both poems appear in translation in Ziolkowski 1993.

[67] Beginning 'conveniunt subito cuncti de montibus altis', these verses (Schaller and Könsgen 1977, no. 2750; Walther 1959, no. 3288) have also been attributed to Alcuin or a member of his circle; the text has been frequently printed (*MGH PLAC* 1.270; *Anthologia latina* 687); see further, Castillo 1973. This and the next item were written before the twelfth century but were turned by attribution into pseudo-Ovidiana at that time.

[68] Beginning 'dulcis amica veni, noctis solatia praestans' (Schaller and Könsgen 1977, no. 3975); see Klopsch 1973, who regards it as most likely a tenth-century product on the basis of metrical peculiarities (174–5). Among pseudo-Ovidiana involving animals belongs also *De lupo* (Walther 1959, no. 17029; beginning 'Sepe lupus quidam per pascua lata vagantes'); as its alternative title, *De monacho*, suggests, though, it might also belong to the anti-religious satires discussed immediately below.

[69] Walther 1959, nos. 8095, 18131; James 1913: 288. James hazarded no guesses as to date or provenance (289). The poem's 126 verses are leonine hexameters, but so widespread is the use of the rhymed verse, especially in its simplest form (*consonans* or *concinnans*), that this offers little help. Is it worthy of mention in this context that the possible author of *De vetula*, discussed below, Richard of Fournival, is known as the author of the *Bestiaire d'amours*?

Ovid was of course a noted naturalist, not only in the *Halieutica* but throughout the *Metamorphoses*.[70] Given the prominence of the latter, it might at first blush seem surprising that Ovid's greatest work – *Ovidius maior* – did not inspire more 'spin-offs', but it would not be easy to create an entire alternative *Metamorphoses*.[71] The forty-four hexameters beginning 'altera sed nostris', first published in 1976 by W. S. Anderson[72] from the margins of a fourteenth-century Vatican manuscript of the *Metamorphoses*, is indeed, as Anderson noted, a metamorphic episode. Following upon what can best be described as a liturgical 'malfunction', the priest (*flamen*) and the priestesses ('vestals') are metamorphosed into a cock and hens, respectively. W. D. Lebek argued four years later,[73] however, that beneath what seemed to Anderson a pathetically ignorant attempt to write about an ancient Roman rite there lies a scandalous tale, whether an actual event (or rumors thereof) or just a fabliau. I compress Lebek's summary of 'the story in plain English':

A bishop (or . . . abbot) came to a nuns' cloister . . . , saw the abbess, [and] . . . fell in love with her. [She] . . . fell in love with . . . him . . . [T]he two ecclesiastics had intercourse.

Even more. To keep the other nuns quiet,

The bishop made love to them, too – omitting none of them: an admirable feat. God . . . changed the bishop into a cock (whom the high dignitary had resembled so much) and the abbess together with her nuns into hens.[74]

---

[70] Cf. Viarre 1966: 8.

[71] Should one consider counting the *Ovide moralisé* among pseudo-Ovidiana? This would cross the Latin/vernacular divide, but there are other candidates for pseudo-Ovidiana that exist only in a vernacular. For example, in the first half of the fifteenth century Juan Rodríguez del Padrón inserted into his Spanish version of the *Heroides* three letters of his own devising, two of them forming an exchange between Troilus and Briseis (Troylos a Brecayda, Brecayda a Troylos), ascribing them to Ovid; Hexter 2007b: 1317. Elsewhere in the present volume there is extensive discussion of the commentary tradition on Ovid; see especially the contribution of *il miglior fabbro* and volume co-editor Frank Coulson. While commentaries are certainly paratexts, and thus Ovid commentaries a subset of para-Ovidiana in one sense of the term, only in a few odd cases in the commentary tradition – and then primarily within the *Metamorphoses* tradition – can one see the lines blur between explanatory texts and poems of the sort I survey here. Even the allegorisations of Arnulf or Bersuire are not in any sense pseudo-Ovidiana (even as they testify to the lability of the text in the face of strong readers). One might be more justified in at least considering the cases of John of Garland's verse *Integumenta Ovidii* (Coulson and Roy 2000, no. 333) or possibly Giovanni del Virgilio's prosimetrical *Allegorie* (Coulson and Roy 2000, no. 424; see also nos. 265 and 427), especially the elegiac verses the latter incorporated (from another source) into his paratext. See Coulson 2007, esp. 44–5, with n. 49 on the verse in del Virgilio, with reference to Rotondi 1934.

[72] Anderson 1974.   [73] Lebek 1978. He dates the poem to the eleventh century or later (120).

[74] Lebek 1978: 113. Lebek points to the conclusion of the Philemon and Baucis story (*Met.* 8.698–720) as the Ovidian passage most likely to be in the anonymous poet's mind (122).

This is satiric in spirit, as is the *De Lombardo et lumaca* from the later twelfth century, likely its last quarter.[75] In twenty-six nicely accomplished elegiac distichs the poet presents a mock-heroic scene in which a Lombard peasant prepares to do battle with the 'monster' that is destroying his fields. Said monster ultimately turns out to be a snail. Lenz argues that the point of the joke is not that all Lombards are stupid. Instead, the poet encourages his fellow citizens to recognise that their enemy, Emperor Fredrick I, who was just in these years campaigning in northern Italy, was not invincible, as evidenced by his defeat at Legnano in 1176. If this interpretation, which has its attractions, is the true one, it will make *De Lombardo et lumaca* the only pseudo-Ovidian poem with so direct a political message.[76]

An allegory of a very different sort lies behind the pseudo-Ovidian *De sompnio*,[77] a poem of thirty-four elegiac couplets that, out of diverse materials and pretexts, some Ovidian, some biblical, presents what is ultimately an apocalyptic vision to the dreamer.[78] The vision itself is of two female figures, utterly different in appearance and demeanour, to which a third figure appears, a man, who explains the significance of the allegorical figures.

The title of Ovid's own *De medicamine faciei femineae* inspired *De medicamine surdi* or *De medicamine aurium*, although an important impulse came from a report in Pliny about a recipe Ovid himself versified for a cure for angina.[79] And there is also *De quattuor*

---

[75] Walther 1959, no. 20072. The best edition is that of Bonacina 1983. It had previously been published by Lenz 1957, who ultimately sets 1176, the date of the Battle of Legnagno, as a *terminus post quem* (222). The poem survives in one thirteenth-century manuscript (the Holkham manuscript, of Italian provenance, noted below, see also n. 89) and then fourteen fifteenth-century texts (206–7), a temporal distribution worth noting (205).

[76] That the poem is mock-heroic is not in debate. I have grave doubts that it in fact parodies Hector's leavetaking of Andromache in *Iliad* 6 (Lenz 1957: 220), as Lenz maintains, or that we should put so much weight on the fact that the peasant's wife refers to Hercules rather than Theseus or Perseus (221). Lenz's major point will stand without such straining.

[77] Walther 1959, no. 12341, best consulted in Smolak 1983. It was first published in Lehmann 1927: 63–5 and then by Lenz 1968, who is by no means shy about complaining about Lehmann's insufficencies in matters of detail (101–2, 106, 108–11, 113). Smolak 1983: 190 in turn takes Lenz to task. This poem begins 'Nox erat, et placido capiebam pectore sompnum' and is to be distinguished from *Am.* 3.5, 'Nox erat et somnus . . .', which, though printed in all standard editions of the *Amores*, is regularly doubted to be Ovid's own poem. As noted above (n. 5), it also appears in medieval manuscripts with the title *De somno* (= *De rustico*), often along with authentic Ovidian poems unmoored from their original context (e.g., *Am.* 1.5 and 2.15).

[78] Ovidian passages include *Amores* 3.1 and 3.5 (see immediately above), *Metamorphoses* 8.788–808; Biblical passages include Pharaoh's dream (Gen. 41.1–7) and Rev. 6–7; non-Ovidian non-Biblical sources include Boethius' *Consolatio philosophiae* and the anonymous *Carmen de ventis* (in several versions); Smolak 1983, especially 199–205; see now also Bertini 1995.

[79] Walther 1959, nos. 1165 and 11701; see the edition of Lenz 1958. This same poem appears under yet other titles, e.g. *De speculo medicinae/medicaminis* and *De herbarum virtutibus*. For Pliny's testimony, see *Natural History* 30.4.12.

humoribus[80] – in several manuscripts, the two poems are closely connected[81] – and, to continue on the theme of the body, albeit with a less medical focus, the *De ventre*, also called the *Altercatio ventris et artuum*, a poem in elegiacs (196 verses) that describes the debate among the body's parts for precedence, a rhetorical set-piece from Livy (2.32.8ff.) to John of Salisbury.[82]

I mentioned above medieval sources that could give us a sense of how medieval students and scholars understood these works, or some of them, to fit into Ovid's life production. The poems of the *Appendix Vergiliana* are generally conceived as juvenilia, the works of the young Virgil prior to his composition of the *Eclogues*, and in the early fifteenth century Sicco Polenton (1375/6–1447/8) places a number of the works we now consider pseudo-Ovidian – in his eyes they are genuine – likewise early in Ovid's career.[83] In contrast, Ovid's medieval biographies generally set the new Ovidian titles after the *Heroides* and the *Amores*.[84]

The contents of extant (and reported) manuscripts provide precious evidence not only of the availability of pseudo-Ovidiana but also of the degree to which they were grouped together, with or without other works of Ovid.[85] The number of manuscripts that contain at least one of the works

---

[80] Edited in Sedlmayer 1884: 149–50 and Pascal 1907: 107–10. Beginning 'Auctor apud grecos medicine primus apollo' (Walther 1959, nos. 1673 and 4670). See also Lenz 1958: 593–4. (After Winter 1986: 21.)

[81] The latter is known also as *De quattuor elementis* or *De quattuor complexionibus hominum* and is edited in Sedlmayer 1884: 149–50 and Pascal 1907: 107–9. Beginning 'Auctor apud grecos medicine primus apollo' (Walther 1959, no. 1673). Lenz 1958: 533–6 discusses the close relation between *De medicamine aurium* and *De quattuor humoribus* and identifies an additional verse at the end of the former and attested by two manuscripts as a transition added by a redactor to create a link between the poems.

[82] Walther 1959, no. 3087. Cf. Lenz 1959b; indeed, Lenz believes John knew this poem before penning his version in the *Policraticus* (6.24).

[83] 'Prima quidem inter studia ingenii, reor, experiendi causa libellos edidisse fertur de Medicamine Faciei, de Medicamine Aurium, de Cuculo, de Culice, de Nuce, de Philomena, de Scachis, de Vetula, de Puellis, de Vino. Haec iuvenis. Maturior autem factus . . . ', Ullman 1928: 66. Polenton seems to suggest these are genuine, although with his term *fertur* he hedges his bet. On Polenton on Virgil see Putnam and Ziolkowski 2008, esp. 321 and 369–70.

[84] E.g. N (Milan, Biblioteca Ambrosiana, MS H 64 sup., *s.* xiv), as summarised by Ghisalberti 1946: 57 claims that, after Ovid wrote the *Heroides*, *De sine titulo (Amores)* and *Medicamina faciei femineae*, he wrote *De nuce*, *De cuculo*, *De pulice* and *De puellis*.

[85] In reception studies, one also regularly looks to *florilegia*, but interestingly, Ovid was not excerpted in any of the known *florilegia* with the single exception of the *Florilegium Gallicum*, which includes excerpts from the *ES* (Richmond 2002: 453). Wilken Engelbrecht has kindly reminded me how important it is to attend to the portions of texts excerpted and the sequencing of authors and texts in each individual manuscript. As he notes, the excerpts from *ES* occur after excerpts from the other single and before excerpts from the double letters on fol. 65v of Paris, BN, lat. MS 7646, hence Heinsius' placement of *ES* as *Her.* 15, while Berlin, SB-PKb, Diez. B Sant. 60, where the excerpts from the *Heroides* lack any snippets from *ES*, follow a radically different ordering of Ovid's works (personal communication).

in the pseudo-Ovidian family is roughly 350. Here I highlight only a few books and patterns that can shed some light on the reception of the pseudo-Ovidiana within the period. It is of interest, for example, that until the very end of the twelfth century,[86] extant texts contain one pseudo-Ovidian poem each (most frequently, either *De cuculo* or *De philomela*). Dated to the turn of the twelfth to the thirteenth century are a very few manuscripts that include several pseudo-Ovidiana, for example, Tours, Bibliothèque municipale, 879, which groups *De somnio*, *De pulice* and *De pediculo* after all Ovid's works (excepting the *Remedia amoris*).[87]

In the thirteenth century, larger groupings of pseudo-Ovidiana become common. Among the most interesting are Bern, Burgerbibliothek, MS 505[88] and Oxford, Bodl., Holkham MS 322.[89] The trend seems only to accelerate. Extensive collections in fourteenth-century books include Berlin, SB-PKb, Diez. MSS B Sant. 1[90] and 4,[91] and Vatican City, BAV, Vat.

[86] For this preliminary review I have had to rely on a variety of sources for the dates of these manuscripts, many of which are ranges rather than dates and often, I fear, at second hand. The dates in particular should not be pressed over much. For simplicity's sake, in this quick review I have omitted texts that contain (as is not infrequently the case) sections of different dates. The most significant of these might well be F, Frankfurt Stadt- und Universitätsbibliothek, Barth. MS 110, well known as the single medieval manuscript witness to the *ES*; see Engelbrecht 1993. The manuscript also contains *Nux, De philomela, De cuculo, De medicamine aurium, De sompnio, Metamorphoses, De vino, Ars amatoria, Remedia amoris, Amores, Ibis, De somnio* (= *Amores* 3.5), *Epistula Sapphus, De quattuor humoribus, De nemore*, the standard medieval *Heroides, Fasti, Epistulae ex Ponto, Tristia* and *Nux*. See Richmond 2002: 453. Of the pseudo-Ovidiana, only *De vino* and the *Epistula Sapphus* (if the latter be pseudo) are in sections of the manuscript written 'towards the end of the twelfth century; the others [are] not earlier than the late thirteenth' (Richmond 2002: 453) Indeed, the *Pulex* may even be a fifteenth-century addition. *De vino = De Baccho* (Walther 1959, no. 18078), a collection of verses by the seventh-century author Eugenius of Toledo, was labelled as Ovidian and circulated in the Middle Ages; see Lenz 1959a: 176–7, Ghisalberti 1946: 37. *De nemore = De luco*. Begins 'Lucus amenus erat quem fons faciebat amenum'; cf. Lehmann 1927: 95, n. 42, Walther 1959, no. 10440, Winter 1986: 15.
[87] Of this manuscript, Richmond 2002: 453 writes that it 'collected all the genuine works with the exception of the *Medicamina*, and added the spurious *de Pulice* and *de Pediculo*'. Another such manuscript would be Naples, Bibl. Naz. IV F 13.
[88] Containing: *Ars amatoria, De pulice, De pediculo, De anulo, De medicamine aurium, De conflictu veris et hiemis, De somnio, Ars amatoria* (the last two items fragmentary).
[89] Containing: *Fasti, Liber puellarum, Epistulae ex Ponto, Ars amatoria, Remedia amoris, Tristia, De Lombardo et lumaca, De quattuor elementis, Amores, Ibis* and a fragment of the *pseudo-Remedia amoris*.
[90] Containing the *Metamorphoses* (with notes), *Fasti, Heroides, Amores, Ars amatoria, Remedia amoris, Tristia, Epistulae ex Ponto, Ibis, De philomela, De pulice, De somno* (= *Amores* 3.5), *De nuce, De medicamine aurium, De quattuor elementis sive de quattuor humoribus hominum, De medicamine faciei, De cuculo, De luco*. See Winter 1986: 13–16.
[91] Dated 1343–4, this remarkable assemblage includes many school standards: *Asinarius, Geta, Pamphilus, Disticha Catonis, Theoduli Ecloga*, Gualterus Anglicus' *Romuleae Fabulae*, Alexander Neckam's *Fabulae dictae novus Aesopus*, Avianus' *Fabulae*, Bernard of Morlaix' *De contemptu mundi, Facetus*, Matthew of Vendôme's *Tobias*, '*Quinque claves sapientiae*', pseudo-*Remedia amoris, Heroides, Tristia, Ars amatoria, Epistulae ex Ponto, Nux, De somno* (= *Amores* 3.5), *De cuculo, De pulice, De anulo*

lat. MS 1602.[92] Of the many fifteenth-century texts, important compilations are represented by Leiden, Bibliotheek der Rijksuniversiteit, Voss. lat. MS o 96;[93] Florence, BML, Plut. MS 36 2;[94] Modena, Biblioteca Estense, Est. lat. MS 157 (alpha o 6 26);[95] and Munich, Bayerische Staatsbibliothek, clm MS 18910.[96]

* * * * * * *

I have reserved for last a work that must take a special place in any survey of pseudo-Ovidiana, for Ovid is not only its putative author but its autobiographical subject: the mid-thirteenth-century *De vetula*,[97] by far the longest work among the pseudo-Ovidiana. The *De vetula* combines virtually all of the strands of Ovid's life and work as fantasised by medieval readers and reflected in the standard biographies but even more in the medieval Ovid they conjured for themselves by producing new Ovidian poetry, amalgamating existing texts to their collections, imitating his style and manner, and transforming him by translating his works into contemporary vernaculars, both prose and verse.[98]

(= *Amores* 2.15), *De medicamine aurium, De quattuor elementis, De philomela, De lupo, De mirabilibus mundi, Ibis, De medicamine faciei,* Maximianus' *Elegiae* (entitled '*Ovidius De senectute*' by the original hand, corrected later), *De vetula, Ilias latina,* 'Notae ad Homerum latinum' (Winter 1986: 18–22). *De lupo,* beginning 'Sepe lupus per pascua lata vagantes' (Walther 1959, no. 17029), has been published in Voigt 1878: 58–62 (Winter 1986: 21). *De lupo* also occurs in the earlier Berlin, Staatsbibliothek, Phillipps MS 1694 (dated 1190–1210).

[92] Dated 1370–1400, it contains: *Amores* (with gaps), *De somnio, De pulice, De medicamine faciei, De quattuor humoribus, De philomela, De psytaco* (= *Amores* 2.6), *Nux, Conflictus veris et hiemis, Conflictus Voluptatis et Diogenis* (= *de luco*), *Amores* 1.13, *Amores* 1.5, *Amores* 2.15, *Amores* 1.10, *De pulchris puellis clero traditis* (= *De distributione mulierum*), *De nuntio sagaci, Contra mulieres, Ibis.* The *De distributione mulierum* has recently received an edition and commentary in Hinz 2006.

[93] Containing: *De pulice* (frag.), *pseudo-Remedia amoris* (frag.; titled *De feminis*), *Nux* (frag.), *De medicamine aurium, De philomela, De Lombardo et lumaca, De ludo scacchorum, Pamphilus* and other items including some from the *Appendix Vergiliana.*

[94] Containing: *Ars amatoria, Remedia amoris, Heroides, Amores* (titled *De sine titulo liber*), *Tristia, Epistulae ex Ponto, Ibis, Nux, Consolatio ad Liviam, De medicamine faciei, De philomela, Ovidii vita.*

[95] Containing: *Ars amatoria, Remedia amoris, De medicamine aurium, De quattuor elementis, De Lombardo et lumaca, Liber puellarum, Ibis, Tristia, Amores.*

[96] *Doctrina mense, De cuculo, Carmen de arte amandi, pseudo-Ars amatoria, pseudo-Remedia amoris, Epistula Sapphus ad Phaonem, Geta.*

[97] Walther 1959, nos. 19615 and 9611 (only Book 3), edited by Klopsch, Pseudo-Ovidius 1967. The following year saw the publication of another edition by Robathan 1968. The poem contains *c.* 2,400 hexameters. Berlin, Diez. B Sant. 4 just described (n. 91, above) is among the not very large number of manuscripts that have both collections of other pseudo-Ovidiana and *De vetula*; by and large, it exhibits its own, sizeable manuscript transmission. See Pseudo-Ovidius 1967: 160–83.

[98] *De vetula* was in turn among the relatively few pseudo-Ovidian works translated into vernaculars: on Jean Le Fèvre's mid fourteenth-century translation (with additions), see Hexter 2007b: 1316; on Bernat Metge's late fourteenth-century partial Catalan prose rendering entitled *Ovidi enamorat*, see Hexter 2007b: 1318.

The frame is provided first by a prose 'Introitus' and verse 'Prefatio'. The latter, covering the first part of the story, describes how Ovid, once he was certain that he would not be recalled from exile, composed this book in which he described what his mode of living was so long as he devoted his life to love, why he changed his lifestyle, how he lived thereafter and what he devoted himself to in the post-love period of his life. He gave this book the title *De vetula* – 'on the old woman' – on account of the reason for his change of lifestyle.[99] And he saw to it that the book was buried with him in his tomb so that, if it should perchance happen that his bones were transferred, the book would be transferred along with them, renewing his fame. But because no one took care of moving his remains, it was neither read as one of the author's official works nor held in common use.[100]

The verse preface already smacks of the schoolroom introduction, and in fact, in virtually all manuscripts the poem is accompanied by at least one of two standard *accessus* to Ovid's works, likely very early and possibly fabrications of the author of *De vetula* himself, indicating that *De vetula* was meant to join the established Ovidian reading and teaching canon, or at the very least ape its protocols. The opening 'Introitus' continues the frame story. Its latter portion describes how:

the king of the Colchians found the book in a certain tomb from the public cemetery located in the vicinity of the city Dioscorus, the capital of his realm; he sent it to Constantinople, where there were many Latins, since the Armenians neither understood the Latin language nor had translators of Latin.[101]

It is the very first sentence that actually completes the narrative, identifying that it was a certain Leo, protonotarius of the palace of Byzantium, who transmitted the text.

While Ovid's relegation to the Black Sea provides a frame for the composition and explains the non-canonical transmission of *De vetula*, 'the body of the poem offers us "Ovid"'s erotic autobiography, which moves (on its own terms) from an *ars amatoria* to a *remedium amoris*'.[102] The first

---

[99] An alternative title is *De mutatione vitae* (as Roger Bacon termed it); Pseudo-Ovidius 1967: 79.

[100] Pseudo-Ovidius 1967: 193–4. The Latin vocabulary of the final verse deserves quotation: 'nec fuit autemptim lectus nec habetur in usu'.

[101] Pseudo-Ovidius 1967: 193. For an excellent review of the topos, see 'Das Buch im Grabe', 22–34 of *op. cit.* At a certain point, this fantastic tale begins to seem a parody of the tropes by which forgeries are meant to take on authenticity, like the unearthing of the Kensington Runestone in 1898. As Grafton 1990: 8 puts it, '[c]laims of faithfulness in copying suggest, and tales of texts discovered in miraculous circumstances directly reveal, the presence of the forger'.

[102] Hexter 2002b: 440. My summary of *De vetula* expands upon and often echoes my account of the work in that earlier study (439–42); I discussed the work yet more briefly and from a particular perspective in Hexter 1999a: 340–2; brief overview also at Knox 2009b: 214–15. In those earlier

book begins with 'Ovid' 's confession that at the start of his erotic career, he was obsessed with women. But the young 'Ovid', like any thirteenth-century swell, was devoted to the full range of evidently popular leisure-time activities, including hunting, fishing, swimming and games of all sorts.[103] Certainly, *De vetula* owed some of its popularity to its inclusion of fields and disciplines of interest to its thirteenth-century readers. Along the way, the 'Ovid' of *De vetula* describes an astonishing range of indoor pastimes, including dice, chess and other contemporary board games.[104]

The second book resumes the narrative of 'Ovid''s erotic autobiography. After a lengthy diatribe against eunuchs (*semiviri*), 'Ovid' goes on to give the actual history of the central love affair of his life. Even if, as noted, this has nothing to do with the *Amores* and Corinna,

we meet figures with analogues in the world of Roman love elegy: a beautiful girl and her older female companion, the *lena* in love elegy, here the old lady (*vetula*) who gives the poem its name. The old lady pretends to be a go-between, but the two women conspire in tricking 'Ovid' out of his longed-for intercourse with the young beauty by substituting the 'hag' herself – the 'bed-trick' of fabliaux.[105] 'Ovid' meets her some twenty years later, after the beautiful young girl has married and born children. Now widowed and of course older, she consents to intercourse, which our 'hero' enjoys moderately, but clearly, the joys of the flesh are not the same at a more mature age.

In the third book, 'Ovid' moves to put these earthly joys and vanities behind him. As 'Ovid' turns successively to scholarly disciplines – philosophy, mathematics, geometry, music, and astronomy – Ovid the poet of learning moves from worldly expertise to more sublime topics... His characteristic cosmological speculations lead him to reflect on the first causes of the world. Ultimately, 'Ovid' arrives at a prophesy of Christ's birth based on astrological lore. Indeed, learned in the tradition of prophesy in the Hebrew Bible, his prophesy includes a virgin birth, even if it – as well as the other Christian mysteries, such as the incarnation and the

discussions of the erotic aspects, I had unfortunately overlooked Godman 1995. On its own terms, the poem is 'fictional' even when reconstructing, as it does, Ovid's love life. As has long been noted, there is no Corinna, no wife, indeed, no emperor of any name within the three books of the poem. Of course, Corinna was already recognised as a fiction, of one sort or another, which opens the door on the possibility of our here reading 'the true story'.

[103] On swimming, n.b. 'hic artem nandi praecipit', Ovid, *Tr.* 2.486.
[104] These accounts involve the author in complex mathematical descriptions that may be responsible for frightening away those who might otherwise contemplate translating the poem. The first book includes much more, such as 'Ovid''s lament on the decline of philosophical learning and his lampooning of lawyers.
[105] To cite my earlier summary: 'Not unwittily, "Ovid" describes this substitution in language drawing on "his own" *Metamorphoses*: "... In nova formas / corpora mutatas cecini, mirabiliorque non reperitur ibi mutatio quam fuit ista, / scilicet, ut fuerit tam parvo tempore talis / taliter in talem vetulam mutata puella" (2.495–9). Bedtricks are not unknown to Ovid; the story of Myrrha in *Metamorphoses* 10 turns on one, but that is a very different motif', Hexter 2002b: 441.

trinity – explicitly escapes his capacity to understand. He ends his book with hopes for salvation and a prayer to the virgin mother of God (*optima virgo*, 3.805).[106]

Our 'Ovid', though not precisely converted,[107] testifies to the Christian story. Clearer still is the moral point of *De vetula*: 'Ovid' has abandoned his licentious ways and reformed. His own disillusionment with the active sexuality he trumpeted at the outset and his turn to the realm of higher speculation supports a revision of Ovid, coinciding roughly with the rise of moralising and allegorising interpretations of the *Metamorphoses* and other of Ovid's works.

To be sure, 'Ovid''s own hints at the coming of Christianity from out of his pagan unknowing are presented in what must seem to us as very unChristian terms, drawing on astrology and, in particular, on Arabic teaching, especially Albumasar's,[108] but it is not so clear that everyone in the thirteenth century would have regarded them as necessarily incompatible. In fact, precisely the degree to which 'Ovid''s argumentation in Book 3 is 'pagan' adds credibility to the Christian prophecy.[109]

Klopsch, whose edition of and introduction to *De vetula* remains the most significant work on the poem to date, also rightly describes the author of *De vetula*[110] as heir to the tradition of the twelfth-century allegorical epics

---

[106] Hexter 2002b: 441–2.

[107] He does not comprehend the references which we understand as referring to Jesus, a youth in the Holy Land in the years Ovid found himself on the Black Sea. Although there was a standard biography for Ovid, many variants and tales circulated in the form of these study aids – para-Ovidiana themselves, and by contributing other dimensions to the picture of Ovid, constituting yet other pseudo-Ovids – and in some Ovid does become Christian. For example, from a manuscript now in Freiburg, Bischoff 1952 published a story where Tomis – as in some other accounts conceived of as an island – was near Patmos so that Ovid could hear St John preach, leading to his conversion.

[108] Abu Ma'shar al-Balkhi (d. 886), a Persian astronomer, astrologer and mathematician. See also Pseudo-Ovidius 1967: 69–72.

[109] 'The poet [of *De vetula*] has his Ovid predict solely on the basis of human science: the [existence of] one creating god, who one day, according to his own will, will mark an end to the world; all of creation and the immortality of the soul; the mechanism by means of which god directs, above the stars, the universe, humanity, and the course of history; and the imminent rise of a new religion and the birth of its divine founder from a virgin mother'; Pseudo-Ovidius 1967: 72–3.

[110] On the question of authorship, see Klopsch in Pseudo-Ovidius 1967: 78–99. The poem must have been completed and published between 1222 and 1268, the former the date of the accession of the emperor Johannes Vatatzes (the Vatachius of the 'introitus', though he ruled at Nicaea rather than Byzantium, which at the time was in the hands of the Latin crusaders), the latter the date of Roger Bacon's *Opus maius*, which refers to *De vetula*. In 1424, a Dutch Dominican, Arnold Gheylhoven, ascribed the work to Richard de Fournival (10 October 1201 – c. 1260) and although there is no clear provenance for this identification, he remains the leading candidate for authorship. While in the end, Klopsch thinks the attribution to Richard 'unlikely' (*unwahrscheinlich*), he admits that it is not possible to exclude it unconditionally (99). See also Lepage 1981. As far as Gheylhoven's ascription goes, Mozley 1938: 53 wrote 'bien qu'elle ne soit à vrai dire appuyée d'aucune preuve externe, n'a rien d'invraisemblable en soi et peut être provisoirement acceptée'. The real author seems to have

by Bernardus Silvestris, Alain of Lille and John of Hauteville; in this genre, Christianity is never mentioned, and the point is to arrive by philosophical speculation – in the case of the twelfth-century Chartrians, Platonising philosophical speculation – at a 'natural' and 'philosophical' position that supports Christian doctrine.[111]

It may seem hard to believe that any medieval reader seriously thought that this poem was written by the Roman Ovid, so much does its fictional nature announce itself – to us, at least – at every turn, but it seems as if this was not universally obvious in the late Middle Ages.[112] Walter Burley and Richard de Bury, both of the fourteenth century, seem to have accepted it as an authentic work of Ovid.[113] Most others were more skeptical, from the thirteenth-century Roger Bacon to Robert Holcot in the fourteenth century.[114] Not a few of the Ovidian lives and even manuscripts of the *De vetula* doubt or even deny outright that the work is Ovid's.[115] Petrarch's rejection of the identification is categorical.[116]

* * * * * * *

The current study cannot follow the course of the pseudo-Ovidiana through the fifteenth and sixteenth centuries, when historical philology (as we have understood it these five hundred years) would shear Ovid of his 'false' plumage and reproduce the 'historical' Ovid, a classical writer reimagined as a modern author.[117] Something is gained, something lost

succeeded in concealing his identity, but if the surgeon and author Richard de Fournival did not write *De vetula*, someone uncannily like him did. Wilken Engelbrecht has recently noted that up to Richard de Fournival, no single *accessus* makes 'authorial' Ovidiana out of pseudo-Ovidiana; Engelbrecht 2006, esp. 212 n. 9.

[111] Indeed, this tradition goes back to Boethius' *Consolation of Philosophy* and likely further (e.g. Minucius Felix's *Octavius*).

[112] Then again Boccaccio and Giovanni del Virgilio also believed, or at least transmitted, the story that Ovid did not die in exile but returned to Rome only to be suffocated by the crowds greeting him (Ghisalberti 1946: 35). Of course belief in authenticity is not required for a work to be influential. The turn of a pagan to Christianity would interest Dante of *La divina commedia*, and echoes of *De vetula* have been identified in *Purgatorio* (Picone 2003: 390, with reference to his earlier studies).

[113] Pseudo-Ovidius 1967: 82.

[114] Pseudo-Ovidius 1967: 78–83.   [115] Pseudo-Ovidius 1967: 83–4.

[116] In a letter with the superscript 'Quid sit peius an sua scriptoribus eripere an aliena iungere' (*Ep. seniles*, 2.4), Petrarch writes: 'Librum cuius nomen est de Vetula dant Nasoni, mirum cui vel cur cuiquam id in mentem venerit, nisi hoc fortasse lenocinio clari nominis obscuro fama operi quaeritur, et quod vulgo fit ut gallinis pavonum ova subiiciant, id ab istis in contrarium vertitur sperantibus ut generosus superincubitor vilia ova nobilitet . . .', cited from Monteverdi 1958: 192; more briefly at Pseudo-Ovidius 1967: 83, where Klopsch also cites Giovani Dominici as one who dismissed Ovid's authorship of *De vetula* in contrast to the later Sicco Polenton (see above, n. 83), who likely accepted it.

[117] Not that the history of pseudo-Ovidiana ends with the sixteenth century. After the establishment of an historical Ovid, a fully fictional one was free to develop, including fictional Ovidian poems, for example, 'L'amour en courroux' by the 'Ovide' in Mme De Villedieu's six-part novel of 1672–3,

in every transformation. The gain in historical authenticity goes hand-in-hand with a loss of seemingly infinite plasticity, an 'Ovid' that could be bent this way and that. I hope that the above survey and attempted 'anatomy' of pseudo-Ovidiana will have suggested something else more clearly. It was not only Ovid who, in the Middle Ages, could change shape with such marvellous variety. 'Forms changed . . . into new bodies':[118] forms were changed and new bodies produced by and for readers, who were themselves thereby subtly changing. Medieval poets, readers writing, in a strange but recognisably Ovidian form of metamorphosis, stretched themselves to assume forms that were part their own, part Ovid's, altering both and blurring the lines between them.

Clearly, some lines are clear. Others are less so, including the one between stylistic exercise and emulative creation, on the one hand, and prosthesis on the other. Para-Ovidiana might well be not just a more capacious category but the name of an entire field, stretching to include commentary and translations as well as stylistic tributes, and imitations in all languages. The pseudo-Ovidiana gain illumination from the broader field, to be sure; indeed, they cannot be fully understood without a sense of that larger terrain. Yet attempting to map the subfield represented by the pseudo-Ovidiana, however disputed the boundaries and the term, is indispensable to filling out our picture of Ovid in the Middle Ages.

Les Exilés de la Cour d'Auguste (Chatelain 2008: 301). Chatelain's in-depth study of a rough half century is, in my view, a paragon among works on classical reception for the richness of cultural contextualisation.

[118] 'In nova fert animus mutatas dicere formas / corpora', *Met.* 1.1–2.

Annotated list of selected Ovid manuscripts

ORIGINALIA

AMORES

Paris, BN, lat. MS 8242 [France, *s.* ix]
Eton College, MS 91 [France?, *s.* xiii]
Oxford, Bodl., Auct. MS F I 17 [England, *s.* xiv*in.*]

ARS AMATORIA

Oxford, Bodl., Auct. MS F 4 32 [England, *s.* x]
Eton College, MS 91 [France?, *s.* xiii]
Oxford, Bodl., Auct. MS F I 17 [England, *s.* xiv*in.*]

EX PONTO

Munich, Bayerische Staatsbibliothek, clm MS 19476 [Germany, *s.* xii]
London, BL, Burney MS 220 [England, *s.* xii*ex.*]
Oxford, Bodl., Rawlinson MS G 109 [England, *c.* 1200]
Eton College, MS 91 [France?, *s.* xiii]
Oxford, Bodl., Auct. MS F I 17 [England, *s.* xiv*in.*]

IBIS

Cambridge, Trinity College, MS O 7 7 (1335) [England, *s.* xiii*in.*]
Oxford, Bodl., Auct. MS F I 17 [England, *s.* xiv*in.*]

FASTI

Vatican City, BAV, Vat. lat. MS 3262 [Italy, *s.* xi]
Cambridge, Pembroke College, MS 280 [England, *s.* xii]
Edinburgh, National Library of Scotland, Advocates Library, MS 18 5 13
    [England, *s.* xii]

London, BL, Cotton MS Titus D XXIV [England, *s.* xii/xiii]
Eton College, MS 91 [France?, *s.* xiii]

HEROIDES

Eton College, MS 150 [Italy, *s.* xi]
Oxford, Bodl., Rawlinson MS G 99 [England, *s.* xii$^{ex.}$]
Eton College, MS 91 [France?, *s.* xiii]
Oxford, Bodl., Auct. MS F I 17 [England, *s.* xiv$^{in.}$]
Oxford, Balliol College, MS 143 [England, *s.* xiv]
Cambridge, Trinity College, MS R 3 18 (598) [England, *s.* xiv ?]

METAMORPHOSES

Naples, Biblioteca Nazionale, MS IV F 3 [Italy, *s.* x]
Paris, BN, lat. MS 12246 (fragment) [France, *s.* ix]
Vatican City, BAV, Urb. lat. MS 342, fols. 77–8 (fragment) [France, *s.* x]
Oxford, Bodl., Auct. MS F 4 30 [England, *s.* xii]
Eton College, MS 91 [England, *s.* xiii]
Leiden, Bibliotheek der Rijksuniversiteit, Vossianus lat. MS Q 61, with some Anglicana glossing [*s.* xiii/xiv]
Oxford, Bodl., Auct. MS F I 17 [England, *s.* xiv$^{in.}$]

REMEDIA AMORIS

Oxford, Bodl., Rawlinson MS G 109 [England, *c.* 1200]
Cambridge, Trinity College, MS R 3 29 (609) [England, *s.* xiii$^{in.}$]

TRISTIA

Eton College, MS 91 [France?, *s.* xiii]
Oxford, Bodl., Auct. MS F I 17 [England, *s.* xiv$^{in.}$]

COMMENTARIES
ARNULF OF ORLÉANS (FL. 1180)

Commentary and allegories to *Metamorphoses*; Commentaries to the *Fasti, Tristia, Amores, Ars amataoria*.

Fasti

Vatican City, BAV, Reg. lat. MS 1548 [*s.* xiii]
Zurich, Zentralbibliothek, Rh. 76 [*s.* xiii]

Tristia

Antwerp, Musaeum Plantin-Moretus, M 85 (lat. 71) [*s.* xiii]

Epistulae ex Ponto (?)

Copenhagen, Kongelige Bibliothek, Gl. kgl. Saml. 2015, 4° [*s.* xii*ex.*]
Wolfenbüttel, Herzog August Bibliothek, 155 Gud. lat. [*s.* xii/xiii]

Amores

Freiburg im Breisgau, Universitätsbibliothek, 381 [*s.* xii*ex.*]

Ars amatoria

Wolfenbüttel, Herzog August Bibliothek, 155 Gud. lat. [*s.* xii/xiii]

Remedia

Wolfenbüttel, Herzog August Bibliothek, 155 Gud. lat. [*s.* xii/xiii]

Metamorphoses (Grammatical commentary and allegories)

Munich, Bayerische Staatsbibliothek, clm MS 7205, [Germany, *s.* xii*ex.*]
Venice, Biblioteca nazionale Marciana, Marc. lat. MS XIV 222 (4007)
[France ?, *s.* xii*ex.*]

WILLIAM OF ORLÉANS (FL. 1200)

Versus bursarii (Commentary on *Amores, Tristia, Ex Ponto, Remedia, Heroides, Ars amatoria* and *Metamorphoses*)

Berlin, SB-PKb, lat. qu. MS 219 [France, *s.* xiii*in.*]
Leiden, Bibliotheek der Rijksuniversiteit, Lips. MS 39 [England, 1255]

FULCO OF ORLÉANS (FL. 1200)

Commentaries to the amatory works of Ovid and his exilic poetry, including the *Amores, Ars amatoria, Remedia* and *Tristia*

Amores

Paris, BN, lat. MS 8207 [*s.* xiii]

Ars amatoria

Paris, BN, MS lat. 8207 [*s.* xiii]
Paris, BN, lat. MS 8302 [*s.* xiii]
Vatican City, BAV, Reg. lat. MS 1563 [*s.* xiii]

Remedia amoris

Paris, BN, lat. MS 8207 [s. xiii]
Milan, Biblioteca Ambrosiana, MS G 37 sup. [*s.* xiii]

Tristia

Paris, BN, lat. MS 8207 [*s.* xiii]

ANONYMOUS COMMENTARY TO THE *ARS AMATORIA* [FRANCE, S. XII]

Copenhagen, Kongelige Bibliotek, Fabricius MS 29 2° [France, *s.* xiii$^{in.}$]

ANONYMOUS COMMENTARY TO THE *HEROIDES* [S. XII]

Munich, Bayerische Staatsbibliothek, clm MS 19475 [*s.* xii]

JOHN OF GARLAND (FL. 1230), *INTEGUMENTA OVIDII*

Oxford, Bodl., Digby MS 104 [England, *s.* xiii$^{ex.}$]
Oxford, Bodl., Auct. MS F 5 16 [England, *s.* xiv]
Leiden, Bibliotheek der Rijksuniversiteit, Vossianus Lat. MS Q 61 [*s.* xiv/xv]
Oxford, Merton College, MS 299 [England, *s.* xv$^{in.}$] fol. 280r

VULGATE COMMENTARY ON THE *METAMORPHOSES* (FL. 1250)

Leiden, Bibliotheek der Rijksuniversiteit, BPL MS 95 [France, *s.* xiii$^{ex.}$]
Sélestat, Bibliothèque humaniste, MS 92 [France, *s.* xiii$^{ex.}$]
Vatican City, BAV, Vat. lat. MS 1598 [France, *s.* xiii$^{ex.}$]

WILLIAM OF THIEGIIS (FL. 1275)

Paris, Bibliothèque nationale de France, lat. MS 8010 [France, *s.* xiv]

GIOVANNI DEL VIRGILIO (FL. 1322/23)

Prose paraphrase (*Expositio*) and allegories (*Allegorie*) on the *Metamorphoses*

Expositio

Rome, Biblioteca Casanatense, MS 1369 (*s.* xiv)
Oxford, Bodl. Canon. misc. MS 457 (*s.* xiv)
Vatican City, BAV, Reg. lat. MS 1676 (*s.* xiv)
New York, Pierpont Morgan Library, MS M 938 (*s.* xv)
Siena, Biblioteca Comunale degli Intronati, MS H IX 51 (*s.* xv)

Allegorie

Milan, Biblioteca nazionale Braidense, MS AF XIV 21 (*s.* xiv)
Oxford, Bodl., Canon. misc. MS 457 (*s.* xiv)

PIERRE BERSUIRE (FL. 1350), *OVIDIUS MORALIZATUS*

Hereford, Cathedral Library, MS O I 9 [England, *s.* xiv*med.*]
Oxford, Merton College, MS 85 [England, *s.* xiv]
Cambridge, University Library, MS Ii 2 20 [England, *s.* xiv*ex.*]
Dublin, Trinity College, MS 115 [England, *s.* xiv*ex.*]
Durham, Cathedral Library, MS B IV 38 [England, *s.* xiv*ex.*]
London, British Library, Royal MS 15 C XVI [England, *s.* xiv*ex.*]
Cambridge, Peterhouse College, MS 237 [England, *s.* xiv/xv]
Cambridge, Sidney Sussex College, MS 56 (Δ. 3. 11) [England, *s.* xv]
Oxford, Merton College, MS 299 [England, *s.* xv*in.*] fol. 1r
Oxford, Bodl., Bodley MS 571 [England, *s.* xv*in.*]
Oxford, St John's College, MS 137 [England, *s.* xv]

THOMAS WALSINGHAM (C. 1340 – C. 1422), *ARCHANA DEORUM*

London, BL, Lansdowne MS 728 [England, *s.* xv]
Oxford, St John's College, MS 124 [England, *s.* xv*in.*]

SOZOMENO OF PISTOIA (EARLY FIFTEENTH CENTURY) COMMENTARY ON
THE *METAMORPHOSES* DRAWING LARGELY ON BOCCACCIO'S *GENEALOGIA*

Pistoia, Biblioteca Forteguerriana, MS A 46 [Italy, *s.* xv]

Cambridge, St John's College, MS D 22 (97) [England, s. xiv] *Metamorphoses*

Oxford, Bodl., Rawlinson MS B 214 [England, *s.* xv] *Metamorphoses*

Oxford, Merton College, MS 299 [England, *s.* xv*in.*] *Narratio fabularum* on the *Metamorphoses*, doubtful attribution to John Seward

*Oxford, Bodl., Bodley MS 571 [England, *s.* xv*in.*]

Oxford, Bodleian Library, Hatton MS 92 [England, *s.* xv]

Paris, Bibliothèque nationale de France, lat. MS 16238, Constructio Ovidii Magni of Jean Bolent, 1348 [France, *s.* xiv]

IMPORTANT MANUSCRIPTS CONTAINING ANTHOLOGIES OF ACCESSUS AND COMMENTARIES TO THE OVIDIAN CORPUS C. 1100 TO 1400.

Munich, Bayerische Staatsbibliothek, clm MS 4610 [Germany, *s.* xii] Contains the earliest known commentary on the *Metamorphoses*, including comments by Manegold of Lautenbach, *fl.* late eleventh century.

Munich, Bayerische Staatsbibliothek, clm MS 14482 [Germany, *s.* xii] Three commentaries on the *Metamorphoses* and one on the *Remedia*

Munich, Bayerische Staatsbibliothek, clm MS 14809 [Germany, *s.* xii] Commentaries on the *Ars amatoria*, *Remedia* and *Metamorphoses*

Munich, Bayerische Staatsbibliothek, clm MS 19474; MS 19475 [Germany, *s.* xii] *Accessus ad auctores* (including Ovid)

Bern, Burgerbibliothek, MS 411 [*s.* xiii*in.*]

Antwerp, Musaeum Plantin-Moretus, MS M 85 (lat. 71); [*s.* xiii] Commentaries to the *Amores*, *Ars amatoria*, *Remedia*, *Metamorphoses*, *Fasti*, *Tristia* and *Ex Ponto*.

Antwerp, Musaeum Plantin-Moretus, MS O B 5 1 (lat. 68) [*s.* xiii] Glosses to the *Amores*, *Ars amatoria*, *Fasti*, *Heroides*, *Remedia* and *Tristia.*

Copenhagen, Kongelige Bibliotek, Fabricius MS 29 2° [northern France or Germany, *s.* xiii*in.*] Commentaries and *accessus* to Ovid, Statius and Claudian.

Frankfurt am Main, Stadt- und Universitätsbibliothek, Barth. MS 110 [Germany, *s.* xiii*in.*] Glosses on nearly the entire Ovidian corpus (including *Heroides* 15 [*Epistula Sapphus*])

Freiburg im Breisgau, Universitätsbibliothek, MS 381 [*s.* xii*ex.*] Contains early commentaries on *Metamorphoses, Heroides* and *Epistulae ex Ponto*; Arnulf of Orléans on the *Amores* and *Remedia amoris*,

Oxford, Bodl., Canon. class. lat. MS 1 [Italian, *s.* xiii] Glosses to virtually
the entire Ovidian corpus

Paris, BN, lat. MS 7994 [*s.* xiv] Contains glosses to virtually the entire
Ovidian corpus

Vatican City, BAV, Vat. lat. MS 1479 [France, *s.* xiv] Commentaries on
the *Metamorphoses* and *Remedia*

London, BL, Cotton MS Titus D xx [England, *s.* xv$^{in.}$] Containing an
anonymous *Libellus deorum* drawing on Bersuire and Ridevall.

Oxford, Bodl., Rawlinson MS B 214 [England, *s.* xv] attributed to Walter
of Peterborough

Wolfenbüttel, Herzog August Bibliothek, Cod. Guelf. MS 5 4. Aug. 4°
[*s.* xiv]

Three *accessus* and a commentary to the *Metamorphoses*

Pseudoepigrapha

Oxford, Bodl., Auct. MS F 2 14 [England, *s.* xii], ps.-Ovid, *Nux*

Cambridge, Jesus College, MS 70 [England, *s.* xv] ps.-Ovid, *De vetula*

Cambridge, Sidney Sussex College, MS 56 (Δ. 3. 11) [England, *s.* xv],
ps.-Ovid, *De vetula*

ILLUSTRATED MANUSCRIPTS OF OVID, METAMORPHOSES AND COMMENTARIES

METAMORPHOSES

Naples, Biblioteca Nazionale Vittorio Emanuele III, MS F IV 3 [Italy, *s.*
xi/xii]

Vatican City, BAV, Vat. MS lat. MS 1596 [Italy or Spain, *s.* xii]

Florence, BML, Plut. MS 36 8 [Italy, *s.* xiii/xiv]

Cesena, Biblioteca Malatestiana, MS MXXV 6 [Italy, *s.* xiv]

Venice, Biblioteca Nazionale Marciana, MS Zan. lat. 449a (1634) [Italy,
s. xiv]

Vienna, Österreichische Nationalbibliothek, MS 127 [*s.* xiv]

Oxford, Bodl., Rawlinson MS B 214 [England, *s.* xv]

Trent, Castello del Buonconsiglio, MS 1364 [Italy, *s.* xv]

Vatican City, BAV, Vat. lat. MS 2780 [Italy, *s.* xv]

METAMORPHOSES IN ITALIAN PROSE TRANSLATION BY SIMINTENDI

Florence, Biblioteca Nazionale Centrale, Panciatichi MS 63 [Italy, *s.* xiv]

OVIDE MORALISÉ IN OLD FRENCH VERSE

Geneva, Bibliothèque publique et universitaire, MS 176 [France, *s.* xiv]
Lyons, Bibliothèque municipale, MS 742 [France, *s.* xiv]
Paris, Bibliothèque de l'Arsenal, MS 5069 [France, *s.* xiv]
Rouen, Bibliothèque municipale, MS o 4 [France, *s.* xiv]
Vatican, BAV, Reg. lat. MS 1480 [France, *s.* xiv]

PIERRE BERSUIRE, OVIDIUS MORALIZATUS

Bergamo, Biblioteca civica Angelo Mai, Cassaf. MS 3 4 [Italy, *s.* xiv]
Treviso, Biblioteca comunale, MS 344 [Italy, *s.* xiv]
Vatican City, BAV, Vat. Reg. lat. MS 1480 [Italy, *s.* xiv]
Ghent, Bisshoppelijke Bibliotheck, MS 12 [Netherlands, *s.* xv]
London, BL, Cotton MS Julius F VII [England, *s.* xv]

Bibliography

PRIMARY SOURCES

Accessus ad auctores, Bernard d'Utrecht, Conrad Hirsau: Dialogus Super Auctores (1970), ed. R. B. C. Huygens. Leiden.

Alain of Lille. (1955) *Anticlaudianus: texte critique avec une introduction et des tables*, ed. R. Bossuet. Paris.

(1980) *De planctu naturae*, ed. J. J. Sheridan. Toronto.

Alfonso el Sabio. (1930) *General Estoria, primera parte*, ed. A. G. Solalinde. Madrid.

(1957–61) *Alfonso el Sabio: General Estoria* (2 vols.), ed. A. G. Solalinde, Ll. A. Kasten and V. R. B. Oelschläger. Madrid.

Alighieri, Dante. (1964a) *Convivio*, ed. G. Busnelli and G. Vandelli, introduction by M. Barbi, 2nd edn., with appendix by A. Quaglio (2 vols.). Florence.

(1964b) *La Divina Commedia*, tr. J. A. Carlyle, rev. H. Oelsner. London.

(1965) *Monarchia*, ed. P. G. Ricci. Vol. v in *Le opere di Dante Alighieri*, edizione nazionale a cura della Società dantesca italiana. Verona.

(1966a) *Dantis Alagherii Epistolae: The Letters of Dante*, ed. and tr. P. J. Toynbee. Oxford.

(1966–7) *La Commedia secondo l'antica vulgata*, ed. G. Petrocchi. Vol. vii in *Le opere di Dante Alighieri*, edizione nazionale a cura della Società dantesca italiana. Milan.

(1967) *Dante's Lyric Poetry*, ed. and tr. K. Foster and P. Boyde (2 vols.). Oxford.

(1979) *Epistole*, ed. A. Frugoni and G. Brugnoli. In Dante Alighieri, *Opere minori*, vol. ii, ed. P. V. Mengaldo *et al.* Milan and Naples.

(1980) *Vita Nuova*, ed. D. di Robertis. Milan and Naples.

(1990) Dante Alighieri. *Convivio*, tr. R. Lansing. Garland Library of Medieval Literature, 65. New York.

(1992) Dante Alighieri. *Vita Nuova*, tr. M. Musa. Oxford and New York.

(1996b) *De vulgari eloquentia*, ed. and tr. S. Botterill. Cambridge.

Anon. (1979) *Curial e Güelfa*, ed. M. Gustà. Barcelona.

Anthologia Latina. (1982–) Ed. D. R. Shackleton Bailey. Stuttgart.

Aquinas, St Thomas. (1964). *Summa theologiae*. Latin text and English tr. Blackfriars edition. New York.

Architrenius. (1974) Ed. P. G. Schmidt. Munich.

Arnulf of Orléans. (1932) F. Ghisalberti, 'Arnolfo d'Orléans: un cultore di Ovidio nel secolo XII', *Memorie del Reale Istituto Lombardo di Scienze e lettere* 24: 157–234.

(1958) *Arnulfi Aurelianensis Glosule super Lucanum*, ed. B. M. Marti. Rome.

(2005) *Arnulfi Aurelianensis Glosule Ovidii Fastorum*. Florence.

Baena, Juan Alfonso de. (1993) *Cancionero de Baena*, ed. B. Dutton and J. González Cuenca. Madrid.

Baudri of Bourgueil (1979) *Baldricus Burgulianus Carmina*, ed. K. Hilbert, Editiones Heidelbergenses 19. Heidelberg.

(1998–2002) *Baudri de Bourgueil: Poèmes* (2 vols.), ed. J.-Y. Tilliette. Paris.

Bene da Firenze. (1983) *Candelabrum*, ed. G. C. Alessio. Padua.

Bernardus Silvestris. (1978) *Cosmographia*, ed. P. Dronke. Textus minores, 53. Leiden.

(1986) *The Commentary on Martianus Capella's De nuptiis Philologiae et Mercurii attributed to Bernardus Silvestris*, ed H. J. Westra. Toronto.

Bersuire, Pierre. (1960–6) *Reductorium morale, liber xv naar de Parijse druk van 1509: Werkmateriaal* (3 vols.). Utrecht.

Biblia sacra iuxta vulgatam versionem. (1969) Ed. R. Weber, *et al.*, 2nd rev. edn. Stuttgart.

Boccaccio, Giovanni. (1939) *Le rime. L'amorosa visione. La caccia di Diana*, ed. V. Branca. Bari.

(1951) *Genealogie deorum gentilium libri*, ed. V. Romano. Bari.

(2001) *Famous Women*, ed. and tr. V. Brown. Cambridge, MA.

Bondéelle-Souchier, A. (2000–6) *Bibliothèques de l'Ordre de Prémontré dans la France d'Ancien Régime* (2 vols.), Histoire des Bibliothèques Médiévales, Documents, Études et Repertoire 58. Paris.

Brunetto Latini (1981) *Brunetto Latini: il Tesoretto (The Little Treasure)*, ed. J. B. Holloway. New York and London.

Chaucer, Geoffrey. (1984) *The Manciple's Tale*, ed. D. C. Baker. Variorum Edition. Norman.

(1987) *The Riverside Chaucer*, ed. L. D. Benson. 3rd edn. Boston.

Chrétien de Troyes. (1965) *Christian von Troyes Sämtliche Werke*, ed. W. Foerster and A. Hilka. Halle 1885–99, repr. Amsterdam.

Philomena. (1909) Ed. C. de Boer. *Philomena conte raconté d'après Ovide par Chrétien de Troyes*. Paris and Geneva.

Conversini da Ravenna, Giovanni. (1989) *Dialogue between Giofanni and a Letter*, ed. and tr. H. L. Eaker, with intr. and notes by H. L. Eaker and B. G. Kohl. Binghamton, NY.

Corpus Inscriptionum Latinarum, consilio et auctoritate Academiae litterarum regiae Borussicae editum. (1863) Berlin.

Enrique de Villena. (1958) *Los doze trabajos de Hércules*, ed. M. Morreale. Madrid.

(1976) *Tratado de la consolación*, ed. D. C. Carr. Madrid.

Folchino de Borfoni. (2003) *Folchini de Borfonibus, Cremonina: (grammatica, orthographica et prosodia)*, ed. C. DeSantis. Turnhout.

Galteri de Castellione. (1978) *Alexandreis*, ed. M. Colker, Thesaurus mundi 17. Patavii.

Gascoigne, Thomas. (1881) *Loci e libro veritatum*, ed. J. E. T. Rogers. Oxford.

Giovanni del Virgilio. (1933) ed. F. Ghisalberti, 'Giovanni del Virgilio espositore dell "Metamorfosi"', *Giornale dantesco* 34: 3–110.

Giraldus Cambrensis. (1974) *Speculum duorum, or A Mirror of Two Men*, ed. Y. Lefevre and R. B. C. Huygens. Cardiff.

Gower, John. (1899–1902) *The Complete Works of John Gower*, ed. G. C. Macaulay (4 vols.). Oxford.

  (1962) *The Major Latin Works of John Gower*, trans. E. W. Stockton. Seattle.

Guibert de Nogent (1984) *Self and Society in Medieval France: The Memoirs of Abbot Guibert de Nogent*, ed. J. F. Benton. Toronto.

Guilelmus Peraldus. (1499) *Sermones*. Tübingen.

Henry of Settimello (1949) *Elegia*. Ed. G. Cremaaschi. Bergamo.

Inscriptiones Latinae Selectae. (1892–1916) ed. H. Dessau. Berlin.

Jean de Montreuil. (1963–86) *Opera*, ed. E. Ornato, G. Ouy and N. Grévy-Pons (4 vols.). Turin.

Jocelin of Brakelond. (1949) *The Chronicle of Jocelin of Brakelond*, ed. H. E. Butler. Oxford Medieval Texts. Oxford.

John of Garland. (1929) The *Integumenta* on the *Metamorphoses* of Ovid by John of Garland: First edited with introduction and translation by L. K. Born. PhD diss., University of Chicago.

  (1933) *Giovanni di Garlanda, Integumenta Ovidii: poemetto inedito del secolo XIII*, ed. F. Ghisalberti. Messina-Milan.

John of Glastonbury. (1985) *Cronica sive antiquitates Glastoniensis ecclesie. The Chronicle of Glastonbury Abbey: an Edition, Translation and Study of John of Glastonbury's Cronica sive antiquitates Glastoniensis ecclesie*, ed. J. P. Carley. Woodbridge.

John of Salisbury. (1991) *Ioannis Saresberiensis Metalogicon*, ed. J. B. Hall and K. S. B. Keats-Rohan, Corpus christianorum, Continuatio mediaevalis 98. Turnhout.

Juan de Mena. (1989) *Obras completas (de) Juan de Mena*, ed. M. A. Pérez Priego. Barcelona.

Juan del Encina. (1996) *Obra completa (de) Juan del Encina*, ed. M. A. Pérez Priego. Madrid.

Knighton, Henry (1995) *Knighton's Chronicle*, ed. G. H. Martin, Oxford Medieval Texts. Oxford.

Leomarte. (1932) *Sumas de historia troyana*, ed. A. Rey. Madrid.

March, Ausias. (1979) *Obra poética completa* (2 vols.), ed. R. Ferreres. Madrid.

Metge, Bernat. (1983) *Lo somni*, in *Obra completa de Bernat Metge*, ed. L. Badia and X. Lamuela. Barcelona.

Metham, John. (1999) *Amoryus and Cleopes*, ed. S. F. Page. Kalamazoo.

Nigel Wireker [alt. Longchamps]. (1960) *Speculum stultorum, Nigel de Longchamps*, ed. J. H. Mozley and R. R. Raymo. Berkeley.

Ovid. (1950) *Heroidas*, tr. with intr. and notes by A. Alatorre. Mexico City.

(1951) *P. Ovidi Nasonis Amores*, ed. F. Munari. Florence.

(1961) *Amores*, ed. E. J. Kenney. *Amores; Medicamina faciei femineae; Ars amatoria; Remedia amoris.* Oxford.

(1964–1983) Ovidio. *Metamorfosis*, ed. with intr., tr. and notes, A. Ruiz de Elvira. (3 vols.). Madrid.

(1965) *Ovidiana Graeca: Fragments of a Byzantine Version of Ovid's Amatory Works*, ed. P. E. Easterling and E. J. Kenney. Cambridge Philological Society, supp. 1. Cambridge.

(1971) *Epistulae Heroidum*, ed. H. Dörrie. Berlin.

(1977a) *Heroides and Amores*, ed. G. P. Goold. Cambridge, MA.

(1977b) *P. Ovidii Nasonis Metamorphoses*, ed. W. Anderson. Leipzig.

(1977c) *Ovid, Ars Amatoria, Book 1*, ed. A. Hollis. Oxford.

(1984) *Metamorphoses*, tr. F. J. Miller and G. P Goold, 3rd edn. (2 vols.). Cambridge, MA.

(1985) *The Art of Love and Other Poems*, ed. G. P. Goold, 2nd edn. Cambridge, MA.

(1986) *Ovidio. Heroidas*, ed. with intr., tr. and notes, F. Moya del Baño. Madrid.

(1987) *L'art d'amours = The art of love*, tr. L. B. Blonquist. New York.

(1988) *Tristia, Ex Ponto*, ed. G. P. Goold, tr. A. L. Wheeler, 2nd rev. edn. Cambridge, MA.

(1989) *Amores. Arte de amar. Remedios contra el amor. Sobre la cosmética del rostro femenino*, tr. with intr., and notes, V. Cristóbal. Madrid.

(1990a) *The Poems of Exile*, tr. Peter Green. Harmondsworth.

(1990b) *Ovid: The Love Poems*, tr. A. D. Melville. Oxford.

(1991) Ovidio. *Obra amatoria 1: Amores*, with intr. and notes, A. Ramírez de Verger (ed.) and F. Socas Gavilán (tr.). Madrid.

(1992) *Sorrows of an Exile: 'Tristia'*, tr. A. D. Melville. Oxford.

(1994) *Heroidas*, tr. with intr. and notes V. Cristóbal. Madrid.

(1995a) *Metamorfosis*, tr. with intr. and notes M. C. Álvarez Morán and R. M. Iglesias Montiel. Madrid.

(1995b) *Amores, Medicamina Faciei Femineae, Ars Amatoria, Remedia amoris*, ed. E. J. Kenney. Oxford.

(1995c) *Ovidio. Obra amatoria II: El arte de amar*, with intr. and notes, A. Ramírez deVerger (ed.) and F. Socas Gavilán (tr.). Madrid.

(1995d) *Heroides: Select Epistles*, ed. P. E. Knox. Cambridge.

(1997) *Ovid's Metamorphoses Books 1–5*, ed. W. S. Anderson. Norman.

(1998) *Ovidio. Obra amatoria III: Remedios de amor. Cremas para la cara de la mujer*, with intr. and notes, A. Ramírez de Verger and L. Rivero (eds.) and F. Socas Gavilán (tr.). Madrid.

(2004) *P. Ovidi Nasonis Metamorphoses*, ed. R. J. Tarrant. Oxford.

(2008) *Ovide du remède d'amours*, ed. T. Hunt. Modern Humanities Research Critical Texts. London.

Ovide moralisé. (1915–38) Ed. C. de Boer. '*Ovide Moralisé*: *Poème du commencement du XIVe siècle, publié d'après tous les manuscrits connus* (5 vols.), Afdeeling Letterkunde 15, 21, 30, 37, 43. Amsterdam.

(1954) ed. C. de Boer. *Ovide moralisé en prose, texte du quinzième siècle.* Amsterdam.

Pamphilus de amore. Pánfilo o el arte de amar. (1977), ed. and tr. L. Rubio and T. González Rolán. Barcelona.

Paulus, Camaldulensis. (1990) *Il 'Donatus' di Paolo Camaldolese*, ed. V. Sivo. Spoleto.

Petrarca, Francesco. (1945) *Rerum memorandarum libri*, ed. G. Billanovich. Florence.

(1951) *Rime, Trionfi e poesie latine*, ed. F. Neri *et al.* Milan and Naples.

(1955) *Secretum*, ed. E. Carrara. Milan.

(1968) *Laurea occidens. Bucolicum carmen* x, ed. G. Martellotti. Rome.

(1973) *Secretum*, ed. U. Dotti. Leiden and Cologne.

(2003) *Invectives*, ed. D. Marsh. Cambridge, MA.

Planoudes, Maximus (1976) *Maximou Planoude metaphrasis ton Ovidiou Epistolon*, ed. M. Papathomopoulos. Ioannina.

Pseudo-Ovidius. (1967) *'De vetula' Untersuchungen und Text*, ed. P. Klopsch. Leiden and Köln.

Richard de Bury. (1950) *Philobiblon*, ed. A. Altamura. Milan.

Rodríguez del Padrón, Juán. (1984) *Bursario*, ed. P. Saquero Suárez-Somonte and T. González Rolán. Madrid.

Ruiz, Juan, Arcipreste de Hita (1913). *Libro de Buen Amor*, ed. J. Cejador. (2 vols.). Madrid.

Santillana, Íñigo López de Mendoza, Marqués de. (1988) *Obras completas*, ed. A. Gómez Moreno and M. P. A. Kerkhof. Barcelona.

Three Middle English Sermons from the Worcester Chapter Manuscript F 10 (1939), ed. R. L. Grisdale Leeds School of English Language Texts and Monographs 5. Kendal.

Tostado de Madrigal, Alfonso de. (1995) *Alonso Fernández de Madrigal (El Tostado): Sobre los dioses de los gentiles*, ed. P. Saquero Suárez-Somonte and T. González Rolán. Madrid.

Virgil. (1999–2000) *Virgil* (2 vols.), ed. and rev. G. P. Goold. Loeb Classical Library 63. Cambridge, MA.

Walsingham, Thomas. (1867–9) *Gesta abbatum monasterii sancti Albani*, ed. H. T. Riley (3 vols.), Rolls Series 28. London.

(1968) *Thomae Walsingham: De archana deorum*, ed. R. A. van Kluyve. Durham, NC.

(2003) *The St Albans Chronicle: The Chronica maiora of Thomas Walsingham, 1376–94*, ed. J. Taylor, W. Childs and L. Watkiss, Oxford Medieval Texts. Oxford.

Wyclif, J. (1887–90) *Sermones*, ed. Johann Loserth (4 vols.). London.

SECONDARY SOURCES

Alatorre, A. (1949) 'Sobre traducciones castellanas de las *Heroidas*,' *Nueva Revista de Filologica Hispanica* 3: 162–6.

(1950b) *Las 'Heroidas' de Ovidio y su huella en las letras españolas*. Mexico.

Alexakis, A. (2008) 'Two verses of Ovid liberally translated by Agathias of Myrina (*Metamorphoses* 8.877–878 and *Historiae* 2.3.7)', *Byzantische Zeitschrift* 101.2: 609–16.

Allen, C. (2002) '*Ovid and art*', in *The Cambridge Companion to Ovid*, ed. P. Hardie. Cambridge: 336–67.

Allen, J. B. (1970) 'An anonymous twelfth-century *De natura deorum* in the Bodleian Library,' *Traditio* 26: 352–63.

(1971) *The Friar as Critic: Literary Attitudes in the Later Middle Ages*. Nashville.

(1982) *The Ethical Poetic of the Late Middle Ages: A Decorum of Convenient Distinction*. Toronto.

Allen, P. (1992) *The Art of Love: Amatory Fiction from Ovid to the 'Roman de la Rose'*. Philadelphia.

Alton, E. H. (1926) 'The mediaeval commentators on Ovid's *Fasti*', *Hermathena* 44: 101–18.

(1931) 'De nuntio sagaci', *Hermathena* 46: 61–79.

Alton, E. H. and D. E. W. Wormell. (1961) 'Ovid in the Mediaeval Schoolroom', *Hermathena* 95: 67–82.

Anderson, R. D., P. J. Parsons and R. G. M. Nisbet (1979) 'Elegiacs by Gallus from Qasr Ibrim', *Journal of Roman Studies* 69: 125–55.

Anderson, W. B. (ed. and tr.) (1980–4) *Sidonius: Poems and Letters* (2 vols). Cambridge, MA.

Anderson, W. S. (1974) 'A new Pseudo-Ovidian passage', *California Studies in Classical Antiquity* 7: 7–16.

(1977) 'Studies on the Naples MS IV F 3,' *Illinois Classical Studies* 2: 255–88.

Angelis, V. de. (1984) 'Magna questio preposita coram Dante et Domino Francisco Petrarca', *Studi Petrarcheschi*, n.s. 1: 103–209.

Arcaz, J. L. (1992) *Las obras amatorias de Ovidio en los manuscritos de España*. Madrid.

(1996) 'Presencia manuscrita de las obras amatorias de Ovidio en España: *Amores, Ars amatoria y Remedia amoris*', in *La obra amatoria de Ovidio: aspectos textuales, interpretación literaria y pervivencia*, ed. J. L. Arcaz, G. Laguna Mariscal and A. Ramírez de Verger. Madrid: 41–62.

(2007) 'La mitología clásica en la poesía castellana del siglo XIV', in *La mitología clásica en la literatura española: panorama diacrónico*, ed. J. A. López Férez. Madrid: 145–64.

Arcaz, J. L., G. Laguna Mariscal and A. Ramírez de Verger (ed.) (1996) *La obra al matoria de Ovidio: Aspectos ltextuales, interpretación literaria y pervivencia*. Madrid.

Armstrong, L. (1981) *Renaissance Miniature Painters and Classical Imagery: The Master of the Putti and his Venetian Workshop*. London.

Arnould, A. and J. M. Massing. (1993) *Splendours of Flanders*. Exhibition catalogue, Fitzwilliam Museum. Cambridge.

Ascoli, A. R. (2008) *Dante and the Making of a Modern Author*. Cambridge.

Ashton, J. R. (1944) Ovid's *Heroides* as translated by Alphonso the Wise: An Experiment in Source Study. PhD diss., University of Wisconsin.

Avril, F. (1996) 'Gli autori classici illustrati in Francia dal XIII al XV secolo', tr. L. Maniaci, in *Vedere i classici*, ed. M. Buonocore. Rome: 87–98.

Badia, L. (1993) 'Per la presència d'Ovidi a l'Edat Mitjana catalana, amb notes sobre les traduccions de les Heroides i de les Metamorfosis al vulgar', in *Tradició i modernitat als segles XIV i XV: estudis de cultura literària i lectures d'Ausias March*. Valencia and Barcelona: 56–67.

Bagnall, R. S. (1993) *Egypt in Late Antiquity*. Princeton.

Bakalian, E. (2005) *Aspects of Love in John Gower's Confessio Amantis*. New York.

Baldwin, B. (1987) 'John Lydos and Ovid', *Museum Philologicum Londiniense* 8: 3.

Baldwin, J. W. (1992) 'L'*Ars amatoria* au XIIe siècle en France: Ovide Abélard, André le Chapelain et Pierre le Chantre', in *Histoire et société: Mélanges offerts à Georges Duby*. Aix-en-Provence, vol. 1: 19–29.

(1994) *The Language of Sex: Five Voices from Northern France Around 1200*. Chicago.

Ballistreri, G. (1976) 'Le *Allegorie ovidiane* e Giovanni del Virgilio', in *Acta conventus omnium gentium ovidianis studiis fovendis*, ed. N. Barbu, E. Dobroiu and M. Nasta. Bucharest: 103–13.

Bandini, A. M. (1774–7) *Catalogus codicum latinorum Bibliothecae Mediceae Laurentianae* (5 vols.). Florence.

Barbieri, L. (2005) *Le epistole delle dame di Grecia nel Roman de Troie in prosa*. Tübingen.

Barchiesi, A. (1997) *The Poet and The Prince: Ovid and Augustan Discourse*. Berkeley.

(2002) 'Narrative technique and narratology in the *Metamorphoses*', in *The Cambridge Companion to Ovid*, ed. P. Hardie. Cambridge: 182–97.

Barkan, L. (1990) *The Gods Made Flesh: Metamorphosis and the Pursuit of Paganism*. New Haven, CT.

Barker, W. W. (2001) *The Adages of Erasmus*. Toronto.

Barolsky, P. (1998) 'As in Ovid, so in Renaissance Art', *Renaissance Quarterly*, 51.2: 451–74.

Barthes, R. (1977) 'The death of the Author', in *Image, Music, Text*, tr. and ed. S. Heath. New York: 142–8.

Basi, C. and C. Guasti (eds.) (1846–50) *I primi V libri delle metamorfosi d'Ovidio: volgarizzate da Ser Arrigo Simintendi da Prato*. Prato.

Baswell, C. (1995) *Virgil in Medieval England: Figuring the 'Aeneid' from the Twelfth Century to Chaucer*. Cambridge.

Battaglia, S. (1959) 'La tradizione di Ovidio nel medioevo', *Filologia Romanza* 6: 185–224.

Baum, A. D. (2001) *Pseudoepigraphie und literarische Fälschung im frühen Christentum*. Wissenschaftliche Untersuchungen zum Neuen Testament 2. 138. Tübingen.

Bayless, M. (1996) *Parody in the Middle Ages: The Latin Tradition*. Ann Arbor, MI.

Beardsley, Th. S. (1970) *Hispano-Classical Translations Printed between 1482 and 1699.* Pittsburgh, PA.

Beck, H. G. (1971) 'Besonderheiten der literatur der Paläologenzeit', in *Art et société à Byzance sous les Paléologues.* Association Internationale des Études Byzantines. Venice: 43–52.

Becker, F. (ed.) (1972) *Prolegomena zum Pamphilus (de amore) und kritische Textausgabe. MLatJb supp. 9.* Ratingen.

Beidler, P. (1982) *John Gower's Literary Transformations in the 'Confessio Amantis'.* Washington, DC.

Bell, D. N. (1992) *The Libraries of the Cistercians, Gilbertines and Premonstratensians*, Corpus of British Medieval Library Catalogues 3. London.

Bent, M. and A. Wathey (eds.) (1997) *Fauvel Studies: Allegory, Chronicle, Image and Music in Bibliothèque Nationale de France, MS Français 146.* Oxford.

Bertini, F. (ed.) (1976–) *Commedie latine del XII e XIII secolo.* Genoa.

(1995) 'Amores III 5 e l'elegia pseudoovidiana "De sompnio"', in *Aetates Ovidianae: lettori di Ovidio dall' Antichità al Rinascimento*, ed. I. Gallo and L. Nicastri. Pubblicazioni dell'Università degli Studi di Salerno, Sezione Atti, Convegni, Miscellanee 43. Naples: 223–37.

Bestul, T. H. (1989) 'Chaucer's Parson's Tale and the late medieval tradition of religious meditation', *Speculum* 64: 600–19.

Bianchini, S. (1989) 'Arrigo da Settimello e una sua fonte oitanica', *Studi Medievali* 30: 855–63.

Billanovich, G. (1958) '"Veterum vestigia vatum" nei carmi dei preumanisti Padovani: Lovato Lovati, Zambono di Andrea, Albertino Mussato e Lucrezio, Catullo, Orazio (*Carmina*), Tibullo, Properzio, Ovidio (*Ibis*), Marziale, Stazio (*Silvae*)', *Italia medioevale e umanistica* 1: 155–243.

Bischoff, B. (1952) 'Eine mittelalterliche Ovid-Legende', *Historisches Jahrbuch* 71: 268–73.

(1994b) 'Libraries and schools in the Carolingian revival of learning', in *Manuscripts and Libraries in the Age of Charlemagne*, ed. B. Bischoff and M. M. Gorman. Cambridge: 93–114.

(1994a) 'Benedictine monasteries and the survival of classical literature', in *Manuscripts and Libraries in the Age of Charlemagne*, ed. B. Bischoff and M. M. Gorman. Cambridge: 134–160.

Black, R. (1996) *Studio e scuola in Arezzo durante il medioevo e il rinascimento: i documenti d'archivio fino al 1530.* Arezzo.

(2001) *Humanism and Education in Medieval and Renaissance Italy: Tradition and Innovation in Latin Schools from the Twelfth to the Fifteenth Century.* Cambridge.

Black, R. and G. Pomaro. (2000) *Boethius's 'Consolation of Philosophy' in Italian Medieval and Renaissance Education: Schoolbooks and their Glosses in Florentine Manuscripts.* Florence.

Blake, N. F. (1981) 'Critics, criticism, and the order of the *Canterbury Tales*', *Archiv für das Studium der neueren Sprachen und Literaturen* 218: 47–58.

Blamires, A. (ed.) (1992) *Woman Defamed and Woman Defended.* Oxford.

Bloch, R. H. (2003) *The Anonymous Marie de France*. Chicago.

Blumenfeld-Kosinski, R. (1997) *Reading Myth: Classical Mythology and its Interpretations in Medieval French Literature*. Stanford.

(2002) 'Illustration et interprétation dans un manuscrit de l'Ovide moralisé (Arsenal 5069)', *Cahiers de recherches médiévales* 9: 71–82.

Boas, M. (1914) 'De librorum Catonianorum historia atque compositione', *Mnemosyne* 42: 27–46

Bode, G. (1834) *Scriptores rerum mythicarum Latini tres Romae nuper reperti* (2 vols.). Celle, repr. Hildesheim, 1968.

Bodnar, E. W. (ed. and tr.) with C. Foss. (2003) *Cyriacus of Ancona: Later Travels*. Cambridge, MA.

Boese, H. (1966) *Die Lateinischen Handschriften der Sammlung Hamilton zu Berlin*. Wiesbaden.

Boissonade, J. F. (ed.) (1822) *Publii Ovidii Nasonis Metamorphoseon libri xv graece versi a Maximo Planude*. Paris.

Bonacina, M. (1983) 'De Lombardo et lumaca', in *Commedie Latine del XII e XIII secolo*, IV, ed. F. Bertini. Genoa: 95–135.

Bond, G. W. (1989) 'Composing yourself: Ovid's *Heroides*, Baudri of Bourgueil and the problem of persona', in *Ovid in Medieval Culture*, special issue of *Mediaevalia*, ed. M. Desmond, 13: 83–117.

(1995) *The Loving Subject: Desire, Eloquence, and Power in Romanesque France*. Philadelphia.

Boutemy, A. (1937) 'Une copie de l'*Ars amatoria* au British Museum', *Revue des études Latines* 15: 92–102.

Brancaforte, B. (1990) *Las Metamorfosis y las Heroidas de Ovidio en La General Estoria de Alfonso el Sabio*. Madison.

Brann, N. L. (1981) *The Abbot Trithemius (1462–1516): The Renaissance of Monastic Humanism*. Leiden.

Braune, J. (1935) *Nonnos und Ovid*. Greifswald.

Brownlee, K. (1986) 'Ovid's Semele and Dante's Metamorphosis: *Paradiso* XXI–XXIII', *Modern Language Notes* 101: 67–82.

Brownlee, M. S. (1997) 'The practice of cultural authority: Italian responses to French cultural dominance in *Il Tesoretto, Il Fiore*, and the *Commedia*', *Forum for Modern Language Studies* 33: 258–69.

(1990) *The Severed Word: Ovid's 'Heroides' and the Novela Sentimental*. Princeton.

Bryan, W. F. and G. Dempster. (1958) *Sources and Analogues of Chaucer's 'Canterbury Tales'*. New York.

Bullough, D. (1964) 'Le scuole cattedrali e la cultura dell'Italia settentrionale prima dei comuni', in *Vescovi e diocesi in Italia nel medioevo (sec. IX–XIII): Atti del II Convegno di storia della chiesa in Italia (Roma, 5–9 sett. 1961)*. Padua.

Buonocore, M. (1994) *Aetas Ovidiana: la fortuna di Ovidio nei codice della Biblioteca Apostolica Vaticana*. Sulmo.

(ed.) (1996) *Vedere i classici: l'illustrazione libraria dei testi antichi dall'età romana al tardo medioevo*. Exhibition catalogue. Vatican City, 1996–7. Rome.

Burger, G. and S. F. Kruger (eds.) (2001) *Queering the Middle Ages*. Minneapolis.

Burgwinkle, W. (2005) *Sodomy, Masculinity, and Law in Medieval Literature*. Cambridge.

Burns, M. (1997) 'Classicizing and medievalizing Chaucer: The sources for Pyramus' death-throes in the *Legend of Good Women*', *Neophilologus* 81: 637–47.

Burrow, J. A. (1983) 'The portrayal of Amans in *Confessio Amantis*,' in *Gower's 'Confessio Amantis': Responses and Assessments*, ed. A. J. Minnis. Cambridge 5–24.

Burton, R. (1983) *Classical Poets in the 'Florilegium Gallicum'*. Frankfurt am Main.

Bury, E. (ed.) (2003) *Lectures d'Ovide: publiées à la mémoire de Jean-Pierre Néraudau*. Paris.

Butinyà, J. (1994) 'Cicerón, Ovidio, Agustín y Petrarca en Lo Somni de Bernat Metge', *Epos* 10: 173–201.

Buttenwieser, H. (1940) 'Manuscripts of Ovid's *Fasti*: The Ovidian tradition in the Middle Ages', *Transactions and Proceedings of the American Philological Association* 71: 45–51.

Butterfield, A. (2002) *Poetry and Music in Medieval France: From Jean Renart to Guillaume de Machaut*. Cambridge.

 (2004) '*Confessio Amantis* and the French tradition,' in *A Companion to Gower*, ed. Sîan Echard. Cambridge: 165–80.

Bynum, C. W. (2001) *Metamorphosis and Identity*. New York.

Calabrese, M. (1994) *Chaucer's Ovidian Arts of Love*. Gainesville, FL.

Callan, N. (1946) 'Thyn owne book: A note on Chaucer, Gower, and Ovid', *Review of English Studies* 88: 269–81.

Camargo, M. (1988) 'Towards a comprehensive art of written discourse,' *Rhetorica* 6: 167–94.

 (1991) *Ars dictaminis, Ars Dictandi*, Typologie des sources du Moyen Âge, Fasc. 60. Turnhout.

 (1995) *Medieval Rhetorics of Prose Composition: Five English Artes Dictandi and their Tradition*. Binghamton, NY.

Cameron, A. (1965) 'Wandering poets: A literary movement in Byzantine Egypt', *Historia* 14: 470–509.

 (1970) *Claudian: Poetry and Propaganda at the Court of Honorius*. Oxford.

 (2004) *Greek Mythography in the Roman World*. Oxford.

Camille, M. (1992) *Image on the Edge: The Margins of Medieval Art*. Cambridge, MA.

Campbell, C. (2007) 'Lorenzo Tornabuoni's History of Jason and Medea Series: Chivalry and Classicism in 1480s Florence', *Renaissance Studies* 21: 1–19.

Canart, P. (1998) 'Quelques exemples de division du travail chez les copistes byzantins', in *Recherches de codicologie comparée: la composition de codex au moyen âge en Orient et en Occident*, ed. P. Hoffmann. Paris: 49–67.

Candlish, J. S. (1891) 'On the moral character of pseudonymous books', *The Expositor* ser. 4, 4: 91–107, 262–79.

Cantavella, R. (1998): 'The meaning of *destral* as "go-between" in the Catalan *Facet* and in Old Occitan', *Medium Aevum* 67: 304–12.

Capellino, M. (1984) 'Note su maestri e scuole vercellesi nel secolo XIII', in *Vercelli nel secolo XIII*. Vercelli: 83–98.

Capello, G. (1943) 'Maestro Manfredo e Maestro Sion grammatici vercellesi del Duecento', *Aevum* 17: 45–70.

Carley, J. P. (1988) *Glastonbury Abbey: The Holy House at the Head of the Moors Adventurous*. Woodbridge.

Carley, J. P. and J. F. R. Coughlan. (1981) 'An edition of the list of ninety-nine books acquired at Glastonbury Abbey during the abbacy of Walter de Monington', *Mediaeval Studies* 43: 498–514.

Carlson, D. R. (2003) 'Gower's early Latin poetry: Text-genetic hypotheses of an *Epistola ad Regem* (ca. 1377–1380) from the evidence of John Bale', *Mediaeval Studies* 65: 293–317.

    (2004) 'The invention of the Anglo-Latin public poetry (circa 1367–1402) and its prosody, especially in John Gower', *Mittellateinisches Jahrbuch* 39: 389–406.

Casagrande Mazzoli, M. A. (ed.) (1996) *I manoscritti datati della provincia di Trento*. Florence.

Casali, S. (2005) 'Not by Ovid', *Classical Review* 55: 530–2.

Casas Rigall, J. (1999) *La materia de Troya en las letras romances del siglo XIII hispano*. Santiago de Compostela.

Cassirer, E., P. O. Kristeller and J. H. Randall. (1948) *The Renaissance Philosophy of Man*. Chicago.

Castiglioni, L. (1920) 'Spogli riccardiani', *Bollettino di filologia classica* 27: 162–6.

Castillo, C. (1973) 'La composición del *Conflictus veris et hiemis* atribuido a Alcuino', *Cuadernos de Filología Clásica* 5: 53–61.

Castro Guisasola, F. (1924) *Observaciones sobre las fuentes literarias de 'La Celestina'*. Madrid.

Castro Jiménez, M. D. (1990) 'Presencia de un mito ovidiano: Apolo y Dafne en la literatura española de la Edad Media y el Renacimiento', *Cuadernos de Filología Clásica*. 24: 185–222.

    (1993) *El mito de Prosérpina: fuentes grecolatinas y pervivencia en la literatura española*. Madrid.

    (2007) 'La mitología en la prosa del siglo XIV', in *La mitología clásica en la literatura española: Panorama diacrónico*, ed. J. A. López Férez. Madrid: 123–44.

Cátedra, P. (ed.) (1989) *Enrique de Villena: traducción y glosas de la Eneida, libros I y II* (2 vols.). Salamanca.

Cerquiglini-Toulet, J. (1997) *The Color of Melancholy: The Uses of Books in the Fourteenth Century*, tr. L. Cochrane. Baltimore.

Cerquiglini-Toulet, J. and N. Wilkins (eds.) (2002) *Guillaume de Machaut: 1300–2000*. Actes du colloque de la Sorbonne, 28–9 Septembre 2000, 700e anniversaire de la naissance du poète-compositeur. Paris.

Chatelain, M.-C. (2008) *Ovide savant, Ovide gallant: Ovide en France dans la seconde moitié du XVIIe siècle*. Paris.

Chance, J. (2000) *Medieval Mythography*, vol. II: *From the School of Chartres to the Court at Avignon, 1177–1350*. Gainesville.

Chesney, K. (1942) 'A neglected prose version of the *Roman De Troie*', *Medium Aevum* 11: 46–67.

Ciaranfi, A. M. Francini (1977) 'Appunti su antichi disegni fiorentini per le "Metamorfosi" di Ovidio', in *Scritti di storia dell' arte in onore di Ugo Procacci*, ed. M. G. Ciardi Dupré Dal Poggetto. Milan.

Ciardi Dupré Dal Poggetto, M. G. (1976) 'Review of exhibition, "L'Uomo, il lavoro, l'ambiente nelle miniature Laurenziana"', *Prospettiva* 7: 72–9.

Cirot, G. (1937) 'La guerre de Troie dans le *Libro de Alexandre*', *Bulletin of Hispanic Studies*. 39: 328–38.

Claassen, J.-M. (2007) 'Literary *anamnesis*: Boethius remembers Ovid', *Helios* 34: 1–35.

Clark, J. G. (2004) *A Monastic Renaissance at St. Albans: Thomas Walsingham and his Circle, c.1350–1440*. Oxford, New York.

Clausen, W., F. Goodyear, E. Kenney and J. Richmond. (eds.) (1966) *Appendix Vergiliana*. Oxford.

Clier-Colombani, F. (2001) 'Prologues en images dans *L'Ovide moralisé*', *Bien dire et bien aprandre* 19: 57–76.

Coates, A. (1999) *English Medieval Books: The Reading Abbey Collections from Foundation to Dispersal*. Oxford.

Cohen, G. (ed.) (1931) *La 'comédie' latine en France au xiie siècle* (2 vols.). Paris.

Comparetti, D. (1997) *Vergil in the Middle Ages*, tr. E. F. M. Benecke, rev. J. Ziolkowski. Princeton. (Italian original first published in 1872.)

Constantinides, C. N. (1982) *Higher Education in Byzantium in the 13th and early 14th Centuries, 1204–ca. 1310*. Nicosia.

Coombe, R. J. (1998) *The Cultural Life of Intellectual Properties: Authorship, Appropriation, and the Law*. Durham, NC.

Coon, R. H. (1930) 'The vogue of Ovid since the Renaissance', *The Classical Journal* 25.4: 277–90.

Cooper, H. (1988) 'Chaucer and Ovid: A question of authority', in *Ovid Renewed*, ed. C. Martindale. Cambridge: 71–81.

(1996) *Oxford Guides to Chaucer: The Canterbury Tales*. 2nd edn. Oxford.

Copeland, R. (1991) *Rhetoric, Hermeneutics, and Translation in the Middle Ages: Academic Traditions and Vernacular Texts*. Cambridge.

Coulson, F. T. (1982) A study of the 'Vulgate' commentary on Ovid's *Metamorphoses* and a critical edition of the glosses to Book One, PhD diss., University of Toronto.

(1985) 'MSS. of the *"Vulgate"* commentary on Ovid's *Metamorphoses*: A checklist', *Scriptorium* 39: 118–29.

(1986a) 'New manuscript evidence for sources of the *Accessus* of Arnoul d'Orléans to the *Metamorphoses* of Ovid', *Manuscripta* 30: 103–7.

(1986b) 'New evidence for the circulation of Valerius Flaccus?', *Classical Philology* 81: 58–60.

(1986c) 'Pierpont Morgan Library Ms. M. 938: A newly discovered copy of Giovanni del Virgilio's prose paraphrase of the *Metamorphoses*', *Scriptorium* 40: 255–6.

(1987a) 'The *"Vulgate"* commentary on Ovid's *Metamorphoses*', *Mediaevalia* 13: 29–62.

(1987b) 'MSS. of the *"Vulgate"* commentary on Ovid's *Metamorphoses*: Addendum', *Scriptorium* 41: 263–4.

(1987c) 'Hitherto unedited medieval and renaissance lives of Ovid (I)', *Mediaeval Studies* 49: 152–207.

(1988) 'An update to Munari's catalogue of the manuscripts of Ovid's *Metamorphoses*', *Scriptorium* 42: 111–12.

(1990) 'New manuscripts of the medieval interpretations of Ovid's *Metamorphoses*', *Scriptorium* 44: 272–5.

(1991) *The 'Vulgate' commentary on Ovid's 'Metamorphoses': The creation myth and the story of Orpheus*. Toronto.

(1992) 'Newly discovered manuscripts of Ovid's *Metamorphoses* in the libraries of Florence and Milan', *Scriptorium* 46: 285–8.

(1994) 'A bibliographical update and *Corrigenda Minora* to Munari's catalogues of the manuscripts of Ovid's *Metamorphoses*', *Manuscripta* 38: 3–22

(1995a) 'A newly discovered copy of the *Vulgate* commentary on Ovid's *Metamorphoses* in an *Incunabulum* in the British Library', *Stud Med* 36: 321–2.

(1995b) 'Addenda to Munari's catalogues of the manuscripts of Ovid's *Metamorphoses*', *Revue d'histoire des textes* 25: 91–127.

(1996) 'A checklist of newly identified manuscripts of the *Allegoriae* of Giovanni del Virgilio', *StudMed* 37: 443–53.

(1997a) 'A checklist of newly discovered manuscripts of Pierre Bersuire's *Ovidius moralizatus*', *Scriptorium* 51: 164–86.

(1997b) 'Hitherto unedited medieval and renaissance lives of Ovid (II): Humanistic lives', *Mediaeval Studies* 59: 111–53.

(1998) 'Two newly identified *accessus* to Ovid's *Metamorphoses* in Oxford, Bodleian Library, MS Rawlinson B.214, and London, British Library, MS Harley 2693', *Manuscripta* 42: 122–3.

(2002) 'Addenda and corrigenda to *Incipitarium Ovidianum*', *The Journal of Medieval Latin* 12: 154–80.

(2007) 'Ovid's transformations in medieval France (ca. 1100–ca. 1350)', in *Metamorphosis: The Changing Face of Ovid in Medieval and Early Modern Europe*, ed. A. Keith and S. Rupp. Toronto: 33–60.

(2008) 'Procne and Philomela in the Latin commentary tradition of the Middle Ages and Renaissance', *Euphrosyne* 36: 181–96.

Coulson, F. T. and U. Molyviati-Toptsis. (1992) 'Vaticanus latinus 2877: A hitherto unedited allegorization of Ovid's *Metamorphoses*', *The Journal of Medieval Latin* 2: 134–202.

Coulson, F. T. and K. Nawotka. (1993) 'The rediscovery of Arnulf of Orléans' glosses to Ovid's creation myth', *Classica et Mediaevalia* 44: 267–99.

Coulson, F. T. and B. Roy. (2000) *Incipitarium Ovidianum: A Finding Guide for Texts related to the Study of Ovid in the Middle Ages and Renaissance*. Turnhout.

Cowdrey, H. E. J. (1983) *The Age of Abbot Desiderius: Montecassino, the Papacy and the Normans in the Eleventh and Early Twelfth Centuries*. Oxford.

Craun, E. (1997) *Lies, Slander, and Obscenity in Medieval English Literature: Pastoral Rhetoric and the Deviant Speaker.* Cambridge.

(2003) '*Fama* and pastoral restraints on rebuking sinners: The Book of Margery Kempe,' in *Fama: The Politics of Talk and Reputation in Medieval Europe*, ed. T. Fenster and D. Lord Smail. Ithaca, NY: 187–209.

Cristóbal, V. (1989) 'Nota crítica al Triunphete de amor del Marqués de Santillana', *Epos* 5: 493–5.

(1991) 'Los *Amores* de Ovidio en la tradición clásica', in *Treballs en honor de Virgilio Bejarano: Actes del IX Simposi de la Secció Catalana de la SEEC*, ed. L. Ferreres, vol. I. Barcelona: 371–9.

(1997) 'Las Metamorfosis de Ovidio en la literatura española: visión panorámica de su influencia con especial atención a la Edad Media y a los siglos XVI y XVII', *Cuadernos de literatura griega y latina* 1: 125–53.

(2007) 'Mitología clásica en la literatura española de la Edad Media y el Renacimiento', *Cuadernos de literatura griega y latina* 6: 37–57.

Crosas López, F. (1995) *La materia clásica en la poesía de Cancionero.* Kassel.

(1997) 'Sobre los primeros mitógrafos españoles: el Tostado y Pérez de Moya', *Actas del VI Congreso Internacional de la Asociación Hispánica de Literatura Medieval*, Alcalá de Henares: vol. 1, 543–50.

(1998) *De diis gentium: tradición clásica y cultura medieval.* New York.

Cuissard, C. (1871) 'Les professeurs orléanais Foulque, Arnoul et Hugues le Primat', *Bulletin de la Société archéologique et historique de l'Orléanais* 10: 417–33.

Cunningham, I. C. (1973) 'Latin classical manuscripts in the National Library of Scotland', *Scriptorium* 31: 64–90.

Curtius, E. R. (1953) *European Literature and the Latin Middle Ages*, tr. W. R. Trask. New York.

(1976) *Literatura europea y edad media latina*, tr. M. Frenk Alatorre and A. Alatorre (2 vols.). Mexico.

Dagenais, J. (1985–6) 'Juan Rodríguez del Padrón's translation of the Latin *Bursarii*: New light on the meaning of tra(c)tado'. *Journal of Hispanic Philology* 10: 117.

(1986–7) 'A further source for the literary ideas in Juan Ruiz's Prologue'. *Journal of Hispanic Philology* 11: 23–52.

Damangeot-Bourdat, M.-F. (2007) 'Lire, annoter, illustrer: l'exemple du manuscrit latin 4935 de la Bibliothèque nationale de France (XIVe/XVe siècle)', in *Quand la peinture était dans les livres: Mélanges en l'honneur de François Avril*, ed. M. Hofmann and C. Zöhl. Turnhout and Paris: 62–77.

Davies, M. (1996) 'Humanism in script and print in the fifteenth century', in *The Cambridge Companion to Renaissance Humanism*, ed. J. Kraye. Cambridge: 47–62.

D'Avray, D. L. (1984) *The Preaching of the Friars: Sermons Diffused from Paris before 1300.* Oxford.

Dean, J. (1979) 'The ending of the *Canterbury Tales* 1952–1976', *Texas Studies in Literature and Language* 2: 17–33.

(1985) 'Dismantling the Canterbury Book', *PMLA* 100: 746–62.

Dean, R. J. (1942) 'MS. Bodl. 292 and the Canon of Nicholas Trevet's Works', *Speculum* 17: 243–9.

(1945) 'The earliest known commentary on Livy is by Nicholas Trevet'. *Medievalia et Humanistica* 3: 86–98.

(1948) 'Cultural relations in the Middle Ages: Nicholas Trevet and Nicholas of Prato', *Studies in Philology* 45: 541–64.

Degenhart, B. and A. Schmitt. (1980) *Corpus der italienischen Zeichnungen, 1300–1450*, Part II: *Venedig; Addenda zu Süd und Mittelitalien*. Berlin.

de la Mare, A. (1992) 'Cosimo and his books', *in Cosimo 'il vecchio' de' Medici, 1389–1464*, ed. F. Ames-Lewis. Oxford: 115–56.

Delany, S. (1968) 'Chaucer's *House of Fame* and the *Ovide moralisé*', *Comparative Literature* 20: 254–64.

(1994) *The Naked Text: Chaucer's 'Legend of Good Women'*. Berkeley.

(1999) 'Chaucer's *House of Fame* and the *Ovide moralisé*', in *Chaucer's Dream Visions and Shorter Poems*, ed. W. A. Quinn, Basic Readings in Chaucer and his Time 2. New York: 209–20.

Delisle, L. (1869) 'Les écoles d'Orléans au douzième et au treizième siècle', *Annuaire: Bulletin de la société de l'histoire de France* 7: 139–54.

Demats, P. (1973) *Fabula: trois études de mythographie antique et médiévale*. Geneva.

Deri, B. (2005) '"... Tenui pendentia filo...": Ovidius-distichon egy Árpád-kori' [An Ovidian distich in a charter], *Levéltári Közlemények: A Magyar Országos Levéltár folyó* 76: 5–12.

Derolez, A. (1979) *The Library of Raphael de Marcatellis, Abbot of St. Bavon's, Ghent, 1437–1508*. Ghent.

Derrida, J. (1978) 'Limited Inc.', *Glyph* 2: 162–254.

(1987) *The Post Card: From Socrates to Freud and Beyond*, tr. A. Bass. Chicago.

Desmond, M. (ed.) (1989 for 1987) *Ovid in Medieval Culture*. Special issue of *Mediaevalia: A Journal of Medieval Studies* 13.

(2006) *Ovid's Art and the Wife of Bath: The Ethics of Erotic Violence*. Ithaca, NY.

(2007) 'The Goddess Diana and the ethics of reading in the *Ovide moralisé*,' in *Metamorphosis: The Changing Face of Ovid in Medieval and Early Modern Europe*, ed. A. Keith and S. Rupp. Toronto: 61–75.

Desmond, M. and P. Sheingorn. (2001) 'Queering Ovidian myth: Bestiality and desire in Christine de Pizan's *Epistre Othea*', in *Queering the Middle Ages*, ed. G. Burger and S. F. Kruger. Minneapolis: 3–27.

(2003) *Myth, Montage, and Visuality in Late Medieval Manuscript Culture: Christine de Pizan's 'Epistre Othea'*. Ann Arbor, MI.

Devlin, M. A. (ed.) (1954) *The Sermons of Thomas Brinton, Bishop of Rochester (1373–89)* (2 vols.), Camden Society, 3rd ser., 85, 86. London.

DeVun, L. (2008) 'The Jesus hermaphrodite: Science and sex difference in premodern Europe', *Journal of the History of Ideas* 69: 193–218.

Dewar, M. (2002) 'Siquid habent ueri uatum praesagia: Ovid in the 1st–5th Centuries', in *Brill's Companion to Ovid*, ed. B. Weiden Boyd. Leiden: 383–412.

Díaz y Díaz, M. C. (1991) *Libros y librerías en la Rioja altomedieval*. Logroño.

Dickinson, R. J. (1973) 'The *Tristia*: Poetry in exile', in *Ovid*, ed. J. W. Binns. London: 154–90.

Dihle, A. (1999) 'Zu den ovid-übersetzungen des Maximos Planudes', in *Ovid: Werk und Wirkung. Festgabe für Michael von Albrecht zum 65. Geburtstag*, ed. W. Schubert. Frankfurt am Main: vol. II, 993–1005.

Dimmick, J. (2002) 'Ovid in the Middle Ages: Authority and poetry', in *The Cambridge Companion to Ovid*, ed. P. Hardie. Cambridge: 264–87.

Ditt, E. (1932) 'Pier Candido Decembrio: Contributo alla storia dell'umanesimo italiano', *Memorie del Reale Istituto Lombardo di scienze e lettere, Classe di lettere scienze morali e storiche*, s. 3, 24: 21–106.

Dobson, R. B. (1973) *Durham Priory, 1400–50*. Cambridge.

 (1991) 'English monastic cathedrals in the fifteenth century', *Transactions of the Royal Historical Society*, 6th ser. 1: 151–72.

Dörrie, H. (1968) *Der heroische Brief: Bestandsaufnahme, Geschichte, Kritik einer humanistisch-barocken Literaturgattung*. Berlin.

Dronke, P. (1974) *Fabula: Explorations of the Uses of Myth in Medieval Platonism*. Leiden and Cologne.

 (1976) 'Pseudo-Ovid, Facetus, and the arts of love', *MLatJb* 11: 126–31.

 (1979) 'A note on *Pamphilus*', *JWI* 42: 225–30.

 (1994) 'Andreas Capellanus', *Journal of Medieval Latin* 4: 51–63.

Durling, R. (2001) 'Mio figlio, dov'è? (Inferno x, 60)', in *Dante: da Firenze all' aldilà: Atti del terzo seminario dantesco internationale (Firenze 9–11 giugno 2000)*, ed. M. Picone. Florence: 303–29.

 (2003) 'Guido Cavalcanti in the *Vita Nuova*', in *Guido Cavalcanti tra i suoi lettori*, ed. M. L. Ardizzione. Florence: 177–85.

Earp, L. M. (1995) *Guillaume de Machaut: A Guide to Research*, Garland Composer Resource Manuals 36. Taylor & Francis: London.

Echard, S. (ed.) (2004) *A Companion to Gower*. Cambridge.

Edwards, R. (2006) 'Ricardian dreamwork: Chaucer, Cupid and loyal lovers', in *The 'Legend of Good Women': Context and Reception*, ed. C. Collette. Woodbridge: 59–82.

Ehrhart, M. (1994) 'Ovid, history and authorial responsibility in a fifteenth-century reception of the *Ovide Moralisé*', *Fifteenth-Century Studies* 21: 87–113.

Elliott, A. G. (1977) 'The *Facetus*: or, the Art of Courtly Living', *Allegorica* 2: 27–57.

 (1980) '*Accessus ad auctores*: Twelfth-century introductions to Ovid', *Allegorica* 5: 6–48.

Engelbrecht, W. (1993) 'Der Francofortanus und die *Epistula Sapphus*', *MLatJb* 28: 51–7.

 (2003) *Filologie de Dertiende eeuw: De Bursarii super Ovidios van Magister Willem van Orléans (fl. 1200 AD)*. Olomouc.

 (2006) '"*Carmina Pieridum multo vigilata labore/exponi, nulla certius urbe reor*": Orléans and the reception of Ovid in the *aetas Ovidiana* in school commentaries,' *MLatJb* 41: 209–26.

Engels, J. (1943), *Études sur l'"Ovide moralisé"*. Groningen.

(1966) *De formis figurisque deorum: Textus e codice Brux., Bibl. Reg. 863–9 critice editus* [Werkmateriaal (3) uitgegeven door het Instituut voor Laat Latijn der Rijksuniversiteit Utrecht]. Utrecht.

(1968) 'Note sur quelques manuscrits mythologiques', *Vivarium* 6: 102–7.

(1969) 'Note complémentaire sur les manuscrits Berchoriens de Worcester', *Vivarium* 7: 73–8.

(1971) 'L'édition critique de l'*Ovidius Moralizatus* de Bersuire', *Vivarium* 9: 19–24.

Erb, P. C. (1971) 'Vernacular Material for Preaching in MS Cambridge University Library II.III.8', *Mediaeval Studies* 33: 63–84.

Farrell, J. (1998) 'Reading and Writing the *Heroides*', *HSCP* 98: 307–38.

(2004) 'Review of Hardie P. (ed.) *The Cambridge Companion to Ovid*', in *Bryn Mawr Classical Review* 2004.12.21 (online publication at http://ccat.sas. upenn.edu/bmcr/2004/2004–12-21.html).

Federico, S. (2003) *New Troy: Fantasies of Empire in the Late Middle Ages*. Minneapolis.

Fernández Vallina, E. (1988) 'Introducción al Tostado: De su vida y de su obra', *Cuadernos Salmantinos de Filosofía* 15: 153–77.

Ferster, J. (2000) 'Chaucer's Parson and the "idiosyncrasies of fiction"', in *Closure in 'The Canterbury Tales': The Role of the Parson's Tale*, ed. D. Raybin and L. T. Holley. Kalamazoo.

Fierville, C. (ed.) (1886) *Une grammaire latine inédite du XIIIe siècle*. Paris.

Fisher, E. A. (1979) 'Ovid's *Metamorphoses*, Planudes and Ausonians', in *Arctouros: Hellenic Studies Presented to Bernard M. W. Knox*, ed. G. W. Bowersock, W. Burkert and M. C. J. Putnam. Berlin: 440–6.

(1990) *Planudes' Greek translation of Ovid's Metamorphoses*. New York.

(1995) 'Innovation through translation: The Greek version of Ovid's amatory poems', in *Originality in Byzantine Literature, Art and Music*, ed. A. R. Littlewood. Oxford: 93–8.

(2002/3) 'Planoudes, Holobolos and the motivation for translation', *Greek, Roman and Byzantine Studies* 43: 77–104.

(2004) 'Planoudes' technique and competence as a translator of Ovid's *Metamorphoses*', *Byzantinoslavica* 62: 143–60.

(2007) 'Ovid's *Metamorphoses*: Sailing to Byzantium', *Classical and Modern Literature* 27.1: 45–67.

Fisher, J. (1965) *John Gower: Moral Philosopher and Friend of Chaucer*. London.

Fleming, J. V. (1990) *Classical Imitation and Interpretation in Chaucer's 'Troilus'*. Lincoln, NE.

(2003) 'The best line in Ovid and the worst', in *New Readings of Chaucer's Poetry*, ed. R. G. Benson and S. Ridyard. Cambridge: 51–74.

Fletcher, J. M. (1992) 'Developments in the Faculty of Arts 1370–1520', in *Late Medieval Oxford*. Vol. II of *The History of the University of Oxford*, ed. J. I. Catto and T. A. R. Evans. Oxford: 315–45.

Fodor, N. (2007) 'Weisheitsliteratur in Übersetzungen vom Westen nach Osten: letztendlich ein Kreis in dem Europäischen Kulturkreis', *Acta Antiqua Academiae Scientiarum Hungaricae* 47: 99–115.

(2008) *Die Übersetzungen lateinischer Autoren durch M. Planudes* (online publication at http://archiv.ub.uni heidelberg.de/volltextserver/volltexte/2008/8700/index.html.

Foucault, M. (1977) 'What is an Author?', in *Language, Counter-Memory, Practice*, ed. D. Bouchard, tr. D. Bouchard and S. Simon. Ithaca, NY: 124–7.

Fowler, D. (1997) 'The Virgil commentary of Servius', in *The Cambridge Companion to Virgil*, ed. C. A. Martindale. Cambridge: 73–8.

Fradenberg, L. (1985) 'The Manciple's servant tongue: Politics and poetry in *The Canterbury Tales*', *English Literary History* 52: 85–118.

Frank, R. W. (1972) *Chaucer and 'The Legend of Good Women'*. Cambridge, MA.

Freckmann, A. (2006) *Die Bibliothek des Klosters Bursfelde im Spätmittelalter*. Gottingen.

Friis-Jensen, K. and J. Willoughby. (2001) *Peterborough Abbey*, Corpus of British Medieval Library Catalogues 8. London.

Fritz, J.-M. (1988) 'Du dieu émasculateur au roi émasculé: métamorphoses de Saturne au Moyen Âge', in *Pour une mythologie du Moyen Âge*, ed. L. Harf-Lancner and D. Boutet. Paris: 43–60.

Fumo, J. C. (2004) 'Thinking upon the crow: The *Manciple's Tale* and Ovidian mythography', *The Chaucer Review* 38: 355–75.

(2007) 'Argus' eyes, Midas' ears, and the wife of Bath as storyteller', in *Metamorphosis: The Changing Face of Ovid in Medieval and Early Modern Europe*, ed. A. Keith and S. Rupp. Toronto: 129–50.

Fyler, J. M. (1979) *Chaucer and Ovid*. New Haven.

(2007) *Language and the Declining World in Chaucer, Dante, and Jean de Meun*. Cambridge.

(2009) 'The Medieval Ovid', in *A Companion to Ovid*, ed. P. E. Knox, Blackwell Companions to the Ancient World. Oxford: 411–22.

Gaertner, J. F. (2007) 'Ovid and the "Poetics of Exile": How exilic is Ovid's exile poetry?', in *Writing Exile: The Discourse of Displacement in Greco-Roman Antiquity and Beyond*, ed. J. F. Gaertner. Leiden: 155–72.

Gagnebin, B. (1976) *L'enluminure de Charlemagne à François I: les manuscrits à peinture de la Bibliothèque publique et universitaire de Genève*. Geneva.

Gaisser, J. H. (2008) 'Apuleius in Florence from Boccaccio to Lorenzo de' Medici', in *Classica et Beneventana: Essays presented to Virginia Brown on the occasion of her 65th Birthday*, ed. F. T. Coulson and A. A. Grotans. Turnhout: 45–72.

Galbraith, V. H. (1937) *The St Albans Chronicle, 1406–20*. Oxford.

Galinsky, K. (1975) *Ovid's Metamorphoses: An Introduction to the Basic Aspects*. Berkeley.

Gallo, I. and L. Nicastri. (eds.) (1995) *Aetates Ovidianae: lettori di Ovidio dall'antichità al Rinascimento*. Pubblicazioni dell'Università degli studi di Salerno: Sezione Atti, convegni, miscellanee 43. Naples.

Gamillscheg, E. (1981) 'Autoren und Kopisten: Beobachtungen zu Autographen byzantinischer Autoren', *Jahrbuch der Österreichischen Byzantinischen Gesellschaft* 31: 379–94.

García Blanco, M. (1944) 'Un Narciso medieval', *Cuadernos de Teatro* 1.1: 23–6.

Gargan, L. (1965) 'Giovanni Conversini e la cultura letteraria a Treviso', *Italia medioevale e umanistica* 8: 97–102.

Garin, E. (ed.) (1958) *Il pensiero pedagogico dello umanesimo*. Florence.

Garrido, R. M. (1991) 'Lectura alfonsí de las *Heroidas* de Ovidio', *Revista Canadiense de Estudios Hispánicos* 15.3: 385–400.

Garrod, H. W. and J. R. L. Highfield. (1978) 'An indenture between William Rede, bishop of Chichester, and John Bloxham and Henry Stapilton, fellows of Merton College, Oxford', *Bodleian Library Record* 10: 9–19.

Gärtner, U. (2005) *Quintus Smyrnaeus und die Aeneis: Zur Nachwirkung Vergils in der griechischen Literatur der Kaiserzeit*. Munich.

Gasca Queirazza, G. (1966) *Documenti di antico volgare in Piemonte*. Fascicolo III: *Frammenti vari da una miscellanea grammaticale di Biella*. Turin.

(1977) 'Le glosse al Dottrinale di Mayfredo di Belmont', *Studi piemontesi* 6.1: 108–11.

Gatti Perer, M. L. (ed.) (1989) *Codici e incunaboli miniati della Biblioteca civica di Bergamo*. Bergamo.

Gehl, P. (1993) *A Moral Art: Grammar, Society, and Culture in Trecento Florence*. Ithaca, NY.

Geiger, J. (1999) 'Some Latin authors from the Greek east', *CQ* 49: 606–17.

Gersh, S. (1982) 'A twelfth-century metaphysical system and its sources', in *Renaissance and Renewal in the Twelfth Century*, ed. R. L. Benson, G. Constable and C. D. Lanham. Cambridge, MA. 512–33.

Gherardi, A. (1881) *Statuti della università e Studio fiorentino*. Florence.

Ghisalberti, F. (1932) 'L'enigma delle Naidi', *Studi danteschi* 16: 105–25.

(1934) 'La quadriga del sole nel Convivio', *Studi danteschi* 18: 69–77.

(1946) 'Mediaeval biographies of Ovid', *JWI* 9: 10–59.

(1966) 'Il commentario medioevale all'*Ovidius maior* consultato da Dante,' *Recondita Istituto Lombardo di scienze e lettere, classe di lettere e scienze morali e politiche* 100: 267–75.

Gillespie, V. (2005) 'From the twelfth century to c. 1450', in *The Cambridge History of Literary Criticism*, vol. II: *The Middle Ages*, ed. A. Minnis and I. Johnson. Cambridge: 145–235.

Ginsberg, W. (1983) *The Cast of Character*. Toronto.

(1989) 'Ovid and the Problem of Gender', in *Ovid in Medieval Culture*, special issue of *Mediaevalia*, ed. M. Desmond, 13: 9–28.

(1998) 'Ovidius ethicus?: Ovid and the medieval commentary tradition,' in *Desiring Discourse: The Literature of Love, Ovid through Chaucer*, ed. J. Paxson and C. Gravlee. Selinsgrove, PA: 62–71.

(1999) *Dante's Aesthetics of Being*. Ann Arbor, MI.

(2002) *Chaucer's Italian Tradition*. Ann Arbor, MI.

Ginzler, J. R. (1987) *The Role of Ovid's 'Metamorphoses' in the 'General Estoria' of Alfonso el Sabio*. Michigan.

Glendenning, R. (1986) 'Pyramus and Thisbe in the medieval classroom', *Speculum* 61: 51–78.

Godman, P. (1985) *Latin Poetry of the Carolingian Renaissance*. Norman, OK.

  (1995) 'Ovid's sex-life: Classical forgery and medieval poetry', *Poetica* 27: 101–8.

Goering, J. (ed.) (1992) *William de Montibus (c. 1140–1213): The Schools and the Literature of Pastoral Care*. Toronto.

Gómez Redondo, F. (1998–2007) *Historia de la prosa medieval castellana* (4 vols.). Madrid.

González Rolán, T. and A. López Fonseca. (2002) *La tradición clásica en España (siglos XIII–XV): Bases conceptuales y bibliográficas*. Madrid.

González Rolán, T. and P. Saquero Suárez-Somonte (1984) 'Las cartas originales de Juan Rodríguez del Padrón', *Dicenda* 3: 39–72.

Gordan, P. W. G. (1974) *Two Renaissance Book Hunters: The Letters of Poggius Bracciolini to Nicolaus de Niccolis*. New York.

Grafton, A. (1985) 'Renaissance readers and ancient texts: Comments on some commentaries', *Renaissance Quarterly*: 38.4: 615–49.

  (1990) *Forgers and Critics: Creativity and Duplicity in Western Scholarship*. Princeton, NJ.

  (1994) 'The scholarship of Poliziano and its context', in A. Grafton, *Defenders of the Text: Traditions of Scholarship in an Age of Science, 1450–1800*. Cambridge, MA: 47–75.

Gransden, A. (1972) 'Realistic observation in twelfth-century England', *Speculum* 47: 29–51.

  (1998) 'Some manuscripts in Cambridge from Bury St Edmunds Abbey: Exhibition catalogue', in *Bury St Edmunds: Medieval Art, Architecture, Archaeology, and Economy*, ed. A. Gransden. British Archaeological Association Conference Transactions 20. Leeds: 228–85.

Greatrex, J. (1990) 'Benedictine monk scholars as teachers and preachers in the later Middle Ages: Evidence from Worcester Cathedral Priory', *Monastic Studies* 2: 213–25.

  (1991) 'Monk students from Norwich Cathedral Priory at Oxford and Cambridge, c.1300 to 1530', *English Historical Review* 106: 555–83.

  (1994) 'English cathedral priories and the pursuit of learning in the later Middle Ages', *Journal of Ecclesiastical History* 45: 396–411.

Green, O. H. (1950) '"Fingen los poetas": Notes on the Spanish attitude toward pagan mythology', *Estudios dedicados a Menéndez Pidal*, vol. 1. Madrid: 75–88.

Greene, R. L. (ed.) (1977) *Early English Carols*, 2nd edn. Oxford.

Gudeman, A. (1888) *De Heroidum Ovidii codice Planudeo*. Berlin.

Guernelli, D. (2007) 'Nicolò di Giacomo: due ulteriori codici', *Rara volumina* 14: 13–21.

Habinek, T. (1977) 'The invention of sexuality in the world-city of Rome', in *The Roman Cultural Revolution*, ed. T. Habinek and A. Schiesaro. Cambridge: 30–1.

Haefner, A. (1934) 'A unique source for the study of ancient pseudonymity', *Anglican Theological Review* 16: 8–15.

Hagedorn, S. C. (2004) *Abandoned Women: Rewriting the Classics in Dante, Boccaccio, and Chaucer*. Ann Arbor, MI.

Hallett, J. P. and M. B. Skinner (eds.) (1997) *Roman Sexualities*. Princeton.

Hamacher, J. (1975) *Florilegium Gallicum: Prolegomena und Edition der Excerpte von Petron bis Cicero, De oratore*. Bern.

Hankey, A. T. (1963) 'Domenico di Bandino', *Dizionario biografico degli italiani*, vol. v. Rome: 707–9.

Hankins, J. (1992) 'Cosimo de' Medici as a patron of humanistic literature', in *Cosimo 'il vecchio' de' Medici, 1389–1464*, ed. F. Ames-Lewis. Oxford: 69–94.

Hanna, R. (2002) *A Descriptive Catalogue of the Western Medieval Manuscripts of St John's College, Oxford, Using Material Collected by the Late Jeremy Griffiths*. Oxford.

Hanna, R. and T. Lawler (eds.) (1997) *Jankyn's Book of Wikked Wyves*. Athens, GA.

Harbert, B. (1988) 'Lessons from the great clerk: Ovid and John Gower', in *Ovid Renewed: Ovidian Influences on Literature and Art from the Middle Ages to the Twentieth Century*, ed. C. A. Martindale. Cambridge: 83–97.

Hardie, P. (ed.) (2002) *The Cambridge Companion to Ovid*. Cambridge.

Harf-Lancner, L. (1985) 'La métamorphose illusoire: des théories chrétiennes de la métamorphose aux images médiévales du loup-garou', *Annales. Économies, Societés, Civilisations* 1: 208–26.

Haskins, C. H. (1924) *Studies in the History of Medieval Science*. New York.

Hauréau, B. (1879) 'Notice sur les oeuvres authentiques ou supposées de Jean de Garlande', *Notices et Extraits des manuscrits de la Bibliothèque nationale et autres bibliothèques* 27: 1–86.

   (1885) 'Additions et corrections', *Histoire littéraire de la France*. Paris.

Haywood, I. (1987) *Faking It: Art and the Politics of Forgery*. New York.

Hearne, T. (ed.) (1715) *Joannis Lelandi antiquarii De rebvs Britannicis collectanea* (6 vols. in 4). Oxford.

Herman, P. C. (1991) 'Treason in the *Manciple's Tale*,' *Chaucer Review* 25: 318–28.

Hermann, H. J. (1929) *Beschreibendes verzeichnis der illuminiertern Handschriften in Österreich*, new series, *Die Italienischen Handschriften des Duecento und Trecento bis zur Mitte des XIV Jahrhunderts*. Vol. VIII, part 5. Leipzig.

Herren, M. (2004) 'Manegold of Lautenbach's scholia on the *Metamorphoses*: Are there more?', *Notes and Queries* 51: 218–23.

Hexter, R. (1986) *Ovid and Medieval Schooling: Studies in Medieval School Commentaries on Ovid's 'Ars Amatoria', 'Epistulae ex Ponto', and 'Epistulae Heroidum'*. Munich.

   (1987) 'Medieval articulations of Ovid's *Metamorphoses*: From Lactantian segmentation to Arnulfian allegory', *Mediaevalia* 13: 63–82.

   (1989) 'The *Allegari* of Pierre Bersuire: Interpretation and the *Reductorium morale*', *Allegorica* 10: 51–84.

(1999a) 'A visit to the museum: The Ovid Galleries', *The International Journal of the Classical Tradition* 6: 75–88.

(1999b) 'Ovid's Body', in *Constructions of the Classical Body*, ed. J. Porter. Ann Arbor, MI: 327–54.

(2002a) 'Narrative and an absolutely fabulous commentary on Ovid's *Heroides*', in *Latin Grammar and Rhetoric from Classical Theory to Medieval Practice*, ed. C. D. Lanham. London: 212–38.

(2002b) 'Ovid in the Middle Ages: Exile, mythographer and lover', in *Brill's Companion to Ovid*, ed. B. W. Boyd. Leiden: 413–42.

(2006) 'Sex education: Ovidian erotodidactic in the classroom', in *The Art of Love: Bimillennial Essays on Ovid's 'Ars amatoria' and 'Remedia amoris'*. Oxford: 298–317.

(2007a) 'Ovid and the medieval exilic imaginary', in *Writing Exile: The Discourse of Displacement in Greco-Roman Antiquity and Beyond*, ed. J. F. Gaertner. Leiden: 209–36.

(2007b) 'Ovid in translation in medieval Europe,' in *Übersetzung Translation/ Traduction*, vol. II, eds. H. Kittel, J. House and B. Schultz. Berlin and New York: 1311–28.

Highet, G. (1949) *The Classical Tradition: Greek and Roman Influences on Western Literature*. New York and London.

  (1978) *La tradición clásica: Influencias griegas y romanas en la literatura occidental*, tr. A. Alatorre (2 vols.). Mexico.

Hinz, V. (2006) 'Kann denn Liebe Sünde sein? Kleriker im Gefolge der Venus beim mittelalterlichen Ovid', *Mittellateinisches Jahrbuch* 41: 35–52.

Hiscoe, D. (1985) 'The Ovidian comic strategy of Gower's *Confessio Amantis*', *Philological Quarterly* 64: 367–85.

Hoffman, R. L. (1966) *Ovid and the Canterbury Tales*. Philadelphia.

Holsinger, B. and D. Townsend. (2000) 'The Ovidian verse epistles of Master Leoninus (1135–1201)', *Journal of Medieval Latin* 10: 239–54.

Holzberg, N. (2002) *Ovid: The Poet and His Work*, tr. G. M. Goshgarian. Ithaca, NY.

  (ed.) (2005) *Die Appendix Vergiliana: Pseudepigraphen im literarischen Kontext*. Classica Monacensia 30. Munich.

Horgan, F. (1994) *The Romance of the Rose*. Oxford.

Horner, P. J. FSC. (1977) 'John Paunteley's sermon at the funeral of Walter Froucester Abbot of Gloucester (1412)', *American Benedictine Review* 28: 147–66.

Humphreys, K. W. (1990) *The Friars' Libraries*, Corpus of British Medieval Library Catalogues, I. London.

Hunt, R. W. (1948) 'The introductions to the *Artes* in the twelfth century', *Studia Mediaevalia in Honorem R. J. Martin, O.P.* Bruges: 85–112.

  (1950) 'Studies on Priscian in the twelfth century, II,' *Medieval and Renaissance Studies* 2: 1–56.

Impey, O. T. (1980a) 'Un dechado de la prosa literaria alfonsí: el relato cronístico de los amores de Dido', *RPh* 34: 1–27.

(1980b) 'Ovid, Alfonso X, and Juan Rodríguez del Padrón: Two Castilian translations of the *Heroidas* and the beginnings of Spanish sentimental prose', *Bulletin of Hispanic Studies* 57: 283–97.

Irmscher, J. (1974) 'Ovid in Byzanz', *Byzantinoslavica* 35: 28–33.

Jacoff, R. and J. T. Schnapp. (eds.) (1991) *The Poetry of Allusion: Vergil and Ovid in Dante's 'Commedia'*. Stanford.

Jaitner-Hahner, U. (1993) 'Die öffentliche Schule in Città di Castello vom 14. Jahrhundert bis zur Ankunft der Jesuiten 1610', *Quellen und Forschungen aus italienischen Archiven und Bibliotheken* 73: 179–302.

James, M. R. (1903) *Ancient Libraries of Canterbury and Dover: The Catalogues of the Libraries of Christ Church Priory and St Augustine's Abbey Canterbury and of St Martin's Priory at Dover*. Cambridge.

(1913) 'Ovidius de Mirabilibus mundi', in *Essays and Studies Presented to William Ridgeway on his Sixtieth Birthday*, ed. E. C. Quiggin. Cambridge: 286–98.

Jeauneau, E. (1957) 'L'usage de la notion d'*integumentum* à travers les gloses de Guillaume de Conches', *Archives d'histoire doctrinale et littéraire du moyen âge* 32: 35–100.

Jordan, M. D. (1996) *The Invention of Sodomy*. Chicago.

Jung, M.-R. (1994) 'Aspects de l'*Ovide moralisé*', in *Ovidius redivivus: von Ovid zu Dante*, eds. M. Picone and B. Zimmermann. Stuttgart: 149–72.

(1996a) 'Les éditions manuscrites de l'*Ovide moralisé*', *Cahiers d'histoire des littératures romanes* 20.3/4: 251–74.

(1996b) 'Ovide, texte, translateur et gloses dans les manuscrits de l'*Ovide moralisé*', in *The Medieval Opus: Imitation, Rewriting, and Transmission in the French Tradition* (proceedings of the symposium held at the Institute for Research in the Humanities, 5–7 October 1995, University of Wisconsin-Madison), ed. D. Kelly. Amsterdam: 75–98.

(1997) 'Ovide Métamorphosé en prose (Bruges, vers 1475)', *Les Lettres Romanes*: 99–115.

Kazhdan, A. P. (2001) 'Latins and Franks in Byzantium: Perception and reality from the 11th to the 12th century', in *The Crusades from the Perspective of the Byzantine and the Muslim World*, ed. A. E. Laiou and R. Mottahedeh. Washington: 83–100.

Keith, A. (2002) 'Ovidian personae in Statius' *Thebaid*', in *The Reception of Ovid in Antiquity*, ed. G. Tissol and S. Wheeler, special issue of *Arethusa* 35: 3: 381–402.

Keith, A. and S. Rupp (2007) *Metamorphosis: The Changing Face of Ovid in Medieval and Early Modern Europe*. Toronto.

Kellogg, J. (1998) 'Transforming Ovid: The metamorphosis of female authority', in *Christine de Pizan and the Categories of Difference*, ed. M. Desmond. Minneapolis and London: 181–94.

Kelly, D. (2002) *Chrétien de Troyes: An Analytical Bibliography*. London.

Kenney, E. J. (1962) 'The manuscript tradition of Ovid's *Amores, Ars Amatoria* and *Remedia amoris*', *CQ* 12: 1–31.

(1963) 'A byzantine version of Ovid,' *Hermes* 91: 213–27.

(1976) 'Ovidius proemians,' *Proceedings of the Combridge Philological Society* 22: 46–53.

(1986) 'Explanatory notes', in Ovid's *Metamorphoses*, tr. A. D. Melville. Oxford.

(1996) (ed.) *Heroides, xvi–xxi.* Cambridge and New York.

Kensak, M. (1999) 'The silences of pilgrimage: Manciple's Tale, *Paradiso, Anti-claudianus*,' *Chaucer Review* 34: 190–206.

Ker, N. R. (1949) 'Medieval manuscripts from Norwich cathedral priory', *Transactions of the Cambridge Bibliographical Society* 1: 1–28.

Ker, N. R., A. G. Watson, I. C. Cunningham and A. J. Piper (eds.) (1969–2002) *Medieval Manuscripts in British Libraries* (5 vols.). Oxford.

Kerby-Fulton, K. (2005) *Books under Suspicion: Censorship and Tolerance of Revelatory Writing in Late Medieval England.* Notre Dame.

Kerby-Fulton, K. and S. Justice. (1997) 'Langlandian reading circles and the civil service in London and Dublin, 1380–1427', *New Medieval Literatures* 1: 59–84.

Keydell, R. (1961) 'Vian, Les *Posthomerica de Quintus de Smyrne*', *Gnomon* 33: 278–83.

Kienast, R. (1929) 'Antiovidianus', in *Aus Petrarcas ältesten deutschen Schülerkreise*, ed. K. Burdach. Berlin.

Kirfel, E.-A. (1969) *Untersuchungen zur Briefform der Heroides Ovids.* Noctes Romanae, Forschungen über die Kultur der Antike 11. Bern and Stuttgart.

Kiser, L. J. (1983) *Telling Classical Tales: Chaucer and the Legend of Good Women.* Ithaca, NY.

Klein, H.-W. (1978) 'Anonymi "Doctrina Mense"', *MLatJb* 13: 184–200.

(1973) 'Carmen de philomela,' in *Literatur und Sprache im europäischen Mittelalter: Festschrift für Karl Langosch zum 70. Geburtstag*, ed. A. Önnerfors, J. Rathofer and F. Wagner. Darmstadt: 173–94.

Kneepkens, C. H. (1991) *Ralph of Beauvais: Liber Tytan.* Nijmegen.

Knorr, W. R. (2004) 'London, John of (*fl. c.*1260)', *Oxford Dictionary of National Biography*, Oxford, 14853.

Knox, P. E. (1988) 'Phaethon in Ovid and Nonnus', *CQ* 38: 536–51.

(2002) 'Ovid's *Heroides*: Elegiac voices', in *Brill's Companion to Ovid*, ed. B. W. Boyd. Leiden: 117–39.

(ed.) (2006) *Oxford Readings in Ovid.* Oxford.

(2009a) 'Commenting on Ovid', in *A Companion to Ovid*, ed. P. E. Knox. Malden, MA and Oxford: 327–54.

(2009b) 'Lost and Spurious Works', in *A Companion to Ovid*, ed. P. E. Knox. Malden, MA and Oxford: 207–18.

Koble, N. (2002) 'Les dieux d'Ovide dans un manuscrit du xve siècle de l'*Ovide moralisé* en vers (Copenhague Kongelige Bibliotek, Thott 399)', *Cahiers de recherches médiévales (xiiie–xve siècles)* 9: 157–75.

Kruger, S. (1992) *Dreaming in the Middle Ages.* Cambridge.

Labande, E.-R. (1981) *Les classiques de l'Histoire de France au Moyen Âge.* Paris.

Lamoureaux, J. (1963) 'A propos de fragments d'Ovide traduit en grec', *Revue des études grecques* 76: 206–9.

Langosch, K. (ed.) (1942) *Das 'Registrum Multorum Auctorum' des Hugo von Trimberg: Untersuchungen und kommentierte Textausgabe.* Germanische Studien 235. Berlin.
Lapesa, R. (1988) 'Sobre el mito de Narciso en la lírica medieval y renacentista', *Epos* 4: 9–20.
Lapidge, M. (2006) *The Anglo-Saxon Library.* Oxford.
Lebek, W. D. (1978) 'Love in the cloister: A Pseudo-Ovidian metamorphosis (altera sed nostris eqs.)', *California Studies in Classical Antiquity* 11: 109–25.
Léchat, D. (2002) 'Héro et Léandre', *Cahiers de recherches médiévales (xiiie–xve siècles)* 9: 25–37.
Leclercq, J. OSB (1982) *The Love of Learning and the Desire for God: A Study of Monastic Culture,* tr. C. Misrahi, 3rd edn. New York.
Lehmann, P. (1927) *Pseudo-antike Literatur des Mittelalters,* Studien der Bibliothek Warburg 13. Berlin and Leipzig.
  (1935) 'Skandinavische Reisefrüchte', *Nordiskstidskrift för bok- och biblioteksväsen* 22: 103–31.
  (1963) *Die Parodie im Mittelalter,* 2nd edn. Stuttgart.
Le Minor, J.-M. (2002) *Catalogue de la Bibliothèque ancienne du Mont-Sainte-Odile: Incunables, Seizième, Dix-Septième Siècles.* Baden-Baden.
Lenz, F. W. (1955) '[P. Ovidii Nasonis] De Pediculo Libellus', *Eranos* 53: 61–74.
  (1956) *P. Ovidii Nasonis Halieutica – Fragmenta – Nux. Incerti Consolatio ad Liviam,* 2nd edn. Turin.
  (1957) 'Das pseudo-ovidische Gedicht De Lombardo et lumaca', *Maia* n.s. 3.9: 204–22.
  (1958) 'Das Gedicht *De medicamine avrivm*', in *Ovidiana: Recherches sur Ovide. Publiées à l'occasion du bimillénaire de la naissance du poète,* ed. N. Herescu. Paris: 526–40.
  (1959a) 'Einführende Bemerkungen zu den Pseudo-Ovidiana', *Altertum* 5: 171–82.
  (1959b) 'Das pseudo-ovidische Gedicht *De ventre*', *Maia* n.s. 3.11: 169–211.
  (1962) 'De pulice libellus', *Maia* n.s. 14: 299–333.
  (1968) 'Das pseudo-ovidische Gedicht "De sompnio"', *MLatJb* 5: 101–14.
Lepage, Y. (ed.) (1981) *L'Oeuvre lyrique de Richard de Fournival.* Publications médiévales de l'Université d'Ottawa. Ottawa Mediaeval Texts and Studies 7. Ottawa.
Levine, R. (1989) 'Exploiting Ovid', *Medioevo romanzo* 14: 197–221.
Levy, B. J. (2004) 'Cheriton, Odo of (1180s–1246)', in *Oxford Dictionary of National Biography.* Oxford
Librán Moreno, M. (1996) 'Colación de Dertusensis 134 (Ov. Metamorphoseon libri xv) I', *Exemplaria* 10: 83–111.
  (1997) 'Colación de Dertusensis 134 (Ov. Metamorphoseon libri xv) (ii)', *Exemplaria* 11: 83–103.
Lida de Malkiel, M. R. (1950) *Juan de Mena, poeta del prerrenacimiento español.* Mexico.
  (1958–9) 'La *General Estoria*: notas literarias y filológicas (i)', *RPh* 12: 111–42.

(1959–60) 'La *General Estoria*: notas literarias y filológicas (II)', *RPh* 13: 1–30.

(1962) *La originalidad artística de La Celestina*. Buenos Aires.

(1973) *Juan Ruiz*. Buenos Aires.

(1974) *Dido en la literatura española*. London.

(1975) *La tradición clásica en España*. Barcelona.

(1977) *Estudios sobre la literatura española del siglo* XV. Madrid.

Liebeschütz, H. (1926) *Fulgentius metaforalis: ein Beitrag zur Geschichte der antiken Mythologie im Mittelalter*, Studien der Bibliothek Warburg. Leipzig and Berlin.

Lobera, F. J.-Serés, G., *et al.* (eds.) (2000) *Fernando de Rojas ('y antiguo autor'), La Celestina*. Barcelona.

López de Bascuñana, I. (1977) 'El mundo y la cultura grecorromana en la obra del Marqués de Santillana', *Revista de Archivos, Bibliotecas y Museos* 80: 271–320.

(1978) 'La mitología en la obra del Marqués de Santillana,' *Boletín de la Biblioteca Menéndez Pelayo* 54: 297–330.

Lord, C. (1975) 'Three manuscripts of the *Ovide moralisé*'. *The Art Bulletin* 57: 161–75.

(1985) 'The *Ovide moralisé* and the Old Testament', in *Tribute to Lotte Brand Philip*, ed. W. W. Clark and C. Eisler. New York: 95–102.

(1995) 'Illustrated manuscripts of Berchorius before the age of printing', in *Die Rezeption der Metamorphosen des Ovid in der Neuzeit*, ed. H. Walter and H.-J. Horn. Berlin: 1–11.

(1998) 'Marks of ownership in medieval manuscripts: The case of the Rouen *Ovide moralisé*', *Source; notes on the history of art* 18: 7 –11.

Lowe, E. A. (1947) *Codices Latini Antiquiores: A Palaeographical Guide to Latin Manuscripts Prior to the Ninth Century*, part IV: Italy, Perugia-Verona. Oxford.

Lowes, J. L. (1918) 'Chaucer and the *Ovide Moralisé*', *PMLA* 33: 302–25.

Lubac, H. de (1954–64) *Exégèse médiévale: les quatre sens de l'Ecriture*. Paris.

Lucas, R. (1970) 'Mediaeval French translations of the Latin classics to 1500', *Speculum* 45: 241–2.

Luscombe, D. (2001) 'Peter Abelard and the Poets', in *Poetry and Philosophy in the Middle Ages: A Festschrift for Peter Dronke*, ed. J. Marenbon. Leiden: 155–71.

Lusignan, S. (1986) *Parler vulgairement: les intellectuels et la langue française aux* XIIIe *et* XIVe *siècles*. Montreal.

Lusignan, S., M. Paulmier-Foucart and M.-C. Duchenne (eds.) (1997) *Lector et Compilator. Vincent de Beauvais, Frère prêcheur: Un intellectual et son milieu au xiiie siècle*. Grâne.

Magistrale, F. (1998) 'L'Ovidio Napoletano: il libro e il testo', in *L'Ovidio Napoletano*, ed. G. Cavallo, P. Fedeli and G. Papporetti, text volume. Sulmona: 41–101.

Mainzer, C. (1972) 'John Gower's use of the "mediaeval Ovid" in the *Confessio Amantis*', *MAev* 41: 215–29.

Manitius, M. (1899) 'Beiträge zur Geschichte des Ovidius im Mittelalter', *Philologus* supp. 7: 723–68.

(1911–1931) *Geschichte der lateinischen Literatur des Mittelalters* (3 vols.). Handbuch der Altertumswissenschaften 9, 1–3. Heidelberg.

Marchesi, C. (1909) 'Le *Allegorie* ovidiane di Giovanni del Virgilio', *Studi romanzi* 6: 85–135.

Marguin-Hamon, E. (2006) 'Tradition manuscrite de l'oeuvre de Jean de Garlande', *Revue d'histoire des textes*, n.s. 1: 189–257.

Marshall, M. H. (1939) 'Thirteenth-century culture as illustrated by Matthew Paris', *Speculum* 14: 465–77.

Martín Fernández, M. A. (1985) *Juan de Mena y el Renacimiento: estudio de la mitología en su obra menor.* Cordóba.

Martinelli, L. C. (1991) 'Sozomeno maestro e filologo', *Interpres* 11: 7–92.

Martindale, C. (ed.) (1988) *Ovid Renewed: Ovidian Influences on Literature and Art from the Middle Ages to the Twentieth Century.* Cambridge.

Martins, M. (1983) 'A racionaliçâo crista de Ovídio na General estoria e no Libro da montaria', *Estudios de cultura medieval*, vol. III. Lisbon: 119–31.

Martos, J. Ll. (ed.) (2001) *Les proses mitològiques de Joan Roís de Corella.* Barcelona.

Mattia, E. (1990–1) 'Due Ovidio illustrati di scuola bolognese', Società di storia della miniatura, Florence, *Miniatura* 3/4: 63–73.

(1996–7) 'L'Illustrazione della "Metamorfosi" di Ovidio nel codice Panciatichi 63 della Biblioteca nazionale di Firenze', *Rivista di storia della miniatura* 1–2: 45–54.

McGill, S. (2005) *Virgil Recomposed: The Mythological and Secular Centos in Antiquity.* Oxford.

McGowan, M. (2005) 'Ovid and Poliziano in exile', *International Journal of the Classical Tradition* 12.1: 25–45 at 38.

McGregor, J. H. (1978) 'Ovid at school: From the ninth to the fifteenth century', *Classical Folio* 32: 29–51.

McHam, S. B. (2005) 'Renaissance monuments to favourite sons', *Renaissance Studies* 19: 458–86.

McKinley, K. L. (1996a) 'Kingship and the body politic: Classical *ecphrasis* and *Confessio Amantis* VII.' *Mediaevalia* 21: 167–93.

(1996b) 'The medieval commentary tradition 1100–1500 on *Metamorphoses 10*', *Viator* 27: 117–49.

(1996c) 'The silenced knight: Questions of power and reciprocity in the Wife of Bath's Tale,' *The Chaucer Review* 30: 40–59.

(1998) 'Manuscripts of Ovid in England, 1100–1500', *English Manuscript Studies, 1100–1700* 7: 41–86.

(2001) *Reading the Ovidian Heroine: 'Metamorphoses' Commentaries 1100–1618.* Leiden.

(2007) 'Lessons for a King from Gower's *Confessio Amantis 5*', in *Metamorphosis: The Changing Face of Ovid in Medieval and Early Modern Europe*, ed. A. Keith and S. Rupp. Toronto: 107–28.

(2008) 'The view from the tower: Revisiting Gower, 1381, and *Vox Clamantis* Book 1', *Mediaevalia* 29: 31–52.

(2011) '*Ekphrasis* as aesthetic pilgrimage in Chaucer's *House of Fame* Book 1', in *Meaning in Motion: Semantics of Movement in Medieval Art*, ed. N. Zchomelidse and G. Freni. Princeton, 215–32.

McLaughlin, M. (1995) *Literary Imitation in the Italian Renaissance: The Theory and Practice of Literary Imitation in Italy from Dante to Bembo*. Oxford.

McLeod, W. (1980) 'Alban and Amphibal: Some extant lives and a lost life', *Mediaeval Studies* 42: 407–30.

McNelis, C. (2009) 'Ovidian strategies in early imperial literature', in *A Companion to Ovid*, ed. P. E. Knox. Oxford: 397–410.

Medica, M. (1999) *Haec sunt Statuta: le corporazioni medievali nelle miniature Bolognesi*. Modena.

Mecklenborg, C. and B. Scheider (2002) *Odyssea: Responsio Ulixis ad Penelopen: die humanistische Odyssea decurtata der Berliner Handschrift Diez. B Sant. 41*. Munich.

Meech, S. B. (1930) 'Chaucer and an Italian translation of the *Heroides*', *PMLA* 45: 110–28.

(1931) 'Chaucer and the *Ovide Moralisé*: A further study,' *PMLA* 46: 182–204.

Meiser, C. (1885) 'Über einen Commentar zu den Metamorphosen des Ovid', in *Sitzungsberichte der Königlichen bayerischen Akademie der Wissenschaften, philosophisch-philologisch- und historische Classe*. Munich: 47–89.

Menéndez Pidal, R. (ed.) (1934) *Historia Troyana en prosa y verso*. Madrid.

Menéndez Pidal, R. and D. Catalán (eds.) (1977) *Primera crónica general de España* (2 vols.). Madrid.

Mews, C. J. (2001) *The Lost Love Letters of Heloise and Abelard: Perceptions of Dialogue in Twelfth-Century France*. Basingstoke.

Meyer, P. (1885) 'Les premières compilations Françaises d'histoire ancienne', *Romania* 54: 1–81.

Michalopoulos, A. N. (2003) 'Ovid in Greek: Maximus Planudes' translation of the double *Heroides*', *Classica et Mediaevalia* 54: 359–74.

Miller, J. M., M. H. Prosser and T. W. Benson (eds.) (1973) *Readings in Medieval Rhetoric*. Bloomington.

Minnis, A. J. (1979) 'A note on Chaucer and the *Ovide moralisé*', *MAev* 48: 254–7.

(1982) *Chaucer and Pagan Antiquity*. Cambridge.

(1988) *Medieval Theory of Authorship: Scholastic Literary Attitudes in the later Middle Ages*, 2nd edn. Philadelphia.

(2001) *Magister Amoris: The 'Roman de la Rose' and Vernacular Hermeneutics*. New York.

Minnis, A. J. and I. Johnson (eds.) (2005) *The Cambridge History of Literary Criticism*, vol. II: *The Middle Ages*. Cambridge.

Minnis, A. J. and A. B. Scott (with the assistance of D. Wallace) (eds.) (1991) *Medieval Literary Theory and Criticism c. 1100 – c. 1375: The Commentary Tradition*. Oxford.

Mish, F. (1973) The influence of Ovid on John Gower's *Vox Clamantis*. PhD diss. University of Minnesota.

Moisan, J.-C. and M.-C. Malenfant (eds.) (1997) *Les trois premiers livres de la 'Métamorphose' d'Ovid*. Paris.

Monfrin, J. (1972) 'La connaissance de l'antiquité et le problème de l'humanisme en langue vulgaire dans France du xve siècle,' in *The Late Middle Ages and the Dawn of Humanism Outside Italy: Proceedings of the International Conference, Louvian May 11–13, 1970*, ed. J. Ijsewijn and G. Verbeke. Leuven: 134–6.

Monteverdi, A. (1958) 'Aneddoti per la storia della fortuna di Ovidio nel medio evo', in *Atti del Convegno internazionale Ovidiano. Sulmona, Maggio 1958*, vol. II. Rome: 181–92.

   (1962) 'Arrigo da Settimello', in *Dizionario Biografico degli italiani*, vol. IV. Rome: 315.

Moog-Grünewald, M. (ed.) (1979) *Metamorphosen der 'Metamorphosen': Rezeptionsarten der ovidischen Verwandlungsgeschichten in Italien und Frankreich im 16 und 17 Jahrhundert*. Heidelberg.

Mora, F. (2002) 'Deux réceptions des *Métamorphoses* au xive et au xve siècles: quelques remarques sur le traitement de la fable et de son exégèse dans l'*Ovide Moralisé* en vers et sa première mise en prose', *Cahiers de recherches médiévales xiiie–xve siècles* 9: 83–98.

Moralejo, J. L. (ed.) (1986) *Cancionero de Ripoll: Carmina Riuipullensia*, with. intr., tr. and notes. Barcelona.

Morel-Fatio, A. (1985) 'Recherches sur le texte et les sources du Libro de Alexandre', *Romania* 4: 7–90.

Morreale, M. (1954) 'Los doze trabajos de Hércules de Enrique de Villena: un ensayo medieval de exégesis mitológica', *Rev. de Literatura* 5: 21–34.

Morris, C. (1972) *The Discovery of the Individual, 1050–1200*. London.

Moss, A. (1982) *Ovid in Renaissance France*. London.

   (1984) *Poetry and Fable: Studies in Mythological Narrative in Sixteenth-Century France*. Cambridge.

   (1998) *Latin Commentaries on Ovid from the Renaissance*. Signal Mountain, TN.

   (2003) *Renaissance Truth and the Latin Language Turn*. Oxford.

Mozley, J. H. (1938) 'Le "De Vetula": Poème pseudo-Ovidien', *Latomus* 2: 53–72.

Müller, C. W. (1969) 'Die neuplatonischen Aristoteleskommentatoren über die Ursachen der Pseudepigraphie', *Rheinisches Museum für Philologie* 112: 120–6.

Müller, H. W. H. (1906) *De Metamorphoseon Ovidii codice Planude dissertatio inauguralis*. Griefswald.

Mulligan, B. (2005) 'An allusion to Ovid in Claudian's *Carmina minora* xxii.56', *Classical Philology* 100: 277–80.

Munari, F. (1957) *Catalogue of the MSS of Ovid's 'Metamorphoses'*. London.

   (1960) *Ovid im Mittelalter*. Zurich.

Munk Olsen, B. (1982–9) *L'étude des auteurs classiques latins au xie et xiie siècles*. Paris.

   (1991) *I Classici nel Canone Scolastico Altomedievale*. Spoleto.

   (1995) 'Les poètes classiques dans les écoles au ixe siècles', in *La Réception de la littérature classique au Moyen Age (ixe-xiie siècle): Choix d'articles publié par des collègues à l'occasion de son soixantième anniversaire*, ed. B. Munk Olsen. Copenhagen: 35–46.

Munzi, L. (1990) 'Una inedita *Summa memorialis* delle *Metamorfosi* ovidiane', in *Dicti studiosus: scritti di filologia offerti a Scevola Mariotti dai suoi allievi.* Urbino: 329–85.

Murphy, J. J. M. (1974) *Rhetoric in the Middle Ages: A History of Rhetorical Theory from Saint Augustine to the Renaissance.* Berkeley.

Murray, H. (1913) *The History of Chess.* Oxford.

Mynors, R. A. B. (1957) 'The Latin classics known to Boston of Bury', in *Fritz Saxl, 1890–1948: A Volume of Memorial Essays from his Friends in England*, ed. D. J. Gordon. London: 199–217.

   (1963) *A Descriptive Catalogue of the Manuscripts of Balliol College, Oxford.* Oxford.

Mynors, R. A. B., D. F. S. Thomson and A. Dalzell (eds.) (1974–) *The Correspondence of Erasmus* (12 vols.). Toronto and London.

Newhauser, R. (2000) 'The Parson's Tale and its generic affiliations', in *Closure in 'The Canterbury Tales'*, eds. D. Raybin and L. T. Holley. Kalamazoo, MI: 45–76.

   (2002) 'The Parson's Tale', in *Sources and Analogues of The Canterbury Tales*, I, eds. R. M. Correale and M. Hamel. Cambridge: 529–613.

Newlands, C. (1986) 'The simile of the fractured water-pipe in Ovid's *Metamorphoses* IV', *Ramus* 15: 143–53.

Newton, F. (1999) *The Scriptorium and Library at Montecassino, 1058–1105.* New York and Cambridge.

Nikitas, D. Z. (ed.) (1990) *Boethius, De topicis differentiis kai hoi Vyzantines metaphraseis ton Manouel Holovolou kai Prochorou Kydone.* Athens.

   (1999) '*Ovidius Allegoricus*: die neugriechische Übersetzung der *Metamorphosen* durch Spyridon Blantzes (1798)', in *Ovid: Werk und Wirkung: Festgabe für Michael von Albrecht zum 65. Geburtstag*, vol. II, ed. W. Schubert. Frankfurt am Main: 1005–19.

Nogara, B. (1910) 'Di alcune vite e commenti medioevali di Ovidio', in *Miscellanea Ceriani: raccolta di scritti originali per onorare la memoria di Mᵉ Antonio Maria Ceriani prefetto della Biblioteca Ambrosiana.* Milan: 413–31.

   (ed.) (1912) *Codices vaticani latini*, vol. III. Vatican City.

Nolan, B. (1989) 'Ovid's *Heroides* contextualized: Foolish love and legitimate marriage in the *Roman d'Eneas*', in *Ovid in Medieval Culture*, special issue of *Mediaevalia*, ed. M. Desmond, 13: 157–88.

Nolan, M. (2004) '"Now wo, now gladnesse": Ovidianism in the *Fall of Princes*', *Journal of English Literary History* 71: 531–58.

Novati, F. (1899) *L'influsso del pensiero latino sopra la civiltà italiana del medio evo.* Milan.

Oberman, P. F. J. (1996) 'The Latin classics in monastic libraries of the Low Countries in the fifteenth century', in *Medieval Manuscripts of the Latin Classics: Production and Use*, ed. C. A. Chavannes-Mazel and M. M. Smith,

Proceedings of the Seminar in the History of the Book to 1500. Los Altos, CA, and London.

OCD³ = *Oxford Classical Dictionary*, 3rd edn. (1996), ed. S. Hornblower and A. Spawforth. Oxford.

ODB = *Oxford Dictionary of Byzantium* (1991), ed. A. P. Kazhdan. Oxford.

O'Gorman, E. (1997) 'Love and the family: Augustus and Ovidian elegy', *Arethusa* 30: 103–24.

Orduna, G. (1984–5) 'La "estoria" de Acteón: Ovidio y la General estoria alfonsí,' *Letras* 11–12: 134–9.

Orgel, S. (ed.) (1976) '*Metamorphoseos libri moralizati*, Lyons, J. Huguetan, 1518', repr. in a facsimile edition in *The Renaissance and the Gods*. New York.

Orme, N. (2006) *Medieval Schools: From Roman Britain to Renaissance England*. New Haven, CT and London.

Orofino, G. (1993) 'L'Illustrazione delle Metamorfosi di Ovidio nel ms IV F 3 della Biblioteca Nazionale di Napoli', *Ricerche di storia dell' arte* 49: 5–18.

(1994) 'Cavalleria e devozione: libri miniati francesi a Napoli e a Bari in età protoangioina', *Il Gotico europeo in Italia*, ed. V. Pace and M. Bagnoli. Naples 375–89.

(1998) 'Il codice napoletano delle "Metamorfosi" come libro illustrato', in *L'Ovidio Napoletano*, ed. Guglielmo Cavallo *et al.*, Sulmona: text volume, 103–9.

Otis, B. (1936) 'The *Argumenta* of the so-called Lactantius', *Harvard Studies in Classical Philology* 14: 131–63.

Pade, M. (1997) 'The fragments of Theodontius in Boccaccio's *Genealogie Deorum Gentilium Libri*,' in *Avignon and Naples: Italy in France, France in Italy in the Fourteenth Century*, ed. M. Pade, H. Ragn Jensen and L. Waage Petersen. Rome: 149–66.

Paetow, J. L. (ed.) (1927) *Two Medieval Satires on the University of Paris: 'La Bataille des VII ars' of Henri d'Andeli and the 'Morale scolarium' of John of Garland*. Berkeley.

Pairet, A. (2002) *Les mutacions des fables: figures de la métamorphose dans la littérature française du Moyen Âge*. Paris.

Panofsky, E. (1960) *Renaissance and Renascences in Western Art*. Stockholm.

Papathomopoulos, M. (1975) 'A propos de la métaphrase planudéene des *Héroïdes* d'Ovid', in *Philtra: Timetikos Tomos S. G. Kapsomenou*, ed. S. Kapsomenos. Thessalonika: 107–18.

Papathomopoulos, M. and I. Tsavare (eds.) (2002) *Ovidiou Peri metamorphoseon: ho metenenken ek tes latinon phones eis ten Hellada Maximos monachos ho Planoudes*. Athens.

Paris, G. (1985) 'Chrétien Legouais et autres traducteurs ou imitateurs d'Ovide', *Histoire Littéraire de la France* 29: 455–525.

Parker, H. N. (1997) 'The Teratogenic Grid', in *Roman Sexualities*, ed. J. P. Hallet and M. B. Skinner. Princeton.

Parker, M. A. (1978) 'Juan de Mena's Ovidian material: An Alfonsine influence?', *Bulletin of Hispanic Studies* 55: 5–17.

Pascal, C. (ed.) (1907) *Poesia latina medievale*. Catania.

Paschalis, M. (2005) 'Introduction', in *Roman and Greek Imperial Epic*, ed. M. Paschalis, Rethymnon Classical Studies 2. Heracleion, Crete: 1–8.

Patterson, L. (1978) 'The Parson's Tale and the quitting of the *Canterbury Tales*', *Traditio* 34: 331–80.

Paulmier-Foucart, M., S. Lusignan and A. Nadeau (eds.) (1990) *Vincent de Beauvais: Intentions et réceptions d'une oeuvre encyclopédique au moyen age. Actes du XIVe colloque de l'institut d'études médiévales, organisé par l'Atelier Vincent de Beauvais (l'université de Nancy II) et l'institut d'études médiévales (Montréal)*. Paris 1990.

Pearsall, D. (1985) *The Canterbury Tales*. London.

(1992) *The Life of Geoffrey Chaucer*. Oxford.

Peck, R. (2004) 'The politics and psychology of governance in Gower: Ideas of kingship and real kings,' in *A Companion to Gower*, ed. S. Echard. Cambridge: 215–38.

Peebles, B. M. (1964) 'The *Ad Maronis Mausoleum*: Petrarch's Virgil and two fifteenth-century manuscripts', in *Classical, Mediaeval and Renaissance Studies in Honor of Berthold Louis Ullman*, ed. C. Henderson, Jr, vol. II. Rome: 169–98.

Pellegrin, E. (1957) 'Les *Remedia amoris* d'Ovide: texte scolaire médiéval', *Bibliothèque de l'école des chartes* 115: 172–9.

Pellegrin, E., J. Fohlen, C. Jeudy, *et al.* (1975–91) *Les manuscrits classiques latins de la Bibliothèque vaticane* (3 vols.). Paris.

Pepin, Ronald E. (2008) *The Vatican Mythographers*. New York.

Percival, F. (1998) *Chaucer's Legendary Good Women*. Cambridge.

Perlman, J. B. (2007) 'Venus, Myrrha, Cupid and/as Adonis: *Metamorphosis* 10, and the artistry of incest', in *Metamorphosis: The Changing Face of Ovid in Medieval and Early Modern Europe*, ed. A. Keith and S. Rupp, Victoria University Centre for Medieval and Renaissance Studies, Essays and Studies, 13: Victoria: 223–38.

Petrucci, A. (1970) 'Censimento dei codici dei secoli XI–XII', *StudMed* II: 1013–1133.

Pette, G. (1991) 'Appendix Vergiliana', in *Enciclopedia Vergiliana*, vol. V.2, ed. A. Salvatore and R. Giomini. Rome: 371–426.

Pfaff, R. W. (1980) *Montague Rhodes James*. London.

Picone, M. (1992) 'Auctoritas classica e salvezza cristiana: una lettura tipologica di *Purgatorio* XXII', *Italianistica* 21: 379–95.

(1993) 'L'Ovidio di Dante', in *Dante e la 'bella scuola' di poesia: Autorità e sfida poetica*, ed. A. Iannucci. Ravenna: 107–44.

(2001) 'Canto XIX', *Lectura Dantis Turicensis: Purgatorio*, ed. G. Güntert and M. Picone. Florence: 287–306.

(2003) 'Ovid and the *Exul Immeritus*', in *Dante for the New Millennium*, ed. T. Barolini and W. Storey. New York: 389–407.

Piper, A. J. (1978) 'Libraries of the monks of Durham', in *Medieval Scribes, Manuscripts and Libraries: Essays Presented to N. R. Ker*, ed. M. B. Parkes and A. G. Watson. London: 213–49.

Pittaluga, S. (ed.) (1976) 'De tribus puellis', in *Commedie latine del* XII *e* XIII *secolo*, vol. I, ed. F. Bertini. Genoa: 279–333.

(1980) 'Pamphilus', in *Commedie latine del* XII *e* XIII *secolo*, vol. III, ed. F. Bertini. Genoa: 13–137.

Poe, E. (2006) 'Marie de France and the *Salut d'Amours*', *Romania* 124: 301–3.

Porter, E. (1983) 'Gower's ethical microcosm and political macrocosm', in *Gower's 'Confessio Amantis': Responses and Assessments*, ed. A. J. Minnis. Cambridge: 135–62.

Possamaï-Pérez, M. (2003) 'La réécriture de la métamorphose dans l'*Ovide moralisé*', in *Lectures d'Ovide: publiées à la mémoire de Jean-Pierre Néraudau*, ed. E. Bury. Paris: 149–64.

(2006) *L'Ovide moralisé: essai d'interprétation*. Paris.

(ed.) (2009) *Nouvelles études sur l'Ovide moralisé*. Paris.

Post, C. R. (1912) 'The sources of Juan de Mena', *The Romanic Review* 3: 223–79.

Purser, L. C. (1898) 'Introduction', in *P. Ovidii Nasonis 'Heroides' with the Greek Translation of Planudes*, ed. A. Palmer. Oxford: ix–lix.

Putnam, M. and J. Ziolkowski. (eds.) (2008) *The Virgilian Tradition: The First Fifteen Hundred Years*. New Haven.

Quain, E. A. (1945) 'The Medieval Accessus ad Auctores', *Traditio* 3: 215–64.

Questa, C. (1959) 'Ovidio nell'Ottoboniano lat. 1469', *Scriptorium* 13: 217–32.

Raby, F. J. E. (1997) *A History of Secular Latin Poetry in the Middle Ages*. Special edn. (2 vols.). Oxford.

Raine, J. (1838) *Catalogi veteres librorum ecclesiae cathedralis Dunelmensis*, ed. Surtees Society I. London.

Rand, E. K. (1926) *Ovid and his Influence*. Boston.

Ratkowitsch, Ch. (1987) 'Baudri von Bourgueil: ein Dichter der "inneren Emigration"', *MLatJb* 22: 142–65.

Reeve, M. D. (1983) 'Appendix Vergiliana', in *Texts and Transmission: A Survey of the Latin Classics*, ed. L. D. Reynolds. Oxford: 437–40.

Reichenberger, A. G. (1969) 'The marqués de Santillana and the classical tradition', *Iberoromania* 1: 5–34.

(1975) 'Classical antiquity in some poems of Juan de Mena', in *Studia hispanica in honorem R. Lapesa*, vol. III. Madrid: 405–18.

Reiff, A. (1959) Interpretatio, imitatio, aemulatio: Begriff und Vorstellung literarischer Abhängigkeit bei den Römern. PhD diss., University of Cologne.

Reydellet, M. (ed. and tr.) (1994–) *Venance Fortunat: Poèmes* (3 vols.). Paris.

Reynolds, L. D. (ed.) (1983) *Texts and Transmission: A Survey of the Latin Classics*. Oxford.

Reynolds, L. D. and N. G. Wilson. (1991) *Scribes and Scholars: A Guide to the Transmission of Greek and Latin Literature*, 3rd edn. Oxford.

Reynolds, S. (1996a) 'Glossing Horace: Using the classics in the medieval classroom,' in *Medieval Manuscripts of the Latin Classics*, ed. C. Chavannes-Mazel and M. Smith, Los Altos Hills, CA: 103–17.

(1996b) *Medieval Reading: Grammar, Rhetoric, and the Classical Text*. Cambridge.

Reynolds, W. D. (1971) The *Ovidius moralizatus* of Petrus Berchorius: An introduction and translation. PhD diss., University of Illinois.

(1978) 'Selections from *De formis figurisque deorum*', *Allegorica* 2: 58–89.

(1990) 'Sources, nature and influence of the *Ovidius moralizatus* of Pierre Bersuire', in *The Mythographic Art: Classical Fable and the Rise of the Vernacular in Early France and England*, ed. J. Chance. Gainesville, FL: 83–99.

Ribemont, B. (2002) 'L'*Ovide moralisé* et la tradition encyclopédique: une approche comparative', *Cahiers de Recherches médiévales (XIIIe–XVe siècles)* 9: 13–24.

Riché, P. (1979) *Les écoles et l'enseignement dans l'Occident chrétien de la fin du ve siècle au milieu du XIe siècle*. Paris.

Richmond, J. A. (ed.) (1962) The *'Halieutica', Ascribed to Ovid*. University of London, Classical Studies 2. London.

(1981) 'Doubtful works ascribed to Ovid', in *Principat: Aufstieg und Niedergang der römischen Welt*, vol. XXXI/4, ed. W. Haase. Berlin and New York: 2744–83.

(2002) 'Manuscript traditions and the transmission of Ovid's works', in *Brill's Companion to Ovid*, ed. B. W. Boyd. Leiden: 443–84.

Rigg, A. G. (1977) 'Medieval Latin Poetic Anthologies (I)', *Mediaeval Studies* 39: 281–330.

(1992) *A History of Anglo-Latin Literature, 1066–1422*. Cambridge.

Rigg, A. G. and E. S. Moore. (2004) 'The Latin works: Politics, lament and praise', in *A Companion to Gower*, ed. S. Echard. Cambridge: 153–64.

Rigotti, G. (1995) 'I. Prologemena', in *Augoustinou Peri Triados: vivlia pendekaideka haper ek tes latinon dialektou eis ten hellada metenenke Maximos ho Planoudes*, vol. I, ed. M. Papathomopoulos, I. Tsavare and G. Rigotti. Athens: xv–cxi.

Rivers, K. (2006) 'Another look at the career of Pierre Bersuire, OSB', *Revue Bénédictine* 116: 92–100.

Robathan, D. M. (ed.) (1968) *The Pseudo-Ovidian 'De vetula': Text, Introduction, and Notes*. Amsterdam.

(1973) 'Ovid in the Middle Ages', in *Ovid*, ed. J. W. Binns. Boston: 191–209.

Roberto, U. (2005) *Ioannis Antiocheni Fragmenta ex Historia Chronica: Text und Untersuchungen zur Geschichte der altchristlichen Literatur*, vol. CLIV. Berlin.

Roberts, M. (2002) 'Creation in Ovid's *Metamorphoses* and the Latin poets of Late Antiquity', in *The Reception of Ovid in Antiquity*, ed. G. Tissol and S. Wheeler, special issue of *Arethusa*, 35.3: 403–15.

Rogers P. (2005) *Pope and the Destiny of the Stuarts: History Politics and Mythology in the Age of Queen Anne*. Oxford.

Rossetti, G. (1980) 'De nuntio sagaci', in *Commedie latine del XII e XIII secolo*, vol. II, ed. F. Bertini. Genoa: 11–128.

Rossi, A. (2004) *Translatio Ovidii: note paleografiche sulle traduzioni medievali delle Metamorfosi*. Bari.

Rothe, H.-W. (1977) *Das Erfurter Kartauserkloster und seine Bibliothek*. Bad Vilbel.

Rotondi, G. (1934) 'Ovidio nel medio evo', *Convivium: rivista di lettere, filosofia e storia* 6: 262–9.

Rouse, R. H. (1963) *Catalogus de libris autenticis et apocrifis*: A critical edition. PhD diss., Cornell University.

(1975) 'The *Florilegium Angelicum:* Its origin, content, and influence', in *Medieval Learning and Literature: Essays Presented to R. W. Hunt*, ed. J. J. G. Alexander and M. T. Gibson. Oxford: 66–114.

(1979) '*Florilegia* and the Latin classical authors in twelfth- and thirteenth-century Orléans', *Viator* 10: 115–64.

Rouse, R. H. and M. A. Rouse. (1991) *Registrum Angliae*, Corpus of British Medieval Library Catalogues 2. London.

(2005) *Catalogus de libris autenticis et apocrifis*, Corpus of British Medieval Library Catalogues 11. London.

Roy, B. (1974) *L'Art d'amours: traduction et commentaire de l'"Ars amatoria" d'Ovide. Edition critique*. Leiden.

Roy, B. and H. V. Shooner. (1985–6) 'Querelles de maîtres au XIIe siècle: Arnoul d'Orléans et son milieu', *Sandalion* 8–9: 315–41.

(eds.) (1996) 'Arnulfi Aurelianensis *Glosule de Remediis amoris*,' *The Journal of Medieval Latin* 6: 135–96.

(1984) *Catálogo de los manuscritos clásicos latinos existentes en España*. Madrid.

Ruiz Esteban, Y. (1990) *El mito de Narciso en la literatura española*. Madrid.

Ruthven, K. K. (2001) *Faking Literature*. Cambridge and New York.

Sabbadini, R. (1905) 'Braciole umanistiche', *Giornale storico della letteratura italiana* 46: 65–81.

Sadlek, G. M. (2004) *Idleness Working: The Discourse of Love's Labor from Ovid through Chaucer and Gower*. Washington, DC.

Saint-Amour, P. K. (2003) *The Copywrights: Intellectual Property and the Literary Imagination*. Ithaca, NY.

Sanford, E. M. (1924) 'The use of classical Latin authors in the *Libri Manuales*', *Transactions and Proceedings of the American Philological Association* 55: 190–248.

Saxl, F. and H. Meier. (1953) *Catalogue of Astrological and Mythological Illuminated Manuscripts of the Latin Middle Ages: Manuscripts in English Libraries*, vol. III, ed. H. Bober. London.

Scattergood, V. J. (1974) 'The Manciple's manner of speaking', *Essays in Criticism* 24: 124–46.

Schaller, D. and E. Könsgen. (1977) *Initia carminum Latinorum saeculo undecimo antiquiorum*. Göttingen.

Schevill, R. (1913) *Ovid and the Renascence in Spain*. Berkeley.

Schiaffini, A. (1922) 'Esercizi di versione dal volgare friulano in latino del sec. XIV in una scuola notarile cividalese', *Rivista della Società filologica friulana* 3: 87–117.

Schiff, M. (1905) *La bibliothèque du Marquis de Santillane*. Paris.

Schmid, W. (1959) 'Ein christlicher Heroidenbrief des 6. Jahrhunderts,' in *Studien zur Textgeschichte und Textkritik: Festschrift G. Jachmann gewidmet*, ed. H. Dahlmann and R. Merkelbach. Opladen.

Schmitt, W. O. (1968) 'Lateinischen literatur in Byzanz', *Jahrbuch der Österreichischen Byzantinischen Gesellschaft* 17: 127–47.

Schnell, R. (1975) 'Facetus, Pseudo-ars amatoria und die mittelhochdeutsche Minnedidaktik', *Zeitschrift für deutsches Altertum* 104: 244–7.

Schotter, A. (1992) 'Rhetoric versus Rape in the medieval Latin Pamphilus', *Philological Quarterly* 71: 243–60.

Schuelper, S. (1979) 'Ovid aus der Sicht des Balderich von Bourgueil, dargestellt anhand des Briefwechsels Florus-Ovid', *MLatJb* 15: 93–118.

Scott, K. L. (ed.) (2002) *An Index of Images in English Manuscripts from the Time of Chaucer to Henry VIII c. 1380 – c. 1509, The Bodleian Library, Oxford*, fasc. iii. London and Turnhout.

Sedlmayer, H. S. (1884) 'Beiträge zur Geschichte der Ovidstudien im Mittelalter', *Wiener Studien* 6: 142–58.

Seznec, J. (1953) *The Survival of the Pagan Gods*, tr. B. Sessions. New York.

(1983) *Los dioses de la Antigüedad en la Edad Media y el Renacimiento*, tr. J. Aranzadi. Barcelona.

Shannon, E. F. (1929) *Chaucer and the Roman Poets*. Cambridge, MA.

Sharpe, R. (1997) *A Handlist of the Latin Writers of Great Britain and Ireland to AD 1540*. Turnhout.

Sharpe, R., J. P. Carley, K. Friis-Jensen and A. G. Watson. (1996) *English Benedictine Libraries: The Shorter Catalogues*, Corpus of British Medieval Library Catalogues 4. London.

Sharrock, A. R. (1994) 'Ovid and the Politics of Reading', *Materiali e discussioni per l'analisi dei texti classici* 33: 97–122.

(2002) 'Ovid and the discourses of love: The amatory works', in *The Cambridge Companion to Ovid*, ed. P. Hardie. Cambridge: 150–62.

(2002) 'Gender and sexuality', in *The Cambridge Companion to Ovid*, ed. P. Hardie. Cambridge: 95–107.

Shooner, H. V. (1981) 'Les *Bursarii Ovidianorum* de Guillaume d'Orléans', *Mediaeval Studies* 43: 405–24.

Shorrock, R. (2001) *The Challenge of Epic: Allusive Engagement in the Dionysiaca of Nonnus*. Leiden.

Signes, J., *et al.* (eds.) (2005) *Antiquae lectiones: el legado clásico desde la Antigüedad hasta la Revolución Francesa*. Madrid.

Silk, E. T. (1935) *Saeculi noni auctoris in Boetii Consolationem Philosophiae Commentarius*. Rome.

Simpson, J. (1995) *Sciences and the Self in Medieval Poetry: Alan of Lille's 'Anticlaudianus' and John Gower's 'Confessio amantis'*. Cambridge.

(1998) 'Ethics and interpretation: Reading wills in Chaucer's *Legend of Good Women*', *Studies in the Age of Chaucer* 20: 73–100.

Sisler, W. P. (1977) An edition and translation of Lovato Lovati's *Metrical Epistles* with parallel passages from ancient authors. PhD diss., Johns Hopkins University.

Smalley, B. (1960) *English Friars and Antiquity in the Early Fourteenth Century*. Oxford.

Smolak, K. (1980) 'Der verbannte Dichter (Identifizierungen mit Ovid in Mittelalter und Neuzeit)', *WS* n.f. 14: 158–91.

(1983) 'Zu Text und Interpretation der pseudo-ovidianischen Elegie De sompnio,' *Wiener Studien* n.f. 17: 189–209.

Solalinde, A. G. (1925) 'La fecha del *Ovide moralisé*', *Revista de Filología Española* 8: 285–8.

(1928) 'El juicio de Paris en el Alexandre y en la *General Estoria*,' *Revista de Filología Española* 15: 1–51.

Solodow, J. (1988) *The World of Ovid's Metamorphoses*. Chapel Hill, NC.

Sowell, M. (ed.) (1991) *Dante and Ovid: Essays in Intertextuality*. Binghamton, NY.

Spargo, J. W. (1934) *Virgil the Necromancer: Studies in Virgilian Legends*. Harvard Studies in Comparative Literature 10. Cambridge, MA.

Spearing, A. C. (2005) *Textual Subjectivity: The Encoding of Subjectivity in Medieval Narratives and Lyrics*. Oxford.

Spence, S. (1996) *Texts and the Self in the Twelfth Century*. Cambridge.

Speyer, W. (1971) *Die literarische Fälschung im heidnischen und christlichen Altertum*. Handbuch der Altertumswissenschaft 1.2. Munich.

Staley, L. (2005) *Languages of Power in the Age of Richard II*. University Park, PA.

Stapleton, M. L. (1996) *Harmful Eloquence: Ovid's 'Amores' from Antiquity to Shakespeare*. Ann Arbor, MI.

Steiner, G. (1951) 'Source editions of Ovid's *Metamorphoses* (1471–1500)', *Transactions and Proceedings of the American Philological Association* 82: 219–31.

Stemplinger, E. (1912) *Das Plagiat in der griechischen Literatur*. Leipzig. Rprt. Hildesheim, 1990.

Stillinger, T. C. (1992) *The Song of Troilus: Lyric Authority in the Medieval Book*. Philadelphia.

Stohlmann, J. (1973) '"Deidamia Achilli": Eine Ovid-Imitation aus dem 11. Jahrhundert', in *Literatur und Sprache im europäischen Mittelalter: Festschrift für Karl Langosch zum 70. Geburtstag*, ed. A. Önnerfors, J. Rathofer and F. Wagner. Darmstadt: 195–231.

(1979) 'Zur anonymen Tischzucht "Doctrina mense": ein Nachtrag', *MLatJb* 14: 282–3.

Stoneman, W. P. (1999) *Dover Priory*, Corpus of British Medieval Library Catalogues 5. London.

Street, F. (1952) 'La paternidad del Tratado de amor', *Bulletin of Hispanic Studies* 54: 15–53.

Strubel, A. (1984) *Guillaume de Lorris, Jean de Meun, 'Le Roman de la Rose'*. Paris.

Swanson, J. (1989) *John of Wales: A Study of the Works and Ideas of a Thirteenth-Century Friar*. Cambridge.

Sweeney, R. D. (1971) 'Vanishing and unavailable books: Latin manuscripts in the Middle Ages and today', in *Classical Influences on European Culture, 500–1500*, ed. R. R. Bolgar. Cambridge: 29–36.

Tafel, S. (1910) *Die Uberlieferungsgeschichte von Ovids Carmina amatoria. Verfolgt bis zum 11 Jahrhundert*. Tübingen.

Tarrant, R. J. (1981) 'The authenticity of the letter of Sappho to Phaon (*Heroides* xv),' *Harvard Studies in Classical Philology* 85: 133–53.

 (1983) 'Ovid', in *Texts and Transmission: A Survey of the Latin Classics*, ed. L. D. Reynolds. Oxford: 257–84.

 (1995) 'The *Narrationes* of Lactantius and the transmission of Ovid's *Metamorphoses*', in *Formative Stages of Classical Traditions: Latin Texts from Antiquity to the Renaissance: Proceedings of a Conference Held at Erice, 16–22 October 1993*, ed. O. Pecere and M. D. Reeve. Spoleto: 83–115.

Taylor, Ch. (1925) *The Mediaeval Mind*. New York.

Taylor, J. (1966) *The Universal Chronicle of Ranulf Higden*. Oxford.

Thiel, E. J. (1968) 'Mittellateinische Nachdichtungen von Ovids *Ars amatoria* und *Remedia amoris*', *MLatJb* 5: 115–80.

 (1970) 'Beiträge zu den Ovid-Nachdichtungen "Pseudo-Ars amatoria" und "Pseudo-Remedia amoris"', *MLatJb* 6: 132–48.

Thomson, R. M. (2001) (ed.) *A Descriptive Catalogue of the Medieval Manuscripts in Worcester Cathedral Library*, with a contribution on the bindings by M. Gullick. Woodbridge.

 (2007) 'Worcester monks and education, *c.*1300', in *The Culture of Medieval English Monasticism*, ed. J. G. Clark. Woodbridge: 104–10.

Tilliette, J.-Y. (1994) 'Savants et poètes du moyen âge face à Ovide: les débuts de l'aetas Ovidiana (v. 1050 – v. 1200)', in *Ovidius redivivus: Von Ovid zu Dante*, ed. M. Picone and B. Zimmermann. Stuttgart: 63–104.

 (1996) 'L'écriture et sa métaphore: remarques sur l'*Ovide moralisé*', in *Ensi firent li ancessor: mélanges de philologie médiévale offerts à Marc-René Jung*, ed. Luciano Rossi *et al.*, vol. II. Alessandria: 543–58.

Toury, M.-N. (2003) 'La Métamorphose d'Ovide au XIIe siècle', in *Lectures d'Ovide: publieés à la mémoire de Jean-Pierre Néraudau*. Paris: 175–87.

Trapp, J. B. (1973) 'Ovid's tomb: The growth of a legend from Eusebius to Laurence Sterne, Chateaubriand and George Richmond', *Journal of the Warburg and Courtauld Institutes* 36: 35–76.

Traube, L. (1909–20) *Vorlesungen und Abhandlungen*, ed. P. Lehmann (3 vols). Munich.

Travis, P. (2003) 'The Manciple's phallic matrix', *Studies in the Age of Chaucer* 25: 317–24.

Trilla Millàs, E. and V. Cristóbal (1996) 'Las *Heroidas* de Ovidio en Joan Roís de Corella,' in *Tradició Clàssica: Actes del XI Simposi de la Secció Catalana de la SEEC*, ed. M. Puig Rodríguez-Escalona. Andorra la Vella: 693–7.

Tsavare, I. (1974) 'He metaphrase ton *Metamorphoseon* tou Ovidiou apo ton Maximo Planoude: he cheirographe paradose', *Dodone* 3: 387–405.

 (1987) 'Deux nouveaux autographs de Maxime Planoude', *Dodone* 16: 225–9.

Turner, J. H. (1977) *The Myth of Icarus in Spanish Renaissance Poetry*. London.

Turyn, A. (1972) *Dated Greek Manuscripts of the 13th and 14th Centuries in the Libraries of Italy*, vol. I. Urbana, IL.

Ullman, B. L. (ed.) (1928) *Scriptorum Illustrium Latinae Linguae Libri* XVIII. Rome.

 (1955) *Studies in the Italian Renaissance*. Rome.

(1963) *The Humanism of Coluccio Salutati*. Padua.

Ullman, B. L. and P. Stadter. (1972) *The Public Library of Renaissance Florence*. Padua.

Van Buuren, A. M. J. (1995) *Medieval Dutch Literature in its European Context*, ed. E. Kooper. Cambridge.

Van T'Sant, J. Th. M. (1929) *Le commentaire de Copenhague de l'"Ovide Moralisé"*. Amsterdam.

Vervacke, S. (1999) Forme et fonction des traductions moralisées des *Métamorphoses* d'Ovide. Le 'De formis figurisque deorum' de Pierre Bersuire (Avignon, 1342) préface à la Bible des poètes (Bruges, Colard Mansion, 1484). PhD diss., Université Laval.

Vian, F. (1959) *Recherches sur les Posthomerica de Quintus de Smyrne*. Paris.

Viarre, S. (1966) *La survie d'Ovide dans la littérature scientifique des xiième et xiiième siècles*. Publications du Centre d'études supérieures de civilisation médiévale 4. Poitiers.

Villa, C. (1996) 'Tra fabula e historia: Manegoldo di Lautenbach e il Maestro di Orazio,' *Aevum* 70: 245–56.

Villaret, F. de. (1876) 'L'enseignement des lettres, et des sciences dans l'Orléanais depuis les premiers siècles du Christianisme jusqu'à la fondation de l'Université d'Orléans,' *Mémoires de la société archéologique et historique de l'Orléanais* 14: 299–440.

Vinge, L. (1967) *The Narcissus Theme in Western European Literature up to the Early 19th Century*. Lund.

Voigt, E. (ed.) (1878) *Kleinere lateinische Denkmäler der Thiersage aus dem 12. Bis 14. Jahrhundert*. Strasbourg: 58–62.

Wallace, D. (1997) *Chaucerian Polity*. Stanford.

(2002) 'Italy', in *A Companion to Chaucer*, ed. P. Brown. Oxford: 218–34.

Wallace-Hadrill, A. (1993) *Augustan Rome*. Bristol.

Wallace-Hadrill, J. M. (1983) *The Frankish Church*. Oxford.

Walsh, P. G. (ed.) (1982) *Andreas Capellanus 'On Love'*, edited with an English translation. London.

Walters, J. (1997) 'Invading the Roman body: Manliness and impenetrability in Roman thought', in *Roman Sexualities*, ed. J. P. Hallett and M. B. Skinner. Princeton: 29–43.

Walther, H. (1959) *Initia carminum ac versuum Medii Aevi posterioris Latinorum*. Carmina Medii Aevi posterioris Latina 1. Göttingen.

Ward, J. O. (1996) 'From marginal gloss to *catena* commentary: The eleventh-century origins of a rhetorical teaching tradition in the medieval west', *Parergon* 13: 109–20.

(1998) 'The *catena* commentaries on the rhetoric of Cicero and their implication for development of a teaching tradition in rhetoric', *Studies in Medieval and Renaissance Teaching* 6: 79–95.

(2001) 'Rhetorical theory and the rise and decline of *dictamen* in the middle ages and early Renaissance,' *Rhetorica* 19: 175–223.

Watson, A. G. (1999) *A Descriptive Catalogue of the Manuscripts of All Souls College, Oxford.* Oxford.

Watson, A. G. and T. Webber. (1998) *The Libraries of the Augustinian Canons.* Corpus of British Medieval Library Catalogues 6. London.

Watt, D. (2003) *Amoral Gower.* Minneapolis.

Weiden Boyd, B. (1997) *Ovid's Literary Loves: Influence and Innovation in the 'Amores'.* Ann Arbor, MI.

Weiss, R. (1977) 'Translations from the Greek of the Angevin Court of Naples', in R. Weiss, *Medieval and Humanist Greek*, Medioevo e umanesimo 8. Padua: 1080–133.

Wendel, C. (1940) 'Planudes, Maximos', in *Paulys Real-Encyclopädie der classischen Altertumswissenschaft*, vol. XL, ed. G. Wissowa *et al.* Stuttgart: 2202–53.

Wenzel, S. (ed.) (1989) '*Fasciculus Morum': A Fourteenth-Century Preacher's Handbook.* University Park, PA and London.

(1995a) 'The classics in late-medieval preaching', in *Mediaeval Antiquity*, ed. A. Welkenhuysen, H. Braet and W. Verbeke. Leuven: 127–43.

(1995b) 'Academic sermons at Oxford in the early fifteenth century', *Speculum* 70: 305–29.

(2000) 'The *Parson's Tale* in current literary studies', in *Closure in 'The Canterbury Tales'*, ed. D. Raybin and L. Tarte Holley. Kalamazoo: 1–10.

(2005) *Latin Sermon Collections from Later Medieval England: Orthodox Preaching in the Age of Wyclif.* Cambridge.

West, D. and T. Woodman. (eds.) (1979) *Creative Imitation and Latin Literature.* Cambridge.

Wetherbee, W. (1984) *Chaucer and the Poets: An Essay on Troilus and Criseyde.* Ithaca, NY.

(1999) 'John Gower', in *The Cambridge History of Medieval English Literature*, ed. D. Wallace. Cambridge: 589–609.

(2005) 'The study of classical authors: From late antiquity to the twelfth century', in *The Cambridge History of Literary Criticism*, vol. II, ed. A. J. Minnis and I. Johnson. Cambridge: 99–144.

(2008) *The Antique Flame: Dante Among the Poets.* Notre Dame.

Wheeler, S. (2002) 'Introduction: Towards a literary history of Ovid's reception in antiquity', in *The Reception of Ovid in Antiquity*, ed. G. Tissol & S. Wheeler, special issue of *Arethusa*, 35.3: 341–7.

Whitby, M. (1985) 'Paul the Silentiary and Claudian', *CQ* 35: 507–16.

(2002) 'The architecture of the *Dionysiaca*', *Classical Review* 52: 283–4.

White, P. (2009) *Renaissance Postscripts: Responding to Ovid's 'Heroides' in Sixteenth-Century France.* Columbus, OH.

Wicksteed, P. H. and E. G. Gardner. (1902) *Dante and Giovanni del Virgilio.* London.

Wilkinson, L. P. (1955) *Ovid Recalled.* Cambridge.

Wimsatt, J. (1967) 'The Sources of Chaucer's "Seys and Alcyone"', *MAev* 36: 231–41.

Winter, U. (1986) *Die europäischen Handschriften der Bibliothek Diez: Teil 1: Die Manuscripta Dieziana B Santeniana, Teil 2: Die Libri impressi cum notis manuscriptis.* Leipzig.

Witt, R. G. (2000) *'In the Footsteps of the Ancients': The Origins of Humanism from Lovato to Bruni.* Leiden.

Wittkower, R. (1939) 'Eagle and serpent: A study in the migration of symbols', *JWI* 2.4: 293–325.

Wolfthal, D. (1999) *Images of Rape: The 'Heroic' Tradition and its Alternatives.* New York and Cambridge.

Woods, M. C. (1996) 'Rape and the pedagogical rhetoric of sexual violence', in *Criticism and Dissent in the Middle Ages*, ed. R. Copeland. Cambridge: 58–86.

Wright, T. (1859–61) 'De victoria belli in Hispania per principem Edwardum', in *Political Poems and Songs*, Rolls Series 14. London.

Yeager, R. F. (1989) 'Did Gower write *Cento*?', in *John Gower: Recent Readings*, ed. R. F. Yeager. Kalamazoo: 113–32.

   (1990) *John Gower's Poetic: The Search for a New Arion.* Woodbridge.

Yerba, V. G. (1987) 'Interlingüística greco-latina en la traducción de las *Metamorfosis* por Planudes', in *Athlon: satura grammatica in honorem Francisci R. Adrados*, vol. II, ed. A. B. Pajares. Madrid: 337–53.

Young, K. (1944) 'Chaucer's appeal to the Platonic deity', *Speculum* 19: 1–13.

Zaggia, M. and M. Ceriana. (1996) *I Manoscritti illustrati delle 'Eroide' ovidiane volgarizzate.* Pisa.

Zak, G. (2007) 'A humanist in exile: Ovid's myth of Narcissus and the experience of self in Petrarch's Secretum', in *Metamorphosis: The Changing Face of Ovid in Medieval and Early Modern Europe*, ed. A. Keith and S. Rupp. Toronto: 179–98.

   (2010) *Petrarch's Humanism and the Care of the Self.* Cambridge.

Zapata, A. (1987) 'Progne y Filomela: la leyenda en las fuentes clásicas y su tradición en la literatura española hasta Lope de Vega', *Estudios Clásic* 92: 23–58.

Zimmermann, M. (ed.) (2001) *Auctor et auctoritas: invention et conformisme dans l'écriture médiévale.* Paris.

Ziolkowski, J. (1993) *Talking Animals: Medieval Latin Beast Poetry, 750–1150.* Philadelphia.

Index locorum

Alfonso X
General Estoria, first part: Genesis, Book 4, ch. 9:91, **237**; Genesis, Book 6, ch. 26:163, **234–5**

Alighieri, Dante
Convivio: 2.2.1–9, **149**; 6.5–6, **150–1**
Epistle 3: **152–3, 154–5**
Inferno: 4.80–90, **125–6, 155**; 4.94–102, **126**; 25.97–102, **126, 156–8**
De monarchia: 2.7.10, **155**; 2.8.4, **155**
Vita Nova: 24.2–5, **143, 147**; 25.6, **150**; 25.9, **144**
De vulgari eloquentia: 1.2.7, **155**; 2.6.7, **127, 155**

Anonymous
Art d'amour: 105–6, **112**; 238, **112**; 920–1, **113**; 1654–63, **114–15**; 2242–70, **113**; 3328–3350, **116**; 3602–4, **114**; 4559–63, **115**; 4695–9, **117**
Commentaries: ad *Met*. 1.1–150, **80–2**; ad *Met*. 1.144, **79**; ad *Met*. 1.190, **78**; ad *Met*. 1.382–98, **79**; ad *Met*. 1.689–723, **75**; ad *Met*. 2.253, **76**; ad *Met*. 2.254–9, **77**; ad *Met*. 2.272–302, **76–7**; ad *Met*. 2.538, **77–8**; ad *Met*. 8.236–59, **79**; ad *Met*. 11.3, **78**
Histoire ancienne: 2.54, **121–2**; 3.89–90, **121**; 5.11–15, **120–1**; 5.133–5, **121**; 8.55–6, **121**; 14.7–10, **122**

Chaucer, Geoffrey
Canterbury Tales: 9.163–362, **223–6**; 9.248–56, **228**; 9.271–80, **224**; 9.359–62, **225**; 10.626–7, **228–9**
Legend of Good Women: 798–801, **211**; 833–49, **211–12**; 862–78, **212–13**; 905–12, **213**; 2120–35, **219–20**; 2211–17, **220**

Gospel According to Mark: 16:4, **169**

Gospel According to Matthew: 4:3, **169**

Gower, John
Confessio Amantis: 3.783–816, **222**; 3.1331–1530, **209**; 5.5230–5504, **215–18**
Vox Clamantis: 1.1021–50, **201–6**

John of Antioch
Historia chronike: Fr. 2, **31**

John of Garland
Integumenta Ovidii: 5–8, **61**; 29–33, **62**; 36–7, **63**; 97, **62**; 99–108, **63–4**; 121–2, **63**; 151–2, **61–2**; 163–4, **64**

Lovato Lovati
Metrical epistles: 215–16, **125**

Nonnos
Dionysiaca: 38.105–434, **29**

Ovid
Amores: 1.5, **243**
Ars Amatoria: 1.5, **2**; 1.214, **169**; 1.277–8, **113**; 1.467–8, **117**; 1.523–4, **114**; 1.755–6, **43**; 2.197, **167**; 2.617, **116**; 3.433–4, **115**; 3.479–82, **117**
Epistulae ex Ponto: 1.1.21–46, **11**; 1.4.21–2, **203, 205**; 2.7.9–10, **132**; 4.3.49–50, **203, 205**
Heroides: 2.65, **121**; 2.123–4, **202–3**; 2.147–8, **166**; 5.5–8, **120–1**
Metamorphoses: 1.1–4, **90, 156, 309**; 1.13, **57**; 1.21, **92**; 1.89–150, **169**; 1.107–46, **91**; 1.163–208, **36**; 1.237–9, **99**; 1.639–40, **53**; 1.669–70, **53**; 1.700–8, **36–41, 57**; 1.747–2.398, **29**; 1.748–54, **95**; 2.1–18, **172**; 2.151–62, **31**; 2.531–632, **221–2**; 2.549–95, **225**; 2.553, **94**; 2.689, **57–8**; 4.55–166, **207–9**; 7.1–158, **69–70**; 8.835–43, **70**; 10.17–39, **243–4**; 13.1–127, **28**; 15.161–2, **174**; 15.878, **3**

Index of manuscripts

Note: Page numbers in italics indicate illustrations.

General index

Abbo of Ramsey, 178
Abélard, Pierre, 10
accessus commentaries on O., 14, 49, 87, 92, 98,
109, 127, 149, 151–2, 178, 185–6, 194, 246,
305; of Arnulf of Orléans, 54; on the
Heroides, 118; on the *Metamorphoses*, 54,
61n; *Orléanais*, 54, 59; of William of
Thiegiis, 72
Actaeon, iconography of, 259–61, 272, 276–7
aetas Ovidiana, 6–7, 19, 160, 177, 178–9, 231,
287, 296
Alain of Lille, 11, 124, 308
Alberic of Montecassino, 123
Albumasar, 307
Alcuin, 178
Aldhelm of Malmesbury, 177, 178
Alexander of Villadei, 9, 68, 127, 131
Alexandria, 28, 30
Alfonso X ('The Wise'), 14, 64–5, 231, 232–9,
249, 255–6; *Estoria de España* of, 232–3;
General Estoria of, 232–9
Alighieri, Dante, 16, 21; *Convivio*, 148, 149, 152,
158; *De vulgari eloquentia*, 147–8, 155; *Epistle
3*, 148, 152–3, 154, 158; exile of, 150–3, 154–5;
illustrations in the manuscripts of, 276;
O.'s influence on, 125–7, 143–59; silencing
of O. by, 156–7; *Vita Nova*, 16, 143–6,
147–8, 149, 150, 153, 157–8; and the Vulgate
commentary, 70
Allegoriae. See Arnulf of Orléans
allegory, in interpretation of O.: 16, 49, 51,
59–65, 67, 68, 80–1, 92, 94, 103, 127–8, 139,
168, 172–3, 249, 250–1, 269–70, 272, 307;
contrasted with irony, 158; and illustration,
86, 269–70, 272; instability of, 103. *See also*
John of Garland; *Ovide moralisé*; *Ovidius
moralizatus*
Alonso de Madrigal, 244–5
amatory poems, of O., 12–13, 33, 45, 182, 190. See
also *Amores*; *Ars Amatoria*; *Remedia Amoris*
Ammianus Marcellinus, 30

amplification. *See* commentaries
Anderson, W. S., 138n, 207n, 284n, 300
anonymous commentaries, on O., 74–82.
See also commentaries
anthologies. *See* florilegia
Apollo, 69, 173; associated with Augustus, 226;
and the crow, 221–30; iconography of,
273–5
Appendix Vergiliana, 130, 285–6, 299, 302
Aquinas, Thomas, 157, 204–5
Archana deorum, 225, 229–30
Arethusa, 156, 157
Argus, 53, 75; iconography of, 259–60, 265–6,
271–2
Ariadne and Theseus: Chaucer's treatment of,
218–21; Gower's treatment of, 215–8, 220;
O.'s treatment of, in the *Metamorphoses*,
216
Aristotle, 204–5
Arnulf of Orléans, 13, 17, 49, 50–5, 58–9, 61, 62,
65, 68, 72, 75, 79, 80, 82, 88, 89, 94, 102n,
103, 127, 128, 186, 191, 225, 237, 300n
ars dictaminis. See *dictamina*
Ascoli, A., 143n, 148, 151
astrology, 10, 306–7
auctor, definitions of, 288–90; O. as, 200
audience: for O., 67, 198; for sermons, 163–4.
See also schools
Augustinian order, 162, 163
Augustus, O.'s conflict with, 151–2, 226. *See also*
authority; exile
authenticity, of texts, 289, 292–3
authority: and *auctores*, 290; Dante's
appropriation of, 158; Dante's attitude
towards, 150–2; O.'s relation to, 1, 150–2,
200, 226

Bacon, Roger, 308
Baebius Italicus, 97
Bakalian, E., 215n
Baldwin, B., 31

364

Printed in Great Britain
by Amazon